Trademark Acknowledgements

Wrox has endeavored to provide trademark information about all the companies and products mentioned in this book by the appropriate use of capitals. However, Wrox cannot guarantee the accuracy of this information.

Credits

Authors
Sing Li
Ronald Ashri
Milé Buurmeijer
Bob Flenner
Eric Hol
Jerome Scheuring
Andrew Schneider

Technical Architect
Gregory Beekman

Development Editors
Tim Briggs
Greg Pearson

Technical Editors
Eleanor Baylis
Andrew Tracey

Additional Editorial
Allan Jones

Project Administrator
Chandima Nethisinghe

Production Coordinator
Pippa Wonson

Design/Layout
Tom Bartlett
Pippa Wonson

Production Manager
Laurent Lafon

Proofreaders
Fiona Berryman
Chris Smith

Technical Reviewers
Ronald Ashri
Danny Ayers
Richard Barnett
Raj Betapudi
Lutz Birkhahn
Carl Burnham
Mark Carlson
Geoff Clements
Jeremy Crosbie
Robert DiFalco
Fredrik Espinoza
Alexander V. Konstantinou
Michael Luck
Phil Powers-DeGeorge
Don Reamey
Andrew Schneider
Iain Shigeoka

Index
Adrian Axinte
Michael Brinkman
Martin Brooks
Andrew Criddle

Cover Design
Shelley Frazier

Managing Editor
Paul Cooper

Author Agent
Emma Batch

Illustrations
Shabnam Hussain

Additional Material
Alexander V. Konstantinou

About the Authors

Sing Li

First bitten by the computer bug in 1978, Sing has grown up with the microprocessor revolution. His first PC was a $99 do-it-yourself COSMIC ELF computer with 256 bytes of memory and a 1 bit LED display. For two decades, Sing has been an active author, consultant, speaker, instructor, and entrepreneur. His wide-ranging experience spans distributed architectures, multi-tiered Internet/Intranet systems, computer telephony, call center technology, and embedded systems. Sing has participated in several Wrox projects in the past, and has been working with (and writing about) Java and Jini since their very first alpha releases, and is an active participant in the Jini community.

Milé Buurmeijer

Educated in Computer Science with a specialization in System Programming and Architecture, Milé has been involved in many key ICT areas in both his educational and professional careers.

His role for the last four years has been as an Advanced Technology Consultant within the Research and Development division of Cap Gemini Ernst & Young in the Netherlands. He has been involved in many Internet related projects, partly as architect/designer/developer, and partly as project leader. The focus of the R&D division is on 'early application development' and he therefore works with 'early adopters' on innovative projects.

Most of these innovative projects have an architecture design phase, which answers questions like 'Is this the right technology to solve a problem that cannot be solved with traditional technology?' In the last four years he has investigated, implemented and propagated knowledge in many technology areas, including: Java technology; applets/servlets; Java technology RMI middleware, multi-tier split in application architecture; Java technology versus ActiveX including CORBA and DCOM middleware; Java technology-based Application Servers; Java Card technology; e-Business; www.bol.com (back end integration); Retail chain (intranet back end integration); Ubiquitous Computing; Jini technology; and Bluetooth.

Milé lives with his wife and son in Arnhem, the Netherlands.

Eric Hol

The first computer Eric ever laid his hands on was an old Wang computer 23 years ago. It was the size of a mainframe, but had only the accomplishments of a WAP phone. Since then, computers and programming have become his hobbies.

This interest eventually lead to a University degree in Medical Informatics. His current role in the Cap Gemini Ernst & Young organization is as Delivery Manager in a business unit called Warp11. SF fans will know that this is a speed faster than Star Trek's Voyager can fly. The reason for calling the unit Warp11 is that it specializes in designing and building state of the art (web)applications at the 'speed of light'. In this role Eric is responsible for the transformation of 'any good idea' into a working solution. The expertise of this unit covers both current and new technologies like Java technology, Jini connection technology, WAP, WML, Bluetooth, Visual Basic, Delphi, and Application Servers.

Another important aspect of his role is investigating new ways of improving software quality and applying the results into the software engineering process. He is also the representative for the

Insurance and Social Security Division of Cap Gemini Ernst & Young Netherlands for Web Legacy integration, Ubiquitous Computing and Mobile E-Commerce. He is also a participant for these subjects in the international Cap Gemini networks, and has been involved in numerous engagements in roles varying from software engineer, architect to project manager. The common denominator between all of these engagements was and is New Technology.

Eric lives with his wife and son in Willemstad, south-west Netherlands.

Ronald Ashri (with Michael Luck)

Ronald Ashri recently graduated from Warwick University, where he obtained a First Class Honours Degree in Computer Systems Engineering. Prior to that he served two years in the Cypriot National Guard where he specialised in cryptography and was responsible for his camp's IT systems. Currently he is working in Adastral Park (BT Research Laboratories), on a project related to distributed technologies (such as Jini), agents and security. This work is a prelude to postgraduate study at the University of Southampton, Department of Electronics and Computer Science in the Intelligence, Agents and Multimedia research group.

Dr Michael Luck is the supervisor of the project described in this book. For several years he has been the head of Agent-Based Systems Group in the Computer Science Department of Warwick University, while now he is part of the Intelligence, Agents and Multimedia group at Southampton University as a Senior Lecturer.

Ronald thanks Photini, Andrea and Katia for their love and support, and also thanks the wonderful people at Wrox who have worked hard to make this book a reality.

Robert Flenner

Robert Flenner is an active author and application architect with Scient Corp. designing innovative e-business systems. He has successfully coordinated architecture strategies and led projects utilizing local as well as geographically dispersed development teams. He has extensive experience consulting with global companies on both strategic and tactical IS development and deployment. His technical consulting experience includes Internet design, CORBA, distributed object modeling, workflow, and high availability transaction processing. He is currently developing a framework for distributed development and collaboration.

Andrew Schneider

Andrew is a technical architect for a consultancy house in the UK. He was originally introduced to the world of computing through the Sinclair ZX-80 and has been hooked ever since. He has been involved in building object oriented systems since 1989, and his current interests are distributed systems, security and aspect oriented programming.

He would like to say thanks to his father for introducing him to computing and for being a source of inspiration ever since. He dedicates his chapter to Justine for being the best thing ever to happen to him, and thanks her for converting his techno-babble into coherent English.

Jerome Scheuring

Jerome Scheuring is the Chief Technology Officer of PersonalGenie, Inc., a leading innovator in lifestyle supporting 'wish fulfilment' technology (http://www.personalgenie.com/).

Born in 1964, Jerome has been actively seeking a career in the software industry since he was nine years old. He carries 20 years of professional experience, beginning with the first commercially successful integrated personal computer systems. He has provided software technology to fields as diverse as the telecommunications industry, real estate, education, securities trading, and professional sports.

He has been working with Jini technology since the first public prototypes became available in November 1998.

He would like to acknowledge the contributions of his co-workers in supporting the PersonalGenie technology, in particular Ayal Spitz, Kelly Quiroz, and Sylvia Scheuring, who advised on sections of the present chapter.

Jerome is married, with two children, and lives in the town of Carmel-by-the-Sea, on the west coast of the USA.

Jini Client or Service	JavaSpaces and Helper Services

Jini Client and Service Support Helper Utilities

Jini Discovery Management Helper Utilities

Jini Protocol Helper Utilities

Jini Network Protocols	RMI and Rich Object Semantics
	Java VM and Networking

Network Protocols

Table of Contents

Table of Contents

Table of Contents

Table of Contents

Table of Contents

Table of Contents

Table of Contents

Table of Contents

Table of Contents

Jini Client or Service	JavaSpaces and Helper Services
Jini Client and Service Support Helper Utilities	
Jini Discovery Management Helper Utilities	
Jini Protocol Helper Utilities	

Jini Network Protocols	
	RMI and Rich Object Semantics
	Java VM and Networking

Network Protocols

Introduction

Welcome

Welcome to *Professional Jini*. This book presents in one single volume everything that a Java programmer will need to start designing and programming with Jini or JavaSpaces technology, including the required confidence and conviction as provided by an exciting survey of current and on-going Jini/JavaSpaces projects.

Who Is This Book For?

This book is for intermediate-to-advanced Java programmers who are interested in network programming, and who are keen to leverage the new power that Jini brings to the distributed computing world.

What's Covered In This Book?

This book is divided into four sections. The first three consist of a set of chapters with a common theme, and the last section contains useful reference material. We outline the first three sections below:

Section 1: Introduction, Background, and Motivation

This section provides the necessary background information on Java's in-built support for network programming because, without it, Jini could not exist. It begins with a description of socket-based communication that leads naturally into a detailed treatment of RMI, Java's Remote Method Invocation, and shows that it is complementary, rather than competitive, to existing distributed technologies such as CORBA.

Section 2: Core Technology

The chapters in this section provide a comprehensive coverage of the Jini and JavaSpaces technologies. Using lots of code examples, it will guide you through the details of all the important concepts for these new technologies, and describe the utilities and tools supplied by Sun that ease their development. By the end of this section, you will already have coded a range of Jini clients and services, and be able to design systems of distributed services and write distributed applications using JavaSpaces.

Section 3: Applying Jini and JavaSpaces in the Real World

In this section, leading developers take us through their design and implementation of Jini and JavaSpaces in their particular problem's domain, and share with us the real-world practical issues they had to deal with. From this section you will see that not only is Jini providing us with a glimpse into the future, but that it is already here and being exploited to its full.

What Do You Need To Use this Book?

Hardware

Make sure you have at least 64MB of memory on your machine before trying this, as we will eventually be starting three lookup service instances on the same machine. This should be your minimum machine configuration for running all of the samples in this book.

Many readers will be using Windows 98, Windows 2000, Windows 95 or Windows NT to test the programs in this book. Most of our code and coverage will be adapted for testing in these Win32 environments. However, there are samples that have been adapted for use on Linux systems.

Software

This book uses Jini 1.1 (currently in beta version at time of writing) and JDK 1.2.2, the Java platform upon which Jini has been thoroughly tested. Jini will not work on versions of Java prior to JDK 1.2.2.

Most of the examples covered in this book will also work using Jini on JDK 1.3, the most recent version of the Java platform. The appendices contain versioning issues, and show how to emulate the required JDK 1.2.2 behavior with JDK 1.3.

- ❑ Jini 1.1 beta can be downloaded from http://www.jini.org/.
- ❑ The Java Development Kit (JDK) Standard Edition can be downloaded from http://java.sun.com/.

The bulk of the book only requires Java and Jini. However, some chapters use additional software tools. Chapter 3 uses the Java Secure Sockets Extension, or JSSE, available at http://java.sun.com/products/jsse. The CORBA discussion in Chapter 4 relies on new features present only in JDK 1.3. It also uses VisiBroker, a Java ORB from Visigenic (http://www.inprise.com/), and Red Hat Linux 6.2 (http://www.redhat.com/, containing a C ORB called ORBit that is also available separately at http://www.labs.redhat.com/orbit/).

Source Code Download

All of the code presented in this book can be freely downloaded from the Wrox web site at

> http://www.wrox.com/

Many useful batch files are provided to ease the running of some of the programs. The code from the case study chapters can also be found here.

On-Line Discussion

When learning another new and exciting technology, you will undoubtedly want to discuss its potential and all its possibilities with other pioneering programmers. P2P provides a Programmer to Programmer   on-line discussion forum on a wide range of programming-related topics, including Jini and JavaSpaces. Find it at http://p2p.wrox.com/.

Conventions

To help you get the most from the text and keep track of what's happening, we've used a number of conventions throughout the book.

For instance:

> **These boxes hold important, not-to-be forgotten information which is directly relevant to the surrounding text.**

While the background style is used for asides to the current discussion.

As for styles in the text:

> When we introduce them, we **highlight** important words.
>
> We show keyboard strokes like this: *Ctrl-A*.
>
> We show filenames and code within the text like so: writeObject()
>
> Text on user interfaces and URLs are shown as: Menu.

Example code is shown:

```
In our code examples, the code foreground style shows new, important, pertinent
code,
while code background shows code that's less important in the present context, or
has been seen before.
```

A Note on Spelling

This book is written in US English, apart from the word 'marshalled'. In US English, it is spelled 'marshaled', with one occurrence of the letter 'l', whereas in UK English it is spelled 'marshalled', with two 'l's. Due to a quirk in the writing of Jini, the MarshalledObject uses the UK spelling of the word. We have also used the UK English spelling of 'marshalled' within the text in order to avoid any potential confusion over its spelling.

Tell Us What You Think

We've worked hard to make this book as useful to you as possible, so we'd like to know what you think. We're always keen to know what it is you want and need to know.

We appreciate feedback on our efforts and take both criticism and praise on board in our future editorial efforts. If you've anything to say, let us know at:

feedback@wrox.com

or

http://www.wrox.com

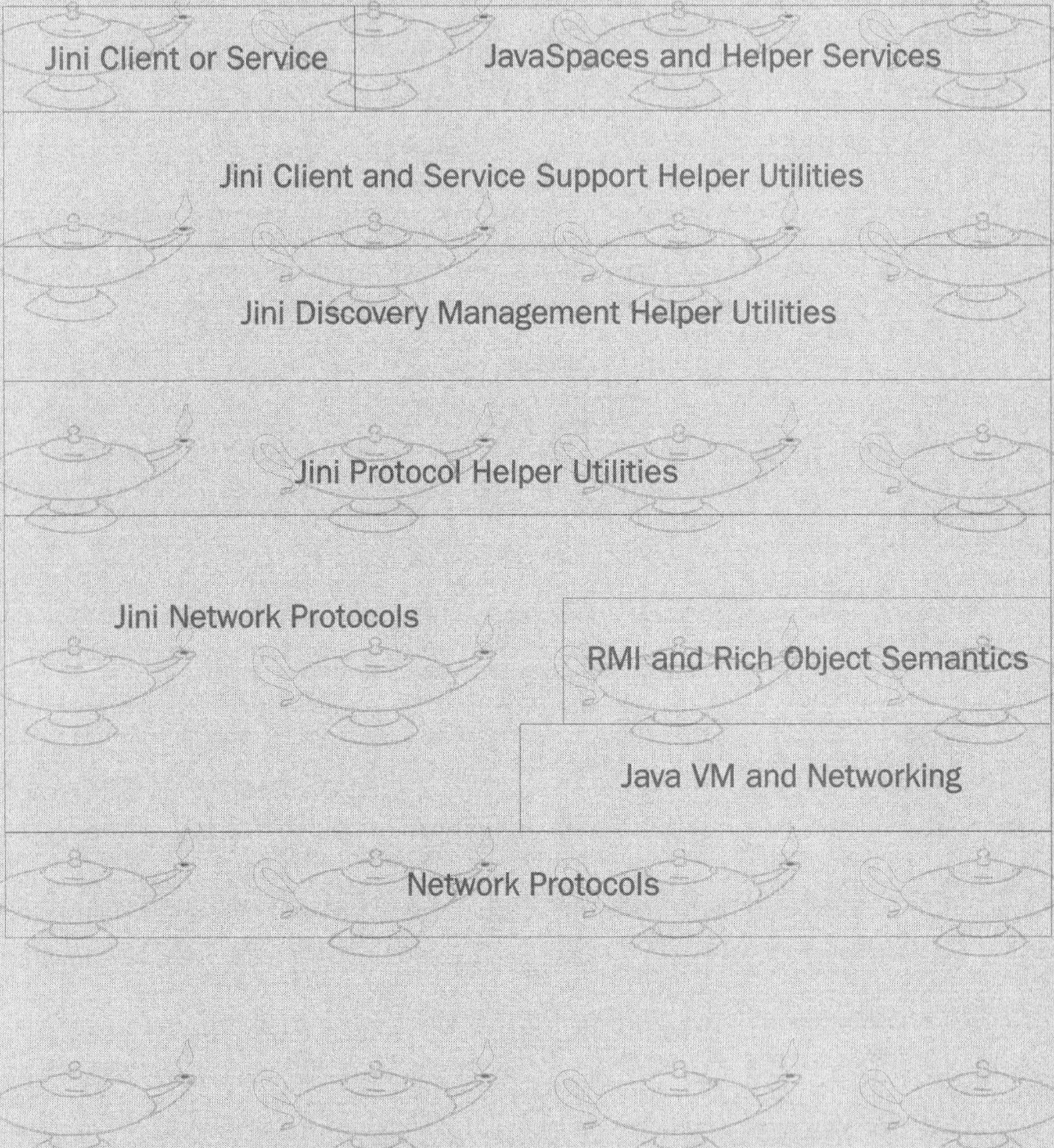

Jini Client or Service
JavaSpaces and Helper Services
Jini Client and Service Support Helper Utilities
Jini Discovery Management Helper Utilities
Jini Protocol Helper Utilities
Jini Network Protocols
RMI and Rich Object Semantics
Java VM and Networking
Network Protocols

Online discussion at http://p2p.wrox.com

Section 1

Introduction, Background, and Motivation

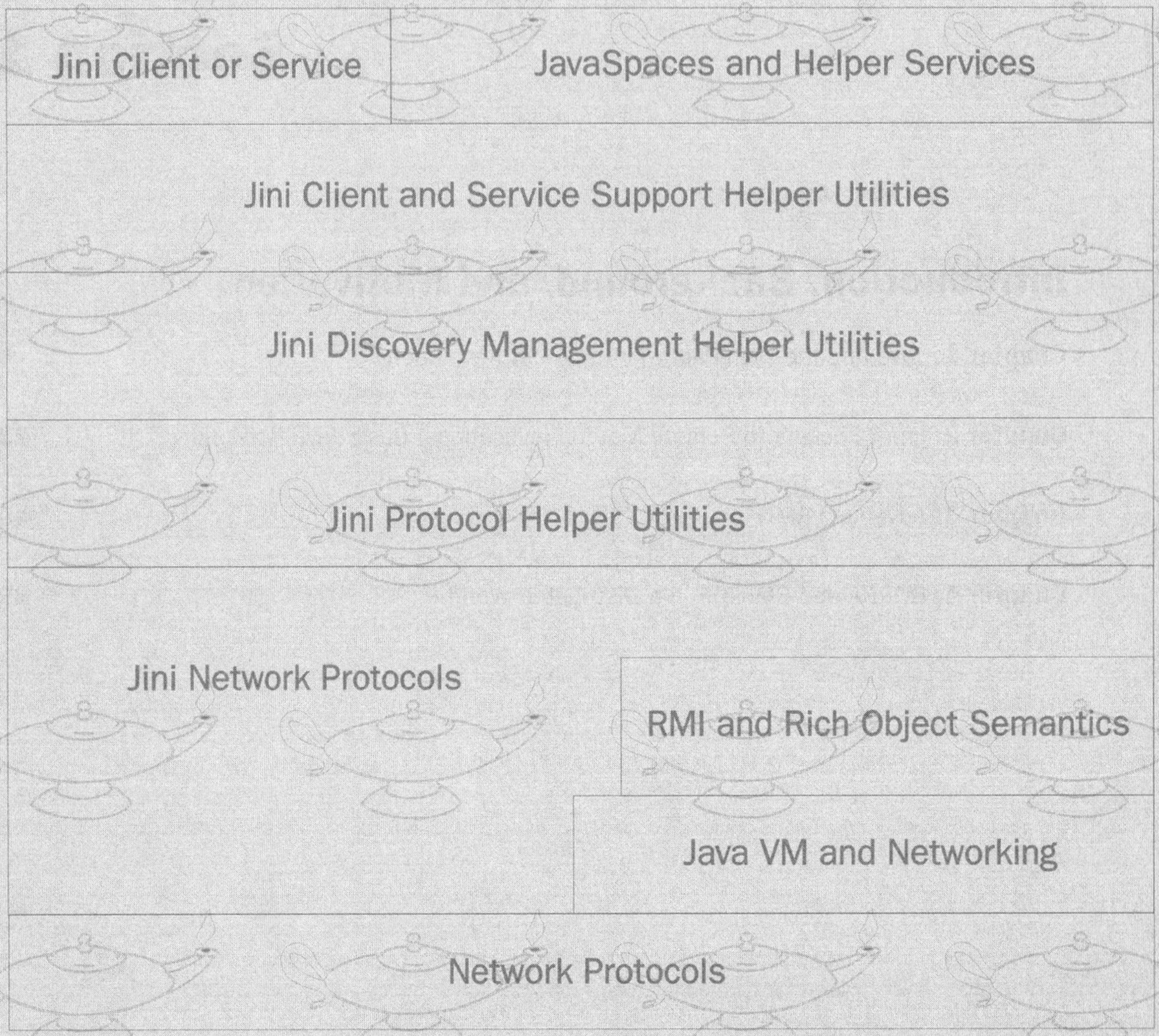

Jini Client or Service	JavaSpaces and Helper Services

Jini Client and Service Support Helper Utilities

Jini Discovery Management Helper Utilities

Jini Protocol Helper Utilities

Jini Network Protocols

RMI and Rich Object Semantics

Java VM and Networking

Network Protocols

Java and the High-Bandwidth Internet Revolution

'You can lead them to water, but you can't make them drink...'

The Internet, connecting millions of people worldwide, simultaneously, around the clock, has dramatically changed the way we live our lives – and will continue to do so. By providing a significantly more efficient information delivery and business transaction infrastructure, it has changed forever the way companies do business, both with customers and one another. As futurists and economists had been portending, the 'networked economy' is finally upon us. Yet, somewhat peculiarly, the software technology created to support it has changed very little since the TCP/IP era of the 1970s. As our understanding of how best to utilize the medium matures, there are gaping holes in the current networking software infrastructure that need to be filled.

Product of the Bandwidth Revolution

We are fast approaching the dream of the telecommunication visionaries of the previous decade, a dream that came about with the convergence of data with telecommunications, of the Internet with TV. These visionaries talked of 'fiber optics to the curb', the dream of bringing unlimited bandwidth, of bringing thousands of TV-channel signals to every home. Although it has arrived about ten years too late, this dream is finally being realized. However, a few key differences should be noted:

❑   The Internet, not the TV, is the driving force behind bringing high bandwidth into the home

❑   It is technology based on existing copper wire (xDSL and cable modems), not on fibre optics, that is carrying this high bandwidth – bandwidth that is TCP/IP data traffic, not digital TV signals

Even though many of us are connecting to the Internet – at work, at least – at 1 Mbps (mega-bits per second) or faster, we tend to spend our time on-line in much the same way as we did in the days of 14, 400 bps connection speeds over analog phone lines: simply downloading files, viewing web pages, perusing bulletin board systems, shopping on-line, joining chat rooms, and so on. Curiously, software is taking its time in catching up with technology, and only very recently have we seen software systems that are specially designed to leverage this new level of connectivity.

Interestingly, even though the evolution of the Internet has progressed through connectivity and networking software technology, the final step of bringing high-speed connectivity to the home is pretty much a revolutionary one. While evolutionary steps simply bring yesterday's software in line with today's requirements, revolutions require that the basics be re-thought, and that the fundamentals re-designed. Responding to this drastic change takes time, and what we are seeing now is only the very tip of the iceberg: **Jini** is a harbinger of things to come in applied distributed computing.

To understand why this is the case, we need to take a brief look at the three decades leading to the final revolution. The following timeline shows how the degree of connectivity between users of computers and computer systems has varied throughout this period.

1960s to 70s

- ❑ The architecture was Dumb Form terminals networked to specialized concentrators networked to mainframes.

- ❑ Financial institutions, the insurance industry, and very large corporations used them.

- ❑ They had to be installed in offices with specialized and monitored cooling rooms for the highly sensitive equipment.

- ❑ The computers had hundreds or even thousands of people using them – in exceptional cases, up to tens of thousands of people would be expected to use the same computer.

Late 1970s

- ❑ The architecture changed to mini-computers or super-microcomputers with dumb terminals, smart terminals, or graphic workstations connected directly or via concentrator boxes. Many of these interacted via the mainframe, but with a less tightly coupled basis than previously; occasionally, they would act as terminal emulators for the mainframe applications.

- ❑ Medium-sized enterprises that could afford and justify the capital outlay in equipment and software licensing joined the larger firms in utilizing this technology.

- ❑ They could now be installed in offices without a specialized computing room. They were even occasionally found on shop floors, warehouses, etc. The smaller size and less stringent environmental requirement of these machines allowed them to be installed almost anywhere. Analog modems allowed remote operation using dumb terminals.

- ❑ In exceptional cases, thousands of people were expected to use the same computer, but usually it was in the tens or hundreds.

Early 1980s

- ❑ By this stage, microcomputers with Graphical User Interfaces were capable of running office applications directly. Word processing, spreadsheets, presentation, and small databases were the mainstay. 'Islands of machines' were connected together via Local Area Networks (LANs) to share large disks, printers and other resources. They may still have connected to mini-computers, super-micro servers, or mainframes in an ad-hoc manner.

❑ Now easily available to small sized enterprises. Almost every business could afford a micro-computer. The allure of starting small and growing to mini or mainframe-like capacity implied that the computing system could easily grow with the business; reassuring the business owner that their apparently incremental investment in software and machinery would not go to waste.

❑ Computers could now be found at work, and on almost every desk. Analog modems allowed remote operation from home or other remote locations. Notebook computers allowed operation at work, on the road, and at home.

❑ Now we'd entered the domain of one person per computer. Hundreds or thousands connect on each LAN. Thousands or tens of thousands would be on each WAN (Wide Area Network), connecting the enterprise as a whole.

Late 1980s to 90s

❑ Easy to use micro-computers with graphical user interfaces running office and home-based applications made computers even more widespread. Many productivity tools and utilities had become available. These home computers were typically not connected in a local area network. Analog modems were used to dial-up and access on-line services.

❑ The ranks of those owning computers expanded to include affluent home users, early adopters of technology, and hobbyists. Some businesses also installed such computers for their VIP employees as an early form of telecommuting.

❑ Notebook computers allowed operation at work, on-the-road, and at home. Telecommuting entered the mainstream.

❑ One or more person per computer. On-line services connected hundreds or thousands of users together on an occasional basis. E-mail, BBS, and Chat rooms flourished.

Year 2000 and Beyond

❑ Inexpensive home micro-computers and digital appliances networked together at home are commonplace. The network is extended via the Internet at high speed to other networks, or to share the vast array of services, information bases and resources that are available through the connected world.

❑ Computers become ubiquitous. Home users, students in schools (all grades), workers in their offices, and more all have access to them.

❑ They can be found at home, in public places such as libraries, airports, cafes, etc. Primary mode of operation is via connection to the Internet.

❑ One person per computer. Dial up or permanent connections to the Internet. Anywhere from tens to hundred thousands, or even millions of users per service on the Internet. Email, BBS and Chat rooms are still the mainstay; but many innovative and new services are adopted rapidly. E-Commerce activities flourish.

It is this final step – the fulfillment of the always accessible, highly connected, wide bandwidth world – that, in effect, makes distributed technologies like Jini inevitable. Clients want to be able to connect to the network anywhere, at any time, and to make use of the services that the network makes available. They need a distributed service network that is robust as well as dynamic, scalable but doesn't get thrown by failing, or indeed potentially abusive, equipment. The Jini services network fulfills these requirements.

Java: Providing the Networking Substrate

Java, in the form of a network computing platform, has brought interactivity to the web through Java applets and middle-tier server technologies such as those provided through J2EE (Java 2 Enterprise Edition).

Java, as a software development platform, has dramatically increased programmer productivity through a simple, well-designed language and execution environment. It allows software engineers to focus on solving application problems, rather than contorting to programming language calisthenics.

Java's support for pure object oriented programming and design has accelerated by leaps and bounds the rate with which a concept can be turned into an implementation. The Java platform's built-in support for networking has single handedly put the power of TCP/IP networking and distributed object programming into the hand of every programmer, engineer, and student; and it did it in such an easy-to-try manner that experimentation was only natural.

This doesn't change the fact, however, that the way distributed systems tend to be constructed – or until very recently, anyway – dates back a couple of decades. Internet-based companies are now directly handling and interacting with millions of customers every single day. Many of these companies are discovering that the conventional distributed computing model has severe scaling limitations, and very primitive robustness properties. The cost of a system that has high scalability and robustness can be exorbitant (due to the requirement of custom expert design and configuration). The conventional way of building distributed systems is too inadequate and inflexible to handle the requirements of the new networked economy that has been brought about by the Internet evolution.

Jini: Towards Truly Distributed Systems

Jini was conceived as the foundation upon which robust, truly distributed systems can be built. Jini is nothing without a network – in fact, by definition, Jini doesn't exist outside of a network.

What is Jini? Jini is a framework for building scalable, robust, distributed systems (using Java). It consists of a set of specifications describing the model of operation for a Jini network, including the related protocols, classes, interfaces, helper utilities and services. A Jini network is a network of many services. Applications are created by dynamically combining these services in groupings called **federations**. The following diagram depicts a Jini network:

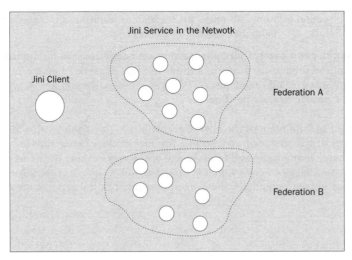

In the figure above, a Jini network consists of a large group of services running on diverse machines throughout a network (represented by circles on the right hand side).

These services are dynamically grouped (via configuration) into two federations: Federation A and Federation B. The Jini client may use the services provided by either federation. Before using a service, the Jini client will join one of the federations, as shown in the following diagram:

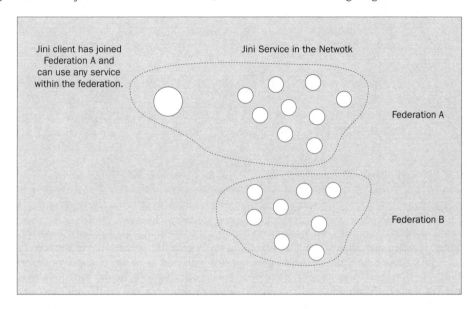

Here, the Jini client has joined Federation A and will have access to any service available within that federation. At a later time, it can decide to leave Federation A and join Federation B, thus gaining access to services and resources available in Federation B.

Inside the federation, the Jini client locates a service through an intermediary service called a **lookup** service. Querying the lookup service is known as lookup, and a client lookup is typically performed based on functionality. That is, the Jini client tells the lookup service what function (or work) it wants the service to perform (using a Java interface, base class, or attached property), and the lookup service will return a service within a federation that satisfies the request. Once located, the client can work directly with the service to get that work done. The figure over shows this in action:

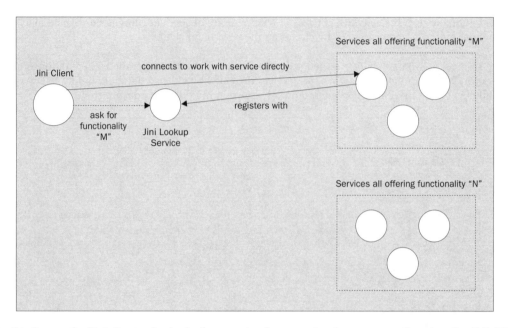

In this figure, the Jini client asks the lookup service for a service that supports functionality 'M'. The lookup service finds a matching service by searching the registrations of available services that it maintains. Every service on a Jini network must register with one or more lookup services within the federation. Note that there may be more than one service offering a particular functionality. This is where some of Jini's fault resilience and scalability comes from. One can easily add new services offering functionality 'M' to the network to scale with client demands. One can also implement robust systems by having multiple services on different hardware providing the same functionality to clients.

Any service in a Jini network may make use of other service(s) in performing its own work. This means that a Jini service can also be a client of another Jini service. The lookup service decouples the client-to-server relationship, enabling distributed dynamic configuration and reconfiguration. Sun provides a reference implementation of a lookup service (called reggie) with the Jini development kit.

Jini provides every programmer, engineer, and student who has mastered Java network programming a place to experiment with solutions to the world's newest and toughest networking problems. It puts an easy to use distributed network construction kit, which positively encourages experimentation, into the hands of those that will most likely benefit from it. The basic concepts encapsulated in the Jini architecture are exactly the same as those that will lead toward the new networked digital economy or, more precisely, a service-based (via Application Service Providers) network economy.

This book will attempt to unravel the apparent mystery surrounding Jini. You will discover that the concepts of Jini are simple, yet powerfully elegant. It models a new way for people to work together – through dynamic collaborations over the Internet. It models how businesses and corporations seek to work more efficiently – by recruiting and making use of resources only when their services are needed, and releasing them immediately afterwards. You will also discover through working with Jini that creating systems based on Jini technology is no more daunting a task than your very first encounter with Java network programming itself.

The Evolution of Java

The networking-centric design of the Java platform had provided the catalyst for application developers to design applications that make use of the network. Java provides a highly productive environment for creating and deploying these network based applications. Java's rich object model is naturally extended by RMI (Remote Method Invocation) across networks and physical Virtual Machine boundaries, enabling design of distributed applications that can leverage the natural model of collaborating networked objects. Jini takes all of this to the next level.

Leveraging on Java, RMI, and years of distributed systems research and design experience, Jini provides the support to build robust distributed computing systems out of a network of collaborating objects. The programming conventions, protocols, libraries, and services that form Jini enable designers to build distributed systems in the very truest sense, in that such a system:

- ❑ Has no single point of failure

- ❑ Is available, once set up, for the foreseeable future: 'once up, never down' operation mode

- ❑ Is tolerant to partial network or software failure

- ❑ Is self-healing, in that it won't grind to a halt because of an unexpected disruption somewhere in the distributed system

- ❑ Combines networked computing resources to boost computing throughput and the system's scalability

- ❑ Utilizes networked computing resources efficiently by federating (that is, forming into a federation, or group) on-demand the services required to solve a computing problem, and then releasing them immediately after completion

By extending the computational capability of a single Java VM to the computational capacity available when all the Java VMs within a network work together, Jini has the capability to transform any network, including the Internet, into a formidable computing resource. One may say that Jini provides the plumbing to convert the network into the computer.

Applying Jini to Networked 'Instant On' Plug-and-Work Device Support

One application of Jini, immediately useful, is in the realm of what Sun refers to as 'instant on' plug-and-work network devices. This is achieved by making each network-accessible device an individual Jini service (either directly via a Java VM on the machine, or via a wrapper or surrogate on the VM connected to the actual device), so that they are instantly 'on the network' as soon as they are plugged in. The following inherent properties of Jini make it ideal for supporting plug-and-work network devices:

- ❑ The ability to add a service and/or client at any time without affecting the operation of the network

- ❑ The ability to remove a service at anytime, either gracefully or abruptly, and have the network self-heal over time

- ❑ The ability for the client and service to move between different physical locations on the same network

❏   The decoupling of client and service via the lookup service enables multiple services to offer the same functionality

Translated into the specific device plug-and-work problem domain, we have the following very desirable networked device-driver features:

❏   Can connect client and devices at any time to the network without affecting the on-going operation of a network

❏   An unanticipated and occasional disruptive client or device disconnection, device failure or network failure, will not have a detrimental impact upon the long term stability of the network and the networked devices

❏   Clients and devices can be moved freely; furthermore, a client can connect to a device that it knows about in advance anywhere in the network as long as the device is connected and operational

❏   It enables a roaming, occasionally-connected client to select from a palette of available services (maybe even presented to a human user through a GUI) all offering the same functionality

Since Jini technology can be applied to plug-and-work networked devices immediately and offers a desirable feature set, most of the promoted mainstream applications of Jini tends to revolve around device connections. Overall, device connection is a very narrow (albeit important) application of the Jini technology.

This book aims to provide an appreciation of what Jini technology can be applied to in the real world, both inside and potentially outside of any immediate revenue-generating commercial ventures. We will also provide some coverage on using Jini for device drivers in Chapter 12. To see many more potential applications of the Jini technology, one needs to visit the Jini site (or 'revolution central') at http://www.jini.org/. Here you will find thousands of designers and application engineers working on a diverse domain of applications using Jini technology. Sun has turned over the source code and much of the evolution of Jini-based technologies to this public group. If you want to help shape the future, then this is the group to join.

What is Covered in this Book?

Our approach to Jini within this book is to build the picture from the bottom up, one step at a time, one layer at a time, each building on the last. The figure below illustrates this layering.

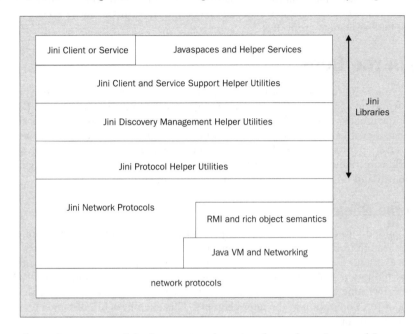

At the lowest layer, just on top of the bare network protocols, we have Java and Java networking. This layer provides programming support on the network protocol level. Programming on this level can be universal. It can be used to program network protocols that will be compatible with any non-Java specific communicating service/device. Jini defines some new protocols on this level. These protocols enable the dynamic discovery and formation of Jini services into federations.

The next level up is unique to Java, and it support Java's rich object semantics over the network protocols. This layer is called the RMI (Remote Method Invocation) layer. It allows one to extend many concepts unique to the Java Virtual Machine (VM) across the network (that is, it enables objects to be passed by value or by reference across different VMs). Jini services can make use of this layer to implement flexible and maintainable networking logic.

Built on top of (and parallel to) the previous layers, Jini provides a rich code library of helper utilities to support the creation of Jini clients and services. The libraries themselves can be divided up into multiple layers. The lowest layer supports Jini programming on the network protocol level. The next layer provides an object-based programming abstraction encapsulating the discovery and federation-forming process. The next layer provides library support for managing many of the network resources (that is, connections). At the highest level, the 'chores' required (by the Jini specifications) of a Jini client or Jini service are completely abstracted. The libraries are role specific, supporting either Jini client programming or Jini service programming. The libraries take care of much of the tedious programming required to build these Jini components, leaving the developer focused on the core logic of the component.

Finally, Jini application design is about distributed systems design. A Jini system takes advantage of all the lower layers of library and protocol support to implement the degree of scalability, robustness, and fault resilience that is appropriate to the application. To help in making such a design easy, Jini has provided a Jini service that offers distributed programming support at a very high level of abstraction. It is called **JavaSpaces**. JavaSpaces supports a distributed systems operation by providing conceptual network-wide stores of objects. These stores can be configured with various degrees of robustness, scalability and fault resilience properties.

Sections in the Book

The book is divided into four sections. In the first section of this book – this section – we will begin with basic Java networking, and discuss the networking features built into JDKs 1.2+ and JDK 1.3. Building upon this solid Java-network grounding, section two thoroughly examines the networked systems architecture that is enabled by Jini technology, and illustrates this with plenty of examples. This section covers all the layers pertaining to the Jini libraries and system design. In the third section, we'll look at some real-world case studies from pioneering engineers already using the technology in their product or design. The fourth and final section includes some useful appendices.

Chapters in the Book

Chapter 2 is a guided tour through the basics of **Java networking**, all the way from raw socket-based programming through to RMI. Although this tour will be a refresher for some readers, it is detailed enough to serve as a fundamental introduction for those new to Java-based network programming. Jini is a technology built on top of basic Java networking, so many of Jini's foundations depend on this technology base. Visiting (or revisiting) the pertinent topics will expedite our discussion and understanding of Jini's operation in the later chapters. This chapter is full of hands-on examples in order to illustrate the discussion.

Chapter 3 will continue our **RMI** coverage, demonstrating several advanced RMI concepts. The main focus will be on the new JDK 1.2 `activatable` objects that are fundamental to Sun's reference Jini services implementations. We will see how `activatable` objects can be used for building services that automatically restart and recover after a crash (once the machine and RMI daemon have been restarted), or to build services that are started only on-demand. The chapter will also cover pragmatic techniques used in real-world Jini network programming. These techniques are used to secure Java network communications, including RMI over SSL, and deal with RMI tunneling through firewalls. We will work with plenty of code samples along with the basic concepts.

Chapter 4 introduces **CORBA** (Common Object Request Broker Architecture) and discusses the premises behind its design, explaining the relationship between RMI, CORBA and Jini. We will look at the areas of functionality overlap between CORBA and RMI, as well as the areas of each that complement and enhance the operations of the other. We will work with the JDK CORBA ORB (Object Request Broker) that has come with every JDK release since the JDK 1.1.x level. Highlighting the cross-vendor heterogeneous interoperability provided by CORBA, we'll create a couple of software components that use ORB, from Visigenic, and have them interoperate with components built using the JDK ORB.

We will also try out the cross-operating system cross-programming language interoperation support by creating a client in the C language, on the Linux operating system, using a third-party ORB called ORBit to interact and work with our Java-based services. Last but not least, the chapter will cover the latest enhancement to RMI and CORBA that has become an integral part of the JDK 1.3 distribution: RMI-IIOP. We will see how RMI and IIOP can work harmoniously alongside each other. This chapter concludes with a comprehensive table that compares the differences and similarities between RMI, CORBA, and Jini. By the end of this chapter, you should have a good understanding of the ways in which RMI, CORBA and Jini complement each other, and the tremendous value that they can add to Java networking.

Having laid the groundwork, *Chapter 5* begins Section 2, and our coverage of the **Jini technology** itself, starting with the very lowlevel protocols. The chapter describes in detail the Discovery and Join protocol suite that is used for the Jini discovery and bootstrap process. We will see the role that lookup services and Jini services are expected to play. We will examine the interaction of the protocols in the suite, and their dependence on IP-multicast will be documented. Through code samples, we will have an on-the wire examination of packets, and we will programmatically intercept and decode these packets.

We'll see how this all ties in with the sockets discussion from the fundamental Java networking chapter, and appreciate how the new protocols are built on top of the familiar ones. The special role of a lookup service, its importance to the entire Jini network – both for getting it together and running in the first place (bootstrapping) and to how it works afterwards – will also be examined in detail. We'll also meet the Join protocol, which stipulates a set of engineering conventions that a Jini service should conform to in order to ensure the smooth functioning of the network as a whole.

Chapter 6 is devoted to another service vital to every Jini network: the **lookup service**. We will examine in detail the role, anatomy, and workings of a lookup service, and also have a detailed discussion of lookup entries, proxies, attributes, and managed sets. This will lead us to appreciate lookup using a template, and understand why it is effective and sufficient for distributed applications. There will be plenty of sample code and small standalone samples throughout this chapter. We will see that a lookup service itself is a Jini service that follows the Join conventions.

Chapter 7 discusses a very important concept for designing Jini systems and working with the Jini libraries: **remote events**. Remote events in Jini extends the standard Java asynchronous notification model across Java VMs. We will see why the Jini specifications and provisions in this area are necessarily so 'thin' and simple. Remote events in Jini involves very few specified interfaces and base classes. Coding samples will illustrate the importance of several remote event details: event IDs and sequence numbers, especially when it pertains to the use of composable (the ability to chain event-processing agents together) third-party event-handling services. We will use a hands-on example to illustrate how to code distributed event receivers as well as senders.

Chapter 8 covers another one of the core concepts in the Jini operation model: **distributed leasing**. Distributed leasing enables services to grant resource allocation on behalf of a client based on a time-limited lease. The importance of distributed leases for ensuring the health of a distributed network will be explained. Using detailed coding examples, we will see how leases can be obtained (and granted). We will study the effects of lease expiration and renewal, both from the consumer and lease granter's perspectives. We will gain an appreciation for why leases are a simple way to solve rather complex distributed resource-management problems. The coverage will be open-ended, allowing us to use Jini to implement our own distributed leasing policies.

Chapter 9 covers **transactions** in Jini: the two-phase commit protocol (2PC), the associated interfaces dissected, and sample code presented that concentrates on interactions. We will discuss the ACID semantics from classic transaction theory, and show how Jini's transactions can be, but are not required to be, consistent with these semantics. We will realize that distributed transaction coordination is useful in many applications with or without the semantics of classic transaction theory. In this chapter, we will work with Sun's reference implementation of a transaction manager, codenamed mahalo. We will also be coding our own participant in a transaction.

Chapter 10 is the first chapter of two in which we provide an in-depth look into the use of Jini's **helper utilities** (libraries) and services. These libraries make the task of programming a Jini application substantially easier. We'll dispel the myth that coding a well-behaved Jini service is an exercise in managing complexity itself. The libraries covered in this chapter are low-level utilities that offer ready-to-use implementations of the basic protocols required by Jini, but yet afford maximum application control. We'll look at all of these helper utilities provided by Jini 1.1, how they work inside, and discover how to code with them. Each utility will be covered in detail and typical usage will be discussed along with sample code. Continuing our examination into the helper utilities, we cover the next level of Jini libraries. This set of libraries assists in managing discovery and federation management information, freeing the application from the management of this task.

Chapter 11 is the final chapter in examining helpers in the Jini library. Here, we look at the highest level libraries available. These libraries assume *all* the responsibility relating to handling the Jini discovery protocols for either a client or a service. These highest level helper utilities truly make creating a Jini service or client a simple affair. We then focus on independent **helper services** that are provided as part of the Jini extended platform. Each helper service is a fully-fledged, independent Jini service that provides assistance to services or other entities that wish to participate in a Jini network. One major use for these services is the support for activatable services that are only started on-demand. The helper services can maintain a Jini identity for these non-active services, even when the service itself is not running. We will show actual coding for each of these helper services. We will also show how to Jini-enable a CORBA service using these helper services as a bridge.

In *Chapter 12*, we will put all the concepts and tools that we have covered to use, by **experimenting** with different strategies that can be used to create Jini services. Techniques used in accommodating legacy systems will also be examined on a coding level. We will cover and present code for Jini services using local proxy objects, remote RMI-based proxy objects, and smart/custom proxy objects. We will demonstrate transitional legacy-service exporting by making an existing CORBA service available within a Jini community (via a custom proxy object). We will also code, from scratch, a custom protocol proxy that doesn't use any RMI at all, but instead uses a low level socket to implement its protocol. On a lower level, we will discuss how you might go about writing distributed device drivers, and show how this relates directly to the problem of writing Jini services. We will examine the Jini Surrogate architecture effort, and discuss how Jini-based network device drivers can be created. The chapter will also summarize the work of the current ServiceUI project, detailing how many distinct user interfaces can be attached to a Jini service (by the service itself or a third party). We will present a complete code example in order to illustrate how to attach and work with user interfaces according to the Service UI specification.

Chapter 13 covers the exciting **JavaSpace** service, and its operation. Its parallel computing heritage will be discussed. The basic operations available via the JavaSpace interface will each be illustrated with sample code. We will demonstrate the ways in which JavaSpace technology is useful as a shared object store in a distributed network. We'll also see how JavaSpaces enables an alternative approach to designing scalable, load-balanced, high throughput distributed systems. We'll also look at how you can utilize JavaSpace technology to build a generalized computational server. The chapter will include the coding of a distributed JavaSpace application.

Chapter 14 **wraps up** the technical chapters, and covers two of the current issues that Jini implementers must be conscious of. We will explain each of these issues in detail, and offer some hints as to how to deal with them in actual Jini system design. We will also talk about how they are likely to change in the near future.

The third section of this book presents various case studies written by modern software practitioners who've put Jini technology to work. They'll show how they've brought this cutting-edge technology into the workplace, and discuss the problems they've encountered along the way.

In *Chapter 15,* **Andrew Schneider** describes his first-hand experience of putting a Jini based system into production. His team had designed and deployed a large scale, dynamic, secure, **remote clinical data access** system in the UK. The system was re-engineered using Jini as a technology base. Andy shares with us how well (and sometimes not so well) some of the fundamental Jini pieces work together in a production environment.

In *Chapter 16,* **Jerome Scheuring** discusses the use of personalization software and digital profiling in the networked home environment. Jerome takes us through his companies reasons for using Jini, comparing it to EJBs (Enterprise Java Beans), and shows how they tackled the big questions of security within Jini.

In *Chapter 17,* **Bob Flenner** takes us through the Jini plumbing of his **JWorkPlace**, a distributed virtual community space for developers to interact, and to share both their code and their experiences. Bob will guide us through JWorkPlace's design rationale, and the role of the various components making up the system. This chapter includes detailed, code-level coverage of how JWorkPlace uses JavaSpaces and XML-based technologies to implement a distributed, globally-sharable code-fragment repository for workgroups.

In *Chapter 18,* **Mil Buurmeijer** and **Eric Hol** take us through their vision of **Jini on Wheels**, where the possible future integration of Jini technology into the car environment is examined. This involves integration with GPS (Global Positioning Service), TMC (Traffic Management Control), navigation systems, route planners and hand-held devices, and presents a glimpse into the future.

In our final case study, *Chapter 19,* **Ronald Ashri** (with **Michael Luck**) will take us through a fascinating system called **Paradigma**. It is an agent implementation environment designed on top of Jini technology. Through their detailed presentation, we will see how XML technology can be used to provide dynamic adaptability in the Paradigma system for agent designs. It will shed some light on how Jini itself can potentially be made more adaptive in the same fashion.

There are tens of thousands of new and yet-to-be-designed case-studies that we think will make Jini one of the most exciting and productive technologies of the new millennium. The material covered in this third section of the book should position you firmly in the driving seat of this new technology.

This book takes you to the water, it is up to you to drink.

Jini Client or Service	JavaSpaces and Helper Services

Jini Client and Service Support Helper Utilities

Jini Discovery Management Helper Utilities

Jini Protocol Helper Utilities

Jini Network Protocols	
	RMI and Rich Object Semantics
	Java VM and Networking

Network Protocols

2

From Sockets to Remote Method Invocation – Basic Java Networking

Jini is built on top of a solid foundation of Java networking technologies. Java networking itself has been available as part of Java since version 1.0 of the JDK Release (although Jini itself only works with JDK versions 1.2 and higher). In fact, Java is the first widely available language/platform that was designed with networking in mind right from day one. If we want to understand and fully explore all the possibilities with Jini/JavaSpaces, we must first be familiar with the networking foundation built into the Java platform.

In this chapter and the next, we will lay down a solid understanding of these foundations. For some readers, this may be a review. However, since our coverage will be brought all the way to the most recent Java 2 release, there may be new features that even the seasoned Java network programmer will find interesting.

Epitome of Java Networking: Sockets

The simplest and most direct way to program network applications using Java is through sockets. In the Java platform, socket programming provides the lowest level of application access to the networking substrate. Coding on the socket level provides the programmer with great flexibility in design, and powerful control over the traffic that actually flows across the network. However, the trade-off is in the complexity of coding. Often, higher-level programming layers – implemented on top of sockets – are the preferred solution since they mask a lot of this complexity.

Endpoint-to-Endpoint Communications

Sockets are conceptually communication endpoints on a network. They typically work across a network that supports the TCP/IP protocol; for example, the Internet. The analogy is rather obvious – a socket is a termination that one can plug into. One can visualize a communication channel as a wire 'plugged' between two sockets. In our case, the 'wire' will be a virtual connection that we can set up by making the appropriate socket library calls. The figure below illustrates this analogy.

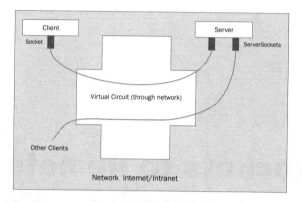

Each end point of the communication channel is associated with a port. One port is distinguished from another port by its number. In TCP/IP, port numbers are 16 bit numbers covering 0-65535. On almost every machine, a range of port numbers (usually between 1 and 1023) is reserved for well-known applications. Port numbers below 1024 are reserved for 'Unix specific' services like rlogin, while those below 256 are for the well know services like FTP, WWW, TELNET, and so on – for example, port 80 is the well-known port for connection to the World Wide Web service.

Communication occurs over the TCP/IP network when a pair of ports – on two separate machines – are connected via a virtual circuit. The port number of the two ports used in the communication need not be identical (or have any relationship at all). The software on one machine (called the **client**) connects to the other (called the **server**) by placing requests with the underlying TCP/IP software layers.

On the server machine, a server program is typically listening on a port for connection requests. The server program is often called a 'service'. Once a client request is received, the service can process the request and send back the result over the virtual circuit via the incoming socket. Thus, sockets are essentially a two-way communication mechanism (although they can be used for one way too).

The idea of using sockets as a programming abstraction originated at the University of Berkeley in the 1970s. It has since been adopted in most major operating systems, and it is an integral part of the Java platform. The sockets API truly simplifies the typically grueling low-level programming required on TCP/IP based applications.

There are actually two major types of TCP/IP connections that one can establish between two networked machines. One is a TCP connection, and the other is a UDP connection. A UDP connection is a datagram based connection. The UDP protocol sends single data packets (called a datagram) between the communicating machines. In a large congested network, the packets may arrive out of sequence, or not arrive at all at the destination machine. It is the responsibility of the software using UDP connection to cater for these problems. UDP is typically used for media streaming (for example, audio or video) applications. With these applications, the loss of packets is not detrimental to the proper functioning of the system. TCP connections are guaranteed as reliable end-to-end connections. All data sent through TCP connections are guaranteed to arrive at the other end, and in sequence – or an error is reported to the application. The sockets we deal with in this chapter are all based on TCP connections.

The JDK Socket Classes

The figure below shows a class diagram for the JDK socket classes. These are basic networking support classes, and have been part of the JDK since JDK 1.0.

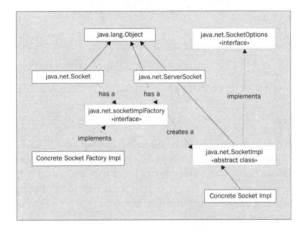

In network programming, we instantiate instances of `java.net.Socket` or `java.net.ServerSocket` directly. The figure above shows that internally they both use a `SocketFactory` to create a `SocketImpl` subclass for operations. This effectively allows the plug-in of different socket implementations at runtime. For example, a socket implementation that provides a secured connection (for example, SSL) can be substituted for the default socket implementation. We will focus our attention on the `Socket` and `ServerSocket` classes here, and will see how `SocketFactory` works in the next chapter.

Creating a Client Socket

One can create a client socket instance in the same way as for any other Java class. The constructor used in the example below specifies the server's host name (or IP address), and the service's connecting port:

```
Socket mySock = new Socket('server.wrox.com',8005);
```

There is no explicit 'open' method in the Socket class (but there is a 'close' method). Therefore, instantiation of Socket also triggers an attempt to establish the virtual circuit. This means that the statement above will cause the client to contact the service across the network at port 8005, and also attempt to establish the virtual circuit. In this case, if a connection is immediately successful, the Socket instance representing the client end of the virtual circuit is returned; otherwise, the operation will block waiting for the connection. Several exceptions may terminate this blocking wait, each for a different reason:

❑ An UnknownHostException may be thrown if the host name cannot be resolved by the network layer

❑ An IOException may be thrown if it is not possible to make the connection (after excessive retries and timeout)

❑ A SecurityException may be thrown if access to the port is not permitted by an installed SecurityManager

Reading and Writing to the Client Socket

As mentioned earlier, a socket supports bi-directional read/write across the network. Reading from an instance of a Socket can be done through a BufferedReader instance (a stream abstraction class from the **java.io** package):

```
BufferedReader myReader = new BufferedReader( new InputStreamReader(
    mySock.getInputStream()));
```

and writing to a socket can be done through a PrintWriter instance:

```
PrintWriter myWriter = new PrintWriter(mySock.getOutputStream(),true);
```

Plain text messages are not the only form of data that can be sent across a socket connection. If one wishes you could also use the InputStream and OutputStream instances to directly read and write bytes over the network, or use other higher level Readers and Writers to perform compression, object serialization, and so on as required. The idea of serializing objects over a virtual circuit and re-constituting it at the other end is a fascinating a lot of practical implications. We will have a lot more to say about this later.

Creating a Server Socket

The ServerSocket class can be used to listen to a specific port (on the local machine) for client connection requests. Upon a client connecting, it will return a Socket instance representing the endpoint of a connection (the server-side endpoint). This is done through the blocking accept() method.

ServerSocket Method	Description
accept()	This method will block waiting for a client to connect to the associated port. Upon a client connecting, it creates a Socket instance that represent the server-side connection of the newly established virtual circuit. The server side port associated with the Socket instance that is returned via the accept() method may not be the same port that the ServerSocket listens to.

A reference to a stream can be obtained from any instance of a `Socket`. There are two methods in the `Socket` class that make this possible:

Socket Method	Description
GetInputStream ()	Obtain an input stream from the socket to read from; data read is supplied directly from the other end point.
GetOutputStream ()	Obtain an output stream from the socket; data written can be retrieved directly from the other end point.

These become the input and output streams of the application. By mapping the network communication to input/output streams, the core logic of the application does not have to deal with the details of low-level communication.

On the coding level, you can create an instance of a `ServerSocket` using its constructor:

```
ServerSocket myServer = new ServerSocket(8005);
```

This will create an instance of a `ServerSocket` associated with port 8005 on the local machine, to be used for client connections. Once you've successfully created a `ServerSocket`, you can use it to listen to the port with:

```
Socket newClient = myServer.accept();
```

This `accept()` method call will be blocked waiting for client connections. Once a client connection has been established, `newClient` will reference the `Socket` instance representing the server-side endpoint of the virtual circuit. You may call its `getInputStream()` and `getOutputStream()` methods to read or write data through the virtual circuit..

Let us now apply the above knowledge in a very simple socket-based application.

A Simple Socket Application

The simple server, called `SockServer`, returns the current server date and time (obtained using the `java.util.Calendar` class) to the client as soon as a connection is made by that client.

Server Side Implementation

You can find the following source in the `SockServer.java` file in the `\ch2\code\socket\basic` directory of the code download which accompanies this book (from the Wrox web site at http://www.wrox.com/).

```
import java.io.PrintWriter;
import java.io.IOException;
import java.net.Socket;
import java.net.ServerSocket;
import java.util.Calendar;
```

```
class SockServer {
  public static void main(String[] args) {
    ServerSocket serv = null;
    Socket aConn = null;
    try {
      serv = new ServerSocket(8005);
```

We create the socket here on the port 8005. This port should be unused on most machines.

```
      while(true) {
        aConn = serv.accept();
        PrintWriter out = new PrintWriter(
          aConn.getOutputStream(), true);
        String curTime =
          Calendar.getInstance().getTime().toString();
        out.println("Connected to Server at " + curTime);
        System.out.println("A client connected at " + curTime);
        aConn.close();
      } // of while
```

The accept() call on the socket will block execution until a client makes a connection. When this happens, we create a PrintWriter from the socket's output stream and write the current server time in text form to the socket (that is, the connected client).

```
    } //of try
    catch (IOException e) {
      e.printStackTrace();
    }
  }
} // of SockServer
```

Client Side Implementation

This simple client will connect to port 8005 on the server system, and print out on the screen anything that the server returns. Our server will only return the current server date and time:

```
import java.io.BufferedReader;
import java.io.InputStreamReader;
import java.net.Socket;

class SockClient
{
  public static void main(String[] args) {
    Socket soc = null;
    String myLine;
    try {
      soc = new Socket("localhost", 8005);
      BufferedReader myIn = new BufferedReader(new
        InputStreamReader(soc.getInputStream()));
      while ((myLine = myIn.readLine()) != null)
        System.out.println(myLine);
    } //of try
    catch (Exception e) {
      e.printStackTrace();
    }
  }
} // of SockClient
```

The code highlighted (in bold) above creates the socket, connects to the server, and then performs `readLine()` until it returns null. This will happen when the server closes its side of the socket.

Testing the Socket Program

You can do the testing on the same machine, or on two machines. The code 'as is' will connect to a server on 'localhost'. This will allow you to test the system on one single machine. If you are trying this on two machines, make sure you have the name of the server host in your client program.

> **Before proceeding further, if you are using Win32, make sure you have an entry in your hosts file that reads:**
>
> **localhost 127.0.0.1**
>
> **You can find the hosts file under <windows>/system on Windows 95/98 or under <windows>/system32/drivers/etc on Windows NT. Some versions of the JDK will not be able to resolve the localhost host name if this is not done. If you are testing on two machines, you should make sure the name and IP address of the other connected machine is also in this hosts file.**

Compile the `SockServer.java` and `SockClient.java` files:

```
javac *.java
```

And then run the server:

```
java SockServer
```

Finally run the client in a separate window:

```
java SockClient
```

You should see output on the server and client consoles similar to the figures below:

> If you encounter 'class not found' exceptions, try to make sure that your CLASSPATH environment variable contains '.' or the current directory in its list.

A Busier Server

That was interesting, but let us now look at simulating a busier server to illustrate a potential problem with this simplistic design. Here is the modification to our SockServer.java code; you can find the modified code in the source code download from the Wrox web site as BusyServer.java under the \ch2\code\socket\busy\ directory.

```
while(true) {
  aConn = serv.accept();
  PrintWriter out = new PrintWriter(
    aConn.getOutputStream(), true);
  String curTime =
    Calendar.getInstance().getTime().toString();
  System.out.println('A client connected at ' + curTime);
  for (int i=0; i< 60; i++)
  {
    curTime =
      Calendar.getInstance().getTime().toString();
    out.println("Message from Server at " + curTime);
    try {
      Thread.sleep(1000);
    }
    catch(InterruptedException e){
      e.printStackTrace();
    }
  }
  aConn.close();
}
```

Instead of writing out the server time to the client just once, it will write it out sixty times and wait one second between each write. This represents a server that is actually doing some useful work that will consume a non-negligible amount of time.

Testing out the Busier Server

Compile this server:

```
javac BusyServer.java
```

Now, run one instance of this server. Then start an instance of the client from the 'basic' program:

```
java BusyServer
java SockClient
```

While the client is printing the time from the server, try to start another instance of the client (in a separate window):

```
java SockClient
```

What you should observe is:

❑   the second instance does not start until the first one terminates

❑   the server can only service one client at a time

❑   new clients are 'blocked' from connecting until the server is free

In fact, one of the constructors of a ServerSocket has the following signature:

```
ServerSocket(int port, int backlog);
```

The second argument to this constructor is the backlog; it controls the number of clients that are allowed to block waiting for the server. If the backlog is ever exceeded, the connection from any additional clients will be refused, causing an IOException on the client end. In our code, since we used a constructor without the backlog argument, the system defaults to allowing up to 50 backlogged clients.

This is an obviously unacceptable design for production. If the service that we have implemented is a web server, this will mean that we can only service one hit per server at any time. What we really need is a way to service multiple requests at the same time. We want to get back to the accept() call as soon as possible in the loop in order to service another customer.

The solution is to design a multi-threaded server.

Servicing Multiple Clients Concurrently

The pseudo-code for a multi-threaded server is:

```
loop
    block and wait for a client connection
    spin off a thread to handle the client
end loop
```

The code that implements this can be found as MtServer.java in the source code download under the \socket\mthread directory for this chapter. It is listed below:

```
import java.io.*;
import java.net.*;
import java.util.Calendar;


public class MtServer implements Runnable {
  Socket sockInst;
```

Note that now the MtServer class implements the Runnable interface: this allows the run() method to contain the actual work that each server thread will perform. Later, when we create the thread to work on the request, we can simply pass an instance of this class as work to do.

```
public MtServer(Socket insock) {
    sockInst = insock;
}
```

The constructor above sets the `Socket` instance that the methods in the class will operate on. We pass it into the constructor because there is no general way of passing parameters between execution threads; otherwise, it would be a different `Socket` instance for each client request.

```
public void run() {
try {
  PrintWriter out = new PrintWriter(
    sockInst.getOutputStream(), true);
  String threadName = Thread.currentThread().getName();
  String curTime =
    Calendar.getInstance().getTime().toString();
  System.out.println(threadName + ": A client connected at "
    + curTime);
  for (int i=0; i< 60; i++) {
    curTime = Calendar.getInstance().getTime().toString();
    out.println(threadName + ": Message from Server at " +
      curTime);
    try {
      Thread.sleep(1000);
    }
    catch(InterruptedException e){
      e.printStackTrace();
    }
  }
  sockInst.close();
} //of try
catch (Exception e)  {
  e.printStackTrace();
}

}
```

We have moved all the work formerly in the service's `main()` method to this `run()` method. This is the work method for each of the threads. Note that the `Socket` instance is closed after work is completed, releasing the virtual circuit and the port.

```
public static void main(String[] args) {
  int threadCounter = 1;
  ServerSocket serv = null;
  Socket aConn = null;
  try {
    serv = new ServerSocket(8005);
    while(true) {
      aConn = serv.accept();
      new Thread(new MtServer(aConn), "Thread #" +
        threadCounter++).start();
    }
  } // of try
  catch(Exception e) {
    e.printStackTrace();
  }
}
}
```

The while loop containing the blocking `accept()` call is still in the `main()` method. However, the server now creates a new thread and a new instance of the `MtServer` class for each request. The loop completes very quickly, and the server is immediately ready to handle another client's request. Note how the new instance of the `MtServer` class is passed into the constructor of the new thread. This is possible because `MtServer` implements the `Runnable` interface that the thread requires.

The second argument for the thread constructor is the (optional) name of the thread. We assign a unique and always increasing number to each thread and put it in its name. This allows us to track the thread that actually serviced our client.

Testing the Multithreaded Service

Now, we can repeat the test we did for the `BusyServer`:

1. Compile all code

2. Start an instance of the server

3. Start two or more instances of the client, one after another

Now all clients will get the attention of the server immediately. You can also see that each client is serviced by a new and different thread (from the thread name that is also printed).

Finally, this implementation is significantly closer to a production service implementation, but there are still problems with this design.

System Failure under Production Torture Test

In production systems, unless the system is relatively lightly loaded (as in our test situation), our multi-threaded service implementation will fail miserably. Why is this the case?

Here are three major reasons:

❑ A new thread is created for each request. Thread creation is a very expensive operation – impacting performance on a highly loaded system.

❑ The design relies on the system doing garbage collection on the 'used threads' as we cycle through them handling user requests. Unfortunately, on a highly loaded system the Java VM may not be able to perform garbage collection in time to reclaim the threads and associated resources.

❑ There is no control on the total number of threads used at any time – the system can be 'drowned' if many requests come in within a very short period of time – all the system resources can be used up in creating threads and holding thread states.

Together, these forces will ensure that our service has a highly dissatisfied user population. In order to solve these problems, most modern production servers actually use this technique: they implement a fixed pool of 'worker threads' to service user requests

Note that this design has the following benefits:

1. Creation of threads is done at the initialization time, when the pool of threads is created – there is no hit in performance during normal operation.

2. The number of threads servicing client requests remains constant, so the system will never be overwhelmed.

3. There is no garbage collection issue with the threads, since no new threads need to be created during service operation.

While fascinating, the coding for a thread-pooled service is beyond the scope of this chapter. The interested reader is encouraged to try their own implementation, since it is a great learning opportunity that also has major production implications (see *Professional Java Server Programming, ISBN 1861002777* from Wrox Press for code samples and an in-depth discussion of thread pooling).

Generic Work Service: Making Our Servers More Flexible

Another limitation of all our service code so far is the fact that all the 'work to perform' logic is hard-coded into the server, requiring server code changes each time the work changes. There are many situations where it would be desirable to code the multi-threaded server only once, and use it for performing different work (depending on the application).

In the following example, we will evolve the multi-threaded server into one that can perform arbitrary pieces of work. Furthermore, we will be able to change the work that is performed without recompiling the service code itself. How will we do this?

The Generic Work Interface

The solution is to use a Java interface to specify, in a generic way, the work that should be performed. In our simple case:

```
import java.io.*;
public interface WorkLoad {
    public void doWork(PrintWriter out);
}
```

This is the WorkLoad.java file in your code distribution under the \ch2\code\socket\wkLdSvr directory. This single interface solves our generic work problem by:

1. Providing an interface that the multi-threaded server can work with (that is, it will call the doWork() method in its threads to perform work).

2. Provide an interface that our class representing 'work to be done' (or tasks) can implement (that is, the work to be done should be coded in the implementation of the doWork() method of the WorkLoad interface).

In this way, we can change or substitute the 'work to be done' class without affecting the multi-threaded server class. In fact, using runtime class loading in Java, we can specify the class of the work to be done by the server as a command line argument!

The Generic Service Itself

Here is the implementation of our generic server. You can find it in the WorkLoadServer.java file in the aforementioned directory:

```
import java.io.*;
import java.net.*;

public class WorkLoadServer implements Runnable {
  Socket sockInst;
  WorkLoad myWork;
  public WorkLoadServer(Socket insock, WorkLoad inWork) {
    sockInst = insock;
    myWork = inWork;
  }

  public void run() {
    try {
      PrintWriter out = new PrintWriter(
        sockInst.getOutputStream(), true);
        myWork.doWork(out);
        sockInst.close();
    } //of try
    catch (Exception e) {
      e.printStackTrace();
    }
  }
}
```

In the `main()` method below, `myWork` will eventually be a reference to the `Class` class specified by the command line argument. The `Class.forName()` method will load the class based on the name in `String` form. The `newInstance()` method of the `Class` class can then be used to create an instance of the class.

```
public static void main(String[] args) {
  int threadCounter = 1;
  String workClassName = args[0];
  try {
    Class myWork = Class.forName(workClassName);
    ServerSocket serv = new ServerSocket(8005);
    Socket aConn;
    while(true) {
      aConn = serv.accept();
      new Thread(new WorkLoadServer(aConn, (WorkLoad)
        myWork.newInstance()), "Thread #" +
        threadCounter++).start();
    }
  } // of try
  catch(Exception e) {
    e.printStackTrace();
  }
}
```

We can see here how the multi-threaded service structure is perfectly preserved. However, we are now dealing with the work to be done purely in terms of the `WorkLoad` interface.

The WorkLoad Class

The server requires some specific work to do. We can create any type of work, as long as the class implements the `WorkLoad` interface.

You can find one such generic workload in the `SomeWork.java` file. You can find this file in the `\ch2\code\socket\wkLdSver` directory.

```java
import java.io.*;
import java.util.Calendar;

public class SomeWork implements  WorkLoad {
  public void doWork(PrintWriter out) {
    try {
      String threadName = Thread.currentThread().getName();
      String curTime =
        Calendar.getInstance().getTime().toString();
      System.out.println(threadName + ": A client connected
        at " + curTime);
      for (int i=0; i< 60; i++) {
        curTime = Calendar.getInstance().getTime().toString();
        out.println(threadName + ": Message from Server at "
          + curTime);
        Thread.sleep(1000);
      }
    } // of try
    catch (Exception e)    {
      e.printStackTrace();
    }
  } // of doWork
}
```

The work being done here is exactly the same as the earlier version with the hard-coded logic. With this new version, however, changing the work performed by the server is as easy as changing the command line.

Testing the Generic Work Service

You can test the generic work service by starting the service with the following command line:

```
java WorkLoadServer SomeWork
```

Start a few instances of the client. You should see no difference, from the client point of view, between this generic work service and the previous multi-threaded service.

Taking a Logical Leap of Faith

There is something very exciting, yet indescribable, about the generic work service example. It goes far beyond the ability to use one generic server for all the workload. Let's flesh this out by doing a mind exercise.

The `WorkLoad` interface is the magical factor that enables the generic loading of work for the server. Now imagine that this interface is actually available on the client side as well. Further, imagine that we now construct the client in such a way that the programming logic directly calls the methods of this interface on the client side. The figure over, shows this in action:

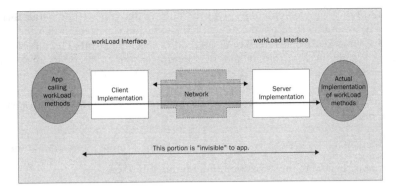

On the client side, we separate the programming logic from the client implementation which is also using the same interface. What we end up with is the ability of an application to call methods on the interface, but have the actual work performed across the virtual circuit on the server. Now, let us enumerate what the client implementation must do above and beyond the basic client:

❑ Implement the interface on the client side

❑ Upon a method call, take the parameters of the method, and ship it across to the server

❑ Upon the server's reply, take any return value and return it to the calling application

The 'server implementation' will now have to:

❑ Determine the method called by the client application

❑ Take the parameters transmitted by the client and call the associated method (from the server-side implementation of that interface) with these parameters as arguments

❑ Obtain the return value and transmit it back to the client

This is extensible to any arbitrary interface. Or, putting it succinctly, we can 'remote' any Java interface (that is, make an interface accessible remotely). If we have to implement all of the above manually, coding method calls across the network will be tedious and error prone. Ideally, we should be able to specify the interface, and then have some tool and/or runtime mechanism to handle all the details. Java offers exactly this capability. It is called Remote Method Invocation (RMI).

Now we will move on to coverage of RMI. Note the client implementation described above is called a stub in RMI.

RMI: Higher Level Network Access for Complex Applications

Most real-world Java applications consist of numerous runtime object instances of classes interacting with each other in intricate ways. If these objects interact with each other across a network boundary, we can implement this interaction by coding a 'client implementation' and a 'server implementation' over sockets. However, given the number and complexity of the interactions, coupled with the possibility of future evolution and changes, custom coding these implementations can be a very expensive proposition.

The combination of these implementations gives the illusion that the methods of an interface are executed remotely by an object across the network. The illusion is perfect in that the client application may not be aware that a particular interface or method is actually executed by a remote object. The calling semantics are identical for remote and local interfaces (remote methods all throw `java.rmi.RemoteException` – this is the only difference observable).

These implementations are candidates for automatic generation. Since these classes, which we will call **stubs** from now on, are:

❑ Code that is fixed (never changed)with respect to the remote interface that they implement

❑ Code that is specific to the corresponding remote interface

We can indeed automatically generate them from an implementation of an interface. A tool called the rmic or 'RMI Compiler' performs this very task during RMI development.

Giving Networking an Object Oriented View

There are many ways to design applications using a set of objects distributed over a network. Most of these applications are called distributed applications. The idea is that system processing is not performed at one single computing resource but is instead performed by an orchestration of machines across a network. A well-designed distributed system can yield the following highly desirable benefits:

❑ **Fault-tolerance**: if some machines in the network fail, the system as a whole still continues to function (maybe at a reduced capacity)

❑ **Scalability**: more client workload can be handled by simply adding computing resources at the server location

❑ **High throughput**: achieved by combining the processing resources of many machines within a network working in parallel

It is possible to design an RMI-based system that exhibits all of the above properties. Good distributed system design demands a lot of effort, time and experience.

Remote Method Invocation is much more than Remote Procedure Calls

RMI delivers capabilities above and beyond legacy distributed computing technology such as RPC (remote procedure call) mechanisms. The table below contrasts the two technologies:

RMI	RPC
has an interface defined in Java for remote operations	has an interface defined in an IDL (Interface Definition Language) language for remote operations
uses separate, automatically generated stubs to perform method remoting	uses IDL, compiled into a language-specific binding which then must be intermixed with implementation code on the source level
has rich object semantics	does not allow object semantics

RMI	RPC
no pointers or C/C++ influence	strong C/C++ influence, depends heavily on pointers to operate properly
works only between Java objects	works with implementations written in any supported programming language
callbacks are done in 'natural' exported object fashion	callbacks requires special handling
arguments to procedures can be objects that carry behavior as well as data	arguments to procedures are data only

In a later chapter, we will compare RMI against CORBA (Common Object Request Broker Architecture). CORBA is an international standard created by OMG (Object Management Group) that provides object semantics on top of RPC.

The above table should make clear the difference between RMI and RPC. We shall now take at a look at some of these features in more detail.

Object to Object Across Networks – Implementing RMI

Let us take a look at a very simple RMI implementation. You can find the source code under the \ch2\code\rmi\basic directory. We will first look at the interface that is 'remoted' (that is, extends remote), contained in the CustWork.java file:

```
import java.rmi.Remote;
import java.rmi.RemoteException;

public interface CustWork extends Remote {
  public String getSvrMsg() throws RemoteException;
}
```

Note two conventions that are necessary here:

❑   the remote interface must inherit from the java.rmi.Remote interface

❑   every method must throw RemoteException

In other aspects, the interface definition is similar to the WorkLoad interface we defined earlier.

The Remote Interface

The java.rmi.Remote interface is a 'marker' interface. It has no method of its own. However, it will allow RMI tools to find the interface(s) that must be remoted. For example, the rmic can locate the interface at compile time and generate the associated stub.

Throwing RemoteException

Any remote method in any remote interface may throw a RemoteException at any time. If we think back to our own socket-based implementation from earlier, the InputStream and OutputStream operations may throw an IOException at anytime, as the action of contacting the server host may result in HostNotfoundException, and so on. The bottom line is that *network-based communication can fail at anytime.*

39

Remote Interface Implementation – Server-Side Object

The role of a client versus the role of a server may not be mutually exclusive, or clear cut in all programming scenarios. One often works with a software component that is the *server* to one remote object, while at the same time being the *client* of another remote object (or even the same one, via a callback). Therefore, please be aware that our reference to a server or a client is *not* an indication of an absolute role for that object: the role will change, depending on the application.

Our code for implementation of the `CustWork` interface can be found in the `\ch2\code\rmi\basic\CustWorkImpl.java` file. This implementation does the same work as our socket server example from earlier: it returns a string message containing the server's current time. The `main()` method of this class will actually bind an instance of the object with the `workObj` name using the RMIRegistry. RMIRegistry is a simple name-to-service mapper that is supplied by Sun as part of the JDK. It can be used by remote clients to find instances of servers by name.

Let us take a detailed look:

```java
import java.rmi.RemoteException;
import java.rmi.server.UnicastRemoteObject;
import java.rmi.Naming;
import java.rmi.RMISecurityManager;
import java.util.Calendar;

public class CustWorkImpl implements CustWork {

  public CustWorkImpl() throws RemoteException {
    UnicastRemoteObject.exportObject(this);
  }

  public String getSvrMsg()throws RemoteException {
    String threadName = Thread.currentThread().getName();
    String curTime =
      Calendar.getInstance().getTime().toString();
    System.out.println(threadName + ": A client connected at "
      + curTime);
    return(threadName + ": Message from Server at " + curTime);
  }

  public static void main(String[] args) {
    try {
      if (System.getSecurityManager() == null)
        System.setSecurityManager(new RMISecurityManager());
      CustWorkImpl myServ = new CustWorkImpl();
      Naming.rebind("workObj", myServ);
      System.out.println("Server ready and waiting...");
    } // of try
    catch (Exception e) {
      e.printStackTrace();
    }
  }

}
```

As can be seen, the server object implements the remote interface, which in this case is `CustWork`. Note that `CustWorkImpl` does not derive from `jara.rmi.server.UnicastRemoteObject`.

We have done this purposely in order to show how to create a remote server that does *not* extend the `UnicastRemoteObject` class. In fact, deriving from this class will make your RMI programming a little easier.

Next, we have the default constructor. A default constructor (with no arguments) is required, and it must throw `RemoteException`, as this one does. Here, the constructor calls the default static `exportObject()` method of the `UnicastRemoteObject` class that will 'export' the object and make it available over the network. We can think of this as 'house work' for the server-side behavior. Remembering our socket-based server-side implementation from earlier, this is equivalent to creating a `ServerSocket` instance (but not yet calling `accept()`).

After this, we have the `getSvrMsg()` method, the only method of the remoted `CustWork` interface. This performs the same trivial functionality as our `SockServer` class from earlier, namely that of sending the server's local time to the client.

We then have `main()`, where we check whether or not a security manager has been installed; if not, we install one. Note that under JDK 1.2.x, because of a sweeping security model enhancement, you must install a security manager to get RMI working properly. The security manager will protect against unauthorized access to protected resources. In most cases, using the default `RMISecurityManager()` will be sufficient. Later, we will also need to define an external security policy that will allow our code to access the TCP/IP ports that are required for RMI operations. The implications of this security model will be discussed in Chapter 14.

Next in `main()`, we create an instance of the server object by using the default constructor (which also exports the object). The `Naming.rebind()` method then submits this instance to our bootstrap naming service. As stated above, Sun's RMI implementation provides such a service, called RMIRegistry. In this particular case, the instance will be associated with the name `'workObj'` on the machine where the RMIRegistry is running. Referring back to our socket-based server implementation, this `rebind()` call is equivalent to starting the server on the blocking `accept()` call, and mapping the port that the server is listening to on to a name – `'workObj'`. If a client implementation now connects to the name service and asks for `'workObj'`, the name service will refer the client implementation to connect to the server's actual port. This functionality is traditionally called 'port mapping'. Therefore the naming service is fundamentally a 'port mapper'.

This final message in `main()` is simply a sanity check, ensuring that everything is working properly and that the server object is ready to accept requests (that is, that the `CustWorkImpl` implementation is blocking on an `accept()` loop).

Working With Remote Interfaces – Client Implementation

On the client side, we need to create an object that will:

❑ obtain a reference to the server-side object over the network

❑ call into the `WorkLoad` interface to obtain the server message

❑ print the server message on the console

Creating an object that makes this call is substantially simpler than coding the server. In fact, other than the initial 'bootstrap' lookup for the first remote object reference, other calls to the remote object are transparent to the calling object – they look like local calls (thanks to the stub object implementing the interface locally).

You can find the basic client code under \ch2\code\rmi\basic\client\RmiClient.java:

Let us take a detailed look:

```java
import java.rmi.Naming;
import java.rmi.RemoteException;
import java.rmi.RMISecurityManager;

public class RmiClient {

  static String servMsg = "";

  public static void main(String[] args) {
    try {
      if (System.getSecurityManager() == null)
        System.setSecurityManager(new RMISecurityManager());
      CustWork servRef = (CustWork) Naming.lookup("workObj");
      servMsg = servRef.getSvrMsg();
      System.out.println(servMsg);
    } // of try
    catch (Exception e) {
      e.printStackTrace();
    }
  }

}
```

The first part of main() deals with installing a security manager if one doesn't already exist. We then use the RMIRegistry service, accessible through the java.rmi.Naming class, to map from the name 'workObj' to the actual server reference that is listening for requests. Note that what we get back in this call is an actual reference to the client side implementation – an instance of the stub object – for the CustWork interface implementation. We can now call the getSvrMsg() method on that interface. The stub will forward the call and respond back with the return value across the network.

RMIC – Generating Stubs

A tool called the RMI Compiler (or the rmic tool) can be used to generate stub classes from the compiled class file; the compiled class file must contain an implementation of a remote interface for this to work. Note that rmic operates on binary class files and generates binary class files.

For example, if (after compiling) we supply our CustWorkImpl.class file as input:

```
rmic -v1.2 CustWorkImpl
```

Then rmic will generate the following class file:

```
CustWorkImpl_Stub.class
```

Here are a few useful command line options for rmic:

Option	Description
`-classpath <path>`	specifies the location of the classes to work on (default is the `CLASSPATH` environment variable)
`-d <directory>`	specifies where to place the generated skeleton and stub classes (default is the current directory)
`-keepgenerated`	do not delete the `.java` source files that are used to generate the stub and skeleton classes
`-verbose`	causes rmic to report what it is doing in more detail
`-v1.2`	generates JDK 1.2 stubs; these are not backward compatible because JDKs before version 1.2 had also generated server side handling code called skeletons (JDK 1.2 and later eliminated this by using reflection to handle the operation automatically)

Testing the Basic RMI Application

We are now ready to test our RMI-based remote server implementation described above. Note that the client directory (`\ch2\code\rmi\basic\client`) is separate from the server directory (`\ch2\code\rmi\basic`) to ensure that the client doesn't simply load the server class locally into its own VM. Instead, we will place only the stub class into the client's directory.

To test our two-object system we need to do the following:

1. In the server directory, compile the interface (`javac CustWork.java`)

2. In the server directory, compile the server code (`javac CustWorkImp.java`)

3. In the server directory, run rmic on the compiled server class to generate the stub class automatically (`rmic -v1.2 CustWorkImpl`)

4. Copy the interface class (`CustWork.class`) to the separate client directory

5. In the client directory, compile the client code (`javac RmiClient.java`)

6. Copy the stub file (`CustWorkImpl_Stub.class`, generated in step 3) into the client directory

7. Create the policy file (discussed below) for the server and client; in this example the file is `\ch2\code\rmi\basic\policy.txt` (a copy must also be placed in the client directory)

8. While in the server directory, run rmiregistry in the background: `start rmiregistry` (start is the DOS command for running a process in the background; Unix/Linux users need only append an & to the end of rmiregisty, as in: `rmiregistry &`)

9. Run the server in the background using the command line below:
`start java -Djava.security.policy= policy.txt CustWorkImpl`
As expected, the server object should be blocked after registering with the rmiregistry (Windows users can run the startsvr.bat file that comes with the code download to do this)

10. In the client directory, run the client using the command line:
`java -Djava.security.policy= policy.txt RmiClient`
(Windows users, use runclnt.bat from code download)

You should see that the behavior is almost identical to our earlier example of socket client and servers. As expected, the server object blocks after registration.

Policy File and Security

Jini security is discussed in Chapter 14, and so a fuller discussion is left until there. However, Jini uses the same fine grained, permissions-based security model as JDK 1.2. A policy file is used to define what operations a class can perform; for security reasons, you obviously want to restrict exactly what a piece of downloaded code can do on your machine.

When testing, it is easier just to use the following policy file (`policy.txt`):

```
grant {
  permission java.security.AllPermission;
  };
```

This policy file grants *unlimited access* to the application, and should only be used when testing. Again, see Chapter 14 for more details.

The RMI Class Tree

The following is a class diagram for the RMI related classes. Most RMI servers will be deriving (or making use of) `java.rmi.server.UnicastObject`, as we have for `CustWorkImpl`. RMI servers that wish to be dormant most of the time, or be activated on-demand, should extend the `java.rmi.server.Activatable` instead. Many of the Jini services extend the `Activatable` class. We will cover the creation of an activatable service in the next chapter.

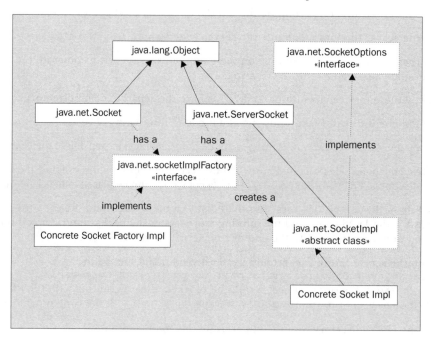

About UnicastRemoteObject

Examining the class diagram above, it reveals the role that `UnicastRemoteObject` plays. First, it is a direct descendent of `java.rmi.server.RemoteServer`. It will handle the server-side behaviors that are required in order to listen and service client requests.

A `UnicastRemoteObject` has the following characteristics:

- ❑ it must be always be running for remote references to be valid

- ❑ communications are point-to-point (one client-to-one server versus one client-to-many servers)

- ❑ it uses TCP based socket streams for communications

Our remote object implementation used the following statement to make itself available over the network:

```
UnicastRemoteObject.exportObject(this);
```

Another way we can implement `CustWorkImpl` is to extend `UnicastRemoteObject` directly:

```
public class CustWorkImpl extends UnicastRemoteObject
    implements CustWork {...}
```

The main difference is that the implementation of `equals()`, `hashCode()` and `toString()` for the remote object will come for free if you extend `UnicastRemoteObject`. More importantly, the semantics of `equals()` and `hashCode()` will be implemented in such a way that two stubs referring to the same remote object will be deemed equal (see Chapter 14 for a discussion on applications where this may be critical).

Networking in Java is Naturally Simple

We have covered a lot of ground in this chapter. We have gone from the very basics of Java networking, from sockets to the very powerful, Java specific, network object transport mechanism known as RMI: remote method invocation.

Our first encounter with sockets was a basic server that allowed clients to connect, which then allowed the server to transmit its current time for display on the client. This client/server setup made use of the `Socket` and `ServerSocket` classes to implement their logic in a simple way. In fact, we saw that `java.io` stream abstraction classes can be used on top of sockets to greatly simplify the transmission and receipt of data over the network: we can simply `read()` or `write()` to the network via the stream classes.

Next, we tried out multiple clients on our basic server and discovered that it was limited in that it can only service one single client at a time – other clients are blocked and made to wait for the server to become free if it is already busy servicing a client. We created a new multi-threaded server that makes use of Java threads support.

The multi-threaded server created one thread for each incoming client request and serviced many requests simultaneously. Then we learned that, while wonderful in sample programs, this multi-threaded server has major shortcomings that will be detrimental in production environment. Finally, we concluded that the best compromise between concurrency and robustness is the use of thread-pooling. Thread-pooling is indeed the bread and butter of production Java server programmers.

Our investigation of the multi-threaded server was followed by the variation of the server that handles dynamically loaded work assignment. We made use of Java's dynamic class loading to enable a user to specify the work that a server should perform at runtime via a command line argument. This technique allows us to create services that have no hard-coded processing logic.

From the server with dynamically loaded work, we took a leap of faith and discovered that the flexible server scenario is a generally desirable one. Furthermore, if any work pieces can be performed by a remote server then the description of the work to be done can be provided in the form of a Java interface. The client and server will only have to agree on the interface in order to work together over the network – the details of the actual implementation are irrelevant. We concluded that if the network support for handling the interface can be generated via a tool, it would greatly facilitate networked programming. Our next discovery was that Java's RMI provides exactly such a tool (the RMIC).

Finally, we rewrote our dynamic work server using Java RMI. We saw how to generate stubs for clients, and how to use the RMIRegistry to map a name to an RMI service. We experienced first-hand how RMI facilitates object to object communications across a network.

Java has truly made networking simple and painless. To cover the equivalent ground in a single book, not to mention a single chapter, would be unthinkable with conventional programming languages and platforms. With the basics of socket and RMI programming in hand, we are now equipped to work with some advanced RMI programming techniques in the next chapter.

Jini Client or Service	JavaSpaces and Helper Services

Jini Client and Service Support Helper Utilities

Jini Discovery Management Helper Utilities

Jini Protocol Helper Utilities

Jini Network Protocols	
	RMI and Rich Object Semantics
	Java VM and Networking

Network Protocols

3

Advanced RMI

RMI provides a high (application) level mechanism for 'object to object' communication over the network. The previous chapter illustrated how RMI is a natural evolution of socket-style programming on an object-oriented platform such as Java. This chapter will examine some of the unique advantages of RMI, as it is implemented today in the Java 2 platform.

We will get some first hand practice with these advanced RMI features:

- ❑ Dynamic download of stubs
- ❑ Transferring behavior as well as state using RMI
- ❑ RMI over Internet Firewalls
- ❑ Using Secure Socket Layer (SSL/TLS) with RMI
- ❑ Creating robust systems using `Activatable` objects

Advanced RMI Features

Serving up Stubs Remotely

RMI supports a variation of the dynamic class-loading feature of Java that distinguishes it from every other language/platform. This is the ability to automatically load a required class across the network. One example of this technology that is seen quite frequently are Java applets on the Internet. When a web page that contains an applet is accessed, the Java classes that make up the applet are downloaded automatically.

This can also be applied to RMI client calls: the stub class that implements the remote interface can be downloaded from a remote source. To specify where the client should look for the stub classes, the system property `java.rmi.server.codebase` must be set for the server-side VM.

We can accomplish this by using the following command (all on one line) to start the server:

```
java -Djava.rmi.server.codebase=http://win98p300:8081/
-Djava.security.policy= policy.all BasicServer
```

This command line sets system properties with the –D option. The codebase is set to
`http://win98p300:8081/`. This means that a web server should be available on the specified host,
listening at port 8081 to support the serving of the stub code. A simple 'class server' is supplied by Sun,
and included as part of the Jini distribution.

We will be using this class server (an HTTP server) from the Jini distribution in our code below. In
Chapter 5, when we start to work extensively with Jini, we will describe in detail how to set up a Jini
network. For now, you need to make sure:

❑   You have JDK 1.2.2 or later installed and operational

❑   You have Jini 1.1 beta or later unzipped into a directory (typically \jini1_1)

Then, in the \ch3\code\bats\ directory, you will need to make some modifications to a file called
setpaths.bat to reflect you own configuration. It contains:

```
set JINIHOME=c:\jini1_1
set WROXHOME=c:\wroxstubs
set STUBHOST=win98p300:8081
```

Make sure you set %JINIHOME% to where you've unzipped the Jini distribution. %WROXHOME% should
point to a directory that the class server can use to store the classes to be downloaded remotely. The
win98p300 host name in %STUBHOST%, should be replaced by your own machine's host name, but take
care not to remove the 8081 port designation.

Under the %JINIHOME%\lib\ directory, the tools.jar archive contains the class server itself. The
port that the class server will listen to is specified by the -port switch (in our case port 8081). The -
dir switch specifies the root directory from which to serve the classes, in this case, we specify
c:\wroxstubs (so be sure to create a directory with this name). The -trees -verbose switches will
print a trace to the console when the server starts up and whenever the server serves a class.

Our code download (from http://www.wrox.com/) includes a batch file to start this class server:
runhttpdstubs.bat.You can find this in the \ch3\code\bats directory. Here is its content:

```
call setpaths
start java  -jar %JINIHOME%\lib\tools.jar -port 8081 -dir %WROXHOME% -trees
-verbose
```

It simply starts the class server at port 8081, and serves the stub code from a directory located at the
directory location specified by the %WROXHOME% environment variable.

Other than the class server, there are actually a couple of other subtle requirements that must be
satisfied before we can get the client to dynamically load the stub class over the network:

Requirement	Reason
The RMIRegistry must be started with a CLASSPATH that does not include the directory where the stub code is located.In fact, it is best to start RMIRegistry with no CLASSPATH environment variable at all.	Ensures that the RMIRegistry loads stub instances via the remote codebase, rather than using a local copy specified via the CLASSPATH.
The client should not find the stub classes in its CLASSPATH.	This is obvious since we want the client to download the stub over the network (we will see how to setup dynamic downloading of stubs later in this chapter).

Passing Parameters in RMI

Parameters passed as arguments in methods of a remote interface follow these rules:

❑ All simple data type variables (int, char) should be passed by value

❑ Any object variable that does not support a remote interface should be passed by copy

❑ Any object variable that supports a remote interface should be passed by reference (that is, the object is not exported – a stub object is sent instead)

The Essential Role of Object Serialization

Object variables that do *not* support a remote interface, called non-remote objects, are passed-by-copy over an RMI connection. What this means is that the object is serialized across the wire and a copy of it is re-constructed at the other end. This applies to both arguments that are passed with the method invocation, and the return value from the method invocation.

This is true regardless of the direction of the call (that is, whether it is a forward call from a client to a server, or a reverse call back into an exported object from a server back to a client). The figure below shows this in action:

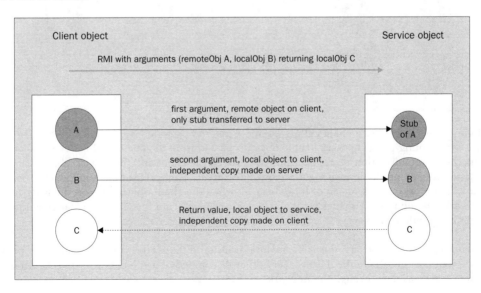

This means that the following must be true:

❑ Arguments to remote methods, and any return value, must implement the `java.io.Serializable interface`

❑ Any fields and members of the object argument must also be serializable

❑ The class file representing the serialized object must be available to the receiving end

Understanding Dynamic Class Loading

Dynamic class loading is one of the most talked-about features of RMI since its conception. It is also one of the most difficult features to understand and configure correctly during any experimentation with the technology.

The idea of Dynamic Class loading, as it applies to RMI, is the ability of an RMI client (not necessarily a client application) to work with classes that it does not know about ahead of time. In fact, the classes need not be on the same machine: they can be dynamically loaded across the network when needed.

The figure below illustrates this scenario.

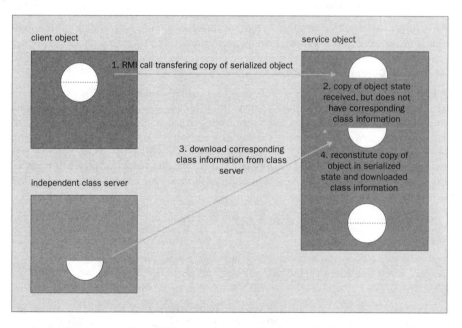

The figure above illustrates a client calling a remote method provided by a service object. During the course of this calling process, a serializable object is passed from the client to the service object. It is actually the state information that is transmitted between the client and the service object. The class information is dynamically loaded via a remote class server. The service object in this case has no idea what it will be working with ahead of time. Instead, when the client object invokes the RMI call across the network, the required class files for the non-remote object from the client are loaded automatically from the independent class server.

As pure OO pundits would say, this is 'behavioral transfer'. Frequently, you will read in the popular technical journals that RMI differs from every other distributed object technology in that it transfers behaviors as well as data through the network.

Object Marshalling

The MarshalledObject is probably one of the least understood classes involved in Java networking. Marshalling refers to the action of serializing one or more objects onto a serial medium (either transmitted over a network or written to a stream-based storage). The serialization procedure involves the serialization of both state and type (class) information. Reading a marshalled object back from the serial medium and re-constituting the object is called unmarshalling.

A MarshalledObject is actually a container for a binary stream of data that represents an object instance. One may think of it is a kind of miniature persistent store for one object. The content of a MarshalledObject is a specific instance of a Java object. Of course, most MarshalledObject instances never end up on a disk, so strictly we cannot call them persistent stores. MashalledObject can also be viewed as an escape mechanism from Java's formal reference structures. Think of it as an envelope to ship objects around in.

Think about the advantage of a MarshalledObject. Anybody who handles the MarshalledObject as a 'middleman' does not have to know what is inside this 'envelope', they just pass it on. Any number of middlemen can pass a MarshalledObject around without serializing and deserialzing its actual content: this is a major time and work saver. Furthermore, the MarshalledObject can even be compared with another *without* having to first deserialize the contained object.

There are a couple of special properties that a MarshalledObject satisfies:

❑   The serialization of a MarshalledObject has the exact same format and semantics used for marshalling RMI parameters and return values

❑   The stream may optionally contain a URL codebase annotation; this allows the unmarshaller of the object to load the corresponding class file if it is not already available to it

Codebase URL Annotation

Setting up a system for Dynamic Class loading is non-trivial. Most of the bandwidth in mailing lists for RMI and RMI-IIOP – and even Jini and JavaSpaces – is concerned with problems relating directly or indirectly to this feature. Because of this, a thorough understanding of this subject matter will make our later sojourn into the Jini JavaSpaces world substantially more pleasant.

In order for the client to locate the stubs that it requires over the network, it must know where on the network they are located. How does a client get this information?

The secret lies in the MarshalledObject instance that it receives, and the codebase URL inside it.

The figure below illustrates this concept:

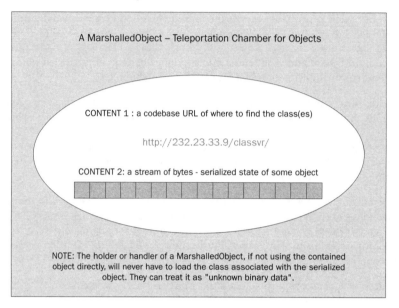

A MarshalledObject – Teleportation Chamber for Objects

CONTENT 1 : a codebase URL of where to find the class(es)

http://232.23.33.9/classvr/

CONTENT 2: a stream of bytes - serialized state of some object

NOTE: The holder or handler of a MarshalledObject, if not using the contained object directly, will never have to load the class associated with the serialized object. They can treat it as "unknown binary data".

When the unmarshalling code on the client finds this codebase URL, it obtains the class information over the network before deserializing the data elements.

At this point, one may wonder: how did the URL annotation get into the `MarshalledObject` in the first place?

The answer is more complicated here. For any stub object that is serviced by the RMIRegistry, the marshalling layer will annotate the object if and only if the RMIRegistry cannot find the class anywhere in its CLASSPATH. You need to remember this, because you can spend many sleepless nights trying to figure this one out.

Therefore, before starting RMIRegistry, you must ensure that you have no CLASSPATH environment variable set; or if you have, that it does not include any of the stub objects that you want to be annotated.

> **When starting the RMIRegistry, make sure that the `CLASSPATH` is not set. If this is not possible, at least make sure the `CLASSPATH` does not include any stub class to be dynamically and remotely loaded, or other classes that the stub depends on. This is the only way to ensure that codebase annotation will occur for the marshalled stub classes.**

Now if the object we are talking about is not a stub registered with RMIRegistry, then it will either be:

❏ A returned value from a method call, or

❏ A parameter returned through a method call

In both of these cases, the responsible marshalling layer will ensure that the codebase annotation occurs.

One obvious question, of course, is: how does the marshalling layer know what the codebase annotation should be? The answer to this is that it is set in the `java.rmi.server.codebase` system property, as we showed in the opening section of this chapter: it is set via the -D switch when starting the Java VM.

Finally, we may ask if we ever need to define `java.rmi.server.codebase` for the client. If we ever pass a remote object to the server, either as a parameter of a method called on the server, or as the return value of a method called by the server, then yes, we will have to.

Dynamic class loading should now start to make sense.

Delivery of Dynamically Loaded Classes

We now know that the client can get the codebase URL annotation that is inside the marshalled object, but how does it actually load the stub classes that it needs? The answer lies in the `java.net.URL` class. This is the class that will be used to load the class information.

The java.net.URL class supports the following protocol access:

- ❑ A file path
- ❑ Over the network via the HTTP protocol
- ❑ Over the network via the FTP protocol

The file protocol is of limited utility in practical applications since it assumes that both the server and client have the same mapping to a shared file system (that is, if the annotation is file:///javaroot/stubs/, then the client must have the same directory at the same path to find the stubs).

While the third alternative is also interesting, it is the HTTP protocol that is most frequently used. Obviously, in order to allow a client to download the class from a URL beginning with http://, you must have an HTTP server serving the class requests over the network.

Behavioral Transfer

The fact that an object can be sent over RMI without the receiving object having the corresponding class files is usually touted as 'behavioral transfer' in RMI. In fact, this is one of the most frequently hyped differentiators between RMI and older distributed technology like CORBA (covered in the following chapter):

- ❑ RMI can be used to transfer both data and behavior

Translated from layman terms, it means:

- ❑ Both object states and object class code can be transferred during an RMI method call

An Example of Behavioral Transfer

Let us take a look at an example where this is actually done, and see why it is such a fascinating concept.

In this example, we will set up a generic work server. This server will perform work on behalf of the client. The unique thing is that the server does not know ahead of time what work it will perform. The client will transfer both the data and the behavior during an RMI method call. The server will perform the client-supplied behavior on the client-supplied data and return.

You will find the following in the `\ch3\code\behav\GenericService.java` file in the source distribution:

```
import java.rmi.Remote;
import java.rmi.RemoteException;

public interface GenericService extends Remote {
   public String doWork(GenericWork inWork) throws RemoteException;
}
```

`GenericService` is the remote interface. Think of it as the prescribed way of submitting arbitrary work to the server. It has only one method, called `doWork()`. The key to the system's operation is the definition of the parameter passed into it. The type for this parameter is `GenericWork`, another interface:

```
public interface GenericWork {
   public String perform();
}
```

The arbitrary work that the client wishes the server object to perform must implement this interface. The figure below shows this relationship. The server object only knows how to perform work from classes that support the `GenericWork` interface. It does so *without* knowing in advance the actual class definition of the 'work' class itself.

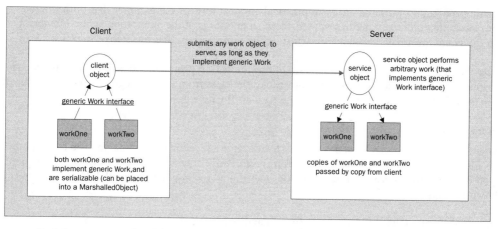

You can find the source code of the server object in `\ch3\code\behav\GenericServiceImpl.java`:

```
import java.rmi.RemoteException;
import java.rmi.server.UnicastRemoteObject;
import java.rmi.Naming;
import java.rmi.RMISecurityManager;

public class GenericServiceImpl implements GenericService {
   public GenericServiceImpl() throws RemoteException {
      UnicastRemoteObject.exportObject(this);
   }

   public String doWork(GenericWork inWork) throws
      RemoteException {
```

```
        // server has no idea what it is doing here
        return inWork.perform();
    }
```

This single call, `inWork.perform()`, will perform the work supplied from the client, regardless of the actual implementation class. The mechanism is a direct consequence of how RMI passes parameters. Recall that:

❑   Remote objects are passed by stub (reference)

❑   Non-remote objects are passed by copy

Since the class that implements the `GenericWork` interface is non-remote, it is passed by copy. This means that the marshalling process will load the class file itself across the network – and thus the behavior transfer.

```
    public static void main(String[] args) {
      try {
        if (System.getSecurityManager() == null)
          System.setSecurityManager(new RMISecurityManager());
        GenericServiceImpl myServ = new GenericServiceImpl();
        Naming.rebind("workObj", myServ);
        System.out.println("Server ready and waiting...");
      }
      catch (Exception e){
        e.printStackTrace();
      }
    }
  }
```

The behavior transfer can be done on a per-call basis. That is, two consecutive calls from the same client can submit different work to the server. This is exactly what we will do in this case with two trivial workloads. Here are the classes that contain the work to be done. You can find these two pieces of work, each defined in its own class, within the same file as the source code of the client application, under \ch3\code\behav\client\ServClient.java.

```
import java.rmi.Naming;
import java.rmi.RemoteException;
import java.rmi.RMISecurityManager;
import java.io.Serializable;

class WorkOne extends Object implements GenericWork,
  Serializable {
```

For it to work as 'a passed-by-copy RMI' argument, we must implement `GenericWork` and `Serializable`.

```
    public String perform(){
      int base = 2;
      for (int i=0; i< 10; i++)
        base += 2;
        return '' + base;
    }
  }
```

Here the work to be done is adding the number 2, a total of 10 times.

```
class WorkTwo extends Object implements GenericWork,
  Serializable{
  public String perform(){
    int base = 2;
    for (int i=0; i< 10; i++)
      base *= 2;
      return '' + base;
    }
  }
```

WorkTwo has exactly the same structure, but the work done is 2 multiplied by itself 10 times. Obviously, these two pieces of work could have been arbitrarily complex – and the server would have performed it just as happily.

Finally, here is the client code that will instantiate and submit the work to the server:

```
public class ServClient {

  static String servMsg = '';

  public static void main(String[] args) {
  try {
    if (System.getSecurityManager() == null)
      System.setSecurityManager(new RMISecurityManager());
    genericService servRef = (genericService)
      Naming.lookup('//' + args[0] + '/workObj');
```

Here, we are explicitly allowing for cross-network operation (instead of single machine). The parameter to the Naming.lookup() method is of the format:

```
'//<hostname>:<port>/<service object name>'
```

In our code, the <hostname>:<port> portion can be supplied as an argument when invoking the client from the command line.

```
GenericWork wk1 = new WorkOne();
GenericWork wk2 = new WorkTwo();
```

The two different instances of work are created here.

```
servMsg = servRef.doWork(wk1);
System.out.println('Performed workload ONE on server,
  with result = ' + servMsg);
servMsg = servRef.doWork(wk2);
System.out.println('Performed workload TWO on server,
  with result = ' + servMsg);
```

We call the server's doWork() method twice, once for each type of work. The unmarshalling of the method arguments will do the behavior transfer automatically.

```
}// of try
catch (Exception e) {
  e.printStackTrace();
```

```
      }
    }

    }
```

Running Our Behavioral Transfer Sample

To run our sample program, we should:

1. First compile the GenericServiceImpl class in the behav directory using the command line:

```
..\bats\buildit GenericServiceImpl.java
```

2. Generate stubs using rmic with the command line:

```
rmic -v1.2 GenericServiceImpl
```

3. Copy the stubs to the root directory to be served by the class server. Use the copystubs.bat batch file (type copystubs in the behav directory). This file contains:

```
call ..\bats\setpaths
copy GenericWork.class %WROXHOME%
copy GenericServiceImpl_Stub.class %WROXHOME%
copy GenericService.class %WROXHOME%
```

4. Compile the client program in the \ch3\code\behav\client directory:

```
..\..\bats\buildit2 ServClient.java
```

5. Copy the workloads to the stubs directory. Use the copywork.bat file in the \ch3\code\behav\client directory (that is, type copywork in the client directory). It contains:

```
call ..\..\bats\setpaths
copy WorkOne.class %WROXHOME%
copy WorkTwo.class %WROXHOME%
```

6. Now, startup a class server using the runhttpdstubs.bat batch file. Find this under the \ch3\code\bats directory.

7. Change directory to \ch3\code\, set the CLASSPATH to nothing (set CLASSPATH=""), and start rmiregistry:

```
start rmiregistry
```

8. Now, start the GenericServiceImpl using the startsvr.bat batch file in the \ch3\code\behav directory. It contains:

```
call ..\bats\setpaths
start java -Djava.rmi.server.codebase=http://%STUBHOST%/ -
Djava.security.policy=policy.all GenericServiceImpl
```

9. Start the client using the startclnt.bat batch file in the \ch3\code\behav\client directory. It contains:

```
call ..\..\bats\setpaths
java -Djava.rmi.server.codebase=http://%STUBHOST%/ -
Djava.security.policy=policy.all ServClient localhost
```

You should see the client submit the two pieces of work to the server, and the result of the two remote computations using behavioral transfer.

Security Managers and Policy Files

Another major obstacle that prevents dynamic class loading from working properly is the ever-changing handling of security throughout the evolution of JDK 1.1 to JDK 1.3. They have rather different security models, and this affects the operation of networking software such as RMI.

Starting with JDK 1.2, one must have security policy files specified for both the server and the client. One must also ensure that a `SecurityManager` is installed for (again) both the client and the server. The only exception to this case is if the client has all the definitions of the stub classes that it will ever access (both directly and indirectly), and that no behavior transfer is performed. This is an exceptional case rather than the norm. Failure to provide the policy file may result in cryptic messages from the client that have no relationship to security.

Bootstrapping using RMIRegistry

RMIRegistry is a 'bootstrap' naming service; it can be used to obtain the first reference to a remote object (that is,. the first reference between two machines). This very first reference can then return additional references to other objects in the network.

RMI Over and Through the Internet

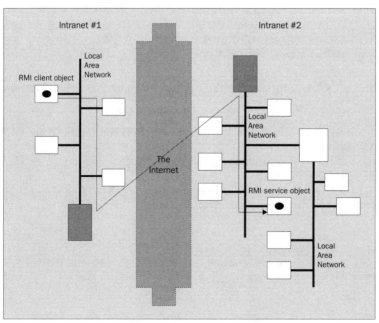

What we have discussed thus far is applicable to using RMI for custom applications across any network, whether it is an Intranet within a corporation, or the Internet itself. However, when an RMI application has to communicate from within an Intranet to the Internet outside, or when an RMI application has to use the Internet as an intervening network (see above figure), we need to be aware of another set of requirements. These requirements can be summed up as:

❑ RMI must be able to pass through common Internet access-control mechanisms such as firewalls

❑ The RMI data transmitted through an untrusted network, such as the Internet, should be encrypted to ensure privacy

❑ There must be a reliable way to ensure that the identity of the end-point connected is authentic, when connecting over an untrusted network

With this in mind, we will look at two RMI supplementary technologies that attempt to fulfill these requirements:

❑ RMI over firewalls

❑ SSL-based RMI connections

RMI over Firewalls

When RMI is deployed in the real world, many situations that are out of the control of the designers of the original system may affect its operation. One lesson learned from RMI in the JDK 1.1.x is the near universal existence of firewalls in corporations. In the early days of limited availability and expensive implementations, companies and businesses that used a firewall were few and far between. Today, you will be hard pressed to find a business or corporation that does not use a firewall for their Internet access. A firewall system typically:

❑ Blocks access from the Internet into the corporate network (or selectively allows very little, tightly controlled access)

❑ Optionally blocks or filters access from inside the firewall to certain resources on the web (for example, sites with questionable virtues)

The figure below illustrates the action of a firewall:

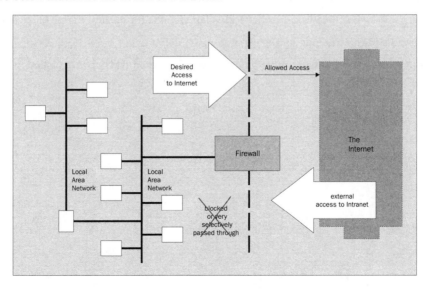

With Java 2 comes a firewall compatible implementation of RMI. Benefiting from the experience from its 1.x cousins, the Java 2 RMI classes are firewall ready. In fact, one can write and design an RMI application, and then enable the firewall compatibility only when necessary. This design defers the decision of firewall tunneling to deployment-time configuration, alleviating the application code-writers from having to write firewall specific code. The configuration for the firewall can be done without access to the original source code, and no recompiling is necessary.

This deployment-time configuration is performed by setting a few system properties. The RMI runtime support code will examine these properties. The system properties that will be used are:

System Property Name	Description
socksProxyHost	Configure the RMI communications layer to use the SOCKS proxy located at the specified host if direct connection fails; default port to use is 1080
socksProxyPort	If socksProxyHost is configured, but the proxy server is not at the standard port 1080, use this system property to specify the actual port
http.proxyHost	Configure the RMI communications layer to use HTTP tunneling through an HTTP proxy located at the specified host if direct connection fails; default port to use is 80
http.proxyPort	If http.proxyHost is configured, but the HTTP proxy server is not at the standard port 80, use this system property to specify the actual port used

Setting Up a Firewall Test Network

To test RMI operations over a firewall, you will need to use enough machines to simulate one if you don't have access to both sides of an actual firewall. In order to properly test RMI over firewall scenarios, you will need the following minimum system configuration:

- ❑ Two separate and configured TCP/IP networks
- ❑ One gateway machine with two network adapters, one for each of the two networks
- ❑ Firewall software running on the gateway machine
- ❑ An RMI server machine running on one network, and an RMI client machine running on the other network

This will dictate a network of at least three machines in the following configuration:

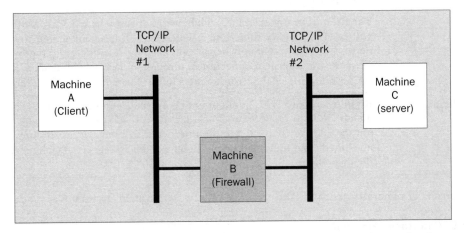

If you have a permanent connection to the Internet, two local machines and a notebook computer with dial-up capabilities, we can configure a test system as follows.

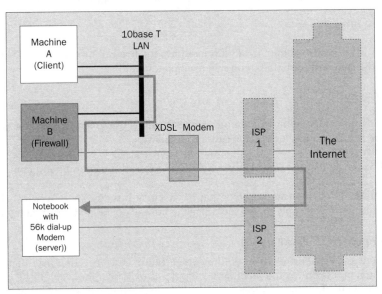

Here, the Internet is used as the external network. Machine A (the client) is accessing the Notebook machine though the firewall(Machine B).

Machine Name	Description
A	Acts as a client, running a Java 2 VM, and configured to connect to the Internet through a firewall located on machine B. Will be connecting to the notebook computer over the Internet via this firewall.

Table continued on following page

Machine Name	Description
B	The firewall proxy machine, which need not run a Java 2 VM. A SOCKS and/or HTTP proxy should be installed here. It has connections to two networks: the internal network where machine A resides, and the Internet. In our case, the Internet connection is through an ISP providing an xDSL connection; the local network connection is through 10-baseT Ethernet.
Notebook	Running a Java 2 VM, configured to connect to the Internet through a direct dialup (56 kbps modem) to a local ISP. This machine will act as the server in our tests. Once connected to the Internet, it will have access to firewall machine B, but there will be no direct way for it to access machine A behind the firewall.

In the remainder of our discussion of RMI over firewalls, we will use this test setup as the reference.

RMI over SOCKS Based Firewall

If you are using a SOCKS compatible firewall, you're in luck. The SOCKS support built into the Java 2 RMI is robust and complete. In fact, simply starting the server with the property:

```
socksProxyHost=myhost
```

will enable the RMI server to automatically find and use the firewall proxy. If your SOCKS firewall is not listening at the standard port 1080, you will also need to add:

```
socksProxyPort=port_number
```

Actually, the RMI implementation will attempt a direct connection over the existing network first, and then look for the proxy and use it only after an initial failure.

This simple fallback scheme makes RMI over a SOCKS firewall transparent and completely automatic.

On a Win32 system, if you are using a proxy that has a 'client installation' or a 'winsock shim (replacement)', the above will apply to you too, since the firewall operation is transparent to the application.

Tunneling RMI Through HTTP Proxy

If you simply have an HTTP proxy firewall, the configuration and/or testing may be a little more complicated. Much of it is due to the fact that no standards exist as to how an HTTP proxy should operate. RMI will do the best job possible to try and 'tunnel through' this proxy, but results will vary depending on your particular firewall and server combination.

Here is the invocation option you should use when starting your RMI server:

```
http.proxyHost=hostname    [http.proxyPort=port_number]
```

You should set the http.proxyPort system property if the proxy is not at the default port 80 (most firewall proxies will *not* be mapped to this port).

Running Firewall Tests

To start testing of the system, we dial in to our ISP on the notebook, and make it the server machine. Since most ISPs give dynamic IP assignments, we must obtain this IP upon dial-in. In our case, we are on a Windows 98 system, and the `winipcfg` utility will show the IP assigned.

Assuming that you have your firewall test system as described earlier, we need to perform some system configuration before proceeding with the test.

Firstly we set up the hosts file, on both the notebook computer and the client machine to reflect the new IP. On a Windows 98 machine, the hosts file can be found at:

```
C:\windows\....
```

On a Windows NT/2000 machine, the hosts file is found at:

```
C:\windows\system32\drivers\etc\...
```

For each of these hosts files, make sure you have added all the machine names and any dynamically assigned IP addresses that you have just discovered.

On the server notebook, we then start the following:

- ❑ The class server to serve up stubs
- ❑ The RMIRegistry to provide lookup
- ❑ The RMIServer program itself

You can test system and configuration sanity by:

- ❑ Pinging from the notebook to the firewall gateway machine
- ❑ Pinging from the client machine to the firewall gateway machine

Next, we can now start the RMI client machine with the RMI client program. Make sure you remember to set the `socksProxyHost` system property.

When RMI over the firewall works, it will take some time for the direct connection to fail, and then you will see the stubs being downloaded from the notebook followed by the actual method call.

HTTP Tunneling Quirks

You can use the same configuration to test HTTP tunneling by simply setting the `http.proxyHost` system property.

With HTTP tunneling, you may encounter the following problems:

- ❑ An attempt to connect may timeout
- ❑ Stubs won't download
- ❑ Stubs will download but unmarshalling fails

To overcome some of these problems, you may try:

❑ Using the IP address directly (instead of the notebook's hostname) when invoking the client program, and in the `java.rmi.server.codebase` property when starting the server program

❑ Using a proven web server installed on the notebook to serve your stub classes rather than the simple class server

❑ A different HTTP proxy firewall implementation, if possible

❑ Copying the stub class directly to the client side

With some HTTP proxy firewalls, the proxy will not entertain requests to connect to an arbitrary port (for example, 1099 for RMIRegistry) on the server. For these types of proxies, you will need to install a special CGI (Common Gateway Interface) program to 'reflect' the call from a request on the standard web server port to your server. See the figure below for an illustration of this action. This CGI program is called:

```
java-rmi.cgi
```

and is ironically only available with JDK 1.1x. The change in security model with Java 2 makes the use of this CGI problematic. Essentially, one needs to configure the global policy file to enable access to the protected ports, thus creating a security risk.

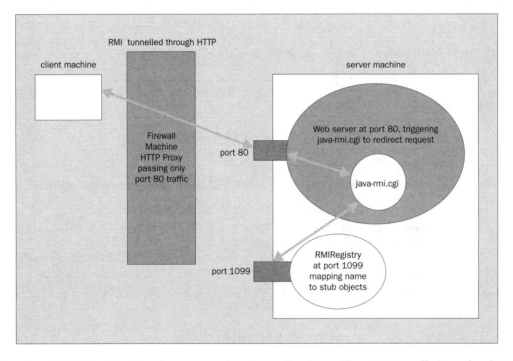

Bear in mind that in all of the above cases, the setup will only enable outgoing calls from the client to the server. This only represents the secure half of the RMI equation.

If you export any local client objects by supplying them as parameters to remote methods, and the server needs to call back through these objects, then you will need to perform your own custom proxying to enable this.

In effect, you will be providing a way for external entities to access resources internal to firewalled organizations. Any solution will involve a firewall by-pass, and you should proceed only with the understanding and permission of the security administrator. Because of this serious security implication, most RMI-through-firewall system designs do not export client side 'remote' objects.

Securely Encrypted Datastreams with RMI Over SSL

Many of us use SSL (Secure Socket Layer) every day without realizing it. Some would recognize it as the little lock that shows up when we access certain web sites over the Internet. Over the past years, we've been trained to trust pages that cause the web browser to show these little locks. We trust the sites that we're connected to (for example, an On-line Stock Trading service, or a Banking Institution, etc.), and we assume that any communications through these connections are encrypted.

An SSL connection gives us three guarantees:

❑ **Server authentication**: the site we connected to is really who they say they are

❑ **Data privacy**: communication between your machine and the server is encrypted – so anyone seeing the transmission will have no way of reading it

❑ **Message integrity**: the data transmitted from the server to the client has not been modified or tampered with mid-stream

With Java 2, we can now also enjoy these benefits when using RMI communications. In effect, we have SSL available as an optional layer beneath the RMI machinery, as the figure below illustrates. At the time of writing, RMI over SSL is enabled through a standard Java extension library called the Java Secure Sockets Extension, or JSSE.

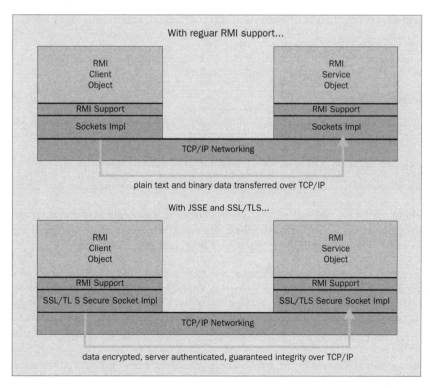

The Java Secure Sockets Extension 1.0

JSSE 1.0 contains a Java implementation of the SSL v 3.0 and TLS (Transport Layer Security) v1.0 protocols; TLS is described later. It enables secure communications over the Internet.
On the application level, JSSE provides socket-based applications (for example, RMI) an easy way of switching over to SSL operation. Underneath, JSSE actually extends the `javax.security` package in JDK 1.2.x and makes use of JCE (Java Cryptography Extension) to perform its work.

Until JSSE becomes an integral part of the base JDK, you can find and download a copy of the latest version of this extension from http://java.sun.com/products/jsse/.

All About SSL

How can SSL make such strong security guarantees? While programming RMI over SSL does not require an understanding of how SSL works, having such an understanding will allow us to make sense of all the steps that are required to get the communication links set up. Furthermore, it will enable us to design and deploy the technology with confidence, and be able to adapt flexibly to changing production scenarios.

SSL and TLS

SSL was originally conceived and implemented by Netscape, and is now a proposed international standard in the form of an IETF draft called Transport Layer Security (TLS) 1.0.

SSL provides:

- ❑   Server authentication
- ❑   Optional client authentication
- ❑   Client/server negotiation of cipher suites (set of 'crypto algorithms' used)
- ❑   Privacy via encrypted links

It makes use of public key encryption to perform authentication.

Public Key Encryption Basics

Public key encryption uses a set of two asymmetric keys to perform the encryption. A key-generating algorithm produces a private key and a public key. The unique properties of these keys are:

- ❑   Given one of the keys, it is almost impossible to determine the other
- ❑   Data encrypted by one of the keys can only be decrypted by the other one (and vice versa)

The idea behind public key encryption is to widely circulate the public key, and then send data encrypted using the closely guarded private key. This way, the source of the data is authenticated (since the public key can only be used to decrypt the data from one single private key).

If the server encrypts the data stream with the server's private key, and the client decrypts it with the server's public key – we're done! Actually, we're not. Public key encryption and decryption are extremely CPU intensive operations. Until we all have supercomputer equivalents on our desks, this is not likely to happen. SSL uses simpler and much faster symmetric key encryption to encrypt the data stream.

SSL Handshaking

Instead of using public key encryption for encryption of data streams, SSL/TLS uses it for the initial 'handshaking' phase.

The protocol has the following phases:

Phase	Description
Phase I: Handshaking	During this phase, the following is performed:
	❑ client connects to server, and server is authenticated to be who it says it is
	❑ client and server negotiate a basic cipher suite to use during the communications to follow
	❑ the server may require authentication of the client
	❑ client and server agree to the use of a session key (shared secret, symmetric keys) for encrypting the data stream; the same key is used for both encryption and decryption, and both the sender and receiver have access to the same key
Phase II: Communication Session	Data is transmitted in encrypted form using the session key resulting from the handshaking phase. Session keys are disposed of once the connection ends.

Certificates and CAs

Certificates are used to distribute public keys in a reliable way. A certificate contains a byte stream. In the byte stream are the certificate's serial number, the expiration date of the certificate, the name of the entity (company), the entity's public key, the name of the certification authority (CA) who issued the certificate, and so on. This byte stream is digitally signed by the CA issuing the certificate.

> **Certificate signing is identical in operation to code signing in Java. Basically, a one-way hash is performed on the byte stream and a message digest is generated. The message digest is then encrypted using the private key of the CA. The byte stream, unencrypted, is then transmitted together with this 'encrypted message digest' or 'signature'. The receiver of the certificate can use the public key of the CA to decrypt the message digest, perform the one-way hash on the byte stream, and compare the results. This will guarantee both the origin of the certificate (that is, the CA), and integrity of the certificate (that is, no tampering has taken place).**

One of the most frequently used standard formats for certificates is the X.509 standard. JSSE 1.0 supports the use of X.509 certificates for SSL operation.

In the real (Internet) world, there are several well known 'trusted' CAs. These include Verisign, Thawte, etc. The certificates of these trusted CAs are included with most browsers and SSL implementations.

These trusted certificates are in turn used to validate the certificates of individual sites during SSL server authentication, as illustrated in the figure below:

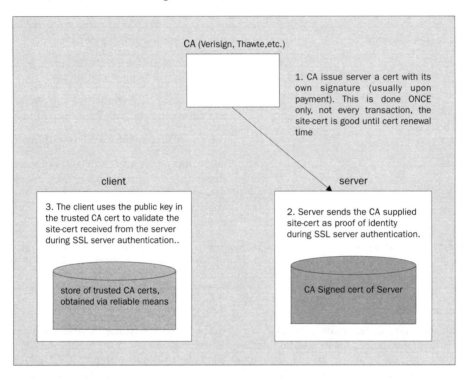

SSL Server Authentication

SSL supports server authentication. This is what ensures that the server is really who it says it is. The server sends the client its certificate during the handshake. The client then does the following:

- ❑ Checks the validity date of the certificate
- ❑ Checks whether or not the CA that issued the certificate is a trusted CA
- ❑ Validates the CA's digital signature on the certificate (this ensures that the certificate is issued by the trusted CA and has not been tampered with)
- ❑ Checks the domain name on the certificate against the domain of the server

Once the server is authenticated, the SSL handshake continues and the client starts exchanging session key information. The session key is typically a symmetric 'shared-secret' key used to encrypt the data stream.

In summary, here are the certificates and keys that are required to establish an SSL session:

Role	Certificates or Keys Required
Client	A set of certificates from trusted CAs.
Server	The site key (both private and public server keys); certificates signed by a trusted CA for transmission to the client during authentication.

Creating Your Own Set of Keys Using Keytool

To test out SSL on our own pair of systems, it is not necessary to contact one of the trusted CAs and purchase a site certificate.

Instead, we can use a 'self-signed' certificate to create an SSL session (of course, if you actually have a trusted CA signed certificate, you can use the real thing).

For a self-signed certificate to work in our test scenario, we need to:

❑   On the server, create a private key and a self-signed certificate and store them in a keystore

❑   Install our certificate as a trusted CA on the client

This way, when server authentication is performed, the client will be using our certificate as the trusted CA certificate to validate the site certificate sent by the server. The figure below illustrates how a self-signed certificate can be used to create an SSL session without obtaining a signed certificate from a trusted CA (compare this to the previous figure):

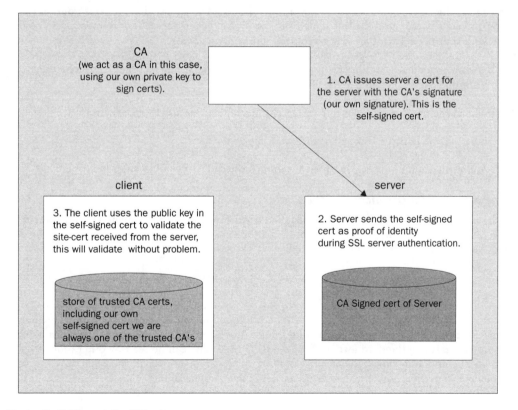

Creating a Self-Signed Certificate

The keytool utility that is distributed with JDK 1.2.x can be used easily to create a self-signed certificate. Here is the command to do so:

```
keytool -genkey -dname 'cn=Sing Li, ou=Java XML, o=Wrox, c=UK'  -alias
wrox -keysize 512  -keystore .\wroxkeys -storepass javarmi -validity 500
```

With `keytool`, the `-genkey` switch indicates that a public/private key pair and self-signed certificate are to be generated; the other switches specify parameters as follows:

Option	Description
-dname	Specifies the X.500 DN (Distinguished Name) information that is part of the X.509 certificate. Can contain parts such as CN (common name), OU (organization unit), O (organization), C (country), etc.
-alias	Specifies an alias that can be used to retrieve the keys after creation.
-keysize	The size of the key, between 512 and 1024 bits in increments of 64.
-keystore	Creates a local store instead of a system store (at a system default location).
-storepass	Sets the password for the keystore.
-validity	The number of days that the certificate will be valid for.

You can use the above command to create a keystore called `wroxkey` that contains your very own public/private key pair, and the self-signed site certificate for our server test. Remember to replace my name with your own. This is all that is required on the server side.

The keystore created above is in JKS format, a binary proprietary format that is used by the `keytool` utility and supported by various JSSE library APIs.

If you like to see the details of the self-signed certificate, you can use the command:

```
keytool -list -v -keystore .\wroxkeys
```

The system will ask for a password after this command: you will need to enter javarmi.

Installing a Trusted CA Certificate on the Client

On the client side, we must install the self-signed certificate that we have created as a trusted CA. To do so, we must first export the X.509 certificate from the keystore on the server side. This can be done using the `keytool` again with the command:

```
keytool -export -alias wrox -rfc -file wroxkey.cer -keystore .\wroxkeys
```

This will export the certificate associated with the key (with alias 'wrox') in a file called `wroxkey.cer` from the keystore called `wroxkeys`. You will be prompted for the keystore password, remember to enter `javarmi` as the password (specified in the `keytool -genkey` command). The format of `wroxkey.cer` is in a standard format (Internet RFC 1421) that can be read by other tools. If you do not use the `-rfc` option to export the certificate, the format will be a binary format that only `keytool` will be able to access. You can view the certificate using the command line:

```
type wroxkey.cer
```

Each JDK installation maintains a keystore (in JKS format) that contains the certificates from well-known, trusted CAs. In fact, you will find trusted certificates from both Verisign and Thawte already in there. You will find the keystore in the following directory:

```
<JDK home>/jre/lib/security
```

The name of this keystore is called `cacerts`. You can view the details of all the certificates (certs) in this store with the command:

```
keytool -list -v -keystore .\cacerts
```

The password to this keystore is, by default, `changeit`.

Assuming that you have the binary certificate from the server available in the `wroxkey.cer` file, you can use the following command to install our certificate as a trusted CA certificate on the client:

```
keytool -import -alias wrox -keystore .\cacerts -storepass changeit
```

When asked if you want to make the certificate a trusted one, make sure you reply yes.

This is the set up necessary before we can establish a test SSL session between a client and server machine. Next, we should make sure that the JSSE 1.0 extension is properly installed on both the client and the server machines.

Installing JSSE 1.0

The distribution of JSSE 1.0 comes in a zip file (for Win32 platforms). You can unarchive it and it will create its own `jsse1.0` directory where the documentation, sample code, etc. will reside.

Installing Security Provider and Extension Libraries

To install JSSE 1.0 into your current copy of JDK, you need to add the provider to the security provider configuration file. You can find this in the file:

```
<JDK install directory>\jre\lib\security\java.security
```

Make sure the following lines are included:

```
security.provider.1=sun.security.provider.Sun
security.provider.2=com.sun.net.ssl.internal.ssl.Provider
```

Next, copy the three extension library JAR files:

```
jsse.jar
jcert.jar
jnet.jar
```

from `jsse1.0\lib` to the directory:

```
<JDK install directory>\jre\lib\ext
```

This is the only installation necessary for the JSSE 1.0 in order to start developing applications using SSL for our purposes.

RMI with Alternate Socket Factory: RMI over SSL

RMI over SSL is implemented in Java 2 using the elegant factory design pattern. Instead of simply using the default socket implementation when an instance of a socket is created, JDK 1.2.x and later allows the programmer to replace the socket factory used to manufacture an instance of a socket implementation. This can be done via the static `setSocketImplFactory()` method of the `Socket` and `ServerSocket` classes. The original version of socket in Java 1.1.x is not socket factory clean, and cannot be easily converted to handle SSL.

Also introduced with JDK 1.2.x, the RMI runtime support code now allows a pair of socket factories (one for the client, and one for the server) to be specified when an RMI server object is exported.

These factories will then be used whenever a socket is created by the RMI based application.

By supplying socket factories that will create SSL server and client sockets, an RMI object can be SSL enabled easily.

Implementing Server-Side Socket Factory

The server-side socket factory is the slightly more involved one. We must set up the server for server authentication. This means that we need to create an SSL context object with a site key and its associated certificate for this purpose.

Using the `wroxkeys` keystore that we created earlier, and the self-signed certificate associated with our own key pair, we can code the server-side socket factory as shown below (`\ch3\code\ssl\ServerSocketFactory.java` in the code download from Wrox):

```
import java.io.*;
import java.net.*;
import java.rmi.server.*;
import javax.net.ssl.*;

import java.security.KeyStore;
import javax.net.*;
import javax.net.ssl.*;
import javax.security.cert.X509Certificate;
import com.sun.net.ssl.*;

public class ServerSockFactory implements
    RMIServerSocketFactory, Serializable {
```

The RMI server socket factory must implement the `RMIServerSocketFactory()` interface. This interface only has one method called `createServerSocket()`. This is implemented next.

```
public ServerSocket createServerSocket(int port) throws
    IOException {
    SSLServerSocketFactory myFact = null;
    try {

      SSLContext myContext;
      KeyManagerFactory myKeyMgrFactory;
      KeyStore myKeyStore;
      String myPassword = 'javarmi';
```

```
    char[] myCharPassword = myPassword.toCharArray();
    myContext = SSLContext.getInstance('TLS');
    myKeyMgrFactory = KeyManagerFactory.getInstance('SunX509');
    myKeyStore = KeyStore.getInstance('JKS');
    myKeyStore.load(new FileInputStream('wroxkeys'),
      myCharPassword);
    myKeyMgrFactory.init(myKeyStore, myCharPassword);
    myContext.init(myKeyMgrFactory.getKeyManagers(), null,
      null);

    myFact = myContext.getServerSocketFactory();
```

We use the `wroxkeys` keystore here, which is password protected ('javarmi'). This code builds the required server-side SSL context, and then uses the `getServerSocketFactory()` method of this context to return the required SSL factory. This factory will create serverside sockets that will:

❑   Send the X.509 certificate in the `wroxkeys` keystore (our self-signed certificate) to the client for server authentication

❑   Use the private key stored in the `wroxkeys` keystore to handle the SSL handshaking

```
    }
    catch (Exception e) {
      e.printStackTrace();
    }
    return myFact.createServerSocket(port);
  }
}
```

Implementing the Client-Side Socket Factory

The code for the client-side socket factory is substantially simpler. Since client authentication is optional in SSL, simply using the default client-side SSL socket factory is adequate. This is done via a static method in the `javax.net.ssl.SSLSocketFactory` class from JSSE 1.0.

```
import java.io.*;
import java.net.*;
import java.rmi.server.*;
import javax.net.ssl.*;

public class ClientSockFactory implements
  RMIClientSocketFactory, Serializable {
  public Socket createSocket(String host, int port)
  throws IOException{
    SSLSocketFactory myFact = (SSLSocketFactory)
      SSLSocketFactory.getDefault();
    SSLSocket s = (SSLSocket)myFact.createSocket(host, port);
    return s;
  }
}
```

Implementing the Serverside Object

The serverside code for our SSL server object is almost identical to the non-SSL implementation we saw earlier. The only difference is the need to specify the server (and client!) socket factories to be used to create the socket used in the communication. We can use a version of the `UnicastRemoteObject.exportObject()` method call to accomplish this.

```
import java.rmi.RemoteException;
import java.rmi.server.UnicastRemoteObject;
import java.rmi.Naming;
import java.rmi.RMISecurityManager;

import java.util.Calendar;

public class SslWorkImpl  implements custWork {

  public SslWorkImpl() throws RemoteException {
    UnicastRemoteObject.exportObject(this, 8022,
      new ClientSockFactory(), new ServerSockFactory ());
  }
```

This is a version of `exportObject()` which takes the two socket factories as parameters. If you are extending `UnicastRemoteObject`, you should call the superclass constructor which takes these parameters.

```
  public String getSvrMsg()throws RemoteException {
    String threadName = Thread.currentThread().getName();
    String curTime =
      Calendar.getInstance().getTime().toString();
    System.out.println(threadName + ': A client connected at '
      + curTime);
    return(threadName + ': Message from Server at ' + curTime);
  }

  public static void main(String[] args) {
    try {
      if (System.getSecurityManager() == null)
        System.setSecurityManager(new RMISecurityManager());

      sslWorkImpl myServ = new sslWorkImpl();
      Naming.rebind('workObj', myServ);

      System.out.println('Server ready and waiting...');
    }
    catch (Exception e) {
      e.printStackTrace();
    }
  }

}
```

The rest of the server logic is exactly the same.

Implementing the Clientside Object

Here, the beauty of dynamic class loading for Java really shines through. Recall that:

❑   The RMI stub object is responsible for creating the socket and communicating back to the server for invocation of methods

❑   RMI stub objects are generated on the server side

❑   RMI stub objects can be dynamically downloaded to the client on an as-needed basis

This means that the client code used does not have to be aware that it is using SSL at all (though JSSE must still be installed on the client machine). Therefore, you can use the earlier basic RMI client to test this system out.

Testing the RMI over SSL system

Here are the steps to start up the RMI over the SSL system:

1. Compile the server and client Java files:

   ```
   ..\bats\buildit SslWorkImpl.java
   ```

2. Use rmic to generate the stub for the SslWorkImpl class

   ```
   rmic -v1.2 SslWorkImpl
   ```

3. Copy the stub file and the CustWork class files to the %WROXHOME% directory (where the class server will be pointed to); use the copystubs.bat batch file:

   ```
   copystubs
   ```

4. Start the HTTP class server:

   ```
   ..\bats\runhttpdstubs
   ```

5. Start rmiregistry, making sure that the CLASSPATH does not point to the stubs:

   ```
   start rmiregistry
   ```

6. Make sure that the wroxkeys keystore is in the server directory

   Start up the secure server; this may take longer than you are used to – wait for the message from the server to appear in the console before proceeding:
   ```
   startsvr
   ```

7. Make sure that cacerts on the client side contains your self-signed certificate as a trusted CA

   Start the RMI client object in the \ch3\code\basic\client directory using the batch file:
   runclnt

The operation and appearance of this system will be identical to a non-SSL system. However, you will notice the considerable delay before a connection between the server and the client can be made. This is the overhead introduced by the SSL handshake phase (and server authentication). Most commercial or production versions of JSSE should be significantly faster than the reference implementation from Sun.

Achieving RMI Immortality – Activatable Objects

Before JDK 1.2.x, RMI objects only lived and worked for the lifetime of an application, and then died. At most, an RMI object could live for the lifetime of the containing VM. With Activatable objects, however, RMI objects can live forever and attain virtual immortality. Activatable objects are unique to Java and are completely new to JDK 1.2.x.

Activatable Objects give the System Hope for Fault Tolerance

Before the availability of the `Activatable` object, your RMI server object would have to have been running when a client made a request through RMI. If the instance of your server object had aborted, or if the machine accidentally rebooted, then the client object would no longer be able to access the server. Any state information that was in the server object was lost forever.

`Activatable` objects in JDK 1.2.x make it possible to create object references to remote objects that appear to be immortal. What this literally means is that a server object can be instantiated once, and virtually last forever. Of course, hardware does fail, and software does crash. It really is impossible to have a single instance of an object last forever. It is not impossible, however, to make the client think that this is the case.

We can understand this by examining exactly how a client sees a server RMI object. First, the client really only has direct access to the stub object. It is this stub object that knows how to communicate with the remote implementation. Now, suppose the remote system actually dies or is no longer there. As long as the stub object can somehow create a new instance of the implementation and then restore the state of the server, there are no other observable changes to the client. In other words, we need:

❑ A way to re-instantiate a server-side implementation object if the system resets or crashes

❑ A way to maintain the state of the server-side implementation in a persistent way that can survive software failure and system reboots

`Activatable` objects provide the above functions. The figure below illustrates this:

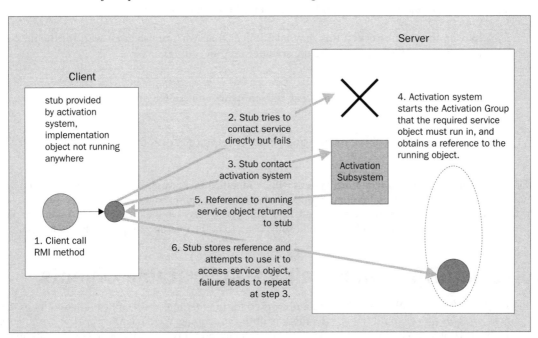

RMID: the Activation Subsystem

How does the `Activatable` object do its magic? The secret lies in a new RMI support service called the RMI Daemon (RMID). A daemon, as those familiar with Unix will know, is a friendly and helpful demon – in other words, a useful background process.

RMID is helpful indeed. It is the single instance of the Java VM that must be restarted whenever the system is reset or rebooted. RMID will then re-create all instances of Java VMs and server objects that had registered with it as `Activatable`, and do so inside one or more VM instances as determined by the grouping of `Activatable` objects into `ActivationGroups`.

In reality, server objects can register with RMID to have either one of the following crash recovery behaviors:

❑ Restart whenever RMID restarts

❑ Restart only when the client makes an actual call to the server object and the server has not yet started (i.e. activated on first call)

To implement the second bullet point, the client must be able to obtain a reference to an object that has not yet been instantiated (or has been instantiated and subsequently died/crashed). `Activatable` objects support exactly this type of object reference.

Robust Persistence: Can it be Done?

When an `Activatable` object is instantiated, the RMID support system can optionally supply it with a `MarshalledObject` as a parameter. By writing this `MarshalledObject` to a persistent store (i.e. the disk drive), and having the server object use this to store any non-volatile state that it wants to maintain, a form of robust persistence can be achieved. This will allow both the server (behavior) and the server state (in the form of a `MarshalledObject`) to survive hardware resets or software crashes.

A Word on Activation Groups

All objects belonging to the same `ActivationGroup` will run in the same Java VM, and will share system properties and environment variables (i.e. the security policy file). This is one good way to save on the number of VMs that are spawned on a system. Depending upon the implementation, multiple `ActivationGroups` may run within the same VM, but a single `ActivationGroup` cannot be split between multiple VMs. Instead of having to spawn one new VM for every new service object class, we can control how service object classes are partitioned on the server side by using `ActivationGroups`.

The figure below illustrates the relationship between the pieces that makes up the activation subsystem:

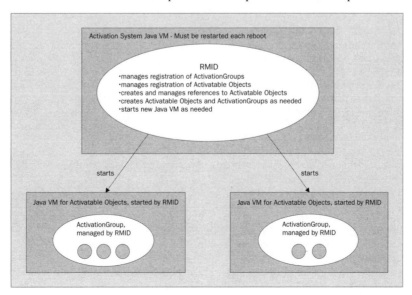

The Road to Immortality

Since an `Activatable` object may be activated on demand, there must be a way to create a reference (stub) to an object instance that is not yet activated. Typically, this is done via a set-up program. This program will perform the following tasks:

❑ Create (or locate) the `ActivationGroup` that the `Activatable` object will belong to

❑ If a new `ActivationGroup` is created, set up the environment of the group using an `ActivationGroupDesc`

❑ Create an `ActivationDesc` that describes:

 ❑ The service object's class name

 ❑ Where the `Activatable` object can be found

 ❑ The `MarshalledObject` persistent state argument that should be passed to the `Activatable` object when it is activated

❑ Register the `ActivationDesc` with RMID and obtain a stub object to the remote interface

❑ Bind this stub object to the service's name with RMIRegistry

Implementing an Activatable Object

We will now implement the service object itself, and the setup program. We will use as a base our trusty `CustWork` RMI service. Here again is the interface definition:

```
import java.rmi.Remote;
import java.rmi.RemoteException;

public interface CustWork extends Remote {
  String getSvrMsg() throws RemoteException;
}
```

The actual service code can be found in `\ch3\code\activ\ActWorkImpl.java`.

```
import java.rmi.RemoteException;
import java.rmi.server.UnicastRemoteObject;
import java.rmi.Naming;
import java.rmi.RMISecurityManager;
import java.rmi.MarshalledObject;
import java.rmi.activation.*;

import java.util.Calendar;

public class ActWorkImpl implements CustWork {

  public ActWorkImpl (ActivationID id, MarshalledObject inObj)
    throws RemoteException  {
    Activatable.exportObject(this, id, 0);
  }

  public String getSvrMsg()throws RemoteException {
    String threadName = Thread.currentThread().getName();
    String curTime =
```

```
                Calendar.getInstance().getTime().toString();
           System.out.println(threadName + ": A client connected at "
             + curTime);
           return(threadName + ": Message from Server at " + curTime);
       }

    }
```

Since we won't be starting this service object from the command line, we do not need a `main()` method. Instead, the activation system (RMID) will be starting this service on our behalf. When this happens, the constructor shown here will be called. The activation system expects us to register our activation with it; the `Activatable.exportObject()` method does this, as well as exporting the object in the RMI sense.

Creating the Setup Program

The setup program does most of the work for an `Activatable` object system.

You can find the code in `\ch3\code\activ\activeSetup.java`.

```
import java.rmi.*;
import java.rmi.activation.*;
import java.util.Properties;

public class ActiveSetup {

  public static void main(String args[]) {
    System.setSecurityManager(new RMISecurityManager());
    try {
      Properties props = new Properties();
      props.put("java.security.policy", "policy.all");
      props.put("java.rmi.server.codebase",
        "http://win98p300:8081/");

      ActivationGroupDesc.CommandEnvironment myEnv = null;
      ActivationGroupDesc myGroup = new
        ActivationGroupDesc(props, myEnv);

      ActivationGroupID myGroupID =
        ActivationGroup.getSystem().registerGroup(myGroup);

      ActivationGroup.createGroup(myGroupID, myGroup, 0);
```

Register an `ActivationGroup` with the activation system (that is, RMID) here. Notice how we set up the environment and codebase for the VM that will host this `ActivationGroup`. The `ActivationGroup.getSystem().registerGroup()` method uses RMID to register our group.

```
        String location =
          "file:///writing/projrew/ch3/code/activ/";
```

This is where the Activation system will find the class file for the service object.

```
        MarshalledObject data = null;
```

Pass in a `MarshalledObject` if you need to preserve state information between activations.

```
        ActivationDesc desc = new ActivationDesc ('ActWorkImpl',
          location, data);

        CustWork myStub = (CustWork) Activatable.register(desc);
        System.out.println('Got the stub for ActWorkImpl');
```

Obtain the stub object from the activatable system, and pass it to the RMI registry so that the remote client can find it.

```
        Naming.rebind('workObj', myStub);
        System.out.println('Registered with RMIRegistry');
      }
      catch(Exception e) {
        e.printStackTrace();
      }
      System.exit(0);
    }
  }
```

Who's got Whose Codebase?

Unlike the clear-cut situation with 'regular' RMI objects, the setting up and running of an `Activatable` object involves many different Java VMs. Since dynamic stub downloading and behavior transfer both depend on the `java.rmi.server.codebase` system property of the service VM, we must be careful to make sure we understand the different Java VMs that are involved.

Java VM	Description
Java VM in which the setup program runs	This VM is temporary (it is only alive during the lifetime of the setup program and will be destroyed when the program is finished. Setting any environment or system properties here will not affect the service object's behavior.
Java VM that hosts the activation group where a particular service object will be activated	This is the VM whose system properties and environment will affect the service object's behavior. The only way to control this is to configure these parameters when creating the activation group.

Client Transparency

Since an `Activatable` object is a purely server-side implementation detail we can use the basic RMI client again for testing. To the client, it will work identically whether the server is using a `UnicastRemoteObject` that must always be running, or if it is using an activatable one that is activated-on-demand. This client transparency is a feature that makes RMI extremely flexible and versatile.

Testing our Activatable Object System

To test our `Activatable` object system, we need to perform the following steps:

1. Compile the service object source files:

```
..\bats\buildit ActWorkImpl.java
```

2. Run rmic on the `ActWorkImpl` to generate the stubs:

```
rmic -v1.2 ActWorkImpl
```

3. Copy the stubs and interface file to the `%WROXHOME%` directory to be served by the class server, use the `copystubs.bat` file for this:

```
copystubs
```

4. Start the class server:

```
runhttpdstubs
```

5. Start the RMIRegistry, making sure that its `CLASSPATH` will not locate the stubs:

```
start rmiregistry
```

6. Start the activation system by running RMID, from the `\ch3\code` directory:

```
start rmid
```

7. Run the `ActiveSetup` program – no service object instance should start at this time:

```
startsvr
```

8. Run the basic RMI client program in the `\ch3\code\basic\client` directory. You should see an object instance start up (in the RMID console) and the server-side message:

```
runclnt
```

Since RMID is the VM that activates the service object, its console is used for output. Now, try running the client a few more times. Since the service object is now activated, the new method invocation will not start new instances.

Now, shut down RMID by killing the task, or pressing *Ctrl-C* while the console is in focus. This will simulate a software failure.

Finally, start RMID again (making sure you're in the same directory as the last time you started it). Now run a client program again. It works; RMID has started a new service object instance! Note that you do not have to run the setup program ever again.

RMID uses a log directory to maintain all the information on `ActivationGroup` and `Activatable` objects. By default, it is created in the directory where RMID is started. This is the way it finds out how to activate the objects. By design, you should never need to delete this log directory (that is, erase all registrations); instead, you can write a program to unregister a service object from the activation system. In practice, however, it is often faster to simply delete this log directory during testing.

Implementing Fault Toleration

For the grand finale project of this chapter, we will create a service object that will purposely commit suicide regularly. This service object will be set up as activatable. We will also write an ignorant client that will simply continually invoke methods on the service object. This will illustrate the fact that while generations of service objects come and go, the client actually believes that the service object is living forever.

You can find the suicidal service object under `\ch3\code\fragile\FragileWorkImpl.java`:

```
import java.rmi.RemoteException;
import java.rmi.server.UnicastRemoteObject;
import java.rmi.Naming;
import java.rmi.RMISecurityManager;
import java.rmi.MarshalledObject;
import java.rmi.activation.*;

import java.util.Calendar;

public class FragileWorkImpl implements CustWork, Runnable {

  public void run() {
    try {
      Thread.sleep(30000);
      System.out.println('****Choke.. Puke... I dieth!****');
      System.exit(0);
    }
    catch (Exception e) {
      e.printStackTrace();
    }
  }
}
```

It spins off a thread that will kill the entire service instance after 30 seconds by calling
System.exit(0).

```
public FragileWorkImpl (ActivationID id, MarshalledObject
  inObj) throws RemoteException {
  Activatable.exportObject(this, id, 0);
  new Thread(this).start();
  System.out.println('Fragile server started...');
}
```

The constructor also sets the service object's lifetime by starting the suicide thread.

```
public String getSvrMsg()throws RemoteException {
  String threadName = Thread.currentThread().getName();
  String curTime =
    Calendar.getInstance().getTime().toString();
  System.out.println(threadName + ': A client connected at '
    + curTime);
  return(threadName + ': Message from Server at ' + curTime);
}
}
```

The Setup Program

The setup program is identical in structure to the previous example. You can find the source in
\ch3\code\fragile\FragileSetup.java file.

```
import java.rmi.*;
import java.rmi.activation.*;
import java.util.Properties;

public class FragileSetup {
```

```java
public static void main(String args[]) {
    System.setSecurityManager(new RMISecurityManager());
    try {
        Properties props = new Properties();
        props.put('jabva.security.policy', "policy.all");
        props.put('java.rmi.server.codebase',
            'http://win98p300:8081/');

        ActivationGroupDesc.CommandEnvironment myEnv = null;
        ActivationGroupDesc myGroup = new
            ActivationGroupDesc(props, myEnv);

        ActivationGroupID myGroupID =
            ActivationGroup.getSystem().registerGroup(myGroup);

        ActivationGroup.createGroup(myGroupID, myGroup, 0);

        String location =
            'file:///writing/projrew/ch3/code/fragile/';
        MarshalledObject data = null;


        ActivationDesc desc = new ActivationDesc
            ('FragileWorkImpl', location, data);

        CustWork myStub = (CustWork) Activatable.register(desc);
        System.out.println('Got the stub for FragileWorkImpl');

        Naming.rebind('workObj', myStub);
        System.out.println('Registered with RMIRegistry');
    }
    catch(Exception e) {
        e.printStackTrace();
    }
    System.exit(0);
    }
}
```

The Happy but Ignorant Client

We modified the basic RMI client program and have it mindlessly loop and call methods on the remote service object. It will wait about 10 seconds between each call. You can find the source in the \ch3\code\fragile\client\RmiClient.java file.

```java
import java.rmi.Naming;
import java.rmi.RemoteException;
import java.rmi.RMISecurityManager;

public class RmiClient {
    static String servMsg = '';
    public static void main(String[] args) {
        try {
            if (System.getSecurityManager() == null)
                System.setSecurityManager(new RMISecurityManager());
            CustWork servRef = (CustWork) Naming.lookup('workObj');
```

```
        while(true){
            servMsg = servRef.getSvrMsg();
            System.out.println(servMsg);
            Thread.sleep(10000);
        }
    }
    catch (Exception e) {
        e.printStackTrace();
    }
  }
}
```

Testing the Fragile System

To test the system, follow the instruction in the previous activatable object sample. You should delete the RMID's log directory (under \ch3\code directory) before you attempt to try this system out, since both servers have the same name.

You will also need to copy the CustWork.class file to the \ch3\code\fragile directory before compilation.

Here are the observable differences to look for:

❑   The client hangs around in a loop and never dies

❑   The server should die every 30 seconds

❑   After the server dies, a new client request activates a new instance of the server

Notice how the client is totally oblivious to the fact that the server:

❑   Uses Activatable object

❑   Has failed and died between method invocations

This is one of the major reasons why one would use Activatable objects.

Java Networking Beyond RMI and Sockets

In this chapter, we have examined several advanced RMI programming concepts. We have seen how dynamic class loading can be extended across the network to provide behavioral transfer for RMI programs. We discussed the importance of MarshalledObject, and its optional URL annotation. We then wrote a flexible work server that accepts arbitrary work from a client and performs it.

Taking a more pragmatic stance, we examined two common problems that production RMI programmer frequently have to deal with:

❑   Making RMI work over a firewall

❑   Encrypting RMI connection to ensure security

Working with actual code, we experimented with RMI through firewalls and discovered that SOCKS based firewalls are automatically supported. Many HTTP based tunneling proxies are also supported, but for outbound calls only. Encrypted RMI connections are creatable via RMI over SSL technology. We examined SSL, TLS, and public key encryption technologies in general. We also coded a complete RMI over SSL example that creates and communicates over an encrypted, secure connection. We've also seen how to install and use the Java Secure Socket Extension (JSSE) library.

Last but not least, we worked with the JDK 1.2+ support for `Activatable` objects. The vital role of RMID as the activator subsystem was examined. `Activatable` objects enable the creation of services that do not need to stay up all the time (that is, they wake on demand); it also facilitates the design of robust services. We then wrote two services that support `Activatable` objects, the final one showing how a robust system can be created using `Activatable` objects.

If only all the systems running in this world were programmed in Java, the sockets and RMI technology that we have described in detail within this chapter could be used to solve all the networking problems. The real world is unfortunately filled with legacy systems – and many of them not object oriented at all.

The jobs of many of today's IT professionals involve makingthese dissimilar and heterogeneous systems work with each other over the network. The standardization of the networking industry (and the Internet) on TCP/IP (versus IPX or XNS, etc) has helped the situation on a very low level.

On the application level, the only universal solution is the Object Management Group's (OMG) CORBA system. CORBA is the Common Object Request Broker Architecture, and it allows a system of objects implemented on heterogeneous systems to interoperate with each other.

In the next chapter we will examine how Java can play a very important role when working with such systems. Our discussion will include coverage of RMI-IIOP where the client written in RMI code (that is, an RMI client) can actually make use of CORBA objects in a heterogeneous network.

Jini Client or Service	JavaSpaces and Helper Services
Jini Client and Service Support Helper Utilities	
Jini Discovery Management Helper Utilities	
Jini Protocol Helper Utilities	

Jini Network Protocols	
	RMI and Rich Object Semantics
	Java VM and Networking

Network Protocols

4

CORBA and RMI-IIOP in a Distributed World

There is a lot of buzz out there comparing Jini to CORBA, the Common Object Request Broker Architecture. CORBA is a decade old, industry standard, object-based technology that allows computer systems to work with each other over a network, regardless of the system's processors, processing power, hardware architecture, programming language, and operating system.

In this chapter, we will introduce CORBA from the ground up for the benefit of readers who may not be familiar with this technology. The history of CORBA, how the technology works, and what the technology is especially good for, will all be covered. Our code development will lead us to discover the CORBA implementation that is built into the JDK distribution since version 1.2. We will code CORBA servers and clients, and witness how it may be similar to, or different from, RMI and Jini. One particular code example will take us to the world where CORBA excels: cross-programming language, cross-operating system object interoperation.

The previous two chapters had a concentrated dose of RMI coverage, so by now you should be amply fluent in the technology, and clear about what it can do for you. By the end of this chapter, you will be equally fluent in CORBA technology, especially in the way it relates to, and compliments, RMI and Java. By the end of this book, you'll be fluent in Jini (and related JavaSpaces) technology as well, and you'll see that Jini, RMI, and CORBA can indeed coexist happily together, complementing each other in the functionality and reach that they provide to the development community..

Regardless, the debate and hype of CORBA versus Jini goes on. Partially because both CORBA and Jini are network-based technologies for distributed computing, and partially due to misunderstanding what Jini really is and does best, these debates inevitably dwell on the fact that Jini can use RMI as a substrate and so have a tendency to disintegrate into RMI versus CORBA discussions. In the context of Java, RMI is very similar to CORBA. In fact, from JDK 1.3 onwards the two are combined, allowing them to inter-work seamlessly. This is only possible because there is a one-to-one mapping between what RMI does for Java programmers, and what CORBA does for Java programmers.

We will work with the very latest technology, called RMI-IIOP, in this chapter. Our examination will reveal how this RMI-to-CORBA mapping technology works under the hood. To gain hands on experience, we will code RMI servers that will become immediately usable by CORBA clients. Then we will take advantage of CORBA and show how a C++ based client running on a Unix system (across differing platforms, operating systems, and programming languages) can take immediate advantage of an RMI server running on a Windows machine – all using this amazing RMI-IIOP technology.

By the end of this chapter, we will understand the implications and differences of CORBA, RMI, and RMI-IIOP technologies. We will also have gained some programming experience with the Java variant of the CORBA technology and the new RMI-IIOP technology, plus cross-platform deployment of interoperating CORBA/RMI systems.

CORBA

CORBA encompasses a suite of specifications from the Object Management Group (OMG). The OMG is a consortium consisting of members from about 800 companies. Founded in October 1989, OMG's mandate is to 'create a component based software marketplace'. The members of OMG accomplish this by generating a suite of specifications that can be used to develop interoperable software projects in heterogeneous environments and across a network. The specifications are freely available over the Internet, and anyone can implement systems conforming to these specifications without paying any royalty or licensing fee. Participation in the OMG is through fee-based membership, and most of the membership consists of individuals who are sponsored by the company that they represent or work for.

Being a specification designed by committee, CORBA was originally very large and all encompassing (circa 1.0). The unwieldy nature of such a large and ambitious specification made actual implementation of the specification expensive and impractical. As a result, there were very few CORBA 1.0 implementations and most of them were not publicly available. Adapting to the shorter project cycles and rapid changes brought upon by the Internet revolution, the newer levels (2.0 and beyond) of CORBA aim to provide instead a universal base with variants for specific applications built on top. The OMG review process itself has also been revised to expedite quick and early adaptation of any technology still under final technical review. Most developers working with CORBA are using one of the level 2.x versions – the specification for CORBA 3.0 is at the finalization stage.

The informing principle behind CORBA is **heterogeneous interoperability**:

> **CORBA software components will work with mainframes, mini-computers, micro-computers and operating systems across a network. CORBA software components can be written in any supported programming language, whether it is object oriented or not.**

Although this is clearly different to the Java-specific RMI technology that we examined in the last two chapters, CORBA's functionality does overlap with the capabilities provided by RMI within the domain of homogeneous Java systems. Outside this realm, however, CORBA allows you to extend the reach of Java-based systems into (new or legacy) hardware, software, operating systems, and programming languages. The figure below illustrates CORBA's additional functionality, and shows how RMI and CORBA do overlap in term of their functionality within the Java world.

The PC server on the left hosts a Java object that is able to access the PC Unix server on the top, the mainframe computer on the right, and the mini-computer on the bottom. This occurs because both RMI, allowing Java VMs on different platforms to work with each other, and CORBA, enabling objects on different operating systems or programming languages to work with each other, are supported. The arrows labeled CORBA/IIOP are connections enabled by CORBA technology (IIOP is the on-the-wire protocol used by CORBA over TCP/IP networks), and those labelled RMI/JRMP are connections enabled by RMI technology (JRMP, Java Remote Method Protocol, is the on-the-wire protocol used by RMI).

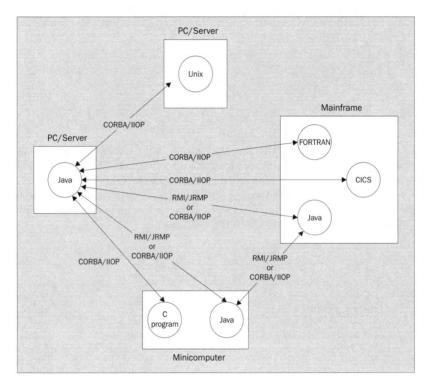

Inside CORBA

We can see how the Java VM supports remote calling syntax simply by introspecting an object reference during an interface call, and looking for the tell-tale `Remote` marker. It can then trigger the appropriate stub call required to extend the object call across the network. So what we need to know now is what CORBA does to create the same effect across such a diverse set of platforms, operating systems, and languages.

The Object Request Broker (ORB)

Unlike RMI, where we can assume the existence of a Java VM, in CORBA we must explicitly specify the pieces that transform a method call into a network packet on the client end, and the pieces that transform the network packet back to a method invocation on the server end. CORBA does this through an **ORB**. An ORB is an Object Request Broker. The figure below shows a client working with an ORB to contact a server.

The ORB is used to get the object reference; once the object reference is obtained, the ORB is not used in subsequent calls to the object.

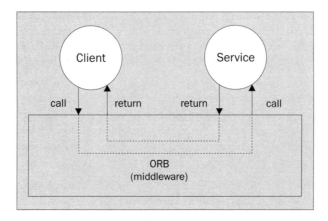

This picture doesn't show how two ORBs, potentially from different vendors and running on completely different hardware/software platforms, work together over a network. The magical glue here is a standard protocol for inter-ORB communications, specified by the OMG. This protocol is called IIOP (Internet Inter-ORB Protocol). IIOP is a well-specified protocol (a specialization of the General Inter-ORB Protocol or GIOP) that runs on top of TCP/IP (thus the Internet designation) network. The figure below shows two ORBs talking together via IIOP:

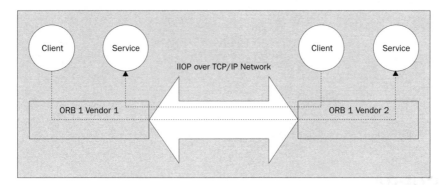

The diagram above shows how a client working with an ORB from vendor 1 (for example, on a Solaris workstation running a Java applet) can work with a service on an ORB from vendor 2 (for example, an IBM mainframe running CICS, their Customer Information Control System).

Notice that the ORB is responsible for transforming the CORBA interface method call into a network packet, and for sending that packet to the server's ORB. The server's ORB is then responsible for decoding the network packet, actually invoking the proper method call, and then transforming the return value back to a network packet for the client – this, of course, is called marshalling. It makes use of a well-specified on-the-wire format called CDR (or Common Data Representation) to marshal data items onto the network. As of CORBA 2.0, IIOP-based interoperation with other ORBs is a requirement for all conformant networked ORB implementations.

The Stubs and Skeletons

When we take a more detailed look at what actually happens, we will see that the CORBA client actually talks through a stub, and the method invocation actually occurs on the server side through a skeleton. The stub is typically generated source code that is specific to the interface being invoked. It is also the client's link to the ORB. In fact, the client communicates through the stub and does not have to be explicitly aware what ORB is being used, or that an ORB is being used at all.

At the server end, the ORB first receives the network packet. It will then call through to the interface's method implementation through what is called a skeleton.

The skeleton adapts the ORB to the method implementation. It hides the ORB details by 'up-calling' into the implementation itself. Up-calling simply means that the implementation will be called from the skeleton (from a conceptually lower layer to a higher layer). The figure below illustrates how the ORB works together with stubs and skeletons to make a networked call:

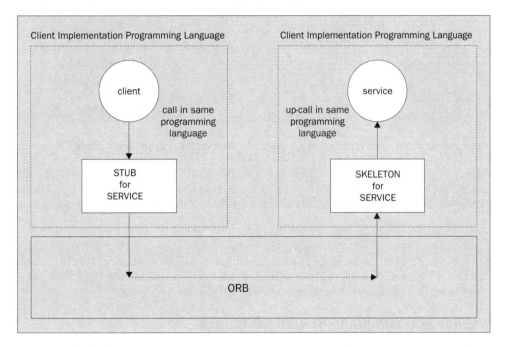

Object Adapters

Although an ORB is typically transparent to the client, it isn't so to the service. A service may need various support functions from the ORB within its implementation. For example, a CORBA service may need to allocate memory or other resources, or it may need to use a specific concurrency-handling strategy to handle client's requests, and so on. So, as you might envisage, a server can become quite ORB specific. CORBA's solution to this is to specify an **object adapter** to handle the calls from the server into the ORB (that is, to provide a set of ORB-based APIs for services to use). The figure over illustrates how a server works with an object adapter:

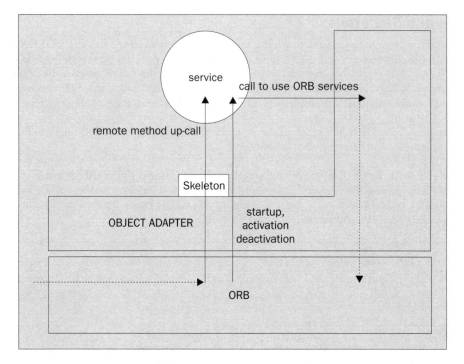

Should an object adapter be required to supply all the necessary support functionality for each and every type of service implementation, it would be enormous, carrying around with it, for many service implementations, redundant baggage that will simply be not used. This is clearly inefficient: object adapters cannot and should not do everything for every type of service. Consequently, CORBA's object adapters come in different shapes and sizes, each suitable for different types of service implementations.

The most commonly used one is the Basic Object Adapter (BOA). The BOA provides method invocation support and will allow one executable to implement a single CORBA method, a service instance (called a CORBA object in CORBA), or multiple instances of the same CORBA object. It will also handle activation and provide persistent support for a small piece of data. Object adapters provided by vendors may do much more than what the OMG defined BOA provides.

IDL Compiler and Language Specific Bindings

Let us look at how stubs and skeletons (equivalent to RMI stubs/proxies) are created in CORBA. The figure below shows this process. First, the objects and their interfaces are mapped out using CORBA's Interface Definition Language (IDL). The IDL description itself is programming language independent, and describes the interface and methods in much the same way as a Java interface file would. This programming language independent IDL file is then put through a programming language specific compiler, called an IDL compiler. The IDL compiler will generate stub code, skeleton code, and sometimes (depending on the implementation) other helper code in the target language being supported. This set of IDL-compiler generated code, specific to one programming language, is called a 'language binding' in CORBA. The stub, skeleton, and helper code can then be combined with one's own service or client logic using the target programming language compiler to produce the final executable.

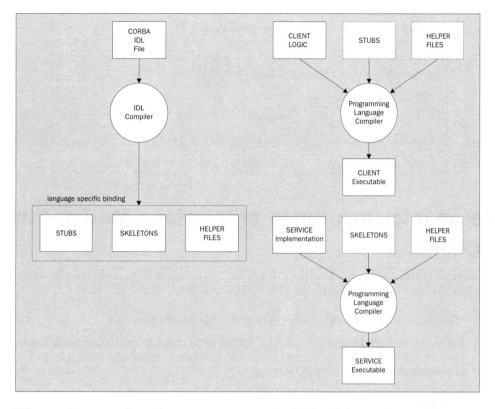

The IDL compiler is specific to the operating system, the ORB and the vendor-specific programming language implementation. In an IDL file, the data types are mapped from the IDL language into each language's data type in the most obvious way. CORBA's IDL specification provides data type translations between CORBA IDL and each of the programming language being used.

As an illustration, here are the mappings between common CORBA IDL data types and Java data types:

CORBA IDL Type	Java Data Type
octect	byte
string	Java.lang.String (all 8 bit characters)
long	int (32 bits)
unsigned long	int
long long	long (64 bits)
unsigned long long	long
boolean	boolean
char	char (value only from 0 to 255 allowed)

Table continued on following page

95

CORBA IDL Type	Java Data Type
wchar	char
wstring	Java.lang.String
short	short
unsigned short	short
float	float
double	double

Skeleton Implementation of Interface Methods and Delegation

The generated skeleton code will bind the ORB to the server object implementation. There are two generally accepted ways to implement an object that supports a CORBA interface:

❑   Directly from the mapped interface, using language binding

❑   Indirectly through delegation via a TIE (a TIE works through a delegate: an object that method calls are forwarded to; note that it has a different inheritance hierarchy and does not directly implement the mapped interface)

Let us look at each case in turn.

Server Implementation via Direct Mapped Interface

The following information is specific to the way the JDK 1.3 implementation of the CORBA ORB works. Other vendor's ORBs and IDL compilers may work slightly differently.

JDK 1.3 supplies a Java IDL compiler called idlj. The IDL-to-Java skeleton generated by the idlj tool uses the first of the methods listed above to implement an object that supports a CORBA interface. For each IDL interface, the following Java-based interfaces are generated:

❑   An Operations interface containing the method to be implemented

❑   An interface (with the same name as the CORBA interface) that extends the Operations interface, and adds CORBA-specific interfaces to its inheritance mix

The generated skeleton's base implementation code will actually make calls through the methods of the second interface listed above. The Java servant object providing the server implementation must implement the method of the Operations interface; default implementations for all the CORBA interface methods are inherited from the base implementation class when we write our code.

The figure below illustrates how all this works. Here, `MyInterface` is the CORBA interface defined in IDL. We see that `MyInterfaceOperations` interface, `MyInterface` interface, and `MyServantImplBase` class is the Java-specific material generated. Notice how `MyInterface` aggregates both CORBA-specific interfaces and `MyInterfaceOperations`. Since `MyServantImplBase` is an abstract class that provides the implementation for any aggregated CORBA-specific interfaces, all that is left to do is implement the methods of the actual CORBA interface. The implementation of the methods of the actual CORBA interface is done by the programmer via the `MyServant` class (inherit from the `MyServantImplBase` and fill in all the missing methods).

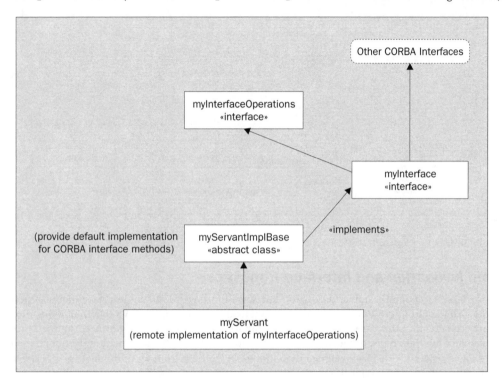

Server Implementation Using a TIE

In the TIE scenario, the Java object implementation need not be aware of CORBA existence at all. Instead, an object instance is *tied* into the CORBA skeleton. Using a TIE, methods calls are delegated directly to the delegate. This is similar in architecture to a common wrapper. In fact, this is how one would wrap legacy systems and coding with Java. Only the outer or wrapper object that implements the TIE will need to know anything about CORBA. The figure below illustrates this TIE scheme.

Here, the TIE inherits from `MyInterfaceOperations` and other CORBA-specific interfaces. It contains a reference to a delegate object that actually implements the CORBA interface methods. All calls through the methods of `MyInterfaceOperations` will be forwarded to the delegate object.

In this way, the delegate object implementing the methods need not have any ancestral relationship to any CORBA-specific classes or interfaces.

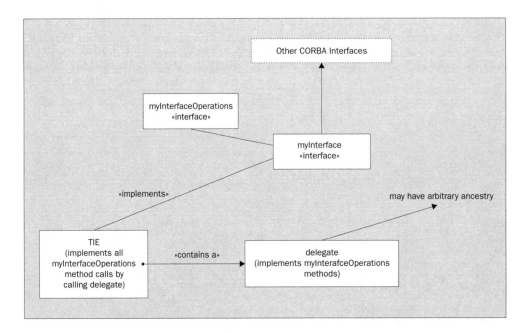

Dynamic Invocation and Interface Repository

You don't have to compile stub and skeleton language bindings to invoke interface methods across the network. You could opt to build a stub programmatically through CORBA's dynamic invocation support. The client in this case must be able to obtain information on the interface, the methods that it contains, and the data types of the arguments and return values. This information, frequently called the meta-data associated with an object, can be obtained at runtime from an optional CORBA specified service called an **interface repository**.

As the name suggests, the interface repository is a service that can be available to both CORBA clients and services. It contains the information associated with interfaces that may be used within the specific CORBA network.

On the server side, a dynamic skeleton interface is used to invoke the appropriate object and method. An interface repository is not a pre-requisite for dynamic invocation in CORBA. The client is free to use any available methods to obtain meta-data associated with an object, including static information that has been compiled inside. Of course, by using this approach we're defeating the original premise of using dynamic invocation. The figure below illustrates how dynamic invocation is performed, and the important role that an interface repository plays.

The service on the right hand side installs all the interfaces that it supports into the interface repository during installation time. The client on the left can then dynamically read this information from the interface repository on an as-needed basis. This interface information is used by the dynamic invocation support to build the required stub and skeleton logic on-the-fly.

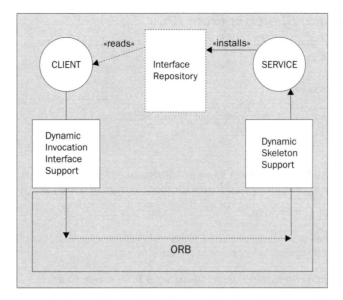

The details of dynamic invocation is beyond the scope of this book; interested readers can consult the OMG's own website at http://www.omg.org/ for definitive information:

Sun's JDK ORB: CORBA, Java Style

Now that we understand the fundamentals of CORBA, let us put it into practice and start creating some CORBA client and servers. This is extremely simple to do with JDK 1.3 and beyond because a CORBA ORB is built-in with the default JDK distribution. The following discussion assumes that you are working with JDK 1.3 Standard Edition or later. If you are working with JDK 1.2 or earlier, you may have to download additional libraries and tools to get the RMI-IIOP portion of the samples working. Check http://ww.java.sun.com for the latest downloads and library information.

Before we get down to the business of server and client, we have to create the CORBA IDL file that describes the interface that they will communicate through. In our first example, the interface has only one method, taking float arguments and a single string argument. The method itself will return the sum of the two input values in float form. The third argument, a string, will be a CORBA output value, whose value will be changed by the return of the method. The figure below illustrates the flow of information through this interface.

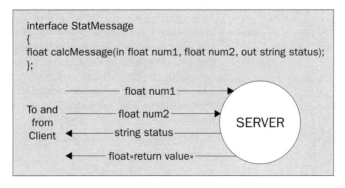

Generating Stub and Skeleton From IDL

In the code download that accompanies this book, you will find the StatMsg.idl file under
\ch4\code\jorb\ directory:

```
interface StatMessage
{
float calcMessage(in float num1, in float num2,
  out string status);
};
```

To compile this CORBA IDL into Java stubs and skeletons, we will need to use the idlj utility. The
command to compile both stubs and skeletons for the StatMsg.idl file is:

```
idlj -fall StatMsg.idl
```

The -fall option generates all the required stubs and skeletons for both the client and server side (you
can use -fclient if you wish to generate the client side only).

Following compilation, the idlj tool generates several Java source files:

File Name	Description
StatMessageOperations.java	This is a Java interface that represents the mapping from the CORBA specific IDL file to the Java language binding. The interface reflects just what is specified in the IDL file, and nothing more.
StatMessage.java	This is a Java interface that extends the actual translated interface. It adds CORBA object specifics to the operations interface. This is the interface that the skeleton will actually implement.
_StatMessageImplBase.java	This is a Java abstract class because not all of its required methods are implemented. It is the skeleton that you use as a base class for the object implementation. It extends a base CORBA ObjectImpl class and implements the StatMessage interface. However, the actual implementation of the StatMessage interface will be provided by your own code when the object implementation is coded.
StatMessageHolder.java	This standard Holder class allows out or in/out arguments to be passed in method calls even when a pass-by-value semantic is enforced by the underlying language. The Holder class includes a member called value which is the type of the holder (in this case, the StatMessage type). This value member can be modified within the holder without disturbing the actual address or value of the holder itself.

File Name	Description
StatMessageHelper.java	Contains various helper methods useful when working with StatMessage. The most frequently used one will always be the narrow() method. This is used to cast a returned CORBA object reference into the StatMessage type. This is the exact way that programming language independent type casting is done in CORBA.
_StatMessageStub.java	This class is the client-side stub implementation for the interface. It converts calls from the Java client of the StatMessage interface into method invocation within the ORB.

The figure under *Server Implementation via Direct Mapped Interface*, seen previously earlier in this chapter, showed the hierarchy of several of these interfaces and classes, showing where they fit together to provide the CORBA functionality.

Let us take a look inside each file generated, remembering that this is both vendor specific and specific to the JDK 1.3 ORB implementation.

Here, we can see the generated StatMessageOperations interface. Note how it is almost identical to the IDL specification:

```
/**
 * StatMessageOperations.Java
 * Generated by the IDL-to-Java compiler (portable), version "3.0"
 * from statmsg.idl
 */

public interface StatMessageOperations
{
  float calcMessage (float num1, float num2,
    org.omg.CORBA.StringHolder status);
} // interface StatMessageOperations
```

Since the status argument is an out parameter and its value needs to be modified within the method call the data type that is used is actually a StringHolder class. The StringHolder class holds a String member inside, called value. This allows us to pass out the changed value.

Next, we have the StatMessage interface. This interface adds a couple of CORBA specific interfaces to our StatMessageOperations interface. The skeleton must implement the methods of all these interfaces. Generating code in this fashion allows us to bypass the single-inheritance only restriction of Java classes:

```
/**
 * StatMessage.Java
 * Generated by the IDL-to-Java compiler (portable), version "3.0"
 * from statmsg.idl
 */

public interface StatMessage extends StatMessageOperations,
  org.omg.CORBA.Object, org.omg.CORBA.portable.IDLEntity
{
} // interface StatMessage
```

The final interesting generated class that we will look at is the _StatMessageImplBase class. This is the skeleton code itself. It needs to implement StatMessage, and gets much of its CORBA-specific implementation from extending the ObjectImpl class. Being an abstract class, it actually leaves the implementation to the methods of the StatMessageOperations interface for you to code in your subclass (the server object implementation).

```
/**
 * _StatMessageImplBase.Java
 * Generated by the IDL-to-Java compiler (portable), version "3.0"
 * from statmsg.idl
 */

public abstract class _StatMessageImplBase extends
   org.omg.CORBA.portable.ObjectImpl
   implements StatMessage, org.omg.CORBA.portable.InvokeHandler
{

   // Constructors
   public _StatMessageImplBase ()
   {
   }

...

// rest of the code not included

...

}
```

Implementing the Server and Remote Object

Our server implementation is in the \ch4\code\jorb\StatMessageServer.java file:

```
import org.omg.CosNaming.*;
import org.omg.CosNaming.NamingContextPackage.*;
import org.omg.CORBA.*;
import Java.io.*;
```

StatServant is the object implementation. It extends the skeleton class to get most of its default CORBA behavior. The only missing method that we must implement from the abstract _StatMessageImplBase class is the method we have defined in the CORBA IDL file: calcMessage. Here, 'out' implementation returns both the sum in float form and in a string message form. We also print out, on the server side, a status message every time we receive a call into this method from a client:

```
class StatServant extends _StatMessageImplBase {
   public float calcMessage (float num1, float num2,
      org.omg.CORBA.StringHolder status) {
      System.out.println("received a client call...");
      float mytotal = num1 + num2;
      status.value = "String result: " + mytotal + ".";
      return (mytotal);
   }
}
```

The actual `StatMessageServer` class is our server implementation. It must initialize the ORB (via the object adapter). It also creates an instance of the `Servant` object (combined stub and our object implementation code) and connects it (exports it) to the ORB:

```
public class StatMessageServer {
  public static void main(String args[]) {
    try {
      // create and initialize the ORB
      ORB orb = ORB.init(args, null);

      // create servant and register it with the ORB
      StatServant myRef = new StatServant();
      orb.connect(myRef);
```

At this point, the instance of the object implementation is ready to take client calls. However, the client must somehow obtain a reference to the object.

Typically, a client will obtain remote object references through:

- ❑   A factory method

- ❑   The return value or `out` arguments from method calls

- ❑   A well-known naming service (such as COSNaming – an OMG defined CORBA service)

- ❑   The string form of the object reference, known as an IOR (Interoperable Object Reference, explained below), via some operating-system based mechanism (for example, within a file or a registry)

In our case, we will choose the second method because it is very simple to implement. Here, we create a text file to write the IOR into. The IOR is a core part of the IIOP protocol, and is used to encode information such as host, port, the object instance location and other potentially ORB-specific information – all into a string of hexadecimal characters. It is meant to be an opaque reference that can be used to locate an object instance anywhere over the CORBA network, even across ORBs (thanks to its IIOP heritage). The `orb.object_to_string()` method returns such an IOR. We write it directly to the `ior.txt` file. The client will use this IOR to locate the service later.

```
      try{
        PrintWriter myFile = new PrintWriter(new FileWriter
          ("ior.txt"), true);

        myFile.println(orb.object_to_string(myRef));
        myFile.close();
      }
      catch (Exception ex) {
        ex.printStackTrace();
      }
```

Finally, we print a status message and wait around for incoming calls:

```
      System.out.println("JDK 1.3 CORBA server ready and
        waiting...");
      // wait for invocations from clients
      java.lang.Object sync = new java.lang.Object();
      synchronized (sync) {
```

```
      sync.wait();
    } // of inner try
  } // of outer try
  catch (Exception e) {
    System.err.println("ERROR: " + e);
    e.printStackTrace(System.out);
  }
 }
}
```

This is all we need to perform on the server side. It is basically the same logic flow as an RMI server. It has to:

❑   Create an instance of the object containing the service logic

❑   Export the object to make it available over the network

❑   Make a reference of the object available for clients to find

❑   Wait around for clients to make calls into the service logic

Creating CORBA Clients Based on IDL Generated Stubs

To create a CORBA client that will use the Java binding generated from the IDL file, we simply write the program that uses the generated and compiled classes. You can find the client source code in \ch4\code\jorb\StatClient.java:

```
import org.omg.CosNaming.*;
import org.omg.CORBA.*;
import Java.io.*;
```

The client logic does not need to create local objects. All of the code is within the static main method for simplicity:

```
public class StatClient {
  public static void main(String args[]) {
    try {
```

The first thing we do is use an instance of a BufferedReader to read the ior.txt file, allowing us to retrieve the string form of the object reference for our server. We also print out a status message with the entire (and very long!) IOR for troubleshooting purposes:

```
      BufferedReader myReader = new BufferedReader(new
        FileReader("ior.txt"));
      String myIOR = myReader.readLine();
      myReader.close();
      System.out.println("Using ... "+ myIOR);
```

Next, we create and initialize an ORB that will help us to locate the object.

```
      ORB orb = ORB.init(args, null);
```

Here, we use the `orb.string_to_object()` method to reconstitute an object reference from the IOR string. The client is oblivious as to how this is done. The IOR should always be handled by the client as an opaque cookie that can easily be transported as text, but can be transformed into a CORBA object reference at anytime through the help of the local ORB. Once we obtain the object reference, we immediately cast it the `StatMessage` type. This is done, as we have mentioned earlier, via the universal CORBA 'narrow' operation. The programmatic way of casting can be performed even on languages that do not natively support the concept of type conversion or casting (for example, the FORTRAN language).

```
// get the root naming context
org.omg.CORBA.Object objRef =
    orb.string_to_object(myIOR);
StatMessage myRef = StatMessageHelper.narrow(objRef);
```

Now we have a reference to a Java object that supports the Java `StatMessage` interface. We can call its `calcMessage()` method to compute the result.

Note that for the 'out' string parameter, we are creating a `StringHolder` instance to pass in a mutable version of the CORBA 'string' data type.

```
// call the Hello server object and print results
StringHolder myMessage = new StringHolder();
float myResult = myRef.calcMessage(2.1233f, 1.1111f,
    myMessage);
```

Once the server completes the calculation remotely, the result is printed to the client computer for display:

```
        System.out.println("The calculated result is " +
            myResult + ". And... " + myMessage.value);
    }
    catch (Exception e) {
        System.out.println("ERROR : " + e) ;
        e.printStackTrace(System.out);
    }
  }
}
```

This is all that has to be done on the server and client side of the CORBA application. In real world implementations, the client or server side usually exists already (if you're working with a legacy mainframe system, for example). It may be implemented in a programming language other than Java. In these cases, all you will be supplied with is the IDL file, and some way to obtain the initial object reference. Following the above general steps, one can easily create either a Java client to use the existing CORBA object and services, or create CORBA services in Java that can be used by all variety of CORBA clients (some of which may be services themselves).

Let us compile the programs and see them work.

Compile the `StatMessageServer` and `StatClient` classes:

```
javac StatMessageServer.java
javac StatClient.java
```

Now, in the background, start the server running on its own console:

```
start java StatMessageServer
```

It should soon start and print out the "waiting..." status message as the screen shot below:

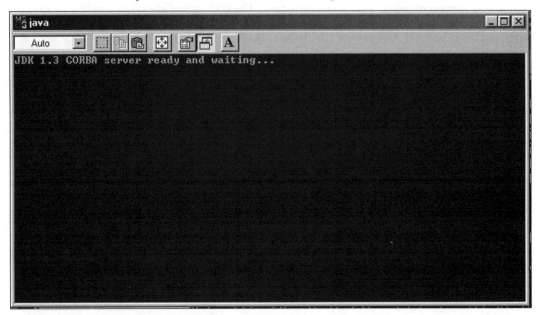

This means that the IOR has already been written to the `ior.txt` file. Those on Windows machines can view the (long) IOR using the command line:

```
type ior.txt
```

You should see a rather long string similar to that in the screen shot below:

If you start the client, this IOR will be converted back into an object reference to the server, and the server used to compute the sum and generate the string message. Use the command line:

```
java StatClient
```

Your output should be similar to that in the screen shot below:

The computation has been carried out remotely on the server. You should see a new status message in the server console indicating that a client call has been serviced, as shown below:

Working with Another Vendor's ORB: Visigenic

The example we've just seen used the default ORB that comes with the JDK. In a former life, this ORB was a commercial product known affectionately as JOE and NEO, so this move, that puts a highly functional ORB within reach of everyone who can download it, is a major plus for developers and CORBA enthusiasts.

We have mentioned that one of the advantages of CORBA is its interoperability between ORBs from different vendors. Since all ORBs must communicate via an interoperable IIOP on-the-wire protocol, calls between different ORBs are almost automatic.

One major force in the creation of robust and efficient ORBs for production use is Visigenic, a company at the forefront of CORBA-on-Java development, as well as C/C++. Visigenic is a part of Inprise – you can download a 90-day trial version of the latest version of the Visigenic Java ORB product, called VisiBroker, from http://www.inprise.com/.

There are many differences between the JDK ORB and the production Visigenic ORB, other than the vendor support you'd expect. Most of the features supplied by Visigenic are geared towards robust production deployments of CORBA-based products; JDK's ORB is more suitable for experimentation and smaller projects. The key differentiation is JDK ORB's lack of support for persistent servers. Objects implemented using the JDK ORB are alive and their references or IOR only valid for as long as the process that they live in stays up and running. Visigenic's ORB supports a persistent server through restarts or network failures.

So we can recreate our StatMessage client and server using the Visigenic ORB and tool set. We'll see how the client and server works with the Visigenic ORB, and how the Visigenic ORB and the JDK ORB can work together, via IIOP, over the network.

The following discussion assumes that you have downloaded and successfully installed the Visigenic VisiBroker Java-based product.

Generating Stubs and Skeleton from the IDL

The source code for the Visigenic versions of the client and server can be found in the `\ch4\code\visigenic\` directory. First, we must generate the stubs and skeletons from the IDL file. The IDL compiler tool for Visigenic is called `idl2java`, and has some differences to the `idlj` compiler we used for the JDK ORB. Since stubs and skeletons source codes are highly ORB specific, an ORB dependent IDL compiler tool must be used to generate them. We have create a `procidl.bat` batch file for this. It contains:

```
idl2java ..\jorb\StatMsg.idl
```

This will generate the following Java source files:

File Name	Description
StatMessageOperations.java	The mapped IDL-to-Java interface as before.
StatMessage.java	The additional inheritance from CORBA-specific interfaces, similar to before.
StatMessagePOA.java	A Portable Object Adapter (POA) implementation of the skeleton. There is a new OMG specification on POA. The goal of POA is to enable source code written for one ORB vendor's ORB to work with another vendor's ORB via a simple re-compile.
StatMessagePOATie.java	An alternate implementation of the skeleton, using a delegate through the POA as a TIE interface.
StatMessageHolder.java	The `Holder` class to support pass-by-value semantics for this new CORBA 'data type'.
StatMessageHelper.java	A set of helper methods useful for interacting with object references and the ORB, including the `narrow()` casting method.
_StatMessageStub.java	The client side stub for accessing the `StatMessage` remote object implementation.

Note that there is great similarity between the JDK ORB's set of generated support files and the Visigenic generated set.

Of special interest here is the alternate TIE skeleton implementation. The `StatMessagePOATie.java` file contains:

```
public class StatMessagePOATie extends StatMessagePOA {
```

There are two constructors; you can either pass in an object that implements just the translated Java interface (that is, no CORBA knowledge or implementation at all), or both the object and your own POA instance. The non-CORBA object that you pass in will be stored internally in the _delegate member. Its method will be delegated to whenever a method is called through the skeleton via the POA:

```
private StatMessageOperations _delegate;
private org.omg.PortableServer.POA _poa;

public StatMessagePOATie (final StatMessageOperations
  _delegate) {
  this._delegate = _delegate;
}

public StatMessagePOATie (final StatMessageOperations
  _delegate, final org.omg.PortableServer.POA _poa) {
  this._delegate = _delegate;
  this._poa = _poa;
}
```

Next, we have a series of access methods for the _delegate and _poa members.

```
public StatMessageOperations _delegate () {
  return this._delegate;
}
public void _delegate (final StatMessageOperations delegate){
  this._delegate = delegate;
}

public org.omg.PortableServer.POA _default_POA () {
  if (_poa != null) {
    return _poa;
  }
  else {
    return super._default_POA();
  }
}
```

Here, the skeleton's implementation of the StatMessage interface's methods delegates (via a TIE) to the embedded object – which does not have to know it is being wrapped via a Java CORBA layer.

```
public float calcMessage (float num1, float num2,
  org.omg.CORBA.StringHolder status) {
  return this._delegate.calcMessage(num1, num2, status);
}

}
```

StatMessagePOATie.java is generated by default when idl2java is executed, and can be quite useful when using CORBA in wrapping existing functionality or legacy systems in general.

Writing a CORBA server for the Visigenic ORB

The server coding can be found in the `\ch4\code\visigenic\StatServer.java` file. You will recognize the logic flow, although the coding details differ slightly.

```
import org.omg.PortableServer.*;
import Java.io.*;
```

We use the POA version of the skeleton directly instead of the TIE version for simplicity. As is the case with the JDK ORB, we declare the servant class that implements the `StatMessage` interface first. The code is almost identical, except that the class inherits from the POA skeleton:

```
class StatServant extends StatMessagePOA {
  public float calcMessage (float num1, float num2,
    org.omg.CORBA.StringHolder status) {
    System.out.println("received a client call...");
    float mytotal = num1 + num2;
    status.value = "String result: " + mytotal + ".";
    return (mytotal);
  }
}
```

Here is the server implementation portion of the code. We initialize the ORB as before. Using the ORB, we locate the `rootPOA` and perform some Visigenic-specific operations for lifespan policy support (that is, support for transient or persistent service):

```
public class StatServer {
  public static void main(String args[])  {
    try {
      // create and initialize the ORB
      org.omg.CORBA.ORB orb = org.omg.CORBA.ORB.init(args,
        null);

      POA rootPOA = POAHelper.narrow (
        orb.resolve_initial_references("RootPOA") );

      // Create policies for our persistent POA
      org.omg.CORBA.Policy[] policies = {
        rootPOA.create_lifespan_policy(
          LifespanPolicyValue.PERSISTENT)
      };

      // Create myPOA with the right policies
      POA myPOA = rootPOA.create_POA("statsServer",
        rootPOA.the_POAManager(), policies);
```

Next, we create an instance of our `Servant` class. We then locate and activate our POA, so that we can talk to the ORB through the POA:

```
      // Create the servant
      StatServant myServant = new StatServant();
      // Decide on the ID for the servant
      byte[] myId = "stats".getBytes();
```

```
        // Activate the servant with the ID on myPOA
        myPOA.activate_object_with_id(myId, myServant);

        // Activate the POA manager
        rootPOA.the_POAManager().activate();
```

Here, using the `servant_to_reference()` method of the POA, we obtain the IOR for our service and then write it out to the `ior.txt` file as we did with the JDK ORB implementation:

```
        // convert servant to an object reference
        org.omg.CORBA.Object object =
          myPOA.servant_to_reference(myServant);

        FileWriter output = new FileWriter("ior.txt");
        output.write(orb.object_to_string(object));
        output.close();
```

We then write out to the server console a message indicating that we are ready and waiting to accept client requests:

```
        System.out.println("Visigenic server ready and
          waiting...");
```

Finally, we wait around – without terminating – for incoming client calls.

```
      }
    catch (Exception e) {
      System.err.println("ERROR: " + e);
      e.printStackTrace(System.out);
    }
  }
}
```

You can compile the server program in the Visigenic environment using the command line (`vbjc` is the VisiBroker Java Compiler wrapper from Visigenic):

```
    vbjc StatServer.Java
```

Creating CORBA Clients Using Visigenic VisiBroker for Java

Being independent and almost oblivious to the details of ORB and server implementations, the coding of the CORBA client for Visigenic is identical to the one for the JDK ORB. The source code is in `\ch4\code\visigenic\StatClient.java`:

```
import org.omg.CORBA.*;
import java.io.*;

public class StatClient {
  public static void main(String args[]) {
    try {
      // create and initialize the ORB
      BufferedReader myReader = new BufferedReader(new
```

```
          FileReader("ior.txt"));
       String myIOR = myReader.readLine();
       myReader.close();
       System.out.println("Using ... "+ myIOR);
       ORB orb = ORB.init(args, null);

       org.omg.CORBA.Object objRef =orb.string_to_object(myIOR);
       StatMessage myRef = StatMessageHelper.narrow(objRef);

       // call the Hello server object and print results
       StringHolder myMessage = new StringHolder("");

       float myResult = myRef.calcMessage(2.1233f, 1.1111f,
         myMessage);

       System.out.println("The calculated result is "
         + myResult + ". And... " + myMessage.value);
     }
   catch (Exception e) {
     System.out.println("ERROR : " + e) ;
     e.printStackTrace(System.out);
   }
  }
 }
}
```

Compile this client using the Visigenic environment:

```
vbjc StatClient.java
```

Testing Visigenic Intra-ORB Operations

To test the CORBA client and server operation through the Visigenic ORB, we must first start an instance of the supplied VisiBroker SmartAgent (see Visigenic's documentation on how to do this). Make sure the SmartAgent is up and running before continuing, as it is a fundamental part of the Visigenic ORB implementation. The screen shot below shows the Visigenic SmartAgent running:

Now, start the server by using the command line:

```
start vbj StatServer.java
```

You should see the "waiting..." message from the server, as shown below:

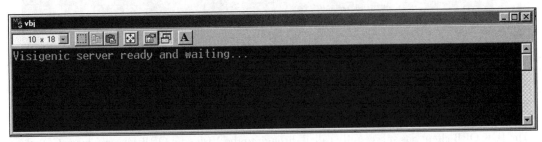

At this time, the IOR has been written to ior.txt, and you can view it with type ior.txt, if you so wish.

Now, we can start the client using the command line:

```
vbj StatClient.java
```

Your output should be similar to that below:

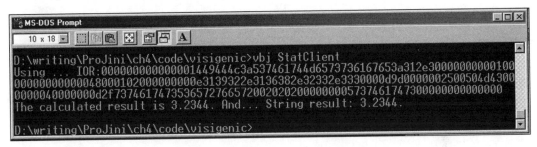

If you check the server console, you will also see that a client call has been serviced. The client has successfully located the service via the IOR, using the Visigenic ORB, and made the call through to the server.

It is now time to do something more exciting. Do *not* exit from the running Visigenic StatServer, as we will now go across ORBs using IIOP and call it from the JDK ORB client!

Testing Visigenic and JDK ORB Inter-ORB Operations

Change directory to the \ch4\code\jorb\ directory. Now copy the ior.txt file from the Visigenic directory:

```
copy ..\visigenic\ior.txt
```

You can replace the old IOR that is still there. Now, start a JDK ORB client instance by using the command line:

```
java StatClient
```

Your output should look like:

Your Visigenic server console should print another client access message as well.

The JDK ORB client has successfully called through to the Visigenic ORB server! This is CORBA at work over IIOP. Recall that Visigenic also has support for C/C++ clients, so any servers implemented using these programming languages will work equally seamlessly.

Terminate the Visigenic server console. We can now reverse the roles. From the \ch4\code\jorb\ directory, run the JDK ORB server in the background:

```
start java StatMessageServer
```

After you see the "waiting..." message, change directory to \ch4\code\visigenic\. Copy over the new ior.txt file:

```
copy ..\jorb\ior.txt .
```

Make sure it replaces the old ior.txt file that may be in the directory. Now, start a client on the Visigenic ORB:

```
vbj StatClient
```

Your output should be similar to that shown below:

A Visigenic ORB client has successfully called through to the JDK ORB server via IIOP. Clients of programming languages supported by Visigenic can make use of Java CORBA servers in the same seamless, easy way.

The figure below illustrates the intra-ORB and inter-ORB calls that we tested in this section. We first tested the `StatClient` and `StatMessageServer` on the JDK 1.3 ORB (shown on the left hand side of the figure), and they worked well over the same ORB. We also independently tested the `StatClient` and `StatServer` on the Visigenic ORB, and they worked superbly within the Visigenic ORB. Finally, we tried the JDK 1.3 `StatClient` to Visigenic `StatServer`, as well as Visigenic `StatClient` with the JDK 1.3 `StatMessageServer`. In these last two cases, inter-ORB operation was triggered, and the JDK 1.3 ORB had to communicate with the Visigenic ORB (over the TCP/IP network via IIOP).

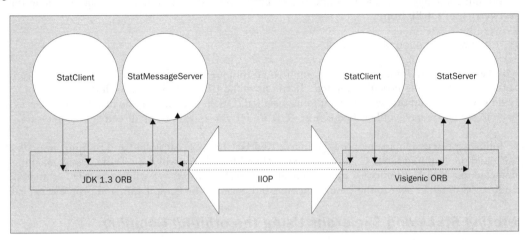

Extreme Inter-ORB Interoperability: ORBit on Red Hat Linux 6.2 using GNU C

The more experienced a software engineer becomes, the more developed their sense of jaded immunity to hype, conjectures, and postulations; experience after experience teaches us to maintain a healthy skepticism of things that we have not seen with our own eyes or touched with our own hands. Earlier in this chapter, we trumpeted the cross machine, cross vendor, cross operating system, cross programming language interoperability of CORBA (enabled by IIOP). The only example we demonstrated so far, though – even though cross vendor – had been using the same operating system on the same machine and using the same programming language.

To regain your trust and confidence, we will now proceed to go 'extreme' on inter-ORB interoperability. We will introduce three new alien elements:

❑ A different operating system: Red Hat Linux 6.2

❑ A different and super-lightweight ORB, implemented completely in C, called ORBit

❑ A different programming language binding, using standard non-object oriented C

I hope that once you seen the successful interoperation on this cross-vendor, cross-platform, cross-operating system, cross-programming language scenario, that you will have faith that any other platforms, operating systems and languages can be similarly adapted.

Getting the ORBit ORB

ORBit is a high performance, small footprint ORB created using the C programming language. ORBit is designed to be compliant with the CORBA 2.2 specification. It is being used by the GNOME project (http://www.gnome.org/), part of the famous GNU FSF (Free Software Foundation) group, in order to communicate between processes and to 'componentize' their development effort for software reuse. There are several language binding sub-projects for ORBit that extends its reach to popular programming languages such as PERL, C++, TCL, Python, Ada, and Eiffel. You can download the latest version of ORBit from:

> http://www.labs.redhat.com/orbit/

If you have Red Hat Linux 6.2, however, then you'll find it as part of the distribution, and you can install it easily from the `rpm` file supplied. If you have the GNOME desktop with the Enlightenment Window Manager and the development tools installed, ORBit may already be installed on your system. Check to see if you have a file called `orbit-idl` under your `/usr/bin/` directory to make sure.

The following discussion assumes that you have Red Hat Linux 6.2 installed and running, and also have ORBit and the required GNU C compiler installed and tested. We will use a Windows 98 machine connected to a Red Hat Linux 6.2 machine over a TCP/IP network. We will use HyperTerminal on Windows 98 to telnet over to the Linux machine and perform the compilation and program execution.

Generating Stubs and Skeletons Using the orbit-idl Compiler

The JDK ORB or Visigenic IDL compiler is clearly useless if you want to compile the IDL for ORBit consumption. ORBit includes its own IDL compiler, called `orbit-idl`. First, FTP the `statmsg.idl` file from the Win98 system over to the Linux system; transfer using `ASCII` mode.

On the Linux system, generate the stubs and skeletons for the C language binding by executing the command:

```
orbit-idl statmsg.idl
```

After the execution, which is quite fast, you should have the following files in your directory:

File Name	Description
statmsg.h	Includes file that has common prototype and data type definitions for the mapped interface.
statmsg-common.c	Similar to the helper class file in Java; contains functions that are common to both servers and clients.
statmsg-skels.c	Skeleton implementation for server-side linkage to the ORB and object adapter.
statmsg-stubs.c	Stub implementation for client-side linkage to the ORB.

Creating a C-Based CORBA Client Using Generated Stub

Both the JDK 1.3 ORB and Visigenic Visibroker are CORBA 2.3 compliant ORBs. The ORBit ORB is only CORBA 2.2 compliant at the time of writing (and probably will remain so for a while to come). While the JDK ORB is incompatible with the ORBit ORB, Visigenic provides compatible interoperation with CORBA 2.2 ORBs (you can also use the JDK 1.2 ORB, as it will support calls from ORBit clients). Here is a summary of the CORBA compatibility levels supported by the various ORBs at the time of writing:

ORB	CORBA Compatibility Level
JDK 1.3 ORB	CORBA 2.3
Visigenic VisiBroker Java ORB	CORBA 2.3 with 2.2 compatibility
ORBit ORB from GNOME	CORBA 2.2

Instead of creating both a C client and server, we will restrict ourselves to the creation of a C-based ORBit client that will work (via IIOP) with a Visigenic Java server.

You will find the source code to the C based client program in the \ch4\code\linuxorbit\statclient.c file. Here is the source:

```
#include "stdio.h"
#include "orb/orbit.h"
#include "statmsg.h"
```

Despite the fact that we are now coding in the C language, the logic flow is very similar to Java's. The client variable is used as an opaque pointer to our object reference, since C is not an object-oriented language.

This pointer is passed into every CORBA object call.

```
StatMessage client;

int
main (int argc, char *argv[])
{
    CORBA_Environment ev;
    CORBA_ORB orb;

    FILE * ifp;
    char * ior;
    char filebuffer[1024];
    char * tpbuf;
    float result;
```

Here, we initialize the ORB, very much the same as in the Java case. The ORBit way of using the local ORB is to specify "orbit-local-orb" in the initialization.

```
    CORBA_exception_init(&ev);
    orb = CORBA_ORB_init(&argc, argv, "orbit-local-orb", &ev);
```

Now, we open up the `ior.txt` file and read in the IOR that we will use:

```
ifp = fopen("ior.txt","r");
if( ifp == NULL ) {
  g_error("No ior file!");
  exit(-1);
}

fgets(filebuffer,1024,ifp);
ior = g_strdup(filebuffer);

fclose(ifp);
```

With the IOR in hand, we call `CORBA_ORB_string_to_object()` to tell the ORB to convert the IOR to an actual object reference for us. The variable client is used to store the pointer to this opaque object.

```
client = CORBA_ORB_string_to_object(orb, ior, &ev);
if (!client) {
  printf("Cannot bind to %s\n", ior);
  return 1;
}
```

We can now invoke the remote object through the reference. Note that we must pass the object pointer as the first parameter to every method. The client pointer points to state information specific to this instance of the object.

```
result = StatMessage_calcMessage(client, 2.1233, 1.1111,
  &tpbuf, &ev );
printf("The sum of  2.121 and 1.111 is %f . And... %s\n",
  result, tpbuf);

if(ev._major != CORBA_NO_EXCEPTION) {
  printf("we got exception %d from server!\n", ev._major);
  return 1;
}
```

Without Java's automatic distributed garbage collection, we must manually release the resources held during the CORBA operations.

```
CORBA_Object_release(client, &ev);
CORBA_Object_release((CORBA_Object)orb, &ev);

return 0;
}
```

To compile this program, we use a `makefile` that is compatible with the GNU make utility:

```
CC = gcc
ORBIT_IDL = /usr/bin/orbit-idl
ORBIT_CFLAGS = -I/usr/lib/glib/include -I/usr/include
ORBIT_LIBS = -L/usr/lib -lORBit -lIIOP -lORBitutil -lglib -lm
CFLAGS = $(ORBIT_CFLAGS)
LFLAGS = $(ORBIT_LIBS)
```

```
all : statclient

statclient : statclient.o statmsg-common.o statmsg-stubs.o
     $(CC) -o statclient statclient.o statmsg-stubs.o statmsg-common.o  -lIIOP -
lORBit -lORBitutil $(LFLAGS)
```

The GNU C compiler, gcc, is used to compile the program. Notice that the client links in statmsg-common.o and statmsg-stubs.o as expected. We also link with IIOP.lib, ORBit.lib, and ORBitutil.lib. At the Linux command line, type:

```
make
```

If your make is successful, you should see something similar to the screen below:

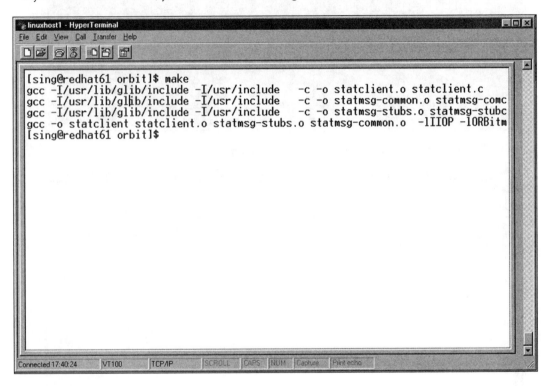

Now, on the Java Win98 machine, change directory to \ch4\code\visigenic\. Start a server by executing the command:

```
vbj StatServer
```

Wait until the "waiting..." message shows up, then FTP the ior.txt file to the Linux machine, in the directory where the client is compiled.

Now, start the client on the Linux machine using the command line:

```
./statclient
```

On the server console, you should see the indication of a successful client call across the operating system and programming language boundary. The output should be similar to that shown below:

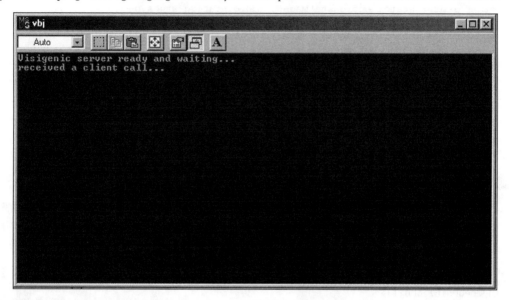

On the HyperTerminal window for the client, we see the input as:

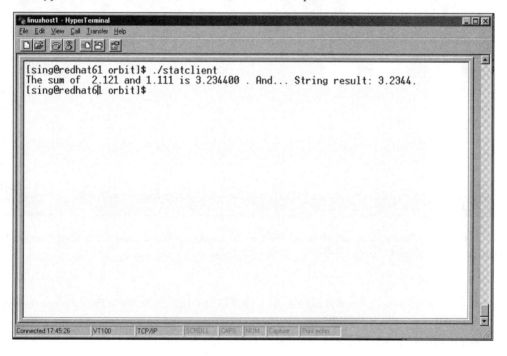

The figure below illustrates what had just happened: cross-operating system, cross-machine, cross-programming language, cross-vendor interoperation via IIOP first hand. The Win32 machine running a Java-based service object on the Visigenic ORB (on the left) was accessed successfully over the network, using IIOP, by the C language client running an ORBit ORB on a Red Hat Linux 6.2 machine.

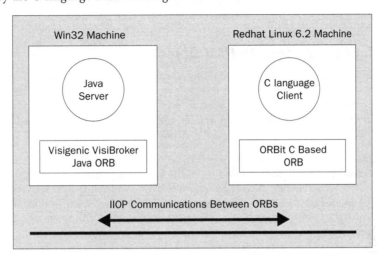

JDK 1.3's No-Work CORBA Support: RMI-IIOP

While it is surprisingly easy to create CORBA servers and clients using the standard JDK, we still needed to map data types, create and maintain IDL files, perform IDL compilation to generate stubs and skeletons, and so on. These tasks are extraneous to the pure and seamless object model that Java offers us. Wouldn't it be great if we could stay within Java's object model, and simply mark certain objects that are going to be available to external CORBA clients?

The new RMI-IIOP support, provided by JDK 1.3 and later, addresses this exact problem and was co-developed between Sun and IBM. This virtually guarantees compatibility with IBM mainframe- and mini-computer-based interoperation over RMI-IIOP – a major market indeed for this product.

Recall that all ORBs communicate with each other over the TCP/IP network via the IIOP standard protocol. By creating RMI stubs that will work with the IIOP protocol instead of (or in addition to) the Sun proprietary JRMP protocol, one can selectively expose RMI objects to be used by CORBA clients.

New RMIC Options Enable RMI-IIOP

The JDK 1.3 version of the `rmic` RMI proxy/stub generating utility has several new options that are useful for RMI-IIOP operation. Here is a summary of the new options and what they will do for us:

JDK 1.3 new `rmic` option	Description
-idl	Generates the CORBA IDL description, in human readable and easy to maintain form, for all remote classes specified or referenced. It is possible to generate IDL directly from a remote RMI interface using this option.

Table continued on following page

JDK 1.3 new `rmic` option	Description
`-iiop`	Generates IIOP-based stub and TIE classes for use in RMI-IIOP operations. TIE classes map (delegates) client requests to the appropriate remote object methods directly.

Enable CORBA Client Access to RMI Objects

The figure below illustrates how RMI-IIOP enables a whole new world of clients on almost any platform to share in the functionality provided by a Java RMI-based server. Remember that CORBA clients may reside on almost any platform, using different operating systems, and coded in many different programming languages. A CORBA service can also be a client, allowing Java-based RMI servers to be integrated as a part of a larger CORBA-based solution.

On the left hand side of the figure, we have a few Java VMs communicating with each other via RMI. RMI uses the proprietary JRMP protocol and has rich object semantics that provides seamless data and behavior mobility through dynamic class loading. Before the availability of RMI-IIOP, the reach of Java stops here – all the platform or machines must support a Java VM in order to play. With the arrival of RMI-IIOP, the big black barrier (thick black vertical line) is broken. The reach of a Java VM is extended to the rest of the world on the right hand side. Now, legacy software written in other programming language can be easily leveraged by Java systems; operating systems or hardware platforms with no Java support (but CORBA support) can interwork with Java networks; and most mainframes and many specialized systems that had long supported CORBA can leverage (or be leveraged by) Java systems immediately.

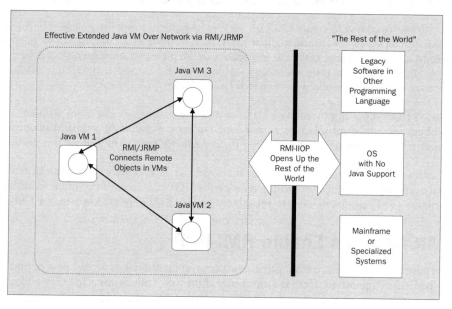

RMI-IIOP Considerations

In fact, using RMI objects as CORBA services becomes a 'no additional work required' feature with JDK 1.3's RMI-IIOP compatible ORB. The only requirement is for the implementation of the RMI-IIOP object to use only the subset of RMI that is compatible with IIOP. Since the JRMP protocol handles more functionality than IIOP provides (much of which is made possible by the homogeneous Java environment), proper RMI-IIOP operation requires adherence to this subset.

Here is a brief list of some restrictions:

- ❑ `Struct, union,` and `inout` of CORBA IDL is not supported

- ❑ Any constant declared within the interface must be resolvable at compile time and be of primitive type or string (no mapping to CORBA IDL otherwise)

- ❑ Case-sensitive, opening up the possibility of name collision

With RMI-IIOP, all the interfaces are defined within Java as RMI (Remote) interfaces. There is no need to create your own CORBA IDL file. OMG has a specification mapping Java to IDL that was drafted in September of 1997, and finalized in March of 1999. Sun's reference RMI-IIOP implementation is compliant with this specification. Note that this is not the same, and is in fact very different from, the IDL-to-Java mapping and associated specification. It is important to distinguish between the two independent mappings. In the IDL-to-Java mapping scenario, we write the programming language-independent IDL description of the CORBA interfaces that we will implement (maybe not using Java). For Java implementations, we compile it with the `idlj` compiler, and we end up with the CORBA stub and skeleton files that we can then use.

> Earlier versions of the `idlj` utility program (called `idltoj`) were not written using Java. Instead, they depended on a C++ pre-compiler. On Win32-based systems, this pre-compiler was only available with the purchase of Microsoft's Visual C++. Starting with JDK 1.3, the `idlj` compiler is completely written in Java and will no longer be dependent on a C++ pre-compiler. At the time of writing the `idlj` compiler is still being finalized and is available as a preview version only.

Using the RMI-IIOP feature, both C++ and Java programmers can define interfaces and/or implement them. RMI-IIOP provides a simple, yet extremely practical interoperability mechanism between these two very frequently used programming languages (even on the same platform).

New CORBA 2.3 Object-by-Value extension

RMI-IIOP requires a new CORBA 2.3 object-by-value extension in order to operate correctly. The initial proposal for this extension was approved by the OMG back in February of 1998, and the specification was finalized in March of 1999. Before this extension, every object reference had to be a remote CORBA reference. From using RMI, we are already used to the fact that non-remote objects, such a `String` argument, are passed-by-value. The CORBA 2.3 extension adds this semantic to CORBA. At the time of writing, this requirement is a minor roadblock for RMI-IIOP to interoperate with ORBs that are not yet CORBA 2.3 compliant. As ORB vendors update their ORBs, and Sun releases new 1.3.x versions, we can expect that interoperability between different vendor's ORBs with RMI-IIOP will be achieved.

Trying out RMI-IIOP

Let's us try out an RMI-IIOP sample. The source code can be found in the `\ch4\code\rmi\` directory. The remote RMI interface that we will expose to CORBA clients is defined in the `RmiCalc.java` file:

```
import java.rmi.*;
public interface RmiCalc extends Remote {
   float calc(float num1, float num2) throws RemoteException;
}
```

This is essentially the same as our earlier StatMessage interface, but without the 'out' String argument that is not supported by RMI semantics.

Coding an RMI-IIOP Server

The code for our implementation of this interface is in the CalcObj.java file. It is similar to regular RMI object implementation; we highlight the differences below:

```
import java.rmi.server.*;
import java.rmi.*;
```

We include the RMI extension to support RMI-IIOP stubs, javax.rmi.*; as well as the new naming extension to support JNDI (Java Naming and Directory Interface) via javax.naming.*.

```
import javax.rmi.*;
import javax.naming.*;
```

Instead of the usual UnicastRemoteObject that we inherit from, RMI-IIOP requires the PortableRemoteObject instead. This new object can work with both JRMP protocol stubs or IIOP protocol stubs, based on a property that one can be set at startup.

```
public class CalcObj extends PortableRemoteObject implements
   RmiCalc {

public CalcObj() throws RemoteException {}
```

Here is our implementation of the calc() method of the remote interface:

```
public float calc(float num1, float num2) throws
   RemoteException {
   System.out.println("A client call has been received...");
   return (num1 + num2);
}
```

The main method has to initialize the ORB, export our object instance, and bind the reference with a name service so that a client will be able to find it. Using the JNDI support (included in JDK 1.3) for CORBA objects and the COSNaming service, this is done quite simply.

```
public static void main(String args[]) {
   try {
      Context initialNC = new InitialContext();
      CalcObj myObj = new CalcObj();
      initialNC.rebind("CalcServer", myObj);
```

This is all that is needed to associate `CalcServer` with the `CalcObj` instance to allow access by CORBA clients.

```
        System.out.println("JDK 1.3 RMI-IIOP server ready and
          waiting...");
      }
    catch (Exception e) {
      System.err.println("ERROR: " + e);
      e.printStackTrace(System.out);
    }
  }
}
```

We do not have to block waiting for client calls – the RMI-IIOP runtime will prevent us from terminating until the last object has been `unexported()`. If we ever want to remove the object from being available for remote calls, we must explicitly `unexport()` the object. The distributed garbage collection algorithm will not work for RMI-IIOP objects (since remote object references can be maintained by completely different non-Java subsystems).

Compiling and Generating RMI-IIOP Stubs and TIEs

Compile the `CalcObj.java` file using the command line:

```
javac CalcObj.java
```

Now, generate the required RMI-IIOP stubs and TIEs using the command line:

```
rmic -iiop CalcObj
```

You will find two binary class files generated:

File Name	Description
_CalcObj_Tie.class	The TIE class used to map/delegate calls to the RMI object on the server end.
_RmiCalc_Stub.class	The client side stub class for invoking remote methods; can work with JRMP or IIOP.

Creating the IIOP Client

The client code can be found in the `\ch4\code\rmi\CalcClient.java\` file. Here is the program:

```
import javax.naming.*;
import java.rmi.*;
import javax.rmi.*;

public class CalcClient {
```

As with the CORBA implementation, the client is very simple. It is made simpler by the fact that JNDI, when working with the COSNaming CORBA service, performs ORB initialization and object export on our behalf. Here, we only need to create the `InitialContext()` – `NameService` in our case – and lookup the `CalcServer` to create our object instance.

Notice how the `PortableRemoteObject.narrow()` method is used to cast the object reference to the instance of RmiCalc that we need:

```java
public static void main(String argc[]) {
  try {
    Context initialNC = new InitialContext();
    RmiCalc myObj = (RmiCalc) PortableRemoteObject.narrow
      (initialNC.lookup("CalcServer"), RmiCalc.class);
    System.out.println("The sum of 2.2333 and 1.1111 is "
      + myObj.calc(2.2333f, 1.1111f));
  }
  catch (Exception ex) {
    ex.printStackTrace();
    System.exit(1);
  }
 }
}
```

Compile the client program using the command line:

```
javac CalcClient.java
```

Testing RMI-IIOP Operation

To test the RMI-IIOP sample, we need to first invoke the transient CORBA COSNaming service that is supplied with the JDK. Use the following command line:

```
start tnameserv
```

This will start the name service listening at port 900. If you want it to listen on another port instead, say port 1090, use this command line:

```
start tnameserv -ORBInitialPort 1090
```

You should see a display similar to that below:

Now, start the server using the supplied `runserv.bat` batch file:

```
start java -Djava.naming.factory.initial
  =com.sun.jndi.cosnaming.CNCtxFactory
  -Djava.naming.provider.url=iiop://localhost:900 CalcObj
```

The `java.naming.factory.initial` property specifies that the COSNaming service should be used. The `java.naming.provider.url` property specifies the host and port where the naming service can be found. By setting these properties to other values, we can cause the same source code to use RMIRegistry and JRMP instead of the COSNaming service and IIOP.

Your server console should look like the screen shot below at this point:

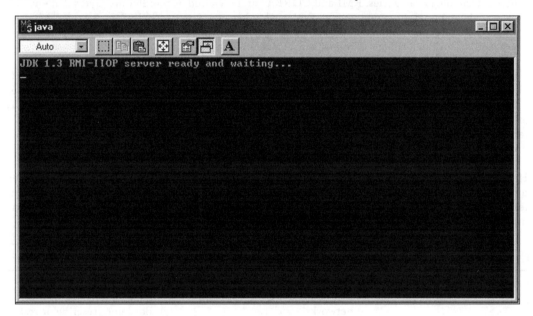

Now, start the client using the supplied `runclient.bat` batch file:

```
java -Djava.naming.factory.initial
  =com.sun.jndi.cosnaming.CNCtxFactory
  -Djava.naming.provider.url=iiop://localhost:900 calcClient
```

On the client console, below, we can see that the client has located the server reference successfully through the naming service, and has called the server successfully to compute the sum:

This concludes our discussion of RMI-IIOP. When interoperable ORBs become available, we can use the –idl option of the rmic compiler to generate CORBA IDL descriptions. The IDL file can then be used by clients on the other ORBs, implemented in potentially another programming language, to access the exposed RMI-IIOP object. Bear in mind, however, that interoperating ORBs still need to obtain the initial object reference in some way. If the ORB can use the COSNaming service, it can then find the initial object reference there.

What Jini Brings to RMI and CORBA

Comparing Jini to RMI or CORBA is a bit like comparing apples to oranges. They are fundamentally different technology categories. RMI and CORBA can be viewed as middleware layers that enable objects and components to communicate with each other over a network. Jini, on the other hand, provides an interaction model and the infrastructure for distributed objects to cooperate with each other, and to work in a coherent, robust, and scalable way.

Jini specifies almost everything to create a functional network of objects that dynamically link together and perform useful work. What Jini does not specify is the communication mechanism between the proxy object (on the client side) and the service. However, this happens to be the very strength of RMI and CORBA, making them an ideal match for working within a Jini network. Not only do the two technologies *not* compete against each other, they are perfectly complementary and can work harmoniously together.

Having said that, this chapter would simply not be complete without contrasting this very fundamental difference against all the features that pundits often insist on forming a comparison of the dissimilar technologies. The following table provides this contrast. As you go through the table, keep in mind the fundamental different intentions, goals, and applications of CORBA/RMI and Jini.

CORBA	RMI	Jini
Middleware technology.	An invisible middleware layer that extends Java objects across networks.	Can use and work with *any* middleware technology or layer. It does not prescribe or restrict applications to a middleware layer itself. In Chapters 9 and 12, we will see examples of this.
Adapts client and server software components (potentially in a heterogeneous hardware and software environment) over a network, letting them work together.	The 'client' versus 'server' distinction is less apparent and often vague in the RMI context. It can work on a heterogeneous hardware environment but only within a network-wide homogeneous software environment – Java.	By itself does not enable clients to talk to a server. It needs a supporting protocol or middleware layer, Jini works equally well with CORBA, RMI, or even a raw socket implementation for communications between clients and services.
Can be coded in any supported programming language, including FORTRAN, C, C++, etc.	Can only be coded in Java, although RMI-IIOP allows clients (CORBA clients) to be coded in any other language.	Services can be implemented using languages other than Java; although Java clients and services make for the most straightforward implementation.

CORBA	RMI	Jini
Programming language independent interface. Definition Language to describe objects and interfaces.	Uses Java's own interface semantics with no special provision required.	The client can find services via the Java interface that they support. This interface can be locally or remote, and its methods may work local or remotely. There are no special semantics or special provisions.
Skeleton and stubs are generated (in the chosen programming language), in chosen source code form, from the IDL.	Proxy and stubs are generated in binary form from RMI interfaces within the binary compiled `.class` file.	Proxy and stubs may or may not exist, depending on the implementation of the proxy object.
Enables a classical approach to distributed computing, allowing objects to find and communicate with each other over a network. How you use such objects together is up to you.	Again a classical model of distributed computing, allowing Java objects to be located remotely on a network. How you use remote objects is up to you.	A new and novel distributed computing model. Provides an infrastructure for objects to find one-another, join together to get work done together, to disconnect and reconnect, and to recover from network or software failures.
Typically depends on what is in fact an optional naming service, in order to locate the initial object reference. Some designs use naming services all the time, even during regular operations. In Java, JNDI can be used to access the CORBA CosNaming service.	Typically uses RMIRegistry to locate initial object references. Designs that use the RMIRegistry all the time, even during non-bootstrap operation, are discouraged. JNDI can be used to access the registry for portability.	Lookup service is an integral part of the Jini specification and any Jini systems. Proxy object lookup, connects, and disconnects are performed routinely and handled as normal operations in a Jini-based system.
Dynamic invocation on an interface is possible. A client can discover how to call an interface at runtime, and access the service object through a dynamically constructed stub.	Behavior similar to dynamic invocation is possible through standard Java introspection. This is useful generally for tools that must work with objects, plug-ins, or extensions that it has no prior knowledge about.	Currently, the interface between a client and a service is fixed and is expected to be well-known and agreed upon in advance. This is the interface that is exposed via a proxy object stored on a lookup service. Java introspection can be used to make dynamic calls once the object is obtained. However, frequently, the interface itself (the type) is used as the common tie.

At this time, we should have quite a clear picture of what RMI provides for the Java platform, what CORBA adds to the picture, and how Jini brings a complete set of different yet complementary values to the table. In the coming chapters, we will learn a lot more about Jini and how to use it effectively. This will include how to leverage RMI and CORBA's value when designing Jini-based distributed systems.

Jini Client or Service	JavaSpaces and Helper Services

Jini Client and Service Support Helper Utilities

Jini Discovery Management Helper Utilities

Jini Protocol Helper Utilities

Jini Network Protocols	
	RMI and Rich Object Semantics
	Java VM and Networking

Network Protocols

Section 2

Core Technology

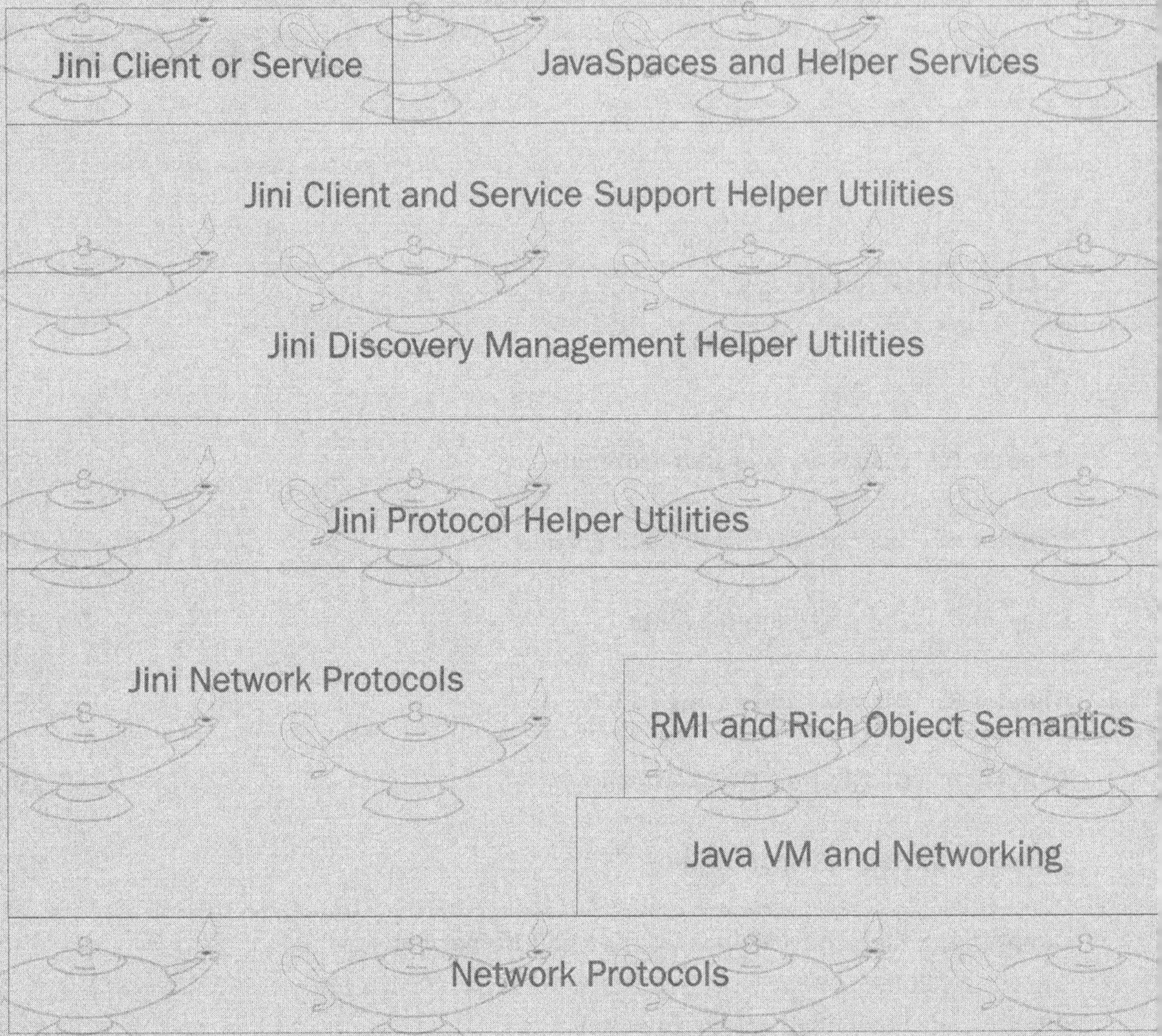

Jini Client or Service | JavaSpaces and Helper Services

Jini Client and Service Support Helper Utilities

Jini Discovery Management Helper Utilities

Jini Protocol Helper Utilities

Jini Network Protocols

RMI and Rich Object Semantics

Java VM and Networking

Network Protocols

Online discussion at http://p2p.wrox.com

Overview

Perhaps the best way to grasp the Jini concept is to regard it as the technology that will eventually realize Sun's "the network is the computer" slogan; a vision of true distributed computing. This perspective makes sense of the design rationale and decisions that have made Jini what it is today.

While using a network-based computer is an attractive idea, the business of transforming the network into the computer is a little more difficult. There are a number of potential pitfalls and obstacles to the real world implementation of this network-based computer, which we'll look at here. The solutions that we'll accumulate as we investigate are very similar to Jini's own feature list.

Let us start by working through a thought experiment in order to look inside this network-based computer. Put aside everything you already know about network computing in today's world: client/server computing, multi-tiered architectures, web based services, etc, and imagine that the Internet is already a formidable network-based computer. What might it look like?

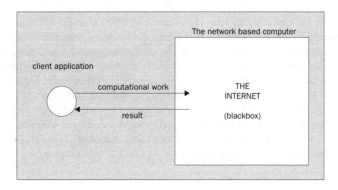

The network-based computer is made up of the network itself, together with every machine that can be reached on that network. Clients of a computing service will, in this ideal world, simply connect to the network-based computer to get some work done.

This work would range from the mundane, such as picking up e mail, to the complex, perhaps predicting enemy submarine attack formations in the 21st century battlefield, for example. Although this interconnectivity scenario is familiar to us because of the client/server computing model, there are some big differences between this model and the Internet model of a network-based service provider:

- ❑ The network-based computer is never down, surviving even major disasters, just as the Internet is never down in its entirety. Although it can't be said that all of the computers in today's Internet are reliably and robustly connected, this futuristic network-based computer will virtually always manage to get work done, as we'll see later.

- ❑ The physical composition of the network-based computer is forever changing. Machines and services come and go continuously, their services and applications being made available or removed as and when they join or leave the network.

There might be hundreds, thousands, or even millions of interconnected computers, reliably and robustly connected inside the black box we're calling a network-based computer. In the following diagram, each dot in the diagram represents a computer

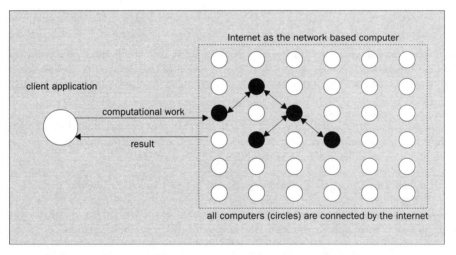

Although the picture so far looks like a pretty close approximation of today's Internet, there is a significant difference. Each computer depicted here is in fact a logical computer, where a number of logical computers can be running on one physical machine. The boundaries that separate each of these independent logical computers are not necessarily associated with the physical machine boundaries – they might be enabled by software (multi-tasking operating systems, for example), hardware (Symmetric Multi-Processing), or a combination of both. One logical computer may be running multiple independent Java VMs, each running within its own process a different application, and communicating with different partner VMs over the network. The following figure shows multiple logical computers residing within one physical computer. From this point on, we will refer to each logical computer as a **computational agent**. These computational agents are the fundamental building blocks in this imaginary network-based computer:

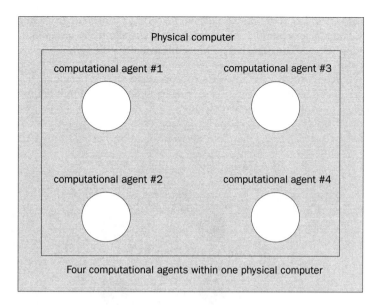

Four computational agents within one physical computer

There are a couple of very good reasons for connecting all these computational agents together – each and every one of them may provide a service that another computer will find useful, just as each and every one of them might find a useful service available. In fact, a group of them can work in unison, each providing their specialty service, together forming a more complex service. In some sense, a complex service can be viewed as a grouping of computational agents to perform one service – appearing to the client as one single computer. This computer, because it is actually a grouping of computational agents, can actually span multiple physical machines. There may be many computers that provide the same or very similar services within the network, which is good news for the client who can then select the 'best-of-breed' service, and even more importantly it provides a high level of fault tolerance. We'll examine fault tolerance later. The following diagram illustrates the client working with simple and complex services:

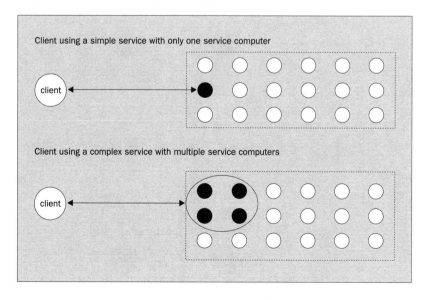

Although in the real world, the client may be driven directly or indirectly (by a human user or by some pre-programmed behavior, for example), we'll remain neutral about the motivation of the client in this scenario so that it applies to all possible cases. More importantly, though, it is easy to see that any computational agent in the network can in fact also act as a client, even while it is participating as part of a complex service. It's perfectly possible for a computational agent providing a service within the network, to simultaneously be making use of a service from another computational agent (or a set of computational agents) in order to get the work done.

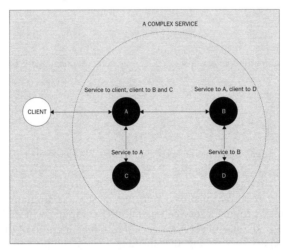

This will be a familiar picture to many readers, being similar to the currently popular tiered application server architecture model that many web based systems use. In this conventional architecture, the client may represent a web browser, and A to D application servers, database servers, transaction server, queuing servers, or something else. In our network-based computer model, however, the details differ significantly from the (more limited) conventional n-tiered architecture.

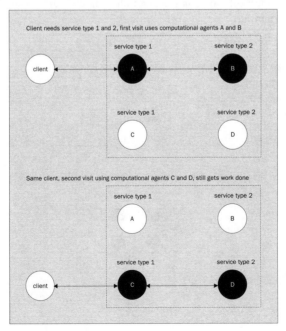

Secondly, any computational agent can join or leave the network at any time, whether it is currently working as a service (or part of a complex service) or not:

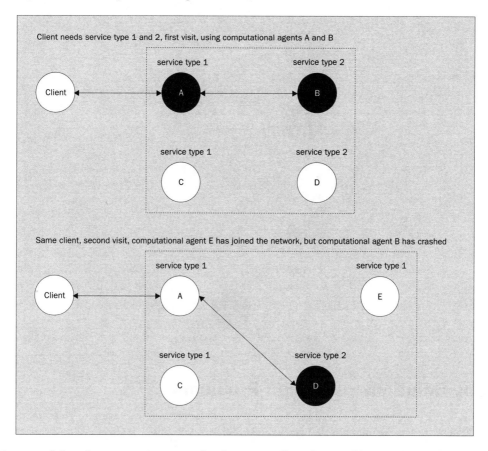

This network-based computer is expected to be practically indestructible – much as TCP/IP is designed to be (in so far as TCP/IP will always connect two machines as long as there is one single route between them). In this scenario, whatever has happened within the network as a whole, a computer requesting a service will get the work done so long as there is a service providing computer/s in there somewhere. The following diagram shows an example:

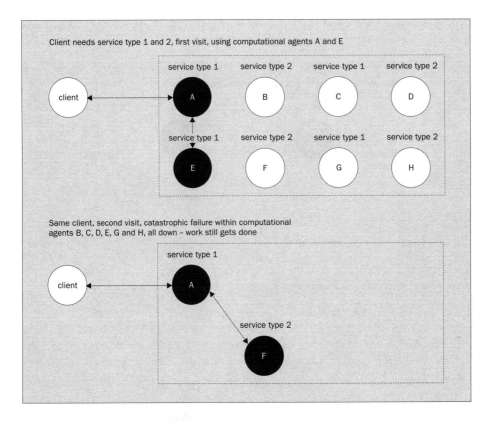

Seeking Solutions to Design Problems

There are some pretty big questions that would have to be addressed if we were to go about designing the ideal network-based computer that we've been looking at:

❑ How is a client going to locate the computer(s) capable of performing the required service?

❑ How is the client going to interact with the service provider?

❑ How will the network deal with, or indeed know about, a new computer offering a service and wanting to join the community?

❑ How is the network going to deal with a computer within the community that fails or disconnects?

❑ How will the network cope when the computer that fails or disconnects while performing a service?

❑ How will the network deal with a client that fails or disconnects while a service is being performed on its behalf within the network?

❑ How do services handle feature enhancements and upgrades?

Let us see what Jini adds on top of the existing Java networking capability (sockets, RMI, etc.) to address each and every point raised here enabling software developers to (one day) create the ideal network-based computer.

Before we continue, we must adopt some Jini terminology. In Jini, the client connects to a service to get work done. This service may be a simple one (only one computational agent), or a complex one (many computational agents).

Locating Services

So how *is* a client going to locate the service capable of performing the required work?

First, the client must know something about the service it requires. This knowledge might be about the type of service it is (what Java interface it supports, what Java class it is an instance of), the attributes associated with the service (Java object instances), or the unique ID that all active services are given. Using one or more pieces of this information, the client can locate the service through a third-party service called the **Lookup service**.

Jini makes pervasive use of the lookup service. This service is a simple process that allows a Jini client to find potential service providers. The client supplies the criterion (type, attribute, or unique ID), and the lookup service locates the service.

There is always at least one lookup service within a Jini network. Most production Jini networks will have multiple lookup services to implement a basic level of redundancy and fault tolerance.

Essentially, the client uses the lookup service to find potential service providers, a list of whom are returned for the client's selection, as depicted in this diagram:

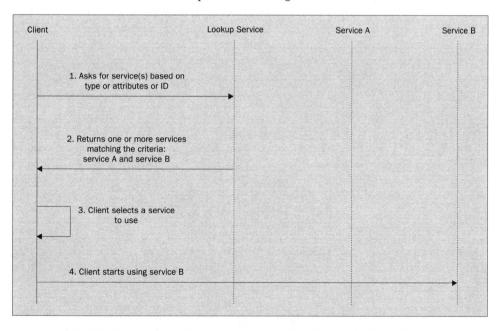

So how does a client find a lookup service in the first place? Lookup service(s) are found through a bootstrap process, the client using either pre-configured knowledge of its whereabouts (when the client already knows the network address of the lookup service(s) required) or through a low-level discovery protocol that uses multicast throughout the network. The client also interacts with the lookup service via a Jini specified well-known interface. We will devote the entire next chapter to cover this bootstrapping process.

Two key points to note here:

❑   The client and the service are coupled extremely loosely, and this allows Jini to survive faults. A client that needs work it has already had done carried out again, doesn't have to use that same service, unless it is the only one on the network.

❑   Lookup provided by Jini is not text based, or based on predefined structures, as is the more conventional naming service. Instead, it is based on Java objects and types as well as actual content. This allows it to be sensitive to inheritance hierarchy (searches can be based on super-class/super-type).

Interacting with Services

Jini enables the client to interact with services able to perform the required work simply by leveraging basic Java networking technology – more specifically, through dynamic class loading. Dynamic class loading enables Java objects to flow between independent Java VMs (see Chapter 3 for more details). In our case, a Java object flows from the service to the lookup service upon registration. This object is called a **proxy** object. This proxy object knows how the work required should be performed, and how to connect back to the service if this is necessary for the work to be done.

When a client looks up a service, the lookup service returns the proxy object that corresponds to the service back to the client. This proxy object is a full-fledged Java object that will be instantiated within the client's Java VM. Any Java class information that is required to re-constitute the proxy will be dynamically loaded over the network through the codebase annotation mechanism. The following diagram illustrates this:

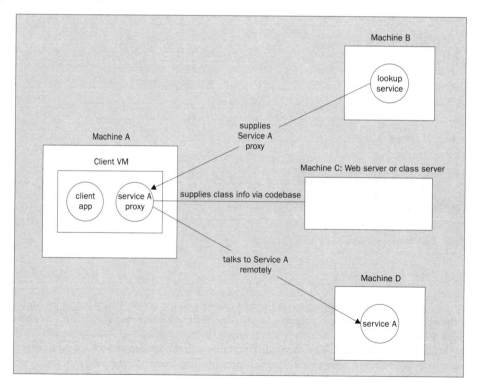

This is very powerful, because the client essentially interacts with a local proxy object alone. It is the proxy object, (the code that is logically a part of the service itself) that gets the requested work done – either carrying it out by itself, or by delegation. At the decision of the proxy object, the services might be performed:

❑ Within the VM of the client where the proxy is running – so in fact the so called proxy is actually providing the service itself

❑ Remotely in the computer that originally offered the service

❑ Through some other division of labor, between the client VM and the remote service provider.

Should either of the last two scenarios listed above require communication with another computer over the network (or indeed the service providing computer), the proxy takes charge, using whatever Java networking protocol or mechanism it likes, and the client is free from this complexity. For example, CORBA may be used to communicate with legacy mainframe systems, or HTTP can be used to access a web based service provider. This is the primary method Jini uses to accommodate legacy systems; the service provider does not have to be Java based at all.

New Services Joining the Network

Jini uses a pre-specified low-level protocol to bootstrap services onto the network. Any service that wishes to join the network must first locate one or more lookup services, using the bootstrap **discovery** protocol, and then submit a proxy object, which might bring with it attached attributes (describing the geographic location of the service, for example, or the department that is hosting the service) that assist lookup. This process is called registration.

A service must follow the Jini specified **discovery and join** protocol. The discovery protocols enable services and clients to find lookup services, in order for them to register and communicate. The join protocol specifies how a service must behave to become a good citizen within the Jini network.

The Jini network itself is partitioned into **groups**, a community of Jini services that work together, using the discovery and join protocol. The client(s) wishing to use a group's capabilities must first join the group. A service can join one or more groups at the same time. A lookup service can provide service for one or more groups at the same time.

Dealing with Machine Failures

Jini uses distributed leases pervasively for reclaiming resources within the Jini network, and in this way deals with computational agents that fail or disconnect within the network.

As we've seen, a computer offering a service must register with a lookup service. The lookup service maintains this registration for a length of time that is negotiated with the service. (There is in fact only one round of this so-called negotiation; the requesting service or client makes a request for a particular lease time, and the granting service complies, denies, or grants a shorter lease.) The requesting service or client is responsible for renewing the lease in order to maintain the registration. Should the service suffer software, machine, or network failure and be unable to renew the lease, it will expire. The lookup service will not return the failed service's proxy to potential clients, and the failed service is no longer considered a member of the Jini network, although it may rejoin later once it is back to better health.

Service implementations are encouraged to grant leases (for the client to hold onto, and renew periodically) whenever a resource is allocated on behalf of a client. This will ensure that sudden failure or disconnection of the client will not result in resources being tied up within the service indefinitely.

Using leases to allocate resources is a really valuable mechanism, ensuring automated cleanup of allocated resources following their expiration or a system failure. The network as a whole is made more robust and reliable.

Dealing with Partial Failures

Jini can also cope with computers failing or disconnecting whether the computer concerned is a performing a service, or a client that fails or disconnects while a service is being performed on its behalf.

There are lots of causes for network failure: software, machine, or network failures can occur while services are being provided to the client. The client may fail internally or disconnect, the service (or one of the computational agents) might fail or disconnect, or the network connection might just go down.

Partial failures can create all sorts of un-determined system states, which, for certain applications, might be disastrous. By specifying a distributed transactions co-coordinator that services can make use of, Jini ensures that orderly transition in the state of the system can be implemented without dealing with even the possibility of partial failure. Services can implement transaction appropriate to their needs.

In many cases, state transitions amongst a distributed set of services (supporting the same transaction semantics) can be reduced to a simple yes or no question – either the work has been completed across all the services involved, or it is not done at all. If work has not been completed successfully across the board, then the system can be restored to the state it held before work began. The transaction co-coordinator provides the management that makes this possible, but the services themselves are responsible for the implementation details. Transactions can be used to ensure that partial failure will not cause the distributed network-based computer system to go into an unknown or potentially unstable state.

Handling Synchronization Issues

There is another interaction scenario between client, service and lookup service that requires design consideration. Taking it as read that a client and its required service typically run on completely separate computers, and that there can be no implicit synchronization between the two parties, it's not likely that the following rather frustrating state of affairs will occur:

- ❏ A client looks up a service
- ❏ The lookup fails because the service isn't available
- ❏ The client leaves, and the required service promptly registers with the lookup service.

Jini specifies a remote event mechanism that allows the client to register its interest with the lookup service. This registration is subject to a leased duration, just in case the client dies or disconnects after registration. Once the client has registered its interest, the lookup service will send an event to the client should the desired service register with it later on.

In this way, a client can keep an eye on the state within the lookup service with regard to services that it is interested in, without having to poll the lookup service for such information.

Upgrade and Enhancement of Service Implementations

The loosely coupled relationship between client and service, together with the distributed leasing scheme, enables a natural and almost automatic way to upgrade or enhance service implementations. This can be done with minimal impact on the system.

In effect, a new version of a service can register itself with all the lookup services while the old version of a service is still in operation, so that the lookup services are populated with new service's proxy. So any client performing a new lookup will retrieve the new proxy with the new service, while clients that keep copies of the old service proxy for a long time still have access to the old service.

In time, all the clients that hold copies of the old service proxy will relinquish their hold, and so all the clients of the service will be working with the new version. At some point the old version of the service will be taken down, and any clients that are still holding the old service proxy will receive an exception when they try to access the proxy and be forced to re-attempt lookup.

Overview of Upcoming Chapters

In the following chapters, we'll go into these aspects of Jini in significantly more detail:

- ❑ Discovery and Join Protocols
- ❑ Lookup Service and Entries
- ❑ Leases, Remote Events and Transactions

We'll also examine some higher level components and services that are built upon the basic Jini framework, but can be very useful for Jini implementers, substantially reducing the work required to implement Jini services and clients.

Finally, we'll implement several styles of Jini services and clients, bringing to fruition everything we have covered in the earlier chapters. We will also discuss the importance of services that actually represent physical devices, and examine the service's role as a device driver.

The last two chapters in this section cover an imminently important Jini service: JavaSpaces, and some issues in the "network is the computer" vision that are not adequately addressed by the current state-of-the-art Jini system.

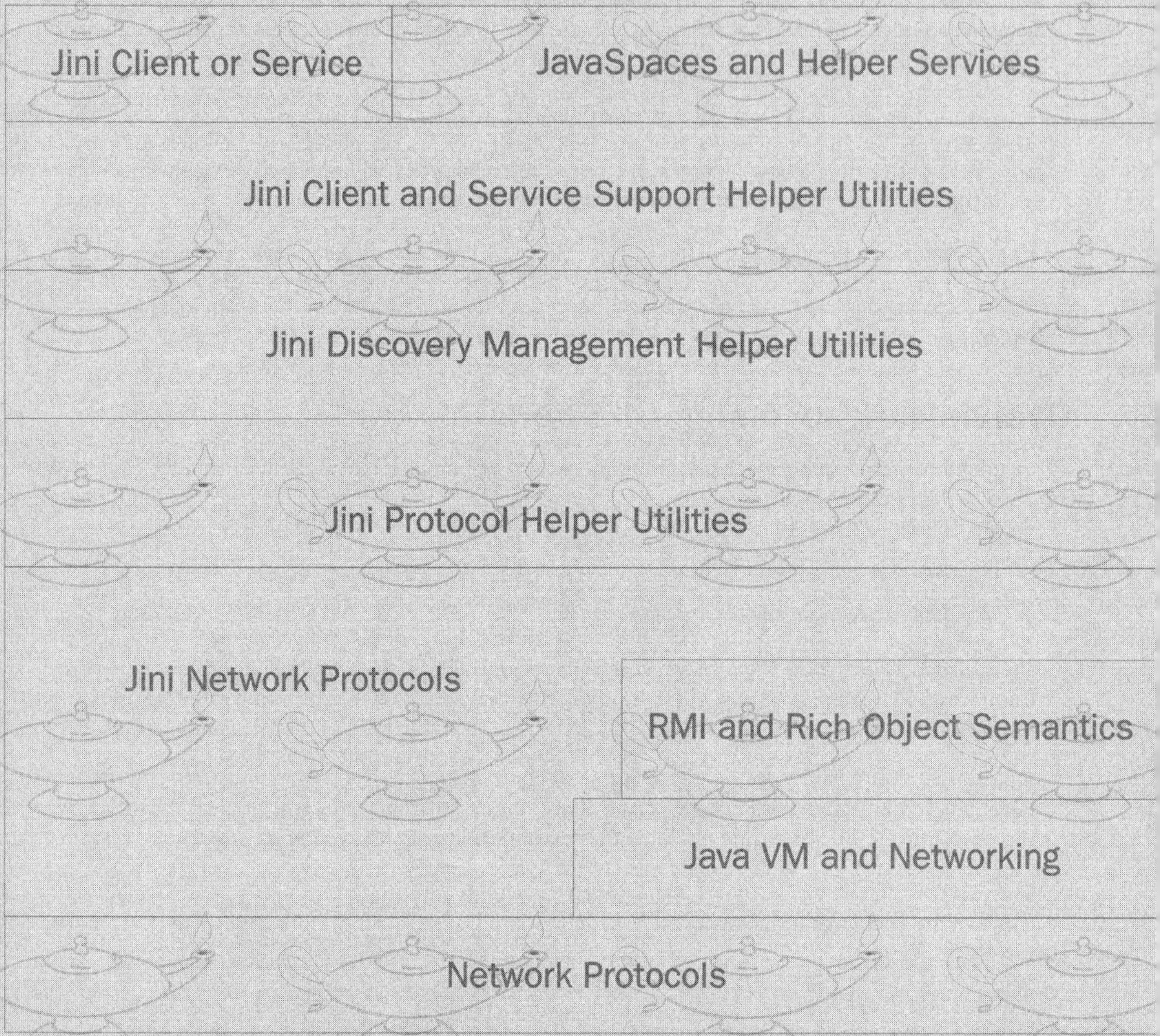

Jini Client or Service
JavaSpaces and Helper Services
Jini Client and Service Support Helper Utilities
Jini Discovery Management Helper Utilities
Jini Protocol Helper Utilities
Jini Network Protocols
RMI and Rich Object Semantics
Java VM and Networking
Network Protocols

Online discussion at http://p2p.wrox.com

5

Discovery and Join Protocols

The suite of protocols known as the **Discovery and Join** protocols govern the way individual computers join, leave and interact with a Jini **federation**. A federation is the collection of Jini clients and services that come together to get work done, (also referred to as a djinn, or Jini community).

Although a federation usually evolves to meet the needs of the various members, it might also come about spontaneously. Once the work is done, all the entities participating in the federation may disengage – ready for another dynamic federation. Given this nature of the federation, the discovery and join protocols are at the heart of a Jini community.

In this chapter, we will be looking at:

❑   Jini's structure: federations and groups

❑   The discovery protocol suite itself: bootstrap protocols implemented using the basic Java networking building blocks you're already familiar with

❑   IP multicast: vital to the current implementation of the discovery protocol, together with a code example

❑   Getting Jini going using either Win32 or Redhat Linux 6.2: setting up our own Jini network, complete with lookup service(s), service and client

❑   Writing our own on-the-wire protocol interceptor

❑   The Join Protocol: although it is part of the discovery and join protocols, is in fact a set of behavioral conventions that hold together a well-behaved Jini network

Jini Groups and Network Partitioning

The limits of today's networking technology being what they are, it would be wishful thinking to imagine that a Jini federation might consist of all the Jini services in the world. There's a little way to go first! Network latency, bandwidth, and computing power are tough limitations that we have to deal with in order to get adequate performance from such networks. If lookup were to be performed over a network as large as the Internet, for example, service startups alone would cause a multicast packet storm fit to saturate a network of almost any bandwidth. A single request/response roundtrip between a client and a service located on a physical computer on the other side of the world would likely take far too long to be practical. Potentially enormous collections of services are, therefore, partitioned into **groups** by imposing boundaries. These boundaries are structured around anything that is logical and meaningful to the Jini network implementers – a company department, for example, or a workgroup.

Groups passively partition the physical Jini network for multicast discovery purposes, and are very different to the active creation of a **federation**. Jini services and clients become members of specific groups within their network upon bootstrapping. A service or client can belong to multiple groups, and a lookup service on a Jini network may service one group or many (or the **public** default group). Any particular service/client on the Jini network can specify the groups that it is interested in joining.

A **federation**, on the other hand, might be quite independent of any group partitioning or any particular discovery protocol. It is the temporary union of Jini clients and services that come together to get work done, and can transcend group boundaries and discovery boundaries imposed by lookup service availability; it can even transcend the boundary of physical Jini network topology.

The list of groups associated with a lookup service, service, or client need not be static – they can even change while the entity itself is live and connected to the Jini network (by an administrator, for example). Although groups logically partition a network, they are not necessarily mutually exclusive. So while the connection of physical machines on a Jini network gives it physical topology, the partitioning of the network using groups gives it logical topology. The following diagram shows how a Jini network might be partitioned through groups:

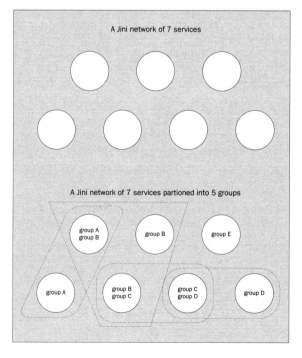

Although the specifics of boundary allocation are not proscribed, most Jini developers are currently using groups and physical network boundaries to partition a large Jini network. Ultimately, as networking and computing technology evolves, one can potentially deploy larger and larger Jini federations. Until then, however, Jini's ability to federate together multiple smaller, potentially remote, federations suffices for most applications, as depicted in the following diagram:

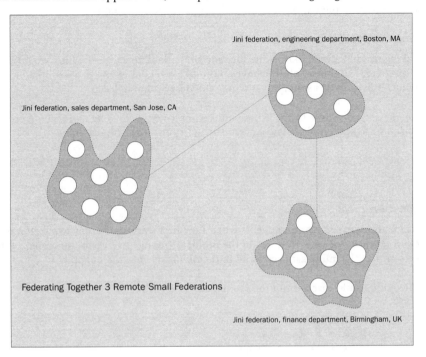

Jini federation, engineering department, Boston, MA

Jini federation, sales department, San Jose, CA

Federating Together 3 Remote Small Federations

Jini federation, finance department, Birmingham, UK

Discovery Protocols

The discovery protocols allow Jini networks to bootstrap themselves. They enable a client or service to obtain an initial remote object reference(s) to the lookup service(s) servicing a community. All subsequent object references are obtained using this (these) initial reference(s), again using lookup.

Unlike conventional client/server systems, in a Jini system clients and services are **loosely coupled** through the lookup service(s). Both clients and services need to locate a lookup service in order to bootstrap into the Jini network. Services **publish** themselves (make their services known to the Jini community) by registering their proxies with one or more lookup services. It's worth bearing in mind that a service usually uses other services in the federation, so in this sense, it is often a client as well.

A client uses the lookup service to locate the service it needs, download the service's proxy object, and start interacting with the service itself. This decoupling is what makes Jini responsive to the dynamic composition of a distributed network. In a properly designed Jini network, each client, service, and even lookup service can start, stop, fail, and restart independently, but the network will continue to stay functional throughout.

There are two distinct discovery methods: **multicast discovery**, used to uncover and contact any and all nearby services, and **unicast discovery**, which is URL based static mapping used when a specific service already known about is being contacted (even if it is quite far away in another sub-network). These discovery methods devolve into three discovery protocols: the **unicast discovery protocol**, the **multicast request protocol**, and the **multicast announcement protocol**. Each of these protocols has a sender, to deal with the initiation of the entity, and a handler for the receiving entity.

Unicast Discovery Protocol

Services and clients that already know the location of the lookup service(s) they would like to contact use unicast discovery. In this much it behaves more like a reconnecting protocol than a discovery protocol, but as it lives in this suite, this is where the description belongs.

This is a pseudo-code example of the syntax unicast discovery uses. The code would connect with a lookup service located at a node called accounting.myco.com, at port 8099:

```
LookupLocator myLoc = new  LookupLocator("jini://accounting.myco.com:8099/");
myLoc.discover();
```

Multicast Request Protocol

This protocol is used by services and clients when they first startup in order to solicit a response from nearby lookup services, 'nearby' in terms of the multicast radius (or maximum reach) of the underlying IP multicast protocol. IP multicast is covered in detail further into the chapter.

This example code would discover all the lookup services within the iguanas group in the current Jini network:

```
String [] myGroups = { "iguanas"};
LookupDiscovery myDis = new LookupDiscovery(myGroups);
myDis.discover();
```

Multicast Announcement Protocol

Lookup services use the multicast announcement protocol to announce their existence to clients and other services. All lookup services, by requirement, must regularly send out multicast announcement protocol packets, as a kind of 'I am here' beacon for lookup services. It functions as a sort of backup protocol, enabling clients and services to find out about lookup services should multicast request protocol fail.

Successful Discovery

A client or service that instigates successful discovery will receive one or more Jini lookup service reference(s) that can handle the group(s) it wishes to join. This lookup service reference is in fact a Java proxy object, called the registrar, which executes within the client or service's VM. The registrar supports a Java interface called ServiceRegistrar, which we'll examine in the next chapter. Exactly how it implements the ServiceRegistrar interface, and how it communicates back to the lookup service, is implementation dependent. The registrar that Sun's reference implementation of the lookup service (**reggie**) uses is in fact a proxy that uses RMI to talk back to the lookup service. So although Jini's discovery process is not RMI dependent, Sun's concrete reference implementation is.

About Service IDs

Every service in a Jini network must have a unique and persistent service ID, because it is simply not possible to tell in advance whether one Jini network will be connected to another. Hypothetically, any Jini networks may be connected to any other, through federations, at one time or another. Under such circumstances, a globally unique service ID is the only way for a client to tell if two services, obtained from two different lookup services, are in fact one and the same.

Before it has been registered, a service carries a service ID with null value, which it passes to the lookup service alongside its proxy object on its initial registration. Every lookup service has the ability to assign globally unique IDs (large algorithm generated numbers) to services during registration. A well-behaved Jini service will use the service ID assigned upon its initial registration throughout its lifetime.

Since lookup services are full-fledged Jini services themselves, they also have unique service IDs. **Reggie** persists its service ID in its own log files, thereby guaranteeing that the same service ID will be used even if the machine crashes and reboots.

The Unicast Discovery Protocol in detail

Like the other discovery protocols, the unicast discovery protocol is used to obtain a reference to a remote lookup service, but you only use unicast when you already know the address of the lookup service that you want to connect to. Unlike the other two protocols, the unicast discovery protocol is based entirely on a TCP connection. It is a straightforward request/response protocol, like the HTTP protocol.

Under this protocol, the handler creates a ServerSocket and listens for TCP connection at port 4160 (which, interestingly, is the operation CAFÉBABE in hex, or equivalent 51966; and 47806 in decimal. The CAFÉ:BABE hex pattern is also used as the magic number for Java class files). This handler portion is implemented on all lookup services.

The sender, implemented by a client or service, simply connects to the address of the lookup service, and sends a request. The handler, implemented by the lookup service, returns a response that includes the desired registrar.

The next figure depicts the workings of this protocol:

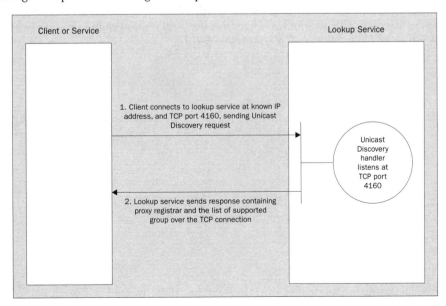

The Unicast Request Format

In the unicast request, the client or service sends the protocol version number over the TCP stream

The Unicast Response Format

The lookup service sends a marshalled object back over the TCP connection in response, containing a reference proxy to the lookup service (the registrar), a count of the number of groups that this lookup service manages, and the list of these groups.

Peer Lookup

Unicast discovery is sometimes used to locate a remote lookup service for **peer lookup**. Peer lookup is a mechanism that federates remote federations together, potentially connecting isolated IP multicast groups in the current implementation. A local service registering with a remote lookup service makes the local service available to the remote federation the lookup service belongs to. If the local service being registered is a lookup service, then the local lookup service, alongside all the services it contains, are made available to the remote federation. This effectively federates together the two remote federations. Note that in this case, the remote lookup service's proxy is **not** obtained by bootstrapping, but through a lookup operation on a local lookup service.

IP Multicast

IP multicast allows a single sender to get information to many receivers without sending individual UDP (User Datagram Protocol) packets to each and every one. Like standard network broadcast, the sender sends packets to a specific IP address (called a multicast group), and reaches interested parties listening to the corresponding multicast group. Unlike standard broadcast addresses used in IP broadcast, however, IP multicast can span beyond a single sub-network, its reach being limited by what is known as the IP multicast **radius**. This parameter is actually the TTL (time to live) parameter in UDP-multicast and it controls how far (usually how many hops) the multicast packets will travel outside of the local sub-network. By adjusting this parameter, a Jini network can expand and/or contract its reach when sending discovery packets.

Many hardware IP routers have a corresponding 'threshold' parameter that can be configured to route only packets with a minimum TTL value. The following diagram illustrates how this works (assuming the routers will route multicast packets with threshold of 1):

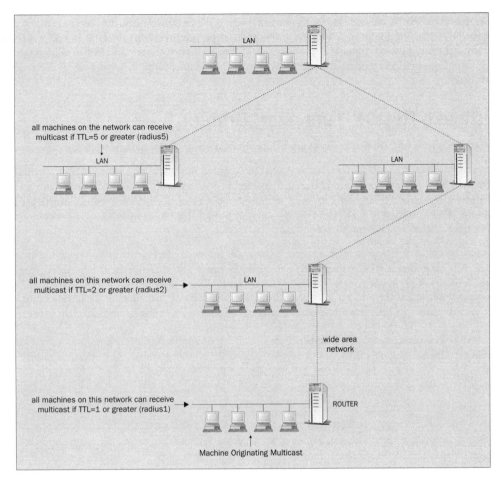

There are frequent references made to 'nearby' services in Jini literature. The term 'nearby' is used fairly loosely to mean 'any node that can be reached using IP multicast in the current network (and therefore within the multicast radius)'. Since IP multicast is used in the physical implementation of the multicast request/announcement protocols, the term 'nearby' also refers to the constraint on the 'range of discovery' imposed by the IP multicast network topology.

Working with IP Multicast

Here we'll extend the examination of basic Java network programming that we looked at in preceding chapters, adding UDP datagram and multicast socket programming. We will code a multicast to UDP datagrams bridge to illustrate how it all works.

UDP is part of the TCP/IP protocol suite, and supports transmission of connectionless datagrams (packets), so UDP datagrams can be transmitted between sender and receiver without a logical connection being established first. These datagrams are also sent without any higher-level control protocols, which means that individual UDP datagrams may arrive out of sequence (having traveled different routes from source to destination, for example), and some datagrams may even be lost in transmission (through partial network crash while a datagram is being routed through the network). Since it does not require the involved handshake, order guarantee, and receipt guarantee provided by protocols like TCP (transmission control protocol), UDP is significantly more operationally efficient.

The sender simply sends it, and the receiver uses whatever it needs in order to receive. Although this might sound like a slightly absurd approach to computer communications, UDP is in fact widely used for streaming time-sensitive data: video, voice, and other scenarios where a packet received late might as well have not been received at all, and a packet that has been dropped doesn't affect the integrity of the application.

A Multicast To UDP Tunneling Bridge

The code we'll look at here is a networking utility that uses both UDP datagram and multicast packets.

Although a large portion of the Internet is multicast enabled, not all ISPs and network providers support multicast within their networks. It is often difficult for people connecting to the Internet to receive programs widely available amongst the multicast enabled part of the Internet (called **Multicast Internet** or **MBone**). The multicast to UDP tunneling bridge utility we'll build here enables users connected to a non-multicast ISP to receive multicast content.

This utility listens at pre-defined multicast groups, and sends any packets received to a specified unicast UDP receiver. A UDP packet can be transmitted through the Internet, and through the ISP networks that don't support multicast, allowing anyone to receive MBone transmissions (or other local multicast broadcasts). Some other applications include 'remote monitoring' for the health of a Jini network, or bridging to allow an applet to participate in a Jini network (currently applet cannot work with multicast sockets).

The figure below illustrates the operation of this tunneling bridge:

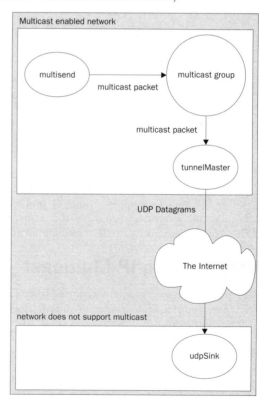

In order to see this tunneling bridge utility in action, we will need to code a **driver** that sends the packets, and a **UDP sink** to receive the re-routed packets. Here are the Java files the system uses with a brief description:

Java Program	Description
tunnelMaster.java	The **tunneling bridge utility** itself. This version will spin off two threads and perform independent tunneling on each one. It prints a message each time a multicast packet is received and subsequently sent via UDP. UDP packets sent with the letter 'X' as its first character will terminate the tunneling thread – this is a mechanism to end the program.
multsend.java	The **driver** program. This program will send multicast packets with fixed content to the two multicast groups that the tunnelMaster is monitoring.
udpSink.java	The **receiver** program. This program spins off two threads and blocks on two predefined UDP ports monitoring for packets (corresponding to the two UDP ports that tunnelMaster sends packets to). It prints a message for each UDP packet received. If a UDP packet is received that has the letter 'X' as its first character, the receiving thread will terminate.

The Tunnel Program

We'll walk through the source code here. The complete source for tunnelMaster.java can be found in the Ch5\code\multcast directory. It begins simply enough:

```
import java.net.*;
```

Next the class tunnelMaster itself implements Runnable, indicating that the work performed in the run() method of the class can be placed on an independent thread for execution:

```
public class tunnelMaster implements Runnable
{
```

The MAXTHREADS constant specifies two threads, each performing an independent forwarding task:

```
// number of ports... must correspond to the index in array below
static final int MAXTHREADS = 2;
```

The MULT_ADDR and MULT_PORT arrays contain the multicast groups and ports that the program will listen to for multicast packets:

```
//listening on these MULTICAST
static final String [] MULT_ADDR = { "229.12.1.12", "229.12.1.13" };
static final int [] MULT_PORT = { 6669, 6670 };
```

The UDP_ADDR and UDP_PORT arrays contains the corresponding UDP host and address that the program will forward the packets to:

```
// send here  (substitute your own IP details)
static final String [] UDP_ADDR = { "192.168.23.30", "192.168.23.30"};
static final int [] UDP_PORT = { 1100, 1111 };

int myIndex = 0;
String interfaceToUse = null;
```

153

The constructor simply assigns the two arguments to members of the class. The first argument, myInterface, is useful for multihomed machines (machines with more than one network adapter or equivalent, such as a dial-up adapter, installed).

On these machines, the operating system designates one of the network adapters as the default, although you can configure this yourself. Which adapter should be designated the default adapter is OS and configuration dependent. By specifying the interface used for multicast, we can make sure that multicast packets aren't sent from the wrong adapter.

The second argument, index, is either 0 or 1 and will select from the array which mapping (from multicast to UDP) to use:

```
public tunnelMaster(String myInterface, int index)


{
    myIndex = index;
    interfaceToUse = myInterface;

}

//Here is the run() method that will be placed on a thread.

public void run()
{
```

MulticastSocket is the class for creating a multicast socket corresponding to a multicast group. It is in fact a special instance of a DatagramSocket, used to create UDP sockets. Both MulticastSocket and DatagramSocket can receive or send DatagramPacket. DatagramPacket is the class representing an actual packet. A DatagramPacket always needs a user allocated buffer for backing store; here we have a byte array called buf for this purpose:

```
MulticastSocket s = null;
InetAddress group = null;
InetAddress dest = null;

byte[] buf;
DatagramPacket recv;
```

We create the multicast socket using the appropriate multicast group in the array and the port number. If this is a multihomed machine, we use the setInterface() method of the MulticastSocket class to select the adapter that will be used in multicasting:

```
try {
        group = InetAddress.getByName(MULT_ADDR[myIndex]);
        s = new MulticastSocket(MULT_PORT[myIndex]);
        if (interfaceToUse != null)
        // select interface for multihomed machines
        s.setInterface(InetAddress.getByName(interfaceToUse));
```

Next, we create the UDP datagram socket, again using the appropriate entries in the associated arrays.

Note how we need to create the buffer using the `buf` byte array. The `joinGroup()` method must be called on a multicast socket to cause it to join a specific multicast group (to associate with an IP address in the multicast range):

```
dest = InetAddress.getByName(UDP_ADDR[myIndex]);

buf = new byte[1000];

s.joinGroup(group);

// get their responses!
recv = new DatagramPacket(buf, buf.length);
String curStr = "";
```

Next, we have a loop where we block on the `receive()` method waiting for multicast packets. This loop will terminate once it has forwarded a packet that has 'X' as its first character:

```
while (buf[0] != 'X')
  {
    s.receive(recv);
```

If we get to this point, then we've received a multicast packet. We now decode the first five characters:

```
curStr = "";
for (int i=0; i<5; i++)
curStr += (char) buf[i];
System.out.println("Got a multicast packet with value=" + curStr + ",
    routing it now...");
```

Next, we change the destination address and port of the packet, and send it along using UDP datagram. Note that the `send()` method is identical for `DatagramSocket` as it is for `MulticastSocket`:

```
    // route it
    recv.setAddress(dest);
    recv.setPort(UDP_PORT[myIndex]);
    s.send(recv);
  }
}
catch (Exception e)
  { e.printStackTrace(); }
    finally {
      try {
          s.leaveGroup(group);
          s.close();
        }
      catch (Exception e) { e.printStackTrace(); }
  }
}
```

The `main()` method parses the command line argument (possibly an IP address selecting an adapter on a multihomed system) and creates two threads to forward the packets:

```
public static void main(String[] args)
{
    String myInterface = null;
    if (args.length > 0)
    myInterface = args[0];

    try {

        for (int i=0; i<MAXTHREADS; i++)
            {
                new Thread(new tunnelMaster(myInterface, i)).start();
                System.out.println("Started thread " + i + " listening on multicast
                    group " + MULT_ADDR[i] + ", port " + MULT_PORT[i] + " , tunnelling
                    to UDP host " + UDP_ADDR[i] + ", port " + UDP_PORT[i]);
            }
        }
    catch(Exception e)
        {
            e.printStackTrace();
            System.exit(1);
        }
    }
}
```

Compile this program using:

```
javac tunnelMaster.java
```

The UDP Receiver Program

The next program we will look at is the udpSink.java file, found under the Ch5\code\multcast directory. This program simply listens for UDP datagrams at two ports and prints the content of the packet received, and like tunnelMaster, the udpSink class implements Runnable:

```
import java.net.*;
public class udpSink implements Runnable
{
```

We set up the two threads listening at the ports used for tunnelMaster:

```
    // number of ports... must correspond to the index in array below
    static final int MAXTHREADS = 2;

    // foreward on these UDP

    static final int [] UDP_PORT = { 1100, 1111 };

    int myIndex = 0;
```

The constructor saves the index into the array for the port to listen at for each thread:

```
public udpSink(int index)
{
    myIndex = index;
}
```

Here, we are using `DatagramSocket`, a superclass of `MulticastSocket`:

```
public void run()
{
    DatagramSocket s = null;
    InetAddress group = null;
    byte[] buf;
    DatagramPacket recv;
    try
        {
            s = new DatagramSocket(UDP_PORT[myIndex]);
            buf = new byte[1000];

            // get their responses!
            recv = new DatagramPacket(buf, buf.length);
            String curStr = "";
```

This loop is also terminated when the 'X' character appears as the first in the packet. Unlike `tunnelMaster`, however, this loop simply prints out the first five characters of the packet, and does not forward it, but sinks it:

```
            while (buf[0] != 'X')
                {
                    s.receive(recv);
                    curStr = "";
                    for (int i=0; i<5; i++)
                    curStr += (char) buf[i];
                    System.out.println("Got a UDP packet at port " + UDP_PORT[myIndex]
                        + " with value=" + curStr);
                }
        }
    catch (Exception e)
        { e.printStackTrace(); }
    finally
        {
            try
                { s.close(); }
            catch (Exception e) { e.printStackTrace(); }
        }
}
```

The `main()` method creates the two threads, and allow them to be blocked, listening for incoming UDP datagrams:

```
public static void main(String[] args)
    {
        try {
            for (int i=0; i<MAXTHREADS; i++)
                {
```

157

```
                        new Thread(new udpSink(i)).start();
                        System.out.println("Started thread " + i + " listening on UDP
                           port " + UDP_PORT[i] + "...");
                     }
                 }
         catch(Exception e)
             {
                 e.printStackTrace();
                 System.exit(1);
             }
     }
}
```

Compile this program using the command line:

```
javac udpSink.java
```

The Multicast Packets Sender Program

The final program of the set that we will look at is multsend.java, in the Ch5\code\multcast directory. This is the program that initially sends the multicast packet. The usage of this utility is:

```
java multsend <multicast group index> <msg to send index>  [<interface for
multihomed systems>]
```

The index will be either 0 or 1, and indicates both the content of the packet, and the multicast group it should be sent to. Note that msg contains the two possible messages. The first one has only 5 characters "HICK5", the second one is a single "X" character used to terminate the tunnel program (and the UDP receiver):

```
import java.net.*;

class multsend {
    static final String [] MULT_ADDR = { "229.12.1.12", "229.12.1.13" };
    static final int [] MULT_PORT = { 6669, 6670 };
    static byte[][] msg = {{ (byte) 'H', (byte) 'I', (byte) 'C', (byte) 'K', (byte)
       '5'} , {(byte) 'X'} };
```

The constructor does nothing:

```
public multsend() {}
```

The startSend() method is where the work is done, and takes three arguments: myAddr, the IP of the interface used in a multihomed system, addressToSend, the index of the multicast group the packet should be sent to and msgToSend, the index of the message (in the msg array) that is to be sent.

```
public void startSend(String myAddr, int addressToSend, int msgToSend)
{
MulticastSocket s = null;
InetAddress group = null;
byte[] buf;
DatagramPacket send;
```

```
//We create a multicast socket, and set the interface to use if necessary.

try {
    group = InetAddress.getByName(MULT_ADDR[addressToSend]);

    s = new MulticastSocket(MULT_PORT[addressToSend]);
        if (myAddr != null)
        // select interface for multihomed machines
        s.setInterface(InetAddress.getByName(myAddr));
        buf = new byte[1000];
```

We associate the multicast socket with the multicast group, prepare the datagram packet, and send it:

```
        s.joinGroup(group);

        DatagramPacket hi = new DatagramPacket(msg[msgToSend],
            msg[msgToSend].length, group, MULT_PORT[addressToSend]);
        s.send(hi);
    }
catch (Exception e)
    { e.printStackTrace(); }
    finally {
            try {
                s.leaveGroup(group);
                s.close(); } catch (Exception e) { e.printStackTrace();
                    System.exit(1); }
            }
        }
```

The main() method parses the command line arguments, and calls the startSend()method with the parsed arguments.

```
public static void main(String[] args)
    {
        if (args.length < 2)
            {
                System.out.println("invalid usage");
                System.exit(1);
            }
        int myHost = Integer.parseInt(args[0]);
        int myMsg = Integer.parseInt(args[1]);
        if ((myHost < 0) || (myHost >1 ) || (myMsg <0) || (myMsg >1))
            {
                System.out.println("group and message must be 0 or 1");
                System.exit(1);
            }

    String myInterface = null;
    if (args.length > 2)
        myInterface = args[2];
```

```
      System.out.println( "Sending multicast message to group " + MULT_ADDR[myHost] +
         ", port " + MULT_PORT[myHost] + ", containing message number " + myMsg );
      multsend aSender = new multsend();
      aSender.startSend(myInterface, myHost, myMsg);
      }
   }
```

Go ahead and compile it:

```
javac multsend.java
```

Testing the Multicast to UDP Tunneling Utility

Begin testing by starting the udpSink program, which does not depend on any other program, using the command:

```
start java udpSink
```

This will start udpSink in another console window. You should get this output:

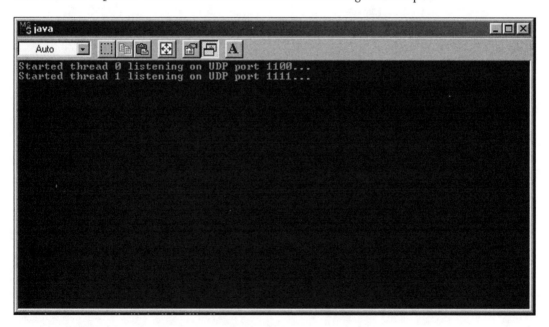

Next, we need to run the tunnelMaster program. Use the command line:

```
start java tunnelMaster
```

Or, if you're using a multihomed system, select the interface to use with an argument:

```
start java tunnelMaster 192.168.23.30
```

`tunnelMaster` should display the following output:

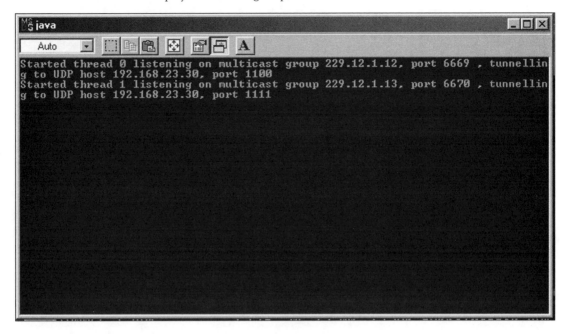

Now, we can send a multicast packet to the multicast group using:

```
java multsend 0 0
```

Or on a multihomed system, specifying one of your adapters:

```
java multsend 0 0 192.168.23.30
```

You should see the first packet being routed in the `tunnelMaster` console, something like this:

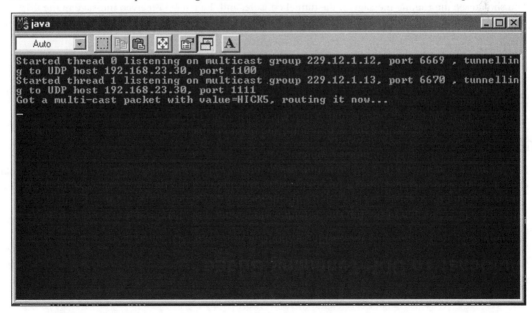

The forwarded UDP packet will appear in the udpSink console:

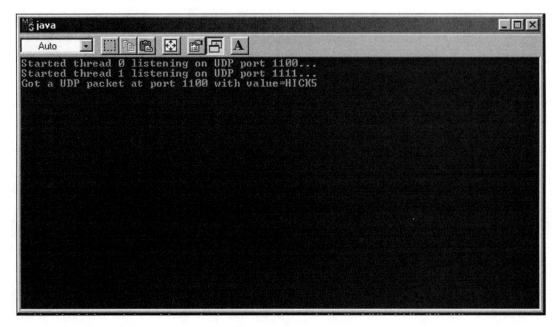

Now try sending a message to the second multicast group using either:

```
java multsend 1 0
```

or:

```
java multsend 1 0 192.168.23.30
```

You should see the routing message in the tunnel console, and the packet received message in the udpSink console. Finally, send the terminating message to each thread of the tunneling utility and the udpSink:

```
java multsend 0 1
java multsend 1 1
```

(Remember to add the interface's IP if you're on a multihomed system.) This should shut down both the tunnelMaster and udpSink program by terminating their receive loops.

The Multicast Request Protocol in detail

Using the multicast request protocol, the client or service initiating discovery can determine the lookup services that are available locally. (Jini 1.1 defines 'local' as equivalent to the IP multicast radius, and the specification recommends a default of 15.)

Mechanics of the Multicast Request Protocol

The mechanics of this protocol are pretty straightforward. On the initiating side (client or service side) a ServerSocket is created, and lookup service connections listened for on an available TCP port. A multicast request packet is sent to multicast group 224.0.1.85, port number 4160, with the following information:

- ❑ IP of the initiator
- ❑ Port at which client's TCP service is listening
- ❑ Set of groups that the client is interested in connecting to
- ❑ Service IDs of the lookup services that the client already knows about

Any responses received from the lookup services are added to the list of lookup services being maintained.

The end of this process is triggered by one of three things; a time-out (the specification recommends 5 seconds), the number of loop iterations (the specification recommends 7), or the number of lookup services located (enough to cover all the groups required).

Should the trigger come before enough lookup services have been located to cover all the desired groups, the initiator must resort to listening for lookup service multicast announcements in order to locate the rest.

On the lookup service side listening at multicast group 224.0.1.85, port number 4160 commences. Multicast packets are examined upon arrival against the list of groups being maintained, to see whether they are already being managed. If so, the list of lookup services already heard is checked to determine if the client/service already knows about this lookup service, and where the group matches, and if the client has not heard from this lookup service, the lookup service will connect to the client's unicast TCP socket and send a reference to its registrar object.

Broadly speaking it looks like this:

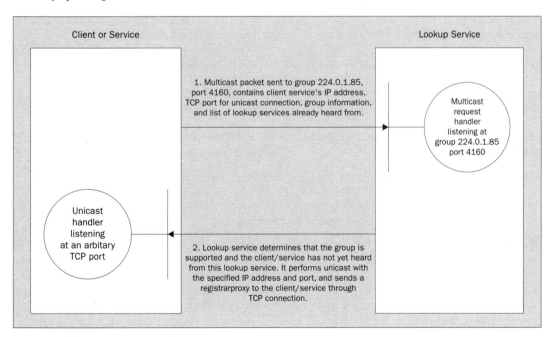

The Multicast Request Packet Format

The format of each element within the packet is specified by the Java library method used to write it (methods of `java.io.DataOutputStream`). This is both machine/hardware independent, and easy to write/read by any Java based client or server.

The host IP of the client is not required in the content of the packet because the envelope within which a UDP packet travels already contains this information. Specifically, the UDP packet header contains the originating host's IP address, the destination host's IP address and port.

These requirements must fit in the maximum UDP datagram packet size of 512 bytes – this is maximum size guaranteed transmission as a single one packet by every TCP/IP implementation. If the request packet cannot be reduced to 512 bytes, by dropping something, then the request must be split into multiple requests. If the client, for example, is interested in more groups than can fit into the 512 bytes, it should break the groups up and perform multiple discovery requests.

If this approach cannot reduce the size packet size enough, then the initiator may drop some of the service IDs in the packet that have already been heard from.

When the lookup service connects back to the initiator, it uses the Unicast discovery response packet format covered in the last section. This TCP based response contains a proxy object, the register itself.

The Multicast Announcement Protocol in detail

Clients and services that want to bootstrap use this protocol as a fallback protocol, following a multicast request failure, or a premature time-out that has left the list of lookup services shorter than required. It is mandatory that every lookup service supports this protocol. Essentially, the initiator sits back and waits to hear from lookup services that are required to announce themselves periodically.

More importantly, though, the multicast announcement protocol is used to announce new lookup services that have started up, and failed lookup services that restart. In this way existing services already running are kept up to date. The announcement is also important when the groups supported by a lookup change.

An existing service that has already registered with the lookup service can then determine if it needs to deregister.

The lookup service sets up the unicast discovery handler listening at a TCP port and regularly (the Jini specifications recommends every 120 seconds) sends multicast announcement packets to the multicast group 224.0.1.84 – port 4160. This contains its own service ID, information about host and port of its unicast discovery server, and a list of groups that it manages.

The client or service creates a UDP multicast socket and listens for packets (from lookup services) on the multicast group 224.0.1.84, port number 4160. As packets come in, the list of lookup services that it carries is checked to see if they have already been heard from, and where they all have the process begins again. Should the packet carry information about a newly discovered lookup service, the unicast discovery protocol is used to connect, using the host and port described in the packet. This is represented in the following diagram:

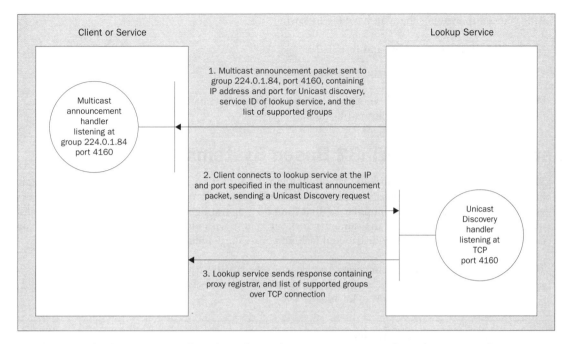

In fact, most lookup services will perform this multicast announcement from the moment they start up to the moment they are shutdown, which ensures that clients started up before the lookup service, or failing multicast requests, might still be able to connect with a lookup service through its multicast announcement.

The Multicast Announcement Packet Format

The lookup service's multicast UDP announcement packets contain:

❏ Protocol version

❏ Host for unicast discovery

❏ Port to use for unicast discovery

❏ ServiceID of the originating lookup service

❏ Count of groups

❏ List of groups serviced by the lookup service

As with the multicast request packets, if the list of groups is too long to fit within the 512 byte UDP datagram limit, multiple announcement packets must be created.

This concludes our coverage of the discovery protocols suite. Now for some hands-on experience with these protocols, and an examination of some code that uses the Jini library.

Setting Up a Jini Network

This is the same setup that we will be using throughout the book to explore the different aspects of Jini. If you have more than one machine available over the network, you should follow these setup instructions, but start the lookup service, client, and service on different machines.

All of our setup assumes that you have the following:

❑ JDK 1.2.2, operational and installed

❑ Jini 1.1 beta or later unzipped into a directory

Please be aware that earlier Jini versions have various bugs and changed utility syntax that will make them unusable with many samples in this book.

Setting Up Jini on Win32 Based Systems

Many readers will be using Windows 95, 98, 2000, or NT to test the programs in this book. Although the code and coverage is primarily geared towards testing in these Win32 environments, there are some samples adapted for the wildly popular Redhat Linux 6.2 operating system. Readers that have machines with both operating systems on the same network (or Win32 with other UNIX operating systems) can use all of the samples, in a truly distributed fashion across these platforms.

To begin with we'll set up a rudimentary Jini system, which will provide the base on which all the samples in the book will run. We will use a set of batch file (.bat files), which you can find in the Ch5\bats\ directory in the source download. They are:

Batch File	Description
runhttpd.bat	Starts a class server to serve the codebase (dynamic class download) required by client code.
runrmid.bat	Starts the RMI activation daemon. Many of the reference implementation of Jini services supplied by Sun are activatable Java services and will require rmid running.
runreggie.bat	Starts Sun's reference lookup service, called reggie. Since it is an RMI activatable service, the setup VM will actually register with rmid and creates an instance of reggie.
setpaths.bat	Sets up the required paths and environment variable that is used by many of the other batch files.
Runjbrowser	Starts the Sun sample Jini lookup service browser application.

This set of batch files can be used to start a Jini network on a single machine, or across a few machines.

Here we'll examine the content of these batch files, and activate them.

> **Important warning for users with multihomed machines:** if the machine that you are
> running on contains more than ONE network adapter – beware! You must use the
> `net.jini.discovery.interface` property to configure the interface to use for
> multicast whenever you run a Jini program that performs discovery. For example:
>
> ```
> java -Dnet.jini.discovery.interface=192.168.23.30 <other
> arguments> myJiniProg
> ```
>
> **Otherwise, the code may fail or hang intermittently, depending on the default adapter
> that it binds to multicasting, and this is operating system, network configuration, and
> Java implementation dependent.**

Do not attempt to run the batch files supplied from a GUI environment. They are designed to be run
within a Win32 command console only.

The first file we will look at is the `setpaths.bat` file – remember to modify the `setpaths.bat` file
to reflect your particular Jini installation. This is what it looks like on our system:

```
set JINIHOME=d:\jini1_1
set DOWNLOADHOST=win98p300:8080
set ADAPTERIP=192.168.23.30
set JINITEMP=d:\temp
```

Change `JINIHOME` to reflect the location of your Jini 1.1 beta installation, `DOWNLOADHOST` to your
own host name and port number, and `JINITEMP` to a `temp` folder. You need to create this folder so
that **rmid** and **reggie** can create and hold onto their log file directories persistently.

The rudimentary Jini system we're going to start up requires (in order of start up):

- ❏ An HTTP server to serve the downloadable client portion of reggie (that is, the class for the
  registrar proxy, etc), called reggie-DL.JAR
- ❏ Rmid running, for RMI activation (reggie depends on it)
- ❏ Reggie running
- ❏ A Jini browser, to monitor the state of the minimal network

You can use the `runhttpd.bat` file to run the simple class server that serves code downloads with the
Jini runtime. The class `server` is distributed in the `tool.jar` file. The batch file simply runs the
HTTP server (at port 8080) and provides it with Jini's lib directory as the root:

```
call setpaths
start java  -jar %JINIHOME%\lib\tools.jar -port 8080 -dir %JINIHOME%\lib  -trees -
verbose
```

If you have run rmid previously and you're not working with winNT or 2000, use:

```
runclean
```

before proceeding. This will delete all old log files (persistent data written by rmid and reggie) that may be hanging around. WinNT and 2000 require you to remove the directory manually.

In a production Jini system, you are unlikely, and certainly not advised, to remove old reggie log files, because they store the persistent information necessary for the lookup service to survive failures. Given that we're testing with many different Jini services and code versions here, however, deleting the files allows us to begin each time with a completely clean slate, as if the Jini system had been booted for the very first time.

Start rmid using:

```
runrmid
```

The `runrmid.bat` file contains:

```
call setpaths.bat
start rmid -log %JINITEMP%\rmid.log
```

We can then start reggie to send some of these packets:

```
runreggie
```

The `runreggie.bat` contains:

```
call setpaths.bat
java -jar -Djava.security.policy=policy.all %JINIHOME%\lib\reggie.jar
http://%DOWNLOADHOST%/reggie-dl.jar policy.all %JINITEMP%\reggie_log iguanas -
Dnet.jini.discovery.interface=%ADAPTERIP%
```

The will start reggie running servicing the group **iguanas**. We also use a grant all security policy file, called `policy.all`, for this casual testing.

Obviously, such a wide-open policy file should never be used during production (security, and production policy file construction, is covered in Chapter 14). When running reggie using the batch file, you need to wait until the setup VM has completed and the command prompt returned to the console. This indicates that reggie is up and running. Once you've started reggie, you should soon see multicast announcement packets from the service.

Next, we can run a Jini Lookup Service browser that is supplied with the Jini distribution:

```
runjbrowser
```

The Jini browser application is part of the `jini-examples.jar` file. The class is called `com.Sun.jini.example.browser.Browser`. Here is the content of the `runjbrowser.bat` file:

```
call setpaths.bat
java -cp .;%JINIHOME%\lib\jini-examples.jar -Djava.security.policy=policy.all -
Djava.rmi.server.codebase=http://%DOWNLOADHOST%/jini-examples-dl.jar
com.Sun.jini.example.browser.Browser -admin
```

Using the `-admin` option gives us control over the administrative interface of the lookup service. Using this interface, it is possible to shutdown a service gracefully (allowing it to cleanup properly). We will see how to work with the administrative interface programmatically in a later chapter. For now, we should be aware that this is the preferred method of shutting down a service in production without deleting the persistent data log files. The browser should startup as a Swing application that looks like this:

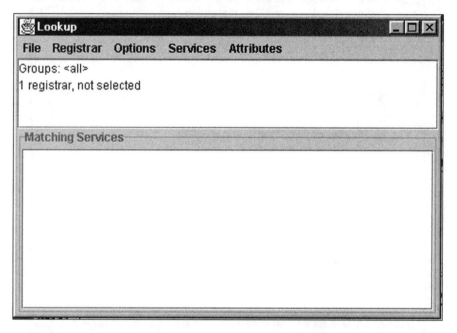

Clicking on the File menu allows us to locate lookup service by group names (the default is to find all groups):

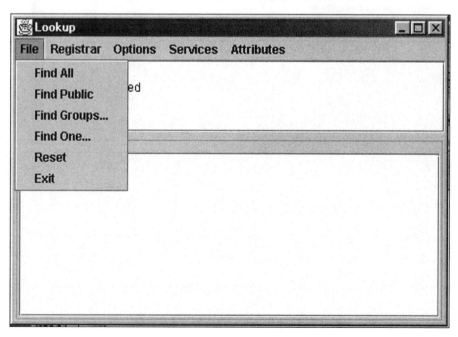

Select Find Groups and enter iguanas into the dialog box. Click on the Registrar menu, and select the only lookup service there. The lookup service, our only instance of reggie, will then appear in the Matching Services list box that comes up:

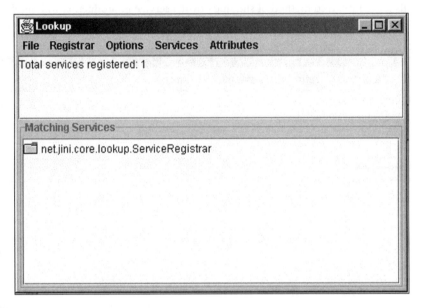

To shutdown reggie, select the service in the bottom window of the browser. Right click on the selection:

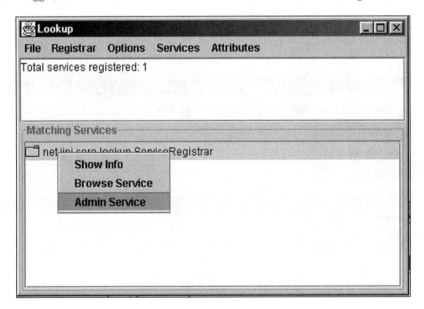

Select Admin Service. A new browser window will popup:

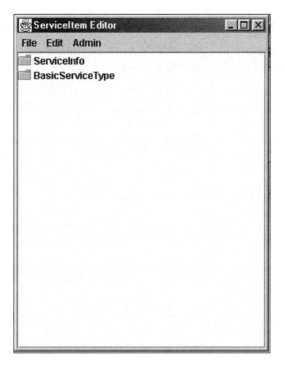

Select the Admin menu, and then Destroy in order to terminate the reggie service, and clean out any current data:

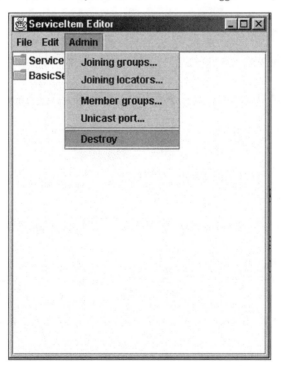

And that's all there is to setting up and testing a rudimentary Jini network that consists of one lookup service and one client browser.

Setting Up Jini on UNIX Systems: Redhat Linux 6.2

For those who may be setting up Jini on a UNIX system, we will use as an example the well-supported and highly popular Redhat Linux 6.2 operating system.

On this system, we assume that you have installed and tested JDK 1.2.2 or later (blackdown.org version or Sun's version). Make sure native threads are used, and not green threads.

We need to set up multicast routing explicitly on Redhat Linux 6.2. The default kernel for Redhat Linux 6.2 has already enabled IP multicast. In order for a Linux node to interoperate with Win32 nodes using Jini, make sure you execute the following multicast default routing command:

```
route add -net 224.0.0.0 netmask 240.0.0.0 dev eth0
```

You may also need to add your hostname to the /etc/hosts file as the very first entry, before the localhost entry if you are going to interoperate with Win32 machines.

You will find the shell script files, equivalent to the BAT files, in the \Ch5\code\unixjini directory. All the shell scripts are based on the default 'bash' Bourne-Again Shell on the Linux platform. If you use any other shell (for example, csh), you will have to modify these shell scripts.

The setpaths.bat file becomes the setpath script and contains:

```
JINIHOME=~/jini1_1
DOWNLOADHOST=redhat61:8080
ADAPTERIP=192.168.23.9
JINITEMP=~/logs
export JINIHOME DOWNLOADHOST ADAPTERIP JINITEMP
```

The runhttpd.bat file becomes the runhttpd script and contains:

```
. .(s)etpaths
java  -jar $JINIHOME/lib/tools.jar -port 8080 -dir $JINIHOME/lib -trees -verbose
```

The runreggie.bat file becomes the runreggie script and contains:

```
. .(s)etpaths
java -jar -Djava.security.policy=policy.all $JINIHOME/lib/reggie.jar
http://$DOWNLOADHOST/reggie-dl.jar policy.all $JINITEMP\reggie_log iguanas -
Dnet.jini.discovery.interface=$ADAPTERIP
```

The runjbrowser.bat file becomes the runjbrowser script and contains:

```
. .(s)etpaths
java -cp .:$JINIHOME/lib/jini-examples.jar -Djava.security.policy=policy.all -
Djava.rmi.server.codebase=http://$DOWNLOADHOST/jini-examples-dl.jar
com.Sun.jini.example.browser.Browser -admin
```

Finally, the runclean.bat file becomes the runclean script and contains:

```
. .(s)etpaths
rm -r $JINITEMP/rmid.log
rm -r $JINITEMP/reggie_log
```

When you create these script files, you will also need to make them executable using:

```
chmod +x <script file name>
```

Otherwise, we usually open a separate terminal for each executed batch file under Linux so we can monitor the execution process. The procedure to start the minimal system is exactly the same as in Win32, and the result is very similar. This is the minimal system running on Linux 6.2:

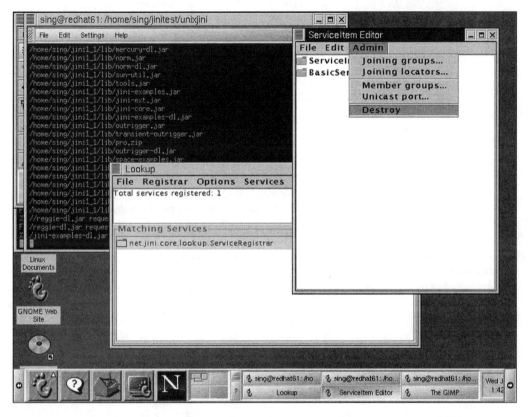

Although the batch files created in this book are Win32 oriented, the user with a UNIX system can adapt them to work with UNIX in this manner.

Analysis of the Discovery Protocols On-The-Wire

We're going to code a simple utility called jintool that will listen on the network for multicast discovery packets. It will listen for both multicast request packets from clients/services and multicast announcement packets from lookup services.

Once a packet has been received, it will decode all the fields of the packet and print them out on the standard output. This tool will allow us to see the discovery protocol in action, and appreciate the timing involved during the discovery process.

We will be using the `java.net.MulticastSocket` class to work with the multicast sockets. In particular, the multicast group and port at which we will be listening for multicast packets are:

Multicast Group	Port	Packet Type
224.0.1.84	4160	Multicast request
224.0.1.85	4160	Multicast announcement

We'll be using some Jini utility classes in the `net.jini.discovery` package to decode the multicast packets that we receive:

Class Name	Description
IncomingMulticastRequest	Takes the multicast request packet in its constructor, and decodes/unmarshalls the packet into its constituents. Provide methods to get the value of the various fields in the decoded packet.
IncomingMulticastAnnoucement	Takes the multicast announcement packet in its constructor, and decodes the packet into its constituents. Provides methods to get the value of the various fields in the decoded packet.

Here is the code of `jintool.java`; the program will create two independent threads, as each thread will block waiting for incoming multicast packets when executing the `receive()` method call of the `java.net.MulticastSocket` class.

```java
import java.net.*;

import net.jini.discovery.*;
import net.jini.core.lookup.ServiceID;


public class jintool implements Runnable
{

  static final int MAXTHREADS = 2;

  static final int MULTICAST_ANNOUNCE = 1;
  static final int MULTICAST_REQUEST = 2;
```

Here, we set up the constant for the multicast group and port address. Thread 1 will listen for multicast announcement packets, and thread 2 will listen for multicast request packets:

```java
    // listening on these multicast sockets
    //  Multicast Annoucement, Multicast  Request
    static final String [] MULT_ADDR = { "224.0.1.84", "224.0.1.85" };
    static final int [] MULT_PORT = { 4160, 4160 };
    static final int [] PACKET_TYPE = { MULTICAST_ANNOUNCE, MULTICAST_REQUEST };
```

`myIndex` will contain our thread index number (0 or 1).

```java
    int myIndex = 0;
```

```
    public jintool(int index)
    {
        myIndex = index;
    }
```

decodePacket is the helper method that will use the net.jini.discovery utility classes to decode the packet. The thread index number is used to indicate the packet type:

```
    public void decodePacket(DatagramPacket inPacket,int inPackType)
    {
        switch (inPackType)
        {
          case MULTICAST_ANNOUNCE:
          {
              IncomingMulticastAnnouncement myPack = null;
              try {
                    myPack = new IncomingMulticastAnnouncement(inPacket);
                  }
              catch(Exception e) { e.printStackTrace(); return;}
              System.out.println("--------------------------------------------------");
              System.out.println("Got a MulticastAnnouncement Packet");
              System.out.println("From host:  " + inPacket.getAddress().toString());
              System.out.println("Service ID: " + myPack.getServiceID());
              System.out.println("Groups:");
              String [] tpGroups = myPack.getGroups();
              if (tpGroups.length == 0)
                 System.out.println("  No group list.");
           else
              for (int i=0; i< tpGroups.length; i++)
                 System.out.println("  #" + i + ": " + tpGroups[i]);
          }
        break;
        case MULTICAST_REQUEST:
         {
            IncomingMulticastRequest myPack = null;
             try {
                myPack = new IncomingMulticastRequest(inPacket);
                }
             catch(Exception e) { e.printStackTrace(); return; }
             System.out.println("--------------------------------------------------");
             System.out.println("Got a Multicast Request Packet");
             System.out.println("From host:  " + inPacket.getAddress().toString());
             System.out.println("Respond to: " + myPack.getAddress().toString() );
             System.out.println("Resp Port:  " + myPack.getPort() );
             System.out.println("Service IDs already heard from:");
             ServiceID [] tpServiceIDs = myPack.getServiceIDs();
             if (tpServiceIDs.length == 0)
               System.out.println(" None yet.");
           else
              for (int i=0; i< tpServiceIDs.length; i++)
                System.out.println("  #" + i + ": " + tpServiceIDs[i]);

             System.out.println("Groups desired:");
             String [] tpGroups = myPack.getGroups();
             if (tpGroups.length == 0
```

```
              System.out.println("  No group list.");
          else
              for (int i=0; i< tpGroups.length; i++)
              System.out.println("  #" + i + ": " + tpGroups[i]);
          }
          break;
      }
  }
```

The `jintool` class itself implements the `Runnable` interface. This `run()` method contains the work for each thread.

```java
public void run()
{
   MulticastSocket s = null;
   InetAddress group = null;
   InetAddress dest = null;

   byte[] buf;
   DatagramPacket recv;
```

Here we create the multicast socket and start waiting for packets, which the `receive()` method inside the `while` loop blocks.

```java
    try {
        group = InetAddress.getByName(MULT_ADDR[myIndex]);
        s = new MulticastSocket(MULT_PORT[myIndex]);
        buf = new byte[1000];
        s.joinGroup(group);

        // get their responses!
        recv = new DatagramPacket(buf, buf.length);

      while (true)
        {
          s.receive(recv);
          decodePacket(recv, PACKET_TYPE[myIndex]);
        }
      }
    catch (Exception e)
        { e.printStackTrace(); }
    finally {
      try {
        s.leaveGroup(group);
        s.close();
        }
      catch (Exception e) { e.printStackTrace(); }
      }
    }
```

The `main()` method simply creates and starts the two threads.

```java
public static void main(String[] args)
    {
        try {

            for (int i=0; i<MAXTHREADS; i++)
            {
```

```
            new Thread(new jintool(i)).start();
            System.out.println("Started thread " + i + " listening on multicast
               host " + MULT_ADDR[i] + ", port " + MULT_PORT[i] );
        }
    }
    catch(Exception e)
       {
          e.printStackTrace();
          System.exit(1);
       }
    }
}
```

Testing the jintool Multicast Packet Decoder

To compile the jintool program, use the supplied batch file called `buildit.bat` using:

`Buildit jintool.java`

```
call setpaths.bat
set CLASSPATH=.;%JINIHOME%\lib\jini-core.jar;%JINIHOME%\lib\jini-
ext.jar;%JINIHOME%\lib\Sun-util.jar
javac %1
```

You will need to test out the jintool on an operational minimal Jini network, following the instructions we worked through earlier in this chapter. Once you have this network going, start jintool (it will come up in a new window) using:

`runit jintool`

(If you find you get an out of environment error, adjust the Initial environment under the Memory tab in the Properties of the window you're working in)

The `runit.bat` file contains:

```
call setpaths.bat
set CLASSPATH=.;%JINIHOME%\lib\jini-core.jar;%JINIHOME%\lib\jini-
ext.jar;%JINIHOME%\lib\Sun-util.jar
start java %1 %2 %3 %4
```

Now jintool is ready to print out any multicast request or multicast announcement packets that it sees.

The following diagram shows a sample run of jintool on a Jini network with a lookup service and one Jini Browser:

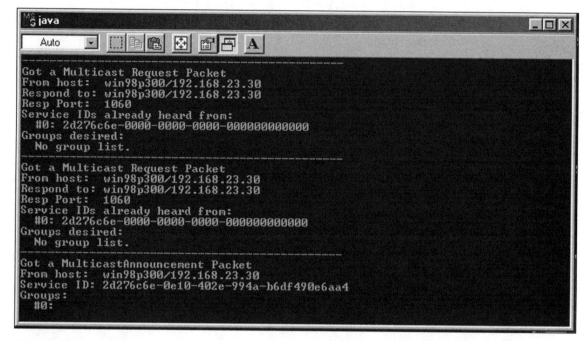

By default, `reggie` will only send a multicast announcement packet, as a UDP datagram, every 120 seconds, so you have to be patient to see them. You can change the interval that reggie will send these packets by modifying the property:

`net.jini.discovery.announce`

We can do this by modifying the `runreggie.bat` file. Here, we set the multicast announcement interval to every 15 seconds:

```
call setpaths.bat
java -jar %JINIHOME%\lib\reggie.jar http://%DOWNLOADHOST%/reggie-dl.jar policy.all
%JINITEMP%\reggie_log iguanas -Dnet.jini.discovery.interface=%ADAPTERIP% -
Dnet.jini.discovery.announce=15000
```

If you do make this change, make sure you run:

`runclean`

on Win98, or delete the logfiles for rmid and reggie manually, before restarting. The arguments for the actual reggie VM is persisted by rmid, and we must kill rmid and delete the persistent store (logfiles) if we want to change these arguments.

The Join Protocol

The join protocol is not a low-level network protocol like the discovery protocol suite. It's a set of design requirements that should be followed for a service to properly join (and leave) a Jini federation. While it cannot be easily enforced, and Jini does not attempt to enforce it, it is important that all service implementations follow the protocol to ensure the long-term consistency and stability of a Jini system.

A Jini system is presented to services and clients alike as a very long-lived system. However, since the lookup services, and our own Jini services all run on machines and networks that will inevitably crash or go down at one point or another, we must provide additional implementation behaviors that will realize the long-lived Jini ideal. This includes behaviors that are necessary to ensure and maintain the consistent and stable state of the system, regardless of how individual services (including lookup services) may fail and restart. These behaviors are part of the join protocol.

To this end, each and every service is expected to keep some persistent state information. This information includes:

- ❑ A service ID

- ❑ Attributes that describe the service, used during lookup (these are properly introduced in the next chapter)

- ❑ A set of groups that the service wants to join

- ❑ A set of specific lookup services that the service should contact by Unicast Discovery

Most of this information (except maybe a set of groups to join) will be unavailable the first time the service starts. It receives its own service ID when it registers with the lookup service. However, once started the service will contain most of the information Jini expects. The join protocol requires that the service persists such information even if the service itself (or the machine hosting the service) crashes. In order to preserve the long-lived nature of the system, the service must re-use this information if it ever has to restart. The join protocol requires a service to maintain all of the above persistent state information.

Should a service restart after a crash, the service must examine the persistent list of lookup services, obtain a reference to each one using the unicast discovery protocol, and try to register with each of them in turn. It can decide to give up if connection is not successful, and it can discard the proxy if it was originally found using multicast discovery (since the lookup service will send multicast announcement when it starts up again anyway). It may not, however, remove the lookup service from the list if the service was originally found using unicast discovery – this is because the lookup service may be remote, and so discovery announcements might never reach the service. Again, this preserves the long-lived Jini system – the service essentially restores its runtime state before the crash. The service must also examine the persistent list of groups it is supposed to join, upon restart, and must try to use multicast discovery to locate lookup servers for these groups. All this is required by the join protocol.

To maintain a system that is always up, administrative changes made to a service (using an administrative interface, as we shall see later) should be reflected immediately without any service downtime. One must be careful to make sure that any 'live' changes to persistent states are performed in such a manner that the network is kept in a consistent state.

If there is a change to the groups that the service should belong to, the service must reflect the change. So, for example, if a service is asked to join a new group, it should first store the group in its persistent set of groups, and then attempt multicast discovery to join the group. If a service is asked to withdraw from a group, it should first remove the group from the persistent store, then remove any lookup services for that group (if the same lookup service does not handle another group of interest) by removing the associated proxy from the persistent store. It should also deregister from the lookup service(s) to be removed prior to disposing with the proxy.

If an administrative change requires a service register or unregister with specific lookup services, it should update the persistent set of lookup services and then register or unregister from the specified lookup service(s).

If there are changes to the set of attributes that are registered with lookup services, consistency must be maintained by saving the change to the persistent store and making the change in every one of the lookup services that the service has registered with.

A final requirement of the join protocol deals with how service should startup. Upon startup, the service should start operation after a random delay (recommended randomized range: from 0 up to 15 seconds). This is done to stagger the firing of multicast request packets for the entire network system/ LAN segment. Otherwise, restarting a system that contains many services may cause a disastrous packet storm to occur.

It's not hard to imagine the reams of complex, tough to debug code that has to be written in order for services to conform to the join protocol. Fortunately, Sun provides a helper class called `net.jini.lookup.JoinManager` that handles the majority of the implementation details required by the join protocol for you. We will see how to use this class in Chapter 8. It is possible to have Jini services that do not fully implement the join protocol. These services are still allowed into a Jini network, since nothing can really enforce that join protocol. However, such badly behaved services may cause the Jini network to enter inconsistent or unstable states while they're active.

Summary

In this chapter, we have dissected the entire Discovery protocol suite, all the way down to the packet format that is transmitted over the wire. We've looked at the way a client or service locates a lookup service in a Jini network, and how the protocols may be implemented using the socket mechanism from basic Java networking (as discussed in Chapters 2 and 3). We started coding, and created a multicast packet monitor and decoder utility that let us observe the discovery protocol in action within any Jini network. Finally, we examined the join protocol and discovered that it is not in fact a low-level network protocol at all, but a set of implementation conventions that every service must follow. Strict adherence to the join protocol is essential to maintain a healthy Jini network. Sun has library code that implements this complex protocol.

In the next chapter, we will move from the low-level protocols up to the lookup service (itself a full fledged Jini service), and look at the code that is involved in lookup and the other interactions that occur between the lookup service and a clients/service.

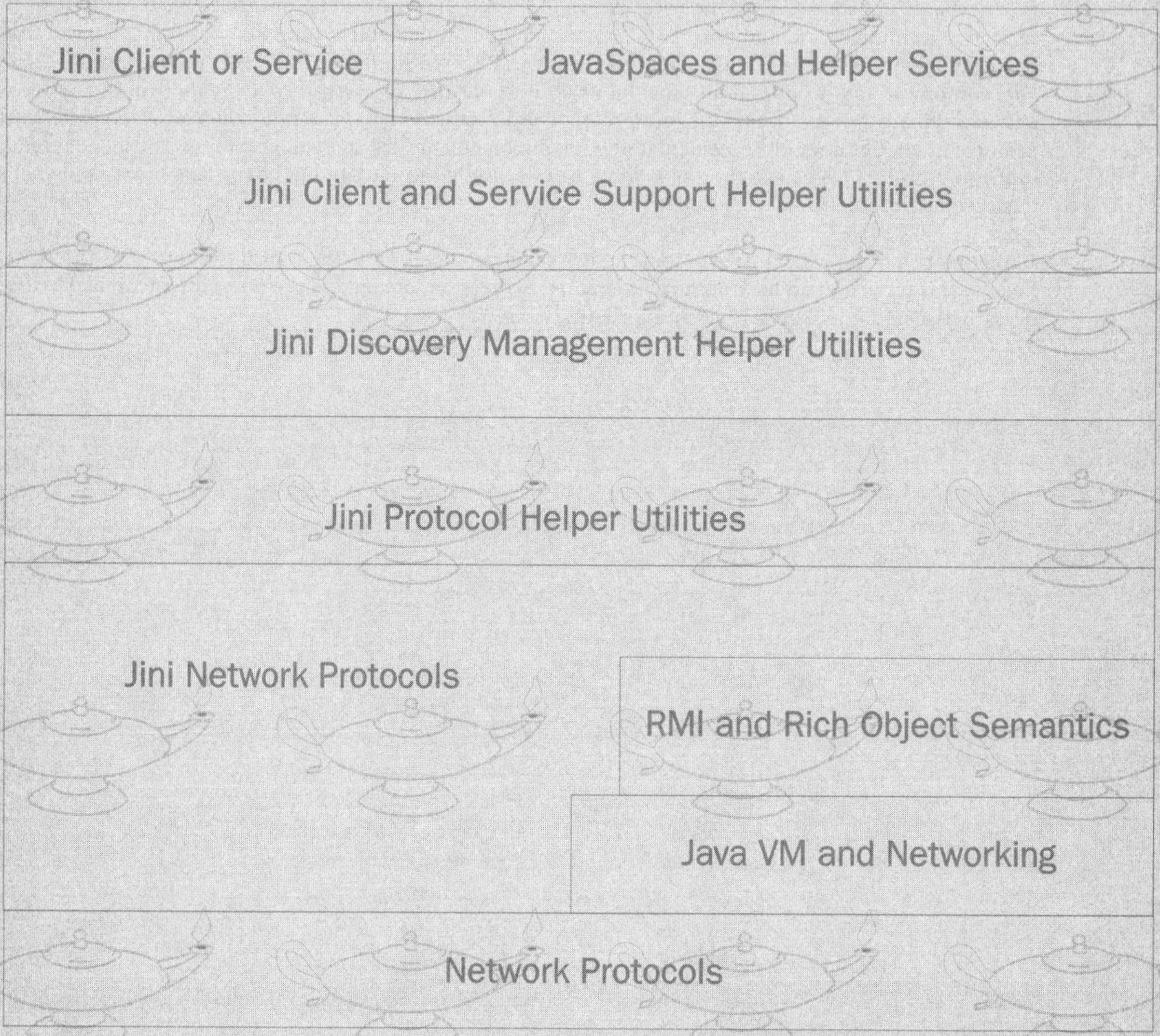

Jini Client or Service
JavaSpaces and Helper Services
Jini Client and Service Support Helper Utilities
Jini Discovery Management Helper Utilities
Jini Protocol Helper Utilities
Jini Network Protocols
RMI and Rich Object Semantics
Java VM and Networking
Network Protocols

Online discussion at http://p2p.wrox.com

6

Jini Lookup Service and Entries

Jini's lookup service enjoys the special status of being the only Jini service that is involved in a Jini federation at its genesis. In fact, without any lookup services, there is no dynamic Jini network. Following a successful bootstrap, as we saw in Chapter 5, the client is handed the lookup service's proxy; the interactions between service and lookup service thereafter, and particularly the behaviors the service exhibits within this interrelationship, are heavily documented in the Jini specifications.

In this chapter we're going to first take an in depth look at the lookup service, the responsibilities it has, and the value it brings to the Jini network. Then we'll design and implement a complex Jini service.

In very broad terms, a Jini lookup service has the following responsibilities:

- ❑ Bootstrap assistance
- ❑ Service location
- ❑ Database maintenance
- ❑ Long-lived, self-healing network maintenance
- ❑ Unique ID dispenser

We are going to investigate these responsibilities, and the essential and independent functional blocks that make a lookup service tick. Many of these functional blocks provide interfaces to, and interaction with, Jini clients and services. We'll look at the significance of a lookup `Entry`, discuss its associated attributes, and examine how the lookup service performs a fast pattern-matching search (called a template search) for service proxies. Finally we'll put some coding examples using the utility and helper classes supplied with the Jini libraries that ease the coding load considerably.

From a network designer/architect perspective, we'll examine how lookup services can be used to partition a network, or connect together separate Jini federations.

Armed with a thorough understanding of what a Jini lookup service actually does, we'll briefly compare and contrast it with the naming and directory services of other popular network technologies, such as CORBA, DNS, and Active Directory.

The Roles of a Jini Lookup Service

The following diagram depicts the interactions between a Jini lookup service and the other entities in a Jini network, all of which we'll look at closely in this chapter.

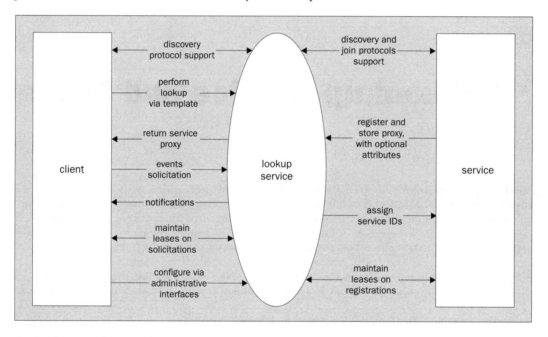

As the diagram shows, a client interacts with the lookup service in the following ways:

Interaction	Description
Supports the discovery protocol	Client finds the lookup service using unicast or multicast discovery. The lookup service must participate in these protocols.
Performs lookup using a template	Client locates services using the lookup service by supplying a search template that contains the lookup criterion (more detailed coverage later in this chapter).

Interaction	Description
Solicits events	Client tells the lookup service that it is interested in being notified when certain changes occurs within the lookup service (when a specified service joins the federation, for example). Lookup service will store this solicitation (registration of interest), and notify the client via a remote event should the change occur.
Maintains lease on solicitations	Event solicitations are leased. The lookup service grants the client a finite duration lease. The client must renew the lease (indicating that it is still interested in the event) before it expires.
Configuration, using administration interfaces	Clients control and configure certain aspects of lookup services (the frequency of transmission of multicast announcement packet, for example).

A Jini service, on the other hand, will interact with the lookup service in these ways:

Interaction	Description
Supports discovery and join protocols	Service locates lookup service using the discovery protocol during bootstrap. After bootstrapping, a Jini service interacts with the lookup service in a manner consistent with the join protocol (as we saw in Chapter 5).
Registers and stores proxies, with attributes if appropriate.	A service registers its own proxy object with lookup service, alongside any attached attributes provided. Lookup services will store these proxies and attributes persistently.
Assigns service IDs	Every service instance in the Jini universe has a unique service ID. The lookup service will generate this unique service ID for a service upon request. Typically, this is only done the first time a service starts up.
Maintains leases on registrations	Proxy registrations are leased. The lookup service grants leases to services, and enforces them. Any service failing to renew the lease on their registered proxy will have the proxy unregistered and removed from the persistent store when the lease expires. This ensures services that abort without deregistering will not hold up resources within the lookup service in the long term.

Basic Lookup Operation

In essence, the lookup service's primary role is that of Jini's registrar, in that it accepts registrations from services. Each registration called a **service item**, and comprises:

❑   Service's proxy object

❑   Service's service ID

❑   A set of attributes, where appropriate, associated with the proxy

The lookup service stores service items persistently, thereby maintaining registrations through restarts.

Clients use the lookup service to lookup up one or more service items. This search is carried out using a client-supplied template, and is, not surprisingly, called **template matching**.

We'll look at how this works in practice and code later on in the chapter; here it suffices to say that matches can made according to:

❑   A specified interface that must be supported by the service's proxy

❑   A specified class or superclass of the service's proxy

❑   Service ID

❑   Attributes associated with the proxy

The following figure shows this template matching mechanism, or simple lookup, in action. The client describes what it wants in a template that it passes to the lookup service, and the lookup service uses the template matching engine to search it's persistent store of service items registered by services. The lookup service then returns a copy of any service items matching the template.

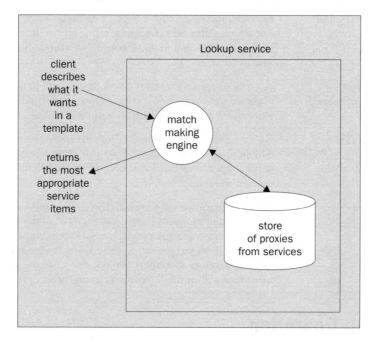

Other Responsibilities of a Lookup Service

Other than acting as a registrar, the Jini lookup service also has the following responsibilities:

❑   Bootstraps the federation: the lookup service is the mechanism through which the Jini network gets up and running

❑   Manages a persistent database storing service items, leases, and registrations

❑ Assists in maintaining a long-lived self-healing network

❑ Acts as a kind of social security dispenser: generates a unique identity service ID upon request

❑ Supports inter-federation communication: services in separate federations can be made available to one another by exporting and importing lookup services

Lookup Service as Bootstrapping Assistant

A lookup service is a full-fledged Jini service. It bootstraps Jini clients and services by delivering its proxy to them using the discovery protocols. All Jini lookup services are required to implement support for discovery protocol, and actively disseminate their proxy object(s) (always implementing the `ServiceRegistrar` interface) to all the clients and services within the federation.

Although bootstrapping might be thought, by definition, to occur only as the system starts up, (when the Jini network is initially powered-up, for example), in the Jini world 'startup' happens anytime and all the time. Jini federations are dynamic. You form them when you need them, and dismantle them when you've finished work (although services are not necessarily shut down). This means that Jini lookup services are required to participate in bootstrapping new clients and services **all the time**, from the very first moment the lookup service itself starts, until the lookup service is shutdown or crashes (and if it crashes, bootstrapping activity resumes upon restart).

A lookup service's constant support for the discovery and join protocol makes it an integral part of the constantly available bootstrapping mechanism in a Jini network. Being a Jini service, it must also maintain its own internal states according to the Join protocol. The next diagram shows the functional blocks inside a lookup service that support the discovery bootstrap protocols:

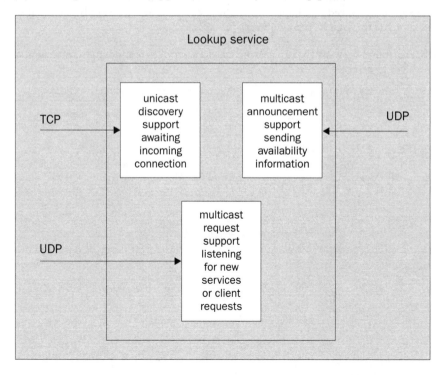

A lookup service supports bootstrapping, in this way, throughout the discovery protocols. On the top left, we can see the unicast discovery support block. A client or service connecting using unicast discovery (via TCP) will be given the lookup service's proxy upon connection. The lower block shows the look up service's support for the multicast request protocol. The block on the upper right is support for multicast announcement protocol, (the beacon packets that announce the availability of the lookup service, and the associated groups that it handles).

Lookup Service's Database Management

A Jini client does not connect to a service directly, but communicates with it through its proxy object, which the client will have obtained from the lookup service. The lookup service is responsible for storing the proxy object (the **service item**), and so the majority of the proxy's life will inevitably be spent inside the database managed by the lookup service.

The lookup service in a Jini network federation acts as a database manager for service items. This behavior effectively de-couples the client from the service. A Jini client does not need to have any apriori knowledge of where the service is. In fact, it does not even need to know which service instance it may be using. All the client needs to know is what it wants the service to do, and it is the duty of the lookup service to supply a proxy for a service that will satisfy the client's need.

De-coupling allows the client to connect to any service in the network that can do the job. In this way it enables fault resilience, ensuring that the client will always get the job done as long as there exists at least one service that can fulfill its needs in the federation.

Some services will not be running all of the time, Jini services implemented as RMI Activatable services, for example (covered in Chapter 3). In these cases the service is only activated when it is used, following a call made through its proxy object.

The figure below shows how the lookup service acts as a service item database manager, allowing Jini client and services to de-couple:

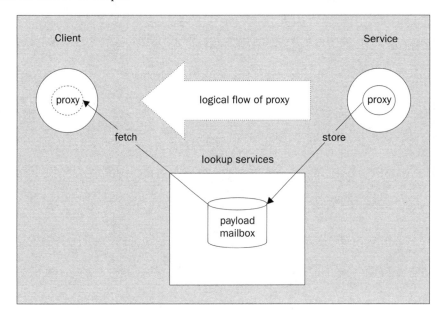

You can see from this figure that the logical flow of the proxy is from the service to the client, but as we have seen, the lookup service de-couples this process, as it stores service proxies in an internal persistent object store, and allows clients to fetch copies of the proxy (service item).

Lookup Service's Maintenance of the Long-lived, Self-healing Network

Turmoil can erupt within a distributed network at any time. Clients can disappear from the network suddenly and never return, badly coded services can crash while clients still hold proxies to them, systems and services can move from one point of the network to another, hardware and network failures do and will occur. While such scenarios require, in a traditional distributed application, special application programming, Jini's solution comes in the form of the lookup services, which help ensure the eventual recovery of resources, and take responsibility for the healing process that follows a system disruption or failure.

The Join protocol (discussed in Chapter 5) ensures that the state associated with the discovery support system is consistent. This contributes to a long-lived, and stable Jini network. A Jini lookup service always conforms to the Join protocol.

Distributed resource leasing contributes to the long-lived, self-healing nature of the network. As all resource allocation is granted based on time-limited leases, then any resources left orphaned following a system crashes or network failure can eventually be reclaimed (when the lease expires). The Jini lookup service uses distributed leases for all the resources that it allocates on behalf of its clients. Service item registrations from services are leased. Failure to renew an expiring lease will cause the service item to be removed from the lookup service.

Event solicitations are also leased. A client can ask (via solicitation) to be notified whenever a service joins, moves, or leaves the group; or when a service item attribute changes. By granting a finite-time lease on these solicitations, the lookup service ensures that the number of clients requiring notification doesn't get out of hand because of stale entries, and time and resources are not wasted notifying clients that no longer exist.

Lookup Service as a Social Security Dispenser

Each service in a Jini network has a unique identity, a globally unique **service ID** . This ID is a random 128 bit number consisting of five fields, generated by an algorithm based on the time at instigation together with the network host address of the machine, which practically guarantees its uniqueness. The globally unique service ID ensures that interested clients can track a service if it moves (as long as the same service is registered with a nearby lookup service at the new location). It also enables clients to determine whether entries from multiple lookup services in fact represent the same service, and to re-locate services that have performed particularly well in the past.

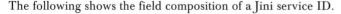

The following shows the field composition of a Jini service ID.

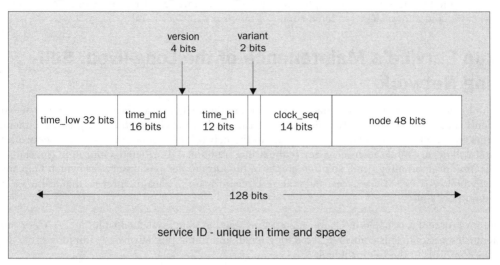

service ID - unique in time and space

Here is a brief description of each of the fields of this 128 bits ID:

Field Name	Length (bits)	Description
time_low	32	Low portion of 60 bit timestamp measured in 100 ns since midnight Oct 15, 1582 UTC
time_mid	16	Middle portion of 60 bit timestamp
version	4	Either 1 or 4; if 1, node field contains IEEE 802 network address; if 4, node field contains a pseudo random number with most significant bit set
time_hi	12	High portion of 60 bit timestamp
variant	2	Always hex 2
clock_seq	14	14 bit random number
node	48	Depends on version, typically contains the network address of the node

Instead of having a centralized service ID assignment mechanism, or a separate tool to generate these service IDs, Jini specifies that every lookup service should be able to generate unique IDs on the initial registration of a Jini service (when a service registers its service item containing a null service ID). A Jini service should only register with a null service ID the very first time it starts up. From this point on, the onus is on the service to maintain its ID whenever it restarts, and use it in all future registrations – across lookup services, reboots or networks moves. If the service does not maintain the same service ID, and uses a newly generated one, the Jini network will treat it as a completely new service instance.

Lookup Service Enabling Inter-Federations Communications

Until networking bandwidth and computing hardware technologies catch up with Jini's model of the network computer, most Jini federations will remain small and tend to follow the traditional, physical Local Area Network boundaries. There are also many application specific advantages to having small, local federations (where all the services and devices are within a workgroup or department, for example). Islands of separate federations will be with us for quite a long time, and while they are, the lookup service provides a link between federations that enables them to communicate, share services, and bridge (federate) two or more federations together, in order to expand the range of services available to clients.

Each federation can have multiple lookup services working for it, and may be logically partitioned through Jini groups. Even though many of these localized federations may be physically connected over the wide area network (the Internet, for example), any service that wants to work for a remote federation needs to export itself directly using a known URL and unicast discovery.

In the figure below, a service, called S1 in federation A, has bootstrapped into a lookup service within federation B across the wide area network. As a result, all clients in federation B have access to the S1 service that actually lives in federation A.

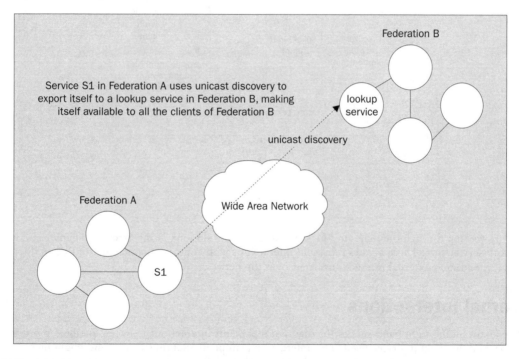

If S1 is a lookup service, it will be providing an inter-federation link. Any client in federation B can lookup S1, and use S1 to lookup any service within federation A.

This concludes our overview of the responsibilities that a Jini lookup service takes on. Now we'll peel away the layers and take a look inside a Jini lookup service, to see how a Jini lookup service actually fulfills these responsibilities.

Anatomy of a Jini Lookup Service

With so many overlapping responsibilities, the inner workings of a lookup service aren't particularly straightforward. In fact, implementing a full-fledged lookup service for Jini is not a simple matter at all. Fortunately, Sun provides **reggie**, (the reference implementation that we used in Chapter 5), as part of the Jini development kit (the extended platform). Reggie provides us with a massive code base that can be customized to build variants of the service.

The following diagram represents the complexity of a Jini lookup service:

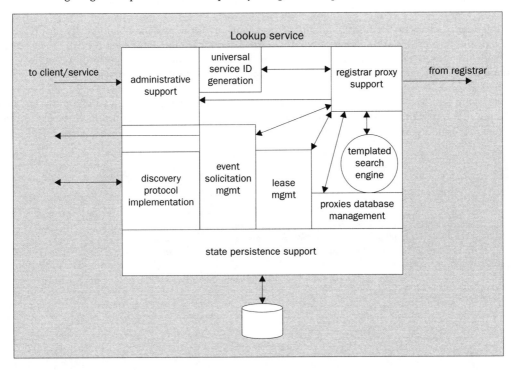

Before we step through the diagram block by block, we should look at the arrows that enter and exit the lookup service box. These arrows represent interactions with components that are outside of the lookup service; and such external interactions occur over the network.

External Interactions

The arrow on the right hand side of the diagram represents interactions between the lookup service's proxy and the lookup service itself. This interaction is implementation specific, and might be a proprietary protocol, or direct RMI. On the left hand side, the arrows represent external interaction with Jini clients and services.

Service Interactions

The interactions between a lookup service and a Jini service include:

❑   Unicast and multicast discovery protocols

❑ Service registration:

❑ Granting and maintaining leases for service item registration

❑ Supporting and joining the protocol

Client Interactions

The interactions between a lookup service and a Jini client include:

❑ Supporting the unicast and multicast discovery protocols

❑ Enabling a client to locate a service based on a template

❑ Enabling a client to solicit for event notification

❑ Sending clients remote events

The major functional blocks within the lookup services are designed to support these interactions.

Major Functional Blocks of the Jini Lookup Service:

These are the major functional blocks of the Jini lookup service:

❑ Implementation of the Discovery protocol

❑ Registrar Proxy Support

❑ Managing the storage of registered service items

❑ Implementing template matching for service lookup

❑ Managing remote event listeners and solicitation

❑ Managing leases

❑ Supporting state persistence

❑ Generating global and persistent Service IDs

❑ Administrative support

Let's look at the work each functional block performs in detail:

Discovery Protocol Implementation

The lookup service supports the three protocols that, as we have seen, comprise the discovery protocols suite, the unicast discovery protocol, the multicast request protocol, and the multicast announcement protocol. The lookup service monitors multicast request protocol packets from new startup clients/services for the groups that it handles.

Registrar Proxy Support

At the end of a successful discovery, the client/service holds one or more lookup service registrar proxies, so the implementer of the lookup service must also implement the registrar proxy.

The registrar proxy supports the `ServiceRegistrar` interface within the Java VM of the client/service. How it actually implements this interface is entirely up to the designer of the lookup service. reggie, Sun's reference implementation, uses RMI for communications between the registrar proxy and the lookup service.

Most of the implementation logic supporting the `ServiceRegistrar` interface is implemented, remote to the client, within the lookup service itself.

Service Items Database Management

As we discussed earlier, the lookup service looks after and persists the service items of the registered services. The maintenance of this database of service items is a key responsibility of the lookup service implementation. The addition and removal of service items should be fast, as should be access to each item. The database needs to be optimized for the template search engine since every lookup handled by the lookup service will make use of both functional blocks.

Template Based Search Engine

The lookup service supports a template search based on any, all or a combination of three criteria: service ID, the type (Java interfaces or classes) that a service supports, and associated attributes. To search for a service, the client fills out a template using only the fields it is interested in. This template is passed to the lookup service. The lookup service compares the template against the service items stored in the database (using the search engine), and returns any service items that match.

While the semantics and expected behavior of the search process are specified, the implementation is not. Lookup services are free to use any technology to implement the search engine (simple data structures, relational database, or even hardware content addressable memory for example).

Client Event Solicitation and Lease Management

A lease is negotiated between a service and a lookup service following the successful registration of the service item. If this lease is not renewed by the service before it expires, the lookup service removes the service item from its database. This means that any service failing to renew its lease – be it because of a broken network connection or system failure – won't be offered to requesting clients. This is just one of the ways in which Jini is reactive to its environment, and thereby eases those all too familiar distributed networking headaches.

A lease is also negotiated between a client and a lookup service when a client solicits for an event, and needs to pass a listener in to the lookup service for storage. If the lease under negotiation is granted by the lookup service, then a listener object is put into storage. (Although it's called negotiation, this is in fact a one step process during which the client requests a lease which is either granted, denied, or allocated a shorter duration than requested.) Should the lease expire before the client renews it, then the lookup service will remove the listener from storage, and the client must begin the soliciting process again if it still wishes to be notified of changes in state.

The lookup service manages event solicitation by saving a reference to a listener object from the client, and tracking the transitions of the managed service items database. If the transition that a registered listener is waiting for occurs, the lookup service sends an event object to the client by calling back on the registered listener object.

The following diagram shows how a lookup service manages event solicitation:

❑ Client registers its listener object with the lookup service, and tells the lookup service the state transition that it would like to monitor: this is the solicitation and is leased

❑ Lookup service monitors for the state transition specified by the client

❑ Following the transition, the lookup service uses the listener object to call back to the client, sending an event object with encapsulated information

❑ Client must renew the lease on the solicitation before it expires

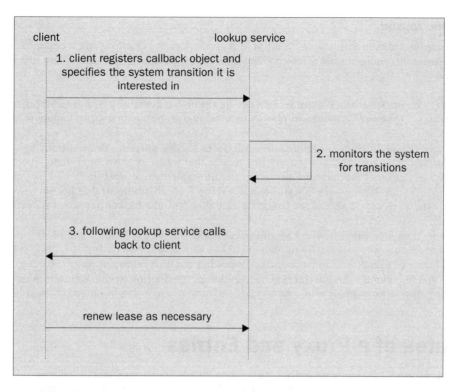

State Persistence and Recovery Support

As a well behaved service, a Jini lookup service conforms to the join protocol conventions and persists its own service ID, the attributes of its own proxy, and the groups that it should belong to if it registers with another lookup service.

In order to comply with the overall system's longevity, the lookup service also persists the groups that it manages, service items, the event listeners registered by client solicitations, and the state of the leases that it manages for service items registrations and event solicitations.

Supporting persistence in a recoverable manner is a complicated business for a typical lookup service. Simply saving state information every time something changes is not going to work because the state changes associated with even a moderate sized dynamic Jini network occur so frequently. Most lookup services will opt for more efficient approaches to the problem (usually varieties of checkpointing).

Universal Service ID Generation

The algorithm that generates globally unique 128 bit service IDs must be implemented by the lookup service. It is the responsibility of the lookup service to assign this service ID when a service initially registers – the lookup service knows that this is the initial registration from the API that the service uses.

Being a well-behaved Jini service, the lookup service also gives itself a unique service ID the first time it executes, which is stored in the files used to implement persistence. In the case of reggie, these files are kept in a user specified log directory. If you remove these files, reggie will think it is being activated for the first time and will generate a new service ID for itself.

Administrative support

There are many configurable aspects of a Jini lookup service: the groups it is a member of, the TCP port used to answer incoming unicast discovery, the location of the store of persistent data (if a file scheme is used), and so on.

It's also very important that a lookup service can be shutdown gracefully without abruptly terminating any processes. This graceful shutdown may include de-registration with nearby lookup services, etc.

The Jini specification includes administrative interfaces for this purpose, some specific to lookup services while others are applicable to any Jini service that wants to implement them. Specifically, all Jini lookup services that support administration should implement at least the net.jini.lookup.DiscoveryAdmin interface. However, all administrable Jini services should implement the net.jini.admin.JoinAdmin interface, and the lookup service is no exception.

Although we'll go into administration at some depth later on, it's important to know, for now, that admin interfaces are **not** necessarily implemented by the registrar object. Instead, the getAdmin() method of the ServiceRegistrar interface is used to obtain a reference to the object (potentially a delegate) that implements the interfaces. One can determine if a Jini service supports administration by testing the registrar for support of the net.jini.Adminstrable tag (no method) interface.

Attributes of a Proxy and Entries

One major function of a lookup service is to provide clients with a template based search facility for its database of registered service items. We will be looking at how exactly this works, after we've examined Jini Entries.

Jini Entry

A Jini entry is actually a marker interface specified as:

```
package net.jini.core.entry;
public interface Entry extends java.io.Serializable { }
```

The java.io.Serializable is already a marker interface without methods, so why do we inherit from it, creating another marker interface without methods?

There are two reasons. First, extending from the Serializable interface makes this object serializable, and so it has a default constructor without arguments, and references all member objects that are also serializable (except for transient or static members).

In the second place, using a different marker interface name – Entry – instigates more constraints. Using Entry, only public, non-static, non-transient, non-final members (called the **field** of an entry) and non-primitive types (int, bool, etc) will be serialized.

Generally speaking, the Entry interface is intended to be implemented by objects that represent a holder for a set of template objects to be matched. In Jini, the attribute associated with a Jini proxy (in the service item) is exactly such a holder.

The following diagram shows a set of attributes attached to a service proxy:

In this diagram, the proxy represents a service at a specific location, which is identified by the Location entry, having fields representing floor, room, and building. The service also has a Name entry with a single Name field. This is used to distinguish between multiple instances of the service at the same location (two compounds synthesizing services within the same laboratory, for example). The Comment entry has a single comment field. This Comment entry is handy for personalizing or attaching comments to a service instance.

The Jini specification states that an entry is typically used by distributed algorithms, and requires exact match semantics. Specifically, it defines the behavior for the store, match and fetch operations.

Storing an Entry

An entry is **stored** through a special serialization process. Each field of the entry is serialized separately and stored as a MarshalledObject (a binary stream with a codebase annotation). The registrar proxy must create this MarshalledObject in the service's VM before passing it over the network to the lookup service.

Matching an Entry

A Jini entry is matched against a template (which is also an entry), field by field, based on the equals() method of the MarshalledObject. If a field is non-null in the template, a match will be attempted, as all null fields in a template represent wildcards and are automatically considered as a match. Essentially, the match is a comparison of the binary stream of each MarshalledObject. Moreover, the actual equals() method of each individual field is not used at all.

Fetching an Entry

When an entry is **fetched** from the lookup service managed database, only the fields are restored, and all other data members ignored. The MarshalledObject fields are transmitted unmodified, in binary stream form, from the lookup service to the registrar proxy. It is the registrar proxy that actually performs the un-marshalling within the VM of the client. As a result, the codebase associated with a field is not accessed until it is un-marshalled. Since un-marshalling occurs in the VM of the client, the entry fields and their associated classes are loaded directly into the client. None of the classes associated with the fields need to be loaded into the lookup service's VM.

197

Service References as Fields

If a field of an entry contains a reference to a service, the serialized references to that service may go stale while the entry is sitting inside the lookup service. These references cannot keep their respective services from garbage collection. As a result, an embedded reference to a service in an entry should only refer to conceptually long-lived, activatable services. This is not detrimental, though, because attributes seldom require embedded service references due to their decorative nature.

Entry Serialization Semantics

A **store** operation followed by a **fetch** operation guarantees that each field will be serialized separately. So should two fields of an attribute refer to the same object instance initially, each will point to a separate copy of the object following de-serialization. This is very different from normal serialization, where object graphs are preserved.

Why is it advantageous to specify entry serialization in this manner? One obvious advantage is that each field can be compared independently, without having to de-serialize **all** of the fields of an entry beforehand.

A rather less obvious advantage lies in the direction that Jini technology appears to be heading. Imagine you have many attributes for match attempts, and that you have a parallel hardware engine that can do many exact matches simultaneously – together with overlapping store and fetch operations. The hardware engine can be used for template searches and dramatically cut down the overall computation time. For the more mathematically inclined, if your proxy has attached M attributes each with (a maximum of) N fields, and you have a hardware engine that has M x N parallel comparison engines, one can perform the required match in a little more time than it takes to compare one single field (the longest one across all the attributes)!

The Service Item

A lookup service maintains a persistent database of service items, registered by Jini services, in the groups it handles. Recall that a service item contains a service ID, the proxy object of the service and a set of (optional) associated attributes.

The service item actually looks like this:

```
public class ServiceItem implements Serializable {
    public ServiceItem(ServiceID serviceID, Object service,
        Entry[] attributeSets) {}
    public ServiceID serviceID;
    public Object service;
    public Entry[] attributeSets;
}
```

Note that the attributes attached to the service proxy, within the `ServiceItem`, are in the array of an entry.

Attaching Attributes

A service item is a proxy with attributes (and a service ID), and each attribute is a holder for multiple separate fields. Each field is an object reference (or null) that will be independently matched (in marshalled form) using a potentially distributed algorithm.

One can attach attributes to a proxy by adding members to the `attributeSets[]` array that is part of every service item.

Attributes are not too useful if clients do not know how to ask for them in searches. A client has to know, ahead of time, what types (the subclasses of an entry) are attributes to a specific service. If you define your own custom attributes, you must publicize them somehow if you want clients other than your own to use them. The `jini.org` community process (http://www.jini.org/) is a good place for groups to define new 'standard' attributes amongst their own industries (printers workgroup, PDA workgroup, for example).

Custom Attributes

If you do define your own custom attributes, you should consider using the `net.jini.entry.AbstractEntry` class, as the attribute's base class:

```
public abstract class AbstractEntry implements Entry {
    public boolean equals(Object o) {…}
    public int hashCode() {…}
    public String toString() {…}
    public static boolean equals(Entry e1, Entry e2) {…}
    public static int hashCode(Entry entry) {…}
    public static String toString(Entry entry) {…}
}
```

The non-static `equals()`, `hashCode()`, and `toString()` methods of this abstract class provide the proper behavior for an entry.

The `equals()` method will do an exact match to compare all fields, the `hashCode()` algorithm combines the hash code of all fields, and the `toString()` will return a string that contains the string representation of all fields (this is especially useful when the fields themselves have a meaningful string-based form).

Note that there are static methods of this class (same name but different parameters). They can be executed without instantiating a subclass of `AbstractEntry`, and will work on entries that are not a subclass of `AbstractEntry` (we can use the static `Entry.equals()` method to compare two entries for equality, using field-by-field binary comparison semantics).

Specifying Who Can Change An Attribute

Attribute values are liable to change during a long-living service's lifetime. In fact, the decorative nature of attributes means that a client may want to change an attribute's value, and potentially attach new attributes to a service during runtime. This can be useful in many situations – for example, distinguishing between multiple installations of the same service, or attaching data meaningful to applications.

In addition to the client, the service itself may change the value of an attribute. Not surprisingly, there are likely to be attributes that have to be protected from changes instigated anywhere other than the service – the attributes that reflect the status of the service, for example. The Jini tag interface for attributes that should only be changed at the service's instigation looks like this:

```
public interface ServiceControlled {
}
```

Although clients should leave these attributes alone, the lookup service can't enforce that they do. The onus is on the client to check before modifying these fields. A registered service is also able to check for modifications that may have been made to service controlled attributes, and override any unauthorized changes.

Standard Attributes

Sun has a pre-defined set of highly generic attributes that any Jini service is able to make ready use of. Since these are pre-defined standard attributes and every Jini client knows about them, their use is highly encouraged.

The attribute Name, for example, is used to give a service instance a specific name, and Comment to attach an annotation/comment to a specific service. Remember that the value of these attributes can be different for each instance of the same service. For example, you may be running two instances of a data research service on your Jini network, but you may want to distinguish them from one another as one is running on an expensive super computer whose computing time you're paying for, and the other is running on an inexpensive PC in the same room:

```
public class Name extends AbstractEntry {
    public Name() {}
    public Name(String name) {…}
    public String name;
}


public class Comment extends AbstractEntry {
    public Comment() {}
    public Comment(String comment) {…}
    public String comment;
}
```

Location and Address are handy attributes that distinguish instances of a service by their physical location. This is especially useful for services that represent or associate with actual physical devices as they indicate the exact location of that device – a typesetting service associated with a typesetter, for example:

```
public class Location extends AbstractEntry {
    public Location() {}
    public Location(String floor, String room, String building) {…}
    public String floor;
    public String room;
    public String building;
}


public class Address extends AbstractEntry {
    public Address(String street, String organization,
        String organizationalUnit, String locality, String stateOrProvince,
        String postalCode, String country) {…}
    public String street;
    public String organization;
    public String organizationalUnit;
    public String locality;
    public String stateOrProvince;
    public String postalCode;
    public String country;
}
```

`ServiceInfo` is controlled by the service only, and is designed to provide specific information about services that manage, or are associated with a specific hardware device, although licensed software services may also find good uses for it:

```
public class ServiceInfo extends AbstractEntry implements ServiceControlled {
    public ServiceInfo() {}
    public ServiceInfo(String name, String manufacturer, String vendor,
        String version, String model, String serialNumber) {…}
    public String name;
    public String manufacturer;
    public String vendor;
    public String version;
    public String model;
    public String serialNumber;
}
```

`Status` is an abstract base class that can be used to implement a status attribute for your own service. It is primarily useful for services that represent devices. The associated `StatusType` class has some pre-defined status that you can use or extend. Note that `Status` does not implement the `ServiceControlled` marker interface. This is to allow for special cases. Should your usage of the `Status` attribute truly reflect the status (a state) of your service (a printer cartridge is out of ink, for example), then you should implement the `ServiceControlled` interface in your subclass. Here are their definitions:

```
public abstract class Status extends AbstractEntry {
    protected Status() {…}
    protected Status(StatusType severity) {…}
    public StatusType severity;
}

public class StatusType implements Serializable {
    private final int type;
    private StatusType(int t) { type = t; }
    public static final StatusType ERROR = new StatusType(1);
    public static final StatusType WARNING = new StatusType(2);
    public static final StatusType NOTICE = new StatusType(3);
    public static final StatusType NORMAL = new StatusType(4);
}
```

The final standard attribute is `ServiceType`. This is useful for clients that present a graphical user interface for a user (through a Jini browser, for example), as it attaches both a graphical icon and human readable descriptions of a service:

```
public class ServiceType extends AbstractEntry implements ServiceControlled {
    public ServiceType() {…}
    public java.awt.Image getIcon(int iconKind) {…}
    public String getDisplayName() {…}
    public String getShortDescription() {…}
}
```

Again, you should make an attempt to use or extend these attributes if your specific requirements overlap with any of these standard attributes. Doing so will allow your service to be as widely useful as possible.

Template Based Matching

We know that an attribute is based on `Entry`, and that `Entry` has special properties with respect to its fields, that lends it to efficient distributed or parallel matching computation. So how does template matching actually work on a coding level?

Clients use a method of the `ServiceRegistrar` interface to perform lookup, creating and supplying a service template, as we'll see in detail in the next section:

```
public class ServiceTemplate implements Serializable {
    public ServiceTemplate(ServiceID serviceID, Class[] serviceTypes,
        Entry[] attributeSetTemplates) {…}
    public ServiceID serviceID;
    public Class[] serviceTypes;
    public Entry[] attributeSetTemplates;
}
```

This template is used to specify the matching criteria. The client can fill in any fields that it wants to match exactly, and leaves any that it does not care about null.

For example:

```
ServiceTemplate myTemplate = new ServiceTemplate(transformerID, null, null);
```

will match only services with the exact `transformerID`s (service IDs), and will return a single unique service if it is registered with the lookup service.

You can also match according to 'type', the class or superclass of service proxy, or by the interfaces that the service proxy supports. The `serviceTypes` array can be populated with classes that you want the service proxy to support. Any class that you specify here dictates that the returned service proxy must be of that class, or a subclass of the specified class, and likewise any interface specified dictates that the returned registrar must support it also. If you specify more than one element in the array, each must match, or there will not be a service proxy (service item) returned.

The `attributeSetTemplates` array contains entries. You can specify attributes by passing them in using the specific entry types (typically subclass of `AbstractEntry`) that you want to match. As discussed before, you need only fill in the fields for each attribute in the array that you want to match exactly. Anything you leave null will act as wildcard and be taken to match all values. If you specify more than one attribute in the array, every one must match in order for a service proxy to be returned.

Lookup Entries and JavaBeans

There are many situations under which a service may want to let a client set the value for an attribute attached to a service, (labeling the location of a printer device, for example). There are also other situations where you may want to associate a specific GUI presentation with a specific attribute (the temperature of an incubator device, adjustable through a drag-and-set graphical usage, for example).

One relatively painless way to deal with this is to associate a **JavaBean** with the attribute. If you're already familiar with JavaBeans you'll see immediately the benefits:

❑ The service can provide an appropriate GUI for displaying and modifying the attribute value with very little coding – just embed the bean and use its property editors

❑ GUI localization is supported

Jini supports entries that have JavaBeans attached. Entries taking advantage of this should also have a bean implemented (using standard JavaBean naming conventions – the class name plus `Bean`, so the class `WroxPrinter` will have `WroxPrinterBean` associated with it) that also implements the `EntryBean` interface:

```
public interface EntryBean {
    void makeLink(Entry e);
    Entry followLink();
}
```

The `makeLink` method attaches the beans to the entry (the bean implementation will store the reference to the entry internally). The `followLink()` method allows us to retrieve an entry associated with a particular bean.

Jini also specifies a helper class called `EntryBeans` (notice the 's') containing only static methods.

```
package net.jini.lookup.entry;

public class EntryBeans {
    public static EntryBean createBean(Entry e) throws ClassNotFoundException,
        java.io.IOException {…}
    public static Class getBeanClass(Class c) throws ClassNotFoundException {…}
}
```

The static `createBean()` method can be used to retrieve the bean associated with an entry. It loads the class using standard JavaBeans naming convention (class name followed by `Bean`), creates an instance, and then hooks it up with the associated entry. It also loads the class using the appropriate class loader – meaning that the codebase URL used to load the entry itself will be used to locate the bean (again a JavaBeans convention). You should place the associated bean class to an entry in the same directory or JAR file as the entry.

The `getBeanClass()` method takes an entry as an argument and returns only the associated bean class itself, without creating an instance (which is useful in, for example, an IDE tool that needs to pre-load JavaBean classes for faster user response).

Using the coding patterns prescribed by the JavaBeans specification, one can easily create associated `BeanInfo` classes, custom property editors, etc.

The Jini library supplies a bean implementation for each of the pre-defined attributes we have covered. These are to be found in the `net.jini.lookup.entry` package. For example, the pre-defined `Location` attribute has the following `LocationBean` associated:

```
public class LocationBean implements EntryBean, Serializable {
    public String getFloor() {…}
    public void setFloor(String s) {…}
    public String getRoom() {…}
    public void setRoom(String s) {…}
    public String getBuilding() {…}
    public void setBuilding(String s) {…}
}
```

Another advantage of associating a bean with an attribute is the ability of many Jini browsers and tools to display the associated bean, thereby providing a more appropriate presentation to the user.

Working with a Lookup Service

As we've pretty much covered everything that you need to know about a lookup service at this point, it's time we got down to some coding. We'll look at some some simple client and service code that interacts with a lookup service.

While we're going to be working with several helper classes in this section in order to write a skeletal service and client, we will not cover the helper classes themselves at length (you can find an analysis of the Jini helper classes in Chapter 11). Our focus here is the programmatic interactions with the lookup service.

Protocol Handling

In order to examine the interaction between the lookup service and clients and/or services, I'm going to show you an application that carries out multicast discovery, and then prints out the lookup services that it hears from in response. Jini provides the net.jini.discovery.LookupDiscovery utility class that encapsulates all of the required low-level Discovery protocol handling.

LookupDiscovery

Here is a simplified synopsis of the LookupDiscovery class.

```
public final class LookupDiscovery {
    public static final String[] ALL_GROUPS = null;
    public static final String[] NO_GROUPS = new String[0];
    public LookupDiscovery(String[] groups) throws IOException {…}
    public void addDiscoveryListener(DiscoveryListener l) {…}
    public void removeDiscoveryListener(DiscoveryListener l) {…}
    public void discard(ServiceRegistrar reg) {…}
    public String[] getGroups() {…}
    public void setGroups(String[] groups) throws IOException {…}
    public void addGroups(String[] groups) throws IOException {…}
    public void removeGroups(String[] groups) {…}
    public void terminate() {…}
}
```

Although we can pass in a string array containing the names of the groups that we want to find lookup service for, there are two constants ALL_GROUPS and NO_GROUPS that can be used instead. ALL_GROUPS will instigate discovery for all lookup services in the local range we are concerned with regardless of the groups that they support. NO_GROUPS will not start the discovery process. It is useful to avoid race conditions since we must register a listener after creation of the LookupDiscovery instance.

The addDiscoveryListener method enables the registration of a listener object. This object must support the DiscoveryListener interface:

```
public interface DiscoveryListener extends EventListener {
    public void discovered(DiscoveryEvent e);
    public void discarded(DiscoveryEvent e);
}
```

The discovered method will be called by the `LookupDiscovery` instance when a set of registrars (lookup proxies) has been discovered. The discarded method will be called when a registrar from the discovered set has been discarded (and so can no longer be reached).

These callback methods are called with a reference to a `DiscoveryEvent` object:

```
public class DiscoveryEvent extends EventObject {
    public DiscoveryEvent(Object source, ServiceRegistrar[] regs) {…}
    public ServiceRegistrar[] getRegistrars() {…}
}
```

The `getRegistrars()` method of this object can be used by the callback object to obtain the list of registrars discovered so far.

The `discard()` method is used to instruct that a lookup service be removed from the cache of discovered service items. This is useful when, for example, a lookup method invocation results in a remote exception, and the lookup service cannot be reached.

The `getGroups()`, `addGroups()` and `removeGroups()` methods manage the set of groups that the `LookupDiscovery` object carries out discovery for. New groups will result in potentially new registrars being discovered, and removal of groups may cause some registrars to be discarded. This behavior is consistent with the Join protocol

Coding a Utility to Discover Lookup Services

We will put our knowledge of Jini lookup services to work here. First, we will start with the code for a very simple utility, demonstrating how a client can locate and work with lookup services.

Creating our DiscoverRegistrars Utility

Here is the code for a utility called `DiscoverRegistrars`. It will discover all the nearby lookup services, and print out their unique service IDs and the groups that they support. The same code skeleton will be used later to create other utilities. You can find the code for the `DiscoverRegistrars.java` source file in the `\Ch6\code\registrars` directory of the source distribution.

```
import net.jini.discovery.*;
import net.jini.core.lookup.ServiceRegistrar;
import java.io.IOException;
import java.rmi.RemoteException;
import java.rmi.RMISecurityManager;
```

Instead of using another listener object to handle the `DiscoveryListener`, we simply implement the required methods within the application class.

```
public class DiscoverRegistrars extends Object implements
    DiscoveryListener {
```

The main method installs a security manager. This is necessary because we will be downloading stubs for the lookup service implementation (reggie). The main method also creates a new instance of `DiscoverRegistrars` and then hangs around forever in a synchronized wait. (In a real world implementation, of course, the service would be either waiting or handling requests from the proxy, instead of hanging around doing nothing.) Since the creation of the `DiscoverRegistrars` instance may throw an `IOException`, it has to locate and talk to the lookup services. We wrap the body of the method in a `try..catch` block.

```
static public void main(String args[]) {
    try {
        if (System.getSecurityManager() == null) {
            System.setSecurityManager(new RMISecurityManager());
        }
        DiscoverRegistrars myApp = new DiscoverRegistrars();
        synchronized (myApp) {
            myApp.wait(0);
        }
    } catch(Exception ex) {
        ex.printStackTrace();
        System.exit(1);
    }
}
```

Much of the work is performed within the constructor.

We create the LookupDiscovery instance, first with NO_GROUPS. Then we add the listener, which is the DiscoverRegistrars instance itself. Finally, we set the groups to ALL_GROUPS enabling the LookupDiscovery to find all local lookup services. This sequence will ensure that the listener is registered before anything can be discovered:

```
LookupDiscovery discover = null;
public DiscoverRegistrars() throws IOException {
    discover = null;
    discover = new LookupDiscovery(LookupDiscovery.NO_GROUPS);
    discover.addDiscoveryListener(this);
    discover.setGroups(LookupDiscovery.ALL_GROUPS);
}
```

The remaining methods are supporting the DiscoveryListener interface. Discovered() is called when the discovery process has resulted in a set of registrars. The set of registrars is accessible from the getRegistrars() method of the DiscoveryEvent reference passed in.

We loop through all the registrars and print out their service IDs (via the getServiceID() method), and the groups supported (via getGroups() method) by the corresponding lookup service:

```
public synchronized void discovered(DiscoveryEvent evt) {
    ServiceRegistrar[] registrars = evt.getRegistrars();
    String [] groups;
    String msg = "";

    for (int n = 0; n < registrars.length; n++) {
        ServiceRegistrar registrar = registrars[n];
        System.out.println( "found a lookup service with service ID:"
            + registrar.getServiceID());
        try{
            groups = registrar.getGroups();
            if (groups.length > 0)
                msg += " Groups: ";
            for (int o=0; o<groups.length; o++) {
                msg += groups[o] + " ";
            }
        }
```

```
                        catch(RemoteException e) {
                            System.err.println(e.toString());
                            e.printStackTrace();
                            System.exit(1);
                        }
                        System.out.println(msg);
                    }
```

The discarded method is an empty implementation, as we are not managing the set of registrars in this application.

```
        public void discarded(DiscoveryEvent evt) {
        }
    }
```

How to Use the Included Batch Files

Before we compile the `DiscoverRegistrars` utility, we'll take a look at their contents. You'll find them in the `\Ch6\code\bats` directory, in the source code distribution.

These batch files are used in subsequent chapters to build and deploy sample programs, they are

> setpaths.bat
>
> buildit.bat
>
> runclean.bat
>
> runhttpd.bat
>
> runhttpdstubs.bat
>
> runrmid.bat
>
> runlookup1.bat
>
> runlookup2.bat
>
> runlookup3.bat
>
> runjbrowser.bat

Next we'll run through each of these batch files, how and when to use them, and what they contain.

The setpaths.bat File

This is the only batch file that you will need to modify. It contains various environment variables to be used within other batch files. It is called and used by almost all other batch files. The one I used to run the code contains:

```
set JINIHOME=d:\jini1_1
set WROXHOME=d:\wroxstubs
set DOWNLOADHOST=win98p300:8080
set STUBHOST=win98p300:8081
set ADAPTERIP=192.168.23.30
set JINITEMP=d:\temp
set JINIJARS=%JINIHOME%\lib\jini-core.jar;%JINIHOME%\lib\jini-
ext.jar;%JINIHOME%\lib\sun-util.jar
```

The following table explains each of variable set in the batch file.

Variable	Description
JINIHOME	The root location of your installation of the Jini distribution from Sun
WROXHOME	The directory where you intend to place all the downloadable stubs from the sample programs. We will set up an HTTP class server to serve the stubs from this directory, enabling them to be downloaded by the clients.
DOWNLOADHOST	The HTTP class server (host and port) that will serve stubs for system library components, such reggie, mahalo, etc.
STUBHOST	The HTTP class server (host and port) that will serve stubs for our sample programs. This server should be serving the stubs from the WROXHOME directory.
ADAPTERIP	The IP address of the network adapter to be used in multicast discovery. This is especially useful on multi-homed machine, to avoid the ambiguity of which adapter to use.
JINITEMP	A temporary directory for creating the log files of reggie, mahalo, etc.
JINIJARS	The JAR files from the Jini library that is necessary to compile and run Jini programs.

Remember to modify the setpaths.bat file to reflect your own installation of Jini.

The buildit.bat File

This batch file is used to compile most of the sample programs. The typical usage, assuming you're in the same directory as the source code you want to run, is:

```
..\bats\buildit <mysample>.java
```

The buildit.bat file contains:

```
call ..\bats\setpaths.bat
javac -classpath .;%JINIJARS% %1
```

The file is straightforward. We include JINIJARS as part of the class path when compiling programs.

The runclean.bat File

Although we will be using this file here to completely cleanup the log files created by rmid and reggie, it can also be used to clear fiddler, mercury and norms log files at a later date. Don't worry about these services yet. The batch file will only work on Win98/95 since it uses the deltree command. These log files and directories will need to be manually removed on Windows NT or 2000 systems. The batch file contains:

```
call setpaths.bat
deltree   %JINITEMP%\rmid.log
deltree   %JINITEMP%\reggie_log
deltree   %JINITEMP%\reggie2_log
deltree   %JINITEMP%\reggie3_log
```

You can also use the Jini Browser tool (started using the `runjbrowser.bat` file) to shutdown any reggie instance independently.

The runhttpd.bat File

This file will start an HTTP based class server instance to serve system component stubs. The class server is provided as part of a JAR file included in the Jini development kit download from Sun: `tools.jar`. The hosting directory is set to the `%JINIHOME%\lib`, the Jini system library directory. The port used by the server is `8080`. Here is what the file contains:

```
call setpaths
start java -jar %JINIHOME%\lib\tools.jar -port 8080 -dir %JINIHOME%\lib
    -trees -verbose
```

We used the `-trees -verbose` command to ensure that we can see what files are available, and which files are served.

The runhttpdstubs.bat File

This file will start an HTTP based class server instance to serve the download stubs and classes for our sample programs. The class server will be serving the stubs from the directory indicated by the `WROXHOME` environment variable. The port used by the server is `8081`, in case you're running both HTTP servers on the same machine. Having a separate HTTP server to serve stubs from that serving the system component stubs, has the advantage that you do not need to add files (or have write access) to the system directory where the system stubs are located. Here is what the file contains:

```
call setpaths
start java -jar %JINIHOME%\lib\tools.jar -port 8081 -dir %WROXHOME%
    -trees -verbose
```

The runrmid.bat File

The file starts an instance of the RMI Activation daemon. The file simply contains:

```
call setpaths.bat
start rmid -J-Djava.security.policy=policy.all -log %JINITEMP%\rmid.log
```

Note that the use of `-J-D` to specify a policy file is only required by JDK 1.3 and later; however, older JDKs can also accommodate this switch, even though they will not use a security policy file. The batch file also specifies the directory for rmid to write its persistent data to, the `%JINITEMP%\rmid.log` directory.

The runlookup1.bat, runlookup2.bat, runlookup3.bat Files

These files are used to start instances of reggie for different groups. The groups that the reggie will handle are:

Batch File Name	Groups the reggie will handle
`runlookup1.bat`	iguanas
`runlookup2.bat`	lizards
`runlookup3.bat`	iguanas and lizards

For example, the `runlookup1.bat` file contains:

```
call setpaths.bat
java -jar %JINIHOME%\lib\reggie.jar http://%DOWNLOADHOST%/reggie-dl.jar policy.all
%JINITEMP%\reggie_log iguanas -Dnet.jini.discovery.interface=%ADAPTERIP%
```

We are starting reggie with the codebase pointing to our DOWNLOADHOST environment variable, log files in the %JINITEMP% directory, and multicast discovery adapter set to %ADAPTERIP%. (See Appendix D for a detailed description of the options available when starting reggie.)

The runjbrowser.bat File

You can use this batch file to start a Jini browser. The Jini browser is supplied as sample with the Jini development kit. We will see how to use this browser at the end of this chapter.

```
call setpaths.bat
java -cp .;%JINIJARS%;%JINIHOME%\lib\jini-examples.jar
-Djava.security.policy=policy.all -Dnet.jini.discovery.interface=%ADAPTERIP%
-Djava.rmi.server.codebase=http://%DOWNLOADHOST%/jini-examples-dl.jar
com.sun.jini.example.browser.Browser -admin
```

Testing the DiscoverRegistrars utility

The following instructions assume that you have stopped rmid and httpd running on your system.

Using the `buildit.bat file`, compile `DiscoverRegistrars.java`:

`..\bats\buildit DiscoverRegistrars.java`

Change directories to `\ch6\code\bats`, and start the HTTP server to serve the proxy for the lookup service using `runhttpd.bat` to start the system stubs server.

Use the `runclean.bat` file to clear reggie and rmid log files, or remove the directories manually under Windows NT or Win2000. Run the `runrmid.bat` file, and an instance of reggie listening for the iguanas groups using `runlookup1.bat` file

Finally, we can test out the `DiscoverRegistrars` utility using a custom batch file, called `rundisc.bat`, located in `\ch6\code\registrars` directory. This file contains:

```
call ..\bats\setpaths.bat
java -classpath .;%JINIJARS%  -Dnet.jini.discovery.interface=%ADAPTERIP%
-Djava.security.policy=policy.all DiscoverRegistrars
```

It includes JINIJARS as the classpath, so the Jini runtime files can be located. We also specify the interface adapter to use for discovery via the net.jini.discovery.interface property.

It is essential that the security policy is specified, otherwise the LookupDiscovery will fail through an access error. We are using the wide-open policy.all file for our experimentation, although, of course, a more restrictive policy file should be used in production.

You should see output like this:

The utility has performed multicast discovery and located the lookup service. The results aren't particularly interesting as we have only one lookup service in the federation, so we'll start up three reggies on our Jini network. We can simulate this network by running multiple reggie instances on a single machine, each with a different set of groups, for those without multiple machines at their disposal.

Setting up multiple reggies

Make sure you have 128 MB of main memory or more on your Win32 machine before trying this, as we will be starting three lookup service instances on the same machine, and ensure the httpd and rmid windows have been terminated. Now, clean out the old log files by running `runclean` (or manually deleting the log files). Start httpd again by running `runhttpd.bat`, and start rmid running using `runrmid.bat`.

The three reggies will each be setup to manage different set of groups, using this partitioning:

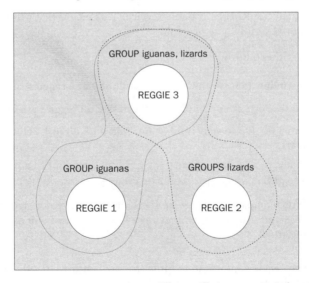

Start the first one by running `runlookup1.bat`. This will start reggie 1, handling the iguanas group, as shown in the diagram above. Wait until the setup VM completes its registration from `runlookup1.bat`, and start the second lookup service by running the `runlookup2.bat` file, which will start reggie 2, handling the lizards group. Once the setup VM has completed its registration from `runlookup2.bat`, start the third lookup service by running `runlookup3.bat` file, which will start reggie 3 that handles both iguanas and lizards groups.

Once the third setup VM returns, all three lookup services have been started. Thanks to the design of reggie, we are able to start all three on the same machine. Reggie will move its TCP port for unicast discovery if it detected that the port is already being use. We make sure that they are each using a different log directory for keeping persistent information.

Now, if you run the `DiscoverRegistrars` utility again (`rundisc` in `registrars` directory), you should see all three lookup services being discovered. This is a screenshot of the output you might expect to see:

We will need the service IDs of the lookup services in order to identify the services again later, so you should make a note of them. We won't be cleaning the log files for little while, but taking advantage of reggie's support for the Join protocol by maintaining persistent state.

Recall that reggie is actually an RMI activatable service. This means that rmid knows how to start the reggie instance and will restart it in case of crashes.

Just to reconfirm this, try the following:

- ❏ Terminate the window that is running rmid (and the three reggies) abruptly, using *Control-C*

- ❏ Run the `DiscoverRegistrars` utility to check that all reggies are terminated

- ❏ Run the `runrmidbat` file to start rmid again, wait until all disk activity stops and the busy cursor disappears

- ❏ Run the `DiscoverRegistrars` utility again, and you should find that all three reggies are running again, and remember the groups that they are responsible for

- ❏ Most importantly, compare their service IDs with the ones you noted earlier – they have been completely preserved. Any client connecting to these services will not know that they have crashed and restarted

So the fact that rmid and reggie conform to the Join protocol ensures that the lookup service can survive unexpected crashes or reboots.

Proxy Registrations by Services

Next we'll create a basic service that shows proxy registration in action. The service will eventually return an index number, first discovering the location of lookup services that support specific groups, then creating a proxy object and registering it with each of the discovered lookup service, and finally maintaining the lease of the registration.

The proxy object created will support a custom interface that we'll define. This is the same interface that a client will use to communicate with the service (through the proxy). In our case, the interface is defined in the `IndexKeeper.java` file in the `\ch6\code\sixpack` directory:

```
import java.rmi.RemoteException;
public interface IndexKeeper {
    public int getIndex() throws RemoteException;
}
```

Even though the `getIndex()` method can throw a `java.rmi.RemoteException`, it won't in our implementation, because we are using a local proxy in our implementation that executes completely within the client's VM and doesn't talk back to the service.

This means that we can use the same code to register multiple proxies, so we'll register six different instances across the three lookup services.

The proxy is implemented by the `IndexKeeperImpl` class. As with all proxies, it must be serializable, which means it must have a constructor that takes no argument, so we'll supply this. The rest of the implementation simply stores an integer as an index. We can use a constructor to pass in the index, and use the `getIndex()` method to get it back. The index is used to differentiate between the six instances that we will be creating.

```
public class IndexKeeperImpl implements IndexKeeper,java.io.Serializable
{
    protected int myIndex = 0;
    public IndexKeeperImpl()
    {}

    public IndexKeeperImpl(int inIndex)
    {
        myIndex = inIndex;
    }

    public int getIndex()
    {
        return myIndex;
    }
}
```

Now, we can compile the interfaces and proxy implementation. Use the command line:

```
..\sixpack\buildit IndexKeeperImpl.java
```

Since the lookup service and the client will need to download the proxy class definitions, we must provide an accessible codebase for them to load it. This can be done by creating a JAR file and copying it in to the directory serviced by the stubs serving HTTPD. The JAR file, in our case, should contain the `IndexKeeperImpl` class and its dependency: the `IndexKeeper` class. The `makejar.bat` file in the `\ch6\code\registrars` directory is created to perform this. It contains:

```
call ..\bats\setpaths.bat
jar cvf SixpackService-dl.jar IndexKeeper.class IndexKeeperImpl.class
copy SixpackService-dl.jar %WROXHOME%
```

Note that the resulting `SixpackService-dl.jar` file is copied to the directory specified by the `WROXHOME` environment variable.

The JoinManager Utility Class

To simplify implementation of the service, we will be using the `net.jini.lookup.JoinManager` utility class (you can find in-depth coverage of this helper utility in Chapter 11). For now, we will learn just enough to use it. This class works together with an instance of `LookupDiscovery` and provides support for all aspects of the join protocol, including managing the set of discovered registrars. The only feature that `JoinManager` does not provide is state persistence, but it makes it easy for the service to implement this itself.

Here is the definition of `JoinManager`:

```
public class JoinManager
{
    public JoinManager(Object obj, Entry[] attrSets, ServiceIDListener callback,
        DiscoveryManagement discoveryMgr, LeaseRenewalManager leaseMgr)
        throws IOException;
    public JoinManager(Object obj, Entry[] attrSets, ServiceID serviceID,
        DiscoveryManagement discoveryMgr, LeaseRenewalManager leaseMgr)
        throws IOException;
    public DiscoveryManagement getDiscoveryManager();
    public LeaseRenewalManager getLeaseRenewalManager();
    public ServiceRegistrar[] getJoinSet();
    public Entry[] getAttributes();
    public void addAttributes(Entry[] attrSets);
    public void addAttributes(Entry[] attrSets, boolean checkSC);
    public void setAttributes(Entry[] attrSets);
    public void modifyAttributes(Entry[] attrSetTemplates, Entry[] attrSets);
    public void modifyAttributes(Entry[] attrSetTemplates, Entry[] attrSets,
        boolean checkSC);
    public void terminate();
}
```

We will only be using the very first constructor of `JoinManager` for our simple service (highlighted above), and not any other methods, as the default behavior of the `JoinManager` is sufficient for our purposes, which are to:

❑ Maintain the discovered set of registrars

❑ Use the registrars to register the supplied proxy object

❑ Maintain the generated service IDs internally (and not generate new IDs)

❑ Maintain leases on the lookup service registration as long as the manager is running

❑ Use a registered callback object as notification of the initial assignation and registration of service IDs

Registering Multiple Proxies with Multiple Lookup Services

The code below is `SixPackService.java`, a service that will create and register six separate proxies with lookup services, and keep them alive. We're setting this up all on one machine, to simplify the experimentation with the Jini configuration, and to allow those of you with only one machine available to try it out.

```
import net.jini.lookup.JoinManager;
import net.jini.core.lookup.ServiceID;
import net.jini.discovery.*;
import net.jini.core.lookup.ServiceRegistrar;
```

```
import java.rmi.RemoteException;
import java.rmi.RMISecurityManager;
import net.jini.lookup.ServiceIDListener;
```

The `IdPrinter` class is a very simple class created to handle the `ServiceIDListener` interface. This interface has only one method called `serivceIDNotify`. When the `JoinManager` has successfully registered a proxy with a lookup service for the first time, it will callback into this object with the associated service ID. Internally, the `JoinManager` will continue to manage the service ID associated with the proxy and use it for any further registrations with other lookup services.

We'll create an instance of `IdPrinter` to be supplied as a parameter to the instance of `JoinManager`. Our implementation simply prints out the instance number of the proxy (since we are creating six separate instances of the `IndexKeeperImpl` proxy) and the service ID that have been assigned. In a production Jini service, the implementation should persist this service ID to permanent storage.

```
class IdPrinter implements ServiceIDListener
{
    int myIndex;
    public IdPrinter(int initIndex)
    {
        myIndex = initIndex;
    }

    // a real service will save the serviceID in persistent store
    public void serviceIDNotify(ServiceID serviceID) {
        System.out.println("instance " + myIndex + " has been assigned service
            ID: " + serviceID.toString());
    }

}
```

This is the actual application class `SixpackService`. The constants specify:

❑   That MAX_INSTANCES (6) IndexKeeperImpl proxies are recreated

❑   Some of them (3 in fact) are registered with GROUPS1 (the iguanas group)

❑   The remaing 3 are registererd with GROUPS2 (the lizards group)

```
public class SixpackService
{
    static final int MAX_INSTANCES = 6;
    static final String [] GROUPS1 = { "iguanas"};
    static final String [] GROUPS2 = { "lizards"};
```

The main method is very similar to `DiscoverRegistrars` in our previous example; it installs an RMI security manager, creates the application instance and then hangs around for the `JoinManager` class to do its work (on the threads that `JoinManager` creates).

```
public static void main(String args[]) {
    try {
        if (System.getSecurityManager() == null) {
            System.setSecurityManager(new RMISecurityManager());
        }
        SixpackService myApp = new SixpackService();
        synchronized(myApp) {
```

```
                myApp.wait(0);
            }
        } catch(Exception e) {
            e.printStackTrace();
            System.exit(1);
        }
    }
}
```

The constructor goes into a loop the number of times specified by MAX_INSTANCES. For each iteration, the constructor:

❑ Creates an instance of a LookupDiscoveryManager helper class (basically carries out lookup discovery with very little user intervention) parameterized with the groups that we want to join

❑ Creates an instance of IdPrinter parameterized with the loop index

❑ Creates an instance of the proxy class, IndexKeeperImpl, and parameterizes it with the loop index

❑ Creates and supplies an instance of JoinManager, with instances of the LookupDiscoveryManager and the IdPrinter as parameters.

This is all that is required for the JoinManager to be able to work. We use a simple algorithm to decide which instances are registered with which groups: the even instances (with odd index) are registered with GROUPS1, and the odd instances (with even index) are registered with GROUPS2. We don't attach any attributes to the proxies with the registrations.

```
LookupDiscoveryManager ldm = null;
JoinManager jm = null;
public SixpackService() throws Exception {

    String [] groupsToDiscover = LookupDiscovery.NO_GROUPS;
    for (int i=0; i< MAX_INSTANCES; i++)
    {
        if ((i % 2) == 0)
            groupsToDiscover = GROUPS1;
        else
            groupsToDiscover = GROUPS2;

        ldm = new LookupDiscoveryManager(groupsToDiscover,
                null /* unicast locators */,
                null /* DiscoveryListener */);
        jm = new JoinManager(new IndexKeeperImpl(i+1),  /* service */
                null  /* attr sets */,
            new IdPrinter(i+1) /* ServiceIDListener*/,
                ldm /* DiscoveryManagement */,
                null /* LeaseManager */);
    }
}
```

Compile the SixpackService.java file with:

..\sixpack\buildit SixpackService.java

Testing Proxy Registrations

Assuming you have been following all along, starting up the three reggies will be second nature by now: run `runhttpd`, then `runrmid` in order to start the three reggies from rmid's persistent states. You may want to run `DiscoverRegistrars` (`\ch6\code\registrars`) again to verify that all three reggies are running managing their assigned groups, and that they've maintained their unique service IDs.

Next, we need to start another HTTP class server to serve the JAR file created for SixpackService. This can be done by running the `runhttpdstubs.bat` file in the `\ch6\code\bats directory`.

We have created a batch file to start the `SixpackService` itself. You should run this batch file only after you've verified all the reggies are up and operational. Here is the `runsix.bat` file:

```
call ..\bats\setpaths.bat
java  -classpath .;%JINIJARS%  -Dnet.jini.discovery.interface=%ADAPTERIP%
-Djava.security.policy=policy.all
-Djava.rmi.server.codebase=http://%STUBHOST%/SixpackService-dl.jar SixpackService
```

Note that the codebase is set to the `STUBHOST` environment variable. In our case, since we are running on one machine, it is the same host, but the port being serviced is 8081.

Once you run the service, you may need to wait a while as the service discovers and registers the proxies. Once it's finished you should see something like this:

Note how each of the proxy instances has been assigned with a unique service ID. Write these service IDs down for future reference.

As long as we keep the services running, the `JoinManager` instances that we have started will continually renew the leases on the registrations across all the lookup services. If we terminate the service, the leases will eventually expire (in 2 to 3 minutes by default) and the system will be purged of unsupported proxies. This way, we can shutdown and restart rmid with the reggies at any point in time without worrying about stale copies of proxies lying around in the lookup services.

Lookup by Clients

Now we'll write a client application that will:

❑   Discover the registrars that support the list of groups provided from the command line

❑   Lookup proxies at each of these lookup services for support of the `IndexKeeper` interface

217

❑ Print out the service ID of each of the proxies downloaded from lookup, invoke their `getIndex()` method and print out their stored instance number

The application will make use of the `net.jini.core.lookup.ServiceRegistrar` interface, which, although we've not seen it until now, is vital to the process: the registrars obtained through discovery will, by definition, support this interface.

The ServiceRegistrar Interface

Here is the definition of the `ServiceRegistrar` interface. The methods that we'll use and discuss here have been highlighted, and the rest will be covered in a later chapter.

```
public interface ServiceRegistrar {
    ServiceRegistration register(ServiceItem item, long leaseDuration)
        throws RemoteException;
    Object lookup(ServiceTemplate tmpl) throws RemoteException;
    ServiceMatches lookup(ServiceTemplate tmpl,int maxMatches)throws RemoteException;
    int TRANSITION_MATCH_NOMATCH = 1 << 0;
    int TRANSITION_NOMATCH_MATCH = 1 << 1;
    int TRANSITION_MATCH_MATCH = 1 << 2;
    EventRegistration notify(ServiceTemplate tmpl, int transitions,
        RemoteEventListener listener, MarshalledObject handback,
        long leaseDuration) throws RemoteException;
    Class[] getEntryClasses(ServiceTemplate tmpl) throws RemoteException;
    Object[] getFieldValues(ServiceTemplate tmpl, int setIndex, String field)
        throws NoSuchFieldException, RemoteException;
    Class[] getServiceTypes(ServiceTemplate tmpl, String prefix)
        throws RemoteException;
    ServiceID getServiceID();
    LookupLocator getLocator() throws RemoteException;
    String[] getGroups() throws RemoteException;
}
```

There are two variations of the lookup method that can either return one, or more than one matching proxy. In our case, we will use the version that can return multiple matches.

Coding the BasicLookup client

The client code is in the `\ch6\code\basiclookup` source distribution directory, called `BasicLookup.java`. You will recognize the code structure as identical to that of `DiscoverRegistrars`. This is maintained to ease our understanding for the new lookup code. We have highlighted the interesting new lines of code below.

```
import net.jini.discovery.*;
import net.jini.core.lookup.*;
import java.io.IOException;
import java.rmi.RemoteException;
import java.rmi.RMISecurityManager;
```

We keep the registrars as a class member to allow member methods access to it. We also limit the maximum number of lookup matches to 10, although in our case the maximum will actually be 6.

```
public class BasicLookup implements DiscoveryListener {
    private  ServiceRegistrar[] registrars;
    static final int MAX_MATCHES = 10;
```

If there aren't any groups specified, a null is passed into `LookupDiscovery`, which is equivalent to `ALL_GROUPS`. Here, we simply pass the entire command line parameter array as the list of groups to be discovered by the `BasicLookup` instance.

```
static public void main(String argv[]) {
    BasicLookup myApp = null;
    try {
        if (System.getSecurityManager() == null) {
            System.setSecurityManager(new RMISecurityManager());
        }
        if (argv.length > 0)
            myApp = new BasicLookup(argv);
        else
            myApp = new BasicLookup(null);

        synchronized (myApp) {
            myApp.wait(0);
        }
    } catch(Exception e) {
        e.printStackTrace();
        System.exit(0);
    }
}
```

`doLookupWork()` obtains information about registrar, prints it out, and then carries out the actual lookup.

```
private void doLookupWork(ServiceRegistrar [] registrars)
    throws RemoteException {
    ServiceMatches matches = null;
    String [] groups;
    String msg = null;
```

Like `DiscoverRegistrars`, the service IDs and groups supported by each lookup service are printed:

```
for (int i=0; i< registrars.length; i++)
{
    msg = "";
    System.out.println("------------------------------------------");
    System.out.println("Registrar: " + registrars[i].getServiceID());
    try {
        groups = registrars[i].getGroups();
        if (groups.length > 0)

            for (int o=0; o<groups.length; o++) {
                msg += groups[o] + " ";
            }

        System.out.println("Groups Supported: " + msg);
        System.out.println("Found IndexKeeper proxies:");
```

Code for Template Matching

The lookup is carried out by class type. Here, we create an array of class types for template matching. A new `ServiceTemplate` is created on the fly with this list, and the effective search query is: every service proxy that implements the `IndexKeeper` interface.

```
                    Class [] myClassType = { IndexKeeper.class };

                    matches = registrars[i].lookup (new ServiceTemplate(null,
                        myClassType ,null), MAX_MATCHES);
```

Working with Multiple Matches

The returned `ServiceMatches` object contains the number of matches, and an array of `ServiceItems` that we iterate through. We delegate the work to be performed on each `ServiceItem` to the `doProxyWork()` method.

```
                for (int j=0; j< matches.totalMatches; j++)
                    doProxyWork( matches.items[j]);
            }
            catch (Exception e) {
                e.printStackTrace();
            }
        }// of for i
    }
```

The `doProxyWork()` method will print out the unique service ID associated with the service proxy instance, and will invoke the proxies `.getIndex()` method to query the instance for its index number.

Both the service ID and the instance number will be printed as output.

```
    private void doProxyWork(ServiceItem inSI) throws RemoteException
    {
        System.out.println(  "  ID: " + inSI.serviceID);
        IndexKeeper  myObj = (IndexKeeper) inSI.service;
        System.out.println(  "        Instance Number: " + myObj.getIndex());
    }
```

The `BasicLookup` constructor takes a list of groups as parameter. These are the groups that discovery will be performed for.

```
    LookupDiscovery discover = null;

    public BasicLookup(String [] ingroups)throws Exception {
        discover = null;

        discover = new LookupDiscovery(LookupDiscovery.NO_GROUPS);
        discover.addDiscoveryListener(this);
        discover.setGroups(ingroups);
    }
```

When the callback occurs, after the local lookup services have been discovered, we simply call `doLookupWork` to iterate through the registrars and perform the lookup by the `LookupDiscovery` instance.

```
    public synchronized discovered(DiscoveryEvent evt) {
        registrars = evt.getRegistrars();
        try {
            registrars = evt.getRegistrars();
            doLookupWork(registrars);
        } catch (Exception ex) {
```

```
                ex.printStackTrace();
        }
    }
    public void discarded(DiscoveryEvent evt) {
    }
  }
```

Compile BasicLookup.java using the batch file:

..\bats\buildit BasicLookup.java

We have created a batch file to run the BasicLookup program. You can find it in the \ch6\code\basiclookup directory. It is called runbasic.bat. and contains:

```
call ..\bats\setpaths.bat
java  -classpath .;%JINIJARS%  -Dnet.jini.discovery.interface=%ADAPTERIP%
-Djava.security.policy=policy.all BasicLookup %1 %2 %3 %4
```

To run BasicLookup, use the command line:

runbasic [group names separated by space]

Testing the BasicLookup Client

The sixpackService will register proxies according to the scheme depicted here:

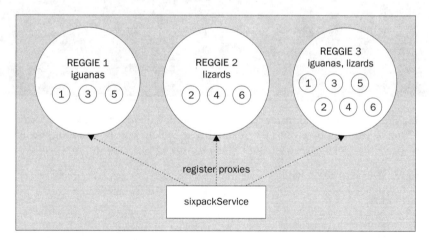

To test the BasicLookup client, first start HTTPD, start rmid and the three reggies by running runrmid.bat as usual. Next, run the HTTPD for the stubs, using runhttpdstubs.bat. Then run the SixpackService service via the runsix.bat batch file and note the service IDs and instance numbers.

Now we can start the BasicLookup client. First lookup by the lizards group using:

runbasic lizards

You should see something akin to this screenshot:

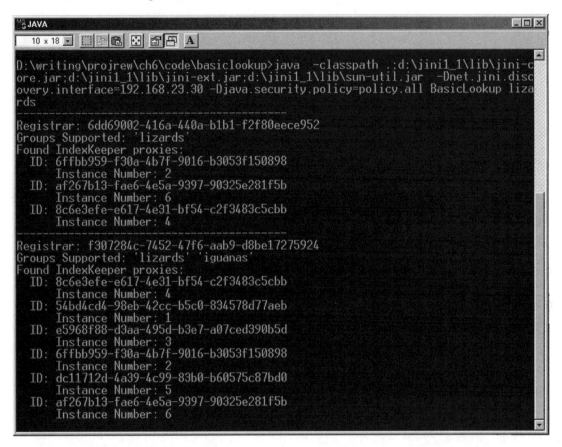

By comparing the service IDs and instance numbers you noted after running the SixpackService, you can see how registration by groups has worked. The lookup service handling the lizards group has 3 registrations, while the lookup service handling the lizards and iguanas group has all 6.

You can also run BasicLookup with:

```
runbasic iguanas
```

This will show the other three proxies that are as yet unaccounted for with the iguanas group.

Now, simulate a disastrous crash and terminate the rmid window using *control-C* on the keyboard to abruptly kill the three lookup services.

Run BasicLookup and confirm that the reggies are dead.

Now, restart the lookup services by running runrmid.bat, and wait for the system to settle.

Run BasicLookup again. Lo and behold, the entire system state is restored! If you carry out discovery and lookup as usual, you'll find that the proxies are still registered with the lookup service and have retained their service ID as if nothing had happened. Essentially, the network has self-healed. This is the beauty of Jini.

Let's inflict a little more pain on the system and terminate the `SixpackService` window. Run `BasicLookup` to check that the proxies are still in the lookup service after the termination of their supporting service. They're there because their leases have not yet expired. If you keep an eye on them for a while using `BasicLookup`, you'll see them being cleaned from the system as their leases expire.

Adding Attributes to the Proxy

Now for a more complex template search, using the service proxy's attributes. We'll use the pre-defined `Location` attribute, which you can find in the `\Sixpack2` directory of the source distribution.

It's pretty much the same `SixpackService` code with some minor tweaks that add the attribute, so I'll just show the changed portions here. First, we must import the entry classes that we will use:

```
...
import java.rmi.RMISecurityManager;
import net.jini.lookup.ServiceIDListener;
import net.jini.core.entry.Entry;
import net.jini.lookup.entry.Location;
```

In the constructor, we create an instance of the `Location` entry and pass it in with `JoinManager` for proxy registration. We will assign the loop index as the floor number, ten times the loop index as the room number, and always use south lab as the `location`.

```
public SixpackService() throws Exception
{
    String [] groupsToDiscover = LookupDiscovery.NO_GROUPS;
    Entry [] attributes = new Entry[1];
    for (int i=0; i< MAX_INSTANCES; i++)  {
        if ((i % 2) == 0)
            groupsToDiscover = GROUPS1;
        else
            groupsToDiscover = GROUPS2;
        attributes[0] = new Location( "" + i /* floor */ , "" + i*10  /* room */,
            "south lab" /* building */);
        ldm = new LookupDiscoveryManager(groupsToDiscover,
                null /* unicast locators */,
                null /* DiscoveryListener */);
        jm = new JoinManager(new IndexKeeperImpl(i+1),  /* service */
                attributes  /* attr sets */,
                new IdPrinter(i+1) /* ServiceIDListener*/,
                ldm /* DiscoveryManagement */,
                null /* LeaseManager */);
    }
}
```

Template Lookup with Attributes

Now that each proxy is adorned with a location attribute, we can do a more complex templated search using `BasicLookup`. Specifically, we will be looking for a proxy that supports the `IndexKeeper` interface and is located in room 30, modifying `BasicLookup` to do it. You can find the source code in the `\BasicLookup2` directory. Here are the changes:

```
import java.rmi.RemoteException;
import java.rmi.RMISecurityManager;

import net.jini.lookup.entry.Location;
import net.jini.core.entry.Entry;
```

We need to import the entry related classes, and we need to modify the `lookupWork` method where the lookup is actually performed.

```
private void doLookupWork(ServiceRegistrar [] registrars) {
    ServiceMatches matches = null;
    String [] groups;
    String msg = null;
    for (int i=0; i< registrars.length; i++)
    {
        msg = "";
        System.out.println("-------------------------------------------");
        System.out.println("Registrar: " + registrars[i].getServiceID());
        try {
            groups = registrars[i].getGroups();
            if (groups.length > 0)

                for (int o=0; o<groups.length; o++) {
                    msg += "\'" + groups[o] + "\' ";
                }

            System.out.println("Groups Supported: " + msg);
            System.out.println("Found attribute match and IndexKeeper proxies:");
```

We'll create both a class array and an entry array. The entry array contains one element: the `location` entry. We parameterized the `Location` with only the "room equals 30" value, leaving the `floor` and `building` values null, to match everything. During lookup, we create a new `ServiceTemplate` instance, passing in **both** the class types and attributes.

```
            Class [] myClassType = { IndexKeeper.class };
            Entry myAttrib[] = new Entry[1];
            myAttrib[0] = new Location(null, "30", null);

            matches = registrars[i].lookup(new ServiceTemplate(null,myClassType
                ,myAttrib), MAX_MATCHES);

            for (int j=0; j< matches.totalMatches; j++)
                doProxyWork( matches.items[j]);
        }
        catch (Exception e) {
            e.printStackTrace();
            System.exit(1); }
    }// of for i
}
```

There is a minor change needed in the `doProxyWork` method in order to print out the attribute value. Thanks to the default `toString()` implementation in the abstract `AbstractEntry` class from which `Location` derives, we can easily display the field values of the `Location` entry.

```
private void doProxyWork (ServiceItem inSI) throws RemoteException
{
    System.out.println( "  ID: " + inSI.serviceID);
    IndexKeeper  myObj = (IndexKeeper) inSI.service;
    System.out.println( "        Instance Number: " + myObj.getIndex());
    System.out.println( "        Attribute: " + inSI.attributeSets[0]);
}
```

Testing Lookup by Attributes

To test the system

❑ Compile `BasicLookup` and `SixpackService` using, copying `buildit.bat` to the appropriate directories:

`..\basicLookup\buildit BasicLookup.java`

`..\Sixpack\buildit SixpackService.java`

in the BasicLookup2 and SixpackService2 directory respectively

❑ Start HTTPD with `runhttpd`

❑ Start the stub server HTTPD with `runhttpdstubs`

❑ Start the three reggies with `runrmid`

❑ Start the `SixpackService` in the `\ch6\code\sixpack2` directory with runsix, and note down the service ID of instance #4

❑ Start the `BasicLookup` client with 'lizards' as the group you want to see

You should see something similar to this:

```
D:\writing\projrew\ch6\code\basiclookup2>java  -classpath .;d:\jini1_1\lib\jini-
core.jar;d:\jini1_1\lib\jini-ext.jar;d:\jini1_1\lib\sun-util.jar  -Dnet.jini.dis
covery.interface=192.168.23.30 -Djava.security.policy=policy.all BasicLookup liz
ards
------------------------------------------------
Registrar: 52a755b8-41c2-459c-a4f7-bfeef6cf9796
Groups Supported: 'lizards' 'iguanas'
Found attribute match and IndexKeeper proxies:
  ID: 4a5e0313-aeaa-4023-b870-cc456680e942
      Instance Number: 4
      Attribute: net.jini.lookup.entry.Location(floor=3,room=30,building=south l
ab)
------------------------------------------------
Registrar: 77365c74-2bfc-45b6-9ef1-83c35b4e7f11
Groups Supported: 'lizards'
Found attribute match and IndexKeeper proxies:
  ID: 4a5e0313-aeaa-4023-b870-cc456680e942
      Instance Number: 4
      Attribute: net.jini.lookup.entry.Location(floor=3,room=30,building=south l
ab)
```

Note that the template search is now more specific, and that only the service proxy with the location attribute of room 30 will be found. This should correspond to the service ID of instance #4 that you jotted down earlier.

Browsing reggies via Jini Browser

The Jini development kit distribution contains a useful utility to browse lookup services. You can start it using the `runjbrowser.bat` file in the `\ch6\code\bats` directory.

Browsing the reggies

If we use `runjbrowser` with the three reggies running, we can get a general idea of what is kept in the lookup service.

For example, with `SixpackService` running, the browser shows three instances of lookup service running:

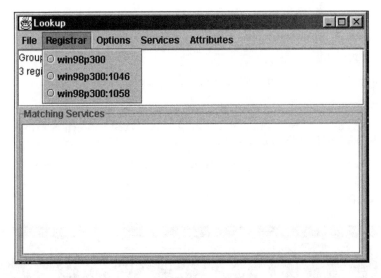

Select one of the registrars; in this case, we have 4 services registered. We call see all the registered services in the list box below. There are 3 `IndexKeeper` proxies and one lookup service proxy:

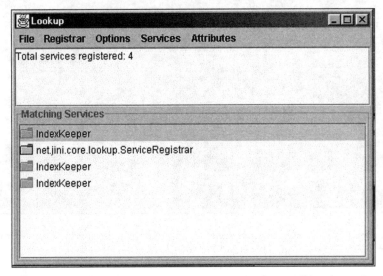

If you double click on one of the `IndexKeeper` proxies, its attribute will be shown in a browser window:

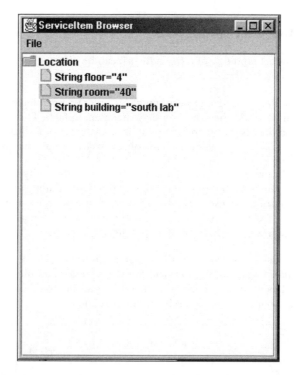

This simple browser can be used to browse any lookup service reachable through discovery on the Jini network. Using the Find One… mechanism, it can also perform unicast discovery to view remote lookup services directly.

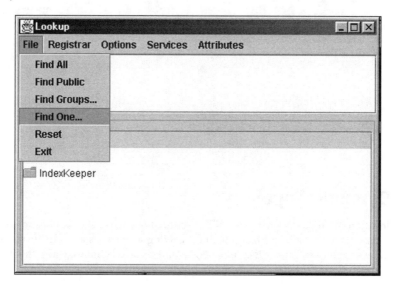

Lookup Service Strategies

Both the logical and physical topology of a Jini network can be affected by the strategic deployment of lookup services and group selection.

As you saw in the simple lizards vs iguanas grouping example, you can logically partition a Jini network within the same physical network (the same physical machine, in fact). The common lookup service that handles both iguanas and lizards group ended up taking registration for all the proxies. This overlapping scheme can be useful as a backup for dedicated lookup services for specific groups in general.

The following diagram illustrates some of the ways you might strategically deploy lookup services. In this figure, the system on the left is setup in star type topology. It emulates a centralized system. The lookup service in the center has access to all lookup services in the entire network, so clients using the centralized lookup service can access every service and resource in the network. This topology may be useful for traditional organizations with centralized control.

The right hand system is designed hierarchically. Clients can traverse from the root lookup service at the top to any intermediate or leaf lookup service, thereby accessing all the services and resources. The resources and services of each sub level are immediately accessible to the parent lookup service in the hierarchy. This topology is natural for hierarchical organizations.

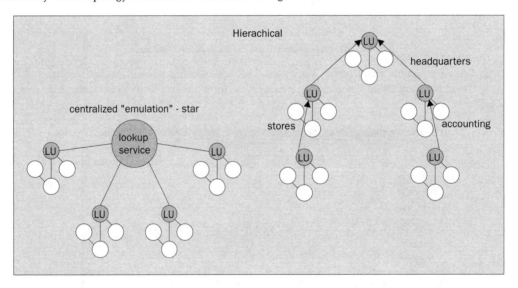

Naturally Dynamic Topology

Although the location of the lookup services will probably have been allocated at some point, the actual network topology will be continually changing and evolving as services and clients come and go, connect, disconnect, reconnect, move locations, crash and restart. In many ways, the exact interaction topology of a Jini based network can never be finalized.

While the physical topology has certainly changed in our example, the logical topology remains the same. The physical network configuration partitioning using groups simply provides the boundaries within which an unlimited set of interaction topologies can occur, and Jini, as we have learn, gives these dynamic interaction topologies the name **federations**.

Natural Fault Resilience

There are many fault resilient facets to a Jini network. Most conventional approaches to fault resilience involve mirroring hardware foundations (keeping two synchronized disk images), some sort of heart beat tracking mechanism (repeated pings between systems and/or over specialized cable and connections), and 'fail-over' support (switching a mirrored system for the failed one).

To realize this within a Jini network is very straightforward – you can simply connect additional services to the network at anytime. Multiple services providing the same functionality happily coexist within the network without conflict, and a client can get work done with complete disregard to the composition of the network, so long as there remains at least one service that can perform the work required. Services that are being used in a distinct logical partition (or even connected physical network) can be easily re-deployed on a troubled partition through a quick 'live' administrative change.

Because of the structure of the Jini network, the set of problems system architects need to resolve in particular network computer implementations are significantly different to those that need resolving in the conventional monolithic or symmetric processing systems. A different mindset is required when you're designing Jini systems – there is a definite paradigm necessary, but it is worth it. Users of the more conventional system are rapidly finding scalability limits that only a distributed platform can economically resolve.

Registering with Multiple Lookup Services

To provide a level of fault tolerance against failure of any one physical machine hosting a lookup service, any particular service can be simultaneously registered on multiple lookup services. Services are registration by groups (unless unicast is involved), and many lookup services can service the same group.

Benefits of Decentralization

The Jini network does not have a centralized database of services available nor does it have a routing topology map indicating how services/clients connect together. Instead, the services available can be viewed at the point of need through a distributed set of the lookup services. The connection paths between clients and services are dynamic, and so there is no single point of failure. A large portion of a Jini network can fail and what little remains will still carry on and perform useful work.

Towards Utopia

To summarize, Jini is designed for creating distributed network systems that are long-lived, so a well designed Jini system will never be down completely (even if part of it fails). Jini is designed to eventually fulfill the network computer vision. Putting these features and goals together, Jini can be used to build distributed computing systems that are logically long-lived today.

So How Does Jini's Lookup Service Compare?

How is Jini lookup service different from other naming and directory services? By now, we should have a very clear picture.

CORBA Naming Service

The CORBA Naming Service allows a hierarchical string name to be resolved to a reference of a remote service. Typically, the ORB (Object Request Broker) is responsible for contacting the naming service (wherever it is) to resolve a name. In this way, the built-in knowledge of where the services are located is very similar to the bootstrapping mechanism in Jini, where a client can locate a lookup service 'auto magically'. While a Jini network by definition will have many lookup services, a CORBA network with a single ORB typically uses only one naming service.

A service must bind itself to a name through the CORBA Naming Service before clients can locate it, and in this, on the surface at least, it is similar to the way a Jini service must register itself with a lookup service before a client can locate the service.

This similarity is very shallow, though. In the first place, searching by attributes or type facility is not readily available in CORBA without additional support or extensions. Furthermore, the service reference delivered by CORBA is very distinct from that Jini delivers. In CORBA, this reference is to a remote interface (specified by IDL) that the client must use to communicate with the service. The work of the service will always be performed on the machine providing the service. In Jini, as you've seen, a reference is given to a **local** proxy object, typically using a local interface. The computation, or work, can be carried out in the client's machine, or across the network on the service machine, or on another different network machine altogether. The protocol used to connect back to the service machine is totally flexible. And, of course, Jini proxies can use CORBA to communicate with a service.

In CORBA, a Naming Service is not strictly required for proper operation. If a client can get a hold of the IOR (a string form of a service with IP address and port encoded) string of a service it can contact the service directly. Jini does not enable clients to contact services directly – they must communicate through the services proxy object using a lookup service. The lookup service is, in Jini, an integral part of what makes a network 'Jini ready'.

Active Directory

The Active Directory Service API allows common API access to various standard directory services (including Microsoft's Active Directory implementation) for generalized lookup. In fact, there is absolutely nothing specific about Active Directory that lends itself to lookup for remote services. It can be used to lookup a user password as readily as an archived company data file. To obtain a reference to a remote service, the Active Directory Service uses an operating system specific mechanism to instantiate it. This is highly unlike Jini, where the output of a lookup is an executable Java proxy object. While, theoretically at least, the output of an Active Directory search can be a binary object executable in the client's machine, in practice the complex dependencies imposed by distinct machine hardware, operating systems and environments render it useless.

The Active Directory is conceptually centralized. That is, a client need not be aware that there are multiple directory services available within the network. The main reason for this is that Active Directory uses replication to distribute its database updates amongst directory services. Active Directory is designed to accommodate very infrequent non-centralized updates. The Jini model, on the other hand, requires that clients are aware of the lookup services available, and is designed for a totally distributed and dynamic system – it can handle very frequent non-centralized updates to lookup service's databases. The dynamic nature of the Jini network is what makes it unique.

DNS

The Domain Name System is used to map string based domain names into IP addresses. The database of the DNS is updated centrally (there may be more than one location depending on namespace partitioning), but replicated throughout the root services. There is only one primary server per domain.

In this way, DNS is traditionally a read-only distributed lookup service (dynamic udpate to primary server is now supported). DNS cannot be used to map arbitrary remote services. For specific applications, however, DNS can be used to locate a corresponding service if the client and service have previously agreed on a port for this use (for example, FTP or TELNET).

Jini and DSN have very little in common. One philosophical parallel is that the Internet is defined partially by DNS – without DNS, there would be no Internet as we know it today. A Jini network is defined partially by its lookup service – without any lookup service, there will be no Jini network.

Fundamental Differences

The key differences between these services lie in their design intent. All of the services mentioned are designed specifically for the type of networks that they work on – CORBA, Microsoft and Internet respectively; and none of them were intended to support a fully distributed, long-lived, dynamic network as Jini was.

Making Connections

Jini, and especially the lookup service, is all about making connections. Once a client has located the services that it needs within a federation, it can carry on oblivious to the Jini lookup service, until the next dynamic union.

In this chapter, we have examined the vital role that a Jini lookup service plays within a Jini network. Essentially, without lookup services, the dynamic nature of a Jini network (the very essence of Jini) disappears.

Our examination of the major building blocks of a lookup service hopefully helped illustrate that the simplicity of its interface, through a singular registrar, in fact covers an extremely complex set of internally implemented subsystems. Thankfully, most of us will never need to write our own lookup services.

We have explored and worked with the programmatic interfaces that interact with a Jini lookup service, both from a service perspective and a client perspective, and experimented extensively with reggie. We have also discussed the importance of properly adding attributes to a proxy and maintaining them – without proper attributes a preferred service may be very hard to find.

As a Jini network architect, the strategy deployment and configuration of Jini lookup services can be the make or break factor for deployment. So we examined various strategies useful in large and small networks, and discussed how to use the key features of a Jini network – dynamism and decentralization – to our advantage.

Last but not least, we re-examined the role of a Jini lookup service and contrasted it with the other naming and directory services that we are already familiar with. We saw the importance of the reverberating theme of decentralization, and the destructive long-term development impact brought upon by architectural complexity. There is an excellent white paper titled **A Note on Distributed Computing**, written in 1994 by some of the key Jini players, that discusses these issues. You can retrieve from http://www.sun.com/research/technical-reports/1994/abstract-29.

In the next few chapters, we examine some of the higher-level elements of Jini: distributed events, distributed leasing, and distributed transactions.

Jini Client or Service	JavaSpaces and Helper Services

Jini Client and Service Support Helper Utilities

Jini Discovery Management Helper Utilities

Jini Protocol Helper Utilities

Jini Network Protocols	
	RMI and Rich Object Semantics
	Java VM and Networking

Network Protocols

7

Jini Distributed Events

Although these next three chapters may well be the toughest in the book, you should find them worthwhile – we will be covering some core cornerstone concepts within Jini: remote events, distributed leasing, and distributed transactions. A thorough understanding of these concepts will enable you to draw from them effectively when developing Jini applications. There is a lot of code spread between the chapters, but we've tried to keep it simple and tightly focused on each of the new concepts being explored. The following is a summary of the coverage in the next three chapters.

Concept	Coverage	Description
Remote Events	This Chapter	Extends the Java event model across the network. Provides a flexible asynchronous communications system. Jini distributed events mechanism is built on top of RMI, making it very simple to use. Designed to be 'chainable' or 'composable', allowing the possibility of using third-party services to process or handle events in the form of a pipeline.
Distributed Leasing	Chapter 8	Associates resource allocation on a remote server with a finite time lease that eventually expires. Distributed leasing allows resources to be automatically reclaimed in case of system or network failure. It forces the client to show 'proof of interest' by renewing the lease on regular interfaces. It contributes to the long-term health of a Jini system by letting the network self-heal, purging itself of resource leaks and zombie allocations, over a long period of operating time. We will examine distributed leasing from both the lease holder (resource user) and lease grantor (resource allocator) point of view.

Table continued on following page

Concept	Coverage	Description
Distributed Transactions	Chapter 9	Provides a 'standard' means of synchronizing the operation or state changes of multiple distributed services. Jini provides the specification for a TransactionManager that can co-ordinate a 'two phase commit' protocol amongst multiple distributed participants. The exact semantics of a transaction in Jini is completely application dependent, the ACID properties of classic transaction theory are not enforced (although they can be for certain applications). We will examine distributed transactions from both the view of an external transaction user, or an internal transaction participant.

In this chapter, our focus will be on distributed events – the main mechanism for asynchronous communications in the Jini world. We will see how Jini extends the model of Java events, one that AWT and Swing programmers will be familiar with, to one that works between remote Java VMs in a distributed network. We will use several code examples to illustrate the concepts. We will see:

❑   How remote events are implemented

❑   The importance of selecting event IDs and sequence numbers for distributed events

❑   The ability – by design – to 'chain' multiple event receivers/senders together, and the advantage of this 'composable' design

❑   How to use third-party event handling service

Remote Events in Jini

It's unlikely, though not impossible, that anyone who's been developing in Java for any length of time has managed to bypass events. Certainly if you've been programming with either AWT, Swing or JavaBeans you'll have come across various forms of listeners and events.

When using AWT events, the event producer (that sends the event) manages a set of objects registered by the event consumer (that receives the event). Each of these objects, supplied by consumers, managed by the producer, implements a 'listener' interface. They are often called listener objects. Once the consumer has registered a listener with the event producer (usually via an addXXXListener() method call of the source object), it can go about its own flow of logic. When the event producer is ready to fire (send) an event, it will go through its list of listeners and call the notify() method (or equivalent) on the listener interface. An XXXEvent object is passed as an argument to the notify() method, the consumer can retrieve event specific information from this XXXEvent object. This procedure is essentially a callback into the sink object. It is up to the sink object, the one that supplies the listener object in the first place, to implement the logic within the notify() method.

Within AWT, Swing, and JavaBeans, all this happens locally within a single VM. Jini extends this across the network, and across multiple VMs. All events thrown are subclasses of net.jini.core.event.RemoteEvent, and all listener objects must implement the net.jini.core.event.RemoteEventListener interface. This is an RMI based remote interface.

Event Concepts in Detail

What we're calling an event is, in real terms, a notification involving an event consumer and an event producer:

❏ The event consumer registers an interest with the producer, usually associated with a state change of the generator (for example, whenever a GUI button is clicked in AWT)

❏ The producer tracks registrations, and monitors for related state changes within its own realm (for example, waiting for a mouse event corresponding to the click of the button)

❏ Should the appropriate change take place, the producer notifies the consumer (for example, the button handling notifies the application code of the 'click')

So it looks something like this:

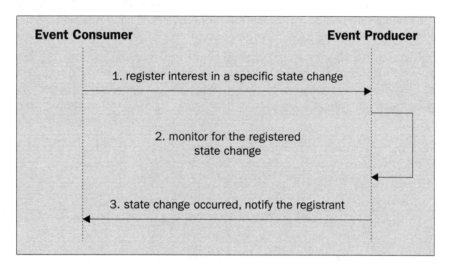

Notification, here, is asynchronous with respect to the normal flow of programming logic of the listener, meaning notifications of state changes in the generator are sent as and when the state changes, not when the interested application checks back for state changes, as is the case with polling. So how does the producer go about notifying the consumer?

Asynchronous Notification

When we take a closer look at how the producer goes about notifying the consumer, we will see that it actually calls the notify() method of the listener interface. This listener interface is implemented by an object that is supplied by the consumer.

In most circumstances, the event generator's method invocation on the event consumer is a synchronous call. Which means that the event generator will be typically blocked while the method is invoked, and not continue with its own logic until the invocation returns. Event generators should protect themselves from listeners with poorly written event handlers, typically accomplished by placing notification into a separate thread to the main event generating program thread. This will ensure that misbehaving consumers (that is, one that takes an exceedingly long time to process an event) cannot stop the main logic of the producer from executing.

Java Event Notification Mechanism

Most Java event notifications are implemented through the familiar listener code pattern.

The interaction is between a consumer and a producer of notifications. A listener is a Java object that implements a listener interface. The consumer passes a listener object to the event producer as a form of registration (indeed, sometimes the event consumer and the listener are the same Java object). The onus is on the event producer to keep track of this registration.

A typical producer can take registrations from many consumers on many state changes of interest, and must manage registration and un-registering appropriately.

When making event notifications, the producer provides an object to the consumer that implements the event interface – this is nearly always a data object. The actual type (subclass) of the event object will give the event handler information about the type of notification, while member variables of the object will provide additional information. One member variable of the event object is the source of the event; this is a reference to the producer itself.

This diagram illustrates the listener coding pattern.

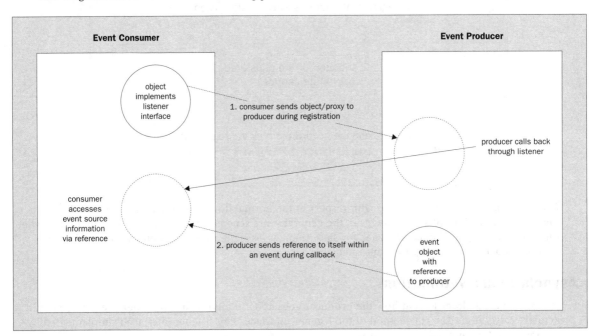

Extending the Model Across the Network

When the event listener code pattern is extended across a network of multiple machines, something interesting occurs. Although the logical concept remains the same, the unreliable nature of the underlying delivery mechanism and infrastructure of a multiple machined network brings heavy-duty complexity to the simple programming paradigm. Jini's remote event API abstracts most of this complexity, and allows the programmer to respond to the new uncertainties.

First, let's look at the way remote events in Jini extend the single machine Java model. The consumer in this case still creates a Java object that implements a listener interface. However, since the event notification will be made remotely, there are really only two choices:

❑   Make the listener interface a remote interface via RMI

❑   Keep the listener interface local, but demand that the consumer supplies a proxy object containing the interface (allowing the consumer to use means other than RMI to communicate with the proxy)

For the provision of event notification, the first choice is by far the simplest, and it is also the chosen path of Jini. Jini defines a specific remote (RMI) interface as the remote event listener:

```
public interface RemoteEventListener extends Remote,java.util.EventListener
{
    void notify(RemoteEvent theEvent) throws UnknownEventException,
            RemoteException;
}
```

So the programmer of the consumer application is responsible for generating RMI stubs for the listener using the rmic tool, and providing a means of downloading the stubs, even though the consumer is really a client on a higher conceptual level. This makes good sense; the client is temporarily an RMI server when event notification is taking place through the remote listener interface.

The event generator supplies an event object as a parameter on the event notification that contains state information: an event ID, a sequence number, a hand-back serialized object (MarshalledObject), and a remote reference back to the producer that fired the event. The hand-back MarshalledObject is one supplied by the consumer itself as part of the listener registration; this can be a reference to state information within the consumer. The event object is an instance of a RemoteEvent subclass. RemoteEvent is defined as:

```
public class RemoteEvent extends java.util.EventObject
{
    public RemoteEvent(Object source,long eventID, long seqNum,
        MarshalledObject handback)
    public Object getSource () {…}
    public long getID() {…}
    public long getSequenceNumber() {…}
    public MarshalledObject getRegistrationObject() {…}
}
```

This means that another RMI stub is required from the listener in order to communicate with the event producer using the source reference contained in the event. However, as you'll usually use listener RMI stubs to make the initial remote event registration possible (assuming that the service/producer chose RMI as the transport mechanism for its service proxy), this simply means that additional class that needs to be in the RMI download server (or JAR file).

The state information from the producer is usually carried in a RemoteEvent subclass that may have additional fields and methods. The consumer uses the hand-back object to attach information to a specific event registration; this MarshalledObject is handed back to the consumer during notification.

An Example of Remote Events

We saw Jini events in action in an earlier example. Recall the `DiscoveryListener` interface that we implemented in Chapter 6. The event handler provides the `discovered()` method call that the `LookupDiscovery` helper class used to inform us when it had discovered lookup services.

```
public interface DiscoveryListener extends EventListener
{
    public void discovered(DiscoveryEvent e);
    public void discarded(DiscoveryEvent e);
}
```

Here, the `discovered()` method invocation is made asynchronously with respect to the normal execution flow of our application. The main program blocks the end of its flow so that the process itself can stay alive to handle the event notification whenever it happens (that is, when the discovery occurs).

The Problems Inherent to Remote Events

If you've worked with RMI, you'll have soon realized that any remote method might throw a `RemoteException` at any time. Which is another way of saying that any message sent between networked machines (and Java VMs of course) is liable to fail.

As either the machines in the network, or the network itself may fail at any time, and for any length of time, event registration should be treated as a type of scarce resource. In other words, event registrations should be leased to ensure the long-lived stability of the Jini system as a whole. This will prevent the producer from keeping too many stale registrations around, or wasting time firing events to consumers who may have either crashed or ceased their interest in the event without de-registering.

When remote event notifications are sent over a network, the following limitations are evident:

❑ Event delivery order cannot be generally assured, especially when there may be intermediary event processors involved

❑ Success of event delivery itself cannot be generally assured

❑ Latency (or delay) in getting an event delivered can be substantial when compared to the actual processing required for the event

These restrictions, combined with the possibility of occasional consumer or producer failure, make the software designer's life significantly more difficult. One must take these constraints into account when designing applications that work with remote events. For example, one could consider batching events together should there be a likelihood of many events traveling between consumer/producer pairs. This can substantially cut down on the average latency time and reduce overall network traffic. One may also provide a reliable event delivery mechanism on top of the basic Jini event infrastructure. Building any of this event processing functionality is beyond the scope of this chapter; however, we will have enough information to attack such a project by the end of this chapter.

Selection of Event ID and Sequence Number

To assist in implementation of intermediary event processing services, Jini has provided the following:

❑   Event IDs

❑   Sequence numbers with each event

❑   Simple event interfaces that are completely composable

The event ID uniquely identifies the type of event, and/or the registration instance, from a producer. Since a single consumer can be registered for many different types of events with a single producer, this will enable the consumer to quickly determine what a specific notification is all about.

Here we see this use of the event ID:

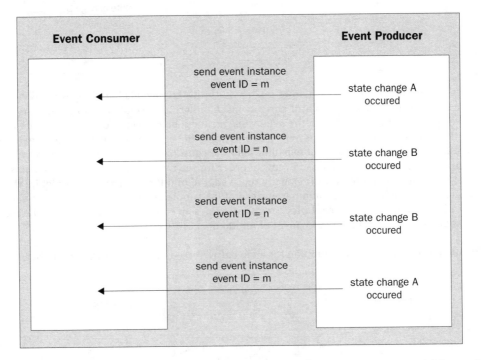

Typically, within one single producer, the same event ID can (but may not necessarily) be used for the same event type across multiple consumers, which allows one-to-one mapping of the event ID and type of event. The following diagram illustrates this use of the event ID by the producer.

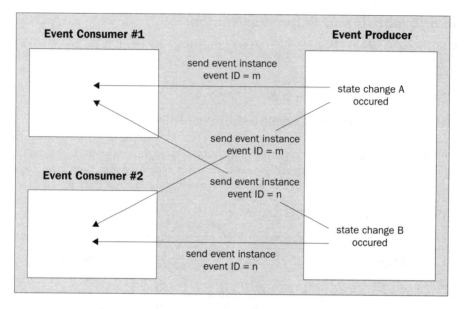

As we will see in the next section when we talk about third-party events handling, we may need more than one event ID per event type. Third-party events handlers are useful, for example, to provide an in-order delivery of events even though the events may actually be delivered out of order (that is, the third-party stores and sorts the events before delivering to the consumer). Such a middleman service may register for event notification on behalf of multiple consumers. These registrations may be with the same consumer for a particular type of event. In order for the middleman service to distinguish between the different clients when the event is actually received, the middleman service will require the event ID to represent a unique 'registration number' instead of the simple event type – which is not unique from the view of the middleman service. In fact, reggie provides an event ID that is based on the registration, and is thus compatible with the deployment of middleman services.

This figure illustrates the implementation for an event ID based on the registration number.

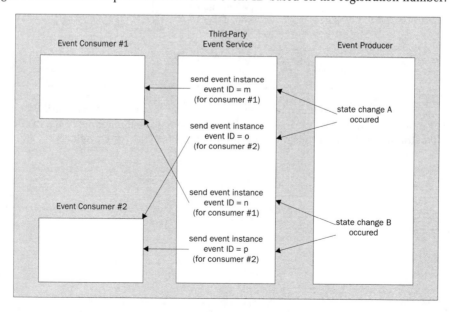

Sequence numbers specify the order in which events were generated by the event generator. It is not guaranteed that the events will arrive at the listener in the order they were generated.

The Jini specification requires that the sequence numbers of events, associated with a specific event ID and from a specific event producer, increase, but it doesn't specify what that increment should be. For example, if you receive two events with the same event ID from the same producer and one contains the sequence number 5 while the other one contains the sequence number 18, you can safely conclude that the event with the sequence number 18 was sent later by the event generator, even if you do receive it before you receive the event with sequence number 5. You can also specify, although the Jini specifications do not require it, a full ordered sequence of numbers. In this case the generator should increment the sequence number by 1 whenever events with the same event ID are fired. Other than providing a means of determining order, this can also keep count of the number of events that may be missing for the consumer (if we know in advance that the increment is 1).

This is vital for applications that cannot tolerate missing events. Our earlier example would have indicated, for example, that there were 18-5 = 13 events that had been generated for the same event ID between the two events that we have on hand.

Third-Party Event Handling

There are plenty of legitimate design scenarios where one might want to make use of third-party events handling, where someone else handles event registrations and/or event handling on your behalf. The following diagram illustrates this:

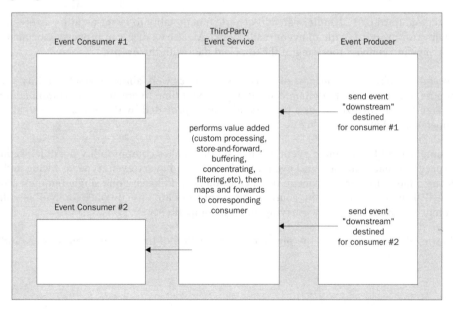

The clients and services that use third-party event handling generally fall into one or more of the following three categories. The event consumers or event producers:

- ❑ Do not want to handle events themselves
- ❑ Cannot handle the events themselves
- ❑ Want the added value that the third-party brings

The service may not want to handle the service because of the complex logic such handling requires, or because it may be positioned badly within the network for event handling – on a slow part of a network, or behind a firewall, for example.

There are actually quite a few examples of services that could not manage events, even if they wanted to: that is a Jini service that runs only on demand (that is, activatable services), services that run on limited Java platforms without RMI support, or even services that run on devices that don't have a Java VM at all. In these cases, a third-party that represents the service and handles events for it allows it to participate fully in a Jini network.

Services might elect to use a third-party for value added reasons: services like event ordering services, for example, event concentrating services, reliable event delivery services, event consolidation services, and so on.

Since version 1.1, the Jini distribution has included a third-party event mailbox service, code-named Mercury. Mercury receives events on behalf of event consumers, buffers or stores them, and allows consumers to retrieve these events at their convenience. We'll examine Mercury's functionality and put it to action in Chapter 11.

Event Routing Through Pipelines

Hooking up third-party event delegates allows you to create a pipeline value-adding model. In effect, a series of specialized third-party handlers can be chained together in both the routing and processing of events.

A value adding, third-party handler can add generic functionality to event handling (store-and-forward functionality, for example, with an event mailbox like Mercury), or it can process associated event data across the pipeline (active processing of the attached data with the event).

This is useful if you're in the business of re-using software as well, allowing **composability** of sorts. You can compose functional blocks dynamically at deployment time to create newly combined functionality. Unix veterans will recognize this as a primary advantage provided by the operating system through the pipe '|' operator and utilities like 'tee'.

It is the simplicity of Jini's remote event mechanism that makes composability possible. Rather than using a specific listener interface and event type for each and every event type, as Swing and AWT do, Jini has one remote listener interface to fit all consumers and likewise one single remote event definition. This means that all event sources and event sinks are directly plug compatible – they can be plugged into one another without worrying about incompatibility.

The following diagram illustrates the plug compatible action of Jini remote event sources and sinks.

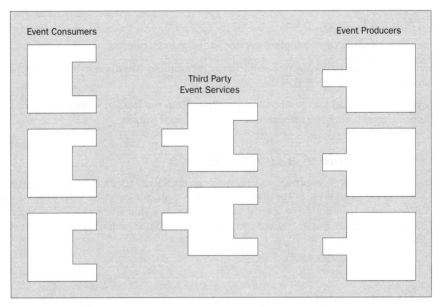

Any third-party event service has to use the event ID to distinguish the information contained in the 'consumer, event type, generator' trio. The service must map the event ID to the trio, and all other services in the pipeline must understand the specific conventions that have been used in order for them to work together.

Implementing an Event Consumer

So let's implement a remote event consumer. You can find the code for this consumer in the ch7\code\EvtClient directory of the source code distribution. We'll be using the same client framework for our later explorations, but for now, this client will be interacting with a lookup service for registration and receipt of remote events. The lookup service will be the reference implementation. Reggie will generate remote events to the client based on the internal state changes in the proxies store. The following illustration shows how EvtClient works.

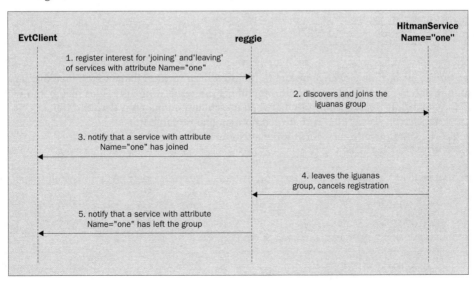

The EvtClient:

❑ Discovers an instance of a lookup service in the group iguanas

❑ Registers with the lookup service in order to be notified when a specific service (with attribute Name="one") joins and leaves the federation

❑ Catches the join and leave remote notifications from the lookup service, and prints the event ID and sequence number information to the standard output

The Event Producer Role of a Lookup Service

A Jini lookup service supports remote event registration directly through the registrar proxy. A client of the service can specify an interest in specific state changes within its service/proxy data store. The registration is performed via the ServiceRegistrar interface that we're already familiar with. There is one specific method in the ServiceRegistrar interface that is responsible for event registration:

```
public interface ServiceRegistrar
{
    ServiceRegistration register(ServiceItem item, long leaseDuration)throws
        RemoteException;
    Object lookup(ServiceTemplate tmpl) throws RemoteException;
    ServiceMatches lookup(ServiceTemplate tmpl, int maxMatches) throws
        RemoteException;

    EventRegistration notify(ServiceTemplate tmpl, int transitions,
        RemoteEventListener listener,MarshalledObject handback, long
        leaseDuration) throws RemoteException;
    ...
}
```

A template can specify the services state changes that can be monitored by the lookup service. The template may contain interface/class types, service IDs, and attributes as in service lookup. The state changes, specified in terms of transitions with respect to the template, are:

```
int TRANSITION_MATCH_NOMATCH = 1 << 0;
int TRANSITION_NOMATCH_MATCH = 1 << 1;
int TRANSITION_MATCH_MATCH = 1 << 2;
```

In other words, every time a change occurs in the proxy registration database, the lookup service will attempt to match the supplied template. It remembers the result of the previous match and will send notification only if the desired transition between match and no match is detected (for TRANSITION_MATCH_NOMATCH), or between no match and match (for TRANSITION_NOMATCH_MATCH), or if some attribute of a service is changed (for TRANSITION_MATCH_MATCH).

This method returns an EventRegistration instance. EventRegistration is a class specified as:

```
public class EventRegistration implements java.io.Serializable
{
    public EventRegistration(long eventID,
    Object eventSource,
    Lease eventLease,
```

```
        long seqNum) {…}
        public long getID() {…}
        public Object getSource() {…}
        public Lease getLease() {…}
        public long getSequenceNumber() {…}
    }
```

Event Consumer Jini Client Coding

Here is the code for the `EvtClient.java` implementation:

```
import net.jini.discovery.*;
import net.jini.core.lookup.*;
import java.io.IOException;
import java.rmi.RemoteException;
import java.rmi.RMISecurityManager;
```

First, we need to import support for RMI calls, leasing, attribute entry, and template matching.

```
import java.rmi.server.UnicastRemoteObject;
import java.rmi.MarshalledObject;
import net.jini.core.event.*;
import net.jini.core.lease.*;
import net.jini.lease.LeaseRenewalManager;

import net.jini.lookup.entry.Name;
import net.jini.core.entry.Entry;
```

Note that `EvtClient` class itself extends `java.rmi.server.UnicastRemoteObject`. This means that any references passed out of `EvtClient` will be automatically 'made' remote by the RMI runtime. We do not have to export the references explicitly.

The implementation of `DiscoveryListener` is created for handling non-remote notifications whenever an instance of a lookup service is discovered within the Jini federation. On the other hand, the implementation of `RemoteEventListener` is for remote notification from the lookup service whenever an instance of a specific service of interest registers with, or leaves, the lookup service/federation, or when its registration with the lookup service changes.

```
public class EvtClient extends UnicastRemoteObject implements
    DiscoveryListener, RemoteEventListener
{
    protected  ServiceRegistrar[] registrars;
    static final int MAX_MATCHES = 5;
```

The `main()` method creates an instance of `EvtClient` and sits dormant while the client waits for remote notifications from the lookup service. Optionally, if a command line argument exists, it passes it into the constructor of `EvtClient`. This command line argument can be use to specify the groups that this `EvtClient` instance should attempt to join (that is, discover lookup services for).

```
        static public void main(String argv[])
          {
            EvtClient myApp = null;
```

245

```
    try
      {
        if (argv.length > 0)
          myApp = new EvtClient(argv);
      else
          myApp = new EvtClient(null);
          synchronized (myApp)
            {
                myApp.wait(0);
            }
      }
    catch(Exception e)
      {
          System.exit(0);
      }
  }
```

The `doLookupWork()` method, like the variations that we have seen in the previous chapter, examines the service item of the registrar (proxy of reggie) and prints out some interesting information such as its service ID and the group that it services.

```
private void doLookupWork()
  {
    ServiceMatches matches = null;
    String [] groups;
    String msg = null;
    if(registrars.length > 0)
      {
        msg = "";
        System.out.println("-------------------------------------------");
        System.out.println("Registrar: " + registrars[0].getServiceID());
        try
          {
            groups = registrars[0].getGroups();
            if (groups.length > 0)

                for (int o=0; o<groups.length; o++)
                  {
                      msg += groups[o] + " ";
                  }
                System.out.println("Groups Supported: " + msg);
          }
        catch (Exception e)
          {
              e.printStackTrace();
              System.exit(1);
          }
      }
  }
```

The constructor creates an `RMISecurityManager` as the client will be downloading proxies from the lookup service. It also starts a `LookupDiscovery` instance to handle discovery of lookup services within the specified groups from the input argument (or null which is the same as `LookupDiscovery.ALL_GROUPS`).

```
    public EvtClient() throws RemoteException
      {
        ClientCore(null);
      }

    public EvtClient(String [] ingroups)   throws RemoteException
      {
         ClientCore(ingroups);
      }

    private void ClientCore(String [] ingroups) throws RemoteException
      {
        if (System.getSecurityManager() == null)
          {
            System.setSecurityManager(new RMISecurityManager());
          }
        LookupDiscovery discover = null;

        try
          {
            discover = new LookupDiscovery(LookupDiscovery.NO_GROUPS);
            discover.addDiscoveryListener(this);
            discover.setGroups(ingroups);
          }
        catch(IOException e)
          {
            System.err.println(e.toString());
            e.printStackTrace();
            System.exit(1);
          }
      }
```

The `discovered()` method is an event notification method on the `DiscoveryListener` interface. It is called when the discovery protocol has produced a set of lookup service proxies. Here we save the reference to the proxies and simply call the `doLookupWork()` and the `doEventReg()` methods.

```
    public synchronized void discovered(DiscoveryEvent evt) {
          registrars = evt.getRegistrars();
          doLookupWork();
          doEventReg();
      }

    public void discarded(DiscoveryEvent evt) {

      }
```

The `doEventReg()` creates a template to specify matches based on attribute `Name="one"`. We submit the template to the `notify()` method of the reggie proxy, and request for notification on both `TRANSITION_NOMATCH_MATCH` and `TRANSITION_MATCH_NOMATCH` transitions by logically ORing them. The consumer in this case is also the listener, therefore we pass the `this` reference for the `RemoteEventListener` argument. RMI runtime will automatically export our server and supply our stub object (`EvtClient_Stub`) to the client via the codebase. For the handback object, we have used a marshalled version of the reggie proxy itself. It is done here just to show how to create a `MarshalledObject`, and is not actually used. We request a permanent lease on the registration, which we know reggie will likely not grant. Whatever duration reggie decides to grant, we will pass the lease returned within the `EventRegistration` instance to a `LeaseRenewalManager` that will handle the 'forever' renewal of lease for us automatically.

```
public  EventRegistration myReg = null;

    protected void doEventReg()
        {
        if (registrars.length > 0)
            {
            Entry myAttrib[] = new Entry[1];
            myAttrib[0] = new Name("one");

          try
             {
                myReg = registrars[0].notify(new
                    ServiceTemplate(null,null,myAttrib) /* tmpl */,
                    ServiceRegistrar.TRANSITION_NOMATCH_MATCH |
                    ServiceRegistrar.TRANSITION_MATCH_NOMATCH,
                    this,
                    new MarshalledObject(registrars[0])   /* handback */,
                    Lease.FOREVER  );
             }
          catch (RemoteException ex)
             {
               ex.printStackTrace();
               System.exit(1);
             }
          catch (IOException ex)
             {
               ex.printStackTrace();
               System.exit(1);
             }

            new LeaseRenewalManager(myReg.getLease(), Lease.FOREVER, null);
          }
        }
```

Finally, the `notify()` method implements the only method on the `RemoteEventListener` interface.
This is essentially the event notification method. Here, we simply dissect and print some interesting
information on the `RemoteEvent` that is supplied. Since we know that the event is actually a subclass of
`RemoteEvent` called `ServiceEvent`, we can obtain the additional information provided by this event.

```
    public synchronized void notify (RemoteEvent inEvt) throws
       UnknownEventException, RemoteException
       {
        ServiceEvent srvEvt = (ServiceEvent) inEvt;
        System.out.println("got a notification from:");
        ServiceRegistrar mySrc = (ServiceRegistrar) srvEvt.getSource();
        System.out.println("   Source service ID: " + mySrc.getServiceID());
        System.out.println("   Event ID: " + srvEvt.getID());
        System.out.println("   Sequence Number: " +
            srvEvt.getSequenceNumber());
        System.out.println("   Due to Proxy: " + srvEvt.getServiceID());

        if (srvEvt.getServiceItem() == null)
           System.out.println("   Proxy Deleted");
        else
           System.out.println("   Attributes: " +
              srvEvt.getServiceItem().attributeSets[0]);
           System.out.println("   Transition: " + srvEvt.getTransition());
       }
    }
```

Run the batch file to compile the code:

```
..\bats\buildit EvtClient.java
```

Next, we need to create the RMI stubs.

Creating RMI Stubs

As we saw earlier, the RemoteEventListener interface is an RMI interface. We create RMI stubs using the rmic utility provided by the JDK. A batch file called makejar.bat is supplied for this purpose; you will find it in the ch7\code\EvtClient directory. The batch file contains:

```
call ..\bats\setpaths.bat
rmic -classpath %JINIJARS%;. -v1.2 EvtClient
jar cvf EvtClient-dl.jar EvtClient_Stub.class
copy EvtClient-dl.jar %WROXHOME%
```

rmic is used to create the RMI stubs required by EvtClient. A JAR file is then created with the stub and copied to the root of the stubs class server.

> **Case-Sensitivity Caveat**
> **Be very careful of case-sensitivity if you're creating JAR files on a Win32 system.**
> **Spelling** EvtClient_Stub.class **as** EvtClient_stub.class **will still work on a**
> **Win32 command line, but create a horrible mess when you get around to debugging: it**
> **will lead to service event notifications that cannot locate the classes it needs.**

Testing the Event Client

To test the event client, we will need to:

❑   Change directory to the ch7\code\bats directory where the startup batch files are located

❑   Delete the log directories for reggie and rmid to clear up previously stored states from other experiments; you can use the runclean.bat file under Windows 95/98 (or manually remove the directories in Win2000 or NT)

❑   Start the HTTP class server by starting runhttpd.bat

❑   Start the stubs serving class server by starting runhttpdstubs.bat

❑   Start the RMI Activation daemon, RMID, by starting runrmid.bat

❑   Start one copy of reggie on the iguanas group by starting the runlookup1.bat file

❑   Wait for the setup VM to complete, now reggie is running properly

❑   Change directory to Ch7\code\EvtClient directory

❑   Start our event client by executing the runevt.bat file in this directory, it contains:

```
call ..\bats\setpaths.bat
java -classpath .;%JINIJARS%  -Dnet.jini.discovery.interface=%ADAPTERIP%  -
Djava.security.policy=policy.all -
Djava.rmi.server.codebase=http://%STUBHOST%/EvtClient-dl.jar EvtClient %1 %2
```

At this point, you should see our client discover the lookup service, and an indication of the registration with the service for event notifications. The output from the client should be similar to this:

Since there aren't any services joining or leaving the federation, there is no transition from the match/no-match states within the lookup service, so we ought to start such a service.

Go to the Ch9\code\hitman directory, we will borrow a service for this purpose. Don't worry about what it does for now, because we will be taking a detailed look at this service in the transaction coverage of this chapter. For now, you only need to know that the proxy registered by this service will have the attribute Name="one" that is necessary to trigger the desired transition. This will cause reggie to send an event to our waiting client. Compile the Hitman service by using:

```
..\bats\buildit HitmanService.java
```

Create the stubs by using:

```
makejar
```

Create a directory for the log files:

```
md hitlogs
```

Finally, start the HitmanService by running the runhit1.bat file.

The following image shows what the HitmanService should look like after it has started. It actually has a GUI. In fact, if you do click on the button, it will do an orderly un-registration with the lookup service by canceling the lease on the proxy registration – but don't click it yet:

Shortly after starting the service, you should see the remote event being caught and decoded by our EvtClient. This shows something close to what you should see:

What's happened is that the search template that specifies the attribute Name="one" has switched from a no_match to match state when the HitmanService proxy is registered. This is exactly what the client registered for.

To observe the event sent when transitioning from match to no_match (numeric value is 2) click the button on the HitmanService GUI to perform an orderly de-registration of the service's proxy.

You should see the EvtClient printing out the details of the new event received. Here we see this new decoded output.

You may want to repeat this and observe the event ID and sequence number being assigned by reggie in this scenario.

Implementing an Event Producer

Now to turn the tables and see how the services implement a remote event producer. As you might expect, this is a bit more complicated than implementing a consumer.

Specifically, the event generator needs to:

- ❏ Provide event registration (Jini does not specify how this should be implemented) and keep track of the registrations
- ❏ Monitor and scan for the state changes
- ❏ Co-ordinate event firing to all the interested consumers
- ❏ Assign eventIDs and sequence numbers to satisfy the application's needs

We'll provide an event registration mechanism for the event generator through a new interface called IndexKeeperRemote. This interface inherits from IndexKeeper, but adds a remote event registration method to it:

```
import net.jini.core.event.RemoteEventListener;
import net.jini.core.event.EventRegistration;

public interface IndexKeeperRemote extends IndexKeeper,java.rmi.Remote
  {
```

```
    public EventRegistration addRemoteListener(RemoteEventListener listener)
        throws java.rmi.RemoteException;

}
```

Note that the interface is also made remote, unlike the original `IndexKeeper` implementation. This means that the proxy object that is stored within the lookup service will be an RMI stub to an implementation of `IndexKeeperRemote` – and not a custom `IndexKeeper` object as we have seen previously.

The state-change we're looking for is simply a specified elapse of time. We'll use a thread that goes to sleep, waking at intermittent intervals to fire events to interested clients. It co-ordinates the firing of events by sequentially scanning the list of registered listeners, and creates a thread that will fire the event. This means that the event producing application will not be blocked by a notification call taking a long time to process (out of order event delivery will also be a distinct possibility).

The event ID is assigned according to the position of the registration in the list of listener registrations. This will be the same for all events from the same registration. The sequence number is implemented globally across all event types, and will increment irregularly should there be more than one type of event registration. In other words, the sequence numbers aren't ordered.

The code for the service can be found in the `ch7\code\EvtService` directory. Here is the `EvtService.java` source code:

```
import java.rmi.Remote;
import java.rmi.server.RemoteObject;
```

We need to import RMI support, lookup entry for attribute management, discovery protocol support and the `JoinManager`.

```
import java.rmi.server.UnicastRemoteObject;
import java.rmi.MarshalledObject;
import net.jini.core.event.RemoteEventListener;
import net.jini.core.event.RemoteEvent;
import net.jini.core.event.EventRegistration;
import java.rmi.RemoteException;
import net.jini.core.event.UnknownEventException ;

import javax.swing.event.EventListenerList;

import net.jini.lookup.ServiceIDListener;
import net.jini.lookup.entry.Name;
import net.jini.core.entry.Entry;
import java.rmi.RemoteException;
import java.rmi.RMISecurityManager;
import net.jini.lookup.JoinManager;
import net.jini.discovery.*;
import net.jini.core.lookup.ServiceID;
```

The `IdPrinter` defined implements the `ServiceIDListener` interface. This is the event notification interface (non-remote) for the service ID assigned by the lookup service. `JoinManager` will make an event notification on the `serviceIDNotify()` method upon a service ID assignment. We print it to standard output as we did before.

```
class IdPrinter implements ServiceIDListener
    {
        int myIndex;
        public IdPrinter(int initIndex)
            {
                myIndex = initIndex;
            }

        // A real service will save the serviceID in persistent store
        public void serviceIDNotify(ServiceID serviceID)
            {
                System.out.println("instance " + myIndex + " has been assigned
                    service ID: " + serviceID.toString());
            }
    }
```

Our `EvtService` class, which implements the remotely callable `IndexKeeperRemote` interface, inherits from `java.rmi.server.UnicastRemoteObject` to make RMI reference handling simple.

```
public class EvtService extends  UnicastRemoteObject implements
    IndexKeeperRemote
        {
            static final int MAX_INSTANCES = 3;
            static final String [] GROUPS1 =  { "iguanas"};
```

`myIndex`, as you might recall from the last chapter, is an instance number given to a specific instance of the service proxy. Since our proxy is actually an RMI stub in this case, the index is assigned to the server-side instance. We maintain a worker thread that will wake up periodically to perform event firing.

The variable `evtSeqNum` holds the global event sequence number, and is initialized to 1. It increments across all events. The worker thread will be incrementing this sequence number by 1 each time it fires an event – regardless of event ID or event type. `meExported` is a temporary holder for the exported instance of the `evtService` itself, and it will be used later by the worker thread to send a remote reference of the source object (within the `RemoteEvent` object) to a listener.

```
            int myIndex = 0;
            Thread worker = null;
            RemoteObject meExported = null;
            long evtSeqNum = 1L;
            protected JoinManager myJM = null;
```

The `main()` method creates an instance of `EvtService`, passing it an integer index that may be supplied as a command line argument. It then sits idle while `JoinManager` and the worker event firing thread goes to work.

```
public static void main(String argv[])
    {
        EvtService myApp = null;
        try
            {
                if (argv.length > 0)
                    myApp = new EvtService(Integer.parseInt(argv[0]));
                else
```

```
            myApp = new EvtService(300);
        }
    catch (Exception e)
        {
            e.printStackTrace();
            System.exit(1);
        }

    synchronized(myApp)
        {
            try
                {
                    myApp.wait(0);
                }
            catch(InterruptedException e)
                {
                    System.exit(0);
                }
        }
    }  // of main()
```

The `EvtService` itself creates an RMI security manager for the `RemoteEventListener` callback.

```
    LookupDiscoveryManager ldm = null;
    JoinManager jm = null;

    public EvtService() throws RemoteException
        {
            StartService(-1);
        }

    public EvtService(int inIndex) throws RemoteException
        {
            StartService(inIndex);
        }
    private void StartService(int inIndex) throws RemoteException
        {
            myIndex = inIndex;
            meExported = this;
            if (System.getSecurityManager() == null)
                {
                    System.setSecurityManager(new RMISecurityManager());
                }
```

It creates the attribute `Name="one"` so that the client will be able to find the service proxy. It also creates the worker thread to fire events occasionally. We will see the sleeper class that implements this thread later. Note that the thread is created in the suspended state at this time. It then creates a `LookupDiscoveryManager` instance to handle discovery protocol for the iguanas group. This `LookupDiscoveryManager` instance, along with the attributes, the RMI proxy, and an instance of the `IdPrinter` class, are supplied as parameters to start the `JoinManager` operation. The `JoinManager` will perform the Join protocol and assure that our service will be available within the iguanas group as long as it is kept alive.

```
                String [] groupsToDiscover = GROUPS1;
                Entry [] attributes = new Entry[1];
                attributes[0] = new Name("one");
                worker = new Thread(new Sleeper(this));
                 try
                    {
                       ldm = new LookupDiscoveryManager(groupsToDiscover,
                                 null /* unicast locators */,
                                 null /* DiscoveryListener */);
                       jm = new JoinManager(this,  /* service */
                                 attributes,
                                 new IdPrinter(myIndex) /* ServiceIDListener*/,
                                 ldm /* DiscoveryManagement */,
                                 null /* LeaseManager */);

                    }
                 catch(Exception e)
                    {
                       e.printStackTrace();
                       System.exit(1);
                    } // catch
                 worker.start();

        }    //EvtService
                attributes[0] = new Name("one");
             worker = new Thread(new Sleeper(this));
                 try
                    {
                       ldm = new LookupDiscoveryManager(groupsToDiscover,
                                 null /* unicast locators */,
                                 null /* DiscoveryListener */);
                       jm = new JoinManager(this,  /* service */
                                 attributes,
                                 new IdPrinter(myIndex) /* ServiceIDListener*/,
                                 ldm /* DiscoveryManagement */,
                                 null /* LeaseManager */);
                    }
                 catch(Exception e)
                    {
                       e.printStackTrace();
                       System.exit(1);
                    } // catch
                 worker.start();

        }    //EvtService
```

The getIndex() method did not change implementation. However, it now retrieves the index for this service instance. This means that every getIndex() call will result in an RMI call from the client to the service.

```
        public int getIndex() throws RemoteException
           {
             return myIndex;
           }
```

Tracking Event Registrations

For convenience, we'll use the general and lightweight `javax.swing.event.EventListenerList` to implement the list of listeners. Although this class can manage heterogeneous lists consisting of listeners of different types, we won't be using this feature of the list in this example.

```
protected EventListenerList myList = new EventListenerList();
```

Here is the event registration handling routine we specified in the new `IndexKeeperRemote` interface. As the Jini specifications don't make recommendations on the correct implementation of registration, we're going to borrow the JavaBeans conventions.

```
public synchronized EventRegistration addRemoteListener(RemoteEventListener
    listener) throws RemoteException
{
    System.out.println("got a registration!");
    myList.add(RemoteEventListener.class, listener);
```

After we have added the listener to the list, we'll find out which position it is actually stored in and note this for the event ID – taking advantage of this specific list implementation and knowing that the position will not change unless the listener element is removed (for this simple example, we will ignore the need to remove listeners).

```
    //find out where it is added to determine event ID
    long tpEventID = 0;
    Object[] listenerList = myList.getListenerList();
    for (int i = listenerList.length - 2; i >= 0; i -= 2)
        {
            if (listenerList[i+1].equals(listener))
                {
                    tpEventID = i+1;
                    break;
                }
        }
    return new EventRegistration(tpEventID, this, null, evtSeqNum);
}
```

Once we have the event ID, we can return the source producer, event ID, current sequence number, and a lease back to the client within an `EventRegistration` instance. We're not creating a lease at this point, but we will later on.

Firing Events

The next method, `fireRemoteEvent()` iterates through the listener list and fires an event for each listener within the list. It will be executed by the worker thread.

```
public void fireRemoteEvent()
    {
        RemoteEvent anEvent = null;
        System.out.println("Checking for listeners...");
        Object[] listeners = myList.getListenerList();

        for (int i = listeners.length - 2; i >= 0; i -= 2)
            {
```

```
          if (listeners[i] == RemoteEventListener.class)
            { // redundant check in      our case
              RemoteEventListener aList = (RemoteEventListener) listeners[i+1];
          try
            {
              if (anEvent == null)
                {
                  anEvent = new RemoteEvent(meExported, i+1,
                            evtSeqNum++, null);
                }
```

Note that the worker thread itself makes use of short-lived threads to fire the events. This will make sure that the worker thread will not be blocked by a `notify()` call on a listener that does not return for a long time. Remember that `notify()` calls are synchronous RMI calls.

```
              System.out.println("Fired one event...");
              // use short temporary threads to avoid blocking
              new Thread(new Notifier(aList, anEvent)).start();
            }
          catch(Exception ex)
            {
              ex.printStackTrace();
            }
            }// of if listener==RemoteEventLister.class
          } // of for i
      }    // of fireRemoteEvent
  }
```

The sleeper class actually implements the logic of the worker thread. It will sleep for 30 seconds, wake up and fire remote events until the service terminates.

```
class Sleeper implements Runnable
  {
    EvtService myService;

    public Sleeper(EvtService inServ)
      {
        myService = inServ;
      }
    public void run()
      {
        int loopCounter = 1;
        while(true)
          {
            System.out.println("in loop... " + loopCounter++);
            System.out.flush();
          try
            {
              Thread.sleep(30000L);
            }
          catch (Exception e) {}
          myService.fireRemoteEvent();
          }
      }
  }
```

The class `Notifier` implements the actual notification for any specific listener. It is a worker thread that is created by the main worker thread. The lifetime of this thread is exactly one single event notification. This is not good production code for most VMs – a more complex thread-pool based implementation would be significantly more efficient. However, we've kept things simple here to help emphasize the event handling and firing logic.

```
class Notifier implements Runnable
  {
    RemoteEventListener myListener;
    RemoteEvent myEvent;
    public Notifier( RemoteEventListener inLis, RemoteEvent inEvt)
      {
        myListener = inLis;
        myEvent = inEvt;
      }
    public void run()
      {
        try
          {
              myListener.notify(myEvent);
          }
        catch (Exception e)
          {
             e.printStackTrace();
          }
      }
  }
```

That is all the code to the service. From the `ch7\code\EvtService` directory, compile the code using:

```
..\bats\buildit EvtService.java
```

Making RMI Stubs

We need to create RMI stubs for the `IndexKeeperRemote` remote interface that we are implementing. These stubs will also be the proxy objects that will be shipped to the lookup service. We can make the RMI stub using the batch file in the `ch7\code\EvtService` directory: `makejar.bat`. it contains:

```
call ..\bats\setpaths.bat
rmic -classpath %JINIJARS%;. -v1.2 EvtService
jar cvf EvtService-dl.jar EvtService_Stub.class IndexKeeperRemote.class
IndexKeeper.class
copy EvtService-dl.jar %WROXHOME%
```

The batch file above will create the JAR file containing the stub and related class. It will also copy the resulting JAR file into the root directory of the HTTP class server for stubs as well.

We are now ready to test the event producer service. However, we do not yet have a client that understands the `IndexKeeperRemote` interface used for this service.

Modifying the EvtClient to use EvtService

Since the `EvtClient` application was first coded to use reggie for event registration, we can quickly adapt it for use with our `EvtService`.

You will find the source code in the ch7\code\EvtClient2 directory of the distribution. We have actually inherited from EvtClient and then made it compatible with EvtService. Because of this, you must copy over EvtClient.class from the ch7\code\EvtClient directory before compiling the source.

In addition, we will also need to copy over the IndexKeeperRemote.java interface file and the IndexKeeper.java file that it is based on.

The doEventReg() method now uses the class type IndexKeeperRemote to find the proxy instead of attributeName="one". It also calls the addRemoteListener() method to add itself as a listener, instead of the notify() method of the ServiceRegistrar as before.

```java
protected void doEventReg()
    {
      if (registrars.length > 0)
        {
            Class [] myClassType = { IndexKeeperRemote.class };

        try
          {
            IndexKeeperRemote myES = (IndexKeeperRemote) registrars[0].lookup(new
                                   ServiceTemplate(null,myClassType,null));
          if (myES != null)
            {
               myES.addRemoteListener(this);
               System.out.println("registered our interest in the event...");
            }
          else
             System.out.println("cannot find any proxy for event service...");
        }
          catch (RemoteException ex)
            {
                ex.printStackTrace();
                System.exit(1);
            }
          catch (IOException ex)
            {
                ex.printStackTrace();
                System.exit(1);
            }
        }
    }
```

The other minor modification required is to change the reference from the ServiceRegistrar to the IndexKeeperRemote interface within the notify() event notification method.

```java
public synchronized void notify (RemoteEvent inEvt) throws
    UnknownEventException, RemoteException
    {
      RemoteEvent srvEvt =  inEvt;
      System.out.println("got a notification from:");
      IndexKeeperRemote mySrc = (IndexKeeperRemote) srvEvt.getSource();
      System.out.println("   Source instance: " + mySrc.getIndex());
      System.out.println("   Event ID: " + srvEvt.getID());
      System.out.println("   Sequence Number: " + srvEvt.getSequenceNumber());
    }
```

Those are all the changes necessary. Follow the steps listed earlier to compile, make stub, and make the necessary JAR file for this new EvtClient.

Testing Our Own Remote Event Producer and Consumer

To test out the new `EvtClient2` and the `EvtService`, we perform the following steps.

- ❏ Change directory to the location of the startup files

- ❏ Clean up the log files by running runclean.bat or remove the log directories manually.

- ❏ Start the class server by running the batch file runhttpd.bat

- ❏ Start the stub class server by running the batch file runhttpdstubs.bat

- ❏ Start the rmid activation daemon by running the batch file runrmid.bat; this should also start the reggie instance from before

- ❏ Change directory to the location of the EvtService by running the runevt.bat file. This file contains:

```
call ..\bats\setpaths.bat
java -classpath .;%JINIJARS%  -Dnet.jini.discovery.interface=%ADAPTERIP% -
Djava.security.policy=policy.all -
Djava.rmi.server.codebase=http://%STUBHOST%/EvtService-dl.jar EvtService %1 %2 %3
```

At this point, you should see the service coming up and a service ID being assigned by reggie

- ❏ Open another command shell with the JDK/Jini environment set, and change directory to Ch7\code\EvtClient2

- ❏ Start an instance of the client using the runevt.bat file in this directory. You should see the client starting up, locate the lookup service, and then make a registration with the service

On the service side, you'll see a message indicating the worker thread has checked the listener list, and you should see the event registration on the service output.

If you wait until the next worker thread sweep, you should see the worker thread announce that it has fired an event.

You can also see in the client output that the remote event notification has been received and decoded. The remote instance number printed (300) was obtained by a call to the getIndex() method which executes on the service side.

So we've successfully created a remote event consumer that works well with lookup services like reggie, by creating an event producer service and modifying the original consumer to work with our service.

Summary

In this chapter, we have thoroughly explored remote events in the Jini context. First, we reviewed and re-examined the Java event model, and saw how remote events extend the same listener code pattern from intra-Java VM to across the network. The unreliable transport across a network has made event implementation across a network more difficult to implement than the local version.

We saw the single interface `RemoteEventListener`, and single class `RemoteEvent` that Jini's remote events are based on. We talked about the ability to compose multiple Jini services together to form an event processing pipeline. The concept of third-party event services was introduced, and the importance of selecting the right algorithm for generating event ID and sequence numbers was discussed.

Through hands-on coding, we worked with the Jini lookup service (reggie) by registering to receive remote events whenever a registered service changes states. Finally, we created our own event notification service that will accept event registrations from clients. We have also modified the original event client to work with our own event notification service.

In the next section, we will cover the one issue that we have purposely avoided in our implementation – distributed leases in Jini.

Jini Client or Service	JavaSpaces and Helper Services

Jini Client and Service Support Helper Utilities

Jini Discovery Management Helper Utilities

Jini Protocol Helper Utilities

Jini Network Protocols	
	RMI and Rich Object Semantics
	Java VM and Networking

Network Protocols

8

Distributed Leasing in Jini

In this chapter, we're going to examine the role distributed leases play in the Jini model, their particular operation model, the code that is used to obtain and maintain leases, and the code one may use to grant leases. We're going to look at:

❑   Granting and receiving leases

❑   Renewing, canceling and expiring leases

❑   The importance of leasing for Jini's resource management

❑   The implementation assistance that Jini provides for both the lease receiver and the lease grantor

Applied Distributed Leasing

In our analysis of the lookup service in Chapter 6, we had a functional block dedicated to granting and maintaining leases. A Jini lookup service grants leases to both service proxy registrations and client event solicitations.

Leases and Distributed Allocation of Finite Resources

We saw the advantages of maintaining service registrations through leases in Chapter 6, when the three reggies we worked with were eventually cleaned up after the SixpackService was terminated. Without leases, service registrations would accumulate – because a Jini service is designed to be long-lived and persists state through crashes and restarts – and eventually result in resource depletion as every registration takes up valuable space in the proxies store and consumes memory with its associated data structures. Therefore, it is a very good idea to lease the allocation of any finite resource in a Jini system.

Resource space is allocated to clients through a very basic negotiation process that enables the system to reclaim resources effectively. Each consumer of these distributed resources must regularly demonstrate an active interest in order to maintain their resource allocation. Should a consumer fail to continue registering interest, crash, or disconnect, the system itself will eventually expire the resource lease.

When Not to Lease

There is an exception to this 'lease all resources' idiom: the service proxy object that is sent from the lookup service to the client is not associated with a lease. This is done for two reasons. Firstly, although the lookup service does return a service item (proxy) to the client, this is in fact a copy of the proxy, which remains registered. Secondly, the lookup service's obligations within that particular loop are completed on return of the proxy copy; the client uses the proxy to communicate directly with the service thereafter. The lookup service doesn't hold any information about the destination of any particular proxy, or any resources of any type associated with the proxy that has been given away. In fact, the lookup service can do anything with its own copy of the proxy with no effect to the consumer who had received the copy. This is fundamentally different from the service registration scenario, where the registration uses memory and storage resources managed by the lookup service, and the event registration scenario, where the registration consumes processing resources as well, to actively monitor transitions within the lookup service.

Negotiating Lease Duration

A lease is granted based on specified time duration, an absolute expiry time being set with respect to the clock of the lease recipient. The negotiation process specified by Jini is simple – a lease is requested for a specified duration, and the lease grantor considers the request, and either grants the duration it wants to, or rejects the request altogether. This is a one-step lease negotiation process, and the lease grantor's decision is final. This is important as the typical Jini client is likely to be the recipient of many leases, and this simple process keeps the number of negotiations over-the-network minimal, and the client coding simple. Here we see this one-step negotiation process:

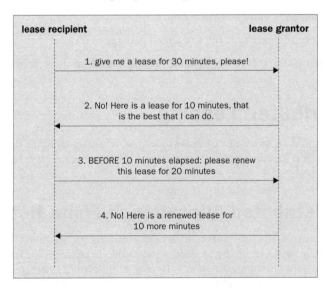

The Jini specifications are not defined in a rigid API for leasing, so the software developer has free rein to implement the method or interface best suited to the application.

Lease Renewal

Once a lease is granted, the onus is on the client to renew the lease for as long as necessary. Lease renewal, also known as 'proof of interest', should take place ahead of expiry time, so that network latency or service loads don't interfere.

The duration of a renewed lease is not added onto the remaining duration of the lease being renewed. Upon successful renewal, a new lease of the desired duration (or some maximum duration imposed by the grantor) is returned. If the renewal fails, the remaining duration left on the lease being renewed will still be effective. This provides the lease recipient with a window of opportunity to retry failed lease renewal.

Although it is possible to ask for service duration to last indefinitely, this effectively disables leasing and introduces the very problems of distributed resource leaks and depletion. Therefore, granting of leases for indefinite duration is to be avoided. Almost all well-behaved Jini services (reggie, and Mercury, for example,) will not grant an indefinite lease request, but will grant a reasonable duration lease (for example, 5 minutes).

There is a design trade-off that the lease grantor must balance; while granting short duration leases keeps the state of the service current, it does so at the expense of increased network renewal processing and traffic. Granting longer duration leases decreases processing and network renewal traffic, but the service will inevitably wind up maintaining stale states for a longer period of time.

A very helpful Jini library class for handling lease renewal for us is called the `LeaseRenewalManager` helper utility. We will provide a detailed coverage of this class in Chapter 11. Interested readers may skip ahead to the detailed coverage of `LeaseRenewalManager` before continuing this examination. The `LeaseRenewalManager` can maintain indefinite leases, and will handle the lease renewal required by the service. You might well be wondering whether this third party manager flouts the best-practice policy of reasonable and repetitive lease allocation.

Oddly enough, it doesn't. The `LeaseRenewalManager` doesn't actually *grant* leases, it merely manages leases that have already been granted by a remote grantor. The value-add that the `LeaseRenewalManager` brings is in allowing a specification of a 'period of employment' when it goes to work and constantly renews the lease on another party's behalf, which is very different from `LeaseRenewalManager` granting leases on resources itself.

What the `LeaseRenewalManager` does do is bring leasing policies in line with the long-lived system. More specifically, the `LeaseRenewalManager` lives within the same VM alongside the user. From the outside, neither the grantor nor anybody else can tell whether the user is using a `LeaseRenewalManager`. Should the VM die or fail for any reason, the `LeaseRenewalManager` instance will go with it. The distributed resources held on behalf of the user will be relinquished afterwards because the `LeaseRenewalManager` will not be renewing it.

The Lease Interface

So far a Jini lease has had the appearance of an object carrying duration information. In reality, Jini has specified `Lease` as an interface, which allows the lease grantor to supply any object, as long as it implements the `Lease` interface, to a recipient as a lease. This means that a typical `Lease` object may have other associated application specific states and methods associated. Here is what the `Lease` interface looks like:

```
public interface Lease
  {
    long FOREVER = Long.MAX_VALUE;
    long ANY = -1;
    int DURATION = 1;
    int ABSOLUTE = 2;
    long getExpiration();
    void cancel() throws UnknownLeaseException, RemoteException;
```

```
    void renew(long duration) throws LeaseDeniedException,
        UnknownLeaseException, RemoteException;
    void setSerialFormat(int format);
    int getSerialFormat();
    LeaseMap createLeaseMap(long duration);
    boolean canBatch(Lease lease);
}
```

The cancel() and renew() methods both throw RemoteException, while the rest of the methods do not. The only information that can be transmitted with the lease, and does not change, is the duration of the lease. This is why operations on the duration are local and do not throw RemoteException.

Only the remote service, which has an overview of resource allocation, can make granting or renewing decisions – therefore the renew() call must be handled remotely by the service. Since the service also maintains all outstanding leases on resources, a cancel operation also must be executed remotely on the service.

The use of RemoteException in this case *does not* imply mandatory support for RMI (unlike the RemoteEventListener case with distributed events). Instead, the object that implements the Lease interface (essentially a proxy object for lease handling) must decide on what mechanism to use for communicating with the actual service. One can readily use CORBA or socket programming to perform this communication. Although RemoteException belongs to the java.rmi package, in practice it should be thought of as a generic network communication error.

Clockskew – Relative and Absolute Durations

Clocks on different machines can and do carry different times – such is the network. Jini leases must, and do, operate given these circumstances.

Synchronizing clocks in a network is a well-known 'hard' problem to solve. If Jini was dependent on network-wide synchronized clocks, it really wouldn't be a terribly useful technology. Thankfully, the distributed leases specified are not dependent on network clock synchronization.

Relative time is used for this purpose. The fluctuation of clocks on machines measured against the reference atomic clock is called clockskew. Clockskew variations on most machines are negligible when leases are expressed in terms of seconds and minutes. That is, in almost all cases, the expiry time for a lease that expires 5 minutes in the future will be more or less the same on all machines. Lease durations should be specified in terms of relative time when transmitted between machines, to prevent clock synchronization problems.

Jini services are required to persist state (if the service is a long-lived one) whenever changes occur, and are therefore written into persistent storage. Currently granted leases must become part of this saved state. Should the service fail, duration based leases persisted to disk are completely useless unless there is some way of remembering when the lease was actually written – equivalent to writing the lease out in absolute time. Therefore lease duration should be always be specified in absolute time when written into persistent storage.

The problem of time synchronization between machines doesn't play a part here, as the machine that reads the leases back from the persistent store is one and the same machine as that which wrote absolute time in the first place.

So, to take a look at the Lease interface again, the remaining methods should make sense:

```
public interface Lease
    {
```

```
long FOREVER = Long.MAX_VALUE;
long ANY = -1;
int DURATION = 1;
int ABSOLUTE = 2;
long getExpiration();
void cancel() throws UnknownLeaseException, RemoteException;
void renew(long duration) throws LeaseDeniedException,
    UnknownLeaseException, RemoteException;
void setSerialFormat(int format);
int getSerialFormat();
LeaseMap createLeaseMap(long duration);
boolean canBatch(Lease lease);
}
```

The constants DURATION and ABSOLUTE are used in the setSerialFormat() method call to control the format that will be used to serialize the lease – DURATION for inter-machine communication or ABSOLUTE for persistence. getExpiration() will always return an absolute expiration time with respect to the local clock of the caller.

Lease Maintenance Optimization: LeaseMap

During normal operation, a Jini client is likely to hold onto and renew many leases from many different producers. Coding this task alone can account for a very large portion of the application logic, and the bandwidth consumed by lease renewal over the network can be significant. Although versatile utility classes like LeaseRenewalManager might simplify the code, they still aren't going to solve the bandwidth consumption problem if LeaseRenewalManager were to renew each lease individually below the surface. Fortunately, it doesn't.

Jini specifies a lease batching mechanism called the LeaseMap that better utilizes network bandwidth.

```
public interface LeaseMap extends java.util.Map
  {
    boolean canContainKey(Object key);
    void renewAll() throws LeaseMapException, RemoteException;
    void cancelAll() throws LeaseMapException, RemoteException;
  }
```

A LeaseMap allows leases to be batched together, enabling multiple renewals and cancellations to be performed at once. The map associates a lease with a duration time (of type long) – the time requested at lease renewal. You can create a LeaseMap instance using the createLeaseMap() method of the Lease interface. The LeaseMap that you obtain from this call will initially contain one single element: the lease instance on which you've called createLeaseMap(), associated with the long argument that you've passed it. Since leases might well have originated from distinct places and generators, it is not always possible or efficient to batch all leases together. The canContainKey() method on a LeaseMap enables you to check if a specific lease can be batched together with the other leases already in the map. The canBatch() method on the Lease interface can be used to test to see if a specific lease can be batched together with another (single) lease.

Why or how to determine if certain leases can be batched together is not specified, because it's liable to be highly application specific. Leases originating from two completely different grantor machines may be batched together sometimes if a common third party is actually performing the lease renewal and cancellation on its behalf, for example.

Thankfully, utility classes like the indispensable `LeaseRenewalManager` remove most of the complexity from managing, batching, and renewing leases. It batches leases into `LeaseMaps` and renews or cancels them efficiently so that the individual developer doesn't have to think about it.

Granting Leases – Jini Landlords

Implementing lease management for a recipient might be complicated and tedious, but it's even worse on the grantor side. An application client/service that decides to grant leases for resources that it holds has a lot to take care of:

- ❏ Managing, allocating and releasing resources on the one hand, while granting and canceling associated leases on the other
- ❏ Managing the leases themselves
- ❏ Designing a lease allocation and renewal policy that makes sense for the application at hand
- ❏ Implementing the proxy object on the client end that supports the `Lease` interface
- ❏ Supporting the proxy object, enhancing efficiency through `LeaseMap` based lease batching

Before we get down to the nitty-gritty of designing and implementing a grantor that fulfils all these requirements, we'll explore the 'non-intrusive' support for building a lease grantor provided by the Jini libraries.

The Jini libraries provide a set of support interfaces and classes for implementation of lease grantor logic following the `Landlord` model. Not all resource allocations can be made to fit this model. However, for those that can, the `Landlord` support classes make granting and management of leases substantially simpler and less tedious. For example, the Javaspace reference implementation (outrigger) uses the `Landlord` support class while reggie doesn't.

What To Take a Lease Out On?

The things that we may want to take a lease out on are as varied as potential Jini applications themselves:

It might be something physical:

- ❏ Disk storage
- ❏ Physical/virtual memory
- ❏ Seats on an airplane

Or something semi-intangible:

- ❏ Computational time
- ❏ An hour-long meeting room booking

Or something completely intangible

- ❏ Temporary bandwidth boost between two components
- ❏ The probability of being served within the next 10 minutes
- ❏ A future right to contend for certain scarce resources

Obviously, all of these have very distinct handling and management requirements. It's almost impossible to even begin providing a general framework without restricting the possible application.

Jini Library Support for Lease Grantors

The Jini support libraries, through the `Landlord` model, attempt to make the implementation of a lease grantor straightforward, without restricting implementation in any way. In no way is a lease grantor implementation required to use Jini's library support – it can freely roll its own implementation from scratch.

The bottom line is that the only interface that your object must support is the `Lease` interface. Since the `Lease` interface contains both local and remote methods, an implementation of a proxy object is necessary – the Jini library provides a pre-built proxy class: `com.sun.jini.lease.landlord.LandlordLease`.

Instances of this class provide complete `Lease` interface implementations to lease recipients, and talks back over-the-wire to a matching object that implements the `Landlord` remote interface (also referred to as the `Landlord` protocol). This effectively reduces a grantor's coding work to the implementation of an object that supports the `Landlord` remote interface.

At the very root of the lease implementation library hierarchy is the `com.sun.jini.lease.AbstractLease`, an abstract class that Jini's `LandlordLease` library proxy inherits from. The `AbstractLease` class handles functionality such as absolute versus relative time, and leaves the rest for its subclasses to handle. If you're implementing your own non-`Landlord` leases, you should consider using the `AbstractLease` as a base class and save yourself some work.

The following diagram illustrates this relationship between the `AbstractLease`, `LandlordLease`, and your own `Landlord` implementation.

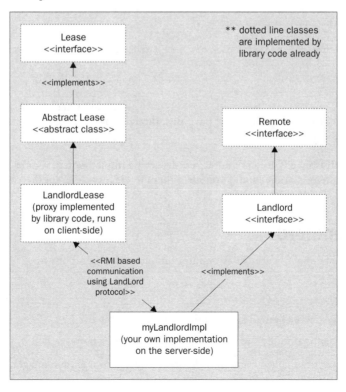

The Landlord Remote Interface

Creating a lease grantor implementation is as easy as implementing a class on the service that implements the remote Landlord interface.

Here it is:

```
public interface Landlord extends Remote
  {
    public long renew(Object cookie, long extension)
        throws LeaseDeniedException, UnknownLeaseException, RemoteException;
    public void cancel(Object cookie)
        throws UnknownLeaseException, RemoteException;
    public RenewResults renewAll(Object[] cookie, long[] extension)
        throws RemoteException;
    public void cancelAll(Object[] cookie)
        throws LeaseMapException, RemoteException;
  }
```

This means that all grantors supporting the LandlordLease proxy only need to implement the renew() cancel() renewAll() and cancelAll() methods. The LandlordLease proxy and its super class take care of the other methods of the Lease interface.

Now, given that you have an object that implements the Landlord interface on the service side, how do you go about creating the LandlordLease proxy? Well, you use the static factory class LandlordLease.Factory provided by the Jini support library:

```
public static class LandlordLease.Factory extends java.lang.Object
    implements LandlordLeaseFactory
  {
    public Lease newLease(Object cookie, Landlord landlord, long duration)
        throws LeaseDeniedException
  }
```

As you can see, this implements the LandlordLeaseFactory interface, which is handy if you ever want to create your own factory. For most purposes, though, the LandlordLease.Factory implementation is just fine.

Although Jini does not specify how a Landlord should be implemented, it does, however, provide a set of interfaces for implementation should you need them to cleanly separate the components within the internal design of a Landlord.

Inside the Landlord

The Landlord package makes certain assumptions about what a Landlord is.

The Landlord:

❑   Owns the resources being leased, and knows the big picture

❑   Does not usually do much work, but delegates to others better suited to particular jobs

❑   May delegate the management of its leased resources to a lease manager

❑   May delegate the granting and renewal of leases and associated management of resources to a policy implementation

❑   Permits direct communications between its two delegates

The Lease Policy Manager manages the renewal of leases and implements a specific policy. Each implementation can contain a different renewal strategy (that is, some may give only a fixed duration lease, other may be sensitive to the current level of resource allocation). The Landlord delegates the `renew()` and `renewall()` operations to it. It will have direct access to the leased resources in order to determine if a lease should be renewed.

The leases themselves are managed by the Lease Manager. The Lease Manager manages the association of lease with the leased resources. The Landlord delegates the `cancel()` and `cancelall()` methods to it. It is assumed that the Lease Policy Manager and the Lease Manager will share the task of managing the leased resources and communicate between themselves to ensure consistent state and handling.

This illustration shows the Landlord and the implied delegation model.

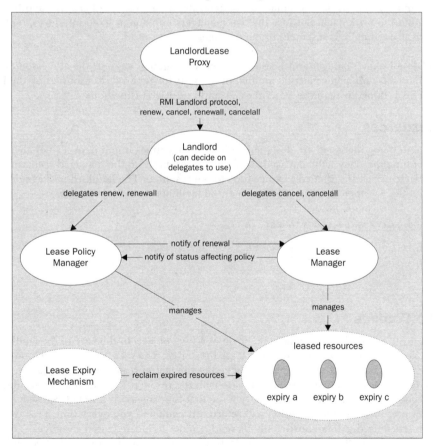

So schematically speaking, the Jini supported internal decomposition consists of a Lease Policy Manager and a Lease Manager. The landlord package in Jini defines interfaces for both of these roles. The Lease Policy Manager may implement the `LeasePolicy` interface:

```
public interface LeasePolicy
{
    public Lease leaseFor(LeasedResource resource, long requestedDuration)
        throws LeaseDeniedException;
    public long renew(LeasedResource resource, long requestedDuration)
        throws LeaseDeniedException, UnknownLeaseException;
    public boolean ensureCurrent(LeasedResource resource);
}
```

The Lease Manager may implement the `LeaseManager` interface:

```
public interface LeaseManager
{
    public void register(LeasedResource resource, long duration);
    public void renewed(LeasedResource resource, long duration,
        long oldExpiration);
}
```

The `Landlord` can also decide to replace these delegates at any time, either using another delegate, or by carrying out the work itself. Because the two managers implement fixed interfaces, replacement will be as simple as creating new instances of the managers.

Since the Lease Policy Manager and Lease Manager will together support the allocation of leased resources, the Lease Manager must be notified of requests for renewal of resources by the Lease Policy Manager. This is done through the `register()` and `renewed()` methods.

Leased Resources

Most resources being managed are designed without expiry times in mind, as it's not always possible to tell ahead of time that they will be leased. To facilitate resources in the managed scenario, you need to implement wrapper classes that add expiry time to the resource. The landlord package defines an interface that the wrapper class should implement to facilitate leased interaction:

```
public interface LeasedResource
{
    public void setExpiration(long newExpiration);
    public long getExpiration();
    public Object getCookie();
}
```

Decorative Cookies

A cookie is arbitrary application data in the form of a Java object. In the case of the landlord model, a cookie can be attached to each instance of a leased resource. The `getCookie()` method of the `LeasedResource` returns a cookie that is attached to the leased resource. Conceptually, the cookie is a decoration for the resource that associates a lease with the resource. The developer decides what to supply as a cookie in each design, and creates it the first time a lease is granted. Subsequently, the `LandlordLease` proxy implementation will return this cookie to you every time a renewal or cancellation is required. All landlord methods send cookies to locate leased resources. Your choice of cookie should allow you to quickly locate the leased resource (a hash map key, for example) and identify the associated lease (some unique number representing the lease).

Lease Expiry Mechanism

There aren't any library interfaces that support a lease expiry mechanism. This is left to the implementation itself. Typically, a background thread, or some sort of lazy reclaim-as-we-go strategy can perform the lease expiry 'sweep' on the lease resources managed by the Lease Manager.

This is the complete Landlord model; if your resource management and lease granting strategy can be factored this way, you'll be able to adopt it for the Landlord model.

A Highly Usable Library Implementation

The landlord package provides a concrete implementation of a Lease Policy Manager, called com.sun.jini.lease.landlord.LeaseDurationPolicy. This class implements the LeasePolicy interface as required. If the client doesn't specify a lease duration, a default one is used. If a duration is specified it is granted if it is less than the maximum duration, otherwise the lease is granted for the maximum duration.

This programmed-in strategy for lease granting can be applicable to many applications (for example, reggie and Javaspaces use a very similar scheme). So, if you can use this Lease Policy Manager implementation, you do not have to write your own.

Here are the methods of the class:

```
public class LeaseDurationPolicy implements LeasePolicy
{
    public LeaseDurationPolicy(long maximum, long defaultLength,
        Landlord landlord, LeaseManager mgr, LandlordLeaseFactory factory);
    public Lease leaseFor(LeasedResource resource, long requestedDuration)
        throws LeaseDeniedException;
    public long renew(LeasedResource resource, long requestedDuration);
    public boolean ensureCurrent(LeasedResource resource);
}
```

One very desirable side-effect of using this implementation is that it knows about the Lease Manager's existence and will co-ordinate its effort with it through the defined interfaces (if you're using them).

The developer supplies the parameters for the LeaseDurationPolicy during its construction, including the maximum grant duration, the default grant duration, the implementation of the Landlord interface, the LeaseManager implementation (if any), and an instance of a factory. Once you've created a LeaseDurationPolicy instance, new leases can be obtained for lease resources by calling the leaseFor() method. This method will call the factory's newLease() method, and also set the leased resource's expiry time appropriately. If you need to renew a lease, use the renew() method of this LeaseDurationPolicy, again it will ensure that the expiry time is updated appropriately on the leased resource. Finally, you can test a leased resource for currency (that is, not yet expired) by using its ensureCurrent() method.

Implementing Your Own Lease Grantor

We will now retrofit our EvtService implementation and lease the remote event registrations that it handles, using the library supplied LandlordLeases and LeaseDurationPolicy to simplify our implementation.

You can find the source code in the ch8\code\LEvtService directory of the source code download.

Lease Negotiation API

Since the interface used for `IndexKeeperRemote` does not know about leases, we must make a modification to the `addRemoteListener()` method to also handle lease negotiation. The new interface is called `EventServiceItf`, and contains:

```
import net.jini.core.event.RemoteEventListener;
import net.jini.core.event.EventRegistration;
import net.jini.core.lease.LeaseDeniedException;

public interface EventServiceItf extends IndexKeeper,java.rmi.Remote
  {
    public EventRegistration addRemoteListener(RemoteEventListener listener,
        long leaseDuration) throws
        java.rmi.RemoteException,LeaseDeniedException;
  }
```

The `addRemoteListener()` method now returns an `EventRegistration` object that will contain a lease. It also has a new argument passing to the service the desired lease duration.

Coding the Service

The code for the service itself is found in the `LEvtService.java` file:

The import list is now more extensive than before, we must also include the leasing specific interfaces and exceptions, as well as the landlord interfaces and packages.

```
import java.rmi.Remote;
import java.rmi.server.RemoteObject;
import java.rmi.server.UnicastRemoteObject;
import java.rmi.MarshalledObject;
import net.jini.core.event.RemoteEventListener;
import net.jini.core.event.RemoteEvent;
import net.jini.core.event.EventRegistration;
import java.rmi.RemoteException;
import net.jini.core.event.UnknownEventException ;

import net.jini.lookup.ServiceIDListener;
import net.jini.lookup.entry.Name;
import net.jini.core.entry.Entry;
import java.rmi.RemoteException;
import java.rmi.RMISecurityManager;
import net.jini.lookup.JoinManager;
import net.jini.discovery.*;
import net.jini.core.lookup.ServiceID;

import com.sun.jini.lease.landlord.*;
import net.jini.core.lease.*;

import java.util.*;

import java.io.Serializable;
```

Our `IdPrinter` did not change, and will still print the assigned service ID to standard output.

```
class IdPrinter implements ServiceIDListener
   {
     int myIndex;
     public IdPrinter(int initIndex)
        {
           myIndex = initIndex;
        }
     public void serviceIDNotify(ServiceID serviceID)
        {
          System.out.println("instance " + myIndex + " has been assigned
             service ID: " + serviceID.toString());
        }
   }
```

Here is our implementation of the `EvtCookie`, consisting of a long `leaseCounter` (`leaseNum`) and a `leaseKey`.

```
class EvtCookie implements Serializable
   {
     protected long leaseCounter;
     protected int leaseKey;

     public EvtCookie() {}
     public EvtCookie(int inKey, long inCounter)
        {
           leaseKey = inKey;
           leaseCounter = inCounter;
        }
     public void setLeaseKey(int inKey)
        {
           leaseKey = inKey;
        }
     public void setLeaseCounter(long inCounter)
        {
           leaseCounter = inCounter;
        }
     public int getLeaseKey()
        {
           return leaseKey;
        }
     public long getLeaseCounter()
        {
           return leaseCounter;
        }
   }
```

`LeasedRegistration` wraps an object implementing the `RemoteEventListener` interface and attaches to it a cookie and expiry time. It implements the `LeasedResource` interface for interactions with the landlord's components. The `LeasedRegistration`'s `notify()` method simply calls the corresponding wrapped listener's `notify()` method.

```
class LeasedRegistration implements RemoteEventListener,LeasedResource
   {
     protected EvtCookie myCookie = null;
     protected long myExpiry = 0L;
     RemoteEventListener assocListener;
     public LeasedRegistration(RemoteEventListener inListener,
        int leaseKey, long leaseCounter)
```

```
            {
                assocListener = inListener;
                myCookie = new EvtCookie(leaseKey, leaseCounter);
            }
        public Object getCookie()
            {
                return myCookie;
            }
        public long getExpiration()
            {
                return myExpiry;
            }
        public void setExpiration(long inExpiry)
            {
                myExpiry = inExpiry;
            }
        public void notify (RemoteEvent inEvt) throws UnknownEventException,
            RemoteException
            {
                assocListener.notify(inEvt);
            }
    }
```

The service class now implements the new lease-aware `EventServiceItf` interface, and it also serves as the landlord for the `LandlordLease` library proxy. By using the service, which is already RMI exported through its inheritance from `UnicastRemoteObject`, we saved the work of defining a separate `Landlord` supporting class.

```
public class LEvtService extends UnicastRemoteObject
    implements EventServiceItf,Landlord
{
    static final int MAX_INSTANCES = 3;
    static final String [] GROUPS1 = { "iguanas"};

    int myIndex = 0;
    Thread worker = null;
    RemoteObject meExported = null;
    public LEvtService() throws RemoteException {}
    private long evtSeqNum = 1L;
    private long leaseNum = 1L;
```

The `leaseKey` is part of the cookie that we will define for leased resources. It will be the key into the exact event registration within a hash map. We will see the other part of the cookie a little later.

```
        private int leaseKey = 3;    // starting registration number at 3

        protected JoinManager myJM = null;
```

We create our own factory instance here using the default `LandlordLeaseFactory` implementation. This factory is passed into the `LeaseDurationPolicy` instance that we will create. We set the maximum duration to grant at 30 seconds, and the default duration to 15 seconds for the policy. Since the service implements the `Landlord` interface, we simply pass the `this` pointer into the `LeaseDurationPolicy` instance to create it. We will not be creating a Lease Manager in this case, since leased resource management can be adequately performed by the `LeaseDurationPolicy` implementation and our own lease expiry thread. We pass in a null to indicate that no Lease Manager is used.

```
        protected LandlordLeaseFactory myFactory = new LandlordLease.Factory();
        protected LeasePolicy myGrantPolicy =
            new LeaseDurationPolicy(30000L,15000L, this, null, myFactory);
```

The `main()` method has not changed from the original code.

```
public static void main(String argv[])
  {
    LEvtService myApp = null;
    try
      {
        if (argv.length > 0)
          myApp = new LEvtService(Integer.parseInt(argv[0]));
        else
          myApp = new LEvtService(300);
      }
    catch (Exception e)
        {
          e.printStackTrace();
          System.exit(1);
        }
    synchronized(myApp)
        {
          try
            {
              myApp.wait(0);
            }
          catch(InterruptedException e)
            {
              System.exit(0);
            }
        }
  } // of main()
```

The constructor is also identical to the original event service. However, as we shall see later, the worker thread now also performs the expiry of leased resources in addition to checking for and firing events to remote listeners.

```
public LEvtService(int inIndex) throws RemoteException
  {
    myIndex = inIndex;
    meExported = this;
    if (System.getSecurityManager() == null)
        {
          System.setSecurityManager(new RMISecurityManager());
        }

    LookupDiscoveryManager ldm = null;
    String [] groupsToDiscover = GROUPS1;
    Entry [] attributes = new Entry[1];

    attributes[0] = new Name("one");
    worker = new Thread(new Sleeper(this));
    try
        {
          ldm = new LookupDiscoveryManager(groupsToDiscover,
                      null /* unicast locators */,
                      null /* DiscoveryListener */);
          new JoinManager(this,  /* service */
                      attributes,
                      new IdPrinter(myIndex) /* ServiceIDListener*/,
                      ldm /* DiscoveryManagement */,
                      null /* LeaseManager */);
```

```
        }
      catch(Exception e)
        {
          e.printStackTrace();
          System.exit(1);
        } // catch
      worker.start();
    }   //LEvtService

  public int getIndex() throws RemoteException
    {
      return myIndex;
    }
```

Notice that we have used JDK 1.2's synchronized collection to implement our listener list instead of Swing's ListenerList. It allows thread-safe access to the list, since renewal requests can come from a lease recipient at any time.

While this is a necessarily heavier weight alternative, it provides us with very simple direct access from a hash key to a listener. By getting rid of the complexity of list management and manipulation, hopefully it will make the rest of the logic a bit easier to understand.

```
protected Map myList = Collections.synchronizedMap( new HashMap());
```

The addRemoteListener() method is also the lease negotiation method. Note that we use as the leaseKey a monotonically increasing number. We check for integer wrap-around and ensure that no other listener registration with the same key exists in the map before continuing.

```
public EventRegistration addRemoteListener(RemoteEventListener listener,
    long inDuration) throws RemoteException,LeaseDeniedException
  {
    System.out.println("got a registration!");
    Integer myKey = new Integer(leaseKey);
    while (myList.containsKey(myKey)) // anticipate overflow
      {
        leaseKey++;
        myKey = new Integer(leaseKey);
      }
```

LeasedRegistration represents our leased resource; it is a wrapper around RemoteEventListener, and attaches a cookie plus expiry time to each listener. We will see the declaration of LeasedRegistration later. Here, we create a new LeasedRegistration by providing the listener being wrapped, and the two components of the cookie: leaseKey for quickly indexing into the leased listener, and leaseNum – a unique number identifying the lease itself.

```
    LeasedRegistration myReg = new
        LeasedRegistration(listener,leaseKey,leaseNum);

    myList.put(myKey, myReg);
```

Since we will not be having too many clients obtaining leases in our test scenarios, one may conclude that leaseKey and leaseNum are redundant. In fact, they are independent and will not be the same in the long run. leaseKey will always reflect a quick location for the LeasedRegistration itself, while leaseNum will uniquely identify a specific lease or registration. Note how we use the leaseFor() method of our LeaseDurationPolicy instance to create and return the requested lease for the client. The lease returned will be the LandlordLease proxy object and will be transmitted across the wire back to the lease recipient.

```
        leaseKey++;

        return new EventRegistration(leaseNum++, this,
            myGrantPolicy.leaseFor(myReg, inDuration) , evtSeqNum);
    }
```

The expireLeases() method is the second job that the worker thread must perform. The code iterates through the map of LeasedRegistrations and removes any that have an expired lease. It uses the fail-fast iterator provided by the JDK 1.2 synchronized map, iterating through the map of leases and stopping expirations if they are detected concurrent with the modification of the underlying listener list. The expireLeases() method resumes the business of sleeping and waking.

Any expired resources that have not been reclaimed will be reclaimed the next time the thread is run.

```
public void expireLeases()
  {
    System.out.println("Checking for expired leases...");
    try
      {
        Iterator myIt = myList.entrySet().iterator();
        while (myIt.hasNext())
          {
            Map.Entry  myEntry =(Map.Entry) myIt.next();
            LeasedRegistration aList = (LeasedRegistration) myEntry.getValue();

            if (aList.getExpiration() < System.currentTimeMillis())
              {
                Integer myKey = (Integer) myEntry.getKey();
                System.out.println("...expiring a lease with key " + myKey);
                myIt.remove();
              }

          } // of while
      } // of try

    catch(ConcurrentModificationException ex)
      {
        // failfast -- break out of the loop, try
        // again later
      }
    catch(Exception ex)
      {
        ex.printStackTrace();
      }
  }
```

fireRemoteEvent() is the initial work performed by the sleeper thread. It follows similar logic, but uses the fail-fast iterator of the synchronized map instead of the former ListenerList.

```
public void fireRemoteEvent()
  {
    RemoteEvent anEvent = null;
    System.out.println("Checking for listeners...");
```

281

```
       try
         {
           Iterator myIt = myList.entrySet().iterator();
           while (myIt.hasNext())
             {
               Map.Entry myEntry =(Map.Entry) myIt.next();

               LeasedRegistration aList = (LeasedRegistration) myEntry.getValue();
               Integer myKey = (Integer) myEntry.getKey();
               if (anEvent == null)
               anEvent = new RemoteEvent(meExported, myKey.intValue(),
                   evtSeqNum++, null);
               System.out.println("Fired one event...");
               // use short temporary threads to avoid blocking
               new Thread(new Notifier(aList, anEvent)).start();

             } // of while

         } // of try

     catch(ConcurrentModificationException ex)
       {
         // failfast -- break out of the loop, try
         // again later
       }
     catch(Exception ex)
       {
         ex.printStackTrace();
       }
   }
```

Coding the Landlord Support Logic

The next set of four methods implement the Landlord interface. Leases that we create and pass to the client are instances of the LandlordLeases proxy object that will call back to this service through the Landlord interface.

For the cancel() operation, we must assert the validity of the cookie, by checking that the leaseKey portion of the cookie is valid. Once the leaseKey has located the LeasedRegistration, we perform an additional check to make sure that the leaseCounter (leaseNum) also corresponds. If the cookie matches, then we remove the actual registration from the map – effectively canceling the lease.

```
public void cancel(Object inCookie) throws
    UnknownLeaseException,RemoteException
  {
    System.out.println("Landlord is cancelling a single lease..");

    if (!(inCookie instanceof EvtCookie))
        throw new UnknownLeaseException("bad cookie");
    EvtCookie myCookie = (EvtCookie) inCookie;

    Integer myKey = new Integer(myCookie.getLeaseKey());

    if (!(myList.containsKey(myKey)))
        throw new UnknownLeaseException("lease not found");
```

```
        LeasedRegistration myReg = (LeasedRegistration) myList.get(myKey);
        if (((EvtCookie) myReg.getCookie()).getLeaseCounter() !=
            myCookie.getLeaseCounter()) throw new
            UnknownLeaseException("lease not found");
        System.out.println("...revoked lease with key " + myKey);
        myList.remove(myKey);
    }
```

The `cancelAll()` method is used primarily for batched leases canceling handling through a `LeaseMap` (that is, by a `LeaseRenewalManager` on the client-side). It repeatedly calls the `cancel()` method and throws a `LeaseMapException` with a map of leases versus exceptions caught if one of the `cancel()` calls actually fails.

```
public Map cancelAll(Object [] inCookies) throws RemoteException
    {
    System.out.println("Landlord is cancelling multiple leases..");
    Map exMap = null;
    LeaseMapException lmEx = null;
    for (int i=0; i<inCookies.length; i++) {
    try
        {
        cancel(inCookies[i]);
        }
    catch (Exception e)
        {
        if (lmEx == null)
            {
            // only on the first exception
            exMap = new HashMap();
            lmEx = new LeaseMapException(null, exMap);
            }
        try
            {
            exMap.put(myFactory.newLease(inCookies[i],this,0), e);
            }
        catch (LeaseDeniedException ex) {}
        }
    }

    if (lmEx != null)
        return (exMap);
    else
        return(null);
}
```

The `renew()` method validates the cookie as before, extracts a reference of the `LeasedRegistration` object from the map, and calls the `LeaseDurationPolicy` instance's `renew()` method to renew the lease. All the maintenance of expiry time on the `LeasedRegistration` is handled automatically by the `LeaseDurationPolicy`.

```
public long renew(Object inCookie, long inExtension) throws
    LeaseDeniedException,UnknownLeaseException,RemoteException
    {
    System.out.println("Landlord is renewing a single lease..");

    if (!(inCookie instanceof EvtCookie))
        throw new UnknownLeaseException("cookie is bad");
    EvtCookie myCookie = (EvtCookie) inCookie;
```

```
        Integer myKey = new Integer(myCookie.getLeaseKey());

        if (!(myList.containsKey(myKey)))
            throw new UnknownLeaseException("cannot find lease");

        LeasedRegistration myReg = (LeasedRegistration) myList.get(myKey);
        if (((EvtCookie) myReg.getCookie()).getLeaseCounter() !=
            myCookie.getLeaseCounter())
            throw new UnknownLeaseException("renew failed");

        // confirmed lease is still in the Hash Map
        return myGrantPolicy.renew(myReg, inExtension);
    }
```

Like `cancelAll()`, `renewAll()` repeatedly calls renew for each of the incoming leases (cookies). It fills out a `Landlord.RenewResults` class, consisting of two arrays to return the renewed leases and any exceptions received during the batch renewal process.

```
public Landlord.RenewResults renewAll(Object [] inCookies, long []
    inExtensions) throws RemoteException
{
    System.out.println("Landlord is renewing multiple leases..");

    // perform batched renew...
    boolean somethingDenied = false;

    long[] granted = new long[inCookies.length];
    Exception[] denied = new Exception[inCookies.length+1];

    for (int  i = 0; i < inCookies.length; i++ )
      {
        try
          {
            granted[i] = renew(inCookies[i], inExtensions[i]);
            denied[i] = null;
          }
        catch(Exception ex)
          {
            somethingDenied = true;
            granted[i] = -1;
            denied[i+1] = ex;
          }
      }
    if (!somethingDenied) denied = null;
    return new Landlord.RenewResults(granted, denied);
}
```

The sleeper worker thread is still the same, except that it sleeps for 10 seconds, fires events, sleeps another 20 seconds, then checks for expired resources and repeats indefinitely.

```
class Sleeper implements Runnable
  {
    LEvtService myService;
```

```
    public Sleeper(LEvtService inServ)
      {
        myService = inServ;
      }
    public void run()
      {
        int counter = 0;
        while(true)
          {
            System.out.println("in loop... " + counter++);
            System.out.flush();
            try
              {
                Thread.sleep(10000L);
              }
            catch (Exception e){}
            myService.fireRemoteEvent();
            try
              {
                Thread.sleep(20000L);
              }
            catch (Exception e){}

            myService.expireLeases();
          }
      }
  }
```

There aren't any changes made to the Notifier class at all.

```
class Notifier implements Runnable
  {
    RemoteEventListener myListener;
    RemoteEvent myEvent;
    public Notifier( RemoteEventListener inLis, RemoteEvent inEvt)
      {
        myListener = inLis;
        myEvent = inEvt;
      }
    public void run()
      {
        try
          {
            myListener.notify(myEvent);
          }
        catch (Exception e)
          {
            e.printStackTrace();
          }
      }
  }
```

The LEvtService.java code can be compiled using the command line:

..\bats\buildit LEvtService.java

Modifying a Client to Test the Landlord

We can modify the EvtClient program for testing this new lease granting event service. Only very minor modifications need to be made. You can find the modified source code in the ch8\code\EvtClient3 directory.

There are copies of the IndexKeeper and EventServiceItf class files in the directory; they are the same as the ones in the LEvtService directory. EvtClient3 actually inherits from EvtClient but with a different implementation around the doEventReg() method:

We perform template lookup by matching a service that implements the new interface. Then we register a listener for remote events, and request a lease. In fact, we start with a 10 second lease request, and step up to 90 seconds. Each time, we will print out the duration that the service has granted us, and we will cancel the lease immediately.

Typical production leases will be substantially longer than 90 seconds (for example, reggie uses 5 minute leases).

```
public EventRegistration myReg = null;

    private void doEventReg()
       {
         if (registrars.length > 0)
           {
             Class [] myClassType = { EventServiceItf.class };

             try
               {
                 EventServiceItf myES = (EventServiceItf)
                     registrars[0].lookup(new
                     ServiceTemplate(null,myClassType,null));

                 if (myES != null)
                   {
                     for (int m=1; m< 10; m++)    // from 10 sec to 90 sec
                       {
                         long durationRequested = m * 10000L;
                         EventRegistration myreg = myES.addRemoteListener(this,
                             durationRequested);

                         Lease myLease = myreg.getLease();
                         System.out.println("  request a lease of " +
                             durationRequested + " ms");
                         System.out.println("  ....received a lease for " + (
                             myLease.getExpiration() -
                             System.currentTimeMillis()) + " ms");
                         myLease.cancel();
                       }
                   }
                 else
                 System.out.println("cannot find any proxy for event service...");

                 }
             catch(Exception e)
               {
                 e.printStackTrace();
                 System.exit(1);
               }
           }
       }
```

Another minor modification is required in the notify method to reflect the new EventServiceItf interface.

```
public void notify (RemoteEvent inEvt) throws
    UnknownEventException, RemoteException
{
    RemoteEvent srvEvt =  inEvt;
    System.out.println("received a notification from:");
    EventServiceItf mySrc = (EventServiceItf) srvEvt.getSource();
    System.out.println("   Source instance: " + mySrc.getIndex());
    System.out.println("   Event ID: " + srvEvt.getID());
    System.out.println("   Sequence Number: " + srvEvt.getSequenceNumber());
}
}
```

Now compile the client:

```
..\bats\buildit EvtClient3.java
```

Create the RMI stubs, the JAR file, and copy them to the class server using the makejar.bat batch file in the ch8\code\EvtClient3 directory. It contains:

```
call ..\bats\setpaths.bat
rmic -classpath %JINIJARS%;. -sourcepath . -v1.2 EvtClient3
jar cvf EvtClient3-dl.jar EvtClient3_Stub.class IndexKeeper.class
copy EvtClient3-dl.jar %WROXHOME%
```

Testing the Landlord Implementation

Change back into the ch8\code\LEvtService directory, to finish setting up our lease granting event service, you need to create RMI and the JAR file using the makejar.bat batch file, The batch file contains:

```
call ..\bats\setpaths.bat
rmic -classpath %JINIJARS%;. -sourcepath . -v1.2 LEvtService
jar cvf LEvtService-dl.jar LEvtService_Stub.class EventServiceItf.class
IndexKeeper.class EvtCookie.class
copy LEvtService-dl.jar %WROXHOME%
```

Note that we must include EvtCookie.class since it is serialized as a member of the LeasedRegistration object.

Start the HTTP class server (runhttpdstubs.bat) and rmid (with the persistent reggie) if you have not already done so (runrmid.bat and runlookup1.bat)

Now you're ready to start the lease granting event service using the runevt.bat file that contains:

```
call ..\bats\setpaths.bat
java  -classpath .;%JINIJARS%  -Dnet.jini.discovery.interface=%ADAPTERIP% -
Djava.security.policy=policy.all -Djava.rmi.server.codebase
=http://%STUBHOST%/LEvtService-dl.jar LEvtService %1 %2
```

You should see the usual service startup message, the service ID printed by the ID printer, and the worker thread waking up to check for event registration and lease expiry.

Go into the `ch8\code\EvtClient3` directory and start a client using the `runevt.bat` batch file.

This batch file contains:

```
call ..\bats\setpaths.bat
java  -classpath .;%JINIJARS%  -Dnet.jini.discovery.interface=%ADAPTERIP% -
Djava.security.policy=policy.all -
Djava.rmi.server.codebase=http://%STUBHOST%/EvtClient3-dl.jar EvtClient3 %1 %2
```

You should see the lookup discovery process, followed by a rapid fire series of event registration and lease cancellations. The client will print out what duration it asked for, and what it got in return. You should see the enforced `LeaseDurationPolicy` at work here.

```
ar;c:\jini1_1\lib\jini-ext.jar;c:\jini1_1\lib\sun-util.jar  -Dnet.jini.discovery
.interface=192.168.1.34 -Djava.security.policy=policy.all -Djava.rmi.server.code
base=http://jini2:8081/EvtClient3-dl.jar EvtClient3
-------------------------------------------------------------
Registrar: 0cbbfe0f-50ae-4770-8eda-cdb9df485a69
Groups Supported: iguanas
  requested for a lease of 10000 ms
  ....received a lease for 9940 ms
  requested for a lease of 20000 ms
  ....received a lease for 20000 ms
  requested for a lease of 30000 ms
  ....received a lease for 30000 ms
  requested for a lease of 40000 ms
  ....received a lease for 30000 ms
  requested for a lease of 50000 ms
  ....received a lease for 30000 ms
  requested for a lease of 60000 ms
  ....received a lease for 30000 ms
  requested for a lease of 70000 ms
  ....received a lease for 30000 ms
  requested for a lease of 80000 ms
  ....received a lease for 30000 ms
  requested for a lease of 90000 ms
  ....received a lease for 30000 ms
```

On the service side, you should also see all the registration and cancellations.

Testing the Lease Expiry Mechanism

The lease negotiation appears to be working so now we will test for lease expiry. This will require the following code change to the EvtClient3.java file in the ch8\code\EvtClient3 directory:

```java
private void doEventReg()
  {
    if (registrars.length > 0)
     {
        Class [] myClassType = { EventServiceItf.class };

        try
         {
            EventServiceItf myES = (EventServiceItf)
            registrars[0].lookup(new ServiceTemplate(null,myClassType,null));

            if (myES != null)
             {

                long durationRequested = 20000L;

                EventRegistration myreg = myES.addRemoteListener(this, 20000L);

                Lease myLease = myreg.getLease();
                System.out.println("  requested for a lease of " +
                   durationRequested + " ms");
                System.out.println("  ....received a lease for " +
                   (myLease.getExpiration() - System.currentTimeMillis()) + " ms");

             }
            else
              System.out.println("cannot find any proxy for event service...");

         }
        catch (RemoteException ex)
        ...
```

You will need to compile the client again, but there is no need to remake stub or jar files. Then you can try to run the client again.

This code change will cause the client to register just one listener, and ask for a lease of just 20 seconds. That should be enough for the client to receive at most one single event. You should see on the service a notice that the client's registration has been revoked when the sleeper thread wakes up.

Our client registration arrived in the middle of loop 14. The worker thread faithfully fired a remote event to our client during loop 15. However, also during loop 15, our 20 second lease has expired and the worker thread removed our registration. From loop 16 onwards, our client will no longer receive remote events.

Implementing Reliable Lease Renewal

Finally, we will unleash our friend, LeaseRenewalManager, on our own Landlord implementation.

Modify the EvtClient3.java file in ch8\code\EvtClient3 directory to contain:

```
private void doEventReg()
  {
    if (registrars.length > 0)
      {
        Class [] myClassType = { EventServiceItf.class };

        try
          {
            EventServiceItf myES = (EventServiceItf)
            registrars[0].lookup(new ServiceTemplate(null,myClassType,null));

            if (myES != null)
              {

                long durationRequested = 20000L;

                EventRegistration myreg = myES.addRemoteListener(this, 20000L);

                Lease myLease = myreg.getLease();
                new LeaseRenewalManager(myLease, Lease.FOREVER, null);
                System.out.println("  requested for a lease of " +
                  durationRequested + " ms");
                System.out.println("  ....received a lease for " +
                  (myLease.getExpiration() - System.currentTimeMillis()) + " ms");
```

```
    }
    else
        System.out.println("cannot find any proxy for event service...");

    }
    catch (RemoteException ex)
    ...
```

This code asks for a lease of 20 seconds with the registration, just like before. However, it then extracts the returned lease (a `LandlordLease` proxy) and hands it over to a `LeaseRenewalManager` instance, asking it to renew the lease indefinitely. Underneath the cover, of course, the `LeaseRenewalManager` instance is dealing with the `Landlord`'s 'no lease greater than 30 seconds' stipulation. Before, it happens silently and we simply receive event notifications from the server as long as we're alive. Now, we can see all the renewal that the `LeaseRenewalManager` is performing on our behalf to keep the listener from expiring.

You can compile the client code and try it out. Here is a sample output from the client, showing just a sustained series of notifications about 30 seconds apart (the maximum lease duration).

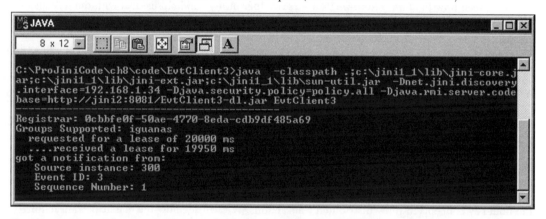

On the service side, it is clear that `LeaseRenewalManger` is doing a lot of work for us. Notice below how our renewal always arrives before the expiry worker thread has a chance to take us away.

Summary

Distributed leasing in Jini allows services to allocate resources on behalf of multiple clients without the risk of resource leaks or depletion. A client negotiates a finite duration lease with the service, and must renew the lease before it expires. This is a way for the client to continually indicate interest in the resource. If a lease expires before a client can renew it, the associated resource may be reclaimed. This scheme also ensures that the system can self-heal after a period of time, when client or services disconnect suddenly.

In this chapter, we have examined leasing from both the point of view of a lease recipient and lease grantor. The role of a lease recipient is considerably simpler to implement, the only requirement is to negotiate a lease duration, and renew the lease before it expires as long as we need the underlying resource. We discovered that lease duration is independent of the absolute time of clocks on the network machines and can exist as a relative duration, or an absolute time with respect to the clock on the lease recipient's machine. Jini applications may use many leases from many grantors during its execution; LeaseMaps can be used to batch multiple leases to make the renewal process more efficient. We have seen how the LeaseRenewalManager helper utility can help us deal with the tedious task of lease batching and renewal.

From the lease grantor point of view, we realized that there is substantially more management coding to perform. Jini does not specify how leases should be granted nor provide any default implementation. Instead, it provides a set of interfaces and abstract classes to support a generic Landlord model of lease management. In this chapter, we have examined the Landlord model in great detail, including the roles and interaction of the Landlord, the Lease Manager, and the Renewal Policy Manager. We have implemented our own lease grantor using the Landlord model to aid in understanding of how to grant leases when resources are allocated on behalf of clients.

In a distributed system, each participating service executes independently of each other. This contributes to the scalability and robustness of the network and improved throughput. However, it also makes synchronization between the systems quite difficult. In the next chapter, we will examine one of the final key concepts in Jini – distributed transactions. We will see how the classical 'transaction' semantics are relaxed to enable a substantially larger class of applications to make productive use of it in Jini systems.

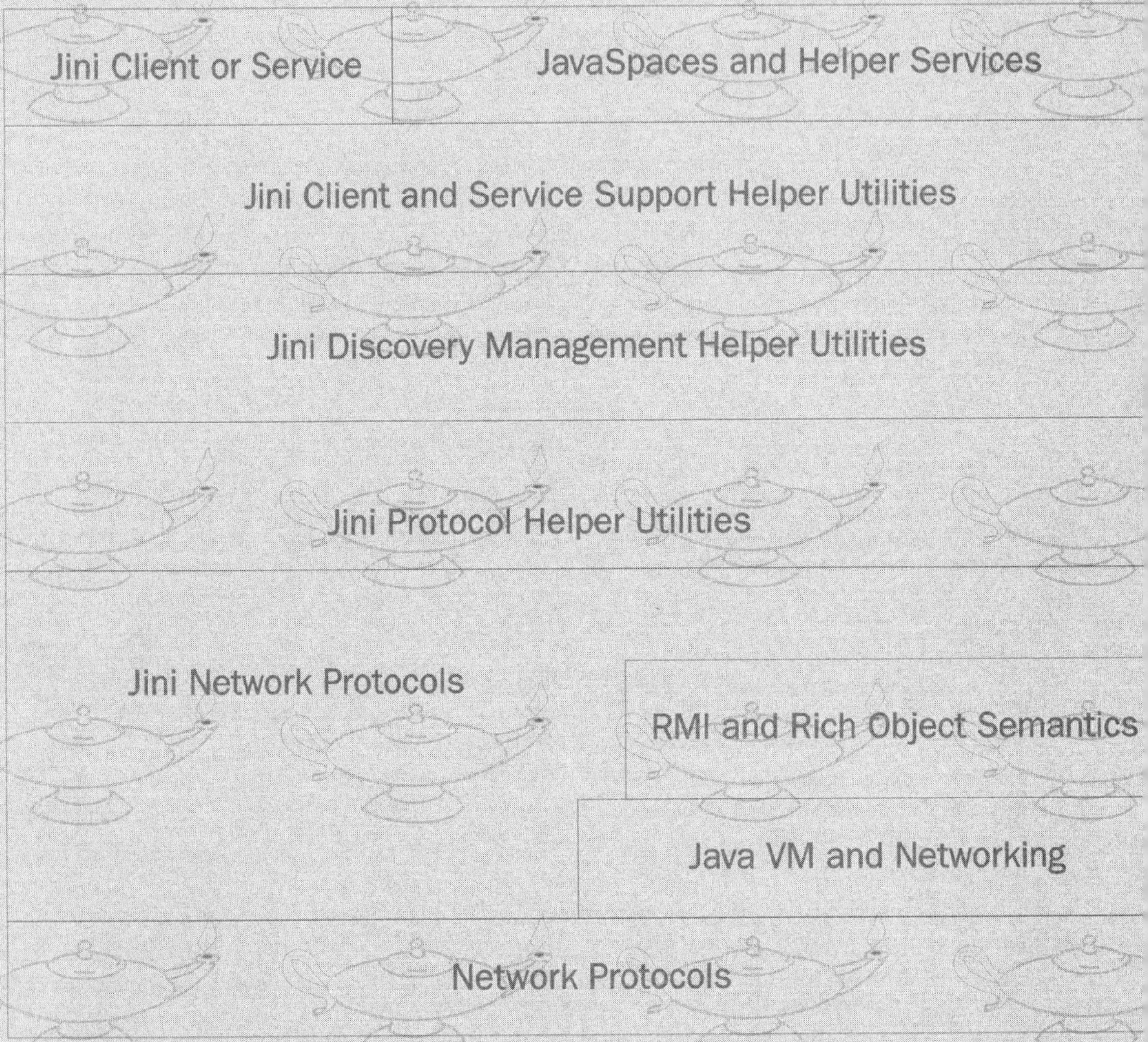

Jini Client or Service
JavaSpaces and Helper Services
Jini Client and Service Support Helper Utilities
Jini Discovery Management Helper Utilities
Jini Protocol Helper Utilities
Jini Network Protocols
RMI and Rich Object Semantics
Java VM and Networking
Network Protocols

Online discussion at http://p2p.wrox.com

9

Distributed Transactions

As we saw in Chapter 5, the Jini infrastructure itself does not have a recovery mechanism to cope with services that fail while they are providing their services. This is because the interaction between the client and the service is entirely application specific, and therefore outside the scope of the Jini network. Failure handling and recovery can't be accomplished without knowledge of the application semantics.

A distributed application is, of course, going to have to handle exactly this sort of failure. For Jini to abstract across application domains and enumerate all the failure possibilities would be a prohibitively complex process, and limit its long-term utility. So instead, Jini provides a **distributed transaction service** that helps any client/server interaction that chooses to make use of it with this sort of failure recovery.

Transaction services are by no means the exclusive domain of Jini. Database management systems have long used transactions to preserve the integrity of a system, and with great success.

The premise is very simple: where there are multiple changes in state encapsulated within a unit of work, the entire unit must complete successfully, or there should be no changes made at all. Although classic transaction management systems and Jini's distributed transaction service are distinct, both share this premise.

In this chapter we are going to investigate:

- ❑ Classical transaction theory, and ACID properties
- ❑ The two-phase commit protocol
- ❑ Coding with transactions, from both the user's perspective and the transaction participant's
- ❑ Using distributed transactions to process synchronization
- ❑ Handling crash recovery and shutdown requests
- ❑ Sun's reference transaction manager implementation: **mahalo**

Jini's distributed transaction service is an 'enabler' technology: it enables the creation of applications that would not otherwise be possible without it (JavaSpaces, which we will examine in Chapter 13, is a good example of an enabler technology).

A Page from Classic Transaction Theory: ACID Properties

ACID stands for the cornerstone properties of transaction theory:

- ❏ Atomicity
- ❏ Consistency
- ❏ Isolation
- ❏ Durability

Atomicity means that if one of more of the operations within the transaction fails, then all the operations that have been carried out will be reversed and the system restored to its initial state. System state restoration, also referred to as a **rollback**, ensures that a transaction will never partially complete.

Consistency means that the state of the system before and after the transaction is always knowable. Whatever takes place within the transaction, whether it fails or succeeds, the system will not be left in an unpredictable or 'blurred' state. It also means that the same action performed in the same conditions, will produce the same result. Although what is meant in coding terms by 'consistency' can be highly application specific, it is possible to deal with every state of any consistent system, as its state will never be unpredictable.

Isolation concerns the visibility of the operations within one transaction: they should not be visible to, or affect, other transactions occurring simultaneously. Other transactions won't be able to see the first transaction's results, or indeed partial results, while the transaction is still in process.

Durability concerns the state of the system following a completed transaction: this should always be stable and robust.

To put these ideas in context, consider an e-commerce web implementation. Items are bought and sold over the web, and money passes between the client and vendor's accounts in a transaction. Atomicity guarantees that the money both leaves the client's account and arrives in the vendor's, or that it stays where it is – there won't be any loose dollars in the system. Consistency means that no matter what happens or who crashes, the system will never be left in an unpredictable state. It is not possible that the system will be in a state where the client's money has been moved but the vendor hasn't received it (the system audit will review a net loss of money in this inconsistent state). Isolation means that any other simultaneous users of the two accounts will not see the effects of either debit or credit until the money has successfully moved and the transaction completed. Finally, durability means that once the money has moved accounts, it has moved forever and the transaction cannot be undone, even if the system falls over.

The following diagram shows the ACID properties of an archetypal transaction moving money between two bank accounts.

You can see the accounts before the transaction, the states they might hold following the transaction, and the inconsistent states that a distributed transaction will prevent.

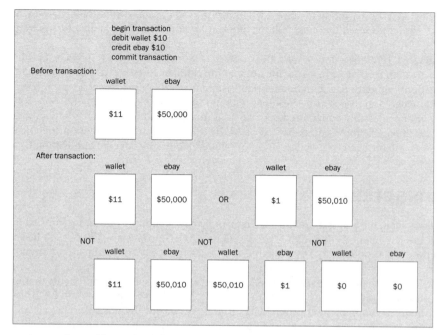

Now that we've explained how the ACID properties of transactions work, it may come as a bit of a surprise to find that the Jini transaction mechanism neither guarantees nor enforces any of them. It does, however, provide a framework that services can use to give transactions ACID properties.

Transactions: Against Partial Failure

The ACID properties of a transaction mean that every interaction between client and server can be handled. Should you divide a unit of work into steps, you could be confident that each of the steps will either complete successfully or not at all, and that the system's state will be predictable between each of the steps. In fact, you might even mandate a nested transaction, where the overall state of the entire system can be restored to its state before the sub-transaction has taken place. A rebate program, for example, may involve withdrawing a large sum from one account and crediting small sums of money to many others; in this case, each of the sub-credits would take the form of a nested transaction, and the large sum withdrawal would fail completely should one of the smaller accounts fail to be credited.

This system is stronger and more reliable than other non-transaction systems, because there is no need to handle bizarre or unexpected partial failure situations: there are only so many known states that the system can end up in, and so they can all be accounted for in the code.

On a single stand-alone system, the beginning transaction is a kind of checkpoint, where the entire state of the system is stored in some way. Individual operations within the transaction are then carried out, and should one of these fail, then the checkpoint state of the system is rolled back.

Should every operation conclude successfully, the checkpoint state will be overwritten and the transaction made durable through the commit stage. While this approach would satisfy AC and D properties of a transaction, the issue of total isolation is still outstanding: an observer could see the incremental changes to the system's state while the transaction is being carried out. Application specific state changes buffering/logging and hiding is necessary to implement the appropriate levels of isolation on a single system.

Implementing ACID on a single machine, whether the system is used simultaneously by many users or not, is fairly straightforward, because failures like system crashes are immediately apparent.

Implementing ACID transactions over a distributed network of multiple systems is, on the other hand, more of an art than a science. In a specific application domain (such as RDBMS servers) implementations can optimize domain and platform knowledge to create such guarantees. Designing a generalized mechanism to perform work that may modify overall system state in some sort of undefined manner would be a terribly convoluted task, and so, in it's overall design drive for simplicity, Jini doesn't insist on an absolute and precise set of ACID transaction implementation specifications. Jini does, however, enable such transactions to be implemented in any specific application domain.

Jini Transactions

So, as we have seen, the Jini transaction mechanism provides support for, and is consistent with, specific application implementations that might well guarantee ACID properties. Jini doesn't insist on these, but the ACID property support it makes available can be useful in certain application domains.

Jini's transaction mechanism provides just enough plumbing for services and clients that want to use transactions to do so, but does not place restrictions on how the plumbing should be utilized, and whether it should be implemented using ACID guarantees or not. By not enforcing classic transaction semantics, the utility of Jini's support is increased impressively. The distributed transaction manager provides multiple system synchronicity, allowing a group of independently computing servers to come together at certain points in time, in known and consistent system states. The co-ordination of such a non-ACID distributed transaction can be applied, in an infinite variety of ways, to many distributed computing problems.

A distributed transaction manager exists to manage and co-ordinate the **two-phase commit protocol**. We'll look at this protocol next:

The Two-Phase Commit Protocol

State changes over multiple systems must be coordinated if a distributed transaction is to be carried out. A specific pattern of interaction (a protocol) must be established between the parties. The two-phase commit protocol, 2PC, is central to the coordination of a distributed transaction, and uses a transaction manager to coordinate the transactions participants.

On a high level, this is what happens during a 2PC transaction:

❑ Transaction participants join up with the transaction manager to perform 2PC

❑ Manager tells every participant to prepare for the commit

❑ Participants prepare by performing the required work in a manner that can be rolled back or committed

❑ Any of the participants that cannot prepare for the commit will signal abort

❑ Should one or more of the participants abort, the entire distributed transaction is aborted, and all participants will be asked to rollback their state.

❑ If all of the participants report successful preparation, the transaction manager will tell every participant to commit

This diagrams illustrates the 2PC in action:

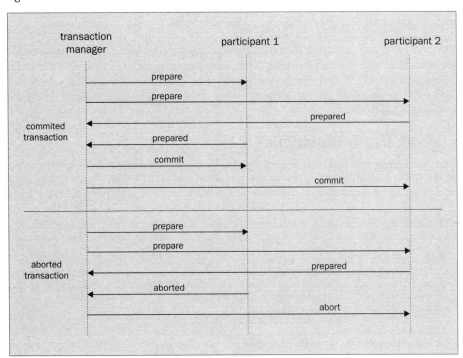

When participants have informed the transaction that they have completed preparation, they must be ready to commit, regardless of intermittent crashes and restarts.

Once the transaction manager has told one participant to commit, it will continue to tell participants to commit until they have all successfully committed. This behavior must also survive crashes and restarts.

Jini leases transactions, so a participant that crashes permanently either before or after reporting a successful preparation won't suspend the transaction indefinitely. The eventual expiry of the dead participant's lease lets the transaction manager know that it should clean up the system.

Jini's Transaction Provisions

Jini specifies interfaces for:

- ❑ Client use of a transaction manager
- ❑ Implementation of a transaction manager
- ❑ Implementation of a transaction participant

The Jini distribution includes a reference implementation of a transaction manager: **mahalo**. This is an activatable service which, like reggie, keeps state information in a log directory.

Jini specifies interfaces (covered in the next section) that enable clients, transaction managers, and transaction participants to coordinate using the 2PC protocol, but doesn't prescribe or enforce any specific semantics. It is up to the application concerned to define what a prepared, committed or aborted state actually is. The interactions between transaction manager, client and participant simply carry out the 2PC dance through the Jini interface, and nothing more.

At one extreme, a sophisticated database and queuing system might use Jini's 2PC support to implement a Java version of their ACID transaction server, forcing application-defined semantics onto all participants, and insisting that they adhere to ACID standards.

At the other extreme, an application may define the prepared, commit and abort states as perishable temporary states that need not be consistent. This setup would break every rule in the ACID transaction rulebook, but 2PC would still perform the undeniably significant role of a distributed synchronization mechanism. Just like Jini itself, the application for Jini's transaction support is limited only by the imagination of the practitioners.

How Jini Clients Use Transactions

A Jini client wanting to perform work within a distributed transaction must first discover a transaction service in the Jini federation – often this will be an instance of mahalo. All transaction services for Jini support the `TransactionManager` interface. The implementation will look something like this:

```
public interface TransactionManager extends Remote, TransactionConstants {
    public static class Created implements Serializable {public final long id;
        public final Lease lease;
        public Created(long id, Lease lease) {...}
    }
    Created create(long leaseFor) throws LeaseDeniedException, RemoteException;
    void join(long id, TransactionParticipant part, long crashCount)
        throws UnknownTransactionException, CannotJoinException,
        CrashCountException, RemoteException;
    int getState(long id) throws UnknownTransactionException, RemoteException;
    void commit(long id) throws UnknownTransactionException, CannotCommitException,
        RemoteException;
    void commit(long id, long waitFor) throws UnknownTransactionException,
        CannotCommitException, TimeoutExpiredException, RemoteException;
    void abort(long id) throws UnknownTransactionException, CannotAbortException,
        RemoteException;
    void abort(long id, long waitFor) throws UnknownTransactionException,
        CannotAbortException, TimeoutExpiredException, RemoteException;
}
```

The following table contains a synopsis of the methods in this interface, and where they're used:

Method	Typically Used By	Description
create()	Client	Specifying the desired lease duration on the call, this method creates a transaction and returns a created object. This object contains a transaction ID (meaningful only to the transaction service) and will be granted a lease.
join()	Participant/Client	Allows a participant to join a specific transaction. A client creates the initial transaction, telling each participant to join by making method calls in to the participant.
getState()	Participant	Obtains the state information (committed, aborted, etc) from a particular manager on a specific transaction, usually called by a participant during crash recovery.

Method	Typically Used By	Description
commit()	Client/Participant	Tells the manager to start and commit a distributed transaction. Two variations exist – one blocking, and the other returning immediately without waiting for all participants to commit or abort.
abort()	Client/Participant	Tells the manager to abort a distributed transaction. Two variations exist – one blocking, and the other returning immediately without waiting for all participants to complete.

Implementing a Client that uses Transactions

The client we will code here uses the HitmanService we used earlier in our exploration of remote events. The interface supported by the HitmanService is called HitmanItf, and has this definition:

```java
import java.rmi.RemoteException;
import java.awt.Color;
import net.jini.core.transaction.server.TransactionManager;

public interface HitmanItf extends java.rmi.Remote {
  public void changeColor(Color color, TransactionManager tm, long transID)
    throws RemoteException;
}
```

The service itself displays a swing panel with a button. Clicking on the button will terminate the service gracefully, by canceling its lease with the lookup service. This service is a full transaction participant: the changeColor() method in the HitmanItf interface can be called within a transaction to change the color of the button. Note how the method has a TransactionManager and a transaction ID parameter. Upon receipt of this call, the service will join the specified transaction with the specified transaction manager.

The behavior of this application is quite straightforward:

❑ Outside a distributed transaction, the button color changes immediately upon the changeColor()from a client

❑ Within a distributed application, the service participates fully in 2PC, so either all instances of the services within a transaction change color together, or none of them do

❑ Support for the transactional color change must be able to survive the crash of any particular Hitman participant

Creating a non-Transactional Base Client

You can find the source code to HitClient.java in ch9\code\hitClient and the ch9\code\hitClient2 directories. The one in the hitClient directory is non-transactional. We'll look at the non-transactional client code first, and then look at the changes necessary for the transactional client code later. Here is the source code to the non-transactional client in the ch9\code\hitClient directory:

```
import net.jini.discovery.*;
import net.jini.core.lookup.*;
import java.io.IOException;
import java.rmi.RemoteException;
import java.rmi.RMISecurityManager;

import net.jini.lookup.entry.Location;
import net.jini.core.entry.Entry;

import java.awt.Color;
```

We have standard discovery and RMI imports, and no need for transactions. The `hitClient` does not support any remote event notification, so there is no need to extend RMI object classes. It also has a 'start instance and wait' `main()` method.

```
public class HitClient implements DiscoveryListener {
    private  ServiceRegistrar[] registrars;
    static final int MAX_MATCHES = 5;

    static public void main(String argv[]) {
      HitClient myApp = null;


      if (argv.length > 0)
        myApp = new HitClient(argv);
      else
        myApp = new HitClient(null);

      try {
          synchronized (myApp) {
              myApp.wait(0);
          }
      } catch(java.lang.InterruptedException e) {
          System.exit(0);
      }
    }
```

The `doLookupWork()` method iterates through the lookup services discovered, looking for proxies that support the `HitmanItf` interface.

These are, as we know, the `HitmanServices`. The client runs the `doProxyWork()` method on the proxy on each service that is discovered:

```
    private void doLookupWork() {
      ServiceMatches matches = null;
      String [] groups;
      String msg = null;
      for (int i=0; i< registrars.length; i++) {
        msg = "";
        System.out.println("--------------------------------------------");
        System.out.println("Registrar: " + registrars[i].getServiceID());
        try {
          groups = registrars[i].getGroups();
          if (groups.length > 0)

            for (int o=0; o<groups.length; o++) {
              msg += groups[o] + " ";
            }
```

```
              System.out.println("Groups Supported: " + msg);
              System.out.println("Found HitmanItf proxies:");
              Class [] myClassType = { HitmanItf.class };
              matches = registrars[i].lookup(new ServiceTemplate(null, myClassType,
                /* myAttrib */ null), MAX_MATCHES);

              for (int j=0; j< matches.totalMatches; j++)
                doProxyWork( matches.items[j]);
            }
          catch (Exception e) {
            e.printStackTrace();
            System.exit(1);
          }
        }// of for i
    }
```

The `doProxyWork()` method prints out the service ID of the `HitmanService` discovered, calls the `changeColor()` method and turns the button red. Since the `doLookupWork()` method discovers all `HitmanService` proxies within the iguanas group, they will all change color:

```
    private void doProxyWork(ServiceItem inSI) throws RemoteException {
        System.out.println(  "  ID: " + inSI.serviceID);
        HitmanItf  myObj = (HitmanItf) inSI.service;
        if (myObj != null) {
            myObj.changeColor(Color.red, null, 0L);
            System.out.println(  "  ** called its changeColor() method! **");
        }
        else
            System.out.println("  ** got NULL pointer ** ");
    }
```

The constructor uses a `LookupDiscovery` utility class to perform the discovery protocol as usual:

```
    public HitClient(String [] ingroups) {
        if (System.getSecurityManager() == null) {
            System.setSecurityManager(new RMISecurityManager());
        }
        LookupDiscovery discover = null;

        try {
            discover = new LookupDiscovery(LookupDiscovery.NO_GROUPS);
            discover.addDiscoveryListener(this);
            discover.setGroups(ingroups);
        } catch(IOException e) {
            System.err.println(e.toString());
            e.printStackTrace();
            System.exit(1);
        }
    }

    public synchronized void discovered(DiscoveryEvent evt) {
        registrars = evt.getRegistrars();
        doLookupWork();
    }


    public void discarded(DiscoveryEvent evt) {

    }
}
```

You can compile the `HitClient.java`, in the `ch9\code\HitClient` directory, using the command:

```
..\bats\buildit HitClient.java
```

There is no need to make any stubs, or export any JAR files in this case. We cannot run this client yet since we have not setup a `HitmanService`.

Now, we should look at the second version of our client, the one that supports transactions.

Changes to Make Client Transactional

So what changes do we need to make `HitClient` transactional? You can find the source code to the transactional client in the `ch9\code\HitClient2` directory.

```java
import net.jini.discovery.*;
import net.jini.core.lookup.*;
import java.io.IOException;
import java.rmi.RemoteException;
import java.rmi.RMISecurityManager;

import net.jini.lookup.entry.Location;
import net.jini.core.entry.Entry;

import java.awt.Color;
```

In the first place we have additional transaction library imports. Since transactions are leased, we must also import the lease library support.

```java
import net.jini.core.transaction.server.TransactionManager;
import net.jini.core.transaction.server.TransactionConstants;
import net.jini.core.transaction.server.TransactionParticipant;

import net.jini.core.transaction.CannotCommitException;

import net.jini.lease.LeaseRenewalManager;
import net.jini.core.lease.Lease;


public class HitClient2 implements DiscoveryListener {
    private  ServiceRegistrar[] registrars;
    static final int MAX_MATCHES = 5;
    protected TransactionManager myTM;
    protected HitmanItf myHit[] = new HitmanItf[MAX_MATCHES];
    protected int myHitCount = 0;


    static public void main(String argv[]) {
        HitClient2 myApp = null;

        if (argv.length > 0)
            myApp = new HitClient2(argv);
        else
            myApp = new HitClient2(null);
        try {
            synchronized (myApp) {
                myApp.wait(0);
```

```
        }
    } catch(java.lang.InterruptedException e) {
        System.exit(0);
    }


}
```

`doLookupWork()` must now search for an instance of mahalo, supporting the `TransactionManger` type, using the lookup registrar. If it finds one, the proxy reference will be assigned to the `myTM` variable. The additional code is highlighted in the code below:

```
private void doLookupWork() {
    ServiceMatches matches = null;
    String [] groups;
    String msg = null;
```

Since we know we only have one lookup service in our network, we assume that only registrars[0] will contain an interesting lookup service.

```
if (registrars.length > 0)
{
    msg = "";
    System.out.println("-------------------------------------------");
    System.out.println("Registrar: " + registrars[0].getServiceID());
    try {
        groups = registrars[0].getGroups();
        if (groups.length > 0)

            for (int o=0; o<groups.length; o++) {
                msg += groups[o] + " ";
            }

        System.out.println("Groups Supported: " + msg);
```

We also know that we have exactly one mahalo running in the network, and here we take advantage of the fact:

```
        // searching for a transaction manager

        if (myTM == null) {
            System.out.println("Searching for transaction manager...");

            Class[] txnClass = new Class[] {TransactionManager.class};
            ServiceTemplate template = new ServiceTemplate(null, txnClass,
                                                                  null);

            try {

                matches = registrars[0].lookup(template, MAX_MATCHES);
                if (matches.totalMatches > 0)
                    myTM = (TransactionManager) matches.items[0].service;
            }
            catch(java.rmi.RemoteException e) {
                e.printStackTrace();
                System.exit(2);
            }
            if (myTM == null) {
                System.out.println("    No transaction manager found.");
```

```
        }
        else {
            System.out.println("Found transaction manager:");
            System.out.println("   ID: " + matches.items[0].serviceID );
        }


    } // outer of myTM == null
```

We have isolated the new transactional work in a `doTransactedWork()` method to keep the logic simple:

```
        System.out.println("Found HitmanItf proxies:");
        Class [] myClassType = { HitmanItf.class };

        matches = registrars[0].lookup(new ServiceTemplate(null,myClassType,
            /* myAttrib */ null), MAX_MATCHES);

        for (int j=0; j< matches.totalMatches; j++)  {
            myHit[j] = (HitmanItf) matches.items[j].service;
            myHitCount++;
            doProxyWork( matches.items[j]);
        }
    }
    catch (Exception e)  {
        e.printStackTrace();
        System.exit(1);
    }
}// of for i


doTransactedWork();
```

In the `doTransactedWork()` method, we first make sure that we have at lease one `HitmanService`, and one valid transaction manager instance. Then we create a transaction using the transaction manager, asking for the longest lease available. The call returns the `tcs` object that includes the transaction ID and a lease.

```
    protected void doTransactedWork() {

      if ( myHitCount > 0  && myTM != null) {
        System.out.println("Located both TXN and hitman service");
        TransactionManager.Created tcs = null;

        System.out.println("Creating transaction");
        try {
          tcs = myTM.create(Lease.FOREVER);
        }
        catch(java.rmi.RemoteException e) {
          myTM = null;
          return;
        }
        catch(net.jini.core.lease.LeaseDeniedException e) {
          myTM = null;
          return;
        }
```

We pull the transaction ID and lease out of the `tcs` object, and give the lease to an instance of `LeaseRenewalManager` for renewal while we stay alive.

```
long transactionID = tcs.id;
new LeaseRenewalManager(tcs.lease, Lease.FOREVER, null);

System.out.println("changing color now...");
```

Next, we loop around each `HitmanService` proxy that has been located, and enlist them in the same transaction, calling them to change the color of their buttons to red. We tell the transaction manager to commit only after all the `HitmanServices` have joined the transaction. Note that the `myTM` parameter is actually an RMI stub object from mahalo, and we are now passing it to our `HitmanService`. RMI runtime will marshall the object correctly and annotate it with mahalo's codebase.

```
try {
  for (int m=0; m < myHitCount; m++)
  {
    myHit[m].changeColor(Color.red, myTM,  transactionID);
    System.out.println("Color change # " + m + " called.");
  }
  System.out.println("Committing transaction...");
  myTM.commit(transactionID);
}
catch (CannotCommitException e)
{
  System.out.println("Commit failed!");
  System.exit(1);
}
catch(Exception e) {
  try {
    myTM.abort(transactionID);
  } catch (Exception ex) { ex.printStackTrace(); }
}
} // of found both


}
...
```

The rest of the code is the same as the non-transactional code. Compile the `HitClient2.java` by using the command:

`..\bats\buildit HitClient2.java`

We do not need to make a stub, or export any JAR files.

Testing the Two Clients

Now would be a good time to try out the two clients and see their differences. We will cover the service a little later, as it involves coding from the perspective of a transaction participant instead of a user.

To test these two clients, we must first set up the service. Go to the `ch9\code\Hitman` directory, and compile the code:

`..\bats\buildit HitmanService.java`

Make the RMI stubs, this is required for the service using:

```
makejar
```

Make sure you have the following three subdirectories in the ch9\code\Hitman directory:

```
hitlogs
hitlogs1
hitlogs2
```

The HitmanService instances will write their log information in these directories.

Now, move to the ch9\code\bats directory and run the HTTPD system class server:

```
runhttpd
```

Run the stub class server:

```
runhttpdstubs
```

Next, run rmid and the associated reggie instance (removing the log files if you need to first):

```
runrmid
```

```
runlookup1
```

Next, run an instance of the reference transaction server, for the iguanas group, using the runmahalo.bat batch file

```
runmahalo
```

This contains:

```
call setpaths.bat
java -jar -Djava.security.policy=policy.all %JINIHOME%\lib\mahalo.jar
http://%DOWNLOADHOST%/mahalo-dl.jar policy.all %JINITEMP%\mahalo_log iguanas
```

As with reggie, wait for the setup VM to finish. Mahalo is an RMI activatable service as well, and uses a setup VM just like reggie. It will print a message to the rmid console. You will not have to start this again unless you want to begin afresh with new states. Like reggie, rmid will restart the transaction service each time it restarts itself.

Now, change directory back to ch9\code\Hitman, and you can start two instances of the HitmanService by starting:

```
runhit1
```

Wait for the GUI to come up, then

```
runhit2
```

You should see two GUIs, with a button each, looking like this:

Change directory to ch9\code\HitClient, the non-transactional client, and run it:

runhit

You will see client output similar to:

You should see all the buttons change color to red almost simultaneously. The service console should not indicate any transactional activities. Mahalo is not involved in this at all.

Dismiss the two HitmanServices by clicking their buttons. Then restart them, while in the ch9\code\hitman directory, with:

runhit1

wait for the GUI to come up, then

runhit2

Now, change directory to ch9\code\HitClient2, where the transactional client resides, and run it. (The very first time that hitman runs you'll get a 'file not found served.per' error. Just run it again – you won't find the error message appears again because the hitman system will recreate it.)

runhit

You will see transactional client output similar to this:

Monitor the output of the services carefully: you will see them enter the prepared state one at a time, and then the commit state. This time, the button colors don't change instantaneously. Instead, mahalo coordinates the 2PC protocol which the `HitmanServices`, as transaction participants, follow.

Implementation of a Transaction Participant

Each of our `HitmanService` instances is in fact a transaction participant. Jini specifies that every transaction participant must implement the `TransactionParticipant` interface:

```
public interface TransactionParticipant extends Remote, TransactionConstants
{
    int prepare(TransactionManager mgr, long id)
        throws UnknownTransactionException, RemoteException;
    void commit(TransactionManager mgr, long id)
        throws UnknownTransactionException, RemoteException;
    void abort(TransactionManager mgr, long id)
        throws UnknownTransactionException, RemoteException;
    int prepareAndCommit(TransactionManager mgr, long id)
        throws UnknownTransactionException, RemoteException;
}
```

The `TransactionParticipant` is a remote interface by specification. This means that a transaction manager (like mahalo) uses RMI to directly call methods on this interface. Each transaction participant must, therefore, export RMI Stubs to support this event notification.

The `prepare`, `commit`, and `abort` methods are instructions from the transaction manager to enter particular states. The `TransactionParticipant` can veto a `prepare()` request by returning a `TransactionConstants.Aborted` status. Once prepared, a `TransactionParticipant` must follow through with either `commit()` or `abort()` upon request by the transaction manager, so the `commit()` and `abort()` methods do not return any values. There is no voting involved: the `TransactionParticipant` must simply carry out requests.

Finally, `prepareAndCommit` is an optimization used by the transaction manager for the last participant to prepare in a transaction. Since all the other participants have completed their prepare phase, this last participant can perform `prepareAndCommit` in one single step.

The HitmanService Implementation

The `HitmanService` is a transaction participant. It uses state persistence in order to be able to meaningfully handle failure across restarts. This is easily one of the most complex examples in the book, so please try to stay with us as we chew through the code and examine the flow, one aspect at a time.

The source code for `HitmanService.java` is in `ch9\code\Hitman`.

```java
import net.jini.lookup.JoinManager;
import net.jini.core.lookup.ServiceID;
import net.jini.discovery.*;
import net.jini.core.lookup.ServiceRegistrar;
import java.rmi.RemoteException;
import java.rmi.RMISecurityManager;
import java.rmi.MarshalledObject;
import net.jini.lookup.ServiceIDListener;
```

The import list for this service is extensive. Not only is it a transaction participant, but also a swing application, an RMI server for `changeColor()` calls, and a discovery protocol user.

```java
import net.jini.lookup.entry.Name;
import net.jini.core.entry.Entry;

import javax.swing.*;
import java.io.*;
import java.awt.Color;
import java.awt.event.*;
import java.rmi.Remote;

import net.jini.core.transaction.server.TransactionManager;
import net.jini.core.transaction.server.TransactionParticipant;
import net.jini.core.transaction.server.TransactionConstants;
import net.jini.core.transaction.UnknownTransactionException;
import java.rmi.NoSuchObjectException;
import net.jini.core.transaction.CannotJoinException;
import net.jini.core.transaction.CannotAbortException;
import net.jini.core.transaction.server.CrashCountException;
```

Persisting States to Permanent Storage

Here is the persistence implementation. The logger class `persist()` method will write any object out to a specified file using `ObjectOutputStream`. It maintains a log directory internally. All persistence data will be written to this log directory (like reggie, rmid and mahalo). One can set the log directory by calling the `setLogDir` method. The `restore()` method is used to read back persisted objects:

```java
class Logger {
    private static String myLogDir = "." + File.pathSeparator;
    public static void setLogDir(String dirname) {
        myLogDir = dirname;
    }
```

```
public static synchronized void persist(String filename, Object item)
  throws IOException {
    ObjectOutputStream os =
        new ObjectOutputStream(new FileOutputStream(myLogDir + filename));
    os.writeObject(item);
    os.flush();
    os.close();
}

public static synchronized Object restore(String filename)
  throws IOException,ClassNotFoundException {
    ObjectInputStream os =
        new ObjectInputStream(new FileInputStream(myLogDir + filename));
    Object retval = os.readObject();
    os.close();
    return retval;
}

} // of class Logger
```

Persisting Service IDs Separately

In this persistence implementation, we're going to persist the service ID in a different place to the other persistent states: the service ID will be saved in the `servid.per` file, while the rest of the state will be saved in the `state.per` file.

This strategy makes debugging and code modification while proxies are still alive in reggie simpler, and means that you don't have to wipe out the log directory all the time. The persistent service ID will ensure that our service proxy in the reggie is always current. On the other hand, any modification of any persistent data structure, or resetting of state, will require us to delete only the `state.per` file in the log directory.

```
interface HitmanConstants {
    static final String IDFILE = "servid.per";
    static final String STATEFILE = "state.per";
}
```

The states that we'll save are bundled in a `SavedStates` class. This facilitates the serialization used during persistence.

Persisting Remote References with Associated Codebase

The `TransactionManager` reference is handled very carefully. We actually **do not** persist the reference of the `TransactionManager` itself – this is transient. Instead, we keep the reference synchronized with a `MarshalledObject` that is persisted with the state. This is necessary because we have to preserve the codebase of the transaction manager reference in order to use it after a crash. Only `MarshalledObject` can contain codebase annotation as we saw earlier in the RMI chapter. `setTM()` and `restoreTM()` methods are used to keep the transient `TransactionManager` reference consistent with the content of the `MarshalledObject` during persistence operations.

```
class SavedStates implements Serializable {
    public Color tmpColor = null;
    public Color currentColor = Color.gray;
    public long crashCount = 0;
    public Color nextColor = null;
    public boolean alwaysAbort = false;
    public transient  TransactionManager myTM = null;
    public MarshalledObject cookedTM = null;
    public long myTID = 0;
    public SavedStates() {}

    public void setTM(TransactionManager inTM) throws IOException {
        myTM = inTM;
        if (inTM != null) {
          cookedTM = new MarshalledObject(myTM);
          java.rmi.server.RemoteObject myRemote =
                                        (java.rmi.server.RemoteObject)inTM;
          java.rmi.server.RMIClassLoader.getClassAnnotation(myRemote.getClass()));
        }
        else
          cookedTM = null;

    }

    public void restoreTM() throws IOException,ClassNotFoundException {
        if (cookedTM != null)
            myTM = (TransactionManager) cookedTM.get();
    }

}
```

Here is the implementation of `IdPrinter` again, but this time with true service ID persistence.

```
class IdPrinter implements ServiceIDListener,HitmanConstants {
    public IdPrinter() {
    }

    public void serviceIDNotify(ServiceID sid) {
        System.out.println("Service has been assigned service ID: "
            + sid.toString());
        try {
            Logger.persist( IDFILE, sid);
            System.out.println("Written to persistent storage.");
        }
        catch (Exception e) {
            System.out.println("Cannot write to persistent storage.");
            System.exit(1);
        }
    }

} //of class IdPrinter Extending from JFrame instead of UnicastRemoteObject
```

The `HitmanService` class needs to implement the remote `TransactionParticipant` interface.
Note that `HitmanService` does not extend the `UnicastRemoteObject`, as some other RMI based
service implementations do.

We are extending it from `Jframe`, with the consequence that any `this` reference within the
`HitmanService` class will not be automatically exported by the RMI runtime. References must be
exported explicitly. Note the `HitmanService` is also an `ActionListener`. This AWT interface is used to
handle the event notification when the GUI button is pressed.

```
public class HitmanService extends JFrame
   implements HitmanConstants, ActionListener, TransactionParticipant {
      static final int MAX_INSTANCES = 3;
      static final String [] GROUPS1 =  { "iguanas"};

      static ServiceID myID = null;
```

We've made the `savedStates` instance static, so that an implicit this reference will not be serialized with the object during persistence operations. `HitmanService` does not implement the `HitmanItf` directly, instead a helper class called `HitmanItfImpl` provides the implementation, which we maintain a reference to in an instance through `myImpl`.

```
      static SavedStates ss = new SavedStates();

      protected JPanel mainPanel;
      protected JButton myButton;

      protected JoinManager myJM = null;

      protected Remote meExported = null;

      static HitmanService myApp = null;
      HitmanItfImpl myImpl = null;
```

The `main()` method does command line processing. The usage syntax is:

```
java hitmanService [<name attribute> [[a | b]
[<log directory ending with \ >]]]
```

The `<name attribute>` will be attached to the service proxy when registering with a lookup service. If "a" is specified as the second argument, the `abortFlag` will be set to true. In this case, the service instance will fail to prepare, causing a distributed transaction abort. It can be used to test for the appropriate behaviors. If "b" is specified as the second argument, the `HitmanService` instance will prepare and commit successfully. Finally, the log directory path can be specified by the third parameter. If specified, it must end with the backslash '\' on a Win32 system.

The main method parses the command line, creates a new instance and builds the simple GUI, but it does not wait around. This is because event handling threads within a swing GUI application will keep the application running without having the `main()` method hanging around forever:

```
public static void main(String argv[]) {
    boolean abortFlag = false;

    // set the root for the persistence directory
    if (argv.length > 2)
        Logger.setLogDir(argv[2]);
    if (argv.length > 1)
        if (argv[1].equals("a"))
            abortFlag = true;
    if (argv.length > 0)
        myApp = new HitmanService(argv[0], abortFlag);
    else
        myApp = new HitmanService("Hitman Service",abortFlag);
```

```
        myApp.pack();
        myApp.show();
        myApp.setLocation(10,10);
    }  // of main()
```

Crash Recovery for 2PC Support

The `restoreAll()` method restores all the persisted states. It keeps the synchronization between the marshalled object and the remote Transaction Manager reference. It also implements the `crashCount` since we only restore states after a restart. `restoreAll` also performs the 2PC crash recovery requirements. It first detects if we're committed into a prepared state. Here is the state mapping in our application:

State	ss.currentColor	ss.nextColor	ss.tmpColor
active	grey	null	red
prepared	grey	red	red
committed	red	null	null
aborted	null	null	null

As we can see, `ss.nextColor` is non-null only when the transaction is in the prepared state. In this case, the restarted participant must query the transaction state using the `getState()` method of the `TransactionManager`. If the return value is `TransactionConstants.COMMITTED`, then the participant must follow through with the transaction commit.

```
    public void restoreAll()  {
        try {
            myID = (ServiceID) Logger.restore(IDFILE);
            ss = (SavedStates) Logger.restore(STATEFILE);
            ss.restoreTM();  // get cooked TM back with codebase
            ss.crashCount++;  // do not persist right the way
```

Here, we determined that we crashed while in the PREPARED state. According to mahalo's implementation of the default transaction semantics, we must now call the transaction manager to get its state for our transaction (either COMMITTED or ABORTED) and proceed to the same state.

```
            // crash recovery if found in PREPARED state
            if (ss.nextColor != null)
            {
                // in prepared mode
                System.out.println("detected PREPARED!");
                boolean done = false;
                while (!done)
                {
                    try {
                        long tState = ss.myTM.getState(ss.myTID);
                        if (tState == TransactionConstants.COMMITTED)
                        {
                            commit(ss.myTM, ss.myTID);
                            done = true;
                        }
                    }
                    catch (UnknownTransactionException ex) {
```

```
                              abort(ss.myTM, ss.myTID);
                              done = true;
                          }
                          catch (NoSuchObjectException ex)
                          {
                              abort(ss.myTM, ss.myTID);
                              done = true;
                          }
                          catch (Exception e)
                          {
                              e.printStackTrace();
                          }
                          try {
                              Thread.sleep(5000);
                          }
                          catch (Exception ex) {}

                      } // of while !done
                  } // of if nextColor

          } // of outter try
          catch (Exception e)
          {   // first time if exception caught
              e.printStackTrace();
              return;
          }
      }  // of restore all
```

Execution Ordering within Constructor

The constructor of the HitmanService sets the default ss.alwaysAbort value, and then loads the RMISecurityManager before calling restoreAll(). This is necessary since restoreAll() needs to reconstitute a remote object in the form of the marshalled TransactionManager reference:

```
public HitmanService(String inTitle,boolean abortFlag) {
    super("Name: " + inTitle);
    ss.alwaysAbort = abortFlag;

    // subtle ordering... this must come first before restoreAll()
    // since restoreAll() requires the RMIClassLoader to work properly
    //
    if (System.getSecurityManager() == null) {
        // need an RMISecurityManager to download proxy from lookup service
        System.setSecurityManager(new RMISecurityManager());

    }
```

We also build the GUI before restoreAll() because if restoreAll() performs crash recovery, it may end up carrying out a commit. Our commit handler performs a RollForward() which sets the color of the button immediately. If we do not create the GUI first, there will be no button to set color on.

```
    // build GUI first, restoreAll() may do a commit
    mainPanel = new JPanel();
    myButton = new JButton("Terminate this service now!");
    myButton.addActionListener(this);
    mainPanel.add(myButton);
    getContentPane().add(mainPanel);

    restoreAll();
```

JoinManager and Persistent Service IDs

The discovery and join handling is pretty standard, like most of the other services we have created so far. However, since we have implemented true persistence, we may use the second form of the JoinManager constructor most of the time. Usually we'll have a service ID already, and won't need the lookup service to assign one.

```
// Discovery and Join through JoinManager
//
LookupDiscoveryManager ldm = null;
String [] groupsToDiscover = GROUPS1;

Entry [] attributes = new Entry[1];

try
{
    myImpl = new HitmanItfImpl(this);

    ldm = new LookupDiscoveryManager(groupsToDiscover, null, null);
    attributes[0] = new Name(inTitle);

    if (myID == null)
    {
        myJM =  new JoinManager(myImpl,
                    attributes ,
                    new IdPrinter() ,
                    ldm,
                    null );
    }
    else
    {
        myJM =  new JoinManager(myImpl,
                    attributes,
                    myID,
                    ldm ,
                    null );
    }
}
catch(Exception e)
{
    e.printStackTrace();
    System.exit(1);
}
```

Joining a Transaction On Demand

The changeColor() method is part of the HitmanItf remote interface. Here, we setup a temporary state variable called tmpColor with the input color, and then we join the specified transaction, placing us into the active state. We also check to make sure that we are not already in the middle of a transaction, or that it is not a non-transactional call. Note the manual exporting of the remote reference using UnicastRemoteObject.exportObject(), which is necessary since the service class does not extend UnicastRemoteObject.

```
    public synchronized void changeColor(Color inColor, TransactionManager tm,
      long trID ) {

        if (ss.myTM != null) {
            System.out.println("already in transaction!");
            actionPerformed(null);  //exit
        }

        if (tm == null) {
            ss.nextColor = inColor;
            rollForward();
        }
        else {
            try {
                ss.setTM(tm);
                ss.myTID = trID;
                if (meExported == null)
                  meExported =
                    java.rmi.server.UnicastRemoteObject.exportObject(this);
                ss.myTM.join(trID, (TransactionParticipant) this, ss.crashCount);
                ss.tmpColor = inColor;

                Logger.persist( STATEFILE, ss);
            }
            catch ( Exception e )  {
              e.printStackTrace();
              actionPerformed(null);
            }

            System.out.println("tranaction joined successfully");
        }  // of else

    } // of changeColor
```

Handling Shutdown Requests

The `actionPerformed()` method is called when the user presses the GUI button. Here, we persist the current state and cancel the registration lease with the lookup service(s) by calling `JoinManager`'s `terminate()` method. We will actually use this to simulate a crash in the middle of a transaction later on.

```
    public void actionPerformed(ActionEvent e) {
        try {
          Logger.persist( STATEFILE, ss);
        } catch (Exception ex) {} // no point to do anything here
        myJM.terminate();
        System.exit(0);
    }
```

TransactionParticipant Interface Implementation

Next we'll look at the `TransactionParticipant` interface implementations, the methods that support the two-phase commit protocol. We also have some private helper methods to make implementation simpler. `RollForward` takes the prepared state information and makes it durable – it makes the color change permanently visible. It also restores the rest of the state variables to null.

```
// support for transacations
//

protected synchronized void rollForward(){
  ss.currentColor = ss.nextColor;
  ss.tmpColor = null;
  ss.nextColor = null;

  myButton.setBackground(ss.currentColor);
  myButton.repaint();


}
```

`rollBack()` restores the state variables to the values they held before the transaction began.

```
protected synchronized void rollBack()    {
  ss.tmpColor = null;
  ss.nextColor = null;


}
```

`prepare()` gets ready for `rollForward()` and `rollBack()`. However, if `ss.alwaysAbort` is set, we will always fail the `prepare()` and return `TransactionConstants.ABORTED`.

```
public int prepare(TransactionManager tmgr, long tid) {
  System.out.println("Preparing...");
  System.out.flush();

  if ((ss.tmpColor != null) && (!ss.alwaysAbort) )
     ss.nextColor = ss.tmpColor;
  else
     try {
        abort(tmgr, tid);
         return TransactionConstants.ABORTED;
     } catch(Exception e) {
        e.printStackTrace();
         actionPerformed(null);
     }
  try {
     Logger.persist( STATEFILE, ss);
     Thread.sleep(5000);
  }
  catch (Exception e) {
     actionPerformed(null);
  }

  return TransactionConstants.PREPARED;
}
```

`commit()` basically does the `rollForward()`. We also implement a delay here so that we can actually watch the state change during testing:

```
public void commit(TransactionManager mgr, long id) {
  System.out.println("committing!");
  System.out.flush();
  try {
      Thread.sleep(5000);
```

```
            rollForward();
            ss.setTM(null);
            Logger.persist( STATEFILE, ss);
        }
    catch (Exception e) {
        actionPerformed(null);
    }

}
```

`abort()` rolls back.

```
public void abort(TransactionManager mgr, long id) {
  System.out.println("aborting");
  rollBack();
  try {
    ss.setTM(null);
    Logger.persist( STATEFILE, ss);
  }
  catch (Exception e) {
    actionPerformed(null);
  }
}
```

`prepareAndCommit()` calls `prepare()` `commit()` to perform the work respectively.

```
public int prepareAndCommit (TransactionManager mgr, long id) {
  int result = prepare(mgr, id);
  if (result == TransactionConstants.PREPARED) {
    commit(mgr, id);
    result = TransactionConstants.COMMITTED;
  }
  return result;
}
}
```

Implementing the HitmanItf Interface

The `HitmanItfImpl` helper class provides the implementation for the `HitmanItf` remote interface. Since it extends `UnicastRemoteObject`, references to it are automatically exported. The lookup service will contain an RMI stub to this class.

```
import java.io.Serializable;
import java.rmi.server.*;
import java.rmi.*;
import java.awt.Color;
import net.jini.core.transaction.server.TransactionManager;

public class HitmanItfImpl extends UnicastRemoteObject
  implements HitmanItf,Serializable {
    HitmanService myServ = null;
    public HitmanItfImpl() throws RemoteException {
    }

    public HitmanItfImpl(HitmanService servRef) throws RemoteException {
      myServ = servRef;
    }
```

During construction of the class, a `HitmanService` instance is passed in. When an RMI `changeColor` call is received, it simply forwards the call to the `changeColor()` method of the `HitmanService` instance.

```
public void changeColor(Color color, TransactionManager tm, long trID)
    throws RemoteException
{
    myServ.changeColor(color,tm,trID);
    System.out.println("called!");
}

}
```

Testing A Transaction Failure Scenario

If you have been following along, you have already compiled and run the `HitmanService` successfully. Now, we'll use the service and the transactional client to test two more scenarios.

First, we will test a case when one of the participants fails to prepare.

Change directory to `ch9\code\bats`

Start the httpd by running:

`runhttpd`

Start the class server for stubs by running:

`runhttpdstubs`

Start rmid, reggie, and mahalo by running (assuming that you left them running before shutting down rmid from the earlier test):

`runrmid`

Change directory to `ch9\code\hitman`.

Start two instances of the `HitmanService` by running:

`runhit1`
`runhit2`

Start an always abort instance of the `HitmanService` by running:

`runhit3`

This batch file, `runhit3.bat` will always abort because it passes "a" as a parameter into the HitmanService instance.

Change directory to `ch9\code\hitClient2` and start a transactional client by running:

`runhit`

Watch the consoles of the services carefully. Notice how they first enter the prepared state, and that the `runhit3` instance aborts. The end result should be abort on all instances and no change in button color. Here is a screenshot of some typical console output from a service instance.

Close down all of the `HitmanServices` by clicking their buttons.

To test a crash recovery scenario, change the directory to `ch9\code\Hitman`, and start two services instances:

```
runhit1
runhit2
```

Now start a transactional client by changing directory to `ch9\code\hitClient2` and running:

```
runhit
```

Watch the progress carefully. After both services have entered prepared, and one service has entered the committed state, quickly click the button on the non-committed service. We have added a delay in the code to make this simpler, but you may have to restart a few times to get the timing right.

We're simulating a participant crash after entering the prepared state, but before the commit request arrived from the manager. Now, you should see the committed button's color turn red. Restart the service that is down, making sure you use the right batch file (runhit1 or runhit2 depending on which one you shutdown). You should see crash recovery go to work, and the button automatically turn to red once it finds that the transaction has already been committed. Here is a typical console output from the crash recovery:

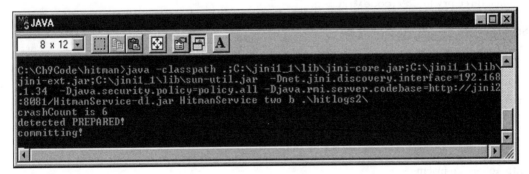

Summary

In this chapter, we examined the classic transaction model and discussed how Jini's transaction model compares with it, and differs from it. Jini's distributed transaction centers around the role of Jini service called the transaction manager. The transaction manager implements the two-phase commit protocol, and co-ordinates state changes between multiple participants. We saw how the two-phase commit protocol can support the ACID properties of classic transaction; and we explored the rigid definition of these properties.

Moving from the concept of generic transactions, to the distributed computing model, we saw that Jini services can benefit from the transaction manager service in many ways that will not involve the rigid ACID semantics of classical transactions. In fact, Jini transaction manager services can be used as a reliable synchronization mechanism between distributed services.

Sun reference implementation of the transaction manager, mahalo, is included with the Jini distribution. We used mahalo to write a client that coordinated a distributed transaction between two participating services, each changing the color of a GUI button.

Next, we examined how to program a Jini transaction participant, a service that a client can ask to join a distributed transaction. Finally, we used our very own transaction client and participants to explore transaction failure scenarios including a participant abort, and a participant crash during the two-phase commit handling.

Now the hard stuff has been dealt with, we can get going with the versatile helper utility and services that the Jini library provides. None of this should prove particularly complex now that you've covered the interactions between clients and services, those built on or around leases, remote events and even transactions.

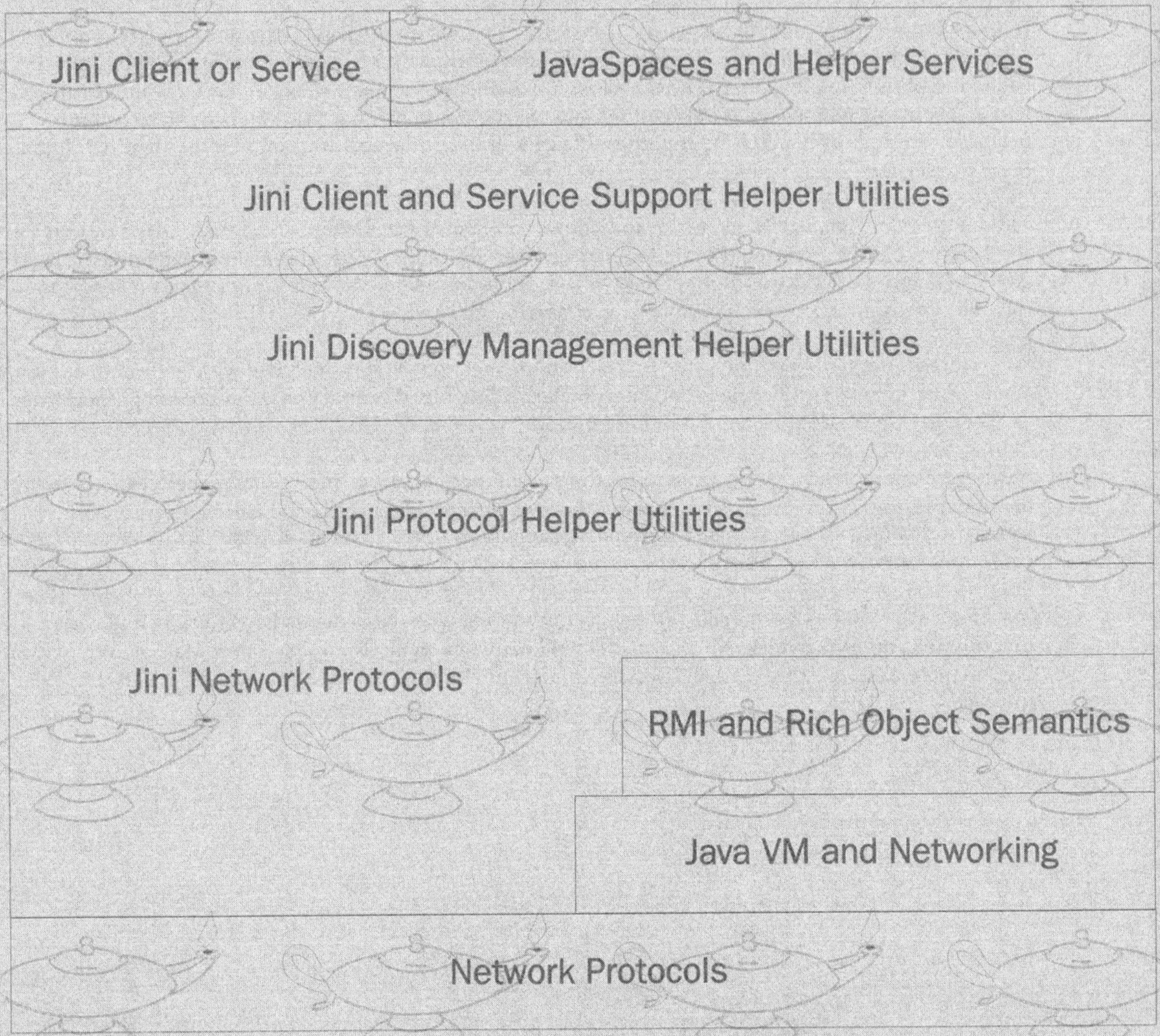

Jini Client or Service	JavaSpaces and Helper Services

Jini Client and Service Support Helper Utilities

Jini Discovery Management Helper Utilities

Jini Protocol Helper Utilities

Jini Network Protocols

RMI and Rich Object Semantics

Java VM and Networking

Network Protocols

10

Basic Helper Utilities

The next two chapters are the cookbook chapters. We'll examine each of the versatile helper utilities and services supplied as part of the Jini library. We will explain the design rationale of each, what it will do for us, and how we can use it. According to the Jini specification, utilities are Java library classes (components) that implement well-defined local (non-remote) interfaces and run *within* the user's Java VM (so developers integrate them into their own code); services, on the other hand, implement well-defined remote interfaces and run within their own independent Java VMs. These independently running helper services are sometimes referred to as 'third-party' services, since they perform tasks such as lease renewal, discovery, etc. on behalf of their client as a 'third-party'. Just like our coverage of the lookup service, we'll construct a schematic diagram of each component, illustrating how it interacts with 'users' (callers for Java library classes and clients for third-party services) and other external pieces. Of course, there will also be a good dose of sample code, tailored to the specific usage of each.

We are going to be examining these utilities and services in some depth, so while this chapter will be useful to you now, we hope that you'll also find it useful as a reference later, when you're developing your own applications. (You can also refer to Appendix I for a higher-level quick reference guide.)

In order to illustrate the concepts introduced here, and run tests with the sample programs we built in earlier chapters, we're going to put together two new utilities, from high-level design through to detailed coding. These utilities are:

- ❑ Reggtool – an extensible command line based utility that finds and modifies Jini lookup services
- ❑ The Instant Jini Service Creation Environment – a simple component that can help turn anything working over a TCP/IP port into a Jini service

We will work on reggtool in this chapter and the next, followed by the Jini Service Creation Environment in the latter part of the next chapter. Hopefully, these tools will be useful to you while you're developing with Jini. They will also both be formally made into jini.org projects, so that you too can contribute to their future evolution – the Jini way.

Jini Library Development Support

There is a wide range of support for Jini developers, many of which you've already seen, within the Jini development kit:

- ❑ The reference implementation of lookup service: reggie
- ❑ The reference implementation of transaction service: mahalo
- ❑ A simple HTTP class server (part of `tools.jar`) for serving RMI stubs
- ❑ Basic specified interfaces and classes presented as part of the API documentation
- ❑ Helper utilities
- ❑ Helper services

We have already seen and worked with the first four quite thoroughly; we haven't looked in depth at the last two, which we'll do here. Helper utilities and services do overlap in terms of functionality, but the big distinction between them is that while utilities are static classes, helper services are independently running third-party Jini services. Helper services are Jini services that contribute to the functioning of an entire Jini network. While the lifetime of a helper utility is the same as the lifetime of its user, the lifetime of a helper service is much longer, as it is part of the long-lived Jini system (like reggie). Helper services must therefore have some additional functionality; they must:

- ❑ Implement persistent mechanisms and handle crash recovery
- ❑ Issue and manage distributed lease(s) whenever a resource is acquired on the user's behalf, ensuring that resources will eventually be reclaimed should the client fail
- ❑ Handle requests from multiple users throughout its lifetime

So, in essence, a helper service is a full-fledged Jini service, while a helper utility is a collection of simple, static, Java library classes.

The Architecture of Helper Utilities and Services

There are different levels of support available in the class library, as each application you build will require support levels according to the nature of that application and the platform it's intended to run on. For example, a device driver will need low-level basic protocol support while a fully-fledged Jini service can readily use the much higher-level do-it-all support of complex library components. To satisfy the needs of this diverse group of users, the Jini library supplies support classes at four different levels:

- ❑ Low-level, basic protocol utilities: handle the low level unicast and multicast discovery protocols
- ❑ Mid-level, protocol utilities: handle the low level protocols and provide assistance in managing the groups and unicast locations
- ❑ High-level, do-it-all manager utilities: handle almost everything that a client or service may need, leaving the application to concentrate on the logic
- ❑ Independent, long-lived, helper services: handle discovery, leasing, and event handling as a third-party on behalf of the actual service/client

The following figure shows the four levels of libraries. The box on the left shows the first three levels of support, provided by helper utilities, being built on top of one another. The box on the right shows helper services as completely independent services providing support for clients/services as a third-party.

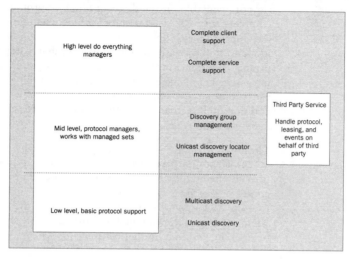

The following is a brief description on these four levels of support, and how they may be used while you're programming.

Classification	Description/Application
Basic protocol utilities	Particularly useful for applications designed for limited platforms and requiring very small footprints, these utilities shield the developer from the tedium of having to use low-level socket calls to control the lower level behavior. They provide no assistance for implementing managed sets (a managed set being a set of objects that is managed by some entity). In this particular instance, multicast discovery requires the management of a set of groups; and unicast discovery requires the management of a set of host:port information. We will devote a complete section working with managed sets later in this chapter.
Mid-level protocol manager utilities	This next level of support gives the developer a little more assistance by taking care of some of the more complex and tedious code used in set management, while still enabling them to access and/or modify protocol handling. It assists in the implementation of managed sets, and is typically used in applications that need some low-level access to the protocol elements but has no need to customize the managed set handling.

Table continued on following page

Classification	Description/Application
High-level, do almost everything, manager utilities	Used by the majority of clients and services, this is the highest level of support available for the discover and join protocols. They provide complete coverage of all required protocol handling, allowing the developer to focus their application entirely on independently implemented service/client logic. It is a reliable implementation of protocol handling, providing full support for, and implementation of, the associated managed sets with the helper utility. The developer can use a substantially simpler interface to interact with the helper utility, and does not need to deal with protocol handling and/or set management details.
Helper Services (independent third-party service)	These services allow devices, services and clients that couldn't otherwise be Jini participants to participate in a Jini network. They provide the good behavior essentials that a Jini participant must conform to. They exist as standalone, long-lived, independently running (third-party) services. They also provide intrinsically volatile clients and services with an 'omnipresence', or 'long-lived point of delegation' within a Jini network.

So each of three levels of helper utility and the independent helper services address a distinct audience. The high-level manager utilities are likely to be the most frequently used of this collection, because they are role-specific (one for client role, and one for service role), and make client or service creation very simple. In this chapter and the next, we will start our detailed coverage with the low-level helper utilities, and proceed up the stack to the higher-level manager utilities. In the next chapter, we will also examine, in detail, the role of the independent helper services.

This table shows each of the helper utilities and helper services that is provided as part of Jini. It also classifies each within the four-level classification scheme. This should give you a better feel for when you may want to use each of the utilities and services in your own applications. The third column indicates where the utility/service will be covered in depth.

Utility/Service Name	Classification	Coverage Chapter
LookupDiscovery	Basic protocol utility	Chapter 10
LookupLocator	Basic protocol utility	Chapter 10
LookupLocatorDiscovery	Mid-level protocol manager utility	Chapter 10
LookupDiscoveryManager	Mid-level protocol manager utility	Chapter 10
LeaseRenewalManager	High-level protocol manager utility	Chapter 11
JoinManager	High-level manager utility	Chapter 11
ServiceDiscoveryManager	High-level manager utility	Chapter 11
LookupDiscovery service	Helper service	Chapter 11
LeaseRenewal service	Helper service	Chapter 11
EventMailbox service	Helper service	Chapter 11

Approach to Learning and Applying Helper Utilities and Services

The better we understand the support level that each utility/service operates on, the easier it will be for us to appreciate their specific design and interface style. With familiarity, we'll find selecting the most appropriate classes or services for our applications much easier. Writing programs using the utilities can be quite easy once we understand the interfaces that they support and why these interfaces are there. Instead of treating these utilities as classic 'black boxes', we will benefit from an in-depth understanding of how these implementations actually work underneath. This understanding will enable us to be flexible, agile, and adaptive in our application of these utilities. The following sections will provide us with this understanding of how the utilities work.

Basic Protocol Utilities in Depth

Using the protocol handling utilities mean that we don't have to program raw Java networking elements on the socket level, as we did earlier in the book, but can instead maintain low-level control over protocol interaction and restrict our coding to a significantly higher level.

In order to construct the `jinTool.java` program in Chapter 5 we coded everything at socket level. Doing so meant that we were repeatedly re-inventing the wheel, and spending a significant amount of time coding around well-specified protocols. Using the protocol handling class effectively delegates these vital yet tedious implementations to Sun's engineering team! For example, the `LookupDiscovery` utility handles the multicast request announcement protocols, and `LookupLocator` the Unicast Discovery protocol.

The Discovery Management Interfaces

While the programming interfaces that access the protocol handling utility classes may appear simple enough, constructing a robust implementation of them is definitely not a simple matter. Fortunately, the original class designers and coders at Sun have handled much of this implementation complexity for us. All we have to contend with is a rather elegant set of unifying interfaces, collectively called the Discovery Management interfaces.

The three discovery interfaces unify the discovery process both conceptually and in practice, each providing simple and intuitive access to a complex set of operations performed by the lower level protocol classes, and allowing the developer to manage specific sets of items vital to the operation of the discovery protocols:

❑   `DiscoveryManagement` – management of discovered lookup service proxy objects (called registrars)

❑   `DiscoveryGroupManagement` – management of groups used during discovery

❑   `DiscoveryLocatorManagement` – management of unicast discovery information

Managed Sets

These interfaces have methods that allow the programmer access to **managed sets**. A **managed set** is a set of items managed by some entity – the set of groups used during discovery, as managed by a utility class, is a managed set. Implementing the `DiscoveryXXXManagement` interfaces allows us to access and modify managed sets, confident that the sets will still be functioning properly within a Jini community. You'll see how powerful this is when we use the `JoinManager` class that handles the join protocol later. In this complex class, each change in the managed set can trigger a multitude of complex operations.

Management of Discovered Registrars

The DiscoveryManagement interface ties together all the methods that are used during the discovery process by the protocol handling classes. It assists in handling the managed set of discovered registrars during the discovery process. The operation model, as it appears to the developer, is relatively straightforward:

❑ User provides a callback in the form of an object supporting the DiscoveryListener interface, calling the addDiscoveryListener() method

❑ Lower-level protocol class performs the actual discovery on-the-wire

❑ On the discovery of one or more lookup services, the protocol notifies the supplied callback object

We're going to look at what goes on behind the scenes and see what is really going on. To begin with, here is the definition of the DiscoveryManagement interface:

```
public interface DiscoveryManagement
{
public void addDiscoveryListener(DiscoveryListener listener);
public void removeDiscoveryListener(DiscoveryListener listener);
public ServiceRegistrar[] getRegistrars();
public void discard(ServiceRegistrar proxy);
public void terminate();
}
```

Here is a brief synopsis of each of the methods:

Method	Description
addDiscoveryListener()	Called by the user to supply a listener/callback object
removeDiscoveryListener()	Called by the user to remove a listener. The implementation will support the management of multiple listeners. All parties registered via the addDiscoveryListener() call will receive callback when discovery succeeds and a new lookup service is located. The application can then use the getRegistrars() method (described next) to see what has been discovered.
getRegistrars()	This method is called by the user to obtain the lookup service registrars that have just been discovered. What this method returns depends on when the call is made (before or after discovery). Note that each implementation will define how many registrars will be returned. Some may return an entire managed set of registrars, while others may simply return the most recently discovered lookup service.

Method	Description
discard()	This is used in the management of registrar sets: should a user (service or client) decide that a previously discovered lookup service should be discarded (because an entity has moved between groups, and the lookup service no longer services these groups, for example), then the user should call this method. Typically, this will result in a flush of the registrar by the protocol handling classes (if they are still holding reference to it). The listeners managed by the object implementing the DiscoveryManagement interface are called to notify them that the lookup service has been discarded
terminate()	Tells the implementation to gracefully end the discovery process. Other methods of this interface should not be called once this method has been called.

There are two significant points that should be made about the DiscoveryManagement interface:

❑ There is no specification as to who actually manages the set of lookup registrars; it can be the interface's implementer, the interface's user, or co-operatively between the two; one must consult the implementation specific documentation to determine this

❑ The listener's registrations are not leased, because this interface is intended to be used and implemented by classes local to the Java VM of the user

The caller of the addDiscoveryListener() registration method must supply an implementation of the DiscoveryListener interface (the callback handling object). Here is a definition of the DiscoveryListener interface:

```
public interface DiscoveryListener extends java.util.EventListener
{
    void discarded(DiscoveryEvent e);
    void discovered(DiscoveryEvent e);
}
```

Note that this is a general interface that discovers arbitrary items. There are only two methods that a listener must implement: the discovered() method, to signify the discovery of one or more items (that is, lookup service registrars), and the discarded() method so that a specific, previously discovered item, can be discarded. If the implementation of this interface is maintaining a cache or managed set of these items, the specified item should be discarded.

There exists another interface that inherits from DiscoveryListener; it is called DiscoveryChangeListener. Applications that are interested in being notified of group membership changes associated with discovered lookup services should implement this interface:

```
public interface DiscoveryChangeListener extends DiscoveryListener
{
    void changed(DiscoveryEvent e);
}
```

The changed() method should be implemented by the listener so it is notified of any group membership changes amongst the discovered lookup services.

The `DiscoveryEvent` class instance that one will receive is defined as:

```
public class DiscoveryEvent extends java.util.EventObject
{
    public DiscoveryEvent(Object source, java.util.Map groups) {..}
    public DiscoveryEvent( Object source, ServiceRegistrar [] regs) {..}
       Map getGroups() {..}
    ServiceRegistrar [] getRegistrars() {..}
}
```

The most useful method is the `getRegistrars()` method. It returns the set of registrars discovered associated with this event. The `DiscoveryListener` interface is not specifically associated with lookup registrars, while the `DiscoveryEvent` object definition that works with it is. The `getGroups()` method returns a `Map`. The keys of the maps are the lookup services that have been discovered, identical to those returned in `getRegistrars()`, while the values of the maps are the corresponding list of groups that each lookup service will handle.

The `DiscoveryManagement` interface that we have just examined is generally implemented by low-level protocol handling classes. Interestingly, even though the higher-level manager classes provide significant internal processing and management functions, they still support this interface and provide an optional direct hook into the innards of the discovery process.

Management of Groups Used During Discovery

As we discussed in Chapter 5, a Jini network is partitioned according to group boundaries. Each participant in the Jini network must keep track of the groups that it wishes to belong to, as well as the groups managed by each and every lookup service it has discovered. Something must then keep track of a set of such groups during runtime. Several library classes provide this function to simplify the Jini programmer's work. The `DiscoveryGroupManagement` interface specifies a collection of methods for working with a managed set of groups.

```
public interface DiscoveryGroupManagement
{
    public static final String[] ALL_GROUPS = null;
    public static final String[] NO_GROUPS = new String[0];
    public String[] getGroups();
    public void addGroups(String[] groups) throws IOException;
    public void setGroups(String[] groups) throws IOException;
    public void removeGroups(String[] groups);
}
```

The two constants, `ALL_GROUPS` and `NO_GROUPS`, may be used as parameters into utility classes that will perform discovery based on groups. `ALL_GROUPS` specifies that the entity is interested in joining/handling `ALL_GROUPS`, while `NO_GROUPS` specifies that discovery/handling should not yet begin.

As you might expect, the `getGroups()` method returns all the groups in the current managed set, `addGroups()` enables the user to add groups to be managed, `setGroups()` replaces the currently managed set of groups, and `removeGroups()` removes a specified set of groups from the managed set.

Note that both `addGroups()` and `setGroups()` throw an `IOException`, indicating that they can fail if the underlying network operation fails. When group composition changes, a Jini service is required to notify lookup services that it has registered with according to the Join protocol.

This notification will involve a network transmission via sockets, and may be subjected to IOExceptions.

Classes that implement this DiscoveryGroupManagement interface either manage the groups themselves, or provide facades to entities that manage the groups. From the perspective of an interface user, the class is providing the managed set functionality.

Management of Unicast Discovery Information

Jini specifies that the unicast protocol be handled as a part of the discovery protocol support. This protocol, as you'll remember from Chapter 5, is used to obtain registrar proxies directly from the local or remote lookup services that are already known.

The Jini library encapsulates the addressing information in a **LookupLocator** object, which is a helper utility. The LookupLocator object for TCP/IP contains the host name/address and the TCP port number used by the unicast discovery listener at the lookup service. It also encapsulates the method to perform unicast discovery, as we will see later in this chapter.

The final discovery management interface of the set, DiscoveryLocatorManagement, deals with a managed set of LookupLocators used typically by protocol handling classes to determine the lookup services on which unicast discovery must be performed. This interface is defined like this:

```
package net.jini.discovery;
public interface DiscoveryLocatorManagement
{
    public LookupLocator[] getLocators();
    public void addLocators(LookupLocator[] locators);
    public void setLocators(LookupLocator[] locators);
    public void removeLocators(LookupLocator[] locators);
}
```

Similar to the groups management interface, one can set, add, and remove LookupLocators. Notice that none of the methods are remote, this is because all protocol handling classes will manage the set of LookupLocators locally – there is no need to send the information across a network. The following section takes a look inside a LookupLocator class.

The main functions of a LookupLocator class are twofold. They encapsulate:

❑   The information associated with a known lookup service (that is, its address and port number)

❑   The connection methods associated with unicast discovery

The following figure shows the action of the LookupLocator utility. The numbers indicate a typical sequence of operation when using the utility. The client or service using the LookupLocator utility will:

❑   First create an instance of the utility and pass its hostname:port information for unicast discovery

❑   Start the discovery process by calling the getRegistrar() method

A variation of the getRegistrar() method allows the client/service to specify a timeout value (in milliseconds) to block while waiting for the discovery.

When using `LookupLocator` on slow networks, this variant of the `getRegistrar()` method can be very handy.

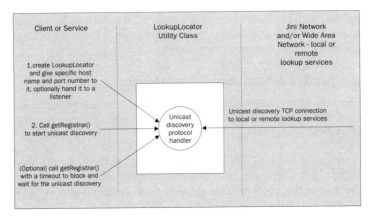

This is its definition:

```
public class LookupLocator extends java.lang.Object implements
    java.io.Serializable
{
    public LookupLocator(String jiniURL) {..}
    public LookupLocator(String host, int port) {..}
    boolean equals(Object loc) {..}
    String getHost() {..}
    int getPort() {..}
    ServiceRegistrar getRegistrar() {..}
    ServiceRegistrar getRegistrar(int timeout) {..}
    int hashCode() {..}
    String toString() {..}
}
```

Note the two different constructors for this class. One uses a URL that may contain both the host and port information (that is, `"jini://myhost.com:4019/"`), and the other takes the host and port information as separate parameters. There is no way to change the host and port assignment once the object is instantiated. This is the expected behavior since each instantiation is the representation of a unique lookup service. The `LookupLocator` can only maintain the identity of the lookup service by its host and port information, so changing the identity does not make sense – a new instance associated with the distinct identity should be created instead.

The `hashCode()` and `equals()` methods inherited from the `Object` root class are redefined to reflect the identity of a `LookupLocator` instance. The two `LookupLocators` are deemed equal when they have the same host and port information. In addition, the `toString()` method will return a Jini URL that contains the host and port information of the `LookupLocator`.

The two `getRegistrar()` methods perform unicast lookup on-the-wire and return the registrar of the associated lookup service (if found). The form with a timeout value is a blocking form, and will wait up to the maximum timeout specified (in milliseconds) for the lookup service to return the registrar object or throw an `IOException` (when the blocking socket times out).

Design Rationale

Encapsulating the information and methods required for unicast discovery protocol handling in one class allows us to use this unicast protocol class in object oriented designs involving higher level management objects. For example, information on multiple known lookup services can be kept in managed sets, and these sets can be used to perform the actual connection to the associated lookup service.

How Do We Use LookupLocator?

We can create an instance of a lookup locator by specifying the hostname and port number:

```
LookupLocator myLoc = new LookupLocator("myhost", 4050);
```

or by using a Jini URL:

```
LookupLocator myLoc = new LookupLocator("jini://myhost:4050/");
```

These two statements connect to the same lookup service through unicast discovery. Should you omit the port specification, the default unicast discovery port, port 4160, will be used automatically. For example, this will connect to port 4160 of myhost:

```
LookupLocator myLoc = new LookupLocator("jini://myhost/");
```

Note that the LookupLocator does not perform any on-the-wire protocol handling during construction, only the host and port information is set.

Following instantiation, one can call a getRegistrar() method to start the discovery process. Once a getRegistrar() method has been called, the LookupLocator object begins discovery.

Let us work through an example of using the LookupLocator helper utility. You can find the code in the lookLocate.java file under the \code\looklocate directory. This is a simple client application that will find a specific lookup service via a LookupLocator.

```
import net.jini.discovery.*;
import net.jini.core.lookup.*;
import net.jini.core.discovery.LookupLocator;
import java.io.*;
import java.rmi.RemoteException;
import java.rmi.RMISecurityManager;

import java.rmi.server.UnicastRemoteObject;
import java.rmi.MarshalledObject;
import net.jini.core.event.*;
import net.jini.core.lease.*;
import net.jini.lease.LeaseRenewalManager;
```

We can see in the following code that myURL contains the information required by the LookupLocator. Our host name is called win98p300, and the port used will be the default CAFÉ-BABE (4160) port.

```
public class lookLocate
{
    LookupLocator myLoc = null;
    static final String myURL = "jini://win98p300/";
```

The lookup will complete within the constructor, so we will not need to wait inside `main()`.

```
static public void main(String argv[])
{
  lookLocate myApp = null;

  if (argv.length > 0)
   myApp = new lookLocate(argv[0]);
  else
    myApp = new lookLocate(myURL);
}

public lookLocate() {}
```

In the constructor, we first load an `RMISecurityManager` to allow us to download registrar stubs from lookup services.

```
public lookLocate(String URL)
{
 if (System.getSecurityManager() == null)
   {
     System.setSecurityManager(new RMISecurityManager());
   }
```

Next, we create the actual `LookupLocator` with the URL as argument.

```
try
  {
    myLoc = new LookupLocator(URL);
    System.out.println("Trying to obtain lookup service directly.");
    System.out.println("   attempting.." + URL);
```

The `getRegistrar()` method will perform the unicast discovery, and we wait for the built-in default time for reply (it is 60 seconds by default, but can be set via the `net.jini.discovery.timeout` property). This is sufficient in our case since the lookup service is actually running on the same machine and we're sure to reach it before the timeout occurs.

```
        ServiceRegistrar myReg = myLoc.getRegistrar();
        if (myReg == null)
        System.out.println("   cannot find locator");
      else
        {
```

We have found the registrar, and we will now print out some information regarding the lookup service. First, we start with the service ID of the lookup service. Next, we find out the groups that are handled by the lookup service and print them.

```
             System.out.println("   found ID: " + myReg.getServiceID());

             String msg = "";
             String [] groups;
             groups = myReg.getGroups();
             if (groups.length > 0)
             for (int o=0; o<groups.length; o++) { msg += groups[o] + " "; }
                System.out.println("   AT host: " + myLoc.getHost());
                System.out.println("       port: " + myLoc.getPort());
                System.out.println("   Groups Supported: " + msg);


             }
          }
       catch(Exception e)
          {
             System.err.println(e.toString());
             e.printStackTrace();
             System.exit(1);
          }
       }
    }
 }
```

You can compile this using:

```
buildit looklocate.java
```

Since this is a client application, and not a remote Jini service, we do not have to create any stubs, and there is no need to build stubs.

Testing the LookupLocator Sample

To test the `LookupLocator` sample, perform the following steps:

- ❑ Change directory to `ch10\code\bats`
- ❑ Clean up any old RMID or reggie logs either manually, or using the `runclean.bat` file
- ❑ Start the class server using `runhttpd.bat`
- ❑ Start the Activation service by running `runrmid.bat`
- ❑ Start a lookup service by running `runlookup1.bat`

At this point, we have a reggie running on the local machine (name in our case is win98p300) at the default TCP port 4160. Now:

- ❑ Change directory to `ch10\code\looklocate`
- ❑ Start the `looklocate` client by executing the `runlook.bat` file

The `runlook.bat` file contains:

```
call setpaths.bat
java    -classpath .;%JINIJARS% -Djava.security.policy=policy.all -
Dnet.jini.discovery.interface=%ADAPTERIP% lookLocate
```

Your output should be similar to this:

```
MS-DOS Prompt
10 x 18
D:\writing\ProJini\Ch8\code\looklocate>java  -Djava.security.policy=policy.all l
ookLocate
Trying to obtain lookup service directly.
    attempting..jini://win98p300/
    found ID: 9e16997e-861f-429f-8385-dbtfe45461e2
    AT host: win98p300
        port: 4160
    Groups Supported: iguanas
```

Notice that the Jini URL "`jini://win98p300/`" has successfully pointed the `LookupLocator` instance to our reggie instance.

Lookup Services Listening On Non-Default Ports

One question naturally comes to mind as we test this simple program. What if there is more than one reggie running on the same machine?

Reggie is designed to be very accommodating. If it finds that the CAFÉ-BABE port is already occupied, it will randomly pick another TCP port to listen at. Unfortunately we can't create `LookupLocator` instances that have Jini URLs pointing to unknown ports.

Thankfully, we can instruct reggie instances to listen to specific ports for unicast discovery. We will take a look at this later, when we design and code the reggtool command line tool.

The next utility we look at is still a low-level utility. While the `LookupLocator` utility handled the client portion of unicast discovery, the `LookupDiscovery` utility discussed next will handle the multicast discovery protocols for a client.

The LookupDiscovery Utility

The `LookupDiscovery` utility is responsible for the on-the-wire handling of the multicast discovery protocols for a client or client-like entity. This includes both the client portion of the multicast announcement protocol (listening for lookup service beacons), and the client portion of the multicast request protocol.

The Design of the LookupDiscovery Utility

The multicast discovery protocols rely on IP multicast performing its work in locating lookup services. As an additional filtering/partitioning mechanism, however, the concept of groups is used. Multicast discovery will not be successful for lookup services that do not handle the group(s) that we want to join. Therefore, unlike unicast discovery, we must supply a set of groups that we are interested in instead of network locations corresponding to host names and ports. Once the `LookupDiscovery` utility has a set of groups, it performs on-the-wire multi-cast discovery to find all the locally reachable lookup services that handle these groups.

This means that one single instance of a `LookupDiscovery` utility can be associated with an entire set of lookup services. Furthermore, the composition of this set may change as the entity using the `LookupDiscovery` changes the groups that it supports, or if the lookup services changes the groups that they service.

What Will LookupDiscovery Do?

The following figure shows what the LookupDiscovery helper utility actually does. The client or service using the utility must:

❏ Create an instance of LookupDiscovery utility and supply a list of groups to look for, as well as registering a listener for callback

❏ Handle the callback to the discovered method, announcing the successful discovery of one or more lookup services

❏ Handle the callback to the discarded method, indicating that a previously discovered lookup service should be discarded

While the LookupDiscovery service does maintain the list of groups internally, it also allows the client/service to directly manipulate this list.

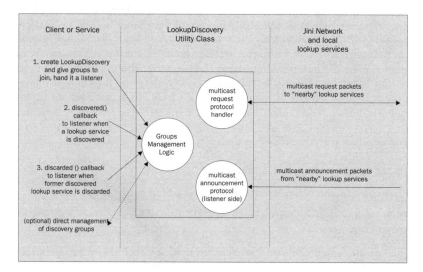

We can see from the figure above that LookupDiscovery will provide callback to the user through a discovered() and discarded() method. This is the familiar DiscoveryManagement interface that we examined earlier. In fact, LookupDiscovery will co-operatively manage the discovery groups with the client (it keeps track of them internally, but will notify the user of changes). This means that one can also access and modify the groups that are managed via the DiscoveryGroupManagement interface that we have seen earlier.

```
public final class LookupDiscovery  implements DiscoveryManagement,
    DiscoveryGroupManagement
{
    public LookupDiscovery(String[] groups) throws IOException{..}
    public void addDiscoveryListener(DiscoveryListener l){..}
    public void removeDiscoveryListener(DiscoveryListener l){..}
    public void discard(ServiceRegistrar reg){..}
    public String[] getGroups(){..}
    public void setGroups(String[] groups) throws IOException{..}
    public void addGroups(String[] groups) throws IOException{..}
    public void removeGroups(String[] groups){..}
    public void terminate(){..}
}
```

All the methods other than the constructor are provided to support the two interfaces. Constructing a `LookupDiscovery`, not surprisingly, requires a `String` array containing the group names. Alternatively, the constants `DiscoveryGroupManagement.ALL_GROUPS` or `DiscoveryGroupManagement.NO_GROUPS` can be used. The `terminate()` method is used to gracefully stop all discovery processes. The methods of the `LookupDiscovery` utility instance should not be called once `terminate()` has been called.

Using the LookupDiscovery Utility

We have already seen many examples of `LookupDiscovery` utility class usage in previous chapters, so here we'll look at a more complex example of the `LookupDiscovery` class. We're also going to take the process a step further, and create the fairly complex reggtool that allows us to monitor and control many aspects of Jini lookup services on a network.

Reggtool – An Extensible, Jini Command Line Tool

The main feature of reggtool is that it is *not* GUI-based. A lot of existing GUI-based Jini tools are so feature laden that the resulting code base is rather convoluted. Achieving clear MVC (Model-View-Controller) separation is easier to sketch on a whiteboard than actually code in Swing and/or AWT (our Paradigma case study will feature such an attempt). Such graphical tools, though admittedly useful, are often limited in that the only person who can extend and maintain it is the author. Would-be contributors may well be discouraged from enhancing and contributing to the tool by the considerable learning curve they first have to struggle with in order to understand the code. A major culprit of such complexity is the coupling of the GUI to the Jini specific logic, such that even a simple browser can involve thousands of lines of code.

We will develop reggtool with the following design rationale:

- ❑ Command structure should be intuitive

- ❑ Text based command will allow scripting to be added easily in the future

- ❑ Freedom from complex libraries (with steep learning curves) brings with it a clean and easy to understand architecture

- ❑ Commands implemented as independent Java classes, with no operative build-in commands, are completely extensible

- ❑ Core code should be simple and easy to follow

The following figure illustrates how reggtool works in practice. The user interacts with reggtool via a command line, text based interface. All output of reggtool is also text based, designed to be used on non-GUI consoles or remotely via TELNET or dumb terminals. The reggtool core code itself is nothing more than an argument parser in the form of command loop, and some support routines for commands. Commands themselves are Java classes that will be dynamically loaded when reggtool starts up. A user can create their own commands according to the reggtool specification (implementing an interface).

This allows users to customize reggtool specifically for their own applications or diagnostic scenarios.

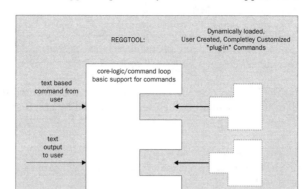

Here is the code, and walkthrough. You can find it in its entirety in the code\reggtool directory, of the reggtool.java file. The structure of reggtool.java is that of a Jini client. You will recognize this structure as we continue with the examination of the code.

```
import net.jini.discovery.*;
import net.jini.core.lookup.*;
import java.io.*;
import java.rmi.RMISecurityManager;
```

We include the low level discovery and lookup packages, and the java.io package with its BufferedReader class and IOException that we will use. We need the RMISecurityManager in order to download the Lookup Service registrar stubs.

The StringTokenizer will be used for parsing the input command. The HashMap will be used to hold the text commands and their dynamically loaded implementation. The ArrayList will be used to hold the list of discovered lookup services.

```
import java.util.StringTokenizer;
import java.util.HashMap;
import java.util.ArrayList;
```

The reggtool class itself implements DiscoveryListener, which, as we will see shortly, provides the LookupDiscovery utility instance (called discover) with a call back. The set of lookup registrars discovered is managed by reggtool, and kept in an ArrayList, part of JDK 1.2's (or later) collections. The commandTable HashMap is used to stores all the commands available to reggtool by mapping the command name String to a reference of an object that implements the commands.

```
public class reggtool  implements DiscoveryListener
{
    private static ArrayList registrars = new ArrayList();
    private static LookupDiscovery discover;
    private static HashMap commandTable = new HashMap();
```

Some constants are defined here, including the version number and the set of dynamically loaded commands that we consider basic. That is, reggtool will fail if it does not find the implementation of these commands.

```
static final int MAX_MATCHES = 5;
static final String CUR_VERSION = "1.0";
static final String [] basicCommands = { "stop", "list" };
static final String BUILTIN_QUIT_COMMAND = "quit";
static final String UNKNOWN_COMMAND_MSG = "Sorry, unknown command.";
static final String SYSTEM_PROMPT = "reggtool> ";
```

Almost all of the work for the basic `reggtool` command parser is performed in the `main()` method. We first set up the standard input for reading the user's command by creating a `BufferedReader` from it.

```
static public void main(String argv[]) {
BufferedReader in = new BufferedReader(new InputStreamReader(System.in));
reggtool myApp = null;
String curCmd = "";
StringTokenizer myTk = null;
String curToken = null;
ReggtoolCommand myCommand = null;
```

Being a client, `reggtool` can be made to work with a specific set of groups. This set of groups can be supplied as part of the command line when invoking `reggtool`. The instantiation of `reggtool` in this case simply starts the multicast discovery (by creating an instance of `LookupDiscovery`) to locate nearby lookup services. Meanwhile, the main thread continues to take command lines from the user at the console. The following code will supply the rest of the command line, `argv`, as the list of groups; or null, which is a synonym for ALL_GROUPS as we shall see shortly.

```
if (argv.length > 0)
  myApp = new reggtool(argv);
else
    myApp = new reggtool(null);
```

Once the `reggtool` instance is created, the welcome tag line is printed, and the commands available enumerated. The `EnumerateCommands()` method scans the current directory for all class files containing objects that implement the `ReggtoolCommand` interface, and adds them to the set of commands supported by `reggtool`, in the `commandTable`. Next, we print a prompt and start the command-parsing loop.

```
try
  {
    System.out.println("Welcome to REGGie TOOL version " + CUR_VERSION);
    myApp.EnumerateCommands();
    System.out.print("reggtool>");
    System.out.flush();
```

Here is the beginning of the command-parsing loop. Unless the quit command terminates the loop, a `StringTokenizer` is used to tokenize the blank delimited command and arguments. The first token is used to match against the commands in the `commandTable`. If a match is found, the rest of the tokens are passed into the `doCommand()` method of the corresponding command object. The `doCommand()` method is actually a method of the `ReggtoolCommand` interface. All command implementation classes must support this interface. The method is provided with the `StringTokenizer` containing command arguments, a copy of the registrars `ArrayList`, and a reference to `reggtool`'s own `LookupDiscovery` instance. This method will perform whatever the command is designed to do, and may operate on the registrars or the `LookupDiscovery` instance. We will see some examples later.

```
        curCmd = in.readLine();
        while(!curCmd.equals(BUILTIN_QUIT_COMMAND))
          {
            myTk = new StringTokenizer(curCmd);
            curToken = null;
            if (myTk.hasMoreTokens())
                curToken = myTk.nextToken();
            if (commandTable.containsKey(curToken))
              {
                myCommand = (ReggtoolCommand) commandTable.get(curToken);
                // pass in a clone of list - command may modify it
                myCommand.doCommand(myTk,(ArrayList) registrars.clone(), discover);
              }
            else
                System.out.println(UNKNOWN_COMMAND_MSG);
            System.out.print(SYSTEM_PROMPT);
            System.out.flush();
            curCmd = in.readLine();
          }
      }
  catch (IOException ex)
      {
        ex.printStackTrace();
        System.exit(1);
      }

    System.out.println("Thanks for using REGGie TOOL!");
  }
```

That's all there is to the `reggtool` 'engine', or the main command processing loop. We will look at some of the subroutines below.

The simple constructor below is not used.

```
    public reggtool() {}
```

The next constructor creates an instance of `LookupDiscovery` as usual, and adds the `reggtool` instance as a `DiscoveryListener`.

```
    public reggtool(String [] ingroups)
      {
        if (System.getSecurityManager() == null)
          {
            System.setSecurityManager(new RMISecurityManager());
          }
        discover = null;

        try
          {
            discover = new LookupDiscovery(LookupDiscovery.NO_GROUPS);
            discover.addDiscoveryListener(this);
            discover.setGroups(ingroups);
          }
        catch(IOException e)
          {
            System.err.println(e.toString());
            e.printStackTrace();
            System.exit(1);
          }
      }
```

Here, the `LookupDiscovery` has discovered a new registrar. In previous code, we simply used the registrar at this point. In `reggtool`, we need to manage the set of registrars since it provides a view of the lookup services available to the commands. Therefore, we need to add each discovered registrar to the `ArrayList` of lookup registrars.

```
public void discovered(DiscoveryEvent evt)
    {
        ServiceRegistrar [] regs = evt.getRegistrars();
        System.out.println("NOTICE: discovery made");
        System.out.print(SYSTEM_PROMPT);
        System.out.flush();
        for (int i=0; i< regs.length; i++)
            if (!registrars.contains(regs[i]))
                registrars.add(regs[i]);
    }
```

In the same way, if a lookup registrar is discarded, it must be deleted from the `ArrayList` that we track. By maintaining the `ArrayList`, we have an accurate view of the lookup services that support our list of groups at any time.

```
public void discarded(DiscoveryEvent evt)
    {
        ServiceRegistrar [] discardedReg = evt.getRegistrars();
        System.out.println("NOTICE - Discarded registrar:");

        for (int i=0; i<discardedReg.length; i++)
          {
              int tpInt = registrars.indexOf(discardedReg[i]);
              System.out.println("   index: " + tpInt);
              registrars.remove(tpInt);
          }
        System.out.print(SYSTEM_PROMPT);
        System.out.flush();
    }
```

Finally, the `EnumerateCommands()` method scans the current directory using the list method of the `File` class, and filter for any file with the '`.class`' extension.

```
public void EnumerateCommands()
{
  File curDir = new File(".");

  String [] fileList = curDir.list(new FilenameFilter() {
  public boolean accept(File dir, String inFile)
    {
        return inFile.endsWith(".class");
    }
});
```

For every file that we find (every Java class file), we look for the support of the `ReggtoolCommand` interface. This interface uniquely identifies dynamically loadable command implementations. Every command found will be added to the `commandTable HashMap` (more details on this later).

```
for (int i=0; i<fileList.length; i++)
    {
     try {
        String baseName = fileList[i].substring(0, fileList[i].length() - 6);
        Class myclass = Class.forName(baseName);
        Class [] allInt = myclass.getInterfaces();
        for (int j=0; j<allInt.length; j++)
        if (allInt[j].getName().equals("ReggtoolCommand"))
           AddToCommandTable(myclass);


        }
      catch (Exception bex)
        { System.out.println(bex);   }
    }
```

After all the dynamically loadable commands are loaded, we check to see if the basic commands are already in the map. We cannot proceed without these basic commands. If a missing basic command is detected, the `reggtool` will exit.

```
// verify that the basic minimal commands are available
for (int i=0; i< basicCommands.length; i++)
if (! commandTable.containsKey(basicCommands[i]))
    {
     System.out.println("Missing basic command :   " + basicCommands[i]);
     System.exit(1);
    }
} // of enumerate commands
```

The last method of `reggtool` is `AddToCommandTable`. Essentially, it instantiates an instance of the command class, and uses the `getCommandWord()` method of the `ReggtoolCommand` interface to get a string representation of the command that is supported. The command word string is then used as the key, and the command object instance itself as the value, for the `commandTable` HashMap.

```
public void AddToCommandTable(Class inCls)
{
  try {
     System.out.println("loading commands extension module - " + inCls.getName());
     ReggtoolCommand myCmd = (ReggtoolCommand) inCls.newInstance();
     String key = myCmd.getCommandWord();
     commandTable.put(key, myCmd);
     }
   catch (Exception e)
     {
     System.out.println(e);
     }
   }
}
```

Extensibility through Dynamically Loaded Commands

`reggtool` without any commands is quite useless – all you can do is quit. However it's pretty easy to implement a command for `reggtool`.

All `reggtool` commands must support the `ReggtoolCommand` interface; you can find the definition in the `code\ch10\ReggtoolCommand.java` file:

```
import java.util.StringTokenizer;
import net.jini.core.lookup.ServiceRegistrar;
import net.jini.discovery.LookupDiscovery;
import java.util.ArrayList;

public interface ReggtoolCommand
{
   public String getCommandWord();
   public String getUsage();
   public String getShortHelp();
   public String getLongDesc();
   public void doCommand(StringTokenizer myTk, ArrayList inRegs,
       LookupDiscovery ld);
   public void initializeSubsystem();
   public void endSubsystem();
   public void nameConflictDetected(Class conflictClass);
}
```

Here is a quick synopsis of what each method is for. There are several methods that are specified, but not implemented currently. These methods are essential to making reggtool a usable command line tool. They provide help facility for the user, we have chosen to leave them out since they do not add to our technical coverage of the helper utility and services.

Method Name	Description
getCommandWord()	Returns the keyword for the command itself ('list', for example, to show the details on each discovered lookup service)
getUsage()	Returns a short string to describe the usage syntax of the command, currently not implemented by reggtool
getShortHelp()	Returns a short help string (should fit within 60 characters) that describes the command, currently not used by reggtool
getLongDesc()	Returns a (long) string that describe the command; it can be up to a page long, currently not used by reggtool
doCommand()	Called by reggtool to request the command be performed, a StringTokenizer is passed in for the arguments to the command, a copy of the ArrayList of registrars and the actual LookupDiscovery instance from reggtool is also passed as arguments
initializeSubsystem()	Called by reggtool upon loading of commands to start any subsystems that the command may require (for example, create new threads, etc.), currently not used by reggtool
endSubsystem()	Called by reggtool before shutdown to terminate any subsystems that the command may have started during initializeSubsystem, currently not used by reggtool
nameConflictDetected()	Called only when another implementation with the same command word has been discovered by reggtool; a reference to the duplicate existing command is provided currently not used by reggtool.

Implementation of Two Simple Commands

This is the coding of two simple commands. The first one is the `'list'` command, found in the cmdList.java file. This command iterates through all the registrars that have been discovered and prints information on each one.

```
import net.jini.discovery.*;
import net.jini.core.lookup.*;
import java.io.*;
import java.rmi.RemoteException;
import java.rmi.RMISecurityManager;
import java.util.StringTokenizer;
import java.util.ArrayList;
import java.util.Iterator;
```

The command word is 'list', and we do not process any arguments here.

```
public class cmdList implements ReggtoolCommand
{
    static final String COMMAND_NAME = "list";
    static final String NOT_LOADED_MSG = "***command not loaded due to conflict";
    static final String COMMAND_USAGE = "list";
    static final String COMMAND_HELP = "List all the lookup services located,
        their index, and service IDs.";

    public cmdList()
{}
```

The getXXX() methods are designed to return constant strings for this command.

```
public String getCommandWord(){ return COMMAND_NAME; }
public String getUsage() { return COMMAND_USAGE; }
public String getShortHelp() { return COMMAND_HELP; }
public String getLongDesc() { return COMMAND_HELP; }
```

The doCommand() method iterates through the ArrayList of registrars and prints out information on each one, using the iterator provided by the collection class. The service ID and the groups that each registrar supports are printed.

```
public void doCommand(StringTokenizer myTk, ArrayList registrars,
    LookupDiscovery ld)
{
    String [] groups;
    String msg = null;
    if( (registrars != null) && (registrars.size() > 0))
        {
            Iterator it = registrars.iterator();
            while( it.hasNext())
              {
                ServiceRegistrar myReg = (ServiceRegistrar) it.next();
                if (myReg != null)
                  {
                    msg = "";
```

```
                        System.out.println("---LOOKUP SERVICE # " +
                            registrars.indexOf(myReg) + " ---");
                        System.out.println("Registrar: " + myReg.getServiceID());
                        try
                            {
                                groups = myReg.getGroups();
                            if (groups.length > 0)

                                for (int o=0; o<groups.length; o++) { msg += "\'" +
                                    groups[o] + "\' ";
                                }

                            System.out.println("Groups Supported: " + msg);
                            }
                catch (Exception e)
                    { e.printStackTrace();
                        System.exit(1);
                    }

                } // of if registrar[i] != null
            } // of while
        }// of if length > 0
      else
      {
          System.out.println("Sorry, no lookup services located.");
      }
}
```

The rest of the interface methods have empty implementations, except nameConflictDetected() which returns a warning message.

```
public void initializeSubsystem() {}
public void endSubsystem() {}
public void nameConflictDetected(Class conflictClass) {
System.out.println(NOT_LOADED_MSG);
    }
}
```

The second command is the 'listogrp' command, or 'list own groups', which lists all the groups currently desired by the reggtool. You can find the source in the \code\reggtool\cmdListogrp.java file. We will focus on its doCommand() method here, since the rest are identical to the 'list' command implementation.

```
public void doCommand(StringTokenizer myTk, ArrayList registrars,
    LookupDiscovery ld)
{
```

We use the LookupDiscovery's getGroups() command to get a list of groups supported by the LookupDiscovery – and hence reggtool itself. We then build a string and print the list of groups out, each separated by a space. A group returning null is equivalent to joining all groups.

```
        String [] myGroups = ld.getGroups() ;
        String msg = "";
        System.out.println("Checking reggtool groups membership:");
        if (myGroups == null)
        {
            System.out.println("  Locating lookup services supporting all groups.");
        }
        else
        {
            for (int o=0; o<myGroups.length; o++) { msg += myGroups[o] + " ";
        }

        System.out.println("  Locating lookup services supporting the groups: " + msg);
    }
}
```

Testing Reggtool and Observing LookupDiscovery at Work

We're going to set up a test for the `reggtool`. First, assuming you still have the old setup with httpd, RMID, and one reggie (started by the `lookup1.bat` file) running. We can:

❑ Change directory to `ch10\code\bats`

❑ Run the `lookup2.bat` file to start a second instance of reggie

❑ Change directory to `ch10\code\reggtool`

❑ Start the `reggtool` by running the `runregg.bat` file, it contains:

```
call ..\bats\setpaths.bat
java -classpath .;%JINIJARS%  -Dnet.jini.discovery.interface=%ADAPTERIP% -
Djava.security.policy=policy.all reggtool %1 %2
```

Including `reggie.jar` should not be necessary. However, at the time of writing, reggie's administrative interface – required by some of our `reggtool` commands – is only available via this jar file; this may be specific to the Jini 1.1 release.

You should see a greeting screen similar to the following screenshot

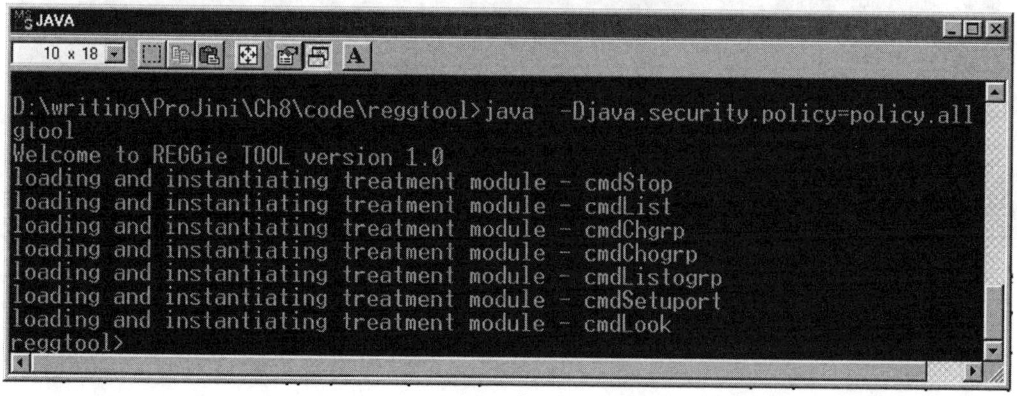

Very shortly, once the `LookupDiscovery` has discovered the lookup service, `reggtool`'s discovered method will be called and we will see the discovery notifications. Notice that we get two distinct and separate notices. By keeping each discovered registrar in an `ArrayList`, we ensure that none of the previously discovered, and as yet undiscarded, registrars are missed. This screenshot shows the discovery notifications.

```
D:\writing\ProJini\Ch8\code\reggtool>java  -Djava.security.policy=policy.all reg
gtool
Welcome to REGGie TOOL version 1.0
loading and instantiating treatment module - cmdStop
loading and instantiating treatment module - cmdList
loading and instantiating treatment module - cmdChgrp
loading and instantiating treatment module - cmdChogrp
loading and instantiating treatment module - cmdListogrp
loading and instantiating treatment module - cmdSetuport
loading and instantiating treatment module - cmdLook
reggtool>NOTICE: discovery made
reggtool> NOTICE: discovery made
reggtool>
```

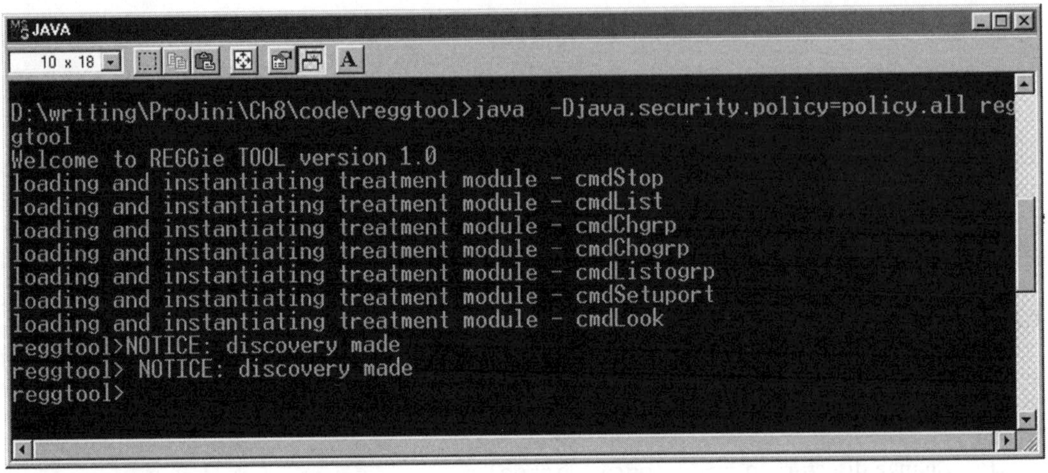

Now, type in the following command:

```
list
```

You should see the details of each of the lookup services that have been discovered. Here we see what the console may look like.

```
reggtool>NOTICE: discovery made
reggtool> NOTICE: discovery made
reggtool> list
----------LOOKUP SERVICE # 0 ----------
Registrar: 9e16997e-861f-429f-8385-dbffe45461e2
Groups Supported: iguanas
Unicast TCP Port: 0
----------LOOKUP SERVICE # 1 ----------
Registrar: a7b3871a-bcdc-4f3e-b91d-8d528663d808
Groups Supported: lizards
Unicast TCP Port: 0
reggtool>
```

To see the groups that are supported by `reggtool`, we can enter the command:

```
listogrp
```

You should see the output shown here:

Now, we can terminate `reggtool`:

```
quit
```

Start it again, but this time with:

```
runregg lizards
```

This will start `reggtool` working with only the lizards group. You should see only one lookup discovery notification. This is because only the reggie instance started by `lookup2.bat` will support the lizards group. Perform a 'list' command to convince yourself that only one registrar has been discovered by the `LookupDiscovery` instance. Now, try the command:

```
listogrp
```

You will now see only the lizards group listed, as shown here:

Recall that the listogrp is actually a direct call to one of the `LookupDiscovery`'s methods that supports the `DiscoveryGroupManagement` interface: `getGroups()`.

What LookupDiscovery Will Not Do For Us

`LookupDiscovery`'s low-level disposition means that its work ends once the discovery protocol has been handled. While it will continue to dynamically monitor transitions in the network with respect to lookup services joining or leaving the groups, it will not manage the set of lookup service registrars for us. Furthermore, while the Jini specification requires that services persist state information such as groups and Jini URLs across restarts, `LookupDiscovery` provides no assistance in this matter. This means that the application will have to take care of:

❑ Tracking the services available within the groups that it supports

❑ Lookup and eliminate duplicate proxies

❑ Persisting states as needed

Mid-Level Protocol Manager Utilities In-Depth

Realistically, both `LookupDiscovery` and `LookupLocator` already make our lives quite a bit easier, but there's a lot more there for the application to do. Lots, lots more. Of course, you can stick with the low-level protocol handling classes like `LookupDiscovery` and `LookupLocator` for maximum control, but if you're working on a project that has highly complex logic, fierce competition, and a short product cycle, you're likely to welcome the next level management utilities.

In general, these utilities make use of the lower level protocol utilities by providing higher level management capabilities – easing the burden and tedious nature of Jini programming.

LookupLocatorDiscovery Utility

`LookupLocatorDiscovery` can be viewed as a manager for multiple instances of `LookupLocators`. Recall that a single `LookupLocator` instance encapsulates all the information of one known TCP-based lookup service, reachable via the TCP based unicast discovery protocol, on the local or some remote networked machine. The `LookupLocatorDiscovery` makes it easy to manage and work with many known lookup services. Instead of managing the set of `LookupLocators`, and performing unicast discovery manually on each and every one of the `LookupLocators`, you can let `LookupLocatorDiscovery` take care of it for you.

Design of LookupLocatorDiscovery

Making it simple to work with multiple `LookupLocator` instances, the `LookupLocatorDiscovery` class eliminates the need for users to initiate discovery on each `LookupLocator` directly, providing a callback model, similar to `LookupDiscovery`. In fact, it implements the very same `discovered()` and `discarded()` methods – in other words, the unifying `DiscoveryManagement` interface!

The following figure illustrates the typical usage sequence of a `LookupLocatorDiscovery` instance. The client or service using the `LookupLocatorDiscovery` helper utility must:

- ❏ Create a set of `LookupLocator` instances, one for each lookup service to be discovered using unicast discovery; create an instance of `LookupLocatorDiscovery` and pass it the `LookupLocator` instances; also register a listener to process discovery event

- ❏ Handle the discover method callback, and save the lookup service(s) discovered

- ❏ Handle the discard method callback, and remove any managed lookup service proxy that needs to be discarded

Note that one can still directly access the `LookupLocators` maintained by the `LookupLocatorDiscovery` utility if necessary.

The dashed boxes in the diagram below are the `LookupLocators` that will actually be used in the unicast discovery process.

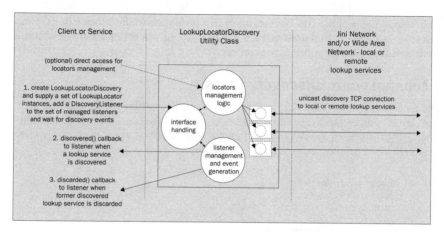

We essentially create a `LookupLocatorDiscovery` by parameterizing it with a set of `LookupLocators`, then we simply monitor for callback via the `DiscoveryManagement` interface as they occur. This completely frees the caller from actively managing the unicast discovery. It also enables the caller to use the exact same support code to handle the lookup registrars found in both multicast and unicast (via the `LookupDiscovery` utility) discovery.

Here is the subset definition of the `LookupLocatorDiscovery` utility, without coverage for the methods that support the `DiscoveryManagement` interface – since we have looked at those methods previously in the `LookupDiscovery` utility coverage.

```
package net.jini.discovery;
public class LookupLocatorDiscovery implements
    DiscoveryManagement,DiscoveryLocatorManagement
{
public LookupLocatorDiscovery(LookupLocator[] locators){...}
public LookupLocator[] getDiscoveredLocators(){..}
public LookupLocator[] getUndiscoveredLocators() {..}

    // support for DiscoveryLocatorManagement interface
public LookupLocator[] getLocators(){..}
public void addLocators(LookupLocator[] locators) {..}
public void setLocators(LookupLocator[] locators){..}
public void removeLocators(LookupLocator[] locators) {..}

    //support for DiscoveryManagement interface
public void addDiscoveryListener(DiscoveryListener listener) {..}
public void removeDiscoveryListener(DiscoveryListener listener) {..}
public ServiceRegistrar[] getRegistrars() {..}
public void discard(ServiceRegistrar proxy) {..}
public void terminate() {..}
}
```

Most of the methods are implemented to support the `DiscoveryLocatorManagement` and the `DiscoveryManagement` interfaces. Two additional methods are worth mentioning, especially when the `LookupLocator` discovery is used for a large set of locations with some of them being remote. Obviously, in this case, the unicast discovery time to reach these lookup services may be significant.

The getDiscoveredLocators() method provides you with an instantaneous view of all the locators that have connected to their corresponding lookup service. The getUndiscoveredLocators() method provides a view of all the locators that are yet to be discovered. Note that this is semantically separate and independent of the DiscoveryLocatorManagement interface since the interface deals mainly with set management, and does not see nor care about whether a locator that it manages has or has not connected to the corresponding lookup service.

Using the LookupLocatorDiscovery Class

We can find an example use of the LookupLocatorDiscovery class in the ch10\code\lookLocDis\lookLocDis.java file. This example will take command line arguments consisting of URLs for LookupLocators, and create a LookupLocatorDiscovery class to unicast discover them all. The complete source code of this simple client is listed below:

```java
import net.jini.discovery.*;
import net.jini.core.lookup.*;
import net.jini.core.discovery.LookupLocator;
import java.io.*;
import java.rmi.RemoteException;
import java.rmi.RMISecurityManager;

import java.rmi.server.UnicastRemoteObject;
import java.rmi.MarshalledObject;
import net.jini.core.event.*;
import net.jini.core.lease.*;
import net.jini.lease.LeaseRenewalManager;
```

The default behavior is just to use the URL of host "win98p300" on the default port (4160). However, if command line arguments are detected, they will be used to create LookupLocators. We can see here that lookLocDis implements the DiscoveryListener interface for callback, in the very same way as our LookupDiscovery example.

```java
public class lookLocDis implements DiscoveryListener
{
    LookupLocator myLoc = null;
    static final String [] myURL = {"jini://win98p300/"};

    static public void main(String argv[])
    {
        lookLocDis myApp = null;

        if (argv.length > 1)
            myApp = new lookLocDis(argv);
        else
            myApp = new lookLocDis(myURL);
    }
```

myLocs contains the set of LookupLocator used to initialize the LookupLocatorDiscovery instance.

```java
    LookupLocator [] myLocs = null;
    LookupLocatorDiscovery myDis = null;
    public lookLocDis() {}
```

In the constructor, we create the array of `LookupLocators`, and instantiate them, one per URL argument from the command line.

```
public lookLocDis(String [] URLs)
{
  if (System.getSecurityManager() == null)
  {
    System.setSecurityManager(new RMISecurityManager());
  }
  myLocs = new LookupLocator[URLs.length];
  try {
    for (int i=0; i< URLs.length; i++)
      myLocs[i] = new LookupLocator(URLs[i]);
```

Next, we create the `LookupLocatorDiscovery` instance using the `Locator` array.

```
myDis = new LookupLocatorDiscovery(myLocs);
```

We will register a listener object that implements the `DiscoveryManagement` interface. In this case, it is the `lookLocDis` instance itself. Immediately after, we simply wait around for enough time for discovery to occur (10 seconds here is plenty for everything running on the same machine) before terminating.

```
myDis.addDiscoveryListener(this);
System.out.println("Waiting a few seconds for discovery....");
Thread.sleep(10000L); // sleep for 10 seconds for it to do
```

We terminate the `LookupLocatorDiscovery` instance gracefully by calling its `terminate()` method.

```
    myDis.terminate();
    }
  catch(Exception e)
    {
      System.err.println(e.toString());
      e.printStackTrace();
      System.exit(1);
    }
  }
}
```

Next comes the implementation of the `DiscoveryManagement` interface. If lookup services are discovered, we simply print out the groups that they support.

```
public void discovered(DiscoveryEvent evt)
{
    ServiceRegistrar [] myRegs = evt.getRegistrars();
    System.out.println("Located " + myRegs.length + " lookup services.");

    for (int i=0; i< myRegs.length; i++)
    {
        System.out.println("------- lookup service # " + i + " ----------");
        System.out.println("  found ID: " + myRegs[i].getServiceID());

        String msg = "";
        String [] groups;
    try {
        groups = myRegs[i].getGroups();
        if (groups.length > 0)
        for (int o=0; o<groups.length; o++) { msg += "\'" + groups[o] + "\' "; }
        }
```

```
                System.out.println("     Groups Supported: " + msg);
            }
        catch(Exception e)
            {
              System.err.println(e.toString());
              e.printStackTrace();
              System.exit(1);
            }
        }   // of for i
      }
    public void discarded(DiscoveryEvent evt) {}
  }
```

You can compile this using:

```
buildit lookLocDis.java
```

In order to test this client with more than one lookup service (and therefore more than one
`LookupLocator`) on the same machine, we need to be able to specify the TCP port at which the
lookup service will listen for unicast discovery – so we'll use `reggtool`.

Adding Two Reggtool Commands to Change Reggie Behavior

The first of the two commands we're going to add changes the groups that a lookup service is handling,
the second allows us to change the TCP port at which the lookup service will work.

Both of these commands work through the administrative interfaces implemented by reggie. More
specifically, reggie provides an administrative object that implements the following administrative interfaces:

❑   `DiscoveryAdmin`

❑   `StorageLocationAdmin`

❑   `DestroyAdmin`

❑   `JoinAdmin`

Let us examine each of these interfaces.

The Jini Administrative Interfaces

`DiscoveryAdmin` is defined as:

```
public abstract interface DiscoveryAdmin
{
    void addMemberGroups(String [] groups);
    String [] getMemeberGroups();
    int getUnicastPort();
    void removeMemberGroups(String [] groups);
    void setMemberGroups(String [] groups);
    void setUnicastPort(int port);
}
```

This interface provides access to a managed set of groups. Note that the built-in semantics for this set of groups is very specific. These are the groups that a particular lookup service will provide discovery support for, as a lookup service, and not the groups that a lookup service will seek to join (this is the domain of another Admin interface as we will see later). So a lookup service can provide discovery support for one set of groups, while joining another set, which is one of the features that makes the Jini network configuration extremely flexible. The other two interesting methods are getUnicastPort() and setUnicastPort(). It is by using these methods that we can get and set the unicast discovery port away from the default CAFÉ-BABE (4160) port. We will be implementing setUnicastPort() in the Setuport command later.

The StorageLocationAdmin interface is defined as:

```
public abstract interface StorageLocationAdmin
{
    String getStorageLocation();
    void setStorageLocation(String location);
}
```

Lookup services (and other third-party services that we will see later) run within their own Java VM on an independent machine. They implement state persistence and have unique service IDs of their own. The StorageLocationAdmin allows the location of the service's store of persistent information to be determined – usually a directory. As we have seen in the case of reggie, multiple instances of a well-designed service can run simultaneously on the same machine if we set their persistence directories to different locations.

The DestroyAdmin interface is defined as:

```
public abstract interface DestroyAdmin
{
    void destroy();
}
```

This is very similar to the terminate() method in the utility class case, expect that it is used to 'shutdown' a remote service by a third-party administrator (external to the service). There is an important distinction to be made between calling destroy() and a system crash – the consequences are drastically different. The intention is that a Jini service, once started, will never shutdown, which means that system failures or crashes are transparently healed when the system restarts again – the service recovers its persistent state information, rejoins groups, and uses the same unique service ID in lookup services, etc. As far as the Jini network is concerned, the same service runs forever, or until it is destroyed using the destroy() method.

Semantically, destruction of a service terminates its existence in space and time. When destroy() is called, the service needs to deregister itself with all the lookup services that it has registered with, complete the work of any clients and clean up its persistent store before exiting. Running the service again results in a new instance. What this means in Jini terms is that calling the destroy() method on a service will invalidate its service ID (that is, its identity) forever. Starting the lookup service again will result in a new unique service ID being generated. If this sounds drastic, it is! In production, the DestroyAdmin interface is used only in exceptional cases.

The `JoinAdmin` interface is defined as:

```
public abstract interface JoinAdmin
{
    void addLookupAttributes(Entry [] attrSets);
    Entry [] getLookupAttributes();
    void modifyLookupAttributes(Entry [] attrSetTemplates, Entry [] attrSets);

    void addLookupGroups(String [] groups);
    String [] getLookupGroups();
    void removeLookupGroups(String [] groups);
    void setLookupGroups(String [] groups);

    void addLookupLocators(LookupLocator [] locators);
    Locator [] getLookupLocators();
    void removeLookupLocators(LookupLocator [] locators);
    void setLookupLocators(LookupLocator [] locators);
}
```

Although we have worked with the `JoinManager` high-level manager utility in previous chapters, and will be examining it thoroughly later in this chapter, a brief overview is warranted here. The `JoinAdmin` interface details how the service use the items that matter to the Join protocol as defined by Jini specification. We will recall that the Join protocol determines what a Jini service must follow to participate in the network immediately after discovery. More specifically, the service must register its proxy with all the lookup services that it wishes to be visible in. To this end, the `JoinAdmin` interface provides control over the attributes that accompany the proxy when the registration is made, the groups that will be used to discover the lookup services to register with, and any `LookupLocators` that the service should used directly.

So should any of the three managed sets, the groups, locators or the attributes associated with proxy be altered via the `addXXX()`, `modifyXXX()`, or `setXXX()` methods, the implementer of this interface will perform all the updates and synchronization that is necessary to comply with the Join protocol. For example, if an attribute of the proxy is modified after discovery via the `modifyLookupAttributes()` method, the implementation must take care to notify every lookup service that the service is currently registered with in order to propagate the change.

The distinct and sensible factoring of the administration task into the interfaces that we have described so far allows a Jini service developer to select the administrative interfaces that apply and implement them.

Reggie, being a well-behaved Jini service as well as a lookup service, implements all of the above interfaces. In fact, it defines its own `RegistrarAdmin` interface, which inherits from all of the above interfaces. Incidentally, since it serves as the reference lookup service implementation, lookup services that support administration may also implement this `RegistrarAdmin` interface. Here is the definition of the `RegistrarAdmin` interface:

```
public abstract interface RegistrarAdmin extends DiscoveryAdmin,
    StorageLocationAdmin, DestroyAdmin, JoinAdmin
{
    int getLogToSnapshotThreshold();
    void setLogToSnapThreshold();

    long getMinMaxEventLease(int threshold);
    void setMinMaxEventLease(long leaseDuration);
```

```
        long getMinMaxServiceLease();
        void setMinMaxServiceLease(long leaseDuration);

        long getMinRenewalInterval();
        void setMinRenewalInterval(long interval);

        float getSnapshotWeight();
        void setSnapshotWeight(float weight);

        .. plus methods implementing all of DiscoveryAdmin, StorageLocationAdmin,
           DestroyAdmin, and JoinAdmin…
    }
```

This class has a lot of methods. Not only does it have all the methods from all four interfaces that we have mentioned so far, but it also has its own specific set of methods for configuring lookup service behavior – specifically for reggie's own implementation. These methods include control for the following properties:

Property Name	Description
LogToSnapshotThreshold	Reggie takes occasional snapshots of the entire system state that it persists to disk. Most of the time, however, state changes are stored as incremental deltas (or differences) with respect to a snapshot. The journal file containing such deltas is called a log file. During crash recovery, the snapshot state is first loaded, and then the deltas in the log file are applied incrementally to restore the state of the system.
	This threshold determines how frequently snapshot capture should occur with respect to anticipated logfile size. The algorithm to determine this seeks a balance between frequency of snapshot dumps and size of log file. Interested readers should consult the reggie documentation on details of this algorithm as it is subject to change and improvement.
MinMaxEventLease	Specifies the minimum duration granted for a lease on event registration, when a max duration is requested. Frequency of client lease renewal can be readily controlled by tuning this parameter.
MinMaxServiceLease	Specifies the minimum duration granted for a lease on a service registration, when a max duration is requested. This is used to tune the frequency of client lease renewal.
SnapshotWeight	The weighting factor used in determining when a snapshot file will be created, works in conjunction with LogToSnapshotThreshold above. Interested readers should consult the reggie documentation on details of this algorithm as it is subject to change and improvement.
MinRenewalInterval	The average minimum client lease renewal duration as issued by the lease granting mechanism. Used in conjunction with MinMaxEventLease and MinMaxServiceLease to tune the lease granting system.

Putting Administration Interfaces to Work

You can find the source code of `Chgrp` command in the `Ch10\code\reggtool` directory. It is in the `cmdChgrp.java` file. Here is the listing of the core `doCommand()` method:

```
public void doCommand(StringTokenizer myTk, ArrayList registrars,
    LookupDiscovery ld)
{
```

This command will process additional arguments from the `StringTokenizer`, containing:

- ❑ The index into the array of registrars, specifying the lookup service whose managed groups should be changed

- ❑ The set of groups to be used

We extract these arguments from the `StringTokenizer`, and place them into `myIdx` and the groups' string array respectively.

```
String nxtToken;
int numTokens = myTk.countTokens();
if (numTokens <= 1)
    return;
String [] groups = new String[numTokens - 1];

int myIdx = Integer.parseInt(myTk.nextToken());
for (int i=0; i<groups.length; i++)
    groups[i] = myTk.nextToken();
```

Now, we check the bounds of the registrar array, and then call `setGroups()` on the user specified registrar (that is, lookup service).

```
if ((myIdx < registrars.size()) && (myIdx >=0))
    {
        ServiceRegistrar myReg =(ServiceRegistrar) registrars.get(myIdx);

        if (myReg != null)
        {
            setGroups(myReg, myIdx, groups);
        }
    }
}
```

The actual work of group changing is done via the `setGroups()` method.

```
private void setGroups(ServiceRegistrar registrar, int Idx, String [] gps)
{
```

This method first tests the lookup service to see if it is administrable. As mentioned in previous chapters, all administrable services implement the `Administrable` interface.

```
      try
       {
          Administrable tpAdmin = null;
          RegistrarAdmin myAdmin =null;
       if (registrar instanceof Administrable)
        {
```

If the registrar in question is administrable, we call its getAdmin() method (supported by the ServiceRegistrar interface that all registrars have) to get a reference to the admin object. This object will support the enormous RegistrarAdmin interface that we saw earlier.

```
          tpAdmin = (Administrable) registrar;
          myAdmin = (RegistrarAdmin) tpAdmin.getAdmin();
```

Once we have the RegistrarAdmin interface, we can call the setMemberGroups() method to change the group that the lookup service will manage. The setMemberGroups() method is part of the DiscoveryAdmin interface discussed earlier. This changes the groups that the lookup service will manage, and not the set of groups that the lookup service will attempt to join upon its own startup.

```
          System.out.println("  Changing lookup service # " + Idx + " now!");
          myAdmin.setMemberGroups(gps);
        }
      } // of try
    catch (Exception ex) { ex.printStackTrace(); }
   }
```

Compile this command using:

```
buildit cmdChgrp.java
```

The setuport Command

The setuport command changes the TCP port used by a lookup service when listening for unicast discovery attempts. Normally, the default CAFÉ-BABE (4160) port is adequate. However, under certain circumstances (for example, running multiple reggies on the same system), one may want control over the port that is actually used.

You can find the source code in the \Ch10\code\reggtool directory, in the cmdSetuport.java file. Here is the core doCommand(), and the helper setPort() method:

```
public void doCommand(StringTokenizer myTk, ArrayList registrars,
    LookupDiscovery ld)
{
```

As in the doCommand() of the chgrp command, this part process the arguments using the StringTokenizer. We expect only two arguments in this case; the first is the index of the registrar to use in the command, and the second is the actual TCP port number to set. We extract them and place them into myIdx and myPort respectively.

```
        String nxtToken;
        int numTokens = myTk.countTokens();
        if (numTokens < 2)
              return;

        int myIdx = Integer.parseInt(myTk.nextToken());
        int myPort = Integer.parseInt(myTk.nextToken());
```

Next, we check array bounds and call the helper setPort() method on the specified registrar (lookup service).

```
        if ((myIdx < registrars.size()) && (myIdx >= 0))
             {
                ServiceRegistrar myReg =(ServiceRegistrar) registrars.get(myIdx);
                if (myReg != null)
                  {
                     setPort(myReg, myIdx, myPort);
                  }
             }
         }

    private void setPort(ServiceRegistrar registrar, int Idx, int port)
    {
        try {
```

Here, we check the lookup service for support for Administrable, and then get a reference to the associated admin object.

```
            Administrable tpAdmin = null;
            RegistrarAdmin myAdmin =null;
            if (registrar instanceof Administrable)
               {
                  tpAdmin = (Administrable) registrar;
                  myAdmin = (RegistrarAdmin) tpAdmin.getAdmin();

                  System.out.println(" Changing port for lookup service #
                     " + Idx + " now!");
```

Finally, we call the setUnicastPort() method, part of the DiscoveryAdmin interface, to change the unicast port used by the lookup service.

```
                  myAdmin.setUnicastPort(port);
               }
           } // of try
        catch (Exception ex) { ex.printStackTrace(); }
    }
```

Compile this command using:

```
buildit cmdSetuport.java
```

Testing LookupLocatorDiscovery Sample and the New Reggtool Commands

Now, we can test the `LookupLocatorDiscovery` sample program. First, set up two instances of lookup services, by:

❑ Changing directory to `Ch10\code\bats`

❑ Cleaning up any old RMID or reggie logfiles manually, or use the `runclean.bat` file on Win98

❑ Starting the class server by running `runhttpd.bat`

❑ Starting the RMID by executing `runrmid.bat`

❑ Starting a reggie for the iguanas group by running `runlookup1.bat` file

❑ Starting a reggie for the lizards and iguanas groups by running `runlookup2.bat` file

❑ Changing directory to `Ch10\code\reggtool`

❑ Starting the `reggtool` using the `runregg.bat` file

You should see two discovery messages. Type in the command:

```
list
```

This screenshot should be similar to the output that you will see. It should contain both lookup services that you have started.

Now, use the new `setuport` command to change the port used by the second lookup service (the one responsible for both lizards and iguanas group). Type in these commands:

```
setuport 0 4160
setuport 1 4166
```

Perform a list command again, and you should see that the first lookup service now listens for unicast at port number 4160, and the second lookup service now listens for unicast at port number 4166 – instead of the random port that it had chosen before.

This screenshot illustrates this:

Finally, we can test our LookupLocatorDiscovery sample by specifying two distinct Jini URLs:

❑ Change directory to Ch10\code\lookldis

❑ Run the utility using URL representing the two lookup services that we have set up; in our case we use the command line:

```
runlook jini://win98p300/ jini://win98p300:4166/
```

This should enable the LookupLocatorDiscovery to find both services directly (using unicast discovery). Your output should be similar to this:

What LookupLocatorDiscovery Will Not Do For Us

The operation of LookupLocatorDiscovery, as we've seen, is completely analogous to its LookupDiscovery cousin – but specifically for managing a set of unicast LookupLocators instead.

Just like the LookupDiscovery, tracking the services available within a federation is in the jurisdiction of the application code, which must also manage the service proxies, including lookup and elimination of duplicate proxies. Furthermore, LookupLocatorDiscovery does not provide any support for state persistence, so this should also be looked after by the application

LookupDiscoveryManager Utility

Now that we have LookupDiscovery to handle all the multi-cast discovery duties, and LookupLocatorDiscovery to handle all the (potentially remote) unicast discovery chores, it's easy to combine the two. All you need to do is write one set of discovery code, and handle one set of discovered registrars.

Inside the LookupDiscoveryManager Utility

Both LookupDiscovery and LookupLocatorDiscovery play major roles inside the LookupDiscoveryManager class. The figure below illustrates this interaction.

The client or service using the LookupDiscoveryManager must first create a set of LookupLocators for unicast discovery, and a set of groups that it desires to locate lookup service for. These are passed as parameters to create an instance of the LookupDiscoveryManager utility. At the same time, the client or service can register a listener. It can then implement the discovered() and discard() methods of the DiscoveryManagement interface to receive the registrars of the lookup services that are discovered.

The LookupDiscoveryManager will handle the following managed sets internally:

❑   Groups to perform multicast discovery for

❑   LookupLocators to perform unicast discovery for

These managed sets can also be manipulated directly by the client/service using interfaces (DiscoveryGroupManagement and DiscoveryLocatorManagement) implemented by the LookupDiscoveryManager utility.

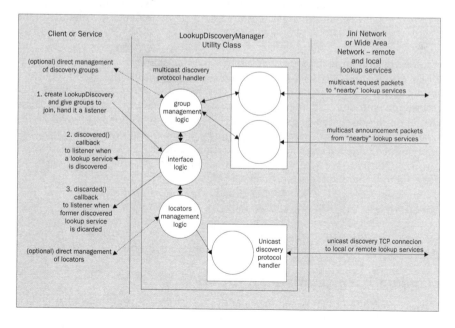

As you can see from this figure, only one set of code has to be written when you're using LookupDiscoveryManager, which handles all the required discovery support duties for a client or service. In fact, using the DiscoveryManagement interface, one can simply code the discovered() and discarded() methods in order to maintain the list of services discovered.

LookupDiscoveryManager provides proper lower level control by giving you access to the multicast discovery groups and the unicast LookupLocators provided by the class. The access to these managed sets are provided the well-defined DiscoveryGroupManagement and DiscoveryLocatorManagement interfaces we have seen previously. Here is the definition of the LookupDiscoveryManager class:

```
public class LookupDiscoveryManager implements DiscoveryManagement,
    DiscoveryGroupManagement, DiscoveryLocatorManagement
{
    static final int FROM_GROUP;
    static final int FROM_LOCATOR;
    public LookupDiscoveryManager(String[] groups, LookupLocator[] locators,
        DiscoveryListener listener) throws IOException {..}
    int getFrom(ServiceRegistgrar proxy){..}

    .. methods implementation the DiscoveryManagement interface..
    .. methods implementation for the DiscoveryGroupManagement interface..
    .. methods implementation for the DiscoveryLocatorManagement interface..
}
```

Note that *all* but one of the methods in LookupDiscoveryManager are implementations of the three interfaces specified. This is not surprising considering that the LookupDiscovery and LookupLocatorDiscovery classes are doing the work internally, and the LookupDiscoveryManager simply delegates the interface implementation method to the internal associated class.

As expected, the constructor takes a set of groups for the internal LookupDiscovery to perform multicast discovery. It also takes a set of LookupLocator for the internal LookupLocatorDiscovery to perform unicast discovery. The final parameter is a DiscoveryListener callback object. This listener is registered with both the internal LookupDiscovery and LookupLocatorDiscovery and will be called upon should multicast or unicast discovery find a new lookup service. To distinguish whether a particular registrar is discovered from unicast or multicast, one can call the getFrom() method supplying the registrar as an argument. A return value of LookupDiscoveryManager.FROM_GROUP indicates multicast, and that the LookupDiscovery instance was used to locate the registrar. A return value ofLookupDiscoveryManager.FROM_LOCATOR indicates unicast, and that the LookupLocatorDiscovery utility was used to locate the registrar.

The LookupDiscoveryManager utility provides the ease-of-use of a high-level discovery class by combining all discovery functions, and control over those functions, within a single class.

Using the LookupDiscoveryManager Utility

Let's now turn our attention to an example use of the LookupDiscoveryManager class. You can find the source code to this program in the \Ch10\Code\lookDisMan.java file.

What this sample program will do is:

- ❑ Instantiate a `LookupDiscoveryManager` class, supplying it with a set of locator URLs for lookup service, and a set of multicast groups
- ❑ Wait a while for discovery to occur
- ❑ Print out each discovered lookup service, and the groups that they are handling

Here is the code:

```
import net.jini.discovery.*;
import net.jini.core.lookup.*;
import net.jini.core.discovery.LookupLocator;
import java.io.*;
import java.rmi.RemoteException;
import java.rmi.RMISecurityManager;
```

The main method simply creates an instance of `lookDisMan`. The constructor takes a string array as argument, this is the actual `argv[]` passed in the command line when the command is invoked. If you do not specify any command line argument, a default of iguanas and the unicast discovery URL jini://win98p300/ are used.

```
public class lookDisMan implements DiscoveryListener
  {
    LookupLocator myLoc = null;
    static final String [] myMix = {"iguanas", "jini://win98p300/"};

    static public void main(String argv[])
      {
        lookDisMan myApp = null;

        if (argv.length > 0)
          myApp = new lookDisMan(argv);
        else
          myApp = new lookDisMan(myMix);
      }

    LookupLocator [] myLocs = null;
    String [] myGroups = null;
    int countLoc, countGroup;
    LookupDiscoveryManager myLdm = null;
    public lookDisMan() {}
```

The `myLocs` and `myGroups` arrays are used to contain the `LookupLocator` to be used for unicast discovery, and groups to be used for multicast discovery respectively. In the constructor, intelligent parsing is performed to separate the unicast URL arguments from the group arguments. Any mix is possible. The algorithm identifies the `LookupLocator` URL via a terminating '/' character. All other arguments are considered groups.

```
public lookDisMan(String [] inMix)
  {
    if (System.getSecurityManager() == null)
      {
        System.setSecurityManager(new RMISecurityManager());
      }
```

```
countLoc =0;
countGroup = 0;
 for (int i=0; i< inMix.length; i++)
   if (inMix[i].substring(inMix[i].length()-1).equals("/")) countLoc++;
   else
      countGroup++;


try
 {
    myLocs = new LookupLocator[countLoc];
    myGroups = new String[countGroup];

    int tpLocs = 0;
    int tpGroups = 0;
    for (int i=0; i< inMix.length; i++)
      if (inMix[i].substring(inMix[i].length()-1).equals("/"))
         myLocs[tpLocs++]= new LookupLocator(inMix[i]);
    else
         myGroups[tpGroups++] = inMix[i];
System.out.println("groups = " + tpGroups + "  locs = " + tpLocs);
```

Once the groups and URLs are separated, the arrays of groups and LookupLocators are used as arguments in the creation of a LookupDiscoveryManager instance. In the case where no group is specified, we need to pass in DiscoveryGroupManagement.NO_GROUPS to prevent the LookupDiscoveryManager from discovering all groups (because null is equivalent to DiscoveryGroupManagement.ALL_GROUPS). We also pass a reference to ourselves (the lookDisMan instance) as a listener.

```
if (tpGroups == 0)
   myLdm = new LookupDiscoveryManager(DiscoveryGroupManagement.NO_GROUPS,
   myLocs, this);
else
   myLdm = new LookupDiscoveryManager(myGroups, myLocs, this);
```

After the creation of the LookupDiscoveryManager instance, we wait for a little while for discovery to occur (in our case, all on one machine, the discovery is typically very short duration).

```
System.out.println("Waiting a few seconds for discovery....");
Thread.sleep(10000L); // sleep for 10 seconds for it to do

myLdm.terminate();
 }
catch(Exception e)
   {
    System.err.println(e.toString());
    e.printStackTrace();
    System.exit(1);
   }
 }
```

In the handling of the callback discovered() method, we synchronize the output so that they do not intermix with one another if callback is performed on multiple threads.

```
  public void discovered(DiscoveryEvent evt)
  {
    ServiceRegistrar [] myRegs = evt.getRegistrars();

    synchronized(this)
      {
      try
        {
          System.out.println("Located " + myRegs.length + " lookup services.");

          for (int i=0; i< myRegs.length; i++)
            {
              System.out.println("------- lookup service # " + i + " ---------");
              System.out.println("    found ID: " + myRegs[i].getServiceID());

              String msg = "";
              String [] groups;
              groups = myRegs[i].getGroups();
              if (groups.length > 0)
              for (int o=0; o<groups.length; o++) { msg += "\'" + groups[o] + "\' ";
                  }

              System.out.println("    Groups Supported: " + msg);
```

The getFrom() method of the LookupDiscoveryManager is used to determine if a particular registrar is discovered from unicast or multicast. The Join protocol requires different handling depending on how a lookup service is discovered.

```
              int tpFrom = myLdm.getFrom(myRegs[i]);
              if (tpFrom == LookupDiscoveryManager.FROM_GROUP)
                System.out.println("    Found from multicast groups.");
              else
                System.out.println("    Found from unicast URL.");
              }   // of for i

          }
      catch(Exception e)
        {
          System.err.println(e.toString());
          e.printStackTrace();
          System.exit(1);
        }

      } // of synchronized

  }
  public void discarded(DiscoveryEvent evt) {}
}
```

Compile the code using:

```
buildit lookDisMan.java
```

Testing the LookupDiscoveryManager Sample

Testing the program will require setup of three different lookup services. They will be setup according to the following:

Lookup Service Number	Groups Handled	Host and Unicast Port
1	iguanas	win98p300 4160
2	lizards	win98p300 4166
3	iguanas,lizards	win98p300 unknown

We can set this up by following the steps (some of these should be looking very familiar by now):

❑ Change directory to Ch10\code\bats

❑ Clean the reggie and RMID logs manually or use the runclean.bat file on Win 98

❑ Start the class server by running the runhttpd.bat file

❑ Start the RMID activation support by running the runrmid.bat file

❑ Start the first lookup service by running runlookup1.bat

❑ Start the second lookup service by running runlookup2.bat

❑ Start the third lookup service by running runlookup3.bat

❑ Change directory to Ch10\code\reggtool

❑ Start our reggtool by running runregg.bat

❑ Type 'list' to find the index of the lookup service supporting the lizards group only

❑ Type setuport <index> 4160 to set the unicast port for the iguanas only server

❑ Type setuport <index> 4166 to set the unicast port for the lizards only server

We are ready to test our LookupDiscoveryManager. Change directory back to Ch10\code\lookdisman, so and type in:

```
runlook iguanas jini://win98p300/ jini://win98p300:4166/
```

Your output should be similar to this:

```
MS-DOS Prompt                                                    _ □ ×
10 x 18                  A
ni-core.jar;d:\jini1_1\lib\jini-ext.jar;d:\jini1_1\lib\sun-util.jar;d
ib\reggie.jar -Djava.security.policy=policy.all -Dnet.jini.discovery.
92.168.23.30 lookDisMan iguanas jini://win98p300/ jini://win98p300:41
groups = 1  locs = 2
Waiting a few seconds for discovery....
Located 1 lookup services.
-------- lookup service # 0 ---------
    found ID: 585934cb-469e-45b4-a02b-8667a2aa8034
    Groups Supported: 'iguanas'
    Found from unicast URL.
Located 1 lookup services.
-------- lookup service # 0 ---------
    found ID: f4277909-b354-4e72-9ee5-9302c1578765
    Groups Supported: 'lizards'
    Found from unicast URL.
Located 1 lookup services.
-------- lookup service # 0 ---------
    found ID: 7d28b834-2bfd-481e-ac26-afe1c7c4edbc
    Groups Supported: 'lizards'  'iguanas'
    Found from multicast groups.

D:\writing\proirow\Ch8\ch8a\code\lookdisman>
```

We have located all three lookup services, one supporting both iguanas and lizards group via multicast, and the iguanas only plus the lizards only group via unicast.

Now try another command line:

```
runlook dummy jini://win98p300/ jini://win98p300:4166/
```

The dummy group is not supported within the Jini network by any lookup services. We end up discovering only two lookup services, both are via unicast discovery (specified by the two Jini URLs on the command line). Here we see the output that you should get.

```
MS-DOS Prompt                                                    _ □ ×
10 x 18                  A
ni-core.jar;d:\jini1_1\lib\jini-ext.jar;d:\jini1_1\lib\sun-util.jar;d
ib\reggie.jar -Djava.security.policy=policy.all -Dnet.jini.discovery.
92.168.23.30 lookDisMan dummy jini://win98p300/ jini://win98p300:4166
groups = 1  locs = 2
Waiting a few seconds for discovery....
Located 1 lookup services.
-------- lookup service # 0 ---------
    found ID: 585934cb-469e-45b4-a02b-8667a2aa8034
    Groups Supported: 'iguanas'
    Found from unicast URL.
Located 1 lookup services.
-------- lookup service # 0 ---------
    found ID: f4277909-b354-4e72-9ee5-9302c1578765
    Groups Supported: 'lizards'
    Found from unicast URL.

D:\writing\proirow\Ch8\ch8a\code\lookdisman>
```

371

Now, try running the `reggtool` again, by changing directory to `\code\reggtool`, and supply the following command:

`chgrp <index of lizards only lookup service> dragons`

Try running `lookdisman` again via:

`runlook iguanas jini://win98p300:4166/`

This time, we have again discovered three lookup services, however the dragons handling lookup service is discovered via unicast only, while the other two are via multicast. Again, here is the output.

```
MS-DOS Prompt                                          _ □ X

10 x 18    ⬜ ▭🗐🗐 ▣ 🗐🗗 A
D.\wiiting\piuji ew\cnoa\coae\iuukuisman/java    ciasspatn .,u.\jin
ni-core.jar;d:\jini1_1\lib\jini-ext.jar;d:\jini1_1\lib\sun-util.jar;d
ib\reggie.jar -Djava.security.policy=policy.all -Dnet.jini.discovery.
92.168.23.30 lookDisMan iguanas jini://win98p300:4166/
groups = 1  locs = 1
Waiting a few seconds for discovery....
Located 1 lookup services.
------- lookup service # 0 ----------
   found ID: 585934cb-469e-45b4-a02b-8667a2aa8034
     Groups Supported: 'iguanas'
     Found from multicast groups.
Located 1 lookup services.
------- lookup service # 0 ----------
   found ID: f4277909-b354-4e72-9ee5-9302c1578765
     Groups Supported: 'dragons'
     Found from unicast URL.
Located 1 lookup services.
------- lookup service # 0 ----------
   found ID: 7d28b834-2bfd-481e-ac26-afe1c7c4edbc
     Groups Supported: 'lizards' 'iguanas'
     Found from multicast groups.
```

What the LookupDiscovery Manager Won't Do For Us

If we are writing a service, the registration of the service's proxy, management of the associated lease, and the handling of the Join protocol is the application's responsibility. State persistence of any sort is not supported either. If we are writing a client, the management of the set of lookup service registrars is still very much the application's responsibility. In summary, the `LookupDiscoveryManager` really just performs the task of locating lookup services.

Moving Onto Higher Level Manager Utilities

In this chapter, we have discovered the large set of versatile helper utilities and services that the Jini library provides. We have seen the three levels that helper utilities come in: low-level protocol utilities, mid-level manager utilities, and high-level manager utilities. We have examined the first two levels of utilities thoroughly, including applying them in actual code.

Also in the chapter, we have presented the core-logic for a useful command line diagnostic tool for Jini called reggtool. reggtool is extensible via dynamic command loading.

We have built several commands for this tool, and used them in testing and examination of the chapter's code samples.

In the next chapter, we will continue our cookbook coverage by examining the remaining level of programming support:

❏ High-Level Manager Utilities

❏ Helper Services

We will build several more commands for reggtool, and will also be designing (and coding) a Service Creation Environment for legacy (or non-Jini) services.

Jini Client or Service	JavaSpaces and Helper Services

Jini Client and Service Support Helper Utilities

Jini Discovery Management Helper Utilities

Jini Protocol Helper Utilities

Jini Network Protocols	RMI and Rich Object Semantics
	Java VM and Networking

Network Protocols

11

High-Level Helper Utilities and Helper Services

The Jini library provides many helper utilities and services to assist in programming Jini clients and services. Helper utilities are Java library classes that implement well-known interfaces locally; they run within the user's (client or service) own Java VM. Helper services, on the other hand, implement well-known interfaces remotely; they run independently within their own VM and handle requests from users (client or service) as a third-party. We saw in the last chapter that helper utilities come on three different levels:

- ❑ Low-level basic protocol utilities
- ❑ Mid-level manager utilities
- ❑ High-level manager utilities

We have seen and worked with the first two levels of utilities in the last chapter. In this chapter, we will start our coverage of the high-level manager utilities as well as the helper services. We will continue our exploration using the reggtool command line tool that we developed in the last chapter. Using the helper services, we will also be creating an 'Instant Jini Service Creation Environment'. This environment will enable non-Jini software systems to participate in a Jini network easily and simply.

Let us now turn our attention to the first high-level helper utility that we will cover. This helper utility can handle repeated lease renewal on our behalf. We have already used it several times in previous examples, it is called the LeaseRenewalManager utility.

The LeaseRenewalManager High-Level Manager Utility

It's impossible to develop Jini services without working with distributed leases, and `LeaseRenewalManager` makes handling these leases almost trivial from the client's perspective.

Design Rationale

Programming lease renewal logic can take up a significant amount of code in a typical Jini application. When working with lookup services, both the service proxy registration and remote event notification registration are leased. When working with other services, there may be many other resources that are leased. In Chapter 8 we saw that leasing helps a distributed Jini network to manage distributed resource allocations (through lease holder's continual proof of interest) and also to heal in case of disruptive failures by cleaning up unused resources upon lease expiry. In order for this to work as intended, most resource owners should not grant leases for a long duration (typically no longer than a couple of minutes). This means that some renewal logic on the leaseholder side must constantly renew leases before they expire. The coding is made more complex in the case where a client holds multiple leases from lease grantors on multiple machines. In order to efficiently renew these leases, they should be batched using the `LeaseMap` grouping mechanism. The coding of lease renewal logic can be both tedious and error prone if littered throughout the lease holder's resource allocation and utilization code, but this can be avoided if we use the `LeaseRenewalManager` helper utility. The `LeaseRenewalManager` implements code to:

❑   Manage the set of leases that are granted to the user by remote lease grantors

❑   Handle the renewal of all leases on behalf of the user

❑   Perform the renewal of leases efficiently, in batch, using the `LeaseMap` mechanism

Inside the LeaseRenewalManager Utility

When an application creates an instance of `LeaseRenewalManager`, it can delegate the tedious duty of lease renewal to it. Since the instance lives within the Java VM of the application, it will have the same lifetime as the application. This means that if the application ever crashes, the `LeaseRenewalManager` will stop renewing leases (since the VM that it is running in has terminated). The distributed network will then be able to 'heal' once the outstanding leases expire.

Here is a figure that describes the functional components within a `LeaseRenewalManager` class. The lease holder first obtains one or more leases with one or more lease grantors; then it creates an instance of the `LeaseRenewalManager` utility – supplying it with a lease to handle with a desired expiration time. Then it continues to add leases to the managed set maintained by the `LeaseRenewalManager`, specifying a desired expiration time for each, and an optional listener for lease renewal failure. The `LeaseRenewalManager` then goes to work and keeps performing the renewal with the actual lease grantor(s) until the desired expiration time has been reached.

If a listener is specified, any failure to renew a lease will result in a notification to the listener.

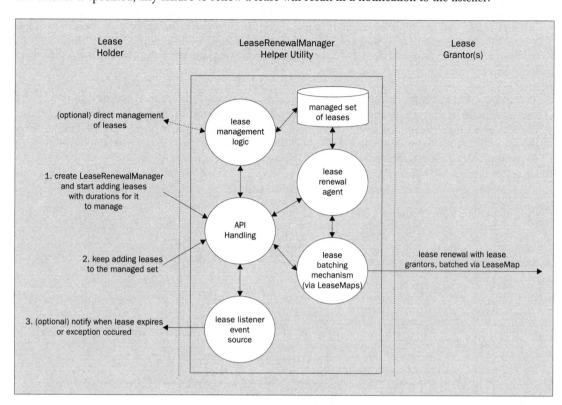

In order to use the LeaseRenewalManager profitably, you need to request a desired expiration time (with the LeaseRenewalManager) that is considerably later than the actual expiration time granted (by the lease grantor). Otherwise, the user may as well renew the lease itself. For example, if a lease grantor is willing to only grant 3 minute leases, we have at least three choices to implement the renewal:

❑ Write our code so that the lease is always renewed with the grantor before the 3 minutes expire, all without using any helper utilities

❑ Use the LeaseRenewalManager utility, hand over the lease from the lease grantor, and ask the LeaseRenewalManager for a desired expiration time of 3 hours in the future

❑ Use the LeaseRenewalManager utility, hand over the lease from the lease grantor, and ask the LeaseRenewalManager for a desired expiration time of 'forever' (until the lease is removed, cancelled, or the current VM terminates)

To assist in this, LeaseRenewalManager manages a desired lease expiration time associated with each lease. When a lease is added to the LeaseRenewalManager, this desired expiration time can be set to any value, or the special values of Lease.ANY or Lease.FOREVER. LeaseRenewalManager will treat either as a request to repeatedly renew the lease until the lease is removed or cancelled. Note, however, that the Lease.ANY or Lease.FOREVER will be passed to the lease grantor upon a renewal – developers may need to be sensitive to which one to use with specific grantors.

Using either `Lease.FOREVER` or `Lease.ANY` with leases handled by the `LeaseRenewalManager` completely delegates the task of renewal to the `LeaseRenewalManager`. There may be cases where this is not desirable and the application needs more control. In such cases, the application can ask for a lease expiry time that is significantly longer than the lease the grantor will be willing to grant. This means that the application can control when it needs to perform lease renewal, rather than having the timing dictated by a grantor.

The application can register a callback object supporting the `LeaseListener` interface with the `LeaseRenewalManager` (associated with the lease). The `LeaseRenewalManager` will then perform all the renewals within the desired expiration time period, and perform the callback, should it fail to renew the lease, before the desired time has elapsed. The application can then decide what to do with the lease renewal problem. Here is the definition of the `LeaseRenewalManager` class:

```
public class LeaseRenewalManager extends Object
{
    public LeaseRenewalManager(){..}
    public LeaseRenewalManager(Lease lease, long expiration, LeaseListener
      listener){..}

    void cancel(Lease lease){..}
    void remove(Lease lease){..}
    void clear(){..}

    long getExpiration(Lease lease){..}
    void setExpiration(Lease lease, long expiration){..}

    void renewFor(Lease lease, long desiredDuration, LeaseListener listener){..}
    void renewFor(Lease lease, long desiredDuration, long renewDuration,
      LeaseListener listener) {..}
    void renewUntil(Lease lease, long desiredExpiration, LeaseListener
      listener){..}
    void renewUntil(Lease lease, long desiredExpiration, long renewDuration,
      LeaseListener listener) {..}
}
```

The first lease is supplied to the `LeaseRenewalManager` through its constructor. The expiration time is specified in terms of absolute time in milliseconds. The `System.currentTimeMillis()` method (plus a duration) is frequently used here if you do not specify `Lease.ANY` or `Lease.FOREVER`. You can also register a `LeaseListener` with the instantiation. Once instantiated, a lease may be removed from the managed set, or cancelled using the corresponding method. The `clear()` method will remove all leases from the `LeaseRenewalManager`, without canceling them. This may be useful if you like to take over the lease renewal task from the `LeaseRenewalManager` at some instance in time.

All subsequent leases other than the first are added to the `LeaseRenewalManager` either using the `renewFor()` or the `renewUntil()` method call. `renewFor()` should be used if you are specifying a desired lease renewal duration , and `renewUntil()` when you are specifying an absolute desired lease expiry time. The desired expiry time or desired duration should typically be longer than the actual renewal duration – putting the `LeaseRenewalManager` to work for you. There are two versions of the `renewFor()` and `renewUntil()` methods, one that takes an additional `renewDuration` argument. The `renewDuration` argument is the actual argument that will be passed by the `LeaseRenewalManager` to the lease grantor. In the case of `renewUntil()`, if the value of `desiredDuration` is `Lease.FOREVER`, then the value of `renewDuration` must be `Lease.ANY`. In the case of `renewFor()`, if the value of `desiredExpiration` is `Lease.FOREVER`, then the value of `renewDuration` can be `Lease.ANY` or any value(in milliseconds). The (desired) expiration time of any managed lease can be changed via the `setExpiration()` and `getExpiration()` methods, this (desired) expiration time is the time when the `LeaseRenewalManager` will stop renewing the particular lease.

If you do register a LeaseListener with the LeaseRenewalManager, the LeaseRenewalManager will make sure that the LeaseListener will be called back if it fails to renew the lease before the desired expiration time has been reached, or if you add an expired lease to the managed set. The LeaseListener interface is defined as:

```
public abstract interface LeaseListener extends EventListener
{
    void notify(LeaseRenewalEvent e);
}
```

And the LeaseRenewalEvent that is passed in the notify() callback method is defined as:

```
public class LeaseRenewalEvent extends EventObject
{
    public LeaseRenewalEvent(LeaseRenewalManager source, Lease lease, long
        expiration, Exception ex);
    Exception getException();
    long getExpiration();
    Lease getLease();
}
```

Note that you can obtain a reference to the lease that is being renewed from the event. The LeaseRenewalEvent returns an exception for the application to examine (for example, network problems in reaching the original lease grantor).

Since we have already seen many examples of using the LeaseRenewalManager class in the previous chapter, we will not repeat one here (see Chapters 8 and 9 for examples).

What LeaseRenewalManager Will Not Do For Us

LeaseRenewalManager performs an extremely thorough job of managing lease renewal. With respect to the lease renewal process, there is very little that it will not do for us. Generally speaking you can hand over the responsibility for leases and forget all about them, using Lease.FOREVER or Lease.ANY. The leases using the LeaseRenewalManager will be renewed as long as the resources are still available and we still need them.

Despite this comprehensive coverage, there are still a few bits and pieces we need to deal with:

❑ Requesting the leases, since the Jini specification has no pre-defined interface for doing so – LeaseRenewalManager cannot do it for us even if it wants to

❑ Assist in lease persistence, in order to survive failure or unintentional restarts

❑ Change the serialization format of leases when necessary, since LeaseRenewalManager will neither transmit leases between machines nor write leases to permanent storage

The LeaseRenewalManager is the first high-level manager utility that we have covered, and we can see that it is quite versatile. The 'do everything' nature is a common trait amongst these high-level utilities. The next high-level manager utility that we will look at is JoinManager – and it takes care of practically everything that a Jini service needs to do other than the core service logic itself.

The JoinManager High Level Manager Utility

A Jini programmer's dream library class would be one that handles every detail of being a well-behaved Jini service, leaving the programmers to code the customized service logic alone. The JoinManager helper utility comes very close to this ideal.

Design Rationale

When coding a Jini service, one may need to write an extensive amount of code to satisfy the need to manage all the registrars from discovered lookup services, and the obligation to conform to the Join protocol. This code is often repeated across Jini services, and is often tedious to code. Instead of having application developers each designing their own high-level library class, or even service construction kits that could handle this tedium, Jini library features JoinManager to handle all the requirements.

What Will the JoinManager Helper Utility Do?

We have already worked with the JoinManager class in Chapter 7, and realized how easy it makes coding a Jini service. Essentially, it provides all of the following functionality – completely freeing up a service builder from Jini infrastructure coding:

The JoinManager will:

- ❑ Manage discovery, both multicast and unicast using a LookupDiscoveryManager instance
- ❑ Maintain a managed set of registrars associated with the discovered lookup services
- ❑ Maintain a managed set of attributes associated with the service's custom proxy
- ❑ Register the service's proxy with all the lookup services that have been discovered, together with attributes specified for the proxy
- ❑ Maintain and renew the leases from the managed set of lookup services for the service proxy registration
- ❑ Implement the Join protocol when the managed set of groups, locators, and attributes are modified
- ❑ Notify the user when a new service ID is assigned by the lookup service

A graphical representation of this formidable set of duties is illustrated in the following figure. The service wishing to use JoinManager has to do the following:

- ❑ Create an instance of JoinManager. The constructor is called by passing in the service's proxy, any attached attributes, and an optional service ID (if the service is restarting). The service can also pass in an instance of an object implementing the DiscoveryManagement interface (that is, an instance of the mid-level LookupDiscoveryManager) and one that implements the LeaseManagement interface (that is, an instance of LeaseRenewalManager).
- ❑ If the service is started for the first time and does not have a service ID yet, it can also listen for notification when the service ID is assigned by a lookup service, and a listener for this notification can be passed in during construction as well. Internally, JoinManager makes use of LookupDiscoveryManager (the dashed box in the diagram below: either user supplied or it instantiates its own) to perform the discovery protocols. The service can have direct access to the discovery groups and locators through JoinManager if it wishes.
- ❑ JoinManager completely hides the management of lookup service registrars from the service. If it wishes, the service can also directly access the managed set of lookup service registrars.

Last but not least, a service can add, delete, or modify the attributes associated with its proxy through the JoinManager. JoinManager adds value in this case by implementing the Join protocol in full, ensuring that any lookup service that has the proxy registered will also get the propagated change in the attributes.

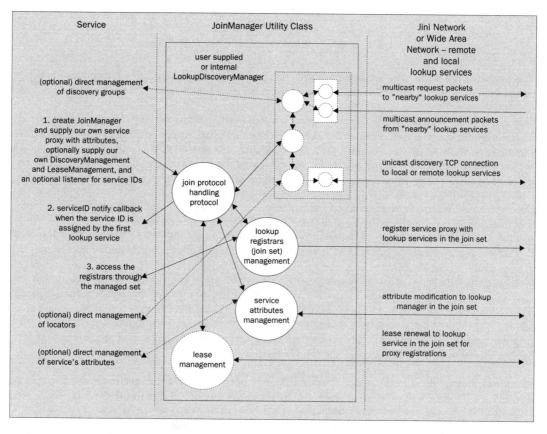

JoinManager performs an incredible amount of grunge work for us, all of which is necessary for a well-behaved Jini service. For a class that does so much, its definition is deceptively simple:

```
public class JoinManager
{
    public JoinManager(Object obj, Entry[] attrSets, ServiceIDListener callback,
        DiscoveryManagement discoverMgr, LeaseRenewalManager leaseMgr) throws
        IOException{..}
    public JoinManager(Object obj, Entry[] attrSets, ServiceID serviceID,
        DiscoveryManagement discoverMgr, LeaseRenewalManager leaseMgr) throws
        IOException{..}

    void addAttributes(Entry [] attrSets){..}
    void addAttributes(Entry [] attrSets, boolean checkSC){..} Entry []
        getAttributes(){..}
    void modifyAttributes(Entry [] attrSetTemplates, Entry [] attrSets){..}
    void modifyAttributes(Entry [] attrSetTemplates, Entry [] attrSets, boolean
        checkSC){..}
    void setAttributes(Entry [] attrSets){..}
```

```
    DiscoveryManagement getDiscoveryManager(){..}
    LeaseRenewalManager getLeaseRenewalManager(){..}

    ServiceRegistrar [] getJoinSet(){..}

    void terminate(){..}
}
```

The following is a more detailed description of what goes on inside this complex utility, tying in the methods in the above interface with the diagram we have seen previously.

The secret of this simplicity is the well-designed reuse of existing library classes. In fact, all of the discovery work is performed using an instance of a class that supports the `DiscoveryManagement` interface (typically an instance of the `LookupDiscoveryManager` class) that can either be supplied by the user or instantiated by default internally. All the lease renewal within the class is performed by an instance of a `LeaseRenewalManager` class that can be supplied by the user or instantiated internally by default. Since the `JoinManager` provides methods to get at both the `LookupDiscoveryManager` and `LeaseRenewalManager` classes directly, the (many) methods implemented by these classes are not duplicated as its own methods. Instead, the user can call `getDiscoveryManager()` or `getLeaseRenewalManager()` to access the instances and operate their methods directly. Most of the `JoinManager`'s own methods are ones that operate on the managed set of attributes for the service's proxy.

Constructing an instance of a `JoinManager` utility can take one of two forms, mainly because it is the duty of a lookup service to assign a unique service ID for a service instance the very first time it starts up. Therefore the `JoinManager` class may be called with a `ServiceIDListener` callback, or with an actual service ID. The first time the service starts, the `ServiceIDListener` is supplied. The object implementing this listener should persist the service ID that is returned. Every subsequent startup of this service should use the second form, using the persisted service ID.

As expected, in addition to the optional service ID, one needs to supply the service proxy, a set of attributes, a `LookupDiscoveryManager` instance (actually any object that implements the `DiscoveryManagement` interface) and a `LeaseRenewalManager` instance. If either of these utility objects are omitted, and null supplied, the `JoinManager` will internally create an instance for use by default. By default, the `LookupDiscoveryManager` instance will be using multicast discovery for all groups; and the `LeaseRenewalManager` will be renewing the lease for the same lifetime as the application (Java VM). The list of attributes can also be null or an empty array if the service does not want to attach any entries to the proxy.

At any moment in time, the `getJoinSet()` method can be used to obtain the registrars from lookup services the `JoinManager` has discovered (via unicast or multicast). This set of registrars is managed by the `JoinManager` according to the Join protocol. The service should not keep its own shadow set of these registrars, as synchronization between the two sets will be difficult. If the service must manage its own set of lookup service registrar due to some design constraints, one should seek out the assistance of lower level utilities instead of using the high-level `JoinManager` utility.

The `addAttributes()`, `modifyAttributes()`, and `setAttributes()` methods can be used to change the attributes attached to the proxy object. Be aware that the requirements of the Join protocols will be satisfied: the `JoinManager` will go through every one of the lookup services that it has registered the proxy with, and ensure that the attributes associated with the proxy will be changed on each one to reflect the new value. This can take a significant amount of time, and the methods will not wait for this to complete before returning. Because of this, it is important that the attributes supplied as arguments to these methods are not modified immediately upon return from the call.

Both the addAttributes() and modifyAttributes() methods have two forms, one with the checkSC (check Service Controlled) boolean flag and one without. The form with the boolean flag should be used by the service when it is modifying attributes on behalf of clients; it will check to make sure the attribute being modified is not a service controlled attribute (that is, implements the ServiceControlled marker interface). If attempts are made to modify these attributes, a SecurityException will be thrown.

The modifyAttributes() method performs modification on attributes through a template based algorithm. It tries to find a match for each element in the attrSetTemplates array, and changes any attribute that matches the template to the attribute provided in the corresponding attrSets. For example, let us take the case where the proxy we are working with has a Location attribute entry, where the fields are: floor, room, and building. If the modifyAttributes() method call has one single element in the attrSetTemplates array, and it is:

```
new Location( "third floor", null /* room */,null /* building */);
```

and the corresponding attrSet's arrays first and only element is:

```
new Location("second floor" , "room 2322", "Lab 1");
```

then this will change all attributes associated with the proxy with Location that has "third floor" as the floor member, to one with 'second floor', 'room 2322', and 'lab 1'.

The terminate() method will gracefully shutdown all the operations of the JoinManager, including the delegate LookupDiscoveryManager and LeaseRenewalManager.

Using the JoinManager Utility

We're going to build a sample program that utilizes the JoinManager class in a different way to the ones we've already seen. This sample will actually use the JoinManager's attributes manipulation methods to modify the service proxy's attributes. By running multiple instances of lookup services, we will be able to see the Join protocol at work when the attributes associated with a service's proxy change. The changes should propagate throughout all the lookup services that the proxy has registered with.

A Jini service can perform any arbitrary work. In this example, our Jini service will perform a rather trivial piece of work – adding two integers together. This service will support a very simple interface called JoinmanItf. It is defined as:

```
import java.rmi.RemoteException;
public interface JoinmanItf extends java.rmi.Remote
{
    public int getSum(int a, int b) throws RemoteException;
}
```

The implementation of the interface will be the Joinman class itself. Therefore, the proxy is actually an RMI proxy that will callback across the network to get the addition performed. The actual getSum() will execute on the service machine, unlike the sixpack example we saw in Chapter 6. You can find the code in the \Ch11\code\joinman.java file.

```
import net.jini.lookup.JoinManager;
import net.jini.core.lookup.ServiceID;
import net.jini.discovery.*;
import net.jini.core.lookup.ServiceRegistrar;
import java.rmi.RemoteException;
```

```
import java.rmi.RMISecurityManager;
import net.jini.lookup.ServiceIDListener;
import java.rmi.server.*;

import net.jini.lookup.entry.Name;
import net.jini.core.entry.Entry;

import java.io.*;
```

We used the same persistence helper class, `Logger`, as we did in our hitman example in Chapter 7. The persist and restore methods will write a serialized object stream to and from hard disk respectively.

```
class Logger
{
    private static String myLogDir = ".\\";
    public static void setLogDir(String dirname)
    {
      myLogDir = dirname;
    }

    public static synchronized void persist(String filename, Object item)
        throws IOException
    {
      ObjectOutputStream os =
          new ObjectOutputStream(new FileOutputStream(myLogDir + filename));
      os.writeObject(item);
      os.flush();
      os.close();
    }

    public static synchronized Object restore(String filename)
        throws IOException,ClassNotFoundException
    {
      ObjectInputStream os =
          new ObjectInputStream(new FileInputStream(myLogDir + filename));
      Object retval = os.readObject();
      os.close();
      return retval;
    }
} // of class Logger
```

The only thing that we will persist in this case is the service ID. This is done so that the first constructor of the `JoinManager` utility will be called initially to get the service ID, and subsequent startup of the service will use the second constructor supplying the assigned service ID. We do not persist the leases maintained by `JoinManager` for simplicity. We already know that reggie will expire outstanding leases within a couple of minutes. The name of the persistence file for the service ID is `'servid.per'`.

```
interface JoinmanConstants
{
    static final String IDFILE = "servid.per";
}
```

When the service is first started and a service ID is assigned by a nearby lookup service, the `JoinManager` utility will notify us of the assignment through the `ServiceIDListener` callback. We use the `idPrinter` class to implement the `ServiceIDListener` interface, and persist the service ID when we're notified the first time our service starts.

```
class IdPrinter implements ServiceIDListener,joinmanConstants
  {
    public IdPrinter()
      {
        public void serviceIDNotify(ServiceID sid) {
        System.out.println("Service has been assigned service ID: " +
          sid.toString());
        try
          {
            Logger.persist( IDFILE, sid);
            System.out.println("Written to persistent storage.");
          }
        catch (Exception e)
          {
            System.out.println("Cannot write to persistent storage.");
            System.exit(1);
          }
      }
  } //of class IdPrinter
```

The `Joinman` class provides the RMI implementation for the `JoinmanItf` interface. It inherits from `java.rmi.server.UnicastRemoteObject` to make stub exporting simple.

```
public class Joinman extends UnicastRemoteObject implements JoinmanItf,
  JoinmanConstants
  {
```

The `Joinman` service will discover all lookup services handling the iguanas group. Notice the declaration of prompt strings; this `Joinman` program will have a command line interface very similar to reggtool, but not as sophisticated. The command line will be used to issue commands that toggle the attribute of the service proxy.

```
    static final int MAX_INSTANCES = 3;
    static final String [] GROUPS1 = { "iguanas"};
    static final String QUIT_COMMAND = "quit";
    static final String UNKNOWN_COMMAND_MSG = "Sorry, unknown command.";
    static final String SYSTEM_PROMPT = "Joinman> ";
    static ServiceID myID = null;

    protected JoinManager myJM = null;

    static Joinman myApp = null;
    JoinmanItf myImpl = null;
```

The `main()` method will sit in a loop and wait for commands from the user, but before doing this it processes the invocation arguments to find the persistence directory, if one exists, and the initial value for the `Name` attribute associated with the proxy, if one is specified. The default general usage of `Joinman` is:

```
java Joinman [<default name attribute> [persistence directory]]
```

where the default name attribute is an attached attribute to the `Joinman` service's proxy when the service is registered with lookup services.

The persistence directory is where `Joinman` will persist its service ID information, and the directory specified must end with '\' on Win32.

```java
public static void main(String argv[])
{
    BufferedReader in = new BufferedReader(new InputStreamReader(System.in));
    String curCmd = null;
    // set the root for the persistence directory
    if (argv.length > 1)
        Logger.setLogDir(argv[1]);
    try
        {
        if(argv.length > 0)
            myApp = new Joinman(argv[0]);
        else
            myApp = new Joinman("Joinman");
```

The user input processing loop starts here. It accepts only three commands: first, second or quit.

The "`first`" command changes the `Name` attribute of the proxy to "`first`" by calling a helper `setFirstAttributes()` method; the "`second`" command changes the `Name` attribute of the proxy to "`second`" by calling a helper `setSecondAttributes()` method; and the "`quit`" command exits the command loop and calls the `wrapUp()` helper method.

```java
System.out.println("Welcome to JoinMan Sample");

System.out.print(SYSTEM_PROMPT);
System.out.flush();

curCmd = in.readLine();
while(!curCmd.equals(QUIT_COMMAND))
    {
        if (curCmd.equals("first"))
            myApp.setFirstAttributes();
        else
            {
            if (curCmd.equals("second"))
                myApp.setSecondAttributes();
            else
                System.out.println(UNKNOWN_COMMAND_MSG);
            }
        System.out.print(SYSTEM_PROMPT);
        System.out.flush();
        curCmd = in.readLine();
```

```
            }
        }
    catch (IOException ex)
        { ex.printStackTrace(); System.exit(1); }
        myApp.wrapUp();
        System.out.print("Thanks for using JoinMan!");

    }   // of main()
```

The `restoreAll()` method is used to persist `Joinman`'s service ID anytime after the very first execution when the ID is assigned.

```
    public void restoreAll()
    {
      try
        {
          myID = (ServiceID) Logger.restore(IDFILE);
        } // of outer try
      catch (Exception e)
        {   // first time if exception caught
          e.printStackTrace();
          return;
        }
    }   // of restore all

  public Joinman() throws RemoteException {}
```

The `Joinman()` constructor takes a parameter that will be used for the initial attribute value for the `Name` attribute of the proxy when it is first registered with the lookup services.

```
      public Joinman(String inTitle) throws RemoteException
      {
        if (System.getSecurityManager() == null)
          {
            // need an RMISecurityManager to download proxy from lookup service
            System.setSecurityManager(new RMISecurityManager());
          }
        restoreAll();
```

We create an instance of `LookupDiscoveryManager`, and set it to discover the iguanas group (GROUPS1).

```
      // Discovery and Join through JoinManager
      LookupDiscoveryManager ldm = null;
      String [] groupsToDiscover = GROUPS1;
```

We create the `Name` attribute for the proxy, and set the value to the argument passed into this method.

```
Entry [] attributes = new Entry[1];
attributes[0] = new Name(inTitle);

try
  {
    myImpl = this;

    ldm =
    new LookupDiscoveryManager(groupsToDiscover,null,null);
```

The very first time we start the service, we will use the `ServiceIDListener` version of the `JoinManager` constructor and supply an instance of `IdPrinter` to persist the service ID assigned. Subsequently, we call the service ID version of the constructor and supply our assigned service ID.

```
if (myID == null)
    {
        myJM = new JoinManager(myImpl, attributes, new idPrinter(), ldm,
            null );
    }
  else
    {
        System.out.println("Using service ID: " + myID);
        myJM = new JoinManager(myImpl, attributes, myID, ldm, null);
    }
  }
catch(Exception e)
  {
    e.printStackTrace();
    System.exit(1);
  }
}
```

This is the only method in the `JoinmanItf` remote interface. A client will call back across the network to execute this.

```
public int getSum(int a, int b) throws RemoteException
  {
    return (a + b);
  }
```

The `setFirstAttributes()` method changes the attribute to a `Name` attribute with value "first" by calling the `setAttribute()` method of the `JoinManager`.

```
public void setFirstAttributes()
  {
    Entry [] attributes = new Entry[1];
    attributes[0] = new Name("first");
    myJM.setAttributes(attributes);
    System.out.println(" Changing attribute name=\"first\"");
    System.out.print(SYSTEM_PROMPT);
    System.out.flush();
  }
```

The `setSecondAttributes()` method changes the attribute associated with the proxy to a `Name` attribute with value "second".

```
public void setSecondAttributes()
 {
     Entry [] attributes = new Entry[1];
     attributes[0] = new Name("second");
     myJM.setAttributes(attributes);
     System.out.println(" Changing attribute name=\"second\"");
     System.out.print(SYSTEM_PROMPT);
     System.out.flush();
 }
```

The `wrapUp()` helper terminates gracefully by calling the `JoinManager`'s `terminate()` method.

```
public void wrapUp()
  {
    myJM.terminate();
    System.exit(0);
  }
}
```

Compile the `Joinman` sample by:

```
buildit joinman.java
```

Since the `Joinman` service supports the remote `JoinmanItf` interface, we must create the RMI stubs required. Use the `makestub.bat` file in the `\ch11\code\joinman` directory. The `makestub.bat` file contains:

```
rmic -v1.2 joinman
```

A JAR file containing the stub and the interface class file should then be moved to the class server's root directory for client downloading. Use the `makejar.bat` file in the `\ch11\code\joinman` directory for this. The `makejar.bat` file contains:

```
call ..\bats\setpaths.bat
jar cvf joinman-dl.jar joinman_Stub.class joinmanItf.class
copy joinman-dl.jar %JINIHOME%\lib
```

Now, we need to add one more custom command to our reggtool before testing this sample.

Extending Reggtool Again

To be able to observe the effect of changing `JoinManager` managed attribute values, we must enhance our reggtool to do actual lookup with the lookup services that it discovers. This can be done by adding a new command, with the command word **look**. The usage syntax is:

```
look <index of lookup service> <value of Name attribute>
```

When executed in reggtool, this command will lookup any service with the specified value in its Name attribute. A special attribute value of "all" will list all the service proxies currently registered with the lookup service. Here is the implementation of the command, its doCommand() method. You can find the source code in \Ch11\code\reggtool\cmdlook.java.

```
public void doCommand(StringTokenizer myTk, ArrayList registrars,
    LookupDiscovery ld)
{
    String nxtToken;
    int numTokens = myTk.countTokens();

    if (numTokens < 2)
        return;
```

We decode the StringTokenizer input into the index, and the desired attribute value.

```
    int myIdx = 0;
    try
        {
        Integer.parseInt(myTk.nextToken());
        }
    catch (NumberFormatException ex)
        {
        System.out.println("Invalid format for first argument: must be a number");
        System.exit(1);
        }
    String attribValue = myTk.nextToken();
```

Next, we verify that the index supplied is not out of range; then we obtain the lookup service proxy and call the helper lookup() method.

```
    if (myIdx < registrars.size())
        {
        ServiceRegistrar myReg =(ServiceRegistrar) registrars.get(myIdx);

        if (myReg != null)
            {
            lookup(myReg, myIdx, attribValue);
            }
        }
    }
```

In the helper lookup() method, we first create a template consisting of the Name attribute with the desired value. We also handle the special "all" value here by creating a null template that will match everything.

```
private void lookup(ServiceRegistrar registrar, int Idx, String attr)
    {
    ServiceMatches matches = null;
    Entry myAttrib[] = new Entry[1];
    myAttrib[0] = new Name(attr);
```

```
System.out.println("Performing lookup on lookup service #
                   " + Idx + " Name=\"" + attr + "\":");
try
  {
    ServiceTemplate myTmpl = null;
    if (attr.equals("all"))
      myTmpl = new ServiceTemplate(null,null,null);
  else
      myTmpl = new ServiceTemplate(null,null ,myAttrib);
```

Then we perform the lookup using the actual registrar.

```
matches = registrar.lookup(myTmpl, MAX_MATCHES);
System.out.println("          .... found " + matches.totalMatches + "
    services...");
```

For every service that we find matching the desired Name attribute, we print out its service ID, class name, and all the interfaces that the service implements.

```
for (int j=0; j< matches.totalMatches; j++)
  {
    if (matches.item[j].service != null)
      {
        System.out.println("        ID: " + matches.items[j].serviceID);
        String msg = "";
        Class myCls = matches.items[j].service.getClass();
        System.out.println("      Class: " + myCls.getName());
        System.out.println("      Interfaces: ");
        Class [] allInt = myCls.getInterfaces();
        for (int k=0; k<allInt.length; k++)
        System.out.println("          " + allInt[k].getName());
      }
  }
} // of try
catch (Exception ex)
  {
    ex.printStackTrace();
  }
}
```

Compile this command extension for reggtool by using:

```
buildit cmdLook.java
```

Testing the Joinman Sample Service

Now we are ready to test the joinman service. Here are the steps:

❑ Change directory to \Ch11\code\bats

❑ Cleanup any reggie and RMID log files by removing them manually, or running the runclean.bat file under Windows 98

- ❏ Start the class server by running the `runhttpd.bat` file

- ❏ Start RMID by running `runrmid.bat` file

- ❏ Start one lookup service for the iguanas group by running `runlookup1.bat`

- ❏ Start another lookup service for the iguanas group by running `runlookup3.bat`

At this point, we have started up two reggies (lookup services) both handling the iguanas group. It is time to startup our `joinman` service.

- ❏ Change directory to `\Ch11\code\Joinman`

- ❏ Create a joinlogs directory under the joinman directory for storing persistent service ID information

- ❏ Start the joinman service using the `runjoin.bat` file; this file contains:

```
call setpaths.bat
java -Djava.security.policy=policy.all -
Djava.rmi.server.codebase=http://%DOWNLOADHOST%/Joinman-dl.jar joinman .\joinlogs\
```

You should see the command prompt of the joinman service, similar to the screenshot below. If it is the first time you have started joinman, you will also get a file not found exception, and the `IdPrinter` calls will persist the assigned service ID to disk.

At this point, the joinman service is started up, and the proxy has been registered with both lookup services. We can start up reggtool and confirm this.

- ❏ In another console, change directory to `\Ch11\code\reggtool`

- ❏ Start the reggtool by executing the `runregg.bat` file

- ❏ Type in the `'list'` command to see the indexes for each of the two lookup services

- ❏ Type in `'look 1 joinman'` to see the details of the registered joinman proxy on the second lookup service

Your output may look like this:

```
reggtool> look 1 joinman
Performing lookup on lookup service # 1 Name="joinman":
      .... found 1 services...
      ID: 6e0caa9f-7e70-4b53-818e-fabc89fd4539
      Class: joinman_Stub
      Interfaces:
            joinmanItf
            java.rmi.Remote
reggtool>
```

Note that the `Name="joinman"` value is passed in via the `runjoin.bat` file command line argument.

You can try lookup on the other service, using the command:

```
look 2 joinman
```

and you will see the identical proxy registered there.

Now, go back to the joinman service console, and type in the `'first'` command. This will cause the `setAttributes()` method of the `JoinManager` to be called. According to the Join protocol, the `JoinManager` will change the attribute on every lookup service that it has registered with.

Now, go back to the reggtool console, and try the same `'look 1 joinman'` command again. You should see something similar to this:

```
reggtool> look 1 joinman
Performing lookup on lookup service # 1 Name="joinman":
      .... found 0 services...
reggtool>
```

There is no longer another service proxy with `Name` attribute of value `"joinman"`. Try the `'look 1 first'` command with reggtool. You should see the proxy now again, as in this screenshot:

```
reggtool> look 1 first
Performing lookup on lookup service # 1 Name="first":
      .... found 1 services...
      ID: 6e0caa9f-7e70-4b53-818e-fabc89fd4539
      Class: joinman_Stub
      Interfaces:
            joinmanItf
            java.rmi.Remote
reggtool>
```

`JoinManager` has propagated the change to both lookup services. Try a lookup on the other lookup service using `'look 2 first'`. You can also try entering `'second'` in the joinman console to change the attribute value yet again. Check with the reggtool to confirm that the joinman service is doing its job, keeping all the proxies in lookup services updated with all the attribute changes.

What JoinManager Will Not Do For Us

The only things we need to focus on when we're using the `JoinManager` are:

❏ Service logic – unfortunately `JoinManager` cannot possibly do this for us

❏ Persistence of service IDs and state is not performed by `JoinManager` – there are many useful Jini service(s) that may not need to persist their state, so the designers of `JoinManager` didn't implement this support.

ServiceDiscoveryManager Class

The `ServiceDiscoveryManager` class does even **more** than `JoinManager`, except it does it for Jini clients or client-like entities (phrases that need careful qualification, given that a Jini service can also be client of other services). The `ServiceDiscoveryManager` can do everything a Jini client might need, with the exception of application logic and persistence. Not only does it do the job, but it also adaptively optimizes work.

Design Rationale

The amount of code required by a typical client to maintain Jini compatibility can be substantial. This is especially true if it needs to make use of many different Jini services to perform its work. Basic Jini support classes require a lot of attention in order to handle the management of both service proxies and state changes in the network. The `ServiceDiscoveryManager` is designed to rid the Jini developer of the need to build around these complexities.

What Does the ServiceDiscoveryManager Do?

The `ServiceDiscoveryManager` does the following tasks on behalf of the client:

❏ Discovery protocol handling, both multicast and unicast

❏ Manages the set of discovered lookup services

❏ Performs lookup on the set of discovered lookup services based on a template

❏ Manages the set of discovered services matching the template, recognizing and eliminating proxy duplication (the consequence of using multiple lookup services)

❏ Registers for, and listens to, remote event notifications from lookup services, issued when services join or leave the federation

❏ May cache the set of discovered lookup services. Using caches optimizes working with service proxies, by preventing the network traffic increase resulting from repeated accessing to the same working set of proxies.

❏ Provides a value-added set of `lookup()` methods, allowing more powerful matching semantics than the existing Jini lookup algorithm (for example, allow > comparisons, etc)

The following diagram shows the interactions supported by this complex library class.

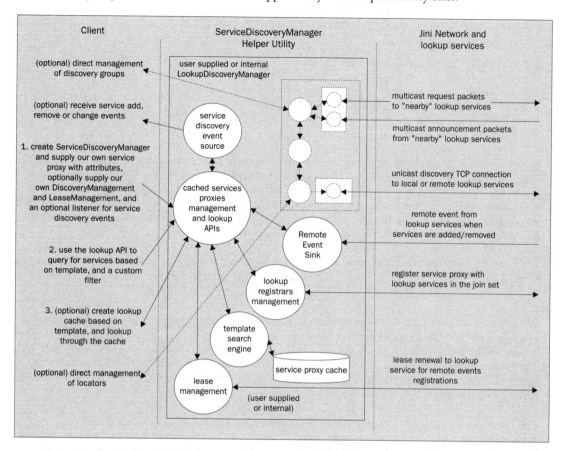

While the under-the-hood logic of `ServiceDiscoveryManager` is complex, the user interface to the class itself couldn't be simpler:

```
public class ServiceDiscoveryManager
{
    public ServiceDiscoveryManager (DiscoveryManagement discoveryMgr,
        LeaseRenewalManager leaseMgr) throws IOException;

    public LookupCache createLookupCache (ServiceTemplate template,
        ServiceItemFilter filter, ServiceDiscoveryListener listener) throws
        RemoteException;

    public ServiceItem lookup(ServiceTemplate tmpl, ServiceItemFilter filter);
    public ServiceItem lookup(ServiceTemplate tmpl, ServiceItemFilter filter, long
        waitDur) throws InterruptedException, RemoteException;

    public ServiceItem[] lookup(ServiceTemplate tmpl, int maxMatches,
        ServiceItemFilter filter);
```

```
    public ServiceItem[] lookup(ServiceTemplate tmpl, int minMaxMatches,
        int maxMatches, ServiceItemFilter filter, long waitDur)
        throws InterruptedException, RemoteException;

    public DiscoveryManagement getDiscoveryManager();
    public LeaseRenewalManager getLeaseRenewalManager();

    public ServiceRegistrar[] getLookupServices();

    public void terminate();
}
```

A ServiceDiscoveryManager instance is created by calling the constructor, with instances of both the LookupDiscoveryManager and the LeaseRenewalManager, exactly as it is with JoinManager. The ServiceDiscoveryManager will create default instances should null be supplied. You can also access these instances through the getDiscoveryManager() and getLeaseRenewalManager() methods respectively. The LeaseRenewalManager instance in this case is used to maintain the lease for the remote event registrations with the discovered lookup services.

The getLookupServices() method can be used to return the registrars from all the lookup services that have been discovered (both unicast and multicast). This set of lookup services is maintained internally by ServiceDiscoveryManager, and should not be duplicated in the application.

We can see that ServiceDiscoveryManager supplies lookup methods that have blocking and non-blocking versions. The blocking version has a timeout specified as the waitDur argument. All of these lookup methods will iterate through the current set of lookup services, performing lookup on each one. The lookup methods that return a single ServiceItem will stop when one service that matches the specified template has been found. The lookup methods that return multiple ServiceItems will continue lookup until the maxMatch number of distinct services has been found.

The low water mark minMaxMatch is specified to allow finer tuning of the lookup process. More specifically, the multiple match blocking version of lookup will stop looking for matching services if at least the low water mark number of matching services are found, and will never return more than MaxMatch number of matched ServiceItems. Note that in each of these lookup methods, one can choose to pass in an object that implements the ServiceItemFilter interface. You can also specify null if you do not want to use a filter.

ServiceItemFilter is defined as:

```
public interface ServiceItemFilter
{
    boolean check(ServiceItem decoratedProxy);
}
```

Every single matched ServiceItem (based on the template) will be passed through the filter. The filter can return false for any ServiceItem that should not be returned to the caller. This is useful to implement more advanced comparison syntax than possible with the Jini template matching. For example, applying this system it is possible to use the filter and find 'all the storage services with at least 2 gigabytes of capacity remaining available', a condition that the Jini template matching mechanism alone cannot detect.

Finally, we come to the rather strange createLookupCache() method:

```
public LookupCache createLookupCache (ServiceTemplate template,
    ServiceItemFilter filter, ServiceDiscoveryListener listener) throws
    RemoteException;
```

Calling this method creates a virtual cache of service proxies that matches the template and filter specified. You can also supply an implementation of ServiceDiscoveryListener in order to catch the callback in a number of circumstances: when the matching services are added initially (and the cache populated with them), when any one of their attributes changed, or when the services are removed (the cache image removed). This approach means that a virtual cache can be created for each template that we need to match on. Here is the definition for ServiceDiscoveryListener:

```
public abstract interface ServiceDiscoveryListener
{
  void serviceAdded(ServiceDiscoveryEvent event);
  void serviceChanged(ServiceDiscoveryEvent event);
  void serviceRemoved(ServiceDiscoveryEvent event);
}
```

And the associated ServiceDiscoveryEvent is defined as:

```
public class ServiceDiscoveryEvent extends EventObject
{
  public ServiceDiscoveryEvent(Object source, ServiceItem preEventItem,
    ServiceItempostEventItem);
  public ServiceItem getPreEventItem();
  public ServiceItem getPostEventItem();
}
```

The data attached to a ServiceDiscoveryEvent contains information for up to two ServiceItem references. In the case of a serviceAdded() notification, the preEventItem() is null, and the postEventItem() is the attributed proxy that is added to the cache. In the case of serviceRemoved() notification, the preEventItem() is the decorated proxy that used to be in the cache, while the postEventItem() is null. In the case of a serviceChanged() notification, the preEventItem() has a copy of the ServiceItem before the change occurred, while the postEventItem() has a copy of the ServiceItem as it exists after the change.

Even though ServiceDiscoveryManager will use the most efficient internal cache implementation, having a separate virtual cache at the application level makes service proxies handling a breeze. The LookupCache interface is used to access a lookup cache instance. LookupCache is defined as:

```
public abstract interface LookupCache
{
  void addListener(ServiceDiscoveryListener listener);
  void removeListener(ServiceDiscoveryListener listener);

  void discard(Object serviceProxy);

  ServiceItem lookup(ServiceItemFilter filter);
  ServiceItem [] lookup(ServiceItemFilter filter, int maxMatches);

  void terminate();
}
```

We can see here that listener management is available should we want to be notified when new services that match the template are added to the cache (from discovery), or when they are discarded. The `discard()` method can be used by the application to discard a particular service proxy from the managed set (that is, the cache). When this occurs, ServiceDiscoveryManager will notify all listeners that the discard has occurred. The two lookup methods will have visibility only into the matched, pre-filtered set of services that the original `createLookupCache()` method has generated and maintained. You can supply another filter to this lookup if you want finer grained filtering capabilities. The ServiceDiscoveryManager will keep the service proxies in the cache synchronized with services available externally via the lookup services by monitoring changes in the lookup service(s) through asynchronous notifications.

Using the ServiceDiscoveryManager Utility

You can find a sample usage of ServiceDiscoveryManager utility in the `\Ch11\code\servdisc.java` file. This simple client program uses ServiceDiscoveryManager to accomplish its tasks. Unlike other uses of ServiceDiscoveryManager that we have seen before, this example will create a service proxy lookup cache based on a template match. It also implements the ServiceDiscoveryListener interface, so that we will be notified whenever a service matching the specified template is added, or removed from the cache. Note that the `serviceAdded()`, `serviceChanged()` and `serviceRemoved()` methods are now working with service proxies themselves, and not the lookup service registrars.

ServiceDiscoveryManager's internal management for the proxies makes it as easy to work with actual service proxies as it is with lookup service proxies. Here is the code for the `servdisc.java` file:

```
import net.jini.discovery.*;
import net.jini.core.lookup.*;
import net.jini.lookup.*;
import java.io.IOException;
import java.rmi.RemoteException;
import java.rmi.RMISecurityManager;

import net.jini.lookup.entry.Name;
import net.jini.core.entry.Entry;
```

Our `servdisc` instance is also a ServiceDiscoveryListener, handling service discovery and discard:

```
public class servdisc implements ServiceDiscoveryListener
```

The `main()` method simply creates an instance of `servdisc` and waits around.

```
{
    static public void main(String argv[]) {
    servdisc myApp = null;

    myApp = new servdisc();

    try
      {
        synchronized (myApp)
          {
            myApp.wait(0);
          }
      }
    }
```

```
        catch(java.lang.InterruptedException e)
          {
            System.exit(0);
          }
      }
```

The constructor arguments are the groups to discover.

```
    public servdisc()
      {
        if (System.getSecurityManager() == null)
          {
            System.setSecurityManager(new RMISecurityManager());
          }
```

We create the simplest ServiceDiscoveryManager possible, using default for both the
LookupDiscoveryManager (that is, discover all groups), and default for the LeaseRenewalManager
(that is, renew indefinitely) arguments.

```
        try
          {
            ServiceDiscoveryManager mySDM = new ServiceDiscoveryManager(null,null);
```

Then, we create a lookup cache that looks for any services with the "first" Name attribute value. We will
not use any filter, since Name="first" adequately describes the matching condition that we want. We
also supply our instance of servdisc as the ServiceDiscoveryListener, to be notified when such a
service is discovered or discarded from the cache.

```
            Entry [] attributes = new Entry[1];
            attributes[0] = new Name("first");
            LookupCache myLUC = mySDM.createLookupCache(new ServiceTemplate
                (null,null,attributes), null, this);
          }
```

And there is all that we will do in this sample. Notice how ServiceDiscoveryManager has really
simplified coding of the logic.

```
        catch(IOException e)
          {
            System.err.println(e.toString());
            e.printStackTrace();
            System.exit(1);
          }
      }
```

Next, the implementation of the ServiceDiscoveryListener interface, starting with
serviceAdded() method. This is called when a service with the Name="first" property is added to the
group (and the cache). We print the service's service ID, and its attributes.

```
    public void serviceAdded(ServiceDiscoveryEvent evt)
    {
      ServiceItem siPost = evt.getPostEventServiceItem();
      System.out.println("** Service added ID: " + siPost.serviceID);
      System.out.println("                    attr: " + siPost.attributeSets[0]);
    }
```

For serviceChanged(), we print out the service ID, and both the attribute (Name) value before and after the change.

```
  public void serviceChanged(ServiceDiscoveryEvent evt)
   {
    ServiceItem siPre = evt.getPreEventServiceItem();
    ServiceItem siPost = evt.getPostEventServiceItem();
    System.out.println("** Service changed ID: " + siPre.serviceID);
    System.out.println("      original attr: " + siPre.attributeSets[0]);
    System.out.println("           new attr: " + siPost.attributeSets[0]);
   }
```

For serviceRemoved(), we print out the service ID and the attribute value of the service just removed from the cache.

```
    public void serviceRemoved(ServiceDiscoveryEvent evt)
    {
      ServiceItem siPre = evt.getPreEventServiceItem();
      System.out.println("** Service removed ID: " + siPre.serviceID);
      System.out.println("                    attr: " + siPre.attributeSets[0]);
    }
  }
```

We can now compile the sample:

```
buildit servdisc.java
```

The servdisc class itself does not implement any remote interface, so it is not necessary to create any stubs. However, the ServiceDiscoveryManager instance itself, when used in the cached mode, must sink remote event notifications from the discovered lookup services. This means that the RMI stubs of the remote event sink must be exported in a JAR file associated with this application.

These stubs are contained in a local class called LookupCacheImpl.LookupListener. We have to extract it manually from the library JAR archives (jini-ext.jar). We do this via the makejar.bat file. The content of this batch file is:

```
ccall ..\bats\setpaths.bat
jar xvf %JINIHOME%\lib\jini-ext.jar
net/jini/lookup/ServiceDiscoveryManager$LookupCacheImpl$LookupListener_Stub.class
jar xvf %JINIHOME%\lib\jini-core.jar net/jini/core/event/RemoteEventListener.class
jar cvf servdisc-dl.jar
net/jini/lookup/ServiceDiscoveryManager$LookupCacheImpl$LookupListener_Stub.class
net/jini/core/event/RemoteEventListener.class
copy servdisc-dl.jar %JINIHOME%\lib
```

The last line moves the new JAR file to the class server's root directory, ready for download by the lookup services whenever they make the listener callback.

The runsdm.bat file can be used to start this sample program, it contains:

```
call ..\bats\setpaths.bat
java -classpath .;%JINIJARS% -Djava.security.policy=policy.all -
Dnet.jini.discovery.interface=%ADAPTERIP% -
Djava.rmi.server.codebase=http://%DOWNLOADHOST%/servdisc-dl.jar servdisc
```

It must set up the codebase for proper download of the stubs.

Testing the ServiceDiscoveryManager Sample Using Reggtool and Joinman

Now, we can test the ServiceDiscoveryManager sample. If you don't have the joinman testing configuration still up and running, fire it up and follow these steps:

- ❑ Start (using runhttpd.bat) or make sure that the class server is started

- ❑ Start (using runrmid.bat) or make sure that RMID is running

- ❑ Start two lookup services (using runlookup1.bat and runlookup3.bat) or make sure that two reggies are already running

- ❑ Start reggtool, perform a list and make sure that both reggies are running

- ❑ Start (using runjoin.bat) an instance of joinman

- ❑ Using reggtool, perform a look <index> joinman to confirm that the joinman has registered with both lookup services

Now, we can start our servdisc example, creating a cache based on Name="first", and monitoring the addition, change, and removal of such proxies to and from the cache. Start it using the runsdm.bat file.

Your output should be similar to this:

There should be no matching service in the cache, and so servdisc remains silent. Now, while servdisc is running, go to the joinman console and type first. This will cause the JoinManager to update the attribute of all registered proxies to Name="first". Notice that servdisc detected this change (through remote events from the lookup services) and the serviceAdded() method of the ServiceDiscoveryListener interface is called. We know, in fact, that the ServiceDiscoveryManager instance will receive one such event from each lookup service – and that it has eliminated the duplicate before calling back on our listener. You should see something similar to this screenshot:

Now, in the joinman console, type in second, and this will change the service proxy's attribute to Name="second" throughout all the lookup services. Note servdisc's reaction:

The name has changed from Name="first" to Name="second" and no longer matches the template of the cache, servdisc detects this and removes the proxy from the cache.

What ServiceDiscoveryManager Will Not Do For Us

There is nothing Jini specific for a Jini client that the ServiceDiscoveryManager doesn't do for us. It's comprehensive coverage makes writing Jini clients very simple.

You only have to code the client logic and make use of ServiceDiscoveryManager whenever it needs the service proxies, to accomplish the work. ServiceDiscoveryManager is a Jini client construction kit in one single easy-to-use bundle.

This concludes our coverage of utility classes that the Jini library provides to make Jini programming simpler. Now we've seen the pretty amazing JoinManager and ServiceDiscoveryManager high-level manager utilities, it's not hard to agree that the Jini library designers have achieved their goal. We will now turn our attention to the last classification of helpers: the helper services.

Helper Services – Making the Impossible Possible

Not all would-be Jini services are fortunate enough to be able to use the JoinManager class. They may not be able to use the library class for the following reasons:

❑ They'd rather be off-line most of the time, and only run when there are requests for their service (via RMI activation)

❑ Java VM limitations or runtime limitations do not allow them to run a JoinManager instance

❑ They are not running in any Java VM at all

The final two bullet points are what the initial hype about Jini tended to center around – even these misfits (services and/or devices) can participate in a Jini network with the assistance of the helper services. In fact, these services/devices can participate in the Jini network without clients knowing anything about their limitations.

The magic that makes this all possible are three third-party services, each performing vital Jini functions on behalf of its client (its client being the service or device: it does get complicated!), even if their client is not capable of communicating with it directly or is not running most of the time. All three of these services run standalone, either on their own VMs or their own physical machines. They can provide third-party, independent, assistance for any service that needs it on the Jini network. These three services are:

- ❑ LookupDiscoveryService
- ❑ LeaseRenewalService
- ❑ EventMailbox

Sun provides a reference implementation for each of these services; they are included in the Jini development kit and are called, respectively:

- ❑ Fiddler
- ❑ Norm
- ❑ Mercury

We'll look at each of these services in detail. Our grand-finale sample will make use of all three of these services to create a kit that can give anything that has the ability to communicate over the network a Jini federation existence. This has, of course, major implications for the integration of legacy systems and limited resource devices into a Jini network.

Fiddler: The LookupDiscoveryService

Fiddler runs as a standalone Jini service. It is in fact an RMI Activatable service. This means that a setup VM is used initially to let RMID know about the existence of the service, before creating another VM to host the service itself. In the \ch11\code\bats directory, we have created a batch file to run this service. You can consult the appendix for a full description of the command syntax. Our runfidd.bat file contains:

```
call setpaths.bat
java -jar -Djava.security.policy=policy.all %JINIHOME%\lib\fiddler.jar
http://%DOWNLOADHOST%/fiddler-dl.jar policy.all %JINITEMP%\fiddler_log iguanas -
Dnet.jini.discovery.interface=%ADAPTERIP%
```

Note that we have to set up the Fiddler's own VM for codebase download, and supply the log directory where Fiddler will persist its state. The group specified, iguanas in this case, is the Jini group that this instance of Fiddler will provide its service for.

Design Rationale

Fiddler is designed to provide compliance to the Jini infrastructure for services that may be Jini-challenged. Services or devices that have no means of their own to implement the multicast discovery and unicast discovery can use Fiddler for these chores. Services that are dormant most of the time can completely delegate the discovery protocol handling duty to Fiddler altogether. Any service that can invoke Fiddler's interface through the network can make use of its services, and inherit the ability to discover lookup services.

What Will LookupDiscoveryService Do?

`LookupDiscoveryService` provides the following services for anyone who calls the method on its interface:

- ❏ Multicast discovery based on a set of groups
- ❏ Unicast discovery based on a set of locators
- ❏ Manages the set of discovered lookup service registrars
- ❏ Manages leased remote event registrations from users
- ❏ Makes remote event callbacks when discovery is made
- ❏ Maintains and sustains state information across multiple restarts

The functionality is very similar to `LookupDiscoveryManager` mid-level manager utility, except the interface between the service implementation and the discovery helper is now remote.

Another interesting difference is that Fiddler provides its own persistence mechanism, remembering all the lease registration, groups and locators even after a service restart.

The following figure illustrates what happens under the hood with Fiddler. The service that wishes to use Fiddler (a client to Fiddler) must first locate an instance of the Fiddler service. This may be done by a setup Jini process that is used only in starting the service (much like the setup VM in RMI Activation). Once a Fiddler service is located, it is given the set of GROUPs that we are interested in (for multicast discovery) and the set of `LookupLocator` information (host:port or Jini URL).

When Fiddler returns, the service will receive a lease for the registration and must renew the lease before it expires in order to continue receiving service. A remote listener is also supplied to Fiddler to receive notification of discovery events. Using Fiddler's remote interface, it is also possible to work with the sets managed by Fiddler – including the set of discovered lookup registrars, the set of discovery groups, and the `LookupLocator` information. Internally, Fiddler resembles the `LookupDiscoveryManager` mid-level utility that we have seen in the last chapter; the major differences stems from its remote and independent nature – additional remote event management logic, lease granting and management logic, persistence handling, and administrative interface support.

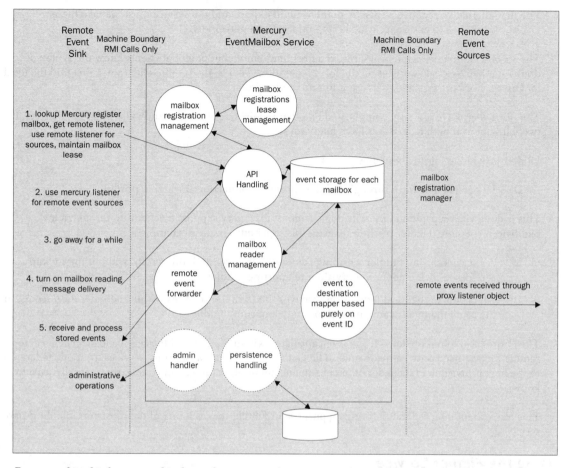

Because of its third-party and independent nature, there is one interesting Jini scenario that can only be accomplished when a service is using Fiddler: forming an inter-federations link.

Fiddler as an Inter-Federations Link

Having the actual service logic separated from the discovery support mechanism over a network boundary is quite an interesting scenario.

In essence, a single `LookupDiscoveryService` (or Norm) can provide remote registrations for many remote client-like entities that will appear as local services to the Jini participants within the local federation.

This is a very interesting use of Fiddler. Imagine for a moment that there is a Jini federation far, far, away in another independent network across the Internet. A conventional Jini service can only be made available to that network in one of these ways:

❑   Knowing the IP and port of a remote lookup service in that faraway federation, and export itself there

❑   Through a local lookup service that may have registered itself with a remote lookup service

❑   Through a tunnel which replicates all registrations and lookup service state changes between the two federations

The first alternative requires a specific point to point export, and the service must manage these LookupLocators to ensure its availability in the remote network(s).

The second alternative, while workable, requires that remote but potential clients know the syntax of double-lookup to locate services on the local federation. That is, the remote client must first find the local lookup service's proxy – and then use it to find the local services.

The third alternative is a very complicated one that requires a very high bandwidth coupling between the two federations if both federations have many services.

Fiddler provides a fourth alternative:

❑　Hyperspace or warp through Fiddler (provide connection through a portal)

This is done via a separation of service logic from its discovery support mechanism, through a low bandwidth coupling. Fiddler provides exactly this capability. In this scenario:

❑　All services using Fiddler (residing remotely) discover and join *locally,* without the lookup services knowing about the invisible teleporting Fiddler

❑　All clients in the local federation discover the (remote) services within the federation *locally*, in the usual manner, again unaware of the teleporting Fiddler

The entire local to remote knowledge is encapsulated within Fiddler and the service logic. The local to remote linkage need only be made once. The fact that Fiddler is transporting services from one federation to the next is invisible to the federation constituents themselves (unless, of course, they actually *want* to know).

This transparent inter-federation bridging purpose of Fiddler makes it one of the most versatile third-party services.

Using the Fiddler Service

Being a full-fledged Jini service, Fiddler registers itself with lookup services of specific groups (controllable via a command line argument upon startup). This implies that the user of Fiddler must act as a Jini client in order to locate it. The necessity for an entity to be a Jini client in order to use the service of Fiddler to become a service has a tone of irony to it. However, in practice, the entity that is client-like and performs the interaction with Fiddler is often *not* the entity that will finally handle service callback across the network. In this case, it makes a lot of sense for the client-like requirement.

In order for a client-like entity to interact with Fiddler, they must agree on a common interface. That interface is, of course, the LookupDiscoveryService interface:

```
public abstract interface LookupDiscoveryService
{
    LookupDiscoveryRegistration register(String [] groups, LookupLocator []
        locators, RemoteEventListener listener, MarshalledObject handback,
        long duration) throws RemoteException;
}
```

The single method, register, is a method that may throw a RemoteException since it needs to communicate back to Fiddler and this may fail.

As expected, the caller supplies the groups to perform multicast discovery for, the locators to perform unicast discovery for, a listener to receive remote discovery callbacks, an optional hand back object to make housekeeping and events co-ordination simpler, and a desired duration for the lease on the remote event registration. The returned object is a `LookupDiscoveryRegistration` object and is defined thus:

```
public abstract interface LookupDiscoveryRegistration
{
    String [] getGroups() throws RemoteException;
    void setGroups(String [] groups) throws RemoteException;
    void addGroups(String [] groups) throws RemoteException;
    void removeGroups(String [] groups) throws RemoteException;

    LookupLocator [] getLocators() throws RemoteException;
    void addLocators(LookupLocator [] locators) throws RemoteException;
    void removeLocators(LookupLocator [] locators) throws RemoteException;
    void setLocators(LookupLocator [] locators) throws RemoteException;

    ServiceRegistrar [] getRegistrars() throws LookupUnmarshalException,
      RemoteException;

    void discard(ServiceRegistrar registrar) throws RemoteException;

    EventRegistration getEventRegistration() throws RemoteExcpetion;

    Lease getLease() throws RemoteException;
}
```

The `LookupDiscoveryRegistration` interface provides the same methods as the `DiscoveryGroupManagement` and `DiscoveryLocatorManagement` interfaces. It does not inherit from these interfaces because all of its methods may throw a `RemoteException` (that is, network communication will be involved). However, the methods to access the managed set of groups and locators are identical. The `getRegistrars()` method can be used to obtain the set of lookup services discovered. The `discard()` method can be used to remove a particular registrar from the set of discovered registrars.

The `getEventRegistration()` method is used to obtain an `EventRegistration` object that will give details on the event registered, the most vital information being the event ID. The client-like entity will need to remember this ID in order to coordinate the remote events received from multiple registrations. These client-like entities will receive `RemoteDiscoveryEvent` when a lookup service is discovered or discarded. The `RemoteDiscoveryEvent` class is defined as:

```
public class RemoteDiscoveryEvent extends RemoteEvent
{
    public RemoteDiscoveryEvent(Object source, long eventID, long seqNum,
    MarshalledObject handback, boolean discarded, Map groups) {..}
    public boolean isDiscarded() {..}
    public ServiceRegistrar[] getRegistrars() throws LookupUnmarshalException {..}
    public Map getGroups();
}
```

This event will be either a discovered or discarded event, as indicated by the `isDiscarded()` value. In either case, `getGroups()` will return a `Map` with the keys being the registrars that are discovered (or discarded) and the values being the groups that each registrar supports.

Finally, the getLease() method of the LookupDiscoveryRegistration interface can be used to obtain the Lease granted by Fiddler for the remote event registration. This implies that we must somehow keep this lease renewed. This may be a strain for a service that wants to be dormant most of the time, or impossible for a service that does not run on a Java VM. Thankfully, there is another third-party service that will take care of all the lease renewal for us. It is called Norm.

Norm: The LeaseRenewalService

Norm performs the same task as LeaseRenewalManager, except that it does it across the network boundary as a helper service. Norm is a lease renewal service that supports the LeaseRenewalService interface.

In the \Ch11\code\bats directory, you will find runnorm.bat that will start the Norm service. It contains:

```
call setpaths.bat
java -jar -Djava.security.policy=policy.all %JINIHOME%\lib\norm.jar
http://%DOWNLOADHOST%/norm-dl.jar policy.all %JINITEMP%\norm_log iguanas -
Dnet.jini.discovery.interface=%ADAPTERIP%
```

Norm is a RMI activatable service. A setup VM is used to register and start it initially. The actual host VM must be set with the codebase, log directory, and 'groups to service' information. In this case, we have the norm-dl.jar codebase, the norm_log persistence directory, and the iguanas group for Norm to service. Note that the set of groups to handle as a service for Norm, is different from the set of groups that each of its clients may want to handle (will vary between each client!).

Design Rationale

Catering to the same set of restricted services (largely dormant and activatable, or services running in constrained environments), Norm enables participation within a Jini network by renewing leases on their behalf. Without such a service, proxy registrations will eventually expire from lookup services if the restricted service cannot regularly renew them. Remote event registrations, such as those issued by Fiddler or reggie, are also leased and require constant renewal.

What Will Norm Do For Us?

As a full-fledged Jini service, Norm will do the following for its client:

- ❑ Manage a set of leases provided by the client

- ❑ Allow manipulation of the set of managed leases

- ❑ Enable the client to specify a desired renewal period (usually long) for each lease, and perform renewal on behalf of the client during this period

- ❑ Grant a lease on the set of leases managed for a client

- ❑ Make remote event notification before the lease-set lease expires

- ❑ Persist all state information, including the managed set of leases in order to survive restarts

Norm also hands out a lease of its own, on the set of leases that it manages for a client, back to the client! This is necessary to keep in line with the self-healing principal of distributed Jini leases.

Should Norm blindly renew leases forever on behalf of the client, the Jini network could, and probably would, end up with many permanently allocated unused resources – the distributed equivalence of a local resource leak. Thankfully, the lease granted by Norm on the set of leases is typically long. The client has a long time to sleep before having to wake up (or be woken up by a remote notification) and renew the lease-set lease.

The following diagram shows the functional blocks within Norm that make it tick. The leaseholder needs to first lookup an instance of a Norm service. Again, a 'setup' Jini client can actually perform this initial lookup on behalf of the actual leaseholder. Once an instance of Norm is located, the leaseholder can create a 'renewal set' of leases to be managed by Norm. It passes this set of leases to Norm. Norm will then take on the duty of renewing the leases in the set. Norm will also handle persistence of its own state, ensuring that it will survive system restarts. The leaseholder can use Norm's remote interface to add new leases to the set at any time. The leaseholder can also register a remote event listener to be notified when the lease on the lease set is about to expire, or when lease renewal fails.

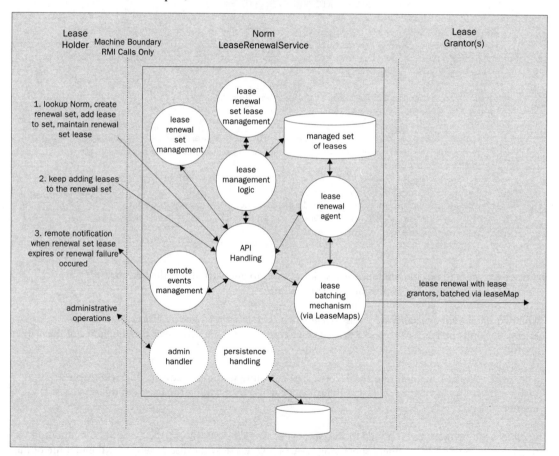

Using Norm, the LeaseRenewalService Service

In order to use Norm, we must obtain a reference to it first. The only proper way to do this within Jini is through a lookup service with which it has registered itself. This means that we must implement client logic to perform discovery, and then lookup Norm. Norm can be looked up based on its type: the LeaseRenewalService interface. This interface is also how the client will first interact with it. Here is the definition of the LeaseRenewalService interface:

409

```
public interface LeaseRenewalService
{
  LeaseRenewalSet createLeaseRenewalSet(long leaseDuration) throws RemoteException;
}
```

Calling the createLeaseRenewalSet() method on Norm's proxy object will result in the creation of a LeaseRenewalSet. We can then add the leases that need to be managed to this set. The desired renewal duration can be specified, and it is usually Lease.FOREVER. The LeaseRenewalSet interface is defined as:

```
public interface LeaseRenewalSet
{
    static final long EXPIRATION_WARNING_EVENT_ID = ..;
    static final long RENEWAL_FAILURE_EVENT_ID = ..;

    Lease [] getLeases() throws RemoteException, LeaseUnmarshalException;
    void renewFor(Lease leaseToRenew, long desiredDuration) throws RemoteException;
    void renewFor(Lease leaseToRenew, long desiredDuration, long renewDuration)
       throws RemoteException;

    void remove(Lease leaseToRemove) throws RemoteException;
    Lease getRenewalSetLease();

    EventRegistration setExpirationWarningListener(RemoteEventListener
        remoteListener, long minWarning, MarshalledObject handback) throws
        RemoteException;
    void clearExpirationWarningListener() throws RemoteException;

    EventRegistration setRenewalFailureListener( RemoteEventListener
        remoteListener, MarshalledObject handback) throws RemoteException;
    void clearRenewalWarningListener();
}
```

Since each method has to communicate back to Norm to get work done, they all throw RemoteExceptions due to possible network failure.

The two static final constants are event IDs for two remote events sent by Norm: ExpirationWarningEvent and RenewalFailureEvent; we will cover the semantics of these events shortly.

The getLeases() method returns all the leases currently in the LeaseSet, and will throw a LeaseUnmarshalException if a problem occur while marshalling the leases in the set across the network.

Each lease to be managed is added to the LeaseRenewalSet by calling the renewFor() method. A desiredDuration is specified; specifying Lease.FOREVER will cause renewal for the lifetime of the LeaseRenewalSet itself (or until an exception occurs during renewal). If you use the variant of renewFor() with the renewDuration argument, you can control the renew duration (in milliseconds) that will actually be passed to the lease grantor to renew the lease with the grantor.

The `remove()` method will remove a specified lease from the managed set. Note that there is no method to obtain or traverse the managed set. The designer of `LeaseRenewalSet` has deemed this unnecessary since the whole purpose of Norm is to provide a 'handover and forget' mechanism for Lease renewal. This also eases some concurrency access considerations should access to the management set be granted remotely.

The lease on the `LeaseRenewalSet` itself can be obtained through the `getRenewalSetLease()` method. A leaseholder that is dormant most of the time will need to call this when it wakes up and renews the renewal set lease.

Each `LeaseRenewalSet` manages only one single instance of a particular listener, therefore the `setXXX()` and `clearXXX()` semantics are used to add and remove the listener. There are two remote listeners that can be registered. The first one is `ExpirationWarningListener`; this listener is called prior to the lease-set lease expiry – the minimum warning time can be specified in the `setExpirationWarningListener()` call. The other one is `RenewalFailureListener`; this listener is called when a lease renewal fails. These listeners will receive `ExpirationWarningEvent` and `RenewalFailureListenerEvent` respectively; each of these events will have an associated `LeaseRenewalSet` that one can examine to determine the cause of the event.

It seems that both Norm and Fiddler make extensive use of remote events in notifying its client of state changes within the service. Fiddler will notify on service proxy changes in its cache, and Norm will notify of lease-set lease expiry as well as renewal failures. There may be many other Jini services on a network that also communicate to a client-like service via remote events. A question remains:

How is a mostly dormant service supposed to be able to handle these remote events (if it wishes to) when it is in a dormant state?

The answer, of course, is yet another third-party service – an event mailbox. This service is called Mercury.

Mercury – The EventMailbox Service

Remote events are used by reggie, Fiddler, and Norm (and probably many other Jini services to come) to provide a client with notification of important state changes in an asynchronous manner, without disturbing the normal flow of application logic. Unfortunately, since there is no way in advance to know when these notifications will occur (hence its asynchronous nature), there can be many scenarios where a client may not be in a situation or state to receive and process remote notification. It would be helpful if a third-party can store-and-hold notification messages until the client is ready to receive and handle them. This is the function of an `EventMailbox` service. Sun's supplied reference implementation of this service is called Mercury.

You can start an instance of Mercury by running the `\Ch11\code\bats\runmerc.bat` file. This file contains:

```
call setpaths.bat
java -jar -Djava.security.policy=policy.all %JINIHOME%\lib\mercury.jar
http://%DOWNLOADHOST%/mercury-dl.jar policy.all %JINITEMP%\mercury_log iguanas -
Dnet.jini.discovery.interface=%ADAPTERIP%
```

Mercury is an RMI activatable service. The above batch file starts the setup VM which will register the service and start an instance. The service instance runs in its own VM, which must be setup with codebase for stub download, security, policy, persistence files directory, and the groups to join.

Design Rationale

Designed for mostly dormant RMI activatable services, and Jini services that may be running on constrained environments, Mercury provides a way for these services to sink remote events without actually running itself at the time the event occurs. When the service is woken or running again, it can contact Mercury to retrieve the stored events and process them in a batch. While Mercury is useful in many cases, some time sensitive events – such as lease expiry notifications – are best not handled in this way.

What Will Mercury Do?

Mercury provides the following functionality to a client-like entity:

❑ A mailbox, in the form of a leased `RemoteListener` object, for the client to use in sinking events

❑ Maintains (and expires) lease on the mailbox

❑ Sinks any incoming remote events on behalf of the client and stores them for later retrieval by the client

❑ Access to the events in the mailbox by sending remote events to the client for processing (when requested)

❑ Persists all state information, including leases and mailbox content for survival across restart

The following figure depicts the operation of Mercury. Mercury acts as an intermediary between a client/service (called the remote event sink), and a remote event source. The remote event sink using Mercury must first discover an instance of Mercury using standard Jini discovery protocols. Once an instance of Mercury is located, the remote event sink can register for a mailbox, and Mercury will return a remote listener. The remote event sink can then use this returned listener for any further registrations with remote event sources. Any events sent from these new registrations will end up in the mailbox within Mercury. When the remote event sink is ready to receive the events, it can ask Mercury to deliver the events in the mailbox to itself via direct remote event notifications. Registrations with Mercury are leased; the remote event sink must renew this lease in order not to lose the mailbox. Mercury will persist its own state in order to survive restarts.

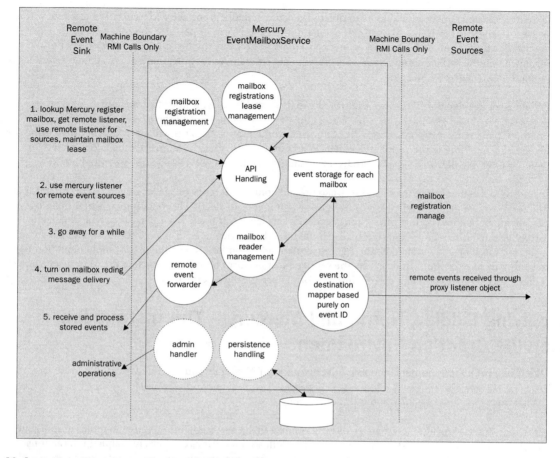

Using the Mercury EventMailbox Service

To use Mercury, a Jini service must first lookup the Mercury service, assuming a client-like state. The Mercury service will support the `EventMailbox` interface, and can be looked up by type. The `EventMailbox` interface is defined as:

```
public interface EventMailbox
{
  MailboxRegistration register(long desiredLeaseDuration) throws RemoteException;
}
```

A call to the register method should also specify the `desiredLeaseDuration` for the mailbox; this is typically `Lease.FOREVER`. The actual lease duration granted can be discovered by checking the `MailboxRegistration` interface that the returned object supports.

```
public abstract interface MailboxRegistration
{
    Lease getLease();
    RemoteEventListener getListener();

    void enableDelivery(RemoteEventListener targetListener);
    void disableDelivery();
}
```

413

The getLease() method allows us to obtain the lease actually granted by Mercury. We can renew this lease ourselves, or, as is more usually done, hand it over to Norm to perform the renewal. The getListener() method returns a reference to the mailbox. It provides a RemoteEventListener instance that the service should use in all subsequent remote event registrations. It is a remote reference to a mailbox managed by Mercury.

When a service decides to retrieve the stored events from Mercury, it must first instantiate its own RemoteEventListener to sink and process the event. Then it will call the enableDelivery() method, passing its own RemoteEventListener as the argument. This will start Mercury delivering the events one at a time to the supplied listener. When the event delivery and processing is completed, or when the service desires to stop the delivery, it should call the disableDelivery() method.

A mostly dormant service may need to wake up and contact Mercury to retrieve events. This means that the service must persist a reference to Mercury when it goes to sleep. This persistence is best done by serializing both a marshalled proxy and Mercury's service ID. If the service persists only a serialized proxy, Mercury may have restarted between the time the service goes to sleep and the service's own waking time. This may invalidate the reference (depending on how smart the proxy implementation is), resulting in an exception. In this case, the service must perform lookup again using the Mercury instance's unique service ID to obtain a correct instance of the proxy to the service.

Applying Fiddler, Norm, and Mercury – The Instant Jini Service Creation Environment

We'll step back for a moment, and ask a deeply philosophical question:

'What does it mean to be *alive* in the Jini universe?'

One may enter a world of alternate reality and realize that a service within a Jini system has a 'soul' but maybe no physical existence at any point in time. Philosophies aside, the loosely coupled interactions between the constituents within a Jini network means that potential clients 'see' or 'feel' the existence of services in rather abstract ways. It does not and cannot determine the well-being of a service via conventional means. Traditional useful information such as 'the service process is running according to the operating system' is meaningless to a Jini client.

In fact, the precise answer to the question consists of three rather simple elements:

❑ The service's registrations (proxy registration or remote event registration) in any lookup services within our multicast radius

❑ The leases that the service may be holding and managing

❑ The events that the service may be sinking (receiving)

These are signs to the Jini system that the service exists and is likely to be running, or at least usable. Interestingly enough, these 'signs' correspond to the functionality of the three helper services that we have covered.

This means that any processing element can, with the combined help of Norm, Mercury and Fiddler, become 'alive' within a Jini network: as a Jini service. Furthermore, it is possible for a 'setup' executable/agent to perform the necessary lookup and registrations with these third-party services on behalf of a more restricted processing element – giving it life within the Jini universe. The actual agent that synthesizes the element's existence really doesn't need to live after performing the registrations. If this sort of 'life giving' were to be handled too carelessly, we could end up with a multitude of problems associated with phantom services littered all over Jini federations. Fortunately, the three helper services incorporate facilities to prevent this chaos, insisting that the agent or the element itself should continually demonstrate proof-of-interest in its own existence by renewing a lease.

The requirement to repeatedly renew a lease may at first appear to defeat the purpose of the original exercise:

❑ Norm renews leases, but the lease on the Norm registration – the `LeaseSet` – itself needs to be renewed

❑ The agent/service cannot delegate the lease renewal duties completely

❑ If an agent is used to launch a processing element that cannot renew leases itself, we may be in a catch 22 situation

In fact, nothing has been violated, and the requirement can be satisfied in a reasonable way. In the first place, the lease duration granted by the third-party services can be substantial in duration – allowing the activatable service (or agent) to be dormant most of the time. Secondly, a simple operating system scheduler, or even batch/shell files, can be used to perform this regular and repetitive lease renewal, thereby releasing the service-providing element from this responsibility.

The Fiddler, Norm, and Mercury trio provide an instant Jini Service Creation environment for any potential Jini service provider. Other than supplying the required discovery, lease renewal, and remote event sinking capabilities to Jini services, they also accommodate a class of services that are unable to participate in a Jini network by themselves.

Legacy System to Jini Service in a Few Minutes

By laying down enough framework code using the combination of Norm, Fiddler, and Mercury, one can create a kit that integrates the legacy systems with the Jini federation. In fact, almost anything that both communicates over the network and can make use of a proxy can become a Jini service. This includes, but is not limited to, CORBA, Perl, C++, HTTP, and Telnet 3270 based services, etc.

The legacy backend providing the 'service logic' does not even have to be Java based: The proxy object, written in Java, can have enough intelligence to locate and communicate with the legacy service.

Designing and Coding the Proxy

Let us get our hands wet and code the skeleton for such a service. First we will code a proxy. You can find the code in the `\Ch11\code\ijsce\myServiceProxy.java` file.

```
public class myServiceProxy implements WroxItf,java.io.Serializable
{
  protected int myIndex = 0;
  public myServiceProxy()
    {}
```

```
   public myServiceProxy(int inIndex)
     {
        myIndex = inIndex;
     }

  public int getIndex()
     {
        return myIndex;
     }
  }
```

This proxy implements the trivial `WroxItf` interface, and provides implementation that will be running on the client's own machine. We are using a very simple proxy in the example, so that we can focus our efforts on the external framework enabling this independent proxy to live as a Jini service. In a real-world production environment, however, you would code a smart proxy that communicates with the service using whatever means the service providing element supports (for example, CORBA, raw socket, terminal screen-scrap, etc.).

The Service Launching and Sustaining Framework

Now, onto the setup logic that will start the Jini service running. You can find the code in the `\ch11\code\ijsce\instantJini.java` file:

```
import net.jini.lease.*;
import net.jini.event.*;
import net.jini.discovery.*;
import net.jini.lookup.*;
import net.jini.lease.*;

import net.jini.core.lookup.*;
import net.jini.core.lease.*;
import net.jini.core.entry.Entry;
import net.jini.core.event.*;

import net.jini.lease.LeaseRenewalService;
import java.io.*;

import java.rmi.RMISecurityManager;
```

We will use the `Logger` class to persist our service ID.

```
class Logger
{
    private static String myLogDir = "." + System.getProperty("file.separator");
    public static void setLogDir(String dirname)
    {
      myLogDir = dirname;
    }

    public static synchronized void persist(String filename, Object item)
        throws IOException
    {
      ObjectOutputStream os =
          new ObjectOutputStream(new FileOutputStream(myLogDir + filename));
      os.writeObject(item);
      os.flush();
      os.close();
    }
```

```
    public static synchronized Object restore(String filename)
       throws IOException,ClassNotFoundException
    {
      ObjectInputStream os =
         new ObjectInputStream(new FileInputStream(myLogDir + filename));
      Object retval = os.readObject();
      os.close();
      return retval;
    }

} // of class Logger

interface instantJiniConstants
    {
      static final String IDFILE = "servid.per";
      static final String STATEFILE = "state.per";
    }

public class instantJini implements instantJiniConstants
   {
     static final long MAX_WAIT = 20000L;
```

The instances of Norm, Mercury, and Fiddler will be held in `myNorm`, `myMercury`, and `myFiddler` respectively. We will be using a `ServiceDiscoveryManager` instance to greatly simplify our Jini client handling duties.

```
static LeaseRenewalService myNorm = null;

static LeaseRenewalSet myLeaseSet = null;
static EventMailbox myMercury = null;
static MailboxRegistration myMbxReg = null;
static LookupDiscoveryService myFiddler = null;
static LookupDiscoveryRegistration myLDReg = null;
static ServiceDiscoveryManager mySDM = null;
static ServiceID myServiceID = null;

public instantJini() {}
```

All of our logic will be in the `main()` method, as this is used to set up our proxy and service logic alone, and won't live as a Jini service itself.

```
static public void main(String argv[]) {
```

`myEvtLease` contains the lease obtained from Mercury, the event mailbox `myEvtListener` is the reference to the mailbox itself. This is the listener that we should supply to services for sinking remote events.

```
    Lease myEvtLease = null;
    RemoteEventListener myEvtListener = null;
```

`myLeaseSet` is the `LeaseSet` managed by Norm, and we will add all our leases from Mercury, reggie, and Fiddler to this set. `myLDLease` is the lease-set lease that Norm will grant; we are responsible for renewing this long-duration lease. However, we will not performing the renewal within this program.

```
    LeaseRenewalSet myLeaseSet = null;
    Lease myLDLease = null;
```

`myImpl` is the proxy that we want to launch. It can locate the (possibly legacy) service-providing element that we have turned into a Jini service.

```
myServiceProxy myImpl = null;
```

We need to install an `RMISecurityManager` to enable download of various service proxies.

```
try
{
   if (System.getSecurityManager() == null)
     {
        System.setSecurityManager(new RMISecurityManager());
     }
}
```

We use the `ServiceDiscoveryManager`'s trivial constructor to create a `LookupDiscoveryManager` that discovers all groups, and a `LeaseRenewalManager` that renews leases for the lifetime of the client.

```
mySDM = new ServiceDiscoveryManager(null, null);
System.out.println("Waiting for discovery....");
```

Next, we wait 10 seconds for discovery.

```
waitForMs(10000L);
```

Finally, we set up class templates for lookup by type. We need to locate Norm, Mercury, and Fiddler service proxies.

```
Class [] myNormType = { LeaseRenewalService.class };
Class [] myMercuryType = { EventMailbox.class };
Class [] myFiddlerType = { LookupDiscoveryService.class };
```

First we lookup Norm, the `validate()` helper method checks the returned pointer to make sure it is not null – and prints out the service that it has located.

```
ServiceItem myTempRet = null;
myTempRet = mySDM.lookup(new ServiceTemplate(null,myNormType, null),
           null, MAX_WAIT);
validate(myTempRet, "lease renewal service");
myNorm = (LeaseRenewalService) myTempRet.service;
```

Next, we lookup Mercury.

```
myTempRet = mySDM.lookup(new ServiceTemplate(null, myMercuryType, null),
           null, MAX_WAIT);
validate(myTempRet, "event mailbox service");
myMercury = (EventMailbox) myTempRet.service;
```

Finally, we lookup Fiddler.

```
myTempRet = mySDM.lookup(new ServiceTemplate(null, myFiddlerType, null),
            null, MAX_WAIT);
validate(myTempRet, "lookup discovery service");
myFiddler = (LookupDiscoveryService) myTempRet.service;
```

With all three services located, we register with Mercury to obtain a mailbox. We also receive a lease for the mailbox that we will store in myEvtLease.

```
// start event service
myMbxReg = myMercury.register(Lease.FOREVER);
myEvtLease = myMbxReg.getLease();
myEvtListener = myMbxReg.getListener();
```

Next, we create a LeaseRenewalSet using Norm. We request the longest lease-set lease available.

```
myLeaseSet =  myNorm.createLeaseRenewalSet(Lease.FOREVER);
```

We add the lease obtained from Mercury to the LeaseRenewalSet, requesting a membership that is the same lifetime as the LeaseRenewalSet itself.

```
myLeaseSet.renewFor(myEvtLease, Lease.FOREVER);
```

Now, we ask Fiddler to perform lookup and discovery on our proxy's behalf. It will discover for all groups, requesting the longest lease possible.

```
// ask fiddler to perform lookup and discovery
myLDReg = myFiddler.register( DiscoveryGroupManagement.ALL_GROUPS, null /*
          locators */, myEvtListener, null, Lease.FOREVER);
if (myLDReg == null)
  {
    System.out.println("*** lookup discovery service does not respond ***");
    System.exit(1);
  }
```

We then extract the returned lease and add it to the managed set from Norm.

```
myLDLease = myLDReg.getLease();
myLeaseSet.renewFor(myLDLease, Lease.FOREVER);

System.out.println("Waiting for fiddler to create our alternate
    identity...");
```

For every registrar (reggie instances) discovered by Fiddler, we need to register our service proxy. Only the very first registration will produce a service ID, which we must use for all subsequent registrations. We also persist this service ID to disk using the Logger class. All the returned ServiceRegistration objects are maintained in the myServiceRegs array.

```
ServiceRegistrar [] registrars = myLDReg.getRegistrars();
ServiceRegistration [] myServiceRegs = new
ServiceRegistration[registrars.length];

System.out.println("Found " + registrars.length + " registrars,
                    waiting for service ID...");

myImpl = new myServiceProxy();
if (registrars.length > 0)
  myServiceRegs[0] = registrars[0].register(new ServiceItem(
                    null, myImpl, null), Lease.FOREVER);

myServiceID = myServiceRegs[0].getServiceID();
System.out.println("Service has been assigned service ID: " +
myServiceID.toString());
      try
      {
         Logger.persist( IDFILE, myServiceID);
         System.out.println("Written to persistent storage.");
      }
      catch (Exception e)
      {
         System.out.println("Cannot write to persistent storage.");
         System.exit(1);
      }

for (int i=1; i< registrars.length; i++)
    myServiceRegs[i] = registrars[i].register(new ServiceItem(myServiceID,
                    myImpl, null), Lease.FOREVER);
```

Next, we iterate through all the `ServiceRegistration` objects and extract their leases, handing them over to Norm for management and renewal.

```
for (int i=0; i< registrars.length; i++)
    if (myServiceRegs[i] != null)
       myLeaseSet.renewFor(myServiceRegs[i].getLease(),Lease.FOREVER);
```

At this point, our proxy has been set up with a lookup discovery mechanism, an event sinking mailbox and a lease renewal mechanism. All of the required leases have been supplied for renewal to Norm. This virtual Jini service is now officially alive. And it will stay alive until the lease-set lease from Norm expires. Here we access the granted duration for this typically long-lived lease and display it.

```
System.out.println("We do not have to wake up for " + (
                    myLeaseSet.getRenewalSetLease().getExpiration() -
                    System.currentTimeMillis())/60000L + " minutes.");


  }
  catch (Exception e)
  {
    e.printStackTrace();
  }
if (myCLM != null)
  myCLM.terminate(); // end gracefully
  }
```

The `validate()` helper checks the `ServiceItem` object returned by a lookup for null.

```
public static void validate(Object obj, String inServiceType)
  {
    if (obj == null)
      {
        System.out.println("** Sorry, cannot find a " + inServiceType + "!");
        System.exit(1);
      }
    else
        System.out.println("...located a " + inServiceType + ".");
  }
```

The `waitForMs()` method is a convenient method to delay the processing thread while lookup and discovery occurs.

```
public static void waitForMs(long msToWait)
  {
    try
      {
        Thread.sleep(msToWait);
      }
    catch (java.lang.InterruptedException ex) { ex.printStackTrace(); }
  }
}
```

That is all the logic necessary to turn any legacy network based service or device into a Jini service, as long as you have created a corresponding proxy to access the service/device. The only remaining thing to do is to renew the lease-set lease granted by Norm before it expires:

❑   Add code to persist the Norm proxy and the lease-set lease reference to disk

❑   Write a utility program that reads these references back from disk and performs renewals

The renewal utility can then be scheduled using an operating systems specific scheduler (for example, AT or CRON on UNIX systems), or a batch file that incorporates a delay. We will not code the elements here – interested readers are encouraged to try it for themselves.

To compile the code, we can use:

`buildit instantJini.java`

We need to make a JAR file for downloading of our proxy implementation. Use the `makejar.bat` file for this. It contains:

```
call ..\bats\setpaths.bat
jar cvf instantJini-dl.jar myServiceProxy.class wroxItf.class
copy instantJini-dl.jar %JINIHOME%\lib
```

Testing the Service Launching Framework

To test the service launching framework, first start up the Jini network:

❑ Start up the class server via `runhttpd.bat`

❑ Start up RMID via `runrmid.bat`

❑ If you've two reggies running on the iguanas group, you're done; otherwise run them using `runlookup1.bat` and `runlookup3.bat`. They will both service the iguanas group

❑ Use the reggtool to verify that the Jini network is running fine and the two lookup services (reggies) are up and running

Now, we will start up our third-party services.

❑ Change directory to `\Ch11\code\bats`

❑ Start Norm by running the `runnorm.bat` file, wait for the setup VM to return

❑ Start Fiddler by running the `runfidd.bat` file, wait for the setup VM to return

❑ Start Mercury by running the `runmerc.bat` file, wait for the setup VM to return

At this point, we have Norm, Fiddler, and Mercury running; all of them should be registered with both of the reggie instances. Verify this by using the reggtool, and use the `"look 1 all"` command. Our reggie produced the following output:

Now, we are ready to launch the trivial proxy as a Jini service using the framework. Change directory to \Ch11\code\ijsce, and run the runinstant.bat batch file. It contains:

```
call ..\bats\setpaths.bat
set ADDPATH=%JINIHOME%\lib\fiddler-cs.jar
java -classpath .;%JINIJARS%;%ADDPATH% -Djava.security.policy=policy.all -
Dnet.jini.discovery.interface=%ADAPTERIP% -
Djava.rmi.server.codebase="http://%DOWNLOADHOST%/instantJini-dl.jar
http://%DOWNLOADHOST%/sun-util.jar http://%DOWNLOADHOST%/reggie-dl.jar"
instantJini
```

You will notice that the java.rmi.server.codebase property is set to include both sun-util.jar and reggie-dl.jar. This is necessary in order to bypass a codebase bug still inherent in the current version of the Norm service at the time of writing. You may want to remove them to see if your version will work without them.

Our execution of the instantJini framework produced the following output. When it completes, our new virtual Jini service is alive. It will stay that way until the lease-set lease expires in almost 2 hours!

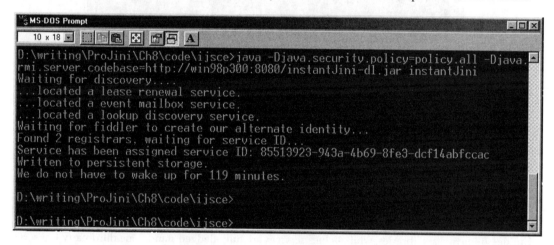

Test to see the service by performing a lookup on the reggies using the reggtool. Enter the command: 'look 1 all'. You should see output similar to the following screenshot. We can see that the service is indistinguishable from any other Jini service. In fact, you might want to check back once in a while to verify that the service does stay alive for 2 hours, thanks to Norm.

Summary

The Jini 1.1 developer libraries provide four principal levels of coding support:

- ❏ Low-level basic protocol helper utilities
- ❏ Mid-level protocol manager helper utilities
- ❏ High-level manager helper utilities
- ❏ Helper services

Utilities are Java class libraries, while helper services are fully-fledged standalone third-party Jini services. In these two chapters, we have examined all the helper utilities and helper services available with the Jini library. We have studied their design rationale, taken peeks underneath to see how each one works inside, and written actual code to work with every one of them. The following table summarizes what we have looked at:

Helper Utility/Helper Service	Description
LookupDiscovery	Low-level protocol utility providing support for multicast discovery through a managed set of groups to perform discovery for.
LookupLocator	Low-level protocol utility providing support for unicast discovery. Each instance is associated with a Jini URL or host:port combination – one remote lookup service to perform unicast discovery for.

Helper Utility/Helper Service	Description
LookupLocatorDiscovery	Mid-level protocol manager utility providing support for unicast discovery. Works with a managed set of LookupLocators and manages the unicast discovery for all of the locators in the set.
LookupDiscoveryManager	Mid-level protocol manager utility providing support for both unicast and multicast discovery. Assumes the combined functionality of LookupDiscovery and LookupLocatorDiscovery via a managed set of discovery groups as well as a managed set of unicast discovery locators.
LeaseRenewalManager	High-level 'do everything' manager utility that can completely take over the tedious lease renewal task for Jini applications. Runs within the Java VM of the user and can continue to renew leases until explicit termination or the VM exits. One can also exert fine grain control over desired lease expiry time, when and how to handle lease renewal failures, etc.
JoinManager	High-level manager utility that assumes the many responsibilities required of a Jini service. This utility will perform both multicast and unicast discovery, manage the resulting set of lookup service registries, register the service's proxy (optionally with attached attributes) with all the desired discovery groups, manage the proxy registration and associated attributes, fully implement the join protocol, and manage the changes in the attributes of the proxy. The JoinManager makes creating new Jini services a breeze.
ServiceDiscoveryManager	High-level manager utility that simplifies the creation of Jini clients. ServiceDiscoveryManager performs everything that a client needs to do in order to discover services. It will perform both unicast and multicast discovery to find lookup services. It manages sets of discovery groups and unicast locators.
LookupDiscoveryService	Codenamed Fiddler, this is a helper service that performs multicast and unicast discovery on behalf of clients. Manages and persists sets of discovery groups, unicast locators, and discovered registrars from lookup services. Works completely independently of its client, and will stay 'alive' even if the client goes to sleep or terminates. Registrations are leased for distributed cleanup should the client crash and never recover.
LeaseRenewalService	Codenamed Norm, this is a helper service that performs lease renewal for its clients. It can renew a complete set of leases, from multiple lease grantors, for its clients. This service persists its state and can survive restarts. It will stay 'alive' even if its client(s) goes to sleep or terminates. The set of leases leased itself in order to cleanup effectively should a client not be able to renew it on time.

Table continued on following page

425

Helper Utility/Helper Service	Description
EventMailboxService	Codenamed Mercury, this is a helper service that sinks and stores remote events for its clients. A client registers for a mailbox and gets a remote listener in return. The remote listener is then used by the client in registering for remote notifications with Jini remote event sources. Events originating from these sources will then be received by Mercury and be stored on the client's behalf. The client can retrieve these events at its leisure. Mercury will stay 'alive' even if its client(s) goes to sleep or terminates. The mailbox registration is leased to assist in effective distributed cleanup.

In this chapter, we have worked with the high-level manager utilities including `LeaseRenewalManager`, `JoinManager`, and `ServiceDiscoveryManager`. We saw how `LeaseRenewalManager` can assume the tedious task of repeatedly renewing leases with lease grantors; how `JoinManager` takes care of almost everything that is required from Jini for the development of a service – except for the service logic itself. We have also seen how `ServiceDiscoveryManager` can make Jini clients rather trivial to write, by providing implementations for most of Jini's requirements.

In the latter part, we have looked inside and worked with the three independent third-party helper services: Fiddler, Norm, and Mercury. These services provide support for special clients who may not be running all the time, or have a restricted environment. They can also be used to integrate legacy or even non-Java services into the Jini network. Through the sample code, we have seen how the three services used together to provide a Jini existence to almost any entity living on the network.

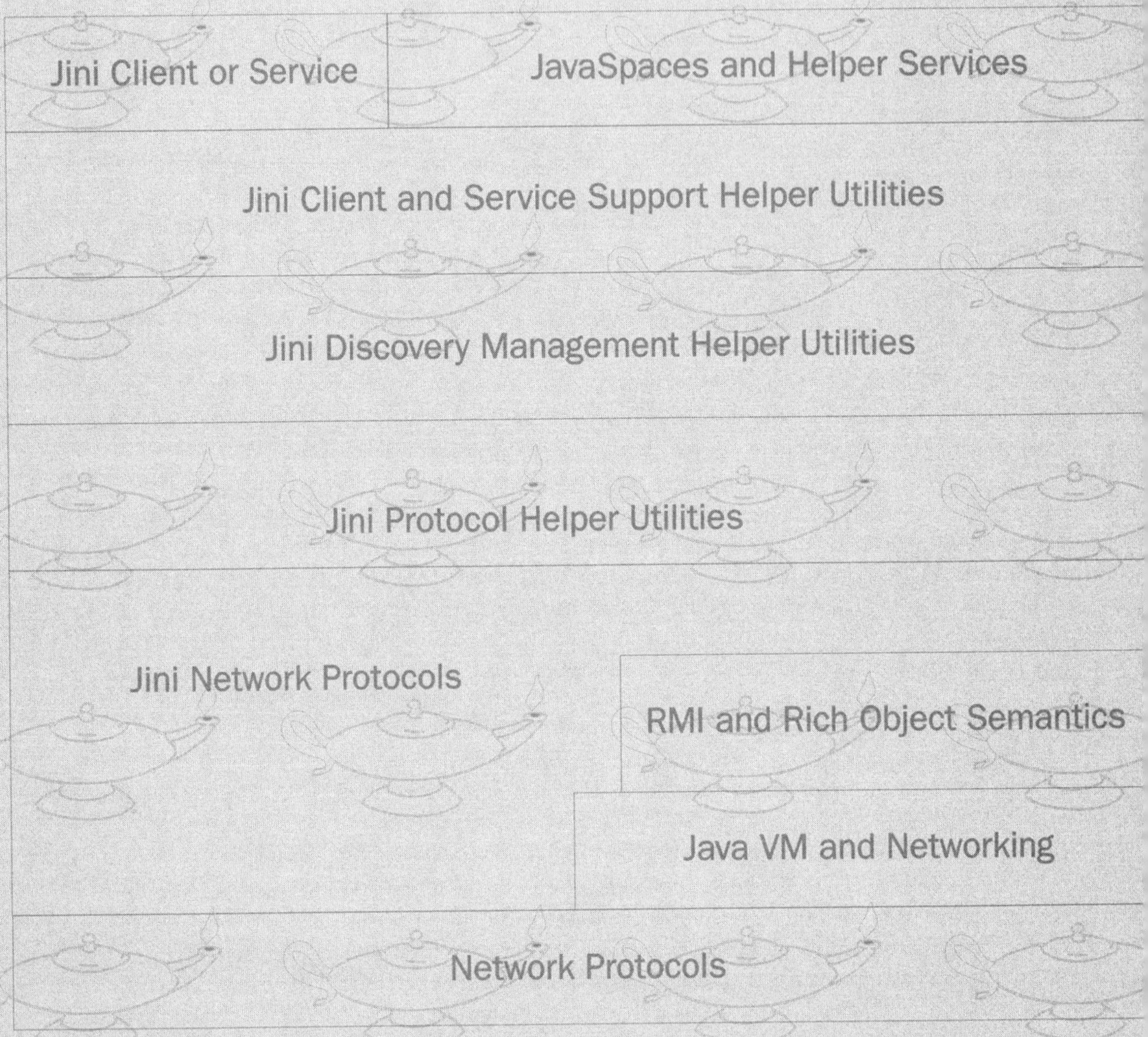

Jini Client or Service	JavaSpaces and Helper Services

Jini Client and Service Support Helper Utilities

Jini Discovery Management Helper Utilities

Jini Protocol Helper Utilities

Jini Network Protocols

RMI and Rich Object Semantics

Java VM and Networking

Network Protocols

12

Implementing Jini Services

We have covered all of the fundamentals of Jini programming. In this chapter, we consider the design of Jini services. Consideration must be given to the final architecture of the resulting system before building Jini services; we will be giving some thought to this at the beginning by examining how a proxy may be implemented. The decision of how a Jini service proxy will communicate with its associated service is a major consideration in the overall service design. There are at least five major ways of creating Jini service proxies, depending on the application:

❑　A proxy that runs entirely local to the client

❑　A proxy that uses an RMI stub to communicate back to the logic on the service

❑　A proxy that has logic on both the client and the service, and uses RMI to communicate between the two

❑　A proxy that has logic on both the client, and the service, but uses a proprietary protocol to communicate back to the service (for example using raw socket based programming)

❑　A proxy that is actually a wrapping for a legacy system service (for example wrapping for a CORBA service)

We will examine each of the above techniques, and provide hands-on coding examples for each one throughout this chapter.

Considering the hype around Jini as being a 'plug-and-play' device technology, we will cover Jini's role for distributed device drivers. In fact, Jini device drivers are only a type of Jini service, whose input and/or output is performed through hardware instead of software. In this light, we will examine the payload launcher model that ties services and device drivers together in Jini. We will examine Jini's support for devices that may not even host a Java VM; we will examine the proposed Jini Surrogate Architecture and see how it will accommodate and give a 'Jini life' to such deprived devices.

Last but not least, part of implementing many services – including Jini based device driver services – is the consideration of providing a user interface associated with the service. This user interface should allow a Jini client device (such as a PDA, GUI terminal, touch phone keypad, etc.) to provide the best interface possible to a user. Jini itself does not provide any guidelines, interfaces, or library for this purpose. Thankfully, a highly successful Jini.org project called ServiceUI addresses exactly this issue. We will see how we can attach a user interface to a Jini service, enabling a client to search by and make use of the attached user interface. Finally, we look towards the near future, and discuss how extending the ServiceUI concept to the distributed environment can bridge Jini with existing web technologies.

Patterns in Jini Service Implementation

As part of the design of a Jini service, or the distributed system that the Jini service is a part of, we must focus our attention on the partitioning of work between a Jini proxy object and the actual service logic. We need to make an architectural decision regarding this partitioning as part of the high-level system design for every service.

To illustrate the possibilities, we will develop an example in which a client calls a Jini service to add three numbers. We will create five different implementations, each with different proxy/service strategies:

❑ The service's work is performed local to the client's VM

❑ The service's work is performed remotely in the service's VM; the proxy is actually an RMI stub to the service's interface

❑ The service's work is split between the client's VM and the service's VM; this is called the 'smart proxy' scenario; the client portion of the work still communicates with the server via RMI (over a separate interface from the service's interface)

❑ The service's work is split between the client's VM and service's VM; this time, the client proxy does not use RMI to communicate with the service, but instead implements its own proprietary protocol using sockets directly

❑ The service's work is actually performed by a CORBA service; this is useful for wrapping legacy CORBA code and making it accessible over the Jini network

The client need not be aware of these varied architectures at all. In fact, the client receives the exact same service, using the exact same proxy interface in all five cases!

One Consistent Client Interface for All Architectures

The Jini proxy object and its associated interface provide a façade (a design pattern) into an arbitrarily complex architecture that gets the required work done.

The interface that we will use is called `CalcItf`; you can find `CalcItf.java` in the `ch9\code\Localpr` directory of the source code download.

```
import java.rmi.RemoteException;

public interface CalcItf
    {
      public double calc(double a, double b, double c) throws RemoteException;
    }
```

Note that while the method of the interface, calc, throws a RemoteException, the interface CalcItf itself is not remote and is not necessarily an RMI interface. In fact, we will be implementing a local version, a CORBA version, and even a non-RMI, custom network protocol version.

The source code to the client program can be found in the CalClient.java file under the ch9\code\CalClient directory of the source code download. It is included below:

```
import net.jini.discovery.*;
import net.jini.core.lookup.*;
import java.rmi.RemoteException;
import java.rmi.RMISecurityManager;
import net.jini.lookup.*;
import java.io.IOException;
```

This client makes use of a LookupDiscovery utility class and handles DiscoveryListener events locally. It discovers local lookup services that handle the 'iguanas' group, and use them to find services that have proxies that support the CalcItf interface.

```
public class CalClient implements DiscoveryListener
    {
        protected ServiceRegistrar [] registrars;
```

The main() method creates an instance of the client, and sleeps about 30 seconds for the discovery to take place. During this time, the client will also call the service's calc() method to compute the sum of the three doubles.

```
static public void main(String args[])
    {
        CalClient myApp = null;
        String tpItf = null;
        myApp = new CalClient();
        try
            {
                Thread.sleep(300001);
            }
        catch (Exception ex)
            {
                ex.printStackTrace();
                System.exit(1);
            }
    }
```

The constructor installs an RMISecurityManager (for downloading stubs that we need), creates a LookupDiscovery, and starts it on the discovery process:

```
public CalClient()
    {
        if (System.getSecurityManager() == null)
        System.setSecurityManager(new RMISecurityManager());
        LookupDiscovery discover = null;
        String [] myGroups = { "iguanas" };
        try
```

```
            {
                discover = new LookupDiscovery(LookupDiscovery.NO_GROUPS);
                discover.addDiscoveryListener(this);
                discover.setGroups(myGroups);
            }
        catch (IOException e)
            {
                e.printStackTrace();
                System.exit(1);
            }
    }
```

The `doCalc()` method performs the actual lookup and also calls the service's `calc()` method to compute the sum. The lookup is purely based on the type of the proxy object. In this case, we fill in a `ServiceTemplate` that indicates it must support the `CalcItf` interface:

```
protected void doCalc()
    {
        Class [] myClass = new Class[1];
        try
            {
                myClass[0] = CalcItf.class;
                CalcItf myItf = (CalcItf) registrars[0].lookup(new
                    ServiceTemplate(null,myClass,null));
```

Once we have located the service via its service object, we can safely call the `calc()` method, yielding the sum of the numbers:

```
                if (myItf != null)
                  {
                    double a = 1.221;
                    double b = 0.232;
                    double c = 2.004;

                    System.out.println("Adding " + a + ", " + b + ",  and " + c
                        + " gives " + myItf.calc(a,b,c) + ".");

                  }
                else
                    System.out.println("Lookup failed.");
            }
        catch (Exception ex)
            {
                ex.printStackTrace();
                System.exit(1);
            }
    }

public synchronized void discovered(DiscoveryEvent evt)
    {
        registrars = evt.getRegistrars();
        System.out.println("discovered " + registrars.length + " registrars!");
        if (registrars.length > 0)
          {
            doCalc();
//          myItem = registrars[0].lookup(new ServiceTemplate(null, myClass, null);
          }
    }

public void discarded(DiscoveryEvent evt) {}

}
```

To successfully compile this client program, we will need the `CalcItf.class` file local to our path; you can copy it from the `ch9\code\Localpr` directory. Use the following command to compile it:

```
..\bats\buildit CalClient.java
```

This client maybe executed via the `runclient.bat` batch file. It contains:

```
call ../bats/setpaths.bat
java  -classpath .;%JINIJARS%  -Dnet.jini.discovery.interface=%ADAPTERIP%
-Djava.security.policy=policy.all  CalClient
```

We will try out this program a little later with one of the services that we will create next.

The Local Proxy Pattern

We have seen this style of implementation before, in the `sixpack` example. Here, the proxy object does not make a connection back over the network. The logic of the service is completely implemented within the serialized service proxy.

Here we see the implementation of such a proxy:

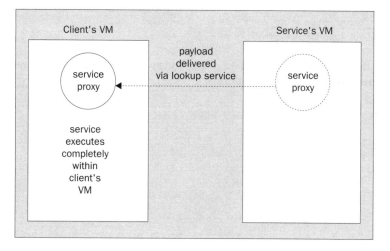

Some actual applications for such a proxy implementation may include:

❑ Cable TV pay-per-view decoding algorithm, or satellite TV descrambling algorithms, etc.; where authorization, auditing, and billing are performed before the network access is allowed

❑ Software or specialized 'algorithm' rental

❑ Distributed software lock or licensing systems

In the code download, you will find under the `ch9\code\Localpr` directory an implementation of the `CalcItf` service using a purely client-local proxy. The proxy that will be downloaded into the client's address space is called `CalcIt.java`:

```
public class CalcIt implements CalcItf,java.io.Serializable
  {
    public CalcIt() {}
    public double calc(double a, double b, double c)
      {
        return (a+b+c);
      }
  }
```

This is the object that will be transferred and executed within the client. The remainder of the service, called `LocalPr.java`, is responsible for finding the lookup services, registering the proxy with them, and keeping the proxy registered by renewing the leases while we are still alive. Here is the code for `LocalPr.java`:

```
import net.jini.lookup.JoinManager;
import net.jini.discovery.LookupDiscoveryManager;
import java.rmi.RMISecurityManager;
import net.jini.lookup.ServiceIDListener;
```

This service makes use of `JoinManager()` to greatly simplify Jini service implementation. The group that we will join is 'iguanas':

```
public class LocalPr
  {
    static final String [] GROUPS1 = { "iguanas" };
    protected JoinManager myJM = null;
```

The `main()` method simply starts an instance of `LocalPr`, and waits around forever – constantly renewing the leases on the proxy registrations:

```
public static void main(String argv[])
  {
    LocalPr myApp = null;
    myApp = new LocalPr();
    try
      {
        synchronized(myApp)
          {
            myApp.wait(0);
          }
      }
    catch(java.lang.InterruptedException e)
      {
        System.exit(0);
      }
  }
```

The constructor installs a security manager (for stubs download) and creates a `LookupDiscoveryManager` instance looking for the 'iguanas' group. This `LookupDiscoveryManager` instance is supplied as an argument to the `JoinManager` instance that we create. Note that the proxy we supply to the `JoinManager` instance is a new instance of the `CalcIt` class. `JoinManager` will ensure that the proxy is registered with all lookup services handling the group, and will keep the leases renewed as long as we are still running.

```
    public LocalPr()
      {
        if (System.getSecurityManager() == null)
            System.setSecurityManager(new RMISecurityManager());

        LookupDiscoveryManager ldm = null;
        String [] groupsToDiscover = GROUPS1;
        try
          {
            ldm = new LookupDiscoveryManager(groupsToDiscover, null, null);
            myJM = new JoinManager(new CalcIt(), null,
                (ServiceIDListener) null,ldm,null);
          }
        catch (Exception e)
          {
            e.printStackTrace();
            System.exit(1);
          }
      }
  }
```

Compile the local program by using the batch file:

..\bats\buildit LocalPr.java

Since the client program needs to be able to download the proxy's class definition, we must create a LocalPr-dl.jar file containing this. The makejar.bat file contains the necessary commands to do this:

```
call ..\bats\setpaths.bat
jar cvf LocalPr-dl.jar CalcIt.class CalcItf.class
copy LocalPr-dl.jar %WROXHOME%
```

Now, we are ready to test the local proxy implementation of the CalcItf service. To set this up, perform the following steps:

- ❑ Change directory to ch9\code\bats
- ❑ Clean up any old rmid or reggie logs manually, or by running the runclean.bat file
- ❑ Start a class server by running the runhttpd.bat file
- ❑ Start a stubs class server by running the runhttpdstubs.bat file
- ❑ Start the rmid by running the runrmid.bat file
- ❑ Start a reggie working in the iguanas group by running the runlookup1.bat file
- ❑ Wait until the setup VM of the reggie returns the command prompt
- ❑ Change directory to ch9\code\Localpr directory, and start the service by running the runlocal.bat file; this file contains the command:

```
call ..\bats\setpaths.bat
java -classpath .;%JINIJARS%  -Dnet.jini.discovery.interface=%ADAPTERIP%
-Djava.security.policy=policy.all -
Djava.rmi.server.codebase=http://%STUBHOST%/LocalPr-dl.jar LocalPr
```

Now, we can start our client program. Open another console, change directory to the `CalClient` directory, and run the batch file `runclient.bat`. The output you see should be similar to that shown below. All of the calculation performed by the service is done local to the client, within the downloaded `CalcIt` object instance.

The RMI Based Proxy Pattern

Since an RMI stub is a fully-fledged Java object, RMI stubs can be directly used as Jini proxy objects. The real benefit of this style of design is the fact that existing Java services or APIs can be rapidly transformed into Jini services – just make the interface remote! In many cases, it can also save coding if there is no need at all to perform any computation local to the client.

The following figure illustrates how RMI stubs acting as a Jini proxy work in practice. On the left hand side, there is the client's VM. A service proxy is delivered from the service to the client by the way of a lookup service. The proxy itself is really an RMI stub; it uses the proprietary JRMP protocol to communicate back to the implementation of the service running in the service's own Java VM.

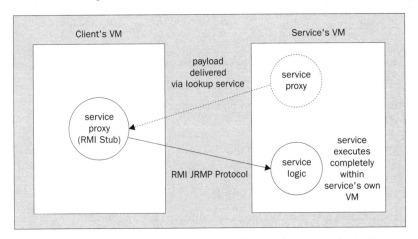

Since RMI stubs are generated from the binary class files using the rmic tool, we will not be able to easily modify their behavior. If this does not present a problem in your application, you may want to consider this simple approach to creating a remote Jini service.

Let us create a RMI stub as a proxy version of our `CalcItf` service. There is a minor problem: even though the `calc()` method itself throws `RemoteException`, the `CalcItf` interface itself is not remote. To alleviate this, we inherit from the existing `CalcItf` interface, and make the new subclassed interface remote instead.

The following diagram shows this technique schematically:

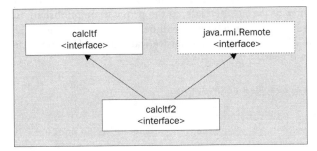

Now, the new `CalcItf2` interface is a remote one and has the exact same method(s) as `CalcItf`. Here is the definition of the `CalcItf2` interface (found in the `ch9\code\Rmipr\CalcItf2.java` file):

```
import java.rmi.RemoteException;
import java.rmi.Remote;

public interface CalcItf2 extends CalcItf,Remote{}
```

Our implementation of the service and this new interface is handled by `RMIPr` class. This class derives from `UnicastRemoteObject`, and therefore instances will be automatically exported (using RMI stubs) when references are passed beyond VM boundary.

```
import net.jini.lookup.JoinManager;
import net.jini.discovery.LookupDiscoveryManager;
import java.rmi.RemoteException;
import java.rmi.RMISecurityManager;
import net.jini.lookup.ServiceIDListener;
import java.rmi.server.UnicastRemoteObject;
```

The class implements the `CalcItf2` interface, but since `CalcItf` is the 'superclass' of `CalcItf2`, a search on `CalcItf` (the non-remote interface) will still catch proxies with the `CalcItf2` (remote) interface.

```
public class RMIPr extends UnicastRemoteObject implements CalcItf2
    {
    static final String [] GROUPS1 = { "iguanas" };
    protected JoinManager myJM = null;
```

The `main()` method starts the instance and hangs around, fielding remote calls from the RMI stub/proxy objects:

```
public static void main(String argv[])
    {
    RMIPr myApp = null;
    try
        {
        myApp = new RMIPr();
        synchronized(myApp)
            {
            myApp.wait(0);
            }
        }
    catch(Exception e)
        {
        System.exit(0);
        }
    }
```

Our constructor installs an `RMISecurityManager`, creates a `LookupDiscoveryManager` to discover the 'iguanas' group, and creates a `JoinManager` instance to handle the Join protocol for us. Note that we pass `this`, an instance of the `RMIPr` class, as the proxy to be published. Since `RMIPr` derives from `UnicastRemoteObject`, the `this` reference will be automatically marshalled as an RMI stub when passed out of the local VM. This is exactly what we want, the RMI stub for the `CalcItf2` interface acting as our Jini proxy object!

```
public RMIPr() throws RemoteException
  {
    if (System.getSecurityManager() == null)
        System.setSecurityManager(new RMISecurityManager());

    LookupDiscoveryManager ldm = null;
    String [] groupsToDiscover = GROUPS1;
    try
      {
        ldm = new LookupDiscoveryManager(groupsToDiscover, null, null);
        myJM = new JoinManager(this, null,(ServiceIDListener) null,ldm,null);
      }
    catch (Exception e)
      {
        e.printStackTrace();
        System.exit(1);
      }
  }
```

Finally, here is the RMI implementation of the `CalcItf2`'s `calc()` method. The client will actually be calling the same method through the `CalcItf` interface.

```
public double calc(double a, double b, double c) throws RemoteException
  {
    System.out.println("A client call was made...");
    return (a+b+c);
  }
}
```

To compile this in the `ch9\code\Rmipr` directory, we need to copy over `CalcItf.class` from `ch9\code\Localpr`, then we can use the batch file:

```
..\bats\buildit RMIPr.java
```

Next, we need to generate the RMI stubs, which are also our Jini proxy objects. This is done as a part of the `makejar.bat` batch file processing. For `RMIPr`, `makejar.bat` contains:

```
call ..\bats\setpaths.bat
rmic -v1.2 -classpath %JINIJARS%;. RMIPr
jar cvf RMIPr-dl.jar RMIPr_Stub.class CalcItf2.class CalcItf.class
copy RMIPr-dl.jar %WROXHOME%
```

The rmic tool is used to create binary stub class files directly from the binary `RMIPr` class file. The `RMIPr-dl.jar` file that we create must contain this stub (proxy object) and the interfaces that it depends on.

To test out RMIPr, we must set up class server, rmid, and reggie as in the LocalPr case. Next, we can start up the RMIPr service using the runrmi.bat file. This file contains:

```
call ..\bats\setpaths.bat
java -classpath .;%JINIJARS%  -Dnet.jini.discovery.interface=%ADAPTERIP%
-Djava.security.policy=policy.all
-Djava.rmi.server.codebase=http://%STUBHOST%/RMIPr-dl.jar RMIPr
```

Now, start CalClient by changing directory to ch9\code\Calclient, and starting the batch file:

```
runclient
```

You should observe on the client's console the numbers to be summed and the total:

This time, however, the calculation is completely done by a remote VM. Looking at the RMIPr's console, you should see an indication that a client has called the remote calc() method:

The Smart Proxy Pattern

Most services do not fit the black and white division of 'all client-side implementation' or 'all server-side implementation'. Instead of fitting these extreme cases, most services require some local processing (data validation, configuration detection, etc.) as well as some remote server-side processing (database access, complex computations, etc.). The smart proxy implementation pattern enables a Jini service to get the best of all these worlds. The following diagram shows how a smart proxy works. On the left hand side, we see the client's VM running. A service proxy 'payload' has been delivered, via lookup service, from the service to the client. This proxy is a smart proxy. It does some processing on the client's machine, and then uses its own RMI interface to communicate back to the service as needed for more processing.

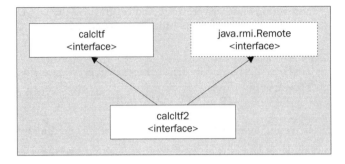

Note that the interface that appears to the client is still local. In this way, the smart proxy appears to be just like a `LocalPr` to the client. The actual remote interface that enables the custom proxy object to talk back to the service may or may not have any direct relationship to the interface that `CalClient` uses to access the service. One way to view this architecture is as a custom proxy object implementation, which happens to be using RMI as its transport to communicate back to the service.

In our implementation, called `SmartPr`, the RMI-based interface actually supports a different method from the one we need for `CalcItf`. Here is `CalcItf3`, our own communications interface between the proxy and the service. You can find the listing in the `ch9\code\Smartpr` directory:

```java
import java.rmi.RemoteException;
import java.rmi.Remote;

public interface CalcItf3 extends Remote
  {
    public double calc(double a, double b) throws RemoteException;
  }
```

Unlike its `CalcItf` cousin, the `calc()` method only adds two double numbers. There are a few ways we can implement the `CalcItf` interface in terms of the `CalcItf3` interface. They include:

❑ Using the `CalcItf3` interface twice

❑ Performing the first sum of two numbers local to the client, and the second sum across the network on the server

Our choice is the second method above. Our smart proxy will not be an RMI stub, but a custom Java object that uses RMI to communicate back to the service. The RMI interface that it will talk back on is the `CalcItf3` interface that will only add two numbers together, not all three.

First, let us take a look at the custom Jini proxy object that will be sent to the client. You can find the source code in the `ch9\code\Smartpr\CalcLoc.java` file:

```java
public class CalcLoc implements CalcItf,java.io.Serializable
  {
    private CalcItf3 myRemote;
    public CalcLoc() {}
    public CalcLoc(CalcItf3 remoteCalc)
```

```
        {
          myRemote = remoteCalc;
        }
        public double calc(double a, double b, double c)
          throws java.rmi.RemoteException
          {
            System.out.println("adding " + a + " and " + b + " locally.");
            double temp = a + b;
            return myRemote.calc(temp,c);
          }
      }
```

We can see that this `CalcLoc` proxy is serializable (required for marshalling the class between services, lookup services, and clients). It also implements `CalcItf`, the only interface that our client understands.

The implementation, however, relies partially on a remote `CalcItf3` interface implementation. The remote object that implements the `CalcItf3` interface can be passed into the `CalcLoc` proxy upon its construction. It is clear from this design that we could:

❑   Do as much work on the client or service side as we want

❑   Use as many RMI interfaces to communicate back to the service as necessary to get the work done

Now, let's take a look at the service itself. The source code is in the `ch9\code\Smartpr\SmartPr.java` file:

```
import net.jini.lookup.JoinManager;
import net.jini.discovery.LookupDiscoveryManager;
import java.rmi.RemoteException;
import java.rmi.RMISecurityManager;
import net.jini.lookup.ServiceIDListener;
import java.rmi.server.UnicastRemoteObject;
```

The `SmartPr` class is an RMI implementation for the 'private' `CalcItf3` interface, used by our proxy implementation. To make this simple, `SmartPr` derives from `java.rmi.UnicastRemoteObject`:

```
public class SmartPr extends UnicastRemoteObject implements CalcItf3
  {
    static final String [] GROUPS1 = { "iguanas" };
    protected JoinManager myJM = null;
    public static void main(String argv[])
      {
        SmartPr myApp = null;
        try
          {
            myApp = new SmartPr();
            synchronized(myApp)
              {
                myApp.wait(0);
              }
```

```
            }
        catch(Exception e)
            {
                System.exit(0);
            }
        }
```

Note that the proxy object that we pass to the `JoinManager` instance is an instance of the `CalcLoc` proxy class. This class will run local to the client. The `CalcLoc` instance, however, contains a reference back to this service. Since the service is a descendent of `UnicastRemoteObject`, the reference will actually be an RMI stub object for the service.

```
public SmartPr() throws RemoteException
    {
    if (System.getSecurityManager() == null)
        System.setSecurityManager(new RMISecurityManager());

    LookupDiscoveryManager ldm = null;
    String [] groupsToDiscover = GROUPS1;
    try
        {
        ldm = new LookupDiscoveryManager(groupsToDiscover, null, null);
        myJM = new JoinManager(new CalcLoc(this), null,
            (ServiceIDListener) null, ldm, null);
        }
    catch (Exception e)
        {
        e.printStackTrace();
        System.exit(1);
        }
    }
```

When the `CalcLoc` instance calls back to the service, it will invoke this `calc()` method. This method only adds together two numbers:

```
public double calc(double a, double b) throws RemoteException
    {
    System.out.println("A client call was made...");
    return (a+b);
    }

}
```

Use the batch file to compile the service:

`..\bats\buildit SmartPr.java`

Again, we need to run the `rmic` tool to create that stub. The `makejar.bat` batch file combines this with creation of the `SmartPr-dl.jar` file:

```
call ..\bats\setpaths.bat
rmic -v1.2 -classpath %JINIJARS%;. SmartPr
jar cvf SmartPr-dl.jar SmartPr_Stub.class CalcLoc.class CalcItf3.class
copy SmartPr-dl.jar %WROXHOME%
```

We need to package up the RMI stub, the `CalcLoc` proxy object class, and the internal `CalcItf3` interface class. These classes will be required by the client and the smart proxy itself once it has been downloaded to the client.

To test out the smart proxy implementation, make sure you have:

- ❑ The httpd class server running (`runhttpd.bat`)
- ❑ The class server for stubs running (`runhttpdstubs.bat`)
- ❑ The RMID activation daemon running (`runrmid.bat`)
- ❑ A reggie working for the 'iguanas' group (`runlookup1.bat`)

Now, change to the `ch9\code\Smartpr` directory and start the service via the `runsmart.bat` file.

Next, start another console, change into the `ch9\code\Calcclient` directory and start the client via the `runclient.bat` file.

You should see the client complete its addition of numbers as usual, as shown below. Note that the proxy object prints out a status message that indicates part of the computation is actually performed on the client's side:

On the service side, we should see the call back to the service by the smart proxy to add two of the three numbers. A message is printed on the service's console, as shown here:

On the service side, we should see the call back to the service by the smart proxy to add two of the three numbers. A message is printed on the service's console, as shown here:

A Remote Service that Does Not Use RMI

RMI is not the only way to perform network-based communications. In fact, there are many real-life design situations where RMI as the communications mechanism between the proxy and the service may not be possible or feasible (where the Java VM at the client and/or service does not support RMI – such as the KVM for PDAs). Jini in no way restricts implementation of remote proxies to using RMI. In fact, the smart proxy scenario was viewed as a custom proxy implementation that happened to use RMI as the communications method between proxy and service.

Now, it is totally possible for us to use another custom protocol instead of RMI. In this case, we will roll-our-own raw by going directly to low level sockets. The following diagram illustrates the freedom to use any protocol we wish to implement for the communications between the proxy and the service. On the left hand side, we have the client's VM, with a proxy that had been delivered from the service via the lookup service. This proxy provides a local interface to the client, but may communicate back to the service via any non-RMI custom protocol. The division of work between the service and the proxy is arbitrary and can vary depending on the application.

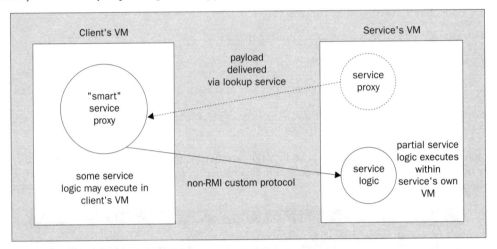

Our custom protocol is straightforward and simple. The server side:

❑   Listens at the well-known TCP port 8001

❑   Upon connection, receives three strings, each ending with a carriage return

❑   Converts each string to `double` and adds them together

❑   Writes the resulting sum as a string (with a carriage return) to the socket

As one can easily deduce, the proxy acting as a client needs to simply:

❑   Open a TCP connection to the server at port 8001

❑   Upon connection, write three double numbers as string, each on its own line, to the socket

❑   Read back a line from the socket containing the sum

Here we see the interactions involved with our custom protocol:

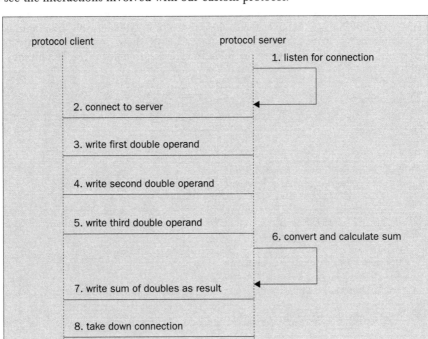

Our proxy object will be a custom (serializable) Java object that will implement the `CalcItf` interface using our custom socket based protocol. This custom proxy is contained in the `ch9\code\Sockpr\SockCalc.java` class:

```
import java.io.*;
import java.net.*;
```

The host and port number of the server (for our custom protocol) are passed as parameters to the constructor of this class. This essentially provides information to the proxy enabling it to contact the service instance during its operation.

```
public class SockCalc implements CalcItf,Serializable
  {
    protected String myHost = null;
    protected int myPort = 0;
    public SockCalc() {}
    public SockCalc(String host, int port)
      {
        myHost = host;
        myPort = port;
      }
```

The `calc()` method of the `CalcItf` interface is implemented by working the client side of our custom protocol. A TCP connection is created, and a `BufferedReader` and `PrintWriter` are created to ease the input and output of lines of text over the socket connection. Note how we are mapping socket connection exceptions to `RemoteExceptions` – this is a case where proxy interface methods throw `RemoteExceptions` (indicating network or communications problems) even though they may not be RMI based.

```
public double calc(double a, double b, double c) throws java.rmi.RemoteException
  {
    double res;
    try
      {
        Socket soc = new Socket(myHost, myPort);
        BufferedReader myIn = new BufferedReader(new
            InputStreamReader(soc.getInputStream()));
        PrintWriter myOut = new PrintWriter(soc.getOutputStream(), true);
        myOut.println("" + a);
        myOut.println("" + b);
        myOut.println("" + c);
        String result = myIn.readLine();
        res = Double.parseDouble(result);
        soc.close();
      }
    catch (Exception ex)
      {
        throw new java.rmi.RemoteException();
      }
    return res;
  }
}
```

Now, back on the Jini service itself. We have the `ch9\code\Sockpr\SockPr.java` service implementation:

```
import net.jini.lookup.JoinManager;
import net.jini.discovery.LookupDiscoveryManager;
import java.rmi.RemoteException;
import java.rmi.RMISecurityManager;
import net.jini.lookup.ServiceIDListener;
import java.io.*;
import java.net.*;
```

The purpose of this service is mainly for setting up the proxy object, registering it with all the lookup services in the 'iguanas' group, and keeping the leases renewed. The only other duty is to handle the server side of our custom protocol. Since it does not handle any RMI calls, there is no need to implement any interface or extend any RMI classes.

```
public class SockPr
  {
    static final String [] GROUPS1 = { "iguanas" };
// Alter the next two lines to your machine's configuration
    static final int MYPORT = 8005;
    static final String MYHOST = "win98p300";

    protected JoinManager myJM = null;
```

The `main()` method starts the instance, and then call the `startService()` method. This method starts the 'accept loop' handling client's request:

```
public static void main(String argv[])
    {
      SockPr myApp = null;
      try
        {
          myApp = new SockPr();
          myApp.startService();
        }
      catch(Exception e)
        {
          System.exit(0);
        }
    }
```

Other than the usual Jini service housekeeping duties, our constructor submits an instance of the `SockCalc` proxy object to the `JoinManager` for registration with all the lookup services that handle the 'iguanas' group. Note that we have initialized the `SockCalc` instance with host and port information, allowing it to callback to our custom protocol handling server.

```
public SockPr() throws RemoteException
    {
      if (System.getSecurityManager() == null)
      System.setSecurityManager(new RMISecurityManager());

      LookupDiscoveryManager ldm = null;
      String [] groupsToDiscover = GROUPS1;
      try
        {
          ldm = new LookupDiscoveryManager(groupsToDiscover, null, null);
          myJM = new JoinManager(new SockCalc(MYHOST,MYPORT),
                              null,(ServiceIDListener) null,ldm,null);
        }
      catch (Exception e)
        {
          e.printStackTrace();
          System.exit(1);
        }
    }
```

We handle the server side of the custom protocol here in the `startService()` method. We will block on port 8001 listening for incoming client requests. Once a request is received, we read the numbers to sum, sum them, and write back the result.

```
public void startService()
    {
      double a, b, c, sum;
      try
        {
          ServerSocket serv = new ServerSocket(MYPORT);
          Socket aConn;
          while (true)
            {
```

```
                aConn = serv.accept();
                System.out.println("Client connected...");
                BufferedReader in = new BufferedReader(new
                    InputStreamReader(aConn.getInputStream()));
                PrintWriter out = new PrintWriter(aConn.getOutputStream(), true);
                String first, second, third;
                first = in.readLine();
                second = in.readLine();
                third = in.readLine();
                a = Double.parseDouble(first);
                b = Double.parseDouble(second);
                c = Double.parseDouble(third);
                sum = a + b + c;
                out.println("" + sum);
                aConn.close();
            }
        }
        catch (Exception e)
        {
            e.printStackTrace();
            System.exit(1);
        }
    }
}
```

To compile this service, first copy over the `CalcItf.class` file from `ch9\code\Localpr` directory, then use the command:

`..\bats\buildit SockPr.java`

Since there is no RMI involved, the `makejar.bat` file is rather simple and contains only the proxy object:

```
call ..\bats\setpaths.bat
jar cvf SockPr-dl.jar SockCalc.class CalcItf.class
copy SockPr-dl.jar %WROXHOME%
```

Make sure that the class server, stub class servier, rmid, and reggie are running. Start the service by executing the `runsock.bat` file; its content is:

```
call ../bats/setpaths.bat
java -classpath .;%JINIJARS% -Dnet.jini.discovery.interface=%ADAPTERIP%
-Djava.security.policy=policy.all
-Djava.rmi.server.codebase=http://%STUBHOST%/SockPr-dl.jar SockPr
```

Now, start another console, change into the `ch9\code\Calclient` directory and execute the client by starting the `runclient.bat` file.

You should see something similar to the screenshot shown below on the client console. The client is again oblivious to the implementation of the Jini service.

The service console should contain output that indicates processing activity:

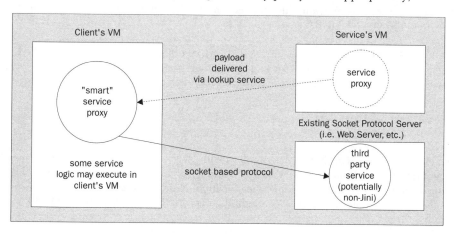

In our example, the Jini service itself is managing the server-side handling of the custom protocol. It is, of course, quite possible to point the proxy object to other third-party services that may already exist. The following diagram shows this possibility. Here, the client VM contains the service proxy as usual. The major difference is that the proxy now uses a socket based protocol to talk back to a server machine. In fact, as the diagram below shows, the server that the proxy connects to need not be the same as the original service's machine (as long as security policy is set appropriately).

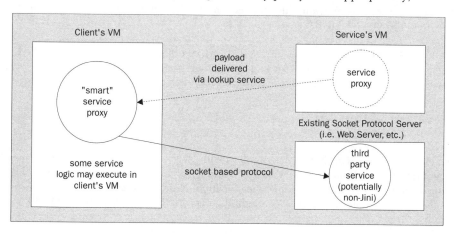

One can easily imagine Jini proxies that use HTTP and can contact multiple websites on the Internet to collect or consolidate information, etc. While this is being performed, the client can be completely oblivious to how the work is being done by the Jini service. Using this technique allows us to bridge the existing TCP/IP Internet world to the distributed world of Jini based technologies.

From CORBA to Jini

One area where bridging can be immediately beneficial is the area of legacy systems integration. The 'any communications protocol' nature of the Jini service architecture allows us to easily integrate systems and functionalities that are accessible via CORBA. In Chapter 4, we examined CORBA and RMI-IIOP and saw how they offer functionality that is complementary to what Jini has to offer. Here, we will illustrate how easy it is to create a Jini service based on CORBA functionality. By creating CORBA based Jini services, one can selectively expose legacy functions for use within the Jini world.

The diagram below illustrates how Jini and CORBA fit together in this respect. Just like our situation with the socket base proprietary protocol client, here the client proxy is actually mapping the Jini interface into CORBA calls across the network. The protocol on-the-wire is CORBA's IIOP.

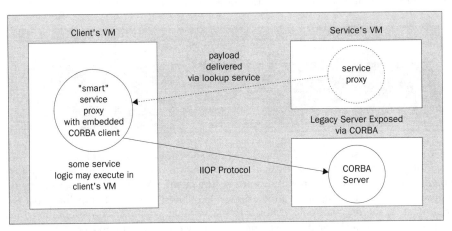

The amazing part is that, once again, the client is completely oblivious to the fact that the functionality is now provided through a CORBA service.

The illusion is performed by our proxy object. This proxy object implements the `CalcItf` that the client knows and loves, and uses CORBA to get its actual calculations done. You can find the source of the proxy object in the `ch9\code\Corbpr\CorbProxy.java` file:

```
import org.omg.CosNaming.*;
import org.omg.CORBA.*;
```

This example uses Sun's ORB that comes standard with JDK 1.3+. We will be using the new RMI-IIOP support built into the ORB that comes with this version. To simplify the example, we will be using the Sun-provided transient name service for service location. Note that our proxy object effectively translates the `CalcItf` interface's `calc()` method code into the corresponding CORBA service method call.

```
public class CorbProxy implements CalcItf,java.io.Serializable
{
    protected ORB orb = null;
    public CorbProxy() {}
```

When the `calc()` method is called, we initialize an ORB, get a `NameService` reference, and use the name service to locate our `CalcService` CORBA object reference:

```
public double calc(double a, double b, double c) throws java.rmi.RemoteException
    {
    double res=0.0;
    try
        {
        String [] args = null;
        ORB orb = ORB.init(args, null);
        org.omg.CORBA.Object objRef =
                        orb.resolve_initial_references("NameService");
        NamingContext ncRef = NamingContextHelper.narrow(objRef);
        NameComponent nc = new NameComponent("CalcService", "");
        NameComponent path[] = {nc};
```

Once located, we cast or narrow the reference to a CORBA interface called `CorCalcItf`. Finally, we call the `calc()` method of this CORBA interface to add the three numbers:

```
        CorCalcItf myRef = CorCalcItfHelper.narrow(ncRef.resolve(path));
        System.out.println("calling CORBA interface...");
        res = myRef.calc(a, b, c);
        }
    catch(Exception e)
        {
        System.out.println("ERROR : " + e);
        e.printStackTrace(System.out);
        }
    return res;
    }
}
```

To try out this example, we assume that JDK 1.3 or later has been installed, or JDK 1.2.2+ with the download and installation of the RMI-IIOP ORB. This is the same requirement for the Chapter 4 CORBA examples.

The actual IDL file that can be used to create stubs and skeletons is found in the `ch9\code\Corbpr\Calc.idl` file:

```
interface CorCalcItf
    {
    double calc(in double a,in double b,in double c);
    };
```

To create stubs and skeletons, assuming you have the idlj IDL compiler installed, requires the command:

```
idlj Calc.idl
idlj -fserver Calc.idl
```

The Jini service doubles as a CORBA service implementation in our case. The source is found in the `ch9\code\Corbpr\CorbPr.java` file:

```
import net.jini.lookup.JoinManager;
import net.jini.discovery.LookupDiscoveryManager;
import java.rmi.RemoteException;
import java.rmi.RMISecurityManager;
import net.jini.lookup.ServiceIDListener;

import org.omg.CosNaming.*;
import org.omg.CosNaming.NamingContextPackage.*;
import org.omg.CORBA.*;
```

We implement our CORBA servant here; the only method we need to implement is the `calc()` method:

```
class CalcServant extends _CorCalcItfImplBase
  {
    public double calc (double a, double b, double c)
      {
        System.out.println("Client CORBA connection...");
        return (a+b+c);
      }
  }
```

Again, no RMI or other interfaces are required to be implemented by the `CorbPr` class here:

```
public class CorbPr
  {
    static final String [] GROUPS1 = { "iguanas" };
    protected JoinManager myJM = null;
    public static void main(String argv[])
      {
        CorbPr myApp = null;
        try
          {
            myApp = new CorbPr();
            myApp.startService();
            synchronized(myApp)
              {
                myApp.wait(1);
              }
          }
        catch(Exception e)
          {
            System.exit(0);
          }
      }
```

The `JoinManager` is provided with an instance of the `CorbProxy` object. We do not need to initialize any host or port information since we're using a name service (except maybe with the host and port of the ORB in some cases).

```
public CorbPr() throws RemoteException
  {
    if (System.getSecurityManager() == null)
        System.setSecurityManager(new RMISecurityManager());
```

```
        LookupDiscoveryManager ldm = null;
        String [] groupsToDiscover = GROUPS1;
        try
            {
              ldm = new LookupDiscoveryManager(groupsToDiscover, null, null);
              myJM = new JoinManager(new CorbProxy(), null,(ServiceIDListener)
                                      null,ldm,null);
            }
        catch (Exception e)
            {
              e.printStackTrace();
              System.exit(1);
            }
      }
```

The `startService()` method initializes an ORB, creates an instance of the servant, connects it to the ORB, and then binds it to the name "`CalcService`" with the naming service.

This `servant` instance can be located by clients through the naming service.

```
public void startService()
    {
      try
        {
          String [] args = null;
          ORB orb = ORB.init(args, null);
          CalcServant myRef = new CalcServant();
          org.omg.CORBA.Object objRef =
                             orb.resolve_initial_references("NameService");
          NamingContext ncRef = NamingContextHelper.narrow(objRef);
          NameComponent nc = new NameComponent("CalcService", "");
          NameComponent path[] = {nc};
          ncRef.rebind(path, myRef);
          orb.connect(myRef);
```

Our servant is now ready to take calls. Finally, we hang around waiting for calls from client:

```
          java.lang.Object sync = new java.lang.Object();
          synchronized(sync)
            {
              sync.wait();
            }
        }
      catch (Exception e)
        {
          e.printStackTrace();
          System.exit(1);
        }
    }
}
```

Copy over the `CalcItf.class` file from `ch9\code\Localpr` directory. Use the `buildit.bat` file to compile it:

```
..\bats\buildit CorbPr.java
```

The `makejar.bat` file for this needs to include the stub and all the classes that the client needs, including the proxy object, of course:

```
call ..\bats\setpaths.bat
jar cvf CorbPr-dl.jar CorCalcItf.class CorCalItfHelper.class _CorCalcItfStub.class
CorCalcItfOperations.class CorbProxy.class
copy CorbPr-dl.jar %WROXHOME%
```

To test out this example, you need to:

❑ Make sure a class server is running (`runhttpd.bat`)

❑ Make sure a class server for stubs is running (`runhttpdstubs.bat`)

❑ Make sure rmid is running (`runrmid.bat`)

❑ Make sure a reggie is working for the 'iguanas' group (`runlookup.bat`)

❑ Run an instance of the CORBA transient name service, using the command line:
`start tnameserv`

You should see the starting up of the name service and its IOR, similar to that shown here:

Now, start the service (and CORBA service) by executing the `runcorb.bat` file. This file contains:

```
call setpaths.bat
java -classpath .;%JINIJARS%  -Dnet.jini.discovery.interface=%ADAPTERIP%
-Djava.security.policy=policy.all
-Djava.rmi.server.codebase=http://%STUBHOST%/CorbPr-dl.jar CorbPr
```

Start another console, change directory into `ch9\code\Calclient`, and start the client by executing the `runclient.bat` file. The client console output will be similar to this:

The service console will also have output indicating the receipt of CORBA calls across the network:

It should be clear from this example that exposing any standalone, API based functionality from legacy systems (for use in Jini networks) is as simple as writing a Jini proxy object for front-ending the legacy system.

The Payload Launcher View

We've seen in all of the five examples above, that the essence of the initial service to client interactions is for the service to launch a payload (the proxy) to a payload receiver (the client). In reality, we know that the task is handled indirectly via a lookup service, using the discovery protocol. The entire discovery protocol suite can be viewed as a distributed payload delivery mechanism.

The following figure illustrates the relationship between the launcher, the launching mechanism, and the receiver. Simply stated, the diagram shows the payload (proxy) being delivered to the receiver (client).

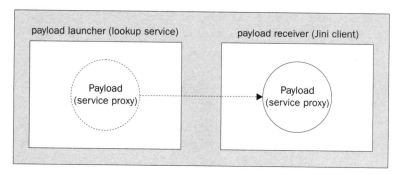

If we consider this simple and abstract view, we will quickly realize that:

❑ The payload launcher, and even the payload launching mechanism itself, need not know anything about the payload that it is launching (it can treat it as a pure binary bundle)

❑ The payload receiver, in order to make adequate use of the payload, must understand how to use it in some way (must be able to execute its content in the case of Jini)

These are rather shocking discoveries when we map them back to Jini:

❑ The payload launcher and mechanism do not need to be written in Java or contain a Java VM

❑ The implementation of the discovery protocol need not be written in the Java language

❑ A Jini client, the receiver, must have access to a Java VM

In fact, these properties are precisely what makes Jini suitable for the deployment of distributed device drivers over a network. Distributed device drivers in the Jini sense are quite different from conventional device drivers that we are used to. First and foremost, they *are* bona-fide Jini services, the very same ones that we have worked with throughout the book. In these cases, the physical device being driven is the 'service' performing the work. Second, they are useful only to Jini clients. However, Jini clients can be embedded in applications and devices as well.

The benefit of using these distributed device drivers/services is clear – they inherit the dynamic, long-lived, self-healing, robust, fault-resilient features of Jini. Let us take a look at this possibility next.

Handling Non-Java Jini Services

In Chapter 11, when we examined the helper services provided by the Jini library, we saw how reggie, Norm, Fiddler, and Mercury can support a long-lived Jini service that may or may not be implemented in the Java language itself.

The following figure shows a Jini service built using these components:

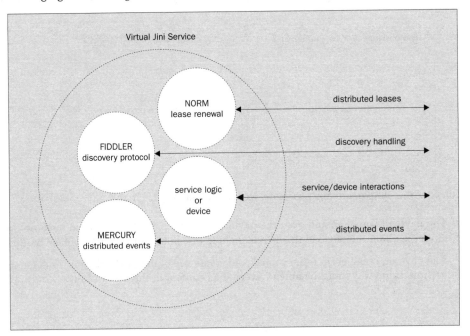

In this case, the implementation of a Jini service is factored into its parts:

❑ The service logic

❑ The discovery and join protocol handling

❑ The lease renewal handling

❑ The distributed events handling

In all of the above, only the service logic is significantly different between different services. The other three parts involve code that is both repetitious and boiler-plate in style. The combination of Norm, Fiddler, and Mercury frees us from having to include this code within our service. This 'service factoring' is, in essence, the distributed equivalent of 'software re-use' in the non-distributed computing world.

Exposing JVM-less Devices as Jini Services

Obviously, the elaborate framework illustrated on the previous page may indeed be used in the support of device drivers for devices that may not have their own Java VM; it does represent a considerably heavyweight framework – requiring multiple long-lived Jini services to support what potentially may be a very simple device. This is undesirable, since the resources (machines, etc.) to host and run these elaborate services may not always be available.

Imagine that you are the designer of a hardware device that is extremely cost sensitive. Instead of fancy 64 bit CPUs with hundreds of megabytes of memory, you're restricted to 32/16 bit CPUs with only hundreds of kilobytes of memory. Your device can be manufactured for a bill of material cost of less than $10 in quantities of 10,000. With the cost, memory, and computational budget that you have available, you cannot possibly accommodate a fully-fledged Java VM. Some form of restricted or 'tiny' Java VM as an alternative is feasible. One potential solution is to use the KVM (but the current version of KVM does not support RMI).

There are two approaches to solve this problem:

❑ Implementing a non-Java service by supporting IIOP.

❑ Using an available VM, somewhere else on a better equipped machine, to host the Jini service' and then having that Jini service communicate with the device directly using whatever means possible (native interface, direct hardware manipulation, socket based custom protocol). This is the essence of the Jini Surrogate Architecture.

We will take a look at the first alternative right now, and discuss the surrogate alternative a little later on in this chapter.

The basic requirements for a non-Java device to become a Jini using service can be summarized as follows:

1. The device needs to perform discovery to locate lookup services, and obtain a registrar object

2. The device needs to be able to register its own proxy using the registrar's `ServiceRegistrar` interface

3. The device needs to be able to renew the lease (using the lookup service provided interface) intermittently to ensure that its proxy object remains available over the Jini network

Step 1 could be implemented using a non-Java alternative – let's say, in our case, an embedded C/C++ language that compiles to the native machine code of the 16-bit CPU that we will be using for the device.

Steps 2 and 3 require a Java VM to load the classes associated with the Java interfaces, and the associated parameters. RMI support is also required to properly communicate with the remote lookup service. Fortunately, through RMI-IIOP support, it is possible to work with a lookup service purely through interacting with the IIOP packets over the wire.

The following diagram illustrates how IIOP interoperability will allow non-Java devices to bootstrap themselves. We can see here that a device can be programmed to monitor, send, and receive IIOP packets directly on the wire. The automatic IIOP support provided by JDK 1.3 and later, enables a device without a Java VM to launch (as a payload launcher) a binary proxy object to an interested Jini client. Regular Jini services can continue to interact with the very same lookup services through the JRMP protocol. Since the device is reading and writing IIOP packets on-the-wire directly, there exists an obvious dependency on IIOP protocol version. Furthermore, any changes in the Jini bootstrap process or interfaces will also necessitate change in the device's implementation.

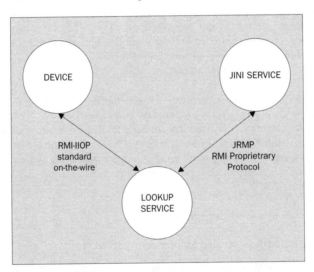

The Surrogate – Providing a Jini Soul for Java-Free Devices

The Jini Technology Surrogate Architecture is a specification in its infancy. It provides a glimpse into the way in which devices that cannot communicate directly with a Jini network may be able to implement Jini compatibility in the near future. You can find the latest version of the specification here:

http://developer.jini.org/exchange/projects/surrogate

The key concept encompasses the use of a 'host capable machine' executing a 'surrogate host'. Translated, we will need a machine capable of running a Java VM to host a helper service that will allow a non-Jini device to participate in the Jini network.

Unlike the elaborate, heavyweight, multi-services system we examined earlier, the same lightweight 'surrogate host' is expected to be able to host and run multiple helper services (called surrogates) – each representing a device. It is assumed that the surrogate host is connected directly to the device in some software accessible way.

Each surrogate itself, being absolutely device specific, is expected to originate from the device itself. One implementation possibility for a surrogate is 'canned' Java bytecodes that will be uploaded from the device to the surrogate host when it contacts the device. The following figure illustrates how a surrogate host obtains a surrogate to host from a device. In this figure, device 1 has just launched a surrogate (just a bunch of binary bits to the device) via a physical interconnect into the surrogate host. The surrogate host is running this surrogate as one of the many services that it supports. It is currently running a surrogate for device 2 as well.

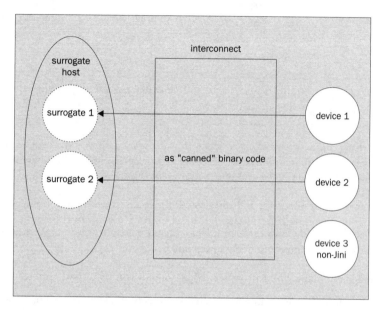

The surrogate host does not have innate knowledge about any device. This would make the surrogate host prone to obsolescence. Instead, the device knowledge is encapsulated in 'interconnect specific' objects known as Interconnect Adapters.

It is easier to understand this if we use a specific example. Imagine an interconnect adapter that adapts the PCI bus to Jini. This will allow any Jini client to access devices connected to the PCI bus, say getting a video capture from a TV tuner card. In this system, when the surrogate host starts up, it will contact the PCI interconnect adapter object, and the PCI interconnect adapter object will in turn enumerate all the devices on the PCI bus. This can be done via software polling, or via other native hardware enumeration means. Each device that supports Jini compatibility will indicate to the PCI interconnect adapter that it has a surrogate available for upload to the surrogate host (or for non-intelligent PCI adapters, the interconnect adapter may need to read the binary surrogate from the adapter's ROM – read-only memory).

The surrogate host will then obtain each of the surrogates in turn, and start them up within their own environment, making them fully-fledged Jini services. The following figure illustrates this interaction. Here, the surrogate host works on a system that features SCSI, USB, and PCI interconnects. It also runs a surrogate for each hardware interconnect. This allows all Jini compatible devices on the system, regardless of whether they are SCSI, PCI, or USB devices, to participate in the greater Jini network.

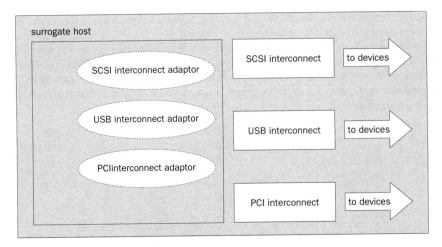

At the time of writing, the protocol used between the surrogate host and the interconnect adapter is not specified. However, it is anticipated that a Surrogate Host Specification will be available in the near future to better specify the interfaces and interaction between these two objects.

The variety of interconnect adapters, and the protocol that each uses to communicate with its associated devices, is also left unspecified. It is anticipated that a future "Interconnect Specification" will be available for each type of hardware interconnect available (USB, firewire, TDMA wireless, Bluetooth, GPIO, etc.). In any case, an interconnect adapter must:

❑   Support the enumeration or discovery of the devices on that interconnect

❑   Have a way to determine when a device disconnects, goes out of range, or becomes non-functional via the interconnect

❑   Have the ability to retrieve a surrogate bundle from the device through the interconnect

The binary package that is delivered from the device as the surrogate in the earlier diagrams is actually a surrogate bundle. A surrogate bundle is specified to be a bundling of resources, as a JAR file, including not only the surrogate Java object, but potentially other resources used in the implementation of the surrogate – including icons, URLs, HTML help files, and support classes. To the device, this bundle is just binary data.

To summarize, the relationship between the various parties is illustrated in the following figure. The surrogate host may activate or deactivate the surrogate. The surrogate can discover and use resources provided by the surrogate host itself. The surrogate communicates with the device only through an interconnect adapter. The interconnect adapter is responsible for discovering any devices that has a surrogate available, retrieving it, and handling it to the surrogate host. The interconnect adapter is also responsible for monitoring the actual device for disconnection, going off-line, or failure. In these situations, the surrogate should be deactivated within the surrogate host.

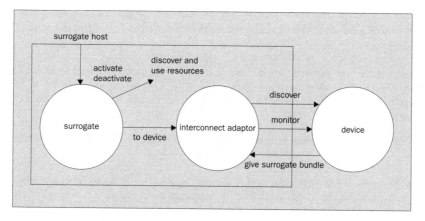

There are a couple of points that we should note:

- ❑ The machine where the surrogate host runs is expected to be the same machine that connects directly to the device (potentially via another hardware bus, interface, network, or other interconnect)

- ❑ The surrogate object is downloaded *and* loaded into the surrogate host through a non-Jini, potentially non-Java related mechanism; it is then executed within the surrogate host as Java bytecode

The protocol between the surrogate host and the surrogate is partially specified. More specifically, a surrogate must implement the SurrogateActivator interface:

```
public interface SurrogateActivator
    {
     void activate(SurrogateContext hostContext, Object interconnectContext)
         throws Exception;
     void deactivate() throws Exception;
    }
```

The surrogate host will activate and deactivate the surrogate through the methods of this interface. When activate() is called, the surrogate is expected to contact the device that it is representing and get things ready. Exactly how this may be done is not described in the current set of specifications.

The first parameter passed into the surrogate is an object that implements the SurrogateContext interface. This interface has only two defined public methods:

```
public interface SurrogateContext
    {
     DiscoveryManagement getDefaultDiscoveryManager();
     void cancelActivation();
    }
```

The surrogate may use this interface to obtain an instance of the discovery manager that is used by the surrogate host. The object would be used to get the ServiceRegistrars that the DiscoveryManagement object has found. The surrogate would then register with each of these ServiceRegistrars (lookup services). The DiscoveryManagement object may implement other DiscoverManagement interfaces such as DiscoveryGroupManagement, which would allow the surrogate to find out what groups it could join. The cancelActivation() method can be used by the surrogate to ask the surrogate host to cancel a previous activation.

The second parameter, the interconnectContext, is a placeholder for future specification on an instance of interconnect information that will be specific to a class of devices.

What is still not clearly specified in the specification, and may be part of the anticipated Surrogate Host Specification, is how a surrogate service appears to the end user over the Jini network. There are at least two possibilities:

❑ The surrogate host presents a well-known interface to special surrogate-aware clients. These clients then use the interface to communicate directly with the devices; in this way, each device does not participate on the Jini network independently – they are dependent on their surrogate host

❑ Each surrogate itself is free to publish its own proxy object to lookup services, and each device exists as an independent service on the Jini network

At the present time, since the specification for the Surrogate Host and the Interconnect Adapter is not yet fully defined, only the latter approach can be productively applied.

ServiceUI – Providing a User Interface for a Jini Service

One of the first successes of the Jini.org Jini Community process is the ServiceUI project, led by Bill Venners of Artima Software.

This project aims to standardize the way that user interfaces will be associated with Jini services/devices (attached to the service proxy).

It is very important to note up front that user-interface, as it is referred to here, is not restricted to the graphical user interfaces (GUIs) that we are used to while using today's PCs and workstations. User interface, as it is defined here, is any adaptive technology that connects a user to a computing service. This opens up the possibility of:

❑ Speech recognition user interfaces, working with the user purely through the microphone

❑ Digital keypad interfaces, as commonly found on telephone handsets world-wide

❑ Terminal based interfaces, using only an 80 column by 24 line screen

❑ Morse code based binary input interfaces, consisting of only one single key with a momentary contact

❑ Other even more bizarre, not necessarily common, ways of connecting to the end-user

It is obvious from the requirements that, instead of subclassing GUI framework libraries, the design exercise is one where the common elements of the following three software layers must be clearly separated:

❑ Control – affecting the operation of the Jini service

❑ Feedback – from the Jini service to the user

❑ The presentation of the feedback (to the user), and the handling of the input (from the user)

Here we see this required separation:

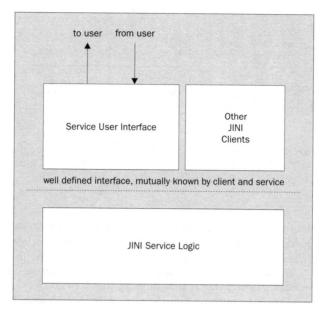

In the figure above, if you trace from the user to the Jini service logic, there is a line where the service logic meets the user interface. ServiceUI is about making a clean definition of this line (see dotted line in the diagram).

This clean separation can be achieved by simply designing and coding the logic of the service with no consideration of the UI from the outset; one can achieve an API-based service that can be accessed purely through the API offered by the interface(s) on its proxy object. A user interface in this case simply becomes a translator (or adapter, as the ServiceUI project calls it) that translates user input into the commands for the Jini service itself.

In the figure, if we trace out from the Jini service logic to the user, the user can accept feedback or status information from the Jini service in several ways:

❑   As return value from API calls

❑   Via distributed event callbacks

The following diagram illustrates the flow of information between the user and the Jini service, through the user interface 'translator'. In this figure, the user sends commands to the service, but uses the service UI as a translator. For example, a user may click a button, which results in the service UI calling a specific method on the interface exposed by the Jini service. The return value from this method call can then be graphically presented to the user (again using the service UI as an adapter) through the user interface.

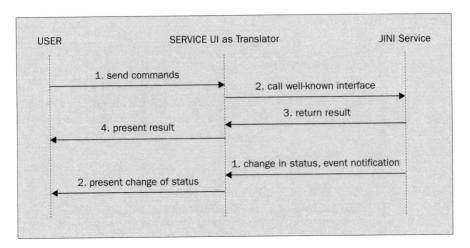

The user interface translates actions of the user (the click of a button, or a speech command, or pressing a specific dial tone sequence, etc.) to the actual API calls of the proxy object of the Jini service. The user interface also wires up the notification or status reporting mechanism of the Jini service to itself. This allows feedback to the user (via a graphical flashing light, a speech synthesized prompt, or a voice message over the phone handset, etc.) via the user interface itself. In this way, each user interface implementation is expected to have intimate knowledge of how to work with the interface(s) provided by the proxy object of the associated Jini service.

Knowing how best to separate the programming logic to enable the plug-in replacement of user interfaces is only part of the battle. One other requirement is to determine how to attach a description of the available user interfaces for a Jini service so that:

❑ The service can attach (one or more) user interfaces to itself

❑ Potential clients can select services based on the user interfaces available (choosing those that they can make use of); or select the best-of-breed/most suitable from a choice of many available services

❑ A service can add value to another by attaching additional user interfaces to it

An object that describes the user interface, and is capable of generating one or more user interfaces, is attached to a Java service through a special attribute (associated with its proxy object within lookup services). This attribute is an instance of the net.jini.lookup.entry.UIDescriptor class. This class actually implements the Entry interface, enabling it to be one of the attributes within an attribute set associated with a service. A UIDescriptor is defined as:

```
public class UIDescriptor extends net.jini.entry.AbstractEntry
{
    public String role;
    public String toolkit;
    public Set attributes;
    public MarshalledObject factory;

    public UIDescriptor() {...}
    public UIDescriptor(String role, String toolkit, Set attributes,
        MarshalledObject factory) {...}
    public final Object getUIFactory(ClassLoader parentLoader)
        throws IOException,ClassNotFoundException  {...}
}
```

The four fields are:

Field Name	Description
role	A `String` describing the role that the UI plays.
toolkit	A `String` describing a library package that the UI depends on ("javax.swing", or "java.awt").
attributes	A set of attributes describing the UI.
factory	A `MarshalledObject`, containing the UI Factory that can be used to create an instance of the UI.

One of the key concepts in the `ServiceUI` implementation is the use of a `MarshalledObject` based `UIFactory` object. UIs can be both large, and potentially have many dependent classes. The use of a `MarshalledObject` UI Factory alleviates the intermediary (the lookup service) from the burden of loading these non-essential classes. The only time when the `Factory` object is unmarshalled and the classes are loaded occurs when a client had decided that it is the right UI to use, and the unmarshalling occurs within the client's Java VM.

The `getUIFactory()` method is useful for unmarshalling the UI factory object without requiring fancy footwork on the part of the client (since the client, at the time of the call, may be using a different class loader from the one necessary to load the class that associated with the marshalled UI factory).

The following figure illustrates this scheme. Note that each service item registered by the service on every lookup service will contain the `UIDescriptor` and its associated fields.

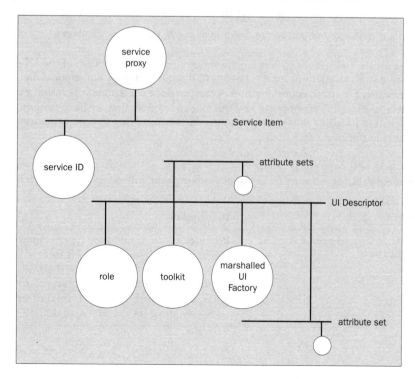

The role string contains the textual name of a Java interface (fully qualified) defining the role of the UI.

Three role types are defined by the current ServiceUI specifications. They are:

Role String (Interface)	Description
net.jini.lookup.ui.MainUI	Presents the main user interface to control the associated Jini service.
net.jini.lookup.ui.AdminUI	Presents a user interface for working with the administrative aspect of a Jini service.
net.jini.lookup.ui.AboutUI	Presents a user interface that shows information concerning the underlying Jini service.

Future ServiceUI specification may specify new UI role strings, but applications can also create application specific UI role strings. The naming of the interface should follow the standard Java naming convention (for example com.wrox.gizmodevice.SetupUI). In this way a client can choose the most appropriate UI based on the UI objects it knows how to use.

The actual user interface object is guaranteed to implement the interface specified in the role string. Now, it is rather un-Java-like to specify interfaces by their textual name. Why can't we just use the instanceOf operator to determine if the user interface object implements a particular interface? Well, the answer turns out to be quite interesting. If you look at the hoops that we need to jump through in order to obtain the actual user interface object, you will see that we are actually performing a double indirection before obtaining the actual user interface object:

❑ Use attributes (the role string) to find the UIFactory object

❑ Use the UIFactory object to create an instance of the actual UI object

It is certainly a substantially more expensive operation to create an instance of the UI object and perform the instanceof operator on it – only to find out that it does not support the required interface. Comparing the string representation of the interface is substantially faster. Furthermore, the 'template matching' mechanism supported by the lookup services that we have examined before is extremely efficient in handling these comparisons – further justifying the performance versus duplicated data tradeoff that has been made.

The attributes field of the UIDescriptor contains a java.util.Set collection of serializable Java objects. Any serializable object may be included, although the following entries are recommended:

Attribute Type	Description
net.jini.lookup.ui.attribute. UIFactoryTypes	Provides a Set of interface types supported by the MarshalledObject in the UI factory field. This allows a client to find the desired UI factory type without unmarshalling the MarshalledObject (and potentially incurring the performance hit of network code-download during unmarshalling).

Attribute Type	Description
net.jini.lookup.ui.attribute. RequiredPackages	Provides information on the minimum required packages (and their version numbers) to run the UI. There is no requirement for this to be exhaustive.
net.jini.lookup.ui.attribute. Locales	Provides information on the locales that are supported by the resulting UI.
net.jini.lookup.ui.attribute. AccessibleUI (only if the UI supports accessibility)	A marker interface indicating that the resulting UI will support the accessibility API (special access technology assisting handicapped individuals).

The very first release of ServiceUI specifies eight UI factory interfaces for creating factories for GUI based UIs. They include:

UI Factory Interface	Creates an UI object based on:
DialogFactory	java.awt.Dialog or subclass
FrameFactory	java.awt.Frame or subclass
JComponentFactory	javax.swing.JComponent or subclass
JDialogFactory	javax.swing.JDialog or subclass
JFrameFactory	javax.swing.JFrame or subclass
JWindowFactory	javax.swing.JWindow or subclass
PanelFactory	java.awt.Panel or subclass
WindowFactory	java.awt.Window or subclass

Any application or service may define specific UI factory interfaces. Unfortunately, this can cause a quick and sudden explosion of UI factory interfaces for any particular new user interface library. It is recommended that the definition of new UI factory types (for non-proprietary user interface libraries) be coordinated through the Jini community process.

Putting ServiceUI to Work

Let us put ServiceUI to work and see how we can actually attach a user interface to a service. Our service will support one single RMI based interface. It has two methods. The interface is called ActionItf. You can find its source code in the ch9\code\Servui directory, in the ActionItf.java file:

```
import java.rmi.*;

public interface ActionItf extends Remote
  {
    public void firstAPI() throws RemoteException;
    public void secondAPI() throws RemoteException;
  }
```

What we would like to do is to attach a two button user interface to this service. When the first button is clicked, the `firstAPI()` method will be called, and the `secondAPI()` method will be called when the second button is pressed.

This simple program will illustrate most of the aspects that are important when attaching a UI to a Jini service.

As of Jini 1.1, `ServiceUI` is not part of the standard library. You may download the latest available libraries from the `ServiceUI` project from http://www.jini.org. The library is distributed in ZIP format. We can add the library to the `JINIJARS` by modifying the `setpaths.bat` file.

```
set JINIHOME=d:\jini1_1
set WROXHOME=d:\wroxstubs
set DOWNLOADHOST=win98p300:8080
set STUBHOST=win98p300:8081
set ADAPTERIP=192.168.23.30
set JINITEMP=d:\temp
set JINIJARS=%JINIHOME%\lib\jini-core.jar;%JINIHOME%\lib\jini-ext.jar;
    %JINIHOME%\lib\sun-util.jar;%JINIHOME%\lib\uiapi100.zip
```

Next, we need to create the two `ButtonUI` classes. You can find this in the `ch9\code\Servui\ButtonUI.java` file. We will base it on a `java.awt.Panel`. This allows us to layout the two buttons and wire up the associated `ActionListeners`.

```
import java.awt.*;
import net.jini.lookup.ui.MainUI;
import java.awt.event.*;
```

This is the `MainUI` of our service, so we need to implement the `net.jini.lookup.ui.MainUI` role interface. Since we will also handle button clicks, we implement the `ActionListener` interface as well:

```
public class ButtonUI extends java.awt.Panel implements
    ActionListener,MainUI,java.io.Serializable
{
    ActionItf myItf;
    Button but1 = null;
    Button but2 = null;
    public ButtonUI() {}
```

The constructor takes as a parameter a service object (we know it implements the `ActionItf` interface by definition). It saves the reference to this service object for later use when the button is pressed. Within the constructor, the buttons are created and the `ActionListener` is hooked up to the same class:

```
public ButtonUI(ActionItf inAct)
  {
    myItf = inAct;
    but1 = new Button("Call first API.");
    but2 = new Button("Call second API.");
    but1.addActionListener(this);
    but2.addActionListener(this);
    add(but1);
    add(but2);
  }
```

To handle the button presses (via the `ActionListener` interface), the `actionPerformed()` method determines which button is pressed and calls the corresponding method of the `ActionItf` interface accordingly:

```
public void actionPerformed(ActionEvent evt)
  {
    try
      {
        if (evt.getSource().equals(but1))
          {
            myItf.firstAPI();
          }
        else
          {
            myItf.secondAPI();
          }
      }
    catch (Exception ex)
      {
        ex.printStackTrace();
      }
  }
}
```

We can now create a factory for our Panel based UI class. The `UIDescriptor` requires a UI factory. Since the UI is Panel based, we should create a factory that is derived from `net.jini.lookup.ui.factory.PanelFactory`. For the `getPanel()` method, we simply create an instance of a `ButtonUI` object. Note that we pass the role object – for `mainUI` it is the service object – into the newly created `ButtonUI` instance. You can find the source code in the `ch9\code\Servui` directory, in the `MyUIFact.java` file:

```
import net.jini.lookup.ui.factory.PanelFactory;
import java.awt.*;

public class MyUIFact implements PanelFactory,java.io.Serializable
  {
    public MyUIFact() {}
    public Panel getPanel(Object roleObj)
      {
        ButtonUI myUI = new ButtonUI((ActionItf) roleObj);
        Panel myPanel = (Panel) myUI;
        return myPanel;
      }
  }
```

Finally, we can now create the Jini service. The source code is found in `ch9\code\Servui\ServicUIPr.java` file:

```
import net.jini.lookup.JoinManager;
import net.jini.discovery.LookupDiscoveryManager;
import java.rmi.RemoteException;
import java.rmi.RMISecurityManager;
import net.jini.lookup.ServiceIDListener;
import java.rmi.server.UnicastRemoteObject;
import net.jini.lookup.entry.*;
import java.rmi.MarshalledObject;
import net.jini.core.entry.Entry;
```

ServUIPr inherits from `UnicastRemoteObject` to make RMI implemention of the `ActionItf` interface simple. Any reference to `ServUIPr` that is exported outside the VM will be referring to the RMI stub instead.

```
public class ServUIPr extends UnicastRemoteObject implements ActionItf
  {
    static final String [] GROUPS1 = { "iguanas" };
    protected JoinManager myJM = null;
    public static void main(String argv[])
      {
        ServUIPr myApp = null;
        try
          {
            myApp = new ServUIPr();
            synchronized(myApp)   {
            myApp.wait(0);
          }
        }
    catch(Exception e)
      {
        e.printStackTrace();
        System.exit(0);
      }
  }
```

The constructor has to register the proxy object (RMI stub for the `ActionItf` interface). It will be done via a `JoinManager` the same way we have done previously. This time, we will also attach a `UIDescriptor` as an attribute, following the `ServiceUI` specifications:

```
public ServUIPr() throws RemoteException
  {
    if (System.getSecurityManager() == null)
      System.setSecurityManager(new RMISecurityManager());

    LookupDiscoveryManager ldm = null;
    String [] groupsToDiscover = GROUPS1;
    UIDescriptor myDesc = null;
    try
      {
```

The `UIDescriptor` is initialized with the role (`ButtonUI`'s role, which is "net.jini.lookup.ui.MainUI"), a toolkit (`myUIFact`'s toolkit, which is "java.awt"), no attached attributes, and an instance of the UI factory within a `MarshalledObject` as the fourth parameter:

```
myDesc = new UIDescriptor(ButtonUI.ROLE, MyUIFact.TOOLKIT, null, new
    MarshalledObject(new MyUIFact()) );

Entry [] attributes = new Entry[1];
attributes[0] = myDesc;
ldm = new LookupDiscoveryManager(groupsToDiscover, null, null);
```

We supply the `JoinManager` with the RMI stub (also the service's proxy object), and attributes that contain the `UIDescriptor` that we have just created:

```
        myJM = new JoinManager(this, attributes,(ServiceIDListener)
                            null,ldm,null);
    }
  catch (Exception e)
    {
      e.printStackTrace();
      System.exit(1);
    }
  }
```

Implementation of the remote `ActionItf` interface means implementing the `firstAPI()` and `secondAPI()` methods. Our implementation will simply print a message when the method is called:

```
public void firstAPI() throws RemoteException
  {
    System.out.println("First API called remotely...");
  }
public void secondAPI() throws RemoteException
  {
    System.out.println("Second API called remotely...");
  }
}
```

Copy over, from the `ch9\code\Servui` directory, the file `ActionItf.class`. Use the command line to compile the service:

`..\bats\buildit ServUIPr.java`

The `makejar.bat` file must create a JAR that includes the following:

❑ The RMI stub (Jini proxy) for the `ActionItf` interface

❑ `ActionItf` interface itself

❑ The `ButtonUI` class

❑ The Panel UI factory class

To create the RMI stub, we need to run the RMIC tool on the `ServUIPr.class` file. The `makejar.bat` file combines all these operations into one batch file:

```
call setpaths.bat
rmic servUIpr
jar cvf servUIpr-dl.jar servUIpr_Stub.class ActionItf.class buttonUI.class
myUIFact.class
copy servUIpr-dl.jar %JINIHOME%\lib
```

Let us now turn our attention to the client that will be looking for the Jini service and its associated user interface. This client will be a `java.awt.Frame` itself. Once it finds a Panel based UI for the service, it will add the UI to its frame. In this way, the user can interact directly with the service using the Panel UI supplied by the service. The following figure illustrates the client and the embedded user interface supplied by the service:

471

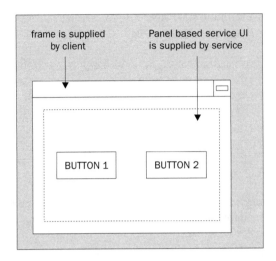

frame is supplied
by client

Panel based service UI
is supplied by service

BUTTON 1   BUTTON 2

The source code for the client can be found in the `ch9\code\Uiclient\UIClient.java` file. Here is the listing:

```
import net.jini.discovery.*;
import net.jini.core.lookup.*;
import java.rmi.RemoteException;
import java.rmi.RMISecurityManager;
import net.jini.lookup.*;
import java.io.IOException;
import net.jini.lookup.ui.factory.PanelFactory;
import net.jini.core.entry.Entry;
import net.jini.lookup.entry.*;

import java.awt.*;
```

The client itself inherits from `java.awt.Frame`. It is used to contain the Panel based user interface that is attached to the Jini service.

```
public class UIClient extends Frame implements DiscoveryListener
    {
        protected ServiceRegistrar [] registrars;
```

The `main()` method creates an instance of the `UIClient` (a `Frame`) and calls its `show()` method to ensure the frame GUI is visible:

```
static public void main(String args[])
    {
      UIClient myApp = null;
      String tpItf = null;

      myApp = new UIClient("Using ServiceUI");
      myApp.show();

      try
        {
          Thread.sleep(200001);
        }
```

```
       catch (Exception ex)
         {
           ex.printStackTrace();
           System.exit(1);
         }
   }
```

The constructor installs an `RMISecurityManager`, and creates a `LookupDiscovery` to discover the 'iguanas' group:

```
   public UIClient(String title)
     {
       super(title);
       if (System.getSecurityManager() == null)
           System.setSecurityManager(new RMISecurityManager());

       LookupDiscovery discover = null;
       String [] myGroups = { "iguanas" };
       try
         {
           discover = new LookupDiscovery(LookupDiscovery.NO_GROUPS);
           discover.addDiscoveryListener(this);
           discover.setGroups(myGroups);
         }
       catch (IOException e)
         {
           e.printStackTrace();
           System.exit(1);
         }
   }
```

The `doAct()` method is called whenever a registrar (handling the 'iguanas' group) is discovered. It will look for a service that supports the `ActionItf` interface and has a UI attached.

```
   protected void doAct()
     {
```

`myClass` contains the type that we are matching on during the lookup, in our case the `ActionItf` interface:

```
   Class [] myClass = new Class[1];
       try
         {
           myClass[0] =  ActionItf.class;
```

`attributes` contains the `UIDescriptor` (an `Entry`) that we are trying to match on during the lookup. We want it to have a toolkit of `java.awt`, and a role of `net.jini.lookup.ui.MainUI`:

```
   UIDescriptor myDesc = null;
       myDesc = new UIDescriptor("net.jini.lookup.ui.MainUI", "java.awt", null,
                                 null );
       Entry [] attributes = new Entry[1];
       attributes[0] = myDesc;
       ServiceMatches myMatch = null;
```

We perform the lookup and try to match at most one entry:

```
myMatch = registrars[0].lookup(new ServiceTemplate
                            (null,myClass,attributes), 1);
Panel myPanelUI = null;
```

If we find one, we need to scan through all its attributes to find the `UIDescriptor` attributes that we need (`role` of `MainUI` and `toolkit` of `"java.awt"`):

```
if (myMatch.totalMatches > 0)
  {
    ServiceItem myItem = myMatch.items[0];
    for (int i=0; i< myItem.attributeSets.length; i++)
      {
        if (myItem.attributeSets[i] instanceof UIDescriptor)
          {
            UIDescriptor mydesc = (UIDescriptor) myItem.attributeSets[i];
```

Once we find the attributes, we will extract (unmarshall) the UI factory and use it to create an instance of the UI that we need. The instance of the Panel UI created by the factory is stored in the `myPanelUI` variable:

```
        if (mydesc.toolkit.equals("java.awt") &&
            mydesc.role.equals("net.jini.lookup.ui.MainUI"))
          {
            PanelFactory myfact = (PanelFactory)
            mydesc.getUIFactory(this.getClass().getClassLoader());
            myPanelUI = myfact.getPanel((ActionItf) myItem.service);
            break;
          }
      } // of outer if
  } //of for int i
```

Finally, we add the newly created UI (`ButtonUI`) to our `Frame`, and call the `Frame`'s `pack()` method to fit the `Frame` around the `Panel` based UI:

```
      if (myPanelUI != null)
        {
          add(myPanelUI);
          pack();
        }
  } // of if totalMatches
else
  System.out.println("Lookup failed.");
}
catch (Exception ex)
  {
    ex.printStackTrace();
    System.exit(1);
  }
}
public synchronized void discovered(DiscoveryEvent evt)
  {
    registrars = evt.getRegistrars();
    System.out.println("discovered " + registrars.length + " registrars!");
    if (registrars.length > 0)
```

```
        {
            doAct();
        }
    }

    public void discarded(DiscoveryEvent evt) {}

}
```

Copy over the `ActionItf.class` file from the `ch9\code\Servui` directory. Compile the client by running the batch file:

`..\bats\buildit UIClient.java`

We can now test this `ServiceUI` based implementation. First, ensure that:

- ❑ A class server is running (`runhttpd.bat`)
- ❑ A class server for stubs running (`runhttpdstubs.bat`)
- ❑ The rmid activation daemon s running (`runrmid.bat`)
- ❑ A reggie handling the 'iguanas' group is running (`runlookup1.bat`)

Change directory to `ch9\code\Servui` and run the batch file `runui.bat`. This starts the `ServUIPr` service.

Open a new console, change directory to `ch9\code\Uiclient`, and run the client by starting the `runclient.bat` file.

Initially, you will see an empty frame (of the client) appear. After a little while, the client will locate the service and its associated Panel based UI. The final UI of the client (combined with the service's UI) will look like this:

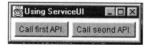

Try clicking on either button. This will result in a remote call through the `ActionItf` remote interface. Each time a button is pressed, the service side should print out a status message. Your output will be similar to that shown here:

Extending the ServiceUI Paradigm to the Distributed Environment

Just as `Norm` extends the `LeaseRenewalManager` into the distributed realm, we can imagine services that extend the ServiceUI paradigm. What will happen then? Instead of translating for a single client that is using the Jini service, we end up with a translation service that is applicable to the entire Jini network! Essentially, one can have a user interface service that provides a specific class of interfaces (such as GUI) to any and all Jini services! Continuing this line of thought, we can see technology that will translate or adapt existing and common user interface technology to the world of Jini.

What existing and common user interface technologies are there that require or will benefit from such translation? Imagine a translation service that maps:

❑   HTTP and HTML to Jini services

❑   Telnet protocol and the VT-100 standard cursor addressing commands to Jini services

❑   Dual tone (DTMF) from 10 digits touch pads and synthesized voice response to Jini services

This essentially provides gateway services from existing worlds into the Jini network. Viewed in the other, more compelling direction, it opens up the Jini network for use by a substantially larger population. It extends the benefit of the distributed 'network becoming the computer' to all of the web browser users of the world, all the users on VT-100 terminals, and all the owners of telephones, respectively.

Now, clearly, not all Jini services can benefit from such translations – just as not all user interface technologies will apply to all applications. It is safe to say, however, that most Jini services will have at least a portion of their functionality (administration, configuration, etc.) that can benefit from having these translation services available.

As it stands today, these are wide-open areas for Jini designers to hone their craft. There are no Sun specified standards in these areas, and the Jini.org community is open for starting these new projects. In fact, much of the work already done in the ServiceUI project can be leveraged and extended effectively to accommodate these translation services.

Summary

In this chapter, we focused our attention on details that need to be worked out when creating Jini services. We started with the partitioning of work, and mode of communications, between the proxy object and the service. Working with actual code examples, we have investigated five distinctly different alternatives.

In the first alternative, the proxy does all the work. This has the advantage that all computing is done on the client, leaving the service free to do almost anything it desires.

In the second alternative, the service does all the work. In fact, the proxy is actually an RMI stub – calling back to the service to get work done.

In the third alternative, we discussed a smart proxy. Some processing is done by the proxy in the client's VM while the rest is done back in the service. An RMI interface, usually not the same as the one that the service supports for client access, provides the communication between the service and proxy.

In the fourth alternative, the processing is still split between the service and the proxy, but the communications between the two is now done via socket level proprietary protocols. This allows rapid integration of socket based protocol servers into Jini.

In the fifth alternative, the processing is split between the service and proxy, and the proxy is actually a CORBA client – mapping calls to its interface into CORBA network calls.

After considering the architecture aspect of creating a Jini service, we looked at special services that are not quite services: device drivers.

Jini is natural for implementing network devices as services. The dynamic federating capability, long-lived fault-resilience, and self-healing properties are ideal for the deployment of devices as Jini services.

Examining the lower level details, we realized that many devices may not have (or be able) to run full Java VMs in order to support Jini. We then looked at three different ways of allowing non-Java devices to participate in a Jini network. Firstly, we can use Norm, Fiddler, and Mercury to provide essential services to a non-Java client; however, this approach is deemed too expensive. Secondly, we can write customized services, even in programming languages other than Java, that will monitor IIOP packets on-the-wire and play back canned responses to them; the JDK 1.3+ support for RMI-IIOP will enable this to occur. The major disadvantage of this approach is that it is prone to obsolescence as soon as the protocol or interface changes. The third, and most feasible, solution was called the Jini Technology Surrogate Architecture. In this case, a surrogate host can host many surrogates, each representing a unique Jini service/device. The surrogate works with interconnect adapters that have hardware technology specific links to control the devices and/or services.

The final portion of this chapter dealt with a common request for Jini services: the ability to attach multiple user interfaces to a service. Clients can then select the most suitable user interface and present it to the end user. A successful Jini.org project called ServiceUI addressed exactly this problem. We examined the details behind ServiceUI and created our very own application working with dynamically attached user interfaces.

At this juncture, the torch is passed onto you – pragmatic programmers. You can now design and build distributed Jini based systems. In the next chapter, we will examine one remaining technology that makes our lives much easier. It is called JavaSpaces, and it is yet another Jini service.

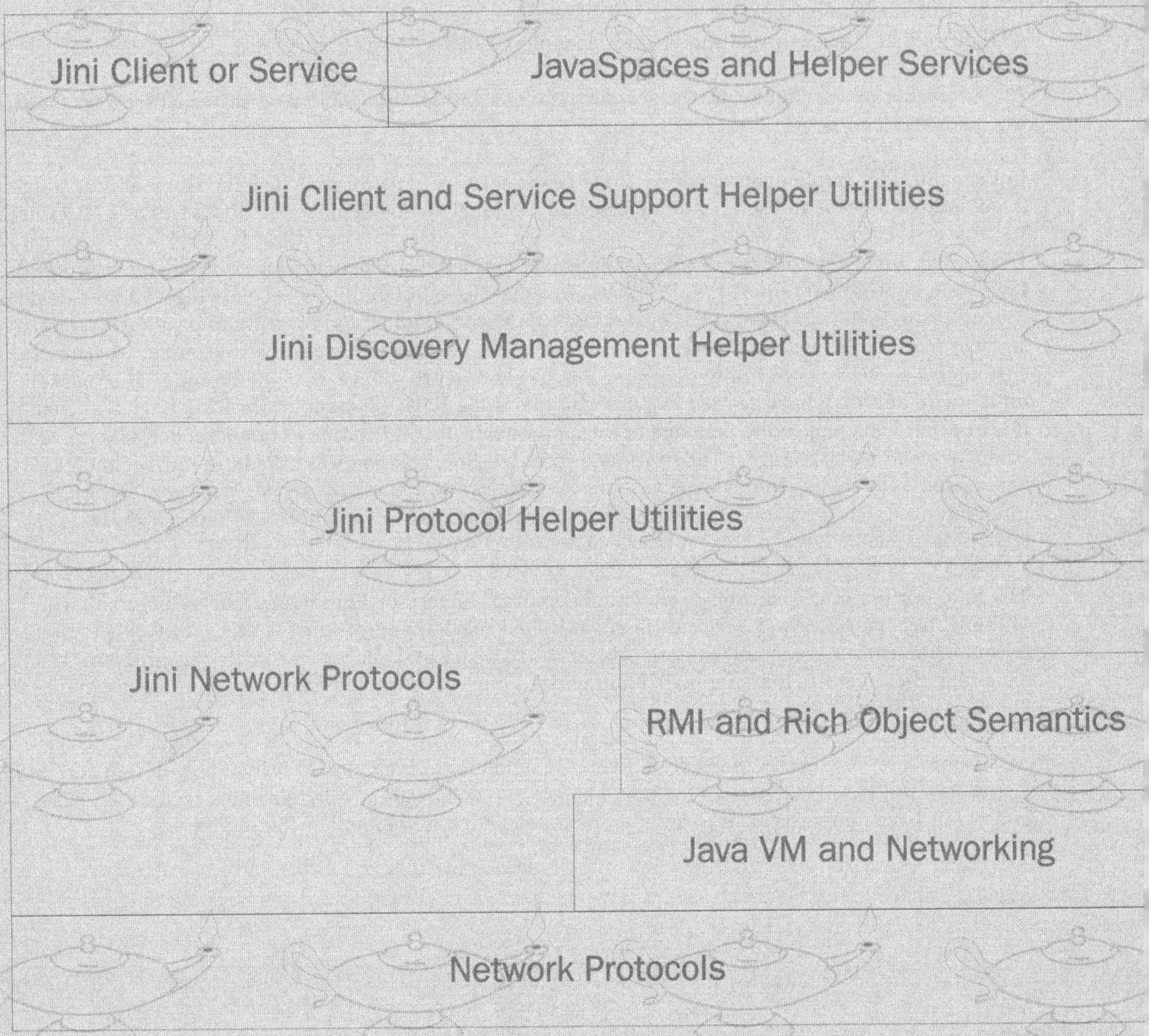

Jini Client or Service	JavaSpaces and Helper Services

Jini Client and Service Support Helper Utilities

Jini Discovery Management Helper Utilities

Jini Protocol Helper Utilities

Jini Network Protocols

RMI and Rich Object Semantics

Java VM and Networking

Network Protocols

13
JavaSpaces as a Jini Service

It's easy to summarize the JavaSpaces technology: JavaSpaces store Java objects. It is a Jini service that allows distributed services to share data and behavior, accessed though the interface `net.jini.space.JavaSpace`. What JavaSpaces should be used for, however, is a rather more complicated question, and best approached by looking at the overriding design principles of Jini Services.

There is a common design principle behind the Jini services: although reggie, mercury, norm, fiddler and JavaSpaces each has specific functionality and design goals, together they form a set of fundamental services that are accessible to virtually any application. They are designed to be generic enough to be useful both to the applications that are around now and those to come.

JavaSpaces stretches this principle even further – it doesn't have a prescribed application. It doesn't even come with 'recommended use' guidelines. You'll come across JavaSpaces being put to a lot of diverse uses – anything from a distributed data store for objects, or a queuing service, to a synchronization point for use in formalized distributed algorithms, for example. Of course, the truth is JavaSpaces can be put to all of these uses, and a lot of others besides (see Bob Flenner's **JWorkPlace** case study in Chapter 17 for a powerful implementation). JavaSpaces adds that little bit more to Jini by making distributed applications really simple.

In this chapter, we will work closely with JavaSpaces, using plenty of code examples. We'll look at:

❑ The interface that defines a JavaSpace, and its key methods

❑ Rigger, the reference implementation

❑ The role transactions play

❑ Some of the uses JavaSpaces might be put to, putting together our own 'compute serve' implementation

❑ Implementing JavaSpaces to solve our own domain problems

This really is a radically different way of designing distributed computational systems!

Jini Services: Facilitatating Distributed Architectures

Jini allows us to build distributed, long-lived, self-healing systems that have no single point-of-failure. The cornerstones of a basic Jini system: loosely coupled lookup services, group partitioning, dynamic federations, remote bridging, distributed leasing, and remote events, allow system designers to dream up all manner of custom distributed system architecture solutions.

No matter how sophisticated a technology might be, designing a distributed architecture that works well for a specific application is always going to involve a lot of work. JavaSpaces significantly eases the process of building adaptable, distributed system architecture. It is made up of:

❑ A conceptual (distributed) working model of service interaction with JavaSpaces (inside or outside transactions)

❑ Interface access to a JavaSpace

❑ Sample starter architectural patterns, to help design systems

Linda Systems, the brainchild of Dr. David Gelernter of Yale University, inspired JavaSpaces technology. Dr. Gelernter discovered that complex distributed computing problems, until then tackled with a complex network of custom coding using low-level languages, could be better and more simply expressed through what amounts to a set of well-defined read/write operations on a shared store. This new direction in thought was monumental in the Massively Parallel Processing (MPP) world.

The UNIX Pipe

Developers, who've been exposed to UNIX, or variants such as Linux, will appreciate the power of the pipe operator. It really wasn't obvious, at first, why simple two-dimensional chaining (processing output together with processing input from different processes) was so powerful and enabling. In the 80s, Dr. Gelernter and his team made sense of this, through their formalization of the concept of an n-dimensional reliable object pipe operator in the form of the Linda system.

Essentially, JavaSpaces can be viewed as a means for distributed processes to transfer their processing results amongst themselves, or to synchronize with each other. More significantly, one can see from the UNIX pipe analogy how different distributed processing services can work dynamically together, without each service anticipating programmatically every possible future use.

JavaSpaces took off from the tuple-based system Linda Systems; leveraging the object mobility enabled by Java and RMI to provide a higher-level abstraction for Jini system designers to use in the creation of their own distributed processing systems. Being a Jini service, JavaSpaces enjoys the potentially long-lived, self-healing, and optionally transacted execution environment.

While some proponents of JavaSpaces insist that the technology can be used to create distributed systems outside the Jini context, it is almost impossible (at the current state of development) to separate the interdependency of the two. Furthermore, we certainly couldn't recommend that developers without in-depth knowledge of Jini and its fundamentals should attempt JavaSpaces implementation.

It is for this very reason that JavaSpaces hasn't been covered until now. You hopefully have a solid understanding of Jini, and have had plenty of hands-on experience with the many facets (and failure models) of Jini-based systems. You are well positioned to begin the theory and practice of JavaSpaces.

There is more than one project at `Jini.org` currently addressing this problem (the most famous of these being **Out-Of-The-Box**). Despite these efforts, simplifying JavaSpaces can only realistically come after the Jini technology itself matures, stabilizes, and gets into the mainstream. In fact, JavaSpace really is **simple** once Jini is understood.

The Remarkably Unremarkable JavaSpace Interface

This is the definition of the JavaSpace interface, in the package `net.jini.space.JavaSpace`:

```
public interface JavaSpace {

  Lease write(Entry e, Transaction txn, long lease) throws RemoteException,
    TransactionException;

  Entry read(Entry tmpl, Transaction txn, long timeout) throws
    TransactionException, UnusableEntryException, RemoteException,
    InterruptedException;

  Entry readIfExists(Entry tmpl, Transaction txn, long timeout) throws
    TransactionException, UnusableEntryException, RemoteException,
    InterruptedException;

  Entry take(Entry tmpl, Transaction txn, long timeout) throws
    TransactionException, UnusableEntryException, RemoteException,
    InterruptedException;

  Entry takeIfExists(Entry tmpl, Transaction txn, long timeout) throws
    TransactionException, UnusableEntryException, RemoteException,
    InterruptedException;

  EventRegistration notify(Entry tmpl, Transaction txn, RemoteEventListener
    listener, long lease, MarshalledObject handback) throws RemoteException,
    TransactionException;

  Entry snapshot(Entry e) throws RemoteException;
}
```

All you need to know in order to work with the JavaSpaces service is how to use this interface. There are really only three operations that you need to be familiar with: **read**, **take**, and **write**, and each operation in this very small set is very straightforward.

The Basic JavaSpaces Premise

JavaSpaces, as we said at the beginning of the chapter, provides a distributed, shared object storage area. Any Jini client capable of obtaining the proxy object to a JavaSpace service can write and read objects to hand from the space. These objects are stored non-hierarchically. They are, in the main, available to everyone all the time (although this is not entirely accurate if you are working with transactions, as we shall see later). A reader obtains the objects that it wants using template matching based on entries, just as lookup is performed by Jini lookup services.

The Simple JavaSpaces Operations

Derived from the Linda System operation, and based on tuples, JavaSpaces define only three different actions, each having two modes of operation: `read`, `write`, and `take`. They implement blocking and non-blocking semantics. There is also an asynchronous notification registration method available, `notify()`, that utilizes Jini remote events.

The following diagram illustrates the basic operations on a JavaSpace, which we'll look into in more detail next:

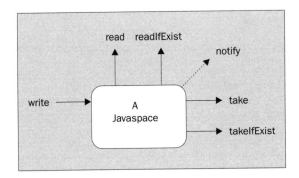

The Write Operation

```
Lease write(Entry e, Transaction txn, long lease) throws RemoteException,
    TransactionException;
```

When an entry (a subclass of a Jini entry) is written to a JavaSpace, its serialized content is stored. The following Java elements are stored within the JavaSpace:

❑   The fields of the entry in serialized form

❑   An RMI codebase annotation that can be used to retrieve the class information on the entry

This information allows the object to be re-constituted for any reader of the JavaSpace. If you write the same entry multiple times, there will be multiple copies of the entry residing in the space. A successful write operation returns a lease, which the writer must renew in order to keep the written entry in the space.

The Read Operation

```
Entry read(Entry tmpl, Transaction txn, long timeout) throws TransactionException,
    UnusableEntryException, RemoteException, InterruptedException;
```

JavaSpaces attempts to match a user-filled template against the entries held in the store. Using an associative search, a copy of the appropriate entry will be retrieved and returned to the reader of the space. Any null fields in the template entry act as wildcards during the match operation.

An entry matched by the search is not removed from the JavaSpace, and another client can read the same entry from the space either concurrently or subsequently. The JavaSpace will return one of any entries that match, but can't make any guarantees about the one that will be returned.

The read method of the JavaSpace interface uses blocking. The caller will be blocked until ether a matching entry becomes available, or a specified timeout period has elapsed. The readIfExist() method provides a non-blocking variant that reads entries only if an immediate match can be made (again, transactions blur this issue, as we'll discuss later).

The Take Operation

```
Entry take(Entry tmpl, Transaction txn, long timeout) throws TransactionException,
    UnusableEntryException, RemoteException, InterruptedException;
```

The take operation works much like the read operation, with the difference that it removes the object from the space. A copy of the entry is re-constituted from the serialized data and codebase annotation.

If more than one client attempts to take the same object from a JavaSpace simultaneously, one of them, and only one, will successfully match and retrieve it. JavaSpaces doesn't guarantee that the client who made the take request first will in fact be successful.

The write and take operations have the very desirable property of being similar to the operation of object-flow implementations. That is, a particular entry can flow from a service into a JavaSpace, and from there to another service, in a robust and tractable manner.

The take() method blocks while it is in operation for specified timeout period. The takeIfExists() variant, however, returns immediately if a match cannot be found (again, transactions are the exception).

Blocking versus Non-Blocking Operations

```
Entry readIfExists(Entry tmpl, Transaction txn, long timeout) throws
    TransactionException, UnusableEntryException, RemoteException,
    InterruptedException;
Entry takeIfExists(Entry tmpl, Transaction txn, long timeout) throws
    TransactionException, UnusableEntryException, RemoteException,
    InterruptedException;
```

Clients that wish to operate in non-blocking mode can use the XXXIfExist() form of the read or take operations. These methods, however, require clients to perform polling (running occasional checks for a matching entry), which is fine when it is an integral part of the applications' design in any case. The blocking call is more appropriate for applications that may not have anything to do unless there is a successful entry read or take. Alternatively, such applications might make use of asynchronous remote events by using the notify method.

As we have seen, both blocking and non-blocking forms of the read/take method have timeout parameters. Their semantics, however, are completely different. The blocking method's timeout stipulates, in milliseconds, the maximum time that operations will block waiting for a match. The non-blocking XXXIfExist() method **will** in fact block, but only when a matching entry actually exists in the space that is currently not visible to the reader, because of a managed transaction lock (implementation of transaction isolation). The timeout indicates how long the XXXXIfExist() caller is willing to wait for the entry to be made visible before giving up.

This brings up a very interesting point, and one that makes JavaSpaces such a simple technology to learn and apply (for Jini developers, anyway).

An Aside: Real Software Progress using Leverage upon Leverage

You'll probably appreciate by now the power of the concurrency abstraction provided by JavaSpaces, and how all the technologies involve leverage abstractions provided by the underlying environment: JavaSpaces leverages Jini which leverages the RMI's transport layer which leverages Java's platform-independence. This leveraging goes far beyond architectural or implementation re-use. The conceptual and pragmatic power of such a distributed system platform is arguably greater than any of its competitors.

The Notify Method

```
EventRegistration notify(Entry tmpl, Transaction txn, RemoteEventListener
    listener, long lease, MarshalledObject handback) throws RemoteException,
    TransactionException;
```

The notify() method, with its associated asynchronous notification, is based on Jini's remote event mechanism. An interested client can register remote listeners to wait for template matching within a JavaSpace. Instead of blocking (or polling on a non-blocked call), the JavaSpace user can elect to be notified when a match on a template occurs.

The manner in which Jini handles remote events means that the client receiving notification must attempt to take or read the matching entry from the space. There is, however, no guarantee that the matching entry will still be in the space by the time client performs this operation.

This means that JavaSpaces-based systems can accommodate a very large number of users, without designers having to deal with the complexity managing concurrency for such a system usually brings with it. Essentially, the JavaSpace implementer solves these tough problems once, and all the users of that space benefit thereafter.

Other Helper Methods

```
Entry snapshot(Entry e) throws RemoteException;
```

The **snapshot** method is used to optimize frequently accessed entries. By capturing a snapshot of such an entry (a commonly used template for matching, for example), this method frees the JavaSpace system from serializing the fields each time the entry is passed into the space. A snapshot entry is equivalent to the originating entry, when it is used as an entry in the operations of the JavaSpace that generated it. Despite this behavior, it is a new and distinct entry (pre-serialized snapshot), and you have to be careful about its identity – an equals comparison will show that it is not the same entry as the original that lies outside of the originating JavaSpace.

A snapshot is only meaningful within its originating context – within the same client Java VM on the same JavaSpace that generated it. It becomes unusable and meaningless outside that context. It's not possible, therefore, to serialize snapshots across VMs, or reuse snapshots across JavaSpaces.

JavaSpaces and Transactions

JavaSpaces leverage the core competency of Jini transactions beautifully, support for Jini transactions being integral to their design. Every operation that we have looked at so far has inbuilt transaction support.

Jini transactions are, as we have seen, indirectly supported by the provision of a distributed transaction co-coordinator, and a specified set of interfaces that a transaction service and participants must implement. Recall that the semantics of Jini transactions aren't specified. The support that ACID (Atomicity, Consistency, Isolation, and Durability) properties provide is not part of these transactions. Instead, the participants are free to implement any degree of ACID support as they see fit, from none at all complete compliance. We looked at the reference implementation of the transaction service, mahalo, which is essentially a distributed 2PC (two phase commit) protocol manager. It is designed to consistently handle the 2PC protocol across a distributed set of participant and able to survive both service and participant failures.

JavaSpaces leverage Jini transactions using the 2PC, and thereby cater for partial failures. The current reference implementation works well with the default semantics supplied by the mahalo. JavaSpace operations that are handled within a transaction are either entirely successful (and therefore committed), or none of them are carried out at all, and they're rolled back. The beauty of this, when applied in the distributed world of Jini and JavaSpaces, is that it will hold true across multiple participating spaces (geographically dispersed or otherwise) in a network. The underlying Jini support ensures that the system is long-lived, self-healing, and recovers from partial failures.

With this robust support, an object taken from one JavaSpace and written into any other JavaSpace (anywhere), within a transaction, can only end up in one of two places: the JavaSpace where it began, or the one it was destined for.

Aside: Resounding JavaSpaces Enthusiasm

WARNING: Many readers may find the following short aside a little over the top and think we're in the business of trying to sell them something. On the other hand, there will hopefully be readers to whom the short discussion that follows will be a real confirmation of their own past experiences of designing and programming activities, affirming the very reasons they've come to Jini and JavaSpaces in the first place. Within this in mind, I'm going to lead a short burst of unabashed JavaSpace cheerleading. Please feel free to skip this section if you're not of a particularly enthusiastic or excitable persuasion.

Many system designers and architects will immediately recognize the power of JavaSpaces' innocently simple guarantee. To better appreciate its significance, consider a conventional, non-JavaSpace system's approach:

> Data is moved from one storage area to another, possibly on a completely different platform
>
> Corresponding code has been matched (where there are different platforms) or transferred (in the case of similar platforms) between the two systems that will access the two different storage systems
>
> State information, a snapshot of execution, has been transferred (and translated in the case of different platforms) between the two systems

Imagine the C/C++ library code this would require, the line count that the necessary code would amass on each platform, in order to handle the circumstances. Consider the huge number of failure scenarios and exception handling code. Think of the concurrency handling, and recovery planning that would have to be taken care of. The implementation of this sizable project would require an experienced team of developers.

There really is an incredible energy and effort expenditure involved in such an implementation, dealing with a moderately complex project and a network of computers. The coding necessary to handle this work, much of which is simply repetitious, can amount to more than half the total development effort.

Using JavaSpaces, a new high-school graduate could code this setup in 5 lines, completing and testing the project in a single afternoon. Because of JavaSpaces' integral support for transactions, there are only ever two outcomes possible, and so there is simply no need for convoluted exception handling code. Moreover, JavaSpaces' integral concurrency support means that interaction between concurrent access and transaction visibility is beautifully handled without a single line of user code!

There is one more nail in the coffin of the more conventional design: interaction of concurrency with failure scenario. Suppose I intended to change the state of a system within a thread of execution, and I eventually failed – how do I ensure that every other concurrent thread that got a glimpse of my change of state 'forgets' what they saw?

One solution might be to hide all the intermediate state changes (essentially implementing our own transaction system), but coordinating this inhibited visibility across multiple network nodes really is fiddly, and anyway, we might want some parties to be able to see the changes while others can't.

The JavaSpace solution maintains a consistent transaction picture in the face of (even massive) concurrency. Only participants within the transaction, wherever they come from on the network, will see the state changes within the transaction. No JavaSpace users outside the transaction will see any effect of the transaction until it commits, regardless of the number and locations of the JavaSpaces involved. Not having to worry about these issues releases developers from the heavy design and coding load that usually accompanies a distributed computing project.

Visibility of State Changes and Transactions

Now is a good time to explain the timeout parameter of the XXXIfExist() method of the JavaSpaces interface. Essentially, a JavaSpace implementation must hide (using a transaction lock) the entries that are written into it within a transaction. These entries must not be made visible to any other client except for those who are part of the same transaction.

This means that entries held under the transaction lock are actually in the JavaSpace, but not visible to any JavaSpace users outside of the transaction. This holds true even when the transaction involves a set of JavaSpaces across a dispersed network. Since each JavaSpace implementation knows about the existence of these entries, the XXXIfExist() method can wait for them to become available, and be made visible to users outside of the transaction.

As we've seen, there are only two possible outcomes for a transaction. If the transaction successfully commits, its effect – including the locked "hidden" entries – will be made visible to the entire JavaSpace. At this point, if there are XXXIfExist() calls waiting, the transaction lock will be unlocked and the XXXIfExist() methods will return successfully with a copy of the entry (or compete for the entry in the case of a takeIfExist() operation). The following diagram illustrates this visibility (transaction isolation) control:

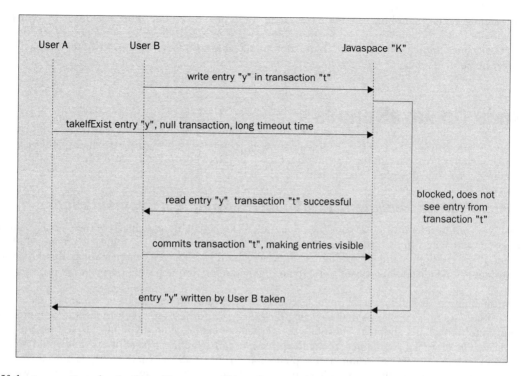

If the transaction aborts, then this entry will cease to exist. If there are other locked matching entries still in the JavaSpace, the XXXIfExist() calls may continue to wait. However, if the abort removes the last hidden matching entry within the JavaSpace, the XXXIfExist() method will return immediately with a failed match.

Using JavaSpaces, we only need to decide on the choice of a blocking or non-blocking call, and select a timeout value appropriate for our application.

Transactions and Distributed Events

Any listeners registered for remote events on a JavaSpace using the notify method will be transaction consistent. This means that, when a matching entry is written to a JavaSpace within a transaction:

❑   A listener registered within the same transaction will be notified as soon as the entry, which will be visible to it, is written (before commit or abort)

❑   A listener registered outside that transaction, or in another independent transaction, will be able to see a matching entry only after the transaction actually commits successfully, and will be notified only at commit time

When a matching entry is written to a JavaSpace outside a transaction, all listeners, either within or outside a transaction, will be able to see to the entry

Listener registrations within a transaction will disappear (be forgotten by the JavaSpace) once that transaction is committed or aborted.

A matching entry might be written in a transaction, and then taken out of the JavaSpace by someone inside the transaction, before it commits. In this case, even though there was a matching locked entry in the space once upon a time, and the transaction finally commits, listeners outside of the transaction will never be notified.

Hands On JavaSpaces

Time to visit some code. To get a JavaSpace running, you need to have Jini 1.1 beta or later installed, which includes JavaSpace in the distribution, on top of JDK version 1.2.2. Earlier releases of Jini required a separate download and install.

Transient versus Persistent JavaSpace Reference Implementations

Two versions of reference JavaSpace implementations are available: **outrigger**, which is persistent and **transient-outrigger**. In the rest of this chapter, we will be working with the transient version. Both of them offer exactly the same programmatic interface, as all JavaSpace implementations should, but the transient one is substantially easier to setup and maintain for simple testing purposes.

Transient outrigger will **forget** all the objects that are in its store upon restart or reboot, so it's particularly useful in scenarios that are using the JavaSpace for testing, synchronization, or non-storage applications. It's fairly simple to substitute the persistent version, should you need to test the full persistent features. To get the best of the long-lived, robust benefits of JavaSpaces, you would really need to look to commercial production implementations of JavaSpaces service (backed up with specialized hardware, fault-tolerant file systems, or relational database systems). There are, however, no such commercial JavaSpace service implementations available at the time of writing.

Starting the Transient outrigger

These are the steps you should follow to get a JavaSpace service running (assuming you're in the `ch13\code\bats\` directory):

- ❑ Clean any old reggie, rmid, and mahalo log files: use `runclean.bat` if you're using Win98, or manually remove the old log files on other systems

- ❑ Start a class server using the `runhttpd.bat` file

- ❑ Start a class server for stubs using the `runhttpdstubs.bat` file

- ❑ Start the rmid daemon using the `runrmid.bat` file

- ❑ Start a reggie instance that will manage the iguanas group using `runlookup1.bat`, and wait for the setup VM to complete its task

- ❑ Start the transaction service using `runmahalo.bat`, and wait for the setup VM to complete its task; (you should see a message on the rmid console)

- ❑ Start an instance of the transient outrigger service, with attribute Name=`"mySpace"`, using the command:

  ```
  runtspace mySpace
  ```

The `runtspace.bat` file contains:

```
call setpaths.bat
start java -jar -Djava.security.policy=policy.all -
Djava.rmi.server.codebase=http://%DOWNLOADHOST%/outrigger-dl.jar -
Dcom.sun.jini.outrigger.spaceName=%1 -Dnet.jini.discovery.interface=%ADAPTERIP%
%JINIHOME%\lib\transient-outrigger.jar iguanas
```

Notice the codebase of `outrigger-dl.jar` must be included, and that
`com.sun.jini.outrigger.spaceName` is used to specify a name for the instance (associated
attributed `name` for the service's proxy). If you do not specify one explicitly, the name `JavaSpace` will
be used. We've also specified in the code that this service should join the `iguanas` group. When you
run it, the transient outrigger will execute in its own console window. You must keep this console
running to keep the transient outrigger functional.

A Framework for JavaSpace Programming

In the `ch13\codespaceWrapper` directory, you will find a straightforward framework created for
simple JavaSpace programming. The sample file is called `SpaceWrapper.java`. All of the samples that
follow use this framework. The `SpaceWrapper.java` class acts as a super class for the majority of our
sample programs: it encapsulates Jini's handling of the discovery and join protocol. It can also be used
to locate a specifically named JavaSpace service. `SpaceWrapper.java` makes extensive use of the
`ServiceDiscoveryManager` utility class that we have covered previously. Here is the source code of
`SpaceWrapper.java`:

```java
import net.jini.core.lookup.*;
import net.jini.lookup.*;
import net.jini.discovery.*;
import java.rmi.RMISecurityManager;
import net.jini.lookup.entry.Name;
import net.jini.core.entry.Entry;
import net.jini.space.JavaSpace;
```

Next we specify some of the constant default values. We will wait for 30 seconds for the lookup operation
with the `ServiceDiscoveryManager`. The default group we are going to join is `iguanas`, and the
default name for the JavaSpace we're looking for is `JavaSpace` (outrigger's default instance name):

```java
public class SpaceWrapper {
  static final long MAX_LOOKUP_WAIT = 30000L;
  static final String DEFAULT_GROUP = "iguanas";
  static final String DEFAULT_SPACE_NAME = "JavaSpace";
  private String  [] myGroups = {DEFAULT_GROUP };
  private String  mySpaceName = DEFAULT_SPACE_NAME;
```

A static initializer will install an RMI Security manager. This allows the application to download outrigger stubs as necessary:

```
static {
  if (System.getSecurityManager() == null) {
      System.setSecurityManager(new RMISecurityManager());
  }
}
```

The `main` method forms a simple test method for the wrapper. It will take two command line arguments, one specifying the group to join, and the other one the name of the JavaSpace to find. It will attempt to join the group, find the JavaSpace, and report the status back to the user:

```
static public void main(String argv[]) {
  SpaceWrapper myApp = null;

  if (argv.length > 1)  {
    System.out.println("Looking for a JavaSpace named " + argv[1] + " within a
      group named " + argv[0]);
    myApp = new SpaceWrapper(argv[0]);
    JavaSpace mySpace =  myApp.locateSpace(argv[1]);
    if (mySpace == null)
      System.out.println("Cannot find space");
    else
      System.out.println("Space located");
  } // of if
}
```

The constructor takes as a parameter the group to be joined (although we're only supporting one group in this simplified version – that's all we need for the test). If the `inGroups` parameter is `null`, then we'll join all available groups in the local network:

```
public SpaceWrapper(String inGroups) {
  if (inGroups != null) {
    myGroups = new String[1];
    myGroups[0] = inGroups;
  }
  else
    myGroups = DiscoveryGroupManagement.ALL_GROUPS;
}
```

The `locateSpace` method performs a lookup for a specifically named JavaSpace service in the federation. It does so by creating a `ServiceDiscoveryManager` instance. The `erviceDiscoveryManager` uses a `LookupDiscovery` utility to join the group we specify:

```
protected ServiceDiscoveryManager mySDM = null;

public JavaSpace locateSpace(String inSpaceName) {

  try {
    LookupDiscovery discover = new LookupDiscovery(myGroups);
    mySDM = new ServiceDiscoveryManager(discover,null);
    if ((inSpaceName != null) && (inSpaceName.length() != 0))
      mySpaceName = inSpaceName;
```

The JavaSpace service is looked up via the Name attribute associated with its proxy object (within the ServiceItem) stored at the local lookup service. Here, we create a template for the lookup, specifying that it must match the name exactly:

```
Entry [] attributes = new Entry[1];
attributes[0] = new Name(mySpaceName);
```

We use the flexible lookup() method of the ServiceDiscoveryManager to search for the JavaSpace service amongst the managed set of lookup services.

```
ServiceItem mySI = mySDM.lookup(new ServiceTemplate(null, null,attributes),
    null, MAX_LOOKUP_WAIT);
if (mySI != null)
    return (JavaSpace) mySI.service;
}
catch(Exception e) {
  System.err.println(e.toString());
  e.printStackTrace();
  System.exit(1);
}
return null;
}
```

The finalize() method is used to shutdown all the additional threads and resources allocated by the instance, before exiting from the application instance:

```
public void finalize() {
  mySDM.terminate();
}

}
```

Compile this wrapper by going into the ch13\code\SpaceWrapper directory and using the command line:

```
..\bats\buildit SpaceWrapper.java
```

You can execute the test routine using the ch13\code\SpaceWrapper\testwrap.bat file that contains:

```
call ..\bats\setpaths.bat
java -classpath .;%JINIJARS%  -Dnet.jini.discovery.interface=%ADAPTERIP%  -
Djava.security.policy=policy.all  SpaceWrapper %1 %2
```

The first argument carries the group we intend to join, and the second the name of the JavaSpace we're looking for. In our case, we can use this command line in a console window:

```
testwrap iguanas mySpace
```

You should see output similar to this screenshot:

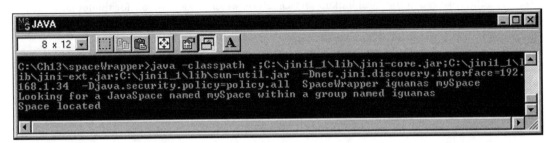

This class, `SpaceWrapper.java`, will be the super class to many of the following samples. Let's put it to use.

Writing to a JavaSpace

Any object within a JavaSpace must be a Jini entry (it must implement the `Entry` marker interface). Recall from our discussion in of entries that `Entry` implies that the fields must be serialized individually and independently – unlike object serialization.

Under the `ch13\codewritespace` directory, we define our own very simple entry, called `MyEntry.java`:

```java
import net.jini.core.entry.Entry;
public class MyEntry implements Entry {
  public String myAddedData = null;
  public MyEntry() {}
  public MyEntry(String inData) {
    myAddedData = inData;
  }
  public String getAddedData() {
      return myAddedData;
  }
}
```

The added value here is the string field `myAddedData`. We also provide a `getAddedData()` method for easy access to the field consistent with JavaBean semantics.

We'll walk through the code that adds instances of this entry to a JavaSpace. The source code can be found in `\code\writespace\Writespace.java`. It begins as you might expect:

```java
import net.jini.space.JavaSpace;
```

`Writespace` inherits from `SpaceWrapper`, which simplifies coding substantially. (You need to copy the `ch13\codespacewrapper\SpaceWrapper.class` file into the local `ch13\codewritespace` directory in order for it to compile properly):

```java
public class Writespace extends SpaceWrapper {
   static final long VERY_LONG_TIME = 60 * 1000 * 30;
   private String itemToWrite = "something";
   private String myGroup = "iguanas";
```

The command line takes four arguments:

- The group to join
- The name of the JavaSpace to find
- The `String` data to put into the `myAddedData` field of the `MyEntry` entry
- The number of instances of the entry to write into the JavaSpace

The `main()` method processes these command line arguments. The first initializes the superclass, and the rest are passed through to a call to the `writeIt()` method:

```
static public void main(String argv[]) {
  Writespace myApp = null;

  if (argv.length > 3) {
    myApp = new Writespace(argv[0]);
    try {
      myApp.writeIt(argv[1],argv[2],Integer.parseInt(argv[3]));
    }
    catch(Exception e) {
      System.exit(0);
    } //of catch
  } // of if
  else
    System.out.println("Incorrect usage!");
}
```

The constructor calls the super class's constructor, initializing the group to join. It also prints a status message out to the console to keep the user posted:

```
public Writespace(String inGroup) {
  super(inGroup);
  System.out.println("Locating group " + inGroup + "...");
}
```

The `writeIt` method is where the crux of the work takes place:

```
protected JavaSpace mySpace = null;
public void writeIt(String inSpaceName, String inData, int repeat)  {
```

First, we must locate the specifically named JavaSpace, using the SpaceWrapper's `locateSpace()` method:

```
try {
  mySpace = locateSpace(inSpaceName);
  if (mySpace != null)    {
    System.out.println("Located JavaSpace called " + inSpaceName);
```

Once we have located the outrigger instance, we use the `write()` method of the JavaSpace interface to write a new instance of `MyEntry` into the space. The command line request indicates the number of instances that will be written. Notice that entries in the space are leased, in order to maintain the long-lived and self-healing properties of the Jini network. We specify 30 minutes for the lease, which should give us enough time for our experimentation. The transaction argument is `null`, because we are not working within a transaction in this example (we will cover transactions in further depth in a later section):

```
        for (int i=0; i< repeat; i++) {
          mySpace.write(new MyEntry(inData), null, VERY_LONG_TIME);
          System.out.println("wrote entry " + (i+1));
        }
      }// of if
    }
    catch (Exception ex)   {
      ex.printStackTrace();
      System.exit(1);
    }
  }
}
```

Compile the code by using the command line:

```
..\bats\buildit Writespace.java
```

We need to create a downloadable JAR file containing the `MyEntry` class, and copy it to the codebase, as it is a custom entry that we have defined. This will enable generic clients and browsers to interpret our custom entry. This JAR file can be created via the `ch13\codewritespace\makejar.bat` file, which contains:

```
call ..\bats\setpaths.bat
jar cvf Writespace-dl.jar MyEntry.class
copy Writespace-dl.jar %WROXHOME%
```

Assuming you have setup the JavaSpace service as detailed earlier, we can now run the `writespace` program using the `\code\writespace\runwrite.bat` file. This file contains:

```
call ..\bats\setpaths.bat
java -classpath .;%JINIJARS%  -Dnet.jini.discovery.interface=%ADAPTERIP% -
Djava.security.policy=policy.all -
Djava.rmi.server.codebase=http://%STUBHOST%/Writespace-dl.jar Writespace %1 %2 %3
%4
```

We must include the codebase in this case, so that tools and browsers can find our custom `MyEntry` class. To execute the program, use the command line:

```
runwrite iguanas mySpace MYfirstENTRY 1
```

This is the output you should see when you execute the program:

The program has written an entry into the JavaSpace. We'll check this using the Sun's JavaSpace browser utility.

Working with JavaSpace's Browser Utility

Sun provides a graphical utility, similar to the Jini Lookup Service Browser that we used previously, to browse the content of JavaSpaces. It is provided as part of the `space-examples.jar` file in the \lib directory, under the Jini install directory. The actual class name is `com.sun.jini.example.spaceBrowser.Browser`. You can run and startup this browser using the batch file we've provided in `ch13\codebats\runjsbrowse.bat`. The file contains:

```
call setpaths.bat
java -classpath .;%JINIJARS%;%JINIHOME%/lib/space-examples.jar -
Dnet.jini.discovery.interface=%ADAPTERIP%  -Djava.security.policy=policy.all -
Djava.rmi.server.codebase=http://%DOWNLOADHOST%/space-examples-dl.jar
com.sun.jini.example.spaceBrowser.Browser -admin iguanas
```

The codebase points to classes that the client must download in the `space-examples.jar` file. Run the browser using the command, from the `ch13\codebats` directory:

`runjsbrowse`

You should see something looking very much like the lookup service browser:

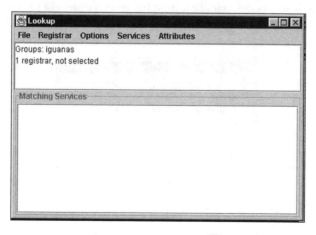

Next, choose the registrar from the **registrar** menu that we're interested in. You should see a line for the JavaSpace service proxy in the bottom list box:

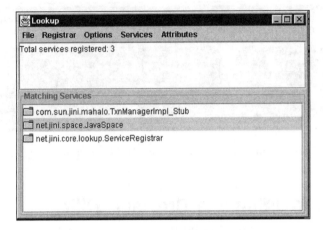

Highlight the JavaSpace service and click the right mouse button. A popup menu appears – select **Browse Entries**. A new window pops up showing all the entries currently in the JavaSpace:

We can see our newly written `MyEntry` instance in the space. In fact, if you double-click on the entry, the browser will download its class definition from the entry's codebase (this is why we needed the JAR file) and inspect, it to provide more information. In our case, we can see the actual value of the `myAddedData` field:

Reading Entries from a JavaSpace

Let's code our own method to read from JavaSpaces. Check the ch13\codereadspace directory for the source code to Readspace.java:

```
import net.jini.space.JavaSpace;
```

We extend SpaceWrapper to save coding. The maximum time we will wait in a blocking read operation is 2 minutes:

```
public class Readspace extends SpaceWrapper {
    static final long MAX_WAIT = 60 * 1000 * 2;
```

The main method processes three arguments: the group to join, the JavaSpace name, and the myAddedData field to match. Our read method will create a template with the specified value for the myAddedData field for matching:

```
static public void main(String argv[]) {
  Readspace myApp = null;
  if (argv.length > 2)
  {
    myApp = new Readspace(argv[0]);
    try {
      MyEntry tp =  myApp.readIt(argv[1],argv[2]);
      if (tp != null)
        System.out.println("successfully read entry");
      else
        System.out.println("cannot read entry");
    }
    catch(Exception e) {
      System.exit(0);
    } //of catch
  } // of if
  else
    System.out.println("Incorrect usage!");
  System.exit(0);
}
```

The constructor initializes the super class, as usual:

```
public Readspace(String inGroup) {
  super(inGroup);
  System.out.println("Locating group " + inGroup + "...");
}
```

The readIt method locates the JavaSpace using the superclass's helper method. It then performs a blocking read for the specified entry.

```
      protected JavaSpace mySpace = null;
      public MyEntry readIt(String inSpaceName, String inData)
      {
        try {
          mySpace = locateSpace(inSpaceName);
          if (mySpace != null) {
            System.out.println("Located JavaSpace called " + inSpaceName);

            return (MyEntry) mySpace.read(new MyEntry(inData), null, MAX_WAIT);
          }// of if
        }
        catch (Exception ex) {
          ex.printStackTrace();
          System.exit(1);
        }
        return null;
      }
    }
```

To compile this program, you will first need to copy `SpaceWrapper.class` from the `ch13\codespaceWrapper` directory, and copy `MyEntry.class` from the `ch13\codewritespace` directory.

Next, use the command line:

`..\bats\buildit Readspace.java`

We can try reading back the entry that we have written earlier using the `runread.bat` file:

```
call setpaths.bat
java -Djava.security.policy=policy.all readspace %1 %2 %3
```

To test the program, use this command line:

`runread iguanas mySpace MYfirstENTRY`

You should see the entry being read back:

Taking Entries from JavaSpaces

Next, we will remove the entry we have written from the JavaSpace. We do this using the `take` operation, essentially a read-and-remove atomic action. You'll find the source code in the `ch13\codetakespace\Takespace.java` file:

```
import net.jini.space.JavaSpace;
```

`Takespace.java` is based on `SpaceWrapper`. We will wait in blocking mode for a maximum of 2 minutes:

```
public class Takespace extends SpaceWrapper {

    static final long MAX_WAIT = 60 * 1000 * 2;
```

The `main` method takes three arguments: one for the group, one for the name of the JavaSpace, and one for the `myAddedData` field that matches the `MyEntry` instance within the space:

```
static public void main(String argv[]) {
  Takespace myApp = null;
  if (argv.length > 2)  {
    myApp = new Takespace(argv[0]);
    try {
       MyEntry tp =  myApp.takeIt(argv[1],argv[2]);
       if (tp != null)
          System.out.println("successfully took entry");
       else
          System.out.println("cannot take entry");
    }
    catch(Exception e) {
      System.exit(0);
    } //of catch
  } // of if
  else
    System.out.println("Incorrect usage!");
  System.exit(0);
}
public Takespace(String inGroup) {
  super(inGroup);
  System.out.println("Locating group " + inGroup + "...");
}
```

The `takeIt` method locates the specified JavaSpace, and then performs the blocking `take` operation:

```
protected JavaSpace mySpace = null;
public MyEntry takeIt(String inSpaceName, String inData) {
  try {
    mySpace = locateSpace(inSpaceName);
    if (mySpace != null) {
       System.out.println("Located JavaSpace called " + inSpaceName);
       return (MyEntry) mySpace.take(new MyEntry(inData), null, MAX_WAIT);
    }// of if
  }
  catch (Exception ex) {
    ex.printStackTrace();
    System.exit(1);
  }
  return null;
}
}
```

Copy `SpaceWrapper.class` and `MyEntry.class` (from the `ch13\codewritespace` directory) into the `ch13\codetakespace` directory. Use the following command line to compile the program:

```
..\bats\buildit Takespace.java
```

The `ch13\codetakespace\runtake.bat` file can be used to run the program; it contains:

```
call ..\bats\setpaths.bat
java -classpath .;%JINIJARS%  -Dnet.jini.discovery.interface=%ADAPTERIP% -
Djava.security.policy=policy.all takespace %1 %2 %3
```

Run the command line:

```
runtake iguanas mySpace MYfirstENTRY
```

Your output will should look like this:

This effectively removes the previously written entry from the JavaSpace. You can try the read operation again by changing directory to `\code\readspace`, and executing:

```
runread iguanas mySpace MYfirstENTRY
```

This time, the read will fail, and the output will be similar, after a short delay, to this:

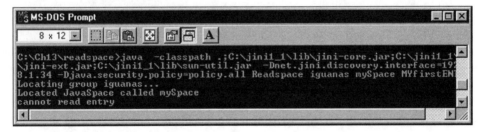

Working with Transactions

We'll try a `write` operation within a transaction, to see how transactions behave. Before doing this, we need to extend the simple `SpaceWrapper` class to include a method that will locate a transaction manager within the group. The new class is called `TrSpaceWrapper`, and the source code is in the `ch13\code\TrSpaceWrapper` directory:

```
import net.jini.core.lookup.*;
import net.jini.core.transaction.server.TransactionManager;
import net.jini.core.transaction.server.TransactionConstants;
import net.jini.space.JavaSpace;
```

All of the existing methods in `SpaceWrapper` are kept. We simply add the additional transaction support in the subclass.

```
public class TrSpaceWrapper extends SpaceWrapper {
```

We include a simple test in the `main` method. It will use the `locateSpace` method to find a JavaSpace service, the `locateTM` method to find a transaction manager, and notify the user of its success or failure through a status message:

```
static public void main(String argv[]) {
    TrSpaceWrapper myApp = null;
    if (argv.length > 1) {
    System.out.println("Looking for a JavaSpace named " + argv[1] + " within a
      group named " + argv[0]);
    myApp = new TrSpaceWrapper(argv[0]);
    JavaSpace mySpace =  myApp.locateSpace(argv[1]);
    if (mySpace == null)
      System.out.println("Cannot find space");
    else
      System.out.println("Space located");

    TransactionManager myTM = myApp.locateTM();
    if (myTM == null)
      System.out.println("Cannot find Transaction Manager");
    else
      System.out.println("Transaction Manager Located");
    } // of if
}


    public TrSpaceWrapper(String inGroups) {
      super(inGroups);
    }
```

`locateTM` is the only new method. It searches for an instance of mahalo using its supported interface, which has value `TransactionManager`:

```
public TransactionManager locateTM()  {
  Class trClass[] = { TransactionManager.class };
    try {
      ServiceItem mySI = mySDM.lookup(new ServiceTemplate(null, trClass, null),
        null, MAX_LOOKUP_WAIT * 2);
      if (mySI != null)
        return (TransactionManager) mySI.service;
    }
    catch (Exception ex) {
      ex.printStackTrace();
      System.exit(1);
    }

    return null;
  }
}
```

Copy over the `SpaceWrapper.class` file from `ch13\codespacewrapper` directory.

Compile the new wrapper using:

`..\bats\buildit TrSpaceWrapper.java`

In the `ch13\codetrspacewrapper` directory, you will find `testwrap.bat` file containing:

```
call ..\bats\setpaths.bat
java -classpath .;%JINIJARS%  -Dnet.jini.discovery.interface=%ADAPTERIP% -
Djava.security.policy=policy.all  TrSpaceWrapper %1 %2
```

Use this batch file to test the `TrSpaceWrapper`:

`testwrap iguanas mySpace`

Your output should look like this:

We can use `TrSpaceWrapper` to help us create a JavaSpaces application that uses transactions. You will find an example in the `ch13\codetrwritespace\TrWritespace.java` file:

```
import net.jini.space.JavaSpace;

import net.jini.core.transaction.server.TransactionManager;
import net.jini.core.transaction.server.TransactionConstants;
import net.jini.core.transaction.*;
import net.jini.core.transaction.Transaction.Created;
```

We extend `TrSpaceWrapper` to get the transaction manager location helper method:

```
public class TrWritespace extends TrSpaceWrapper {
   static final long VERY_LONG_TIME = 60 * 1000 * 30;
   static final long MAX_READ_WAIT = 30 * 1000;
   private String itemToWrite = "something";
   private String myGroup = "iguanas";
```

The `main` method processes four arguments, using parameters identical to the `writespace` program:

> The group to join
>
> The JavaSpace name
>
> The `myAddedData` field value for the instance that is written to the space
>
> The number of entries to write

The `writeIt` method does all the service location, transaction creation, and JavaSpace operations:

```
static public void main(String argv[]) {
  TrWritespace myApp = null;
  if (argv.length > 3) {
    myApp = new TrWritespace(argv[0]);
    try {
      myApp.writeIt(argv[1],argv[2],Integer.parseInt(argv[3]));
    }
    catch(Exception e) {
      System.exit(0);
    } //of catch
  } // of if
  else
    System.out.println("Incorrect usage!");
}

public TrWritespace(String inGroup) {
    super(inGroup);
    System.out.println("Locating group " + inGroup + "...");
}
```

We are now keeping track of both the transaction and the `TransactionManager`, as well as the JavaSpace instance that we are already tracking:

```
protected JavaSpace mySpace = null;
protected TransactionManager myTM = null;
protected Transaction myTransaction = null;
public void writeIt(String inSpaceName, String inData, int repeat) {
   try {
     mySpace = locateSpace(inSpaceName);
     if (mySpace != null) {
       System.out.println("Located JavaSpace called " + inSpaceName);
```

Use the `locateTM` method of the `TrSpaceWrapper` class to find a transaction manager:

```
myTM = locateTM();
if (myTM != null) {
  System.out.println("Located a transaction manager...");
```

Create a transaction indirectly using the `TransactionFactory` semantics object. We keep a reference to the transaction that is created and use it in our JavaSpaces operations:

```
              Transaction.Created tc = TransactionFactory.create(myTM,
                VERY_LONG_TIME);
              myTransaction = tc.transaction;
          }
          else {
            System.out.println("Cannot locate transaction manager,
              terminating.");
            System.exit(1);
          }
```

First, we perform the write operation(s) in the transaction. Notice that the transaction is leased (as we saw in Chapter 9), so we simply use a lease here that we think will be long enough:

```
          for (int i=0; i< repeat; i++) {
            mySpace.write(new MyEntry(inData), myTransaction, VERY_LONG_TIME);
            System.out.println("wrote entry " + (i+1));
          }
```

Next, we try to read one of the written entries within the transaction:

```
          System.out.println("Try reading entry within the trasnaction...");
          myEntry tpEntry = (myEntry) mySpace.read(new myEntry(inData),
            myTransaction, MAX_READ_WAIT);
          if (tpEntry != null)
            System.out.println("Read successful.");
          else
            System.out.println("Read failed.");
```

Next, we keep the transaction open and asleep for a minute:

```
          System.out.println("Sleeping for 60 seconds before commit.");
          Thread.sleep(60 * 1000);
```

Finally, we commit the transaction:

```
          myTransaction.commit();
          System.out.println("Transaction committed.");
        }// of if
      }
      catch (Exception ex)
      {
        ex.printStackTrace();
        System.exit(1);
      }


    }
  }
```

Copy over, from the ch13\codetrspacewrapper directory, the following files to the ch13\codetrwritespace directory:

> myEntry.class
>
> spaceWrapper.class
>
> trSpaceWrapper.class

Use the command line to compile the program:

..\bats\buildit TrWritespace.java

We can create a JAR file containing the MyEntry class required to access the written entry. We can use the makejar.bat file for this. The file contains:

```
call ..\bats\setpaths.bat
jar cvf TrWritespace-dl.jar MyEntry.class
copy TrWritespace-dl.jar %WROXHOME%
```

Make this JAR file:

makejar

The runwrite.bat file can be used to execute the program. It contains:

```
call ..\bats\setpaths.bat
java -classpath .;%JINIJARS%  -Dnet.jini.discovery.interface=%ADAPTERIP% -
Djava.security.policy=policy.all -
Djava.rmi.server.codebase=http://%STUBHOST%/TrWritespace-dl.jar TrWritespace %1 %2
%3 %4
```

Before we test this transacted write program, let us create one more class. This one we will use as a monitor to see the effect of the write within the transaction.

Using takeIfExists() Variation to Determine Transaction Visibility

The source is in the ch13\codetakeie directory, in the TakeIE.java file:

```
import net.jini.space.JavaSpace;
```

We will wait up to two minutes here, not for a matching entry to be written, but for a transaction locked entry to be freed. Since we are outside any transaction ourselves, we only need to inherit from SpaceWrapper:

```
public class TakeIE extends SpaceWrapper {
    static final long MAX_WAIT = 60 * 1000 * 2;
```

The `main()` method process the three arguments: name of group, name of JavaSpace, and the `myAddedData` value of the `myEntry` to take:

```
static public void main(String argv[]) {
  TakeIE myApp = null;
  if (argv.length > 2) {
    myApp = new TakeIE(argv[0]);
    try {
      MyEntry tp = myApp.takeIt(argv[1],argv[2]);
      if (tp != null)
        System.out.println("successfully took entry");
      else
        System.out.println("takeIfExists failed");
    }
    catch(Exception e) {
      System.exit(0);
    } //of catch
  } // of if
  else
    System.out.println("Incorrect usage!");
  System.exit(0);
}


public TakeIE(String inGroup) {
    super(inGroup);
    System.out.println("Locating group " + inGroup + "...");
}
```

The `takeIt` method locates the JavaSpace, and then calls `takeIfExists` on the entry that we want to find. This is normally a non-blocking call:

```
protected JavaSpace mySpace = null;
public MyEntry takeIt(String inSpaceName, String inData) {
  try {
    mySpace = locateSpace(inSpaceName);
    if (mySpace != null)  {
      System.out.println("Located JavaSpace called " + inSpaceName);
      return (MyEntry) mySpace.takeIfExists(new MyEntry(inData), null,
        MAX_WAIT);
    }// of if
  }
  catch (Exception ex) {
    ex.printStackTrace();
    System.exit(1);
  }
  return null;
}
}
```

You will need to copy `MyEntry.class` and `spaceWrapper.class`, from the `ch13\codespacewrapper` directory, to the `ch13\codetakeie` directory. Compile the program by using the command line:

`..\bats\buildit TakeIE.java`

Now we are ready to run the program using the batch file `runtake.bat`, which contains:

```
call ..\bats\setpaths.bat
java -classpath .;%JINIJARS% -Dnet.jini.discovery.interface=%ADAPTERIP% -
Djava.security.policy=policy.all TakeIE %1 %2 %3
```

Try running the program now, using the command line:

`runtake iguanas mySpace TESTTransaction`

Since a matching entry does not exist in the space, the program returns immediately, even though the timeout is up to two minutes. Now, change directory to `\code\trwritespace`, and run the program:

`runwrite iguanas mySpace TESTTransaction 1`

The output should look like this:

Note that the read within the transaction is performed successfully, so the entry has been written to the space. While the `trwritespace` program is sleeping and holding the transaction open, run the `takeie.java` program again. This time, even though no matching entries are visible yet, the `takeIfExists` method actually blocks and waits for the transaction to commit. Once the transaction commits, `takeIfExists` will return successfully with the matching entry. It should look like this:

Applying JavaSpaces

The list of uses that JavaSpaces could be put to grows and grows. There are so many potential applications that to suggest specific cases is like saying that microprocessors should only be used to control robot frogs. In the next few pages we'll introduce some generic application concepts that will leverage specific aspects of JavaSpaces. Hopefully, you will be inspired by one or more of these generic concepts, and apply JavaSpaces to your own application domain.

Leveraging Robust Persistence: JavaSpaces as Network Object Storage

The simplest way to use JavaSpaces is to use them as Jini accessible data stores. Even used in this limited fashion, JavaSpaces gives you many features of added value on top of the functionality that a typical operating system could provide:

❏ An object store, without the need to map objects to flat files or relational databases

❏ Any number of additional attached attributes (member fields) for any object in the store that may be interesting to a service seeking application; allowing intelligent searches based on these attributes

❏ A template based object location mechanism, exactly like the Jini lookup service

❏ Automatic contention resolution and concurrency control when multiple clients are accessing the same object store

❏ Transactions to protect system integrity during object transfers, should stored objects be moved between JavaSpaces at different places in the network

❏ A long-lived, self-healing, and (possibly) persistent storage; we can treat persistent versions of JavaSpaces as a data store that will never fail

Even when you're using JavaSpaces in a limited capacity, and not pulling into play the full power of it's functionality, it will still store objects that are used by multiple short-lived clients, and operate as a network accessible store for collaborative clients. It can also be used to store shared state information in a distributed processing environment involving multiple concurrently executing services.

Leveraging Networked Concurrency Support: JavaSpaces for Synchronization Across Time and Space

Most of us are familiar with the concepts of semaphores, mutexes, monitors, and other concurrency control mechanisms typically provided by the operating system or platform. These mechanisms enable several concurrent threads of execution to synchronize with each other. Being on a single machine (even if it is SMP based), synchronization is a point in time when two or more threads of execution meet simultaneously.

With a distributed system, the picture becomes less clear. Multiple threads of execution can execute simultaneously and independently across multiple machines. In order for these simultaneous threads of execution to rendezvous, we must consider a different distributed mechanism – a JavaSpaces mechanism, for example!

JavaSpaces provides this complex synchronization (in both space and time) in an almost trivial way. Logical Thread A wishing to synchronize with Thread B calls `take()` on a JavaSpace with a long timeout. Logical Thread B eventually call `write()` on the JavaSpace, writing an entry, and so synchronizing with Thread A and passing an object/data at the same time.

Multiple logical threads can synchronize using Logical Thread B at the same time by using the blocking `read()` operation or the `take()` operation.

In designing distributed systems, it is often necessary to create synchronization points in order to "checkpoint" independently operating software systems. This leaves an entire system, or a portion of the system, in a known state. In other cases, the more classic use of synchronization to protect shared data against concurrent modification is applicable. JavaSpaces serves equally well in both design scenarios.

JavaSpaces for Object Flow Systems Design

In classic data processing and structured analysis theory, we learnt about idealized dataflow machines. In such an idealized machine, the data flows along one or more pipelines of processors (not microprocessors, but simple processing agents), each one performing a special transformation or task on the data, and each one potentially combining some built-in or external data to the job being performed. The flow of this data between the processing agents is similar to an assembly line in a factory. At the end of this assembly line is the processed result. More than an entire decade of programmer and designer energy has gone into structured analysis, trying to perfect methodologies based on this pipelined model, the basis of which was that the dataflow machine was not likely to be ever achievable, until now.

The machines in the dataflow model, when mapped to a network of collaborating computers, become the processors, and the network becomes the conduit that connects the processors together to form the pipelines.

In order to build a robust and scalable data processing system, one needs to cater for the varying capacity, resources, and processing power of the processors. Typically in the conventional design, a durable queuing system is used to loosely couple the processors to cater for this difference. Theoretically, queues are used to ease the throughput (and processing) mismatch between consumers and producers. IBM MQ Series and Microsoft's MSMQ are example of such queuing systems.

In the following figure, each circle represents the processing agent that is performing a particular value-added activity to the data along the pipeline. The system on the left is the classical message queue system. Here, each processing agent takes work from a queue, performs its task, and places the work in another queue for other processing agents downstream. The system on the right is a JavaSpace system. We can see that, on an architectural level, a JavaSpace system can be used to emulate a classic queuing system:

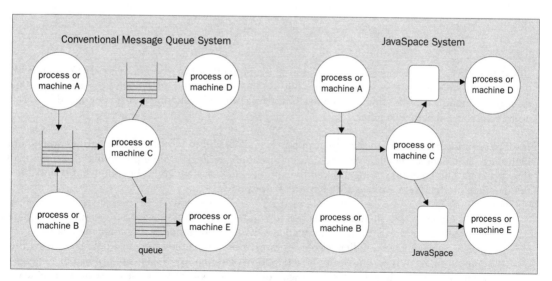

To ensure data integrity and system state consistency, transaction services are added to the mix. Combining a transaction service with a durable queuing service will ensure that no data will be lost, even in the face of partial network failure. The following diagram illustrates this. The processors themselves can use the transaction service to co-ordinate operations and state changes.

Entry "n" is taken from JavaSpace A and written into JavaSpace B. With the assistance of a transaction, we can guarantee that either the entry is transferred to B, or remains in A. This guarantee is valid regardless of how the distributed system may crash or fail in the intervening time. In a classic system, transaction queuing services are used to provide the same system integrity guarantee:

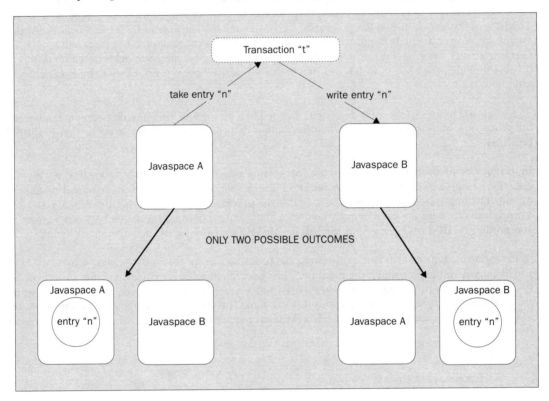

In its simplest form, JavaSpaces can be used as a dataflow machine. After all, if we write an entry that contains data only to the JavaSpace, and do not use the object's method, we have essentially produced a transacted queuing system (albeit with more powerful template matching ability) that has the same architecture as a dataflow system.

JavaSpaces adds much more to the equation however. The ability to store and forward complete objects, including static data, code and dynamic state information, gives rise to the possibility of designing object flow systems. The possibilities engendered by an object flow system go far beyond what is possible with the dataflow model. Here are two of the more obvious ones:

> Data, together with the operations that act on that data, flows through a system of distributed computing resources. In this case, we have the dataflow model without any dedicated processing agents. A smaller set of processors can handle the same data-flow by sharing their computing resources. For example, a data-flow that requires 8 dedicated processing agents can be processed in a JavaSpace system with only 4 processors. Essentially, the processing agents can "change personality", by inheriting behavior associated with the object (we look at how this can be achieved in the next section).

A system that has only bootstrapping ability acquires the latest and newest operating functionality, congregating the flow of objects from JavaSpaces into the main system each time the system is started up. Imagine a distributed OS using components and commands that are assembled at runtime over the network, and over various JavaSpaces. Although this sounds remarkably like the workings of Jini federations, the difference is that the objects obtained are full-fledged objects that provide functionality, rather than proxies to a service that performs the functionality (although nothing prevents them from being proxies communicating to other services or devices). Take an extreme example – Windows NT, Jini Edition was the "red hot" thing in December of 1999. You subscribed to the OS-of-the-month-club and when you turned on your machine, it is running Windows NT, Jini Edition. Linux 2000, Jini Edition became the "red hot" thing a month later, you simply turn on your machine and Linux 2000 was now running with the same data and applications that you were running before.

Distributed Messaging Systems (Chatline for Services)

This is one application area where the long-term persistence of space content may not be a requirement. JavaSpace can be used as a messaging system between concurrently executing entities on a network. Messages can be written to the JavaSpace using the recipient's address as a Jini entry field. The recipient can pick up messages as needed, or register for remote event notifications with the JavaSpace. The following diagram illustrates this style of multi-user messaging system.

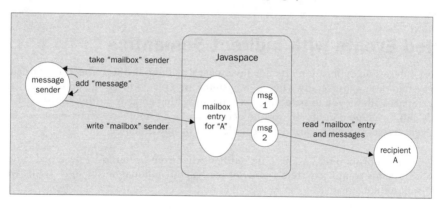

In some applications it may be more appropriate to create one JavaSpace entry per possible recipient, and use that entry as a mailbox by repeatedly attaching new data to it. The message senders add messages to the mailbox by taking the entry out of the JavaSpace, adding the message as an attribute to the entry, and writing the entry back to the JavaSpace. The recipient simply reads its own (single) mailbox entry and takes the messages from the field that contains the list. Doing it this way will ensure the order of messages being delivered to the recipient.

The following diagram illustrates this style of multi-user messaging system. Here, we see the mailbox entry in the JavaSpace in the center; the messages are fields of the mailbox entry. The sender on the left takes the entire entry out of the JavaSpace, adds a message to the entry, and writes it back to the JavaSpace. The receiver reads the mailbox entry from the JavaSpace, and accesses any of the messages attached to it in order.

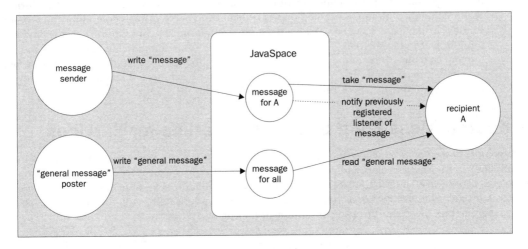

Distributed Events with Indirect Semantics

This is a very interesting application area for JavaSpaces, as there is often a need for this capability in distributed system design, especially when new systems are created to bridge or adapt existing legacy systems. JavaSpaces allows you to be notified when a matching entry is written to the space. This functionality can be adapted indirectly for the occurrence of a remote event, by name, or even before the actual event triggering mechanism has been defined or implemented.

For example, our application may want to be notified whenever a soon-to-be designed complex system has terminated. As this complex system is not yet ready, conventional design and coding wisdom would advise us to wait until it's ready.

Not so with JavaSpaces: we can start work right away. We will register for an event whenever an entry, with a field containing the string "soon-to-be-defined system has shutdown", is written to the space. Our application can be easily tested using a program that writes the triggering entry. When the other team has completed the new system, they only need to make sure that an entry is written to the JavaSpace once their system has completed shutdown.

The very loose coupling enables us to use very thin Java based adapters to trigger remote events based on legacy system state changes. The handlers of these state changes can be coded completely in Java and before the code-complete time of the Java based adapters.

Of course, this really can be viewed as another application where a JavaSpace behaves as a synchronization mechanism across time and space, but it happens so frequently in design that it is worthy of special mention.

Dynamic Producer/Consumer Based Systems

The simple template based matching ability of JavaSpaces is definitely a winning feature for dynamic producer/consumer applications. You might have a commodity exchange system, for example, where sellers are matched with buyers, based on types of items. Sellers can write the quantity that they have available alongside the asking price. Buyers can monitor the JavaSpace for entries denoting products that they are interested in buying, and examine each one for quantity and asking price.

Obviously, a single seller can break up its lot and sell to multiple buyers, or a single buyer can be buying from multiple sellers to fill its orders. This is a perfect match for the ability to transfer behavior with the object stored in a JavaSpace. Rules, as to when to break up, can be specified and made part of the behavior included with the object that contains price and quantity.

Another scenario might take the shape of an online auctioning system. Items up for auction are written to a space as they become available. Bidders search the space for products they are willing to bid on. They can then use the behavior included with the items to place a bid or find out the current bidding price. Alternatively, the serial bidding process can be handled by repeatedly taking and writing an entry back to the JavaSpace.

JavaSpaces for Building Compute Servers

There is an effort afoot to standardize a set of interfaces that use JavaSpaces to create a distributed, generic computational engine using networks of inexpensive computers. This project is called 'Compute-server', and is led by Eric Freeman.

Compute server, in this context, is a generalized computing engine that uses JavaSpaces technology for its front-end. The compute engine can consist of tens, hundreds, or even thousands of machines on a network all performing computational work. The real benefit of using JavaSpaces in this scenario is its ability to store behavior with the data. This means that the tasks individual machines will perform do not have to be fixed in advance.

Before Java, Jini, and JavaSpaces, most compute servers were built using dedicated massively parallel processing hardware (Cray supercomputers, for example) and software supporting dedicated tasks had to be created and installed. With JavaSpaces, the network becomes the interconnection between the processing resources (individual machines) and the Java VM becomes a generic processor that can be programmed on the fly, loading the Java objects from JavaSpaces.

A **master** manages typical compute server operations, by dropping many computing tasks into one (or more) JavaSpaces. A bank of workers monitors this JavaSpace, looking for work to perform, and picking up work by taking the object out of the space and executing work methods. The resulting objects are then either written back to the originating JavaSpace, or to another one.

The master (or another result co-coordinator) retrieves the results from the space. Immediately after performing the work for one task, the worker (assuming each resides on a different VM and/or physical machine) can immediately fetch another piece of work from the JavaSpace and start computing again.

In this way, a large set of computational resources can be harnessed (any idle computers within an intranet, for example) to compute anything that requires many independent parallel computable steps.

The following diagram shows a typical compute server in operation. Although there is only one JavaSpace at work here, in actual production there might be a bank or hierarchy of such JavaSpaces. On the left side there is the controlling master that writes work into the JavaSpace, and takes any completed results out of the space. Meanwhile, the a bank of worker machines looks for work in the JavaSpace, taking any that is available, performing it, and writing results back to the JavaSpace. Each piece of work fetched by a worker may be different, and the throughput of this system, if properly designed, is proportional to the number of workers in the system. If more throughput is needed, then more hardware (servers) should be added:

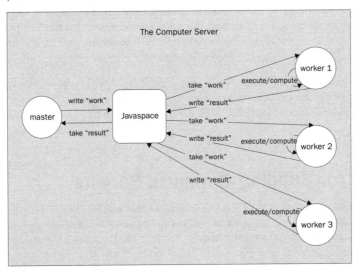

There are a few things worth noticing here:

Simply adding worker machines/VMs increases throughput, because each worker is able to do the work of another. A variant of this approach might be implemented when a particular configuration of worker machines is required (using a JDBC connection to the corporate database, for example). The scalability feature is still applicable within each set of workers – just add another one of the same sort.

Load balancing is completely automatic. No need to hire system tuning experts or operating system gurus. Workers pick up another piece of work after they have finished the last. As long as there is work available in the JavaSpace, the computing facility of the entire compute server will be kept saturated: Zen for tunable conventional systems. This is a simple example, though, and one can envisage more elaborate self-tuning schemes involving different "classes" of workers, using multiple JavaSpaces with workers that have special capabilities (special math processors, or communications links).

The JavaSpace façade effectively decouples the master from the workers. The master does not need to know how the work is performed, or by whom, and the workers need not know where the work comes from, or what larger system it is a part of.

So it's not completely beyond the realms of reason to envisage a scenario that harnesses the entire computing power of a nation in order to compute a complex problem affecting national security during time of war (with very securely encrypted workload and behavior, of course). Less dramatically, you could also harness the computation power of Los Angeles for the next great Hollywood animation movie.

The essence of a piece of work can be abstracted from an interface. The following Command interface illustrates this abstraction. We will use this very interface in our own implementation of a JavaSpace based compute server next:

```
import net.jini.core.entry.Entry;

public interface Command extends Entry {
    public void execute();
}
```

Now we'll put together our own compute server using JavaSpaces.

Building a JavaSpace Based Compute Server

The computational work that will be performed is packaged as an entry that will be written to a JavaSpace by one or more masters. The Command interface is defined in the ch13\codemaster\Command.java file:

```
import net.jini.core.entry.Entry;
public interface Command extends Entry
{
    public void execute();
}
```

The Work Entries

Workers wanting to work with these work entries need to be able to create templates for lookup within the JavaSpace. But as Command is an interface – currently being considered as a standard interface by the compute server workgroup – we will need to define a non-specific intermediate class. We have defined the MyTask class (ch13\codemaster\MyTask.java) for this purpose:

```
public class MyTask implements Command {
    public String workerClass = null;
    public String myStatus = "notdone";
    public Object myResult = null;
    public MyTask() {}
    public MyTask(String inClass, String inStatus,Object inResult)    {
        workerClass = inClass;
        myStatus = inStatus;
        inResult = myResult;
    }

    public Object getResult() {
        return myResult;
    }
    public void setDone() {
        myStatus = "done";
    }
    public void execute() {
        // must override in subclass
    }
}
```

The workerClass field can be used to segregate different classes of workers (those with some database connection to the intranet, from others with special processing hardware, for example). The myStatus field contains either notdone (it has been written by the master) or done (it has been taken by the worker, executed, and written back to the JavaSpace). The myResult field will contain the actual return value of the computation.

Our master will actually submit one of two different types of work. The first one, called `MyWork1.java`, is in the `ch13\codemaster` directory. It simply requires two long numbers to be added:

```
public class MyWork1 extends MyTask  {
  private Long a = new Long(343231);
  private Long b = new Long(123331);

  public MyWork1() {}
  public MyWork1(String inClass,String inStatus,Object inResult)  {
    super(inClass, inStatus,inResult);
  }

  public void execute() {
      myResult = new Long( a.longValue() + b.longValue());
  }
}
```

The `execute()` method is implemented, to execute on the worker's machine. We're also making use of the `getResult()` method to retrieve the result.

The other piece of potential work is a string concatenation. It is contained in the `MyWork2.java` file:

```
public class MyWork2 extends MyTask  {
  private String a = "first";
  private String b  = "second";

  public MyWork2() {}
  public MyWork2(String inClass, String inStatus,Object inResult) {
    super(inClass, inStatus, inResult);
  }
  public void execute() {
    myResult = a + b;
  }
}
```

The Master

The master program is responsible for submitting work to the JavaSpace. The source code is in the `ch13\codemaster\Master.java` file:

```
import net.jini.space.JavaSpace;
```

Our master inherits from `SpaceWrapper` to make Jini work and JavaSpace location easier:

```
public class Master extends SpaceWrapper {
  static final long VERY_LONG_TIME = 60 * 1000 * 30;
  private String myGroup = "iguanas";
```

The main() method processes these three arguments:

The group to join

The JavaSpace name

The work to submit (work1 or work2)

It will call the writeTask() method to write the work to the JavaSpace:

```
static public void main(String argv[]) {
  Master myApp = null;
  if (argv.length > 2)
  {
    myApp = new Master(argv[0]);
    try {
      myApp.writeTask(argv[1],argv[2]);
    }
    catch(Exception e) {
      System.exit(0);
    } //of catch
  } // of if
  else
    System.out.println("Incorrect usage!");
}


public Master(String inGroup) {
  super(inGroup);
  System.out.println("Locating group " + inGroup + "...");
}
```

Depending on the argument, the writeTask() method will create a new MyWork1 or MyWork2 instance and submit it to the compute server (JavaSpace):

```
protected JavaSpace mySpace = null;
protected Command myCommand = null;
public void writeTask(String inSpaceName, String inWork) {
  try {
    mySpace = locateSpace(inSpaceName);
    if (mySpace != null) {
      System.out.println("Located JavaSpace called " + inSpaceName);
      if (inWork.equals("work1"))
        myCommand = new MyWork1("simple","notdone",null);
      else
        myCommand = new MyWork2("simple","notdone",null);
      mySpace.write(myCommand, null, VERY_LONG_TIME);
```

Immediately after writing the work, it starts monitoring the space for a completed work entry. If it finds the matching completed work, it will take it out of the JavaSpace and report the result:

```
            System.out.println("wrote task to space, now wait for result");
            MyWork1 tp1 = null;
            MyWork2 tp2 = null;
            if (inWork.equals("work1")) {
                tp1 = (MyWork1) mySpace.take(new MyWork1("simple","done",null),
                  null,VERY_LONG_TIME);
                System.out.println("Result is " + tp1.getResult());
            }
            else {
                tp2 = (MyWork2) mySpace.take(new MyWork2("simple","done",null),
                  null, VERY_LONG_TIME);
                System.out.println("Result is " + tp1.getResult());
            }
        }// of if
    }
    catch (Exception ex) {
        ex.printStackTrace();
        System.exit(1);
    }
  }
}
```

Copy the `SpaceWrapper.class` from the `ch13\codespacewrapper` directory, to the `ch13\codemaster` directory. Compile the program using the command line:

```
..\bats\buildit Master.java
```

In order to allow clients and browsers to access the work entries, we must create a downloadable JAR file at the codebase. Use the `makejar.bat` file to create this:

```
call setpaths.bat
jar cvf master-dl.jar myWork1.class myWork2.class myTask.class Command.class
copy master-dl.jar %JINIHOME%\lib
```

The Worker

Source code for the worker can be found in the `ch13\codeworker\Worker.java` file:

```
import net.jini.space.JavaSpace;
public class Worker extends SpaceWrapper {
    static final long MAX_WAIT = 60 * 1000 * 2;
    static final String CLASS_TO_SERVICE = "simple";
```

The worker only needs two arguments, one for the group that it is to join, and the other taking the name of the JavaSpace where it will monitor for work:

```
static public void main(String argv[]) {
    Worker myApp = null;

    if (argv.length > 1)    {
        myApp = new Worker(argv[0]);
```

In this case, the location of the JavaSpace and the actual `take` of the work entry are separated. This is because we will be looping around, monitoring the space for any new work to execute. There is no need to repeatedly locate the space in the loop:

```
        try {
          myApp.setSpace(argv[1]);
          while(true)
            myApp.doWork();
        } catch(Exception e) {
            System.exit(0);
        } //of catch
      } // of if
      else
        System.out.println("Incorrect usage!");
      System.exit(0);
    }


    public Worker(String inGroup) {
      super(inGroup);
      System.out.println("Locating group " + inGroup + "...");
    }
```

The `setSpace()` method locates the space using the corresponding method in the `SpaceWrapper` class:

```
    protected JavaSpace mySpace = null;

    public void setSpace(String inSpaceName) {
      mySpace = locateSpace(inSpaceName);
      if (mySpace != null)  {
        System.out.println("Located JavaSpace called " + inSpaceName);
      }
    }
```

The `doWork()` method blocks on a `take` operation, waiting for work that is not done. It calls the work entry's `execute()` method, and writes the completed work back into the JavaSpace:

```
    public void doWork() {
      try {
        System.out.println("Waiting for work....");
        MyTask tpTask = (MyTask) mySpace.take(new MyTask(CLASS_TO_SERVICE,
          "notdone",null), null, MAX_WAIT);
        System.out.println("Got a piece of work.");
        tpTask.execute();
        System.out.println("Finished working on it.");
        tpTask.setDone();
        mySpace.write(tpTask, null, MAX_WAIT);
        System.out.println("Placed finished work back to space.");
      }
      catch (Exception ex) {
        ex.printStackTrace();
        System.exit(1);
      }
    }
  }
```

Before compiling this class, first copy `SpaceWrapper.class`, `Command.class`, and `MyTask.class` from the `ch13\codemaster directory`. Compile with:

`..\bats\buildit Worker.java`

Execute worker programs using the batch file `runworker.bat`. This file contains:

```
call ..\bats\setpaths.bat
java -classpath .;%JINIJARS%  -Dnet.jini.discovery.interface=%ADAPTERIP% -
Djava.security.policy=policy.all Worker %1 %2
```

Start a worker using the command line:

`runworker iguanas mySpace`

Now, change the directory to the master directory, and run the master using the command line:

`runmaster iguanas mySpace work1`

In our case, the master successfully submitted the work and retrieved the result:

The output of the worker console looks like this:

You can also monitor what is going on in the JavaSpace by running the JavaSpace browser using the `ch13\codebats\runjsbrowse.bat` file.

JavaSpaces in Review

In this chapter, we've seen how Jini can be put to use with JavaSpaces, a distributed, network-accessible object store technology with far reaching implementation possibilities, both now and in the future. The JavaSpaces technology is a Jini service, and supports the `net.jini.space.JavaSpace` interface. Its design came from the area of research that developed MPP, tuple spaces, and Linda Systems. JavaSpace deploys the same concepts, but with more simplicity, bringing them to the fingertips of Java/Jini/JavaSpace developers. They're also simpler to understand, and easier to work with.

We examined each method in the JavaSpace interface. We covered the four simple JavaSpace operations: read, write, take, and notify, implementing them and observing their interactions with the JavaSpace.

We also looked at transactions, working on a transacted write operation. We saw that entries written into a JavaSpace are only visible within the transaction itself until committed.

As a foundation technology, JavaSpaces can be used for many, many different applications, and we considered certain system architecture and processing patterns that lend themselves to a JavaSpace solution. We examined a very simple JavaSpace implementation that operated as a shared network storage for objects, and a more complex scenario where JavaSpaces synchronized independently running Jini services across multiple machines. JavaSpaces can be used to support the classic dataflow machine architecture, functioning as a transacted queuing service, or it can deliver much more functionality, providing, for example, a computational system based on flows of objects (data plus behavior). Non-persistent JavaSpace services are still extremely useful for services to communicate with each other, through a sort of chatline for services. The double-indirect decoupling provided by the JavaSpace notify mechanism can be put to good use; interfacing otherwise tightly coupled subsystems together. Dynamic consumer and producer relationships, such as commodity exchange and auction sites, can be implemented readily using JavaSpaces. Even though we took our time looking at possible JavaSpaces implementations, we barely scratched the surface.

Last but not least, we examined the way in which a JavaSpace can be used to build a completely generic compute server out of a network of computers. We worked through the coding and tried out an implementation of such a compute server.

Jini and JavaSpaces

Jini is really exciting because it breaks new ground in enabling a new way of designing and creating robust, long-lived, self-healing distributed systems. JavaSpaces is even more exciting in that it makes building these systems extremely simple.

By the time you reach this point in the book, we hope your interest is thoroughly peaked by the sheer volume of uses you can apply this technology to.

Jini Client or Service	JavaSpaces and Helper Services

Jini Client and Service Support Helper Utilities

Jini Discovery Management Helper Utilities

Jini Protocol Helper Utilities

Jini Network Protocols	
	RMI and Rich Object Semantics
	Java VM and Networking

Network Protocols

14

Jini System Issues and Future Developments

Jini and JavaSpaces are cutting-edge enabling technologies situated at the forefront of engineering and application possibilities. Being new and progressive technologies, they bring with them some issues that call for discussion:

- ❑ Security, namely Jini's integration with the existing Java security model.
- ❑ Speed to mainstream acceptance. There has been a certain sloth about the uptake of these technologies, which is not surprising given the steep learning curve they demand, and the new conceptual model they utilize.
- ❑ Development and debugging tools.

More specifically, there are two as yet unresolved problems that can be found from time to time in an operational Jini system:

- ❑ Duplicated meta-data
- ❑ Serialized object identity

We'll look at these problems, and discuss where one might find solutions to them.

The aim of this chapter is both to suggest something of the future direction that Jini, JavaSpaces, and even Java technologies might take, and to give you a fuller picture of Jini/JavaSpaces development today.

Security and Jini Systems

Jini is consistent with JDK 1.2's fine-grained, permission-based security model. An all-encompassing discussion of the security model is beyond the scope of this book, but there are many excellent books on the subject of Java Security on the market today, and interested readers are referred to these resources for more information.

In most of our examples in this book, we've used the `policy.all` file to enable uninhibited access to all system resources. What this file effectively says is: 'grant all permissions present and future for access to all system resources to any code coming from any machine written by anyone'. Clearly this isn't much of an option for production deployment. It's probably quite familiar by now:

```
Grant
    {
    permission java.security.AllPermission "", "";
    };
```

The `policy.all` is effective VM wide, on every process running on one VM at the same time.

It is possible, however, to limit the groups that your service or client may attempt to join using this policy file. The code that performs the access control check is built into the Jini `LookupDiscovery` utility class. This example restricts an application's scope of discovery to the `iguanas` group:

```
Grant
    {
    permission net.jini.discovery.DiscoveryPermission "iguanas";
    };
```

This would enable any group to be discovered:

```
Grant
    {
    permission net.jini.discovery.DiscoveryPermission "*";
    };
```

When you're working with Jini clients, you can create security policy files (using the standard Java 2 security model) to restrict the activity of downloaded proxy objects. You can also be selective about the access permissions you grant to proxy objects, restricting them according to codebase or code signings.

Under Java 2, you must explicitly install a security manager in order to perform privileged access, even when the executable itself is an application. Applications do not install security managers by default. An access controller object that has been delegated all policy checking by a security manager controls access to privileged resources. The default implementation of the access controller will read the policy file to determine accessibility. This is the reason for installing an `RMISecurityManager` in order to download and execute stub code. The system-wide default policy is specified in a `java.policy` file, found in the `JDKHOME/lib/security` directory. This default policy does not allow code from foreign codebases to execute. Forgetting to install `RMISecurityManager` in code that requires download and execution of remote code (which includes every Jini service and client, as they download lookup service proxies) can give you some very obscure errors during code execution.

Things are a little less clear on the service side. Folks anticipating some sort of authentication and access control at the lookup service level will be disappointed – there isn't anything. Not only does the Jini specification not cover this aspect, but authentication and authorization is still not part of the JDK platform as of release 1.3 (it is available only as a standard extension). Almost anyone having access to a Jini network can perform lookup discovery and download proxies on that Jini network. You can get a minimal level of protection by creating a Java 2 policy file that sets up `java.net.SocketPermission` to restrict the hosts (either by name or by IP) that may connect to the ports on the Java VM hosting a lookup service. In fact, it can be argued that authentication at the lookup service level would be ineffective anyway, as any determined attackers would easily mimic the proxy's protocol to access the service (bypassing the lookup service).

Only authentication and access control at the service level itself is meaningful. Jini 1.1 leaves access control to the services. At the time of writing, neither Jini nor the standard JDK 1.2.2 release provides access control mechanisms for this. Instead, it is left to the service itself to perform its own authentication and access control at application level where necessary. It is anticipated that Jini will incorporate new features of the underlying Java Security Model as it continues to mature. Since the JAAS (Java Authentication and Authorization Service) is not yet part of the standard JDK distribution, users needing this service have to create their own for the time being.

Conceptual Roadblock: Jini is Only for Connecting Devices

There is a general consensus out there that Jini is only for devices. This misconception is widespread, prevalent in the mainstream technical press, software developer communities, and investment analysts. While Jini is a technology that is *applicable* to the shared utilization of networked devices (and a device can certainly appear as a service), I think you will agree by now that this particular implementation of Jini definitely represents a very small part of this generalized distributed network technology.

Jini certainly has been marketed as a substrate for creating instantly available devices anywhere, and it is sometimes labeled and dismissed as a plug-and-play device driver technology for networks. The misconception runs pretty deep, and it's almost impossible to convince the pundits otherwise. The fact that most public Jini presentations with any exposure are punctuated with a Jinified toaster or Jini driven Lego robots doesn't really advance the cause much either.

There are a couple of very good indicators that Jini will shrug off this misconception, and be re-discovered for what it really can do (much like the Linuxes of this world).

First off, Jini leverages Java's unique ability to move objects around a network. Most competing technologies are heavily reliant on specific hardware platforms, and can't provide Java's object flow substrate. The more distributed our networks, the more important this becomes.

Secondly, Jini encompasses distributed systems design approaches and philosophies that are radically different from those currently accepted. It is going to take time for engineers and architects to get comfortable with the paradigm shift (just as it took an incredibly long time for object orientation to go mainstream – and where would we be without that now!).

Thirdly, the current market for component-based network solutions dominates what is currently thought of as the distributed computing market, and it is both well established and extremely lucrative. There is really no valid reason, business or otherwise, to spoil the party while things are going great. So there's no great hurry to exploit distributed computing the Jini/JavaSpaces way. Yet!

Unfortunately, this misconception often manifests itself as a conceptual roadblock for potential Jini developers. Understandably a 'device driver technology' is not very often on their portfolio wish lists – device driver development tends to be thought of as a niche market specialty.

It is uncertain, at the time of writing, when we'll see a real marketing push for Jini in its true colors. There is little urgency to do so in today's marketplace – so this is a great opportunity for those who see what Jini is really all about to explore, experiment and innovate at a comfortable pace.

Coinciding with the increasing popularity of free software and open source, Jini's public disposition (through WWW.Jini.org and SCSL) may indeed herald the software development, design and production of the future.

Tools for Design, Development, and Debugging

This is an area just waiting for someone to step up to the plate. It is unlikely that Sun will address these issues until a critical mass of mainstream applications are applying Jini technology. In the public domain, and within Jini.org, you can find various efforts being made towards creating browsers, status monitors, and the like for Jini networks.

Distributed system design is greatly simplified by Jini. However, because is it a new approach to solving distributed networking problems, there is little formalized methodology supporting complex Jini system design. The potential of Jini style distributed systems is largely unrealized to date, and may require new simulation technology to analyze. This is a kind of 'Hotspot' for distributed systems.

Integrated Development Environments (IDEs) would greatly simplify the development and maintenance tasks a Jini based distributed system entails. At the time or writing, none of the major vendor's IDEs supports integrated Jini development and design (Sun's own Forte is only previewing early support).

Debugging and tuning distributed systems like Jini is, unfortunately, likely to remain more art than science for the foreseeable future. The simple elegance of Jini suggests that something formalized and pervasive *can* be built into its infrastructure, to make debugging and tuning systematic. This would not only be an extremely useful and pragmatic feature for Jini developers, but it would also be something of a breakthrough in applied distributed systems design.

Some of these features will come from Sun as they must; Sun reserves the stewardship of the evolution of the core Jini components. Others will be developed in the form of third-party products, and still others will come from the community projects evolving at Jini.org.

Design Issues

Initially it might appear that Jini's main problem might be that it requires a minimum of 3 megabytes of code. This really isn't practical for most devices – many small devices can't hold this much information. As long as Jini plays the role of a bridge between devices, however, and isn't implemented in the base code of the devices themselves, there isn't much to worry about; it's simply something to be aware of. New APIs could be written to communicate with different devices and legacy systems (if that is in any way practical).

There are two further interesting design issues that can crop up in Jini system designs. These are fairly generalized and non-specific, but if you don't design around them, they might give you operational and maintenance headaches in the long term, particularly as your system scales.

Duplicated Meta-data

This stems from the fact that even though Java provides a seamless object oriented model, and some very simple ways to manipulate objects, it still sits on top of conventional (typically non-object oriented) operating systems that facilitate the necessary functionality.

We are forced into making a choice between the overall 'size' of a transmitted object (and the bandwidth consumed as it transfers), and maintaining duplicated meta-data information. This choice is forced upon us by the constraints imposed by designing a Java based networked system, and in particular, Jini systems. Such restraints are clearly in evidence in the design of the components supplied with Jini (reggie, for example).

When an object is transmitted over the wire, the serialization process marshals the object and annotates it with a codebase (as we saw when we looked at RMI operations). This means that the physical object at the receiver end is unmarshalled from two separate streams:

- ❑ State information
- ❑ Class information from the codebase (and any other dependent class information), potentially requiring network access to another system

The following diagram depicts the dual streamed transmission of an object. Here, the object on the lower left is being conceptually re-constituted. The process requires both the state information that is actually transmitted (lower right), and significant additional traffic in the form of the class information download (upper right):

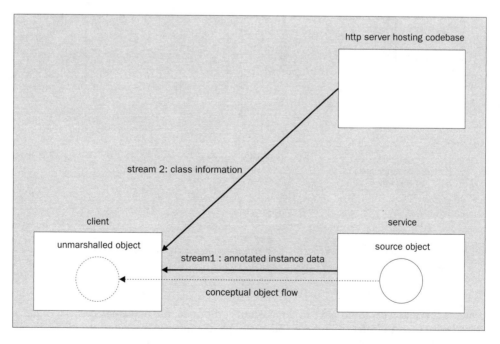

Because of this second point, it's very unwise for certain types of store-and-forward services to keep objects in their normal form. Doing so would mean that the service would have to load all the class information for all the objects that they temporarily hold. Instead, these services typically keep the object in a `MarshalledObject` while they hold it before forwarding to the final recipient. The recipient can then unmarshall the object from the stream, and download the class information that it needs.

Unfortunately, an instance of a `MarshalledObject` is completely opaque. There is no way you can know what is in it before you unmarshall it, and in unmarshalling it you are forced to take the download hit for the associated class information. On the other hand, it is quite useless (and pretty silly) to store a bunch of nameless, faceless objects that you know nothing about; client retrieval would be impossible.

The design solution is almost always to attach descriptive attributes to the objects stored within the service with information. We have seen this in the Jini lookup service (the `ServiceItem`), the JavaSpaces entry, and the `ServiceUI` entry, and will no doubt continue to see this solution implemented in years to come.

The dilemma occurs when one of the attached attributes is actually part of the meta-data information that describes the object within the `MarshalledObject`, has shown in the following diagram. Here, the `MarshalledObject` is one that implements an interface called `myInterface`. There is no way anyone handling this object will ever know that it supports such an interface – a `MarshalledObject` is just a binary blob! Unfortunately, there are many situations where one *must* know that `myInterface` is supported by the object. So, we attach an attribute (a kind of descriptor, or decoration in 'pattern speak') that describes it precisely. Bingo – duplicated meta-data!

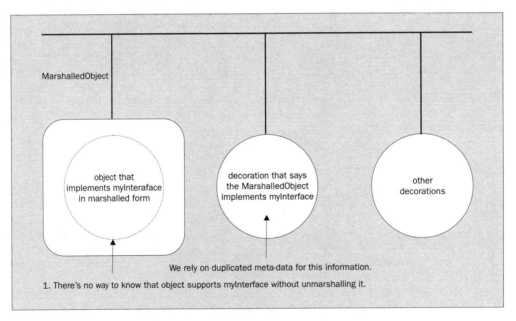

It's a catch 22. We don't want to have to unmarshall and inspect the object inside the `MarshalledObject` in order to find out about its type, the interfaces it supports, methods, and so on, because it might turn out to be of no use to us, and then we're wasting time and bandwidth. But we do need at least some, if not all, of this information before we can decide whether to use the `MarshalledObject` or not.

An external descriptor can solve this problem. The attached attributes, in this situation, usually consist of strings containing the fully qualified Java interface name(s) that the object supports, and/or string names of the classes and superclasses that it is an instance of. What we have here is essentially a replication of the meta-data information. Should the system evolve, becoming larger and more complex, management and synchronization of the data between the true meta-data source (the codebase class information itself) and the duplicate will get pretty convoluted – it's a recipe for disaster. The usual way around this is to relax the requirement that these descriptions should specify the object inside the `MarshalledObject`. In most cases, this is enough, since the client can always release the unmarshalled object if it doesn't do what its descriptor promises. While this represents a workable solution, it still entails wasting bandwidth, which might not necessarily be a problem, but it was what we were trying to alleviate! It is, currently, an uneasy decision that is left to the designer's discretion.

The source of the `MarshalledObject` – those responsible for the marshalling the object instance in the first place, do, of course, know exactly how much meta-data information ought to be exposed outside it, and that duplicating meta-data will only lead to maintenance and operational nightmares. While this issue currently lies with them, then, it would be good to see Jini and Java providing a mechanism that enforces use of a single source of meta-data information.

Serialized Object Identity

Remote object method invocations, using RMI, are made through local Java objects called stubs. Stubs are objects that know how to marshal the required parameters, contact the server, and return values for the method calls. One unique characteristic of RMI stubs is that they override `equals()` and `hashcode()` members inherited from the object. This ensures that proper semantics are used in stub comparison. There are two methods that can be implemented to ensure that two remote objects are deemed equal if, and only if, they refer to the same remote object instance. This allows operational transparency when you're working with a collection of remote and non-remote objects. One can deduce that the methods must somehow map the hostname, port, and a VM object instance number of some sort to the `hashcode()` and `equals()` methods.

When we use RMI stubs as proxy objects for a service in Jini, we automatically inherit this very desirable property. There are, however, plenty of other ways to implement a proxy object, and most of them don't involve using RMI stubs as proxies. In such cases, if we do not carefully override the `equals()` and `hashcode()` methods of the objects, we could be in for some interesting problems. Let me illustrate with a sample scenario:

We have two instances of a Jini service, SERVICEA and SERVICEB. Both of them use the same (non-RMI stub) proxy object. They register with the lookup services in a group called iguanas:

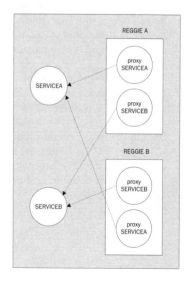

There are actually two lookup services in the `iguanas` group, REGGIEA and REGGIEB. What ends up happening is that both REGGIEA and REGGIEB have a copy of both SERVICEA's proxy and SERVICEB's proxy.

While they are residing in the lookup service, the proxy objects are attached to a `ServiceItem`, and the `ServiceItem` contains a globally unique `ServiceID` that can distinguish the proxies from the two services.

Now, imagine that CLIENTA is looking for Jini services to perform a special task, and both SERVICEA and SERVICEB qualify (as they are the same). CLIENTA will end up retrieving a total of four proxy objects from the two lookup services that match the criterion. If CLIENTA maintains complete records of the `ServiceItem` (a potentially expensive operation), it will be able to determine the duplicated SERVICEA and SERVICEB entries.

If, on the other hand, CLIENTA has only obtained the proxy object from the lookup services (the most likely case, as it is considerably more efficient), CLIENTA just can't distinguish between the duplicated proxies. It will not know whether the four proxies in fact represent one, two, three, or four unique Jini services. Using `equals()` will always return false!

This is still the case even if both services' proxies contain instructions about how the services should be read. CLIENTA can only rely on the `equals()` method to determine if the two proxies refer to the same service. Since the `equals()` method has not been appropriately overridden, there is no way for CLIENTA to tell without additional attached information.

This problem can manifest itself in many other forms, especially if you're working with third party services that may store proxy object instances. The solution is to ensure that the `equals()` and `hashCode()` methods are always overridden for any Jini proxy object that is not based on an RMI stub. Typically, implementations of `equals()` and `hashCode()` can internally use a host address, port, and instance number to ensure uniqueness; in Jini, the alternative way is to use the globally unique Service ID itself in the implementation of these methods.

Coming Changes?

The problems we've looked at so far are not only difficult to debug and work around, but the problem statements themselves are quite difficult to articulate and to understand. Combine this with a semi-satisfactory work-around, and you may not end up with a pretty picture. Such issues force us under the hood to get a thorough understanding of what the Java VM considers an object, how it implements object mobility, and so on. If you have been working with Jini for any significant length of time, you're bound to have come up against one or both of these issues. So, how do we solve them?

It is quite clear that what constitutes a Java object is changing significantly as technologies like RMI and Jini rapidly mature. The identity of a Java object within this extended context of VMs federating across the network is a different beast to that of a Java object working with a single VM.

Should the next generation of distributed, network-ready VMs acknowledge this duality (that we require Java objects to be both what they are today, but that they *may* also need to contain a unique network personality) then the problem will disappear. Meta-data will travel with the serialized state information in an efficient manner, and proxy objects will be different simply because they were created by different services at different times. Once again, we will be able to code object flow applications fearlessly across the extended world as a VM model. Don't hold your breath, though; this state of networked Java Zen may not arrive for a while.

Jini Client or Service	JavaSpaces and Helper Services
Jini Client and Service Support Helper Utilities	
Jini Discovery Management Helper Utilities	
Jini Protocol Helper Utilities	

Jini Network Protocols	
	RMI and Rich Object Semantics
	Java VM and Networking

Network Protocols

Section 3

Applying Jini and Java Spaces to the Real World

Andrew Schneider

Remote Access to Clinical Data

This chapter shows a short case study of how a company provided secure remote access to clinical data. The chapter will cover:

❑   The basic requirements for the system

❑   The impact the introduction of Jini had on the architecture

❑   The construction of Jini services and clients

❑   Providing access to Jini services over the Internet

Background

A patient normally receives medical care via their local medical practice. A Medical Doctor working at one of these the practices is referred to as a General Practitioner (GP). There will be one or more GPs working at this practice and the patient is required to register with one of them. The majority of practices are computerized. A patient's medical history is stored in a database and accessed via a proprietary clinical system. Outside normal practice hours the UK's National Health Service (NHS) provides access to GPs through a network of "Out of Hours (OOH) Centres". When a patient visits an OOH center it is likely the GP they see will not be familiar with their medical history and will not have access to their records.

This project aimed to provide the GP working at an OOH with fast, secure, reliable, simple, and cheap access to a patient's clinical data, wherever that patient might be registered within the country. This case study relates some of the experiences gained while developing and deploying such a system.

Requirements

For the purposes of this case study the product under discussion will be referred to as "RACD" (Remote Access to Clinical Data). The basic requirements of the system are:

❑ For various ethical and political reasons the system has to be de-centralized. Each practice maintains its existing clinical system and database and patients' medical data must not be cached at other locations within the network.

❑ Each practice should be able to define who can access medical data and how that data should be presented.

❑ The system should be tolerant of failure. If a practice's computing facilities fail, then access to other practices' data should not be affected.

❑ The system should be secure. Although NHS has its own private WAN (NHSNet) it is still important that data transfer is encrypted and access to data logged.

❑ It should take significantly less than a minute to retrieve the clinical data and display it.

❑ The system should have a low impact. Its installation and use should not affect existing clinical systems or add significant maintenance overheads.

❑ The system has to be simple to use. GPs may only have ten minutes to spend with a patient; if five minutes of that is taken interacting with RACD it will be of little use.

❑ The system has to be inexpensive. The NHS is notoriously cash poor. Database and application servers with run-time licences had to be avoided where possible. In addition, budgetary constraints on the project meant that products with developer licenses costing several thousand US dollars were also out of scope. For example, database servers from companies like ORACLE were entirely out of the range of normal GP practices' budgets.

RACD in Action

RACD serves views on a patient's clinical data to a browsing GP. A view is a particular subset of a patient's clinical data displayed on the browser. A view may be a patient's full medical record, a summary of their record, or perhaps just a patient's allergies and current medication.

A patient visits a GP at an OOH centre. To obtain access to that patient's data the GP uses a web browser to access a well-known URL. To obtain access to RACD the GP supplies a username and password. Once logged on, the GP searches for the patient using their name and address. The result is a list of the most likely patients. Each patient name is hyperlinked. When a hyperlink is selected RACD interrogates the patient's practice to find out what data views are available. The list of available data views is determined by the following factors:

❑ The access rights of the GP.

❑ The amount of data the practice has decided to make available.

❑ Restrictions the patient has placed on available data. This allows patients to have control over what aspects of their medical record are made available outside the practice they are registered with.

The GP then selects the view they are interested in to see the patient's clinical data.

The Initial Architecture

Phase 1 of RACD was to provide OOH centers access to patient data within the local area. This area may contain a million or so patients and at least 100 users (GPs and nurses). The well-known URL mentioned above provides a gateway to the clinical data at a **central location**. This central location and the service provision at this point are the single source of failure in the system. There are a number of ways to reduce the risk of system outage. Two basic options are:

❑ Use techniques such as fail over hardware, fail over software, replicated servers, redundant servers, and others to provide a high availability service

❑ Replicate the system across two or more physical sites and provide users with multiple URLs

We chose the first option. The details of this, except for where it impacted on our architecture, are outside the scope of this case study. It should be noted that cost was a major issue and so reliability was traded against deployment costs.

The Static Model

The central location would normally be one of the larger and IT literate practices. Software has to be installed at each practice to serve clinical data to the central location. The basic architecture (minus encryption and authentication services) is shown below:

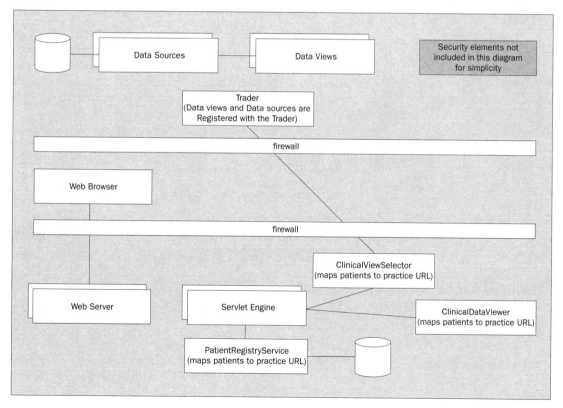

All the services in RACD sit behind firewalls. A web server and servlet engine are deployed at the central location, along with an index (the `PatientRegistryService`) that maps patients to their practices. Each local practice has one (or more) clinical **data views**. A clinical data view (a realization of the `ClinicalDataView` interface) is responsible for providing a view onto a (possibly) disparate set of clinical data. In other words, a clinical data view "dices and slices" data for presentation. A clinical data view accesses clinical data via a **clinical data source** (a realization of the `ClinicalDataSource` interface). A data source provides access (within the practice LAN) to data stored in the local clinical system.

A patient may wish that certain elements of their record were not available for viewing outside of the practice. The clinical data source is responsible for removing those elements from any data sent in response to a request for clinical information. This ensures that an incorrectly coded clinical data view cannot access data a patient doesn't wish viewed. An example of a clinical data source would be `SummaryDataSource`, a data source that provides summary data from the patient's medical record. There are a number of other data sources. These may provide access to the full medical record, data held on a secondary clinical system, x-rays, etc. Each service (view or source) registers itself and some attributes with the trader. These attributes include access permissions. The `ClinicalViewSelector` provides a list of data views available to the user by querying the trader. The `ClinicalDataViewer` servlet then liaises directly with the appropriate data view to obtain the information required to render the data into HTML for display to the user.

The Dynamic Model

The user searches for a patient thus:

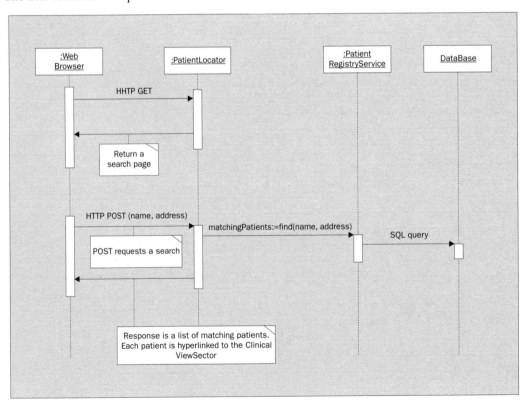

Each local practice has one or more **data views**. Once a patient has been found, a user selects a patient. RACD queries the patient's practice for available data views and presents the list back to the user:

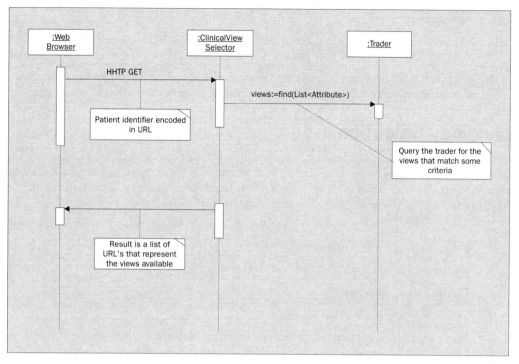

When a user selects a view, the data view is contacted and provides the servlet with data to that is displayed on the user's browser:

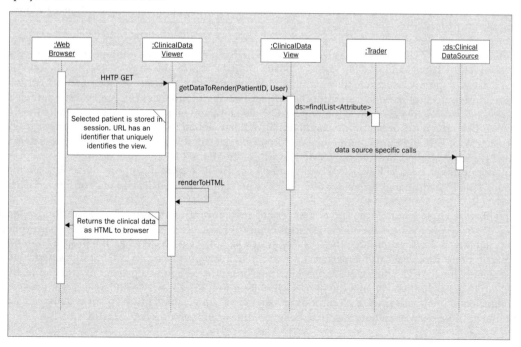

This architecture has a number of advantages:

❏ The `ClinicalDataViewer` does not have to know in advance which views are available at each practice.

❏ The list of views available at a practice is dynamic. Since the trader is consulted each time a list of views is required a practice may add new views and expect them to be available "immediately".

❏ If a practice suffers some catastrophic IT systems failure, access to other practices is not affected since clinical data and the views on the data are not centralized.

Technology Selection

With the initial architecture, requirements, and user interaction model in place, appropriate technologies were selected. The target platforms for RACD were Windows NT and Linux. Linux provides a reliable, fast, and low cost implementation platform for RACD. The development was to be designed and implemented utilizing OO techniques. The target implementation language was Java (JDK 1.2). The decision was influenced by:

❏ The cross platform requirement

❏ The support for building multithreaded servers

❏ The security architecture

❏ The network-centricity of the language

❏ The availability of application servers and other middleware at a low cost

❏ The comprehensive class libraries

At product inception, the Blackdown JVM for Linux wasn't stable enough for commercial products. Linux support was therefore delayed until the next phase of the project, giving the Linux JVM time to stabilize (which it did).

Initially, Enterprise Java Beans was considered a suitable platform for development. It supports both stateful (entity beans) and stateless (session beans) models. It provides simple access to the relational databases commonly in use and also a simple programming model. However, commercial EJB servers were outside the cost parameters set for the project and open source developments were in their early stages and not reliable enough. While the RACD development team could have contributed to an open source EJB server, the organization would not have been willing to spend development time on such a project. With EJB and other commercial middleware rejected, it was decided to build the system using RMI (Remote Method Invocation)/JRMP (Java Remote Method Protocol), and for WAN communications, RMI/HTTP. JRMP was chosen over IIOP because it supports dynamic class loading and is fast. The additional scalability offered by some commercial ORBs was not considered necessary.

The obvious choice for the web server and servlet engine was from the Apache consortium. Apache Server (www.apache.org) and JServ (java.apache.org) have an excellent reputation for performance and stability and are, as importantly, free. (Tomcat was not yet released when the project started.) The Apache Consortium caveats the performance and reliability of Apache on NT but it has performed excellently for RACD. During the technology selection process Sun was promoting Jini and its dynamic networking capabilities. Though the hype surrounding Jini was all to do with having your toaster connected to the house LAN, a closer look showed it was applicable to the type of system we were building. If the documentation was to be believed, Jini would provide RACD with:

❏   Dynamic service discovery

❏   Service location independence

❏   Selection of services based on a trader model

❏   Self-healing networks via a leasing model

❏   Support for WAN access (via the `LookupLocator`) as well as LAN access; the `LookupLocator` is used because multicast is neither available (tends to blocked at routers) nor desirable over a WAN

Interbase (www.interbase.com) was chosen as a database server because our company had previous experience with it (it was already deployed at many local practices) and it was to become an Open Source development. The database would be connected to via JDBC so that RACD was relatively database independent.

These were all elements that would have to be built into RACD, so Jini looked like a perfect fit. Having selected Jini the final technology choices looked like this:

❏   Distributed object protocol: RMI and Jin.

❏   Implementation language: Java

❏   Database access: JDBC and Interbase

❏   Servlet Engine: Apache/Jserv

❏   Web Server: Apache Server

The Impact of Jini on the Initial Architecture

Jini had several immediately obvious impacts on the initial architecture outlined above. Firstly, the `Trader` could be abandoned in favor of the `ServiceRegistrar`. The introduction of the `ServiceRegistrar` meant that the `Attribute` interface could be replaced by `Entry` interfaces. The Jini lookup service provided all the functionality that the trader had been imbued with. Additionally, all services that could be distributed were made Jini services.

Unreliability

A less concrete effect of Jini on the architecture was its philosophy. Jini pushes two elements to the front of every developers mind:

❏   Every connection to a remote service is, by its nature, unreliable

❏   All clients must deal with the unreliability of the connection in a sensible manner

Architectures have been built that try to mask the unreliability of remote connections by making remote and local access to services uniform. In effect, the designer is stating that distribution is orthogonal to the design. This is clearly not a valid statement, since the effect of distribution in terms of reliability, network latency, and security is significant. Jini, with its explicit support for handling unreliability, brings these issues to the fore.

Jini's support for managing unreliability can be seen in the features the lookup service provides. The ability to have a client notified when a matching service becomes available, allows a client to work in two modes. Firstly, when all is well, the client discovers and uses a service. Secondly, when a remote invocation to a service fails, the client can attempt to rediscover a service providing the same interface. If such a service is discovered within a finite time period the client can continue as usual by processing using the new service. If a service is not found in a timely fashion, the failure can be considered fatal to the operation in progress. This pattern of behavior is one that has been exploited to great effect in RACD. Servers fail in many ways. They throw exceptions due to run-time errors, server hosts crash and restart, and JVMs crash. In all cases the RACD services restart (using RMI activation) and participate in the join protocol. Thus all clients can attempt to rediscover services if remote communication related errors occur, in the hope the offending service will restart or another suitable service is available. To improve RACD's ability to cope with failure, multiple instances of a service may be run in multiple JVMs on multiple hosts. When a client switches into discovery mode it will locate another service capable of supporting its request in a short period of time and will not have to wait for the faulty service to restart.

Scaling

Multiple services can provide crude load balancing by allowing the discoverer to choose, on some basis, between services offering the same functionality. A simple system would be for a discoverer to wait for *n* services to be discovered and then randomly pick one. An alternative model would be for the services to register with an associated LoadEntry that defines the current load on the service averaged over some period of time. The service would periodically update this entry. The service with the lowest load could then be selected from a number of discovered instances. For a small system, the central location would have one servlet engine and one PatientRegistry instance. To support more users, the system would have additional PatientRegistry services started within multicast distance of the lookup service. None of the RACD services holds conversational state on behalf of their clients. As such, multiple instances of the services do not have to keep their state in sync. However, the persistent data they access does have to be in sync. This can be achieved by the multiple instances sharing one database server or have a number of replicated databases in use. In addition Apache and JServ support load balancing across multiple hosts and servlet engines. See java.apache.org for details.

Security

There were three aspects to security that needed to be considered:

- ❑ A data view must only be viewable by those authorized
- ❑ Clinical data must be encrypted when transmitted across the WAN
- ❑ Firewalls

The RACD development made the following assumptions:

- ❑ The LAN is secure; if root accounts are compromised RACD provides no protection
- ❑ Since RACD security is based on SSL the private key for the certificate issuer has to be secure
- ❑ The WAN is insecure
- ❑ RACD must be able to operate through several firewalls

Choosing the Sun reference implementation of Jini meant that RMI/JRMP was now the distributed object protocol within the system. The connections between a practice and the central location were via a WAN link. There could be multiple firewalls, of both the router and proxy types, between a client at a central location and a service at the practice. RMI supports this with HTTP tunnelling and proxy support.

Clinical data is, by its very nature sensitive, and the transmission of such data is a hot topic within the NHS. RMI and Jini enabled the RACD architecture to provide secure access quite simply. RACD services use custom socket factories to generate SSL aware sockets for use by the RMI runtime. To ensure a reasonable level of security high strength encryption is used. As RACD is deployed in the UK this meant that cryptographic implementations had to be sourced from a country without export restrictions on encryption systems. (The JCE and SSL implementations were obtained from the IAIK Java Group (jcewww.iaik.at.) Services also advertise their support for SSL via a Jini service attribute. This gave the client a mechanism for restricting its choice of services to those that advertised support for secure transmission and reception.

In any secure system a web of trust needs to be defined. In RACD any application that connects across a WAN via SSL v3 to an RACD service and has a valid client-side certificate is considered trusted. Any application that connects to an RACD service from inside the same LAN is considered trusted. If the latter trust is too insecure the addition of SSL to all RMI communication is trivial but does affect performance.

Restriction of access to particular users is achieved in the following way. The central location has a list of authorized users. Each user has a number of roles. A Jini service advertises itself with a set of `RoleEntry` instances:

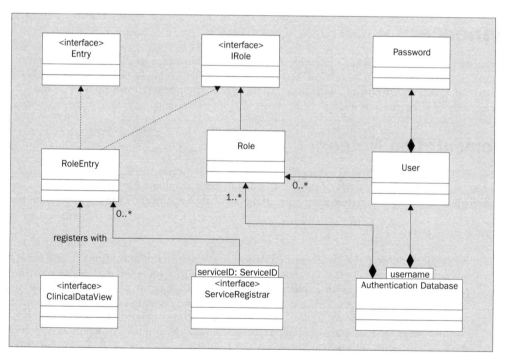

Each `RoleEntry` represents one role allowed to access the view. When a user requires a list of views, the `ServiceRegistrar` is queried for the available views. The `ServiceTemplate` used in the query contains a `RoleEntry` representing the users role. Therefore, the query only returns views that have registered themselves along with a matching `RoleEntry`.

This ensures users only get to see views that they have permission to access. `ServiceTemplates` that include a list of `Entry` objects specify a search based on the existence of all the `Entry` objects, not just one of them. If a user has more than one role, then multiple lookups must be performed, one per role. It would have been much simpler if `ServiceRegistrar` supported a more sophisticated lookup mechanism that allowed a `ServiceTemplate` to specify a match based on the existence of one or more `Entry` objects (supported an OR match as well as an AND match).

The purpose of the role based lookup model is to allow applications to select services based on their users role, not to protect the data against access by rogue software. The lookup model is voluntary. It is assumed that a trusted application will voluntarily use the role based lookup model.

An advantage of this model is that a practice decides which role has access to what information. There is no central security policy (other than the agreement of what roles are to be used across all practices). Each practice enforces differing restrictions by running its Jini services with differing `RoleEntry` instances. The autonomy of practices in defining the security restrictions made GPs more comfortable with the technology because, in most respects, GPs are autonomous and see themselves as the guardians of a patient's clinical data.

Experience

This section describes how RACD (Remote Access to Clinical Data) was structured and what infrastructure was required. The section starts with infrastructure relating to Jini, builds on this infrastructure, and shows how this infrastructure was used. The primary example will be the development of a logging service.

Implementation Notes

Rather than try to show contrived examples, production code (warts and all) has been included. The only concessions to this case study are that the code has been condensed by removing some comments and exception handling. Where exception handling is not shown, the code segment will indicate that.

Several general points to note:

❑ An implementation of a given method may throw a number of exceptions. These exceptions are part of the interface. To ensure the stability of the interfaces the exceptions thrown must not change. However, as an implementation changes so may the exceptions it is required to throw. To avoid this, nearly all exceptions in RACD are encapsulations or subtypes of implementation specific exceptions. This allows the implementation to change with no perturbation of the interface, so long as it can map the exceptions thrown in its operation to the RACD specific exceptions.

❑ Public methods are thread safe when required. Private methods tend not to be. This avoids more synchronization than is necessary to fulfil the public interface's contract with its clients.

❑ Interface names are prefixed with an `I` (the naming convention used in COM).

Building Jini Services

RACD has a number of services:

❑ Data sources. Provides data from clinical systems in a canonical form containing patient notes, patient allergies, summary of patient notes, and medication.

❑ Data views. Dices and slices data from a data source. A data view may take just the medication a patient is currently using and pass that to the client.

❑ Patient lookup service (`PatientRegistry`). A searchable index that maps patients to their registered practice. The practice is represented as a URL. The URL provides the central location with the information needed to connect to the practice RACD servers (the domain name of the practice).

❑ Authentication service. Provides an authentication service for RACD users.

❑ Remote logging. Provides a logging service for the components of RACD. This helps debugging and provides information such as access logs.

These services could be categorized on two axes; type of service (business component, infrastructural component) and location (central location and/or practice). However, they all have some common requirements:

❑ Communications may or may not be encrypted in some form

❑ Services have to restart and rejoin the local Jini community if they or the host system crashes.

❑ Services have to be well-behaved Jini citizens

Each service is an activatable Jini service. Each service needs to go through an initial registration process with the activation system. On activation, services initialize and participate in the discovery/join protocol. To provide this basic infrastructure two design options were considered. First:

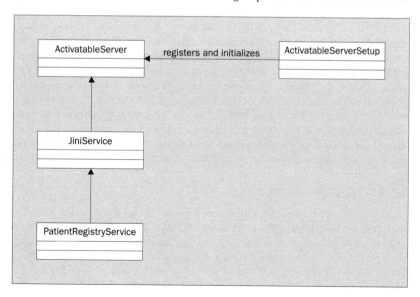

This option provides support to services through inheritance of abstract base classes. The
`ActivatableServer` class provides the code required to export the service to the RMI runtime,
handle any firewall issues, and provide support for custom socket factories. The `JiniService`
provides support for all aspects of the join protocol. The initial registration of a service with the
activation system is provided by an additional class, the `ActivatableServerSetup`. The key
advantage of this design is its simplicity, both in terms of the ease of comprehension and the ease with
which the business component can become Jini enabled. For example, a service only has to inherit from
`JiniService` to participate in the Jini community. Its disadvantage is that every Jini service has to be
activatable. Also, the inheritance relationship is being used to express extension.

Extension can often be more usefully expressed with interfaces and delegation as it tends to yield more
flexible designs. Option 2, shown below, follows this approach.

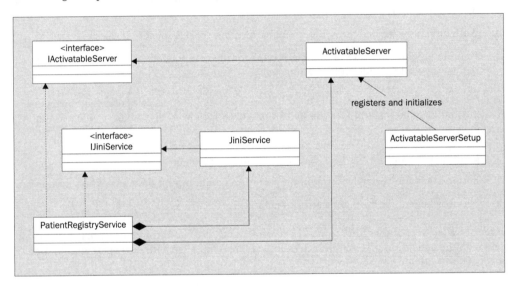

This second option has an advantage in terms of flexibility. A Jini service no longer has to be
activatable. In addition, Jini enabled business components (like the `PatientRegistryService` in
this example), don't inherit from a base class, they just implement the appropriate interface. The Jini
and activation plumbing is provided by the `JiniService` and `ActivatableServer` classes (as in
option 1). Unlike option 1, the connection to the business component is implemented using associations
rather than inheritance. The disadvantage of this design is its complexity. An activatable Jini service
must be composed with `JiniService` and `ActivatableServer` instances. These instances must be
passed `this`, since the service implements `IJiniService` and `IActivatableService`. On
reflection it seemed the additional flexibility wasn't worth the additional complexity. Since all Jini
services in RACD are activatable (how else would they restart on failure) the simpler option was chosen.

Implementing ActivatableServer

The implementation was initially simple. The server is exported on a particular port. This port is
configurable and defaults to 0. 0 has special meaning in RMI; an object exported on port 0 is allocated
an anonymous port. Configurable properties are obtained from a class called `ConfigLoader` and not
`System.getProperties()`. The `ConfigLoader` class allows properties to be defined in terms of
other properties, which were defined in terms of other properties and so on. This feature allows
configuration files like this:

```
RACD.dburl=jdbc:interbase://{RACD.dbDirectory}
RACD.PatientRegistry.db=${RACD.db}{/}patreg.gdb
# ${var} is a reference to a configuration variable named var.
```

The RACD configuration contains information such as:

- The port a service listens on

- Whether a service uses SSL or not

- What activation group a service should belong to

- What roles can access a service

- The location of any databases

- The location of the patient registry

A deployed configuration file has several hundred parameters in it, most of which are never changed but exist to allow the installer to fine tune the behavior of the system at installation time. Whenever there was a question as to what value should be used in a situation, the value was loaded from the configuration file rather than defined as a compile time constant.

`ActivatableServer` looked like this:

```
/**
 * Base class of exceptions relating to this ActivatableServer.
 */
public class ActivatableServerException extends RemoteException {…}

/**
 * Thrown when there is a problem creating a socket factory.
 */
public class SocketFactoryException extends ActivatableServerException {…}

public class ActivatableServer
{
  public static final String PORT_PART = ".port";

  protected ActivatableServer (ActivationID activationID, MarshalledObject data)
      throws ActivatableServerException
  {
    init (activationID, data);
  }

  /**
   * No initialisation.
   * Derived classes that wish to delay initialisation until after some other
   * construction work should use this constructor and then call
   * <code> init (ActivationID, MarshalledObject)</code>.
   */

  protected ActivatableServer ()
  {
  }
```

```
/**
 * If you have extra initialisation proceses override this
 * but always call <code>super.init (ActivationID, MarshalledObject)</code> first
 * in your overriden method.
 * <BR>Threadsafe: No (only called from constructor so it doesn't matter)
 * @param activationID, The activation ID of the object
 * @param data, any marshalled data (not used at the moment)
 */
protected void init (ActivationID activationID, MarshalledObject data)
    throws ActivatableServerException
{
  initRmi (activationID);
}


/**
 * Initialise RMI.
 * <BR>Threadsafe: No (only called from constructor so it doesn't matter)
 * @param activationID, The activation ID of the object
 * @param data, any marshalled data (not used at the moment)
 */
protected void initRmi (ActivationID activationID) throws
    ActivatableServerException
{

  try
  {
    final String ROOT_PART = this.getClass ().getName ();

    // Now we bind to some port.
    int port = ConfigLoader.getIntegerConfigProperty (ROOT_PART + PORT_PART, 0);

    Activatable.exportObject(this, activationID, port);
  }
  catch (RemoteException e)
  {
    throw new ActivatableServerException ("Failed to activate server", e);
  }
}
}
```

To support SSL or other forms of encryption `ActivatableServer` needs to support custom socket factories. The `ActivatableServer` is provided with methods (derivations are expected to override the default implementation) that return socket factories. Sun's JSSE would have simplified this. However, JSSE was not available when RACD was being developed.

```
protected RMIServerSocketFactory makeServerSocketFactory () throws
  SocketFactoryException
{
  return defaultFactory;
}

protected RMIClientSocketFactory makeClientSocketFactory () throws
  SocketFactoryException
{
  return defaultFactory;
}
```

The call to exportObject is modified so that, if required, the custom factories are used:

```
RMIClientSocketFactory clientSocketFactory = makeClientSocketFactory ();
RMIServerSocketFactory serverSocketFactory = makeServerSocketFactory ();
if (clientSocketFactory == null || serverSocketFactory == null)
{
  Activatable.exportObject(this, activationID, port);
}
else
{
  Activatable.exportObject(this, activationID, port, clientSocketFactory,
    serverSocketFactory);
}
```

This performed as expected. The only wrinkle is that the client socket factory must be serializable. If not then the factory cannot be sent to the client and the client will not be able to communicate with the server.

Implementing ActivatableServerSetup

Most of the work in setting up an activatable service isn't in the post-activation constructor (as above), but in the registration with the activation system. This is the province of ActivatableServerSetup. This class initially had a fairly simple implementation that created an activation group, registered the server with the activation group and then quit. It became apparent that this wasn't a workable strategy. RACD may have many services running: a couple of data sources, several views, a logging daemon, and the patient registry. Since each activation group runs in its own JVM this results in a large memory overhead. A single JVM can have a footprint of around 2–4MB. With 8 JVMs running, RACD consumed a huge amount of memory. To reduce this memory footprint, the number of JVMs running needed to be lowered. This required ActivatableServerSetup to be enhanced, allowing different servers to register with the same activation group. The trade off is that, if all servers (on one machine) run in one JVM and it crashes, then all the servers go down. The question is, what allocation of servers to JVMs gives the best balance of memory footprint and reliability? Instead of making a hard coded decision the following approach is used:

❑ When a server of class C is set up a property named *C.group* is read. This property resolves to a filename. This file is known as the **group file**.

❑ The group file is opened.

❑ If the file does not exist, a new activation group is created. The server is registered with it and the activation group ID is written back to the file.

❑ If the file does exist, then the activation group ID is read from the file. If the activation group exists the server is registered with it. Otherwise, a new activation group is created, the ID is written back to the file and the server is registered with the new group.

The purpose of ActivatableServerSetup is that registering an activatable service would be as simple for a developer as:

```
public void main (String args[])
{
  try
  {
    // Register the activatable service, PatientRegistryService.
    new ActivatableServerSetup (PatientRegistryService.class);
  }
```

```
    catch (Exception e)
    {
      e.printStackTrace ();
    }
    System.exit (0);
  }
```

`System.exit(0)` ensures the JVM exits, even if some non-daemon threads are still running. This did happen with the RACD Jini services, since a number of the threads spun off during discovery weren't marked as daemon threads.

The `ActivatableServerSetup` constructor creates a `ServerDescriptor` and assigns the descriptor to a member variable. It then calls `registerServices()` to perform the registration.

```
    public ActivatableServerSetup (Class c) throws ActivatableServerSetupException
    {
      if (System.getSecurityManager () == null)
        System.setSecurityManager (new RMISecurityManager ());

      ServerDescriptor sds[] = { new ServerDescriptor ( c ) };
      serverDescriptors = sds;

      registerServices ();
    }
```

`registerServices()` is responsible for performing the activation registration. The important part of the registration is the location of the activation group:

```
  // Exception handling not shown.
  protected void registerServices ()
      throws ActivatableServerSetupException
  {

    // For each JiniService, register it with the
    // activation daemon.

    for (int i = 0; i < serverDescriptors.length; i++)
    {
      ServerDescriptor sd = serverDescriptors[i];
      if (sd == null)
        throw new IllegalArgumentException (
        "All elements of server desciptor array must be non-null at element " + i);
      // Create the activation group.
      ActivationGroupID agi = null;
      agi = locateActivationGroup (sd);
```

The activation group is either located or created during the call to `locateActivationGroup()`. `ServerDescriptor` is responsible for creating the `ActivationDesc` and other objects such as the `CommandEnvironment`. This allows the knowledge of what properties are needed for the construction of these entities to be kept within the `ServerDescriptor`. The `ActivationDesc` is configured with the `restart` flag set to `true`. This is important as it means the services are always started immediately. This avoids problems with activatable Jini services where a service may crash, lose its lease, and therefore become inaccessible and hence not activatable.

```
      ActivationDesc desc = sd.createActivationDescriptor (agi);
      // IactivatableServer is a marker interface indicating an activatable service.
      IActivatableServer service = (IActivatableServer)Activatable.register(desc);
   }
}
```

`locateActivationGroup()` does all the work relating to activation groups outlined above:

```
   // Exception handling not shown unless part of the fundamental logic.

   protected ActivationGroupID locateActivationGroup (ServerDescriptor sd)
      throws ActivationException, RemoteException
   {
      // Obtain the filename of the file that holds the activation group ID.
      File activationGroupInfo = sd.getGroupActivationFilename ();
      if (activationGroupInfo != null)
      {
         try
         {
            ObjectInputStream inp = new ObjectInputStream (new FileInputStream
               (activationGroupInfo));
            ActivationGroupID id = (ActivationGroupID)inp.readObject();
            inp.close ();

            ActivationGroupDesc desc =
               ActivationGroup.getSystem().getActivationGroupDesc(id);

            return id;
         }
         catch (ClassNotFoundException e)
         {
            throw new ActivationException ("Class " + e.getMessage ()
               + " not found", e);
         }
         catch (UnknownGroupException e)
         {
            // Here there is a group ID in the file but it's not
            // registered with the activation system.
            System.out.println ("got to register and create group");
            // Pass through
         }
         catch (IOException e)
         {
            System.out.println ("no file - got to register and create group");
            // Pass through
         }
      }

      // Standard RMI activation setup
      Properties props = new Properties();
      props.put("java.security.policy", sd.getPolicyFile ());
      ActivationGroupDesc.CommandEnvironment ace = sd.createCommandEnvironment ();

      ActivationGroupDesc group = new ActivationGroupDesc(props, ace);

      // Once the ActivationGroupDesc has been created, register it
      // with the activation system to obtain its ID
      //
      ActivationGroupID agi =
         ActivationGroup.getSystem().registerGroup(group);
```

The Sun RMI activation tutorial indicates that the group must be explicitly created. The following code is therefore needed:

```
ActivationGroup.createGroup(agi, group, 0);
```

In the Javadoc for `java.rmi.activation` it is said that the group will be created implicitly. However, this resulted in Jini services that activated, but for a reason never understood, the join protocol could never find the `ServiceRegistrar`. Simply removing the call to `createGroup()` and allowing the group to be created implicitly, resulted in a service which found the `ServiceRegistrar`. This problem is repeatable in JDK 1.2.2.

```
  // Write the activation group ID back out.
  if (activationGroupInfo != null)
  {
    try
    {
      ObjectOutputStream out = new ObjectOutputStream (new FileOutputStream
        (activationGroupInfo));
      out.writeObject (agi);
      out.close ();
    }
    catch (IOException e)
    {
      throw new ActivationException ("IO problem writing activation details",
        e);
    }
  }

  return agi;
}
```

The problem with the above approach is access to the group file is not protected in any way. Several setup processes could all end up trying to write to the group file if they all began at the same time and no group file or activation group existed. In RACD's case, this could not happen since all the servers start in serial. However, if this wasn't the case then a co-operative file lock could be used to lock the group file using `File.createNewFile ()`.

Sun recommends that `File.createNewFile()` is used to build co-operative file locking mechanisms since the `createNewFile()` operation is atomic. Testing this theory on NT4 SP4 (dual processor) with JDK 1.2.2 and 100 threads creating and deleting the lock file, showed the operation is not atomic. If the file is being deleted at the same time `createNewFile()` is called in another thread, then an `IOException` is thrown from `java.io.Win32FileSystem.createFileExclusively ()`.

This brings to light an issue found during RACD's development. Many 3rd parties claimed their code was threadsafe and when running on a multi-processor machine the software was found to be sadly lacking. The moral of this tale is to never assume code is thread safe, even when provided by a reliable supplier. The testing on a dual processor box was far more successful in identifying these issues than the same testing on a single processor box.

Implementing JiniService

The framework is in place to assist the construction of activatable servers and their registration. JiniService extends this framework to support the construction of well-behaved Jini services. The Jini service has to perform a number of operations when activated:

❑   Create the proxy to register with the `ServiceRegistrar`.

❑   Build the `Entry` objects to register along with the proxy.

❑   Possibly load the service's state from a checkpoint log.

❑   Participate in the discovery/join protocol. This protocol to participate on three occasions:

    ❑   When the service is started.

    ❑   When the service is activated after a JVM crash.

    ❑   When the service is restarted after RMID has been restarted.

❑   Save any `ServiceID` obtained after registering with a `ServiceRegistrar`.

The initial idea for this was taken from Keith Edwards "Core Jini" book. `JiniServices` support multiple proxies. This allows a single `JiniService` instance to support a number of Jini services. This simple idea reduces the footprint of RACD by allowing one RMI server to support a number of Jini services. To successfully register multiple proxies the `JiniService` must ensure that each proxy is allocated a unique `ServiceID`. To ensure that each proxy obtains a unique `ServiceID` from the `ServiceRegistrar`, each proxy must have at least one field that is different from any other proxy registered with the `ServiceRegistrar` that supports the same interface.

Sometimes, during development, a check of the `ServiceRegistrar` using the Jini browser would reveal proxies that were null. In all cases this was a result of either:

❑   The codebase of the `JiniService` registering the proxy was incorrect.

❑   The proxy was not serializable (either directly, or referenced some non-serializable object).

❑   Having a proxy with a automatically generated `serialVersionUID` and upgrading the proxy with additional fields/methods and not completely restarting the system.

Registering a proxy, registering another one, and finding only one registered was caused by either:

❑   Both proxies registering with the same `ServiceID`.

❑   Both proxies being equal in the sense that their marshalled forms were the same, even if the service IDs were the same.

The interface for the `JiniService` looked like this:

```
public abstract class JiniService extends ActivatableServer
{
  // Attributes returned must be immutable.
  protected void getJiniAttributes (List entries, int proxyNumber);
  // Proxies returned must the same on each call.
  protected Object[] getProxies ();
}
```

A Jini service inheriting from `JiniService` overrides `getProxies()` to return the proxies to register. Since each proxy may have a different set of `Entry` instances, `getJiniAttributes()` is overridden to provide the `Entry` instances on a proxy-by-proxy basis. `getJiniAttributes()` is called once for each proxy in the array returned by `getProxies()`. `getJiniAttributes()` adds any `Entry` instance to the `entries` list. The proxy is identified by the `proxyNumber`, the proxy's index into the array returned by `getProxies()`. A sub-class of a Jini service must always call `super.getJiniAttributes()` so that the base class can submit some entries. This allows subclasses to "inherit" attributes from their superclasses.

The activation constructor of `JiniService` calls `init()`. This method checks for the existence of a checkpoint file. If it exists, the checkpoint file is opened and the last known state of the service is read from it. If the state includes a non-null `ServiceID`, then the service registers with the `ServiceRegistrar` using that ID.

Otherwise, it registers with the `ServiceRegistrar` and waits for a `ServiceID` to be allocated. At that point, the `ServiceID` and other state is saved to the file. `init()` looks like:

```
protected void init (ActivationID activationID, MarshalledObject data)
  throws ActivatableServer.ActivatableServerException
{
   super.init (activationID, data);
   try
   {
     try
     {
       final int MAX_DELAY = 10 * 1000;
       // Delay in milli-seconds to avoid packet storm.
       Thread.currentThread ().sleep ((long)Math.random () * DELAY);
     }
     catch (InterrupedException ignore)
     {
     }
     final String ROOT_PART = this.getClass ().getName ();
     checkPointLogFile = new File (ConfigLoader.getConfigProperty (
                                   ROOT_PART + CHECKPOINT_LOG_DIR)
                                   + File.separator + ROOT_PART +
                                   ".log");

     // Restore from the log file or, failing that the properties passed in
     // as marshalled data.
     if (checkPointLogFile.exists ())
     {
       joinWithStateFromCheckPointLog ();
     }
     else
     {
       joinForFirstTime ();

       // Save whatever state we initialised with.
       checkPointState ();
     }
   }
   catch (ConfigLoader.ConfigurationException e)
   {
     throw new ActivatableServer.NoPropertyException (e.getMessage ());
   }
}
```

A problem with lazy activation is that a service can die, its lease with the `ServiceRegistrar` can expire and clients can no longer get a handle to the service to activate it. To avoid this Jini services are registered with an `ActivationDesc` that has its restart flag set to `true`. This ensures that the Jini service is activated immediately after a JVM or RMID restart and has the opportunity to register itself with any `ServiceRegistrars`.

The join/discovery protocol is performed by either `joinWithStateFromCheckPointLog()` or `joinForFirstTime()`. Both these methods are similar in that each proxy is taken in turn, any `Entry` objects are obtained and then a new `JoinManager` is created to handle the join protocol. The `MultiProxyServiceIDListener` object provides the callback required to allow this Jini service to save the `ServiceID` obtained from the `ServiceRegistrar`.

```
protected void joinForFirstTime ()
{
  try
  {
    Object[] proxies = getProxies ();
    Entry[] attributes = null;
    Vector attrs = new Vector ();

    // Obtain attributes and create a JoinManager for
    // each proxy.

    for (int i = 0; i < proxies.length; i++)
    {
      attrs.clear ();
      getJiniAttributes (attrs, i);
      attributes = new Entry [attrs.size()];
      Iterator j = attrs.iterator ();
      int k = 0;

      while (j.hasNext ())
      {
        attributes[k++] = (Entry)j.next ();
      }
      joinManagers[i] = new JoinManager (proxies[i], attributes,
          new MultiProxyServiceIDListener (this, i), null);
    }
    catch (IOException e)
    {
      Log.logMessage ("Failure to join proxy " + i, e, ILog.ERROR);
    }
  }
}
```

`joinWithStateFromCheckPointLog()` differs in that each `JoinManager`'s state has previously been serialized to a file, therefore each `JoinManager` can be re-hydrated from disk. The components of the persisted state are:

```
/**
 * The ID of the services.
 * @serial
 */
ServiceID[] serviceID = null;
/**
 * The attributes the services are registered with.
 * @serial
```

```
*/
Entry[][] attributes = null;
/**
* The groups discovered for each service.
* @serial
*/
String[][] groups = null;
/**
* Lookup objects, one per service.
* @serial
*/
LookupLocator[][] locators = null;
```

When this class was tested it was found that the service never registered with the ServiceRegistrar. This was because the activation daemon does not automatically activate the service. As mentioned earlier, when an activatable service is exported with the restart flag set to true, this indicates that when RMID is *restarted* or the JVM is restarted after a crash the service will be activated. The Jini service needed to be activated immediately to register itself with the ServiceRegistar, or the registration had to be performed in some derivation of ActivatableServerSetup. The first option was considered tidier, but how to activate the service for the first time? There are two ways to activate the object:

❏   Call a method on the service, which will automatically activate the object

❏   Call ActivationGroup.activateObject (ActivationID, MarshalledObject)

The ActivationID can be obtained by replacing the call to Activatable.register with a call to ActivationSystem.registerObject(). This method returns the ActivationID. However, a reference to the ActivationGroup is needed so that activateObject() can be called. The only way to obtain a reference to ActivationGroup is via ActivationGroup.createGroup(). Calling this caused problems with the join protocol (see above). So, instead of the elegant solution, the hack is deployed. A method is added to IActivatableServer (previously just a marker interface), called postRegistrationActivation() and an empty implementation is provided in ActivatableServer. ActivatableServerSetup now calls this method directly after registration to force activation and hence allow the Jini service to start the join protocol. The method now looks like this:

```
// Exception handling not shown.

protected void registerServices ()
    throws ActivatableServerSetupException
{
    // For each JiniService, set-up the marshalled data and register it with the
    // activation daemon.

    for (int i = 0; i < serverDescriptors.length; i++)
    {
        // Code remove to improve clarity
        ActivationGroupID agi = null;
        agi = locateActivationGroup (sd);
        ActivationDesc desc = sd.createActivationDescriptor (agi);
        IActivatableServer service = (IActivatableServer)Activatable.register(desc);
        service.postRegistrationActivation ();
    }
}
```

Supporting SSL with JiniService

To provide support for SSL, the `ActivatableServer.make(Client|Server)SocketFactory` methods are overridden to return `SSLServerSocketFactory` and `SSLClientSocketFactory` instances:

```
protected RMIServerSocketFactory makeServerSocketFactory ()
    throws SocketFactoryException;
protected RMIClientSocketFactory makeClientSocketFactory ()
    throws SocketFactoryException;
```

The JCE and SSL toolkits from IAIK are used to provide the required `SSLSockets` and support for encryption. Sun's JCE was not available due to the US export restrictions of the time. (The new JCE architecture provides better support for export restrictions so this statement is not longer the case.) The support for SSL is needed if the communication between client and servers over the Internet is to be secure.

Building Jini Clients

Jini clients have to perform two common tasks:

❑ Participate in the discovery protocol to find a service

❑ Provide intelligent error handling if a problem is encountered when the service is called

It was decided to provide some supporting infrastructure that would support the above activities. This infrastructure would come in two forms. The first form would allow the client to hook into the discovery process and decide what to do when services were discovered. The second form would perform a blocking request for Jini services. That is, while discovery was taking place, the client would be waiting.

It is important to note that when there are a number of Jini services and some are dependent on others it is not appropriate to assume that a service will start before the service it's dependent on begins. With Jini's dynamic networking facilities this type of design is not necessary. A better approach is to use Jini's discovery protocol asynchronously to wait for the required service to appear. While that service is not available requests that rely on it can either be blocked or rejected; if blocking is chosen then a time-out is used.

RACD provides two classes to support interactions with a Jini service:

❑ `JiniServiceClient`. This provides low-level support for the discovery of Jini services. The discovery of services is asynchronous and does not block the client.

❑ `JiniServiceConnection`. This provides higher-level support for the discovery of Jini services. It provides a degree of fault tolerance. Additionally, it provides a blocking model. When a connection is accessed the caller is blocked until the appropriate Jini service is located, or a time-out occurs.

Implementing JiniServiceClient

The `JiniServiceClient` is used like this:

```
JiniServiceClient connection = new JiniServiceClient (new ServiceTemplate
(...), serviceListener);
```

`serviceListener` is an instance of a class that implements
`JiniServiceClient.JiniServiceListener`. It will accept callbacks from `JiniServiceClient`
each time a service matching the `ServiceTemplate` is found. Of course, a user of
`JiniServiceClient` may not want discovery to continue forever, so the callback method has to be
capable of signalling to the `JiniServiceClient` to stop discovery. In addition it is useful to restart
discovery after it has stopped. Consider the case where a connection to a service is lost (signalled by a
`RemoteException`), during a remote method invocation. In this case, discovery could be restarted to
find another service able to perform the failed operation.

> *As a rule, `RemoteExceptions` in RACD are only thrown when a problem relating to the
> distribution infrastructure is encountered. Catching a `RemoteException` is a sure sign that
> there is a network problem or the server has just crashed. Often programmers use
> `RemoteExceptions` to report all sorts of errors. This blanket use of `RemoteException`
> leads to an inability to differentiate between errors that are a result of communication failures and
> those resulting from non-remote problems.*

`JiniServiceClient` won't work over the Internet for the following reasons:

❑   Callbacks from the `ServiceRegistrar` do not work because HTTP requests can only be
    initiated in one direction through a firewall a client cannot export its own remote objects
    outside the firewall, because a host outside the firewall cannot initiate a method invocation
    back on the client

❑   It uses multicast

The basic outline of the `JiniServiceClient` is below:

```
public class JiniServiceClient
{
    // The template that is used to match services against
    private ServiceTemplate template;
    // The object that does the lookup and discovery
    private LookupDiscovery disco = null;
    // The object listening for state transitions on services
    private ServiceEventListener registrarListener = null;
    // Lease manager for the listener
    private LeaseRenewalManager leaseManager = new LeaseRenewalManager ();
    // Service listener
    private JiniServiceListener serviceListener = null;
    // Discovery lock
    private Object discoLock = new Object ();
```

Clients interested in being notified when services matching a specific template are discovered should
implement the `JiniServiceListener` interface. When `foundService()` is called, it may return
`true` to indicate that the discovery process is to be terminated. This allows for clients only interested in
the first match found. `lostService()` is called when a service that did match the specified template
no longer matches. Currently RACD ignores this, assuming that even if the proxy is re-registered with
entries that don't match the template, the functionality offered remains the same.

```
public interface JiniServiceListener
{
    public boolean foundService (ServiceItem service);
    public void lostService (ServiceItem service);
}
```

An implementation of a discovery listener that calls `foundRegistrar()` when a new registrar is discovered is also included:

```
class Discoverer implements DiscoveryListener
{
  public void discovered(DiscoveryEvent ev)
  {
    ServiceRegistrar[] regs = ev.getRegistrars();
    for (int i = 0 ; i < regs.length; i++)
    {
      foundRegistrar (regs[i]);
    }
  }
  public void discarded(DiscoveryEvent ev)
  {
  }
}
```

The main constructor calls `init()`. Code is split out into `init()` to allow for a further constructor that does nothing. This supports derived classes that don't wish to start the discovery process until some further initialisation has been performed. At that point the derived class can call `init()`:

```
public JiniServiceClient(ServiceTemplate t, JiniServiceListener serviceListener)
  throws java.io.IOException
{
  init (t, serviceListener);
}

protected JiniServiceClient()
{
}
```

`init()` instantiates an instance of `LookupDiscovery` to locate `ServiceRegistrars`. In addition, it saves the template the services are required to match:

```
protected void init(ServiceTemplate t, JiniServiceListener serviceListener)
  throws java.io.IOException
{
  this.serviceListener = serviceListener;
  registrarListener = new ServiceEventListener (serviceListener);
  disco = new LookupDiscovery(LookupDiscovery.ALL_GROUPS);
  template = t;
  disco.addDiscoveryListener(new Discoverer());
}
```

`foundRegistrar()` responds to a `ServiceRegistrar` being discovered:

```
private void foundRegistrar(ServiceRegistrar reg)
{
  try
  {
    EventRegistration er = reg.notify (template,
                ServiceRegistrar.TRANSITION_NOMATCH_MATCH |
                ServiceRegistrar.TRANSITION_MATCH_NOMATCH,
                registrarListener,  null, 10 * 60 * 1000);
```

An event handler is registered with the discovered `ServiceRegistrar`. This event handler is notified when a service is registered that matches the saved template, or an existing match updates its registration details so it no longer matches. On notification, the event handler invokes the appropriate methods defined on the reference to `JiniServiceListener` passed in via the constructor:

```
leaseManager.renewUntil (er.getLease (), Long.MAX_VALUE, null);
// We don't tidy the lease up when this instance is deleted since
// the lease will expire in 10 minutes and get cleaned up by the registrar.
```

Each `ServiceRegistrar` is then queried for matching services. Each matching service results in a call to `foundService()` on the inner interface `JiniServiceListener`:

```
ServiceMatches matches = reg.lookup(template, Integer.MAX_VALUE);
boolean abandonIteration = false;
for (int i = 0; !abandonIteration && i < matches.totalMatches; i++)
{
  abandonIteration = serviceListener.foundService (matches.items[i]);
}
```

Discovery can be terminated by the listener returning `true`:

```
if (abandonIteration)
{
  synchronized (discoLock)
  {
    disco.terminate ();
  }
}
}
catch (RemoteException e)
{
```

If a remote problem occurs then the registrar is discarded:

```
synchronized (discoLock)
{
  disco.discard (reg);
}
}
}
```

The final facility available to a client is `restartDiscovery()`. This allows a client to restart discovery for reasons discussed above:

```
public void restartDiscovery () throws java.io.IOException
{
  synchronized (discoLock)
  {
    disco.terminate ();
    disco = new LookupDiscovery(LookupDiscovery.ALL_GROUPS);
    disco.addDiscoveryListener(new Discoverer());
  }
}
}
```

Implementing JiniServiceConnection

`JiniServiceConnection` is a higher level abstraction than `JiniServiceClient`. It exists to simplify accessing a Jini service in a fault tolerant manner. A client instantiates a `JiniServiceConnection` to provide a persistent connection to a Jini service that matches a supplied `ServiceTemplate`. Nearly all the Jini clients in RACD use this class to access Jini services.

```
// Construct a connection to a Jini service. At this point all that happens is
// the discovery process is started in another thread.
JiniServiceConnection connection = new JiniServiceConnection (
                        new ServiceTemplate (…);
```

`JiniServiceConnection` provides a method named `performRemoteTask()` that allows a client to invoke an operation on the Jini service:

```
// To use the connection you define a remote task for the connection to execute.
connection.performRemoteTask (new JiniServiceConnection.RemoteTask () {
    public Object execute (Object service)
    {
        ISomeServiceProxyInterface proxy =
            (ISomeServiceProxyInterface)service;
        proxy.doSomething ();
    }
});
```

`JiniServiceConnection` assumes the service required is stateless (holds no conversational state on behalf of the client); and so it doesn't guarantee which Jini service receives each method call, only that the service invoked will match the supplied `ServiceTemplate`. All RACD services provide interfaces that are stateless, so the assumption holds. This loose guarantee means that if a remote operation fails, the `JiniServiceConnection` instance can attempt to discover another service matching the template and retry the request. This technique provides a simple mechanism for providing both redundancy and retry semantics for remote operations. If a service cannot be discovered after some period of time then the operation is deemed a failure. The period of time that worked best for RACD was 30 seconds. The time out was a trade off between giving the service enough time to restart, granularity of the retries and not frustrating the user. A retry is only attempted if the failure (caught `exception`) is considered indicative of a remote communications problem. For this to happen it has to be one of:

❑ `RemoteException`: The general RMI exception thrown to indicate remote problems. Even if a connection is refused it is worth retrying since RMID maybe in the process of restarting and hasn't yet put down a listen socket.

❑ `UnknownObjectException`: An activation exception thrown to indicate the reference to the activatable object no longer exists. This can occur if a service crashes and doesn't restart or the administrator removes all the checkpoint logs and restarts all the services (services get new `ActivationIDs`).

❑ `InvocationTargetException`: Thrown when a method invoked by reflection throws an exception. This exception only indicates a remote communication problem if the target exception is one of the above two exceptions. This exception covers the case where reflection is used to invoke methods on the service.

```
public final class JiniServiceConnection implements
JiniServiceClient.JiniServiceListener
{
  // Collection of discovered services that match the template.
  Map discoveredServices = new HashMap ();
  // The Jini service
  private ServiceItem service = null;
  // The template to find a service with
  private net.jini.core.lookup.ServiceTemplate template = null;
  // The time out for each attempt to find a matching service
  static private final int DISCOVERY_TIME_OUT =
    ConfigLoader.getIntegerConfigProperty (JiniServiceConnection.class.getName ()
    + ".timeout", 30*1000);
  // The max number of times the RemoteTask is attempted.
  static private final int MAX_TASK_RETRIES =
    ConfigLoader.getIntegerConfigProperty (JiniServiceConnection.class.getName ()
    + ".taskretries", 4);
  // Count of current discover retries
  private int retries = 0;
  // Looks for Jini Services of the correct type and call us when a service has
  // been found. (call in async from another thread).
  private JiniServiceClient client = null;
```

The exception thrown to indicate a general `JiniServiceConnection` related exception:

```
public class JiniServiceConnectionException extends RemoteException
{
  public JiniServiceConnectionException (String s, Exception e)
  {
    super (s, e);
  }
  public JiniServiceConnectionException (String s)
  {
    super (s);
  }
}
```

Anonymous subclasses of the class below are used to define the operations to invoke on the remote service. Subclasses override `execute()` to access operations on the service passed in as the single argument. Any resulting exceptions from `execute()` are caught and checked against the above list. If the caught exception indicates a remote failure then the operation is retried, otherwise it is abandoned.

```
public static abstract class RemoteTask
{
  /**
   * Override this to specify the task to be executed. If this method throws
   * a RemoteException it is considered to have failed for remote connection
   * reasons and an attempt is made to retry the task.
   * Moral: Do not throw RemoteExceptions
   * to signify a user error.
   * @param service The Jini service JiniServiceConnection is connected to.
   * @return Anything you like.
   */
  public abstract Object execute (Object service) throws Exception;
}
```

Determine if the current connection has discovered a service:

```
synchronized public boolean hasCurrentConnection ()
{
  return service != null;
}
```

The constructor initializes an instance of `JiniServiceClient` with the specified template. The discovery is started and this instance saves any discovered service asynchronously:

```
/**
 * Set the template to be used when locating a service.
 */
public JiniServiceConnection(net.jini.core.lookup.ServiceTemplate template)
  throws IOException
{
  client = new JiniServiceClient (template, this);
}
```

The method below is invoked by this class to handle an exception caught while executing a method on the service. If the exception indicates a remote failure then discovery is restarted, otherwise the exception is thrown. Since `InvocationTargetException` returns a `Throwable` and clients don't want to have to handle critical errors such as subclasses of `Error`, the class wraps exceptions that are not subclasses of `Exception` in `RuntimeExceptions` and throws those. It's a hack, but having clients catch `Error` exceptions was too onerous.

```
protected void handlePotentialRemoteProblem (Throwable e) throws Exception
{
  // Handle an exception caused by a method invoked with reflection.
  if (e instanceof InvocationTargetException)
  {
    e = ((InvocationTargetException)e).getTargetException ();
    if (!(e instanceof Exception))
    {
      throw new RuntimeException ("Critical error :" + e.getMessage ());
    }
  }
  // Determine if the problem is due to remote failure, if it is then
  // restart discovery. Otherwise rethrow the exception.
  boolean isRemoteProblem = (e instanceof RemoteException ||
                       e instanceof UnknownObjectException);
  if (isRemoteProblem)
  {
    problemUsingService (); // Attempt to find another service.
  }
  else
  {
    throw e;
  }
}
```

When a remote failure occurs the collection of discovered services is checked to see if another service is available. If one is, then that service is used. If not then, the only thing to do is null the reference to the service and hope the discovery process finds another service within the time out period.

```
  synchronized protected void problemUsingService () throws java.io.IOException
  {
    if (service != null)
    {
      // Discard the current service
      discoveredServices.remove (service.serviceID);
      // If we have another service up our sleeves we'll use that.
      if (discoveredServices.size () > 0)
      {
        Log.logMessage ("Problem with service " + service.service
          + " using a previously discovery service...", null, ILog.ERROR);
        service = ((ServiceItem)
          discoveredServices.iterator ().next ()).service;
      }
      else
      {
        Log.logMessage ("Problem with service " + service.service
          + " continuing with discovery...", null, ILog.ERROR);
        service = null;
      }
    }
  }
}
```

getServiceProxy() returns the current discovered service proxy or blocks until an appropriate Jini service is discovered. After a time-out a JiniServiceConnectionException is thrown and another retry is attempted. The blocking semantics allow this connection class to try to re-establish a connection with a service matching the supplied template.

```
  synchronized protected Object getServiceProxy () throws
    JiniServiceConnectionException
  {
    if (hasCurrentConnection ())
    {
      Log.logMessage ("HasProxy: " + service.service, null, ILog.DEBUG);
    }
    else
    {

      Log.logMessage ("HasNoProxy: ", null, ILog.DEBUG);
      long timeOut = DISCOVERY_TIME_OUT;
      // Block until the time out is exceeded or a service is discovered.
      // The discovery thread will notify this waiting thread if a service
      // is discovered that matches the template.
      Log.logMessage ("Waiting: " + DISCOVERY_TIME_OUT/1000 + "s", null,
        ILog.DEBUG);
      while (timeOut > 0 && !hasCurrentConnection ())
      {
        long startTime = System.currentTimeMillis ();
        try
        {
          wait (timeOut);
          timeOut = 0;
        }
        catch (InterruptedException e) // Ignore and carry on waiting.
        {
          long wakeupTime = System.currentTimeMillis ();
          timeOut = timeOut - (wakeupTime - startTime);
        }
```

```
      }
      if (service == null)
      {
        Log.logMessage ("TimeOut: ", null, ILog.DEBUG);
        throw new JiniServiceConnectionException ("Timed out waiting for
          connection.");
      }
      Log.logMessage ("WaitedForAndGotProxy", null, ILog.DEBUG);
    }
    return service.service;
  }
```

This method is the heart of the connection class and provides the retry characteristics. It attempts to execute a remote method call on the discovered Jini service. If it fails it tries to find another service to perform the operation. It will retry a failed operation MAX_TASK_RETRIES times (RACD found 4 to be a good default) before giving up.

```
  public Object performRemoteTask (RemoteTask t) throws Exception
  {
    int retries = 0;
    Exception lastException = null;
    // Attempt the operation up to MAX_TASK_RETRIES times before
    // admitting defeat.
    while (retries < MAX_TASK_RETRIES)
    {
      try
      {
        // This may block if this class hasn't discovered a service yet.
        Object retValue = t.execute (getServiceProxy ());
        return retValue;
      }
      catch (Exception e)
      {

        // If this exception is indicative of a remote problem then the
        // current service is discarded and another service is obtained
        // (all being well)
        handlePotentialRemoteProblem (e);
        retries++;
        lastException = e;
      }
    }
    Log.logMessage ("Failed  to invoke remote operation. Throwing exception.",
                lastException, ILog.ERROR);
    throw lastException;
  }
```

The two methods below maintain a list of discovered services during the lifetime of the connection class:

```
  public synchronized boolean foundService(ServiceItem service)
  {
    Log.logMessage ("Found service: " + service.service, null, ILog.DEBUG);
    // Save the discovered service
    discoveredProxies.put (service.serviceID, service);
    // If we don't have an existing connection, then we set the
    // newly discovered service as the "current service".
```

```
    if (!hasCurrentConnection ())
    {
      Log.logMessage ("Saved service: " + service.service, null, ILog.DEBUG);
      this.service = service;

      // We got a service so wake up any threads waiting on this object.
      notifyAll ();
      Log.logMessage ("Waking up threads for: " + service.service, null,
        ILog.DEBUG);
    }

    return false;
  }

  // Remove a service if it's in the map so it cannot be used if there is a
  // problem with the existing service.
  public synchronized void lostService(ServiceItem service)
  {
    discoveredProxies.remove (service.serviceID);
  }
```

A Fault Tolerant Jini Logging Service

RACD has a remote logging service. Remote logging adds a significant overhead to a distributed system. However, a centralized logging mechanism is essential if the state of the overall system is to be readily available in one location. The logging service discussed attempts to minimize any overhead when logging is reduced or turned off. To facilitate simple logging of messages the following semantics were adopted:

❑   A call to log a message will never throw an exception. If logging a message might throw an exception the developer would have to bracket logging calls in `try catch` blocks. In my experience this discourages developers from writing logging code and results in a system with patchy logging.

❑   As a corollary of the above, the logging daemon does not guarantee a message will be logged. For instance, if a disk is full then the log call will quietly fail.

These semantics, though lax, allow a developer to insert logging calls and not worry about any error handling. Logging is a core service in a distributed system. Without a logging facility it can be very hard to diagnose problems. Any failure may occur on any node in the system and for any number of reasons. One failure may be the failure of the logging service itself. In this situation, a useful response for a client would be to log messages to the local file system until such times as the remote logging service becomes available. This class of requirement is easily facilitated by Jini and the JiniClient.

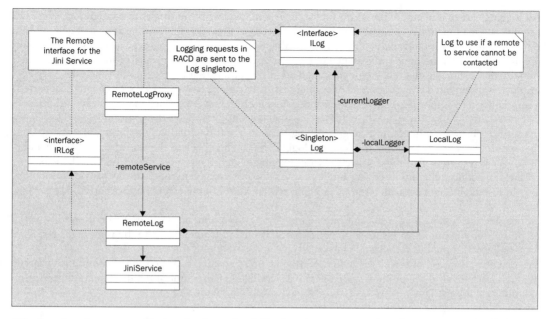

The logging classes provide two basic methods for logging messages (via the `ILog` interface). These are:

```
public void log (String msg, String location, String stackTrace, int severity)
    throws RemoteException;
public void log (String msg, String location, Throwable exception, int severity)
    throws RemoteException;
```

Users of the `Log` object may use these methods or the static `logMessage()` method. All the RACD code uses `logMessage()`. What is the point of `Log` implementing `ILog`? Completeness. If code is added to RACD that relies on use of `ILog` then the `Log` singleton may be passed to it. In addition it means `Log` is in its expected place in the type hierarchy.

The first method logs a message, the location in the code the message is associated with, and optionally, a string stack trace. In addition, the client indicates how severe the event is by passing one of `ILog.WARNING`, `ILog.DEBUG`, `ILog.INFORMATION`, and `ILog.ERROR` as the value of the severity argument. A logger is expected to read from some configuration a bit mask (severity mask) that indicates what severity of messages should be logged and which should be ignored. This bit mask can be obtained via the method:

```
public int getSeverityMask () throws RemoteException;
```

All logging classes implement the ILog interface. The main class is the singleton named Log. This class provides all the functionality discussed above. Log needs to provide access to the remote logger and then, if the remote logger is unavailable, it needs to be able to switch to local logging. To achieve local logging the instance of Log maintains an instance of LocalLog. LocalLog is responsible for logging to a file. Initially this instance is the "current logger" and all log requests are forwarded to it. When the Log instance is instantiated it starts the discovery process. Any ServiceRegistrar discovered is queried for a remote logger (supporting ILog). Log also registers itself to receive service match events. If Log discovers a remote log (by query or via a service match event), it updates the "current logger" to reference the service proxy from the remote logger. All log requests are forwarded via the proxy, to RemoteLog. If the remote log requests fail, then the "current logger" is switched back to the LocalLog instance and discovery is restarted. This mechanism provides logging even if the remote logger isn't available or crashes. In addition the Jini discovery and ServiceRegistrar event mechanisms provide a way for the Log to re-establish contact with a remote logging service after remote errors have occurred.

Notice that the remote logger doesn't implement ILog, it implements IRLog. The reason for this is related to serializtion. If an instance of Throwable is passed from a client to the remote logger, it will be serialized and then deserialized. The stack trace associated with the Throwable is marked transient, so it is not serialized with the instance of Throwable. When the exception is deserialized its stack trace is set to the point at which it was deserialized. This is not much use to an administrator examining the logs. This means the remote logger's implementation of :

```
public void log (String msg, String location, Throwable exception, int severity)
    throws RemoteException;
```

would leave something to be desired in that the stack trace of the exception passed does not reflect what was caught by the client. Rather than confuse the semantics of ILog, the remote logger simply implements an interface specialized for RMI as below:

```
public interface IRLog extends Remote
{
    public int getSeverityMask () throws RemoteException;
    public void log (String msg, String location, String stackTrace, int severity)
        throws RemoteException;
}
```

This differing interface isn't a problem because the remote logger's service proxy acts as an adapter.

The proxy implements calls to:

```
public void log (String msg, String location, Throwable exception, int severity)
    throws RemoteException;
```

by obtaining a string representation of the exception's stack trace and calling the only log() method defined on IRLog. Both the local (ILog) and remote (IRLog) interfaces' methods throw RemoteExceptions. Without this, the remote proxy service would have to consume RemoteExceptions in some way. Since an implementor of ILog doesn't guarantee its implementation will not involve some remote communication, it is appropriate that it includes RemoteException in its throws clauses.

One performance consideration relates to the severity mask. If a remote logger is only logging messages with severity ILog.ERROR and ILog.INFORMATION (the normal case), it is inefficient to have all the messages that won't be logged sent to the remote logger. Smart proxies come to the rescue again. The logic to accept or reject messages based on their severity is placed in the smart proxy, so that only messages that will be logged are sent to the remote logger. It's clear from this example that smart proxies are a valuable tool for partitioning a distributed system to ensure good performance. In addition, since RMI and Jini are based on interfaces, the partitioning can be changed without updating the clients.

The Implementation

RemoteLog is a subclass of JiniService. This ensures it's a good Jini citizen. Its constructor creates an instance of LocalLog to write messages locally and also determines the default severity mask:

```
public class RemoteLog extends JiniService implements ILog.IRLog
{
```

The constants that define the properties looked up via the ConfigLoader:

```
static public final String PROP_ROOT = RemoteLog.class.getName ();
static public final String LOGFILE = PROP_ROOT + ".logfile";
static public final String LOGMASK = PROP_ROOT + ".debug";
```

The constructor, called on activation:

```
public RemoteLog(ActivationID id, MarshalledObject data)
  throws RemoteException, JiniServiceException, ClassNotFoundException
{
  super (id, data);
  try
  {
    String logfile = ConfigLoader.getConfigProperty (LOGFILE);
    log = new LocalLog (new PrintWriter (new FileOutputStream (logfile, true)),
                  ConfigLoader.getIntegerConfigProperty (LOGMASK));
  }
  catch (IOException e)
  {
    throw new JiniService.JiniServiceException ("Failed to open logfile for
                                        writing.");
  }
  catch (ConfigLoader.ConfigurationException e)
  {
    throw new JiniService.NoPropertyException (e.getMessage (), e);
  }
}
```

The basic implementation of IRLog just delegates to the LocalLog instance:

```
public int getSeverityMask () throws RemoteException
{
  return log.getSeverityMask();
}

public synchronized void log(String msg, String location, String stackTrace,
  int severity) throws RemoteException
{
    log.log (msg, location, stackTrace, severity);
}
```

The proxy, shown as an outer class in the design, is an inner class in the implementation. Note how the severity mask is cached in the proxy so that client-side filtering of messages can be performed:

```
public static class Proxy implements ILog, Serializable
{
  public Proxy (ILog.IRLog backend)
  {
    this.backend = backend;
    this.severityMask = backend.getSeverityMask ();
  }

  public int getSeverityMask () throws RemoteException
  {
    return severityMask;
  }

  public void log(String msg,String location,String stackTrace,int severity)
    throws RemoteException
  {
    if (severity & severityMask)
    {
      backend.log (msg, location, stackTrace, severity);
    }
  }
```

This method takes a `Throwable`, which must be converted into a string stack trace before it's serialised to the server. `LocalLog` provides a static helper method to assist with this task:

```
  public void log (String msg, String location, Throwable t, int severity)
    throws RemoteException
  {
    if (severity & severityMask)
    {
      String stackTrace = null;
      if (t != null)
      {
        stackTrace = LocalLog.getStackTrace (t);
      }
      backend.log (msg, location, stackTrace, severity);
    }
  }
  /**
   *
   * @serial
   */
  private ILog.IRLog backend;
  /**
   *
   * @serial
   */
  private int severityMask;
}
```

The following code is the standard implementation required by subclasses of `JiniService`:

```
public Object[] getProxies ()
{
  return new Object [] {new Proxy (this) };
}


protected void getJiniAttributes (List entries, int proxyNumber)
{
  super.getJiniAttributes(entries, proxyNumber);
  entries.add (new net.jini.lookup.entry.ServiceInfo ("Remote Log", "RACD Co.",
     "RACD Co.", "0.4", RemoteLog.class.getName (), "N/A"));
}
private LocalLog log;
```

`main()` provides the initial registration of the service with the activation system:

```
public static void main (String[] args)
{
  try
  {
    new ActivatableServerSetup (RemoteLog.class);

  }
  catch (Exception error)
  {
    error.printStackTrace ();
  }
  System.exit (0);
}
}
```

The `Log` class implements both `ILog` and `JiniServiceClient.JiniServiceListener`. It implements the latter, so it can receive notification each time a new remote logger registers with a `ServiceRegistrar` in the Jini community. Note that most of the singleton related code has been removed to improve clarity.

```
public class Log implements ILog, JiniServiceClient.JiniServiceListener
{
```

The `JiniServiceClient` provides the high level interface between the `Log` and a remote logger service:

```
private JiniServiceClient remoteLogClient = null;

/**
 * Points to the current logger
 */
private ILog logger = null;
/**
 * Local I/O if needed.
 */
```

```
private LocalLog localLog = null;
/**
 * The singleton
 */
private static Log instance = null;
```

The current call stack can be examined crudely using the following technique:

```
Exception e = new Exception ();
e.fillInStackTrace ();
ByteArrayOutputStream baos = new ByteArrayOutputStream ();
PrintStream ps = new PrintStream (baos);
e.printStackTrace (ps);
ps.close ();
baos.close ();
String stackTrace = baos.toString ();
// Now the stack trace can be manipulated as required.
```

The method below is called by `remoteLogClient` each time a new remote logger service is found. If the `Log` instance is currently logging to the local log, the `Log` switches to remote mode and starts logging to the newly discovered remote logger. This method returns `true`, which instructs the `JiniServiceClient` to stop the discovery process as a remote logging service has been found.

```
public boolean foundService (ServiceItem service)
{
  if (logger == localLog)
  {
    switchToRemoteMode ((ILog)service.service);
    Log.logMessage ("Switched to remote mode", null, ILog.DEBUG);
  }
  return true;
}
```

In the case that a remote logger service no longer matches the criteria being used to find a remote logger, the method below is called. The method does nothing since `Log` considers a remote logger, once in use, to always be a remote logger, irrespective of any change in its registration details. This works because we'll find out if the service is no longer available when the next remote call fails.

```
public void lostService (ServiceItem service)
{
}
```

`Log` provides a static convenience method that provides a simpler mechanism for logging a message.

Unlike the methods in `ILog`, it does not require a location string. Instead it determines from where it was called by examining the current call stack.

This is the technique that `LocalLog.getLocationRelativeTo()` uses to work out, for a given calling method and class, where that method was called from.

This information is passed as the location argument to `log()`. `RemoteExceptions` are ignored, as the semantics of logging are such that exceptions are not to be thrown to the client.

```
static public void logMessage (final String msg, final Throwable t,
  final int severity)
{
  try
  {
    instance ().log (msg,
            LocalLog.getLocationRelativeTo (Log.class, "logMessage"),
            t, severity);
  }
  catch (RemoteException e)
  {
  }
}
```

`init()` is called from the singleton's constructor. This method creates the `JiniServiceClient` and initializes it, so it looks for Jini services that implement `ILog`. It then switches to local mode and logs messages to the local file.

```
protected void init () throws RemoteException
{
  try
  {
    // Always start in local mode.
    switchToLocalMode ();

    // It has been suggested that we sleep here to give the discovery a chance
    // to work. Without a sleep we always get a burst of messages to local log.
    // This is a good idea, but not currently implemented in RACD.

    remoteLogClient = new JiniServiceClient (
            new net.jini.core.lookup.ServiceTemplate (null,
            new Class [] { ILog.class }, null), this);
  }
  catch (IOException e)
  {
    e.printStackTrace ();
    throw new RuntimeException ("CRITICAL ERROR starting log");
  }
}
```

Switching to local mode involves setting the current logger to reference the instance of `LocalLog` and restarting the discovery process in the hope that a remote logger may be found:

```
/**
 * Switch to local logging mode.
 */
private void switchToLocalMode ()
{
  try
  {
    if (localLog == null)
    {
```

```
        // We override any existing log files.
        localLog = new LocalLog (
        new PrintWriter (new FileOutputStream (LOCAL_LOG_FILE + hashCode ()
        + ".log")),
        LOCAL_SEVERITY_MASK);
      }
      logger = localLog;
      remoteLogClient.restartDiscovery ();
    }
    catch (IOException e)
    {
      e.printStackTrace ();
      logger = null;
    }
  }
```

Switching to the remote mode requires nothing more than the logger being set to reference the newly discovered service.

```
/**
 * Switch to remote logging mode.
 */
private void switchToRemoteMode (ILog log)
{
  System.out.println ("Switching to remote mode");
  logger = log;
  updateSeverityMaskCache ();
}
```

Log uses itself to log messages. For this reason, recursion has to be handled. This is done by having re-entrant calls to Log treated as NOPs. Below are helper methods to support re-entrance detection in the log methods. None of these methods need to be synchronized as they are atomic operations.

```
protected boolean logCalledRecursively ()
{
  return off != 0;
}

protected void logCallStarted ()
{
  off++;
}

protected void logCallEnded ()
{
  off--;
}
```

The requests for logging functionality are all delegated to the current logger.

```
public int getSeverityMask () throws RemoteException
{
  return logger.severityMask ();
}
```

```
public void log (final String msg, final String location,
  final String stackTrace, final int severity) throws RemoteException
{
  if (!logCalledRecursively ())
  {
    try
    {
      logCallStarted ();
      logger.log (msg, location, stackTrace, severity);
    }
    catch (Exception e) // Any exception results in us switching to local mode
    {
      switchToLocalMode ();
    }
    finally
    {
      logCallEnded ();
    }
  }
}

public void log (final String msg, final String location, final Throwable t,
                 final int severity) throws RemoteException
{
  log (msg, location, LocalLog.getStackTrace (t), severity);
}

/**
 * Set to severity mask for the first time we are in local mode
 */
private static final int LOCAL_SEVERITY_MASK =
  ConfigLoader.getIntegerConfigProperty (Log.class.getName () + ".debug", 0);

/**
 * Set to local log file
 */

private static final String LOCAL_LOG_FILE =
  ConfigLoader.getConfigProperty (
  Log.class.getName () + ".logfile", java.io.File.separator + "local.");
}
```

Servlets as Jini Clients

RACD's user interface is provided by plain HTML. This allows RACD to be viewed with any browser that supports HTML 3.0. The HTML is provided by servlets operating within a servlet engine. For the servlet engine to provide an environment in which Jini can be used, two things must be true:

❑ The thread that invokes `Servlet.service()` must have its context class loader set to a class loader for which a call to `findLoadedClass(this.getClass())` will return a non-null value. Without this the JDK 1.2 RMI class loader has no parent class loader to delegate to. The end result is that the RMI class loader may load a class that is already available in the VM; it just can't find it because no context class loader is set. This means that objects loaded by JServ with class name X will have a different type from those downloaded from the RMI server with classname X. This is not a desirable situation for obvious reasons.

❑ The servlet engine must provide a security manager that supports a configurable security policy or allow a new security manager to be set. Without a security manager classes cannot be downloaded from an RMI server.

JServ (implements Servlet API 2.0) allows the setting of a security manager (as it doesn't set one itself) but, since it was developed with JDK 1.1 and not JDK 1.2, it doesn't set the thread's context class loader. Since Jini relies on JDK 1.2, JServ must run using a JDK 1.2 JVM. To ensure the thread's context class loader is set, the servlets must set the thread's context class loader themselves. RACD servlets all inherit from a superclass that provides the appropriate support. The super class is shown below:

```
public class BaseServlet extends HttpServlet
{
  /**
  * Initialise the servlet. Override and call super.init and then
  * supportRmi if you want to support RMI.
  */
  public void init (ServletConfig cfg) throws ServletException
  {
    System.setSecurityManager(new RMISecurityManager());
  }


  /**
  * <code>service ()</code> does the work before
  * <code>do</code><i>Xxx</i><code>()</code>.
  * This implementation makes sure the thread context class loader is in place.
  * Needed because
  * JServ is based on Java 1.1 and we are using Java 2.
  * @param request  The HTTP request posted.
  * @param response The HTTP response that will be returned.
  * @throws <code>IOException</code> if an IO exception occurs
  * @throws <code>ServletException</code> if a servlet exception occurs
  */
  protected void service (HttpServletRequest request,
                          HttpServletResponse response)
    throws ServletException, IOException
  {
    Thread.currentThread ().setContextClassLoader (
      this.getClass ().getClassLoader ());
    super.service (request, response);
  }
}
```

JServ has to be configured with the appropriate Jini class paths and a security policy file. The only part of the JServ configuration that needed to be setup explicitly to support RMI was `jserv.properties`.

The codebase, java executable and security policy were set as follows:

```
wrapper.bin=E:\jdk1.2.2\bin\java.exe
wrapper.bin.parameters=-Djava.rmi.server.codebase=http://ice.clouds.com/classes/
                       -Djava.security.policy=E:/RACD/security/java.policy
```

This ensures the security policy is set correctly and that servlets can serialize objects with the correct annotation. In addition, the classpath needs to be specified. This is done in the same file with the additional settings:

```
wrapper.classpath=E:/RACD/lib/jini-core.jar
wrapper.classpath=E:/RACD/lib/jini-ext.jar
wrapper.classpath=E:/RACD/lib/sun-util.jar
```

From the above settings, it is clear that the correct operation of RACD relies on the Apache web server being up and running and serving class files from http://ice.clouds.com/classes/ (ice.clouds.com is the RACD development machine). A common mistake when the system failed was to start debugging the source code, without ensuring that the web server was up and running. A number of times, after an hour of fruitless debugging, someone worked out the web server wasn't configured correctly. A list of common items to check before starting the debugging process became very useful. This list follows:

❑   Can we ping the web server?

❑   Can we browse to the codebase?

❑   Can we browse to `http://<web server host>/servlets/IsItWorking` (the JServ test servlet)?

❑   Does `java.rmi.server.codebase` point to a .jar file or end with a trailing slash (/)?

❑   Does the Jini browser show the correct number of registrars and services?

❑   Does checking the Apache access logs reveal the classes are being loaded successfully?

❑   Does the policy file exist in the location specified by `java.security.policy`?

❑   Has the policy file got the correct contents?

❑   Is RMID running?

❑   Does the system account Apache and JServ run under have appropriate access permissions?

❑   Has the proxy changed so that its serialized form is no longer compatible with currently running services?

Jini and the Internet

RACD's user interface is composed of HTML rendered by servlets. For the system to display the clinical data required, it had to obtain this from a `ClinicalDataView` (discussed earlier). This involves the user first obtaining a list of available views and then selecting one. The following diagram outlines the flow of requests:

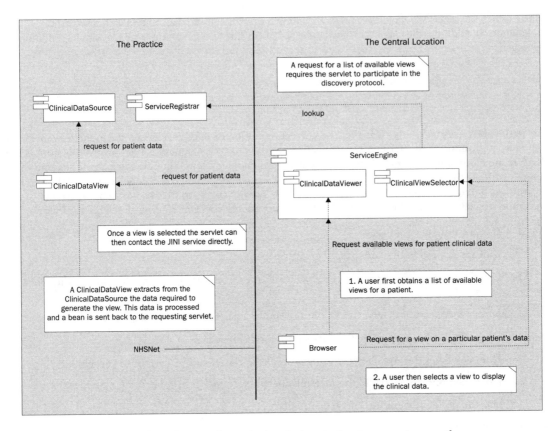

For the user to obtain a list of views, the `ClinicalViewSelector` must query the `ServiceRegistrar` at the practice where the patient's data is located. Once a list of matches has been found, displayed, and the user has selected one, the `ClinicalDataViewer` servlet contacts the service directly and obtains the data to render into HTML. This HTML may take the form of a read-only page or an HTML form. To process the HTML form will require access to services at the central location as well as the practice. This means any HTML conversion and form handling must take place at the central location. We wished to enable differing practices to dictate different styles of HTML output and form interaction (to preserve the practices, autonomy). To this end the central location must obtain an object capable of converting the clinical data to HTML (and handling form based interaction) from the practice. To facilitate this, the `ClinicalDataViewer` requests (once only) an object from the selected service that is capable of handling the interaction between the user and the form. Normally this interaction includes validation of input data, as well as write access to clinical data sources. To connect over the Internet (or NHSNet) to a `ServiceRegistrar` at the practice, a `LookupLocator` is used. This allows the `ServiceRegistrar` to be contacted directly.

The user, servlet engine and practice are all behind firewalls. The make of firewall differs across customers and may be either a proxy or router firewall. These firewalls may operate at the packet or application level. The initial plan was to open specific ports on the firewalls. At the practice this would be 1099 for the `ServiceRegistrar` and a number of ports for the Jini services. This solution was not acceptable for two reasons. Firstly, administrators did not always agree to open new ports on their firewalls. Secondly, binding the Jini services to specific ports caused a major problem. When a Jini service's JVM crashed, the activation daemon would restart it. The Jini service would then wish to bind to its port again. However, on NT the port was still marked as TIME_WAIT and so the bind failed. While the TIME_WAIT time out can be adjusted on NT using the registry editor, it was unclear what all the ramifications of modifying this time-out were. In addition not all administrators approved of their TCP/IP settings being changed in such a way. Using anonymous ports solved this problem but their use would have required opening all ports above a certain number on the firewalls. This was an unacceptable solution.

The second approach was to utilize RMI's HTTP tunneling (SOCKS was not used because the installation of yet more software on the client site was to be avoided). When a direct connection to an RMI server cannot be established the RMI runtime attempts to connect to the same port and embed the request in HTTP. If that fails the runtime attempts to forward the request to the target via a proxy. This proxy is a servlet (or CGI script) running at the destination named `/cgi-bin/java-rmi.cgi`. The request is embedded in HTTP, and sent to the servlet, which unpacks it and sends it to the RMI server behind the firewall. The response from the RMI server is then embedded in HTTP and sent back to the requesting runtime. The runtime unpacks it and returns it to the user. The process is slow but it's supposed to work. The behavior of RMI in a simulated WAN setting was tested like this:

❑   A `ServiceRegistrar` and Jini service ran on one host.

❑   A client program, running on another host, would spawn 20 threads.

❑   Each thread would use `LookupLocator` to locate the Jini service.

❑   Each thread would then invoke a method (`ping()`) on the Jini service.

❑   This method returned a string and the result was tested to ensure it was correct.

❑   If all 20 threads found the service and got the correct result back then the test had passed.

These tests were run using a number of different firewalls. Using RMI's default mechanism for handling firewalls resulted in two problems. Connections would be established but clients would sometimes never receive responses, and sometimes connections could not be established. Poor connection establishment was particularly acute with Raptor firewalls, something reflected in the RMI-USERS mail list. Browsing the Sun RMI-USERS mail list showed that many people had similar problems.

A few users of RMI had found that the switching between different connection modes did not seem to work for particular makes of firewall.

The Sun specific solution to this is to set the default socket factory to use the Sun socket factory that produces HTTP tunneling sockets. Running the tests again showed that all clients could connect to `java-rmi.cgi`, but still clients were blocking (waiting for a result from the Jini service) on a random basis. Upgrading to JDK 1.3 RC1 made no difference. The next step was to download the JDK 1.3 source code and inspect it. In a vain attempt to improve its behavior, the source code was amended to augment the HTTP headers with Expires and pragma directives to ensure proxy caching wasn't happening. This made no difference.

Coincidentally, there was a thread on RMI-USERS discussing people's experiences with RMI and HTTP tunneling. This thread had a number of people, none successful, attempting to get RMI working over the Internet. At no point in this thread did any Sun staff interject to explain what errors people were making. On reading this it was clear that getting RMI working over the Internet was going to be a problem. Reflecting on the problem further, it was decided that RMI wasn't an appropriate tool for the job. It was felt that the ideal protocol for the unreliable and often slow Internet was simple, easy to debug and stateless. These attributes could not be used to describe RMI. RMI uses distributed garbage collection locally or over the Internet, so it isn't stateless. It is not simple to debug either. The next option was to use the Simple Object Access Protocol (SOAP). SOAP is an improvement over XML-RPC for a number of reasons. The most significant for RACD were:

❑ SOAP uses XML Schema. In the author's opinion, schemas are a great improvement over DTDs. A discussion of the reasons is outside the scope of this chapter.

❑ SOAP supports more complex types than XML-RPC.

❑ SOAP messages have a description of what they are going to invoke in the headers. In the future this allows firewalls to better filter remote requests.

At this time a SOAP server could not be found that was based on Java and free. There was a free SOAP client library but it didn't support arrays and, naturally, it didn't support the dynamic class loading that RACD relied on. With time running out it was decided to grow a specific protocol for RACD. With RMI out of the frame, `LookupLocator` could no longer be used. A solution that handled general remote requests needed to be provided. The design for this su-system is below:

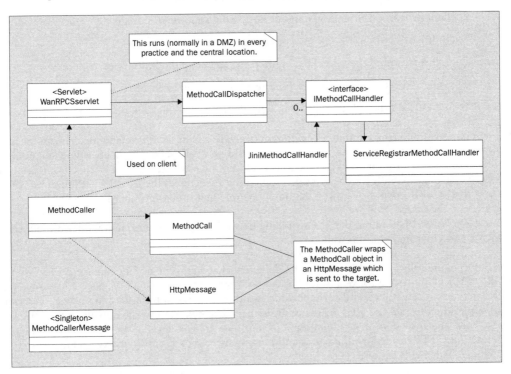

The `WanRPCServlet` acts as the gateway to the services behind the firewall. A request is characterized by the method to invoke and its destination. The destination is represented in this system as a URL to the host with the `WanRPCServlet` and a target. The target is a subclass of `Object` that is used to define which service the method is to be invoked on. RACD has three forms of target:

❑ A string, `"ServiceRegistrar"`, which specifies that a lookup is to be performed on the Jini communities `ServiceRegistrars`. In this case the method is "lookup".

❑ An object that encapsulates an array of `ServiceTemplates`. The first Jini service discovered that matches one of the templates is used to perform the request.

❑ A `ServiceID`. The Jini service with the supplied `ServiceID` is used to perform the request.

In all cases, the service discovered is cached so that future requests do not incur a lookup.

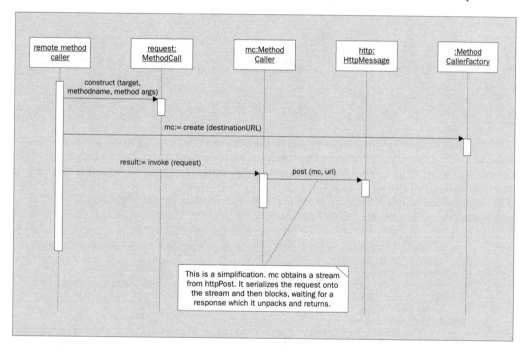

A remote method call is represented by a `MethodCall` object. This object contains the target, the method name and its arguments. The `MethodCall` is invoked by passing it to a `MethodCaller`. A factory creates `MethodCaller` instances, one per URL. `MethodCaller` embeds the `MethodCall` instance in an HTTP message and POSTs it to the `WanRPCServlet` at the specified URL.

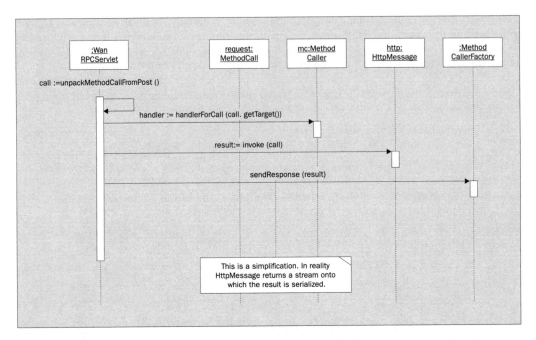

This is a simplification. In reality HttpMessage returns a stream onto which the result is serialized.

When the WanRPCServlet receives a request it unpacks the MethodCall instance and passes it to the MethodCallDispatcher to handle. The MethodCallDispatcher locates a handler for the MethodCall's target, and hands off invocation to the handler. The handler performs the operation and returns the result or throws an exception. WanRPCServlet serializes the result or exception into an HTTP response and sends it back to the client. Using this mechanism the main body of the ClinicalViewSelector class looks like this:

```
// pd.getURL () returns the URL for the practice. This is where the
// lookup must be sent.
URL remoteLookupURL = new URL (pd.getURL ());
// Obtain a caller for the specific URL. The factory only creates one
// caller per URL, returning the cached caller if one has already been
// created.
MethodCaller caller =
            MethodCallerFactory.getInstance ().getCaller (remoteLookupURL);
```

The ClinicalViewSelector displays a list of views the user may examine. The list returned is governed by the user's role, such as Doctor or Nurse. To determine the available views a lookup is executed for each role associated with the user. Smart matching by defining a new Entry implementation that overrides equals() won't work. This is because the ServiceRegistrar considers an Entry to be equal to another one if the marshalled forms of both Entry instances are the same. The only way to obtain the list of views available for all the users views was to either add a higher level protocol for view lookup or invoke lookup multiple times. The latter option was selected for no other reason than time pressure. The following code creates the list of ServiceTemplates that is used to perform the lookups:

```
      // Build up the parameters to the method call.
      Object args [] = new Object [roles.size()];

      roles = roleList.iterator ();

      for (int i = 0; i < args.length; i++)
      {
        IRole role = (IRole)roles.next ();
        args[i] = new ServiceTemplate (null,
          new Class [] { IPatientOrientatedDataView.class },
          new Entry[] { new RoleEntry (role) });
      }

      // Instantiate the lookup MethodCall.
      MethodCall lookup = new MethodCall ("ServiceRegistrar", "Lookup", args);

      // Do a call - embedded in HTTP - across to the WanRPC servlet to access
      // the ServiceRegistrar
      ServiceMatches services = (ServiceMatches)caller.invoke (lookup);

      ServiceItem items[] = services.items;
      // The available views are then displayed on the users web browser.
```

The MethodCall class is nothing more than a wrapper around the arguments, method name, and target. WanRPCServlet looks like this:

```
// ExceptionHandlingHttpServlet simply catches exceptions and displays user
// friendly error messages, nothing more.

public class WanRPCServlet extends ExceptionHandlingHttpServlet {

  // The dispatcher
  private MethodCallDispatcher dispatcher = new MethodCallDispatcher ();
  // Whether the TX/RX counter is to be used.
  public static final boolean bandwidthCounter =
    ConfigLoader.getBooleanConfigProperty(
    WanRPCServlet.class.getName () + ".bandwidthcounter", false);

  /**
   * Called once, before the servlet is used, by the servlet engine.
   * We use it to register any renderers we may need.
   */
  public final void init (ServletConfig cfg) throws ServletException
  {
    super.init (cfg);
    System.setSecurityManager(new RMISecurityManager());

    // Instead of registering the method call handlers "by hand" the servlet reads
    // a list of class names from a configuration property and creates the
    // handlers using reflection.

    String handlers = ConfigLoader.getConfigProperty(
      this.getClass ().getName () + ".handlers", "");
    getServletContext ().log ("Loading: " + handlers);
    StringTokenizer st = new StringTokenizer (handlers, ",");
    while (st.hasMoreTokens())
```

```
    {
      String className = st.nextToken ().trim ();
      try
      {
        // Registers the handler.
        dispatcher.register ((IMethodCallHandler)Class.forName
          (className).newInstance ());
        getServletContext ().log ("Loaded " + className);
      }
      catch (Exception e)
      {
        getServletContext ().log (e, "Failed to load " + className);
      }
    }
  }
```

As an aid to performance measurement this servlet keeps a count of the number of bytes it receives and the number it transmits. These figures are displayed when the servlet responds to a GET rather than a POST request. This information enables bandwidth calculations to be made.

```
private long tx = 0;
private long rx = 0;

/**
 * Display the number of bytes TX'ed/RX'ed and then resets the counters.
 * We only handle GET or POST. The default Servlet class will send an error
 * message back to the HTTP client if a different type of request is received.
 */
public final void doGet (HttpServletRequest request,
                         HttpServletResponse response,
                         PrintWriter writer,
                         ByteArrayOutputStream htmlOutputStream)
                         throws Exception
{
  writer.println ("<HTML><HEAD><TITLE>Bytes transferred since last
    GET</TITLE></HEAD><BODY><H1>Bytes transferred since last GET</H1>");

  if (bandwidthCounter)
  {
    writer.println ("<H2>RX: " + rx + "</H2>");
    writer.println ("<H2>TX: " + tx + "</H2>");
    rx = 0;
    tx = 0;
  }
  else
  {
    writer.println ("<H2>Disabled</H2>");
  }
  writer.println ("</BODY></HTML>");
}
```

The POST operation is interpreted as a request for an operation to be invoked on a server inside the firewall. This is handled in the following code:

```
public final void doPost (HttpServletRequest request,
                     HttpServletResponse response,
                     PrintWriter writer,
                     ByteArrayOutputStream htmlOutputStream)
                     throws Exception
{
  response.setStatus(response.SC_OK);
  response.setContentType ("java-internal/serialisation");
  try
  {
```

The thread's context class loader needs setting since JServ doesn't do this:

```
Thread.currentThread ().setContextClassLoader (this.getClass ().
  getClassLoader ());

getServletContext ().log ("Got RPC request ");
```

`HttpMessage.createMarshallingInputStream()` returns a marshalling stream capable of unpacking the object serialized onto the request stream. If byte counting is enabled, the size of the object (serialized) is determined by writing it to an equivalent output stream and determining the size of the serialized form:

```
ObjectInputStream inp =
  HttpMessage.createMarshallingInputStream (request.getInputStream ());
Object o = inp.readObject ();

if (bandwidthCounter)
{
  ByteArrayOutputStream sizer = new ByteArrayOutputStream ();
  ObjectOutputStream out =  HttpMessage.createMarshallingOutputStream
    (sizer);
  out.writeObject (o);
  out.close ();
  rx += sizer.size();
  sizer.close ();
}
```

The object is expected to be a `MethodCall` instance that describes which method to invoke, its arguments, and what to invoke it on. A handler is obtained that can support the target and the handler is invoked. The handler then does what is required to invoke the operation on the target and either throws an exception or returns the result:

```
MethodCall call = (MethodCall)o;
IMethodCallHandler handler = dispatcher.handlerForCall (call.getTarget ());
getServletContext ().log ("Got method call " + call.getTarget () + " "
  + handler);

Object result = null;
try
{
  result = handler.invoke (call);
}
catch (Exception e)
{
  result = e;
}
```

Serialise the result back onto the output stream and write it out as a response:

```
        ObjectOutputStream out = HttpMessage.createMarshallingOutputStream
          (htmlOutputStream);

        out.writeObject (result);

        out.close ();

        tx += htmlOutputStream.size ();

        getServletContext ().log ("Responded to RPC request." + result);
      }
      catch (IOException e)
      {
        handleException (writer, htmlOutputStream,
          "Problem marshalling RPC call", e);
      }
    }
  }
}
```

The method dispatcher is little more than an index of method handlers against targets. The method handler for `ServiceRegistrar` lookups looks like this:

```
public class ServiceRegistrarMethodCallHandler implements IMethodCallHandler
{
/**
  * The URL of reggie
  */
  private String url = null;

  public final static String PROP_ROOT =
    ServiceRegistrarMethodCallHandler.class.getName ();
  /**
  * Property name for setting the URL
  */
  public final static String PROP_SERVICE_REGISTRAR_URL = PROP_ROOT
    + ".serviceregistrarurl";

  /**
  * Property name for the listening port
  */
  public final static String PROP_LISTEN_PORT = PROP_ROOT + ".listenport";

  public ServiceRegistrarMethodCallHandler()
  {
    // We get the URL for the Jini service registrar and the port on which we'll
    // listen.
    // The handler is pre-configured with the ServiceRegistrar to use.
    url = ConfigLoader.getConfigProperty (PROP_SERVICE_REGISTRAR_URL,
                                          "jini://localhost");
  }

  // Returns true if this handler can handle the target.
  public boolean canHandle (Object target)
  {
    return target.equals ("ServiceRegistrar");
  }
```

```
    // Invoke the lookup
  public Object invoke (MethodCall call) throws MethodFailedException
  {
    try
    {
      Object[] args = call.getArguments ();

      if (args.length < 1)
        throw new IllegalArgumentException (
          "ServiceRegistrar.Lookup takes one or more arguments in method");

      if (!call.getMethod ().equals ("Lookup"))
        throw new IllegalArgumentException (
            "ServiceRegistrar." + call.getMethod () + " not supported");
```

The lookup accepts an array of `ServiceTemplates` to improve performance for multiple lookups. The result returned is the union of all the matches found:

```
      // Every match we find is placed in this vector so we
      // can assemble a union of all matches at the end.
      Vector matches = new Vector ();

      for (int i = 0;  i < args.length; i++)
      {

        if (!(args[i] instanceof ServiceTemplate))
          throw new IllegalArgumentException (
            "ServiceRegistrar.Lookup takes ServiceTemplates as its arguments");

        ServiceTemplate template = (ServiceTemplate)args[i];
        Log.logMessage ("Tunneling to Service Registrar at " + url, null,
          ILog.DEBUG);
        LookupLocator unicastLocator = new LookupLocator (url);
        ServiceRegistrar reg = unicastLocator.getRegistrar ();

        ServiceMatches match = reg.lookup (template, Integer.MAX_VALUE );

        if (match.totalMatches  != 0)
        {
          matches.addAll(Arrays.asList(match.items));
        }

        Log.logMessage ("Found " + match.items.length + " matches for argument "
          + i, null, ILog.DEBUG);
      }

      // Assemble all the items into one array
      ServiceItem items[] = new ServiceItem [matches.size ()];
      Iterator iter = matches.iterator ();
      for (int i = 0; i <items.length; i++)
      {
        items[i] = (ServiceItem)iter.next ();
      }

      Log.logMessage ("Returning " + items.length + " matches", null, ILog.DEBUG);

      // Return all the service matches
      return new ServiceMatches (items, items.length);


    }
```

```
        catch (MalformedURLException e)
        {
          Log.logMessage ("Tunneling to Service Registrar at " + url, e, ILog.ERROR);
          throw new MethodFailedException ("Problem connecting to reggie, bad URL: ",
              e);
        }
        catch (ClassNotFoundException e)
        {
          Log.logMessage ("Tunneling to Service Registrar at " + url, e, ILog.ERROR);
          throw new MethodFailedException ("Problem connecting to reggie,
                                        class not found: ", e);
        }
        catch (RemoteException e)
        {
          Log.logMessage ("Tunneling to Service Registrar at " + url, e, ILog.ERROR);
          throw new MethodFailedException ("Problem connecting to reggie: ", e);
        }
        catch (IOException e)
        {
          Log.logMessage ("Tunneling to Service Registrar at " + url, e, ILog.ERROR);
          throw new MethodFailedException ("Problem connecting to reggie: ", e);
        }
      }
    }
  }
```

This class only throws `MethodFailedExceptions`. `MethodFailedException` stores its stack trace. It also overrides the `printStackTrace()` methods to return the string stack trace. This allows the exception to be serialized and deserialized, yet still maintain the original stack trace. This makes debugging much simpler. Normally exceptions passed back via serialization lose this information.

Another handler is provided for invoking arbitrary methods on Jini services. The handler uses the method name and arguments within the `MethodCall` instance along with reflection, to call the correct method on the Jini service.

`MethodCaller` is similarly simple. It is a basic wrapper around an HTTP POST message. The constructor decomposes the URL provided and recomposes it with the pathname to the `WanRPCServlet`:

```
public class MethodCaller
{

  /**
   * The URL we'll connect to
   */
  private URL url = null;
  /**
   * The underlying object used to communicate with the servlet.
   */
  private HttpMessage message = null;

  /**
   * Construct a method caller connected to a specific URL
   * @param url The URL. Legal URLs are [http|https]//host:port/
   */
  MethodCaller (URL url)
  {
    try
```

```
    {
      this.url = new URL (url.getProtocol (), url.getHost (), url.getPort (),
                  "/eer/servlets/uk.co.racd.wanrpc.WanRPCServlet");
    }
    catch (MalformedURLException ignored)
    {
      // We ignore it because we construct it from an already constructed URL,
      // hence we don't expect
    }
  }
}
```

The connection to the HTTP server is built lazily. The `MethodCaller` is designed to be used in a multi-threaded environment where many threads share the same caller. As `HttpMessage` is thread safe, parallel requests are supported. This improves throughput.

```
/**
 * Call to get the HttpMessage object
 * <BR>Threadsafe: Yes
 */
synchronized protected HttpMessage getMessage ()
{
  if (message == null)
    message = new HttpMessage (url);
  return message;
}
```

Invoking the method is just a case of serialising the `MethodCall` as a POST and waiting for a response. If an exception is returned it's re-thrown. `printStackTrace()` prints the stack trace on the server side (since it's an instance of `MethodFailedException`) which results in the expected stack trace:

```
public Object invoke (MethodCall call) throws IOException, MethodFailedException
{
  // Post the call object to the servlet and wait for a response.
  ObjectInputStream inp = getMessage ().sendPostMessageWithMarshalling (call);

  // Read the returned object off the input stream and return it.
  // If the remote method threw an exception it's serialised as
  // an instance of MethodFailedException.
  try
  {
    Object result = (inp == null) ? null : inp.readObject ();

    if (result != null && result instanceof MethodFailedException)
    {
      MethodFailedException e = (MethodFailedException)result;
      e.fillInStackTrace ();
      throw e;
    }

    return result;
  }
  catch (ClassNotFoundException e)
  {
    throw new MethodFailedException ("Failed to deserialise response", e);
  }
  finally
```

```
    {
      inp.close ();
    }
  }
}
```

`HttpMessage` was originally implemented on top of Sun's `HttpUrlConnection`. Performing the same tests as detailed above resulted in the same intermittent client-side blocks. After some trial and error, it was found that reducing the number of threads down to 4 stopped the problems. The conclusion drawn from this was Sun's `HttpUrlConnection` (or the `sun.net.www.http.HttpClient` class that underlies `HttpUrlConnection`) is not fully thread safe – at least on NT, where it was tested. Switching to `HTTPClient` (http://www.innovation.ch/java/HTTPClient/) resulted in an improvement in concurrency; up to 10 threads would run before clients started to block. Investigation showed that `HTTPClient` has some thread safety issues. The author is aware of this and is fixing them for a future release. Once the major thread safety issues were fixed in `HTTPClient`, RACD finally had a fully working remote invocation protocol that worked across all manner of firewalls. We had lost dynamic class loading. We could add this back in by developing an `HTTPClient` backed version of `URLClassLoader` and having the `HttpMessage` load the classes for objects serialized in the HTTP response from the new class loader. Timescales meant that we didn't add this.

Since RACD has been written, someone on RMI-USERS mail list has managed to get RMI over HTTP working. The proviso is that it used a dedicated proxy (they used Squid). With hindsight, RMI should never have been chosen for internet work and the development project should have prototyped the WAN sub-system earlier rather than later.

Conclusions

The problems relating to RMI and the Internet shed doubts on Sun's ability to deliver a Jini reference implementation that works, as advertised, over the Internet. Without this, the vision of a businessman in Japan connecting to their hard disk back in the UK is nothing but a pipe dream.

Performance has been excellent. RACD practice servers are based on 400Mhz Pentium processors with 128Mb RAM. The central location needs no extra processing power, just more RAM. The primary bottleneck has been the connections between the central location and NHSNet. Compression has eased this problem considerably. It is anticipated that the move to Linux will reduce the size of PC needed to run RACD. This is important, as the NHS is so cost sensitive.

Other than the Internet related issues, Jini and RMI have turned out to be an excellent framework for building a reliable low cost scalable system. Deployment raised no major issues, but confirmed that copious message logging, though not a reliable mechanism, makes the system easier to diagnose. With no network management tools available, administration can be complex when things go wrong. Set-up on client site was straightforward since there were no firewall related issues. If a client could browse to a web site then RACD could connect to it. Jini's dynamic networking has enabled new views to be added and existing ones to be removed without any changes outside the modified practice.

Jerome Scheuring

16

Large-scale Wish Fulfilment Support

PersonalGenie is an application service provider offering the next generation of personalization software: intelligent 'wish fulfillment'. Through a simple and involving user interface process, end users create a Digital Portrait™ of themselves describing their personalities, interests, and intentions. PersonalGenie then uses a person's Digital Portrait™ to recommend products, services, and information that the user would like; to automatically configure networked devices to the user's preferences, and to help users plan complex events like vacations, weddings, and births.

To the end user, PersonalGenie's ability to make uncannily correct predictions and recommendations is magical. This illusion is made possible by a rather ingenious combination of Hollywood entertainment, cognitive psychology... and Jini connection technology architecture.

In this case study, we of PersonalGenie will share with you why we settled upon using Jini as the foundation of our infrastructure, some of the ways we used Jini in our product development, and some of the hurdles we had to overcome. We hope that the lessons we have learned, and the success stories we have to offer, will serve to promote the widespread use of Jini connection technology as the architecture of choice for robust, distributed computing.

While reading this chapter, keep in mind that PersonalGenie, as a company, operates as a completely distributed working environment. Every employee of PersonalGenie works principally out of their home, and physical gatherings of more than two PersonalGenie personnel are rare.

The specifics we'll look at involve our use of Jini as the basis for an innovative time tracking and communications tool, how we've used it in our server architecture, and some of the things we had to do to build in user security. We'll also take a look at a diagramming or presentation notation that PersonalGenie developed to encourage developers to think about the system in a more dynamic, non-linear way.

Involvement in the Jini Community

One of the elements of our success as a business, and our ability to successfully deploy Jini technology, has been the Jini Community (see http://www.jini.org/). We value our participation in the Community, which gives us ever-expanding opportunities in business, and the opportunity to collaborate with other companies and individuals to promote and support Jini technology.

PersonalGenie has been involved in the Jini Community since the first Jini Community Meeting in May of 1999, and we have had an executive presence at each of the subsequent meetings. Our Chief Executive Officer, Sylvia Tidwell Scheuring, is a member of the Technical Oversight Committee (TOC) of the Jini Community, whose current mission is to derive the process for the 'ratification' of standards accepted by the Community.

In addition to participation in the Community meetings and TOC, PersonalGenie has led discussions, appeared on panels, and contributed concepts and code to developing specifications in the Community. The Community has provided introductions to several potential business partners and to personnel who have eventually come to PersonalGenie as full-time employees.

Time Tracking

One of the innovative uses of Jini and JavaSpaces technologies at PersonalGenie is in our model Time and Task Tracking system, affectionately referred to as *Time Warp*.

There are a number of commercial time tracking packages available for small- to medium-sized businesses. When we evaluated these packages in the fall of 1998, we realized that none of them matched the distributed and highly flexible nature of PersonalGenie's projects and work style; they were inevitably tied either to a single workplace, or to a strongly hierarchical management structure, neither of which applies to PersonalGenie. This led, inevitably, to the decision to write our own.

Part of the attraction of Jini is that it presents a generic API for service discovery and control, and can therefore be adapted to many situations. One of the early realizations in the Jini Community was that the provider of a service need not be a computer or hardware entity at all; the Jini protocols might easily communicate with a user interface that presents the service request to a person, rather than to a software entity.

The example usually given of this use of Jini services is document translation services. In this example, the 'service object' represents a means of transmitting a document to the provider of the service, in this case a person skilled in the language of the document, and in the language into which it should be translated. The 'underlying' protocol used by the Jini service object might simply be an e-mail communication with the person. The translator's time would be 'leased' in the Jini sense, and the completed document mailed back to the service object, without the caller of the service being aware that a human being had been involved at all.

The PersonalGenie *Time Warp* system generalizes this notion to all sorts of tasks that can occur in PersonalGenie's day-to-day operations, such as the production of code modules, or of artwork, or the conduct of meetings and appointments, and many other such tasks that are typically fulfilled by people. The Jini service architecture allows us a great deal of flexibility in how we present the services offered by each of our workers.

Each person under this scheme is represented as a Jini service. The availability of each 'person/service' in the central lookup service is equivalent to an 'in/out' board in a typical office environment.

Tasks can be generated and assigned by the workers themselves, or by persons with managerial privileges in the system. Tasks can also be generated on a per-role basis, so that it does not necessarily matter who fulfills them.

Tasks are placed in a JavaSpace, and the service proxy representing the *TimeWarp* user interface on the worker's desktop picks up the request from the space. This user interface allows workers to select their current task from the list of pending tasks and automatically marks the task instance with the amount of time they spend bringing it to completion. Task updates are regularly written back to the space to keep managers and executive personnel aware of the progress of the various projects and tasks.

Since each of the worker's user interfaces is reachable – or, more specifically, addressable – as a Jini service, this mechanism can also function as an 'instant messaging' or chat environment. While instant messaging systems such as ICQ are freely available, and interoperate throughout the Internet, they are not secure, and they are notoriously difficult to integrate with other tools.

PersonalGenie's distributed nature requires tools that approximate the immediacy of personal contact in an office environment. For us, instant messaging is the functional equivalent of poking one's head into someone else's cubicle in a more traditional environment.

Such contacts can be carried out entirely through instant messaging – the conversation optionally being recorded through the *TimeWarp* mechanism – or can lead to a chat session or telephone call for progressively higher levels of interactivity.

For example, some workers have only the basic messaging and time tracking modules, while others have modules for administration of the *TimeWarp* system, or for managing specific groups within the system; the list of assignable tasks for an engineering manager is different, for example, from the list of assignable tasks for an art or graphics manager; both of these are very different again from the interface for managers in, say, the Psychology and Localization department.

Note that not all workers in an instant-messaging or time-tracking environment can act as clients to these advanced capabilities. Many activities – particularly for our sales and executive staff, most of whom are away from their desks most of the day – are connected to the system via two-way pagers or other low-bandwidth, partial-connection devices.

Many of these devices are capable of hosting a small Java utility for time and task tracking, and most of them have some sort of capability that corresponds to instant messaging. Unfortunately, most of them are not capable of streaming connections or multimedia services. How these devices and services are handled is simply a matter of the appropriate advertisement in the central *TimeWarp* Jini lookup service.

Jini makes possible several even higher-level services that may be incorporated into a time tracking application. For example, modules making use of the Java Shared Data Toolkit, Java Media Framework, and Java Telephony API may be employed to add shared whiteboard, video conferencing, and telephone session management. Another feature that Jini makes possible is the ability to automatically detect the source of messages from a particular worker, and adjust their available services automatically. Finally, Jini also enables device mode detection and adjustment for one's current environment – on the road, in meetings, at home, after hours, etc.

Server Architecture

PersonalGenie's server architecture is based strongly on the notion of a fully distributed system; it ties together numerous processes and entities that may only occasionally be present. It employs both Jini and JavaSpaces technologies, the former directly and the latter as the message passing mechanism between components.

One of the questions we are frequently asked when describing this architecture is 'why JavaSpaces and not a commercial message queue?' Almost as frequent is the question 'why Jini and not Enterprise Java Beans?'

There are actually a number of reasonable answers to both of these questions. In the end, however, there are three forces involved:

❑ Independence

❑ Simplicity

❑ Control

We'll discuss each of these in the following sections.

Independence

Independence is a function of writing the infrastructure ourselves, and not relying any more than necessary upon third parties for components of our core business systems: we know and have access to all of the functionality of the system to analyze or modify at our discretion. Since Jini source code is provided as part of the Jini distribution, we can rely on it for our complete solution; the same is true of JavaSpaces technology.

If we were to rely on a vendor of a commercial LDAP or message queue product, we would in essence be at the mercy of such a vendor and their service agreements and technical support. In most cases, it is simpler and faster to act as our own technical support when a developer needs to know about some critical library at 3:00 a.m. in the morning.

Simplicity

Simplicity is the simplicity of the Jini architecture and core libraries themselves; there is a great deal to be said for not providing the feature-richness of a full Java 2 Enterprise Edition or Enterprise Java Beans environment. Jini contains the minimal set of features necessary to accomplish its goals; this allows the environment to focus on adding the appropriate pieces of functionality without the burden of features and components that are not necessary to the application.

Control

Control is related to independence and to simplicity, in that it is a function of our having built the system in-house, but it goes deeper than that: it represents the notion that Jini services – even JavaSpaces – are not deep in complexity, and very little of the functionality of the system is implemented for us by the library, as is certainly the case with most commercial, proprietary software.

Further, many of these software packages make tacit assumptions about the quality of service to an enterprise environment.

For instance, there is an assumption made in CORBA that the connection between the stub code for an object and the ORB is an always-on connection; it is difficult at best to recover from connectivity failure in these environments, and it is frequently difficult to diagnose failure because the cause of the failure is hidden within multiple layers of complexity.

Jini systems are extremely lightweight. The causes of failure are either explicitly carried through the system or are discovered at the application level, with very little hidden functionality.

What can we achieve with these systems?

❑ 100% Uptime

❑ Fault Tolerance

❑ High Performance

Let's look at how we achieve each of these in turn.

100% Uptime

Each of the components of the PersonalGenie server system is an independent module that communicates with other components through a JavaSpace. Some components are also connected to our web server or other communications facilities and serve as our gateways to the outside world.

Since it does not matter to the system which instance of a component processes requests or messages coming from other components, we can take components off-line without interrupting the functionality of the system; if for some reason we have taken all components of a given type off-line, the messages for them will simply stack up until one or more matching components are brought back on-line.

However, this is rarely the case. Even in situations where we need to make revisions to running code, it is simply a matter of starting up their replacements with the updated code, then taking the original components off-line one at a time. This procedure results in no apparent interruption of service from the perspective of the calling components.

In addition to communicating with one another through a JavaSpace, each of the components registers itself as a Jini service with one or more lookup services. The Jini service aspect of each component is its control or administrative feature, allowing various options to be set for the component, such as whether or not it should be producing tracing or error messages of various types.

Options such as these are typically command-line options in most execution environments, and require the component to be shut down and then re-started. Using a Jini control mechanism however, we can perform these types of operations in a distributed and event-driven fashion that allows the component to continue execution even as we modify its parameters.

Of course, it would be possible to send these types of control messages via the JavaSpace inter-component communications mechanism as well, but this was rejected for reasons that will be explained in the next section.

Fault Tolerance

As we and others have mentioned, Jini systems are extremely fault tolerant. Part of the reason for this is that Jini systems have built in the notions of leasing and of redundancy: there is typically no reason not to run two or three different instances of a service performing a task specifically so that if one fails, there are other services available that can perform the needed function, or to gracefully shut down resources devoted to a system or subsystem whose lease has expired.

Redundancy is present at several levels. First, there are redundant components; in general, there is more than one instance of any given component running. One key type of component is the system management component, which oversees the other components and keeps them functioning smoothly. For instance, one of the service attributes advertised for most components of our system is the current load of the given component, typically expressed as the number of requests it is currently processing.

The system management component monitors this value via a listener registered with `ServiceRegistrar.notify()` and spawns new instances of a component if the existing instances reach some threshold value for load. Similarly, the system management component will instruct components to terminate if they fall below a certain threshold value for load – but there will always be at least two instances of each component running and known to the central lookup services, whether the components are on the same physical machine or not.

We provide our network with a number of servers, each capable of taking over the tasks of the others should any of them fail.

Since communication in our server system is handled through a JavaSpace, components need not all be on the same machine. With the system running over a VPN, the components need not even be in the same physical area, allowing location redundancy as well as component redundancy. This further reduces the chance that the failure of any one component – even a key component – will catastrophically impact the performance and stability of the system.

Finally, there is redundancy in the communications mechanism itself: though most inter-component communication is handled through a JavaSpace, control messages and direct monitoring of components is not. The reason for this is fairly simple: the JavaSpace mechanism itself may be the cause of failure. By being able to communicate with components through a separate mechanism, we retain the ability to diagnose the system and terminate it gracefully in the event of catastrophic failure of the messaging subsystem.

Transaction support is another key element of fault tolerance. Transactions are supported throughout Jini, including the JavaSpace implementation, and are used to provide reasonable guarantees of system integrity in the event of the failure of some logical operation. Note that this could be for any number of reasons, not necessarily related to catastrophic failure of a component. For example the arguments provided to some function by the user could be outside a valid range, and the set of operations using the entered value could be rolled back as the value was found to be invalid.

PersonalGenie uses transaction support, for example, in the processing of requests that enter the system from our web-based interfaces. We want to be reasonably certain that any request we make into the system will receive a response that we can then present to the calling system as an HTTP response. We are currently using the mahalo Jini transaction manager, but are also actively exploring the issues involved in writing our own.

Without transaction support, we could send messages in essence into the ether with no assurance that they would either be read or fail completely. Transaction support in Jini allows us to address that question and handle it gracefully in the event that some part of the request fails to complete.

Typically, in such situations, the request is re-tried on a redundant JavaSpace, addressing the potential failure of the JavaSpace itself. If this transaction also fails, the request itself is failed back to the caller. There are a number of other options that we can take at this point, such as caching the request to be re-tried at a time when the system is fully operational. This allows the request to be interpreted by a human, thus leveraging the human's greater capacity for insight into the potential or actual problem with the request.

The most telling element of fault tolerance in a Jini system is the pervasive support for leasing. Leasing provides Jini systems with the notion that, all else being equal, some component of the system must notify the system that it is still operational. If it does not, the system will assume that it has failed, and will take steps to repair the breach.

For example, we mentioned the system manager component earlier – its monitoring function keeps track of services that are approaching their load limit and starts or stops additional redundant services as needed. However, this monitor is also notified when a service's lease with the lookup service has expired, and the service can be treated as no longer present in the system.

The system manager service then probes to see if the service is in fact unavailable. If it is available, but for some reason has stopped renewing its leases with the lookup service, the system manager takes steps to shut the wayward component down, making sure that a replacement exists in the system. This is typically accomplished through a `terminate()` method on the component's administration object, the object returned by `Administrable.getAdmin()`.

In other cases, such as when components of the system are running on remote platforms such as residential gateways, connectivity failure is a frequent cause of failure to renew a lease.

By noting that the lease has expired, the system can take appropriate action to deal with the failure, such as directing future messages for that remote component to a cache or mailbox similar to the Jini Technology Kit's mercury event mailbox, to be retrieved when the component comes back on line.

High Performance

End users of high-bandwidth systems have come to expect certain things of the systems to which they connect, and reasonable response times are chief among these. PersonalGenie's server systems achieve high performance in a variety of ways: some of these mechanisms serve a fault tolerance capacity as well, and we have already mentioned some of them, such as the system manager component.

System components are only loosely related to one another, coupled principally by messages passed in a JavaSpace environment. This looseness allows us to take advantage of computing and storage resources wherever we can find them on the network, rather than being bound to some relatively fixed set of resources in the local machine or server group. This distribution includes our two 'data centers' and a number of other facilities. Though the production systems are generally found within these data centers, we have found that this mechanism also works well in development, where services are typically running on our developers' own machines, which are located throughout the United States.

Components can be stopped and started wherever network metrics are favorable. For example, in a fully deployed system – we have the architecture, but have not yet deployed such a system – we might start components on servers progressively across the world as people woke up and began their day, in one time zone after another, then shut resources down as they were no longer needed while night makes its way around.

This is a simple emergent behavior of the system, based on starting and stopping resources where they are needed in response to demand and network metrics; when a request for a service enters the system, the system can determine the 'closest' processor capable of handling that request, and start the service at that location.

Simply put, our overall architecture follows roughly this pattern:

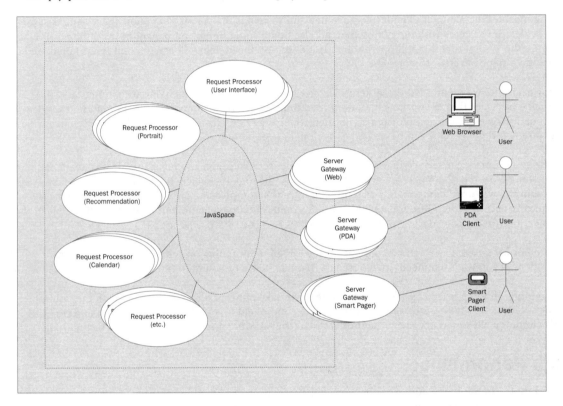

It is important to note that all of the components connected to the coordinating JavaSpace are themselves Jini services. This adds an extra dimension to the control capability of the system; specifically, each of the modules handling requests placed in the JavaSpace can be controlled and monitored as a Jini service independently of the normal inter-component JavaSpace mechanism. This architecture allows for normal message passing to occur within the JavaSpace, but avoids the JavaSpace being a single point of failure. This is accomplished by having each component report JavaSpace communication failures or exceptions directly to the system management components. The system management components in turn may try to restart the JavaSpace, or – depending on the severity of the problem – escalate the notification to a human being.

Device Control Systems

While the PersonalGenie back-end architecture depends heavily on Jini for failure handling and scalability, the PersonalGenie front-end system depends upon Jini technology in other ways. Sun Microsystems' original marketing plan for Jini strongly emphasized the use of Jini in device control. The notion was that devices connected to TCP/IP networks in various ways would advertise themselves with a lookup service, allowing potential consumers of the devices' services to discover and connect to them.

Rather than providing simply yet another collection of callable services, PersonalGenie's emphasis is on the use of our Digital Portrait™ technology to understand the end user's device or automation environment and provide control or automation for the user's available devices and services.

Home automation, or home device control, frequently implies that the user of the device is presented with a specific set of control interfaces to it, with which the user interacts to control the device. These interfaces can be of many different types, for example, a Sony Home Theater Remote Control can be used to control many different types of devices directly. In this era of inter networking, a device control interface might also manifest as a web page, or possibly a Java applet, instead of or in addition to a specialized device such as a remote control.

PersonalGenie takes the approach that simply presenting a user interface to a device, allowing the user to control it remotely, is not sufficient to deal with the number and types of devices found in the typical 'smart home' of tomorrow, or even in the well-equipped home of today.

Presenting the user with the numerous options and possible minutiae of device management is not an approach to simplifying one's life! Instead, PersonalGenie uses its Digital Portrait™ technology and processes to reduce the required interaction with the device's direct user interface to a minimum.

There are two means that we use to accomplish this: **aggregation** and **automation**. There is some overlap in these areas, but together they accommodate the basic functions of device control.

Note that in this discussion we frequently refer to the home environment; although much of our focus at PersonalGenie is on residential and family lifestyle support, there is nothing that prevents these mechanisms from being applied in a corporate or institutional environment.

Aggregation

Aggregation presents some set of device controls as a group. One excellent example of this is the PersonalGenie trip-planning interface: the user is presented with the option to set their house in 'vacation' mode while the family is away. This option allows control of numerous devices at the same time, aggregating control so that each of the various systems of the house does not have to be set individually.

The understanding of what 'vacation' mode means to each device involved is established by the PersonalGenie registry of devices and the range of settings each device can have.

For example, in vacation mode, heating or cooling systems could be set to whichever values result in lowest use during the period the family is away, while still maintaining such things as appropriate watering of the garden through the automated sprinkler system. The house security system might be set to provide warnings to neighbors or other relatives, rather than the immediate occupants of the house in the event of a security breach, and so on.

Similarly, there are several other modes or aggregate settings that the house or office can adopt from time to time. These are normally established on the basis of time, for example 'good night' mode, when everyone in the house is nominally asleep.

Automation

Obviously related to this concept of aggregation is the concept of automation. Many systems, when referring to device or home automation, refer to the user's ability to set the various programs or options of the device up once, and then to 'forget' about them until the program needs to be changed.

PersonalGenie asserts that based on one's personal data and a basic description of one's lifestyle, many of these settings and programs can be established with *no* other user intervention. When a user brings a new 'smart' device home, and plugs it in, its presence in the network triggers a cascade of events as the PersonalGenie Digital Portrait™ of the house and its inhabitants is updated to include the new device.

In a typical scenario, the discovery of a device or service triggers a callback from the lookup service to a planning component. The planning component in turn generates a kind of binary script – referred to in the PersonalGenie nomenclature as a 'wish' – that lists the principal steps necessary to include the device and its range of settings in the library of ongoing or typical scripts (or 'wishes') for this end user or family.

The end result of this process is that PersonalGenie derives an automation scheme for the device. Depending on whether or not it is appropriate – or has been established for this family – PersonalGenie may offer the automation scheme for approval or adjustment to family members authorized to make such decisions.

In many cases, families simply defer to the PersonalGenie understanding of the device, and allow new automation schemes to be enacted automatically, without the requirement of user intervention. Note that this is not fundamentally different from accepting the defaults in any software process. The difference is that in this case, the defaults apply to a wide variety of devices and systems.

Integration of Disparate Systems

One of the points that is frequently overlooked by interested parties reviewing Jini for the first time is that it does not establish a protocol for control of devices and systems *per se*; instead, it establishes a common API that can be easily mapped onto a variety of discovery and control protocols.

Such mappings are typically accomplished through the use of what are called 'bridges' (or 'surrogates'). A bridge is a piece of software that presents a Jini 'front end' to a system running a non-TCP/IP or non-Java-aware networking environment. Bridges are typically written by companies or consortia that wish to allow their device discovery and control services to be integrated into a Jini environment.

Two commonly encountered bridge examples are the Jini/X10 bridge and the Jini/HAVi bridge, where X10 is one of the most common of the general home device control protocols, and HAVi is a standard for communication and control of home audio-visual equipment.

Both of these standards specify their communications protocol down to the wire level. Jini, on the other hand, demands a much higher level of abstraction. It presents a *software* based protocol – an Application Programming Interface – that all of these devices can share in common, allowing a single system to 'talk' to all of the devices in the same way, without concern for what wire-line or signalling protocol each device actually employs.

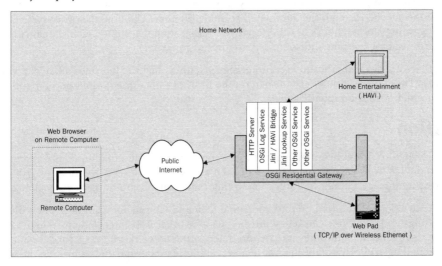

Integration of these disparate devices and communication mechanisms in a hardware sense is the province of the residential gateway, exemplified by the Open Services Gateway Initiative (OSGi), located on the Web at http://www.osgi.org/.

The expectation of most residential gateway manufacturers and resellers – certainly of OSGi members – is that the residential gateway will be exactly that: a collection of services managing communications between networks in the home and between the home and the public Internet. PersonalGenie expects that the residential gateway will contain our proxy for device planning and control services.

Obviously, the most difficult part of this process for PersonalGenie is to establish the mapping of what each type of setting *means* to each device. This process begins with our business relationship with the device manufacturers and consortia. We work with them to gain an understanding of their devices, and to build a library of the range of settings any given device can adopt, then model those settings in the context of the composite Digital Portrait™ of the family and their home.

Note that this process can proceed without the explicit cooperation of the device manufacturers, if – as in the case of CEBus, or X10 – the specifications for their protocols are well established and open. In the case of several device manufacturers – who rely on proprietary protocols that are frequently not in use by other manufacturers – a closer relationship is required to develop Jini bridging technology. The goal of this effort is to provide a consistent mechanism for managing devices and software services.

This notion of Jini as the *lingua franca* of service discovery and control systems has been only slowly adopted, but is gaining momentum as home builders, residential gateway manufacturers, and others discover the need for a common software infrastructure that can address multiple protocols and multiple device domains.

Making it Work

Part of the difficulty with Jini technology is that a number of issues are explicitly left unaddressed in the specification, and a number of issues are specified as implementation dependent. As a result, in order to use Jini as the basis of our software infrastructure, we had to make some adaptations to the system in the following domains:

❑ Security

❑ Class Services

❑ Diagram Techniques

The primary area where Jini technology requires some sort of assistance is in the area of security. The designers of Jini – rightly so – felt that security was an issue to be dealt with by the infrastructure over which Jini technology runs, and that security implementation within Jini should be a matter of implementation.

As a result, one of the principal efforts within PersonalGenie has been to develop a security mechanism for Jini services – the Jini lookup service, specifically – and a set of APIs and helper services that enable and support the construction of secured services. This was principally necessary since – at the time we began implementation of the PersonalGenie system in early 1999 – there was no mechanism for *user* security in Java. Code security has been present in Java for several years, but only recently with the introduction of the JAAS (Java Authentication and Authorization Services) has user security been addressed. The PersonalGenie security model for Jini is intended to complement JAAS, and will be updated as JAAS is fleshed out and more fully integrated into the Java environment.

603

Alongside the secured lookup service has been the development of a secured JavaSpaces implementation, which draws upon the same security mechanism. The secured JavaSpaces allows the use of JavaSpaces for communication of confidential information in a dynamic and flexible way, combining the expressive power of JavaSpaces with the confidence of state-of-the-art cryptographic systems.

A second development is the construction of a class loading mechanism that does not rely upon a server outside the Jini service architecture. As Jini technology examples are provided 'out of the box,' there is a requirement to run a separate web server process to provide the compiled class information to the consumer of a Jini service, that is to provide the class backing up the data contained in the Jini service object.

One of the mechanisms we found extremely useful to write was a service that provides compiled class information to the consumer, thus freeing the system from the responsibility of providing the class information through a separate facility; we'll examine this in greater detail below.

We also found that traditional diagramming techniques did not do justice to the distributed and highly ad hoc nature of a Jini and JavaSpaces environment. In particular, classic flow-of-control and class diagrams did not capture the 'many transmitters – many receivers' model of a JavaSpace with more than a handful of transmitters and receivers.

We'll take a look at some of these points in more detail in the sections that follow.

Security

We've mentioned that security has been one of the concerns of Jini users and potential Jini users for some time. When we began to explore Jini technology for use in home networking environments, we noticed immediately that security was completely an implementation dependency, with no support for the security functions of Authentication and Authorization.

It was clear that while it was certainly possible to implement each of the services in which we were interested with its own – possibly common – security mechanism, it would be considerably more effective in terms of both overall security and the time to implement these services if security were present throughout the Jini service infrastructure.

Further, we were concerned about the possibility of compromise in the communications mechanisms employed between the service object and service provider in situations where these were distributed across the Internet, particularly in the case where a program running on a residential gateway or device made use of a JavaSpace process running on a centrally located server; the transmission between the JavaSpace proxy and the JavaSpace server must be secure in that instance.

We were presented with several options. The official solution to security in the Jini environment involves the larger question of RMI user security – as opposed to the code-level security currently present in RMI – and will be fully integrated with the overall Java security model. Unfortunately, this comprehensive and transparent solution is waiting on developments to be included in the JDK version 1.4, which is not expected until the third quarter of 2001, possibly later. On the other hand, consumers are interested in solutions that can be deployed sooner rather than later. The only real alternative was a non-transparent solution that can be merged into the forthcoming framework of a future JDK version.

We eventually settled on a model where security information was required along with the conventional information in calls to the system that involved securable activity, including registering a service with the lookup service, querying the lookup service for services, and requesting notifications from the lookup service about changes in the status of known services registered with it.

Security information was also attached to methods involved in obtaining or renewing a lease. One choice we made in this area may eventually conflict with the model that the Jini engineers at Sun Microsystems Inc. are building. In the Jini environment, leases are frequently deferred to lease renewal managers or, since the release of Jini 1.1, to lease renewal services.

The security model currently under consideration by Sun engineers suggests that the security information of the current user or authorized agent should be passed to the lease renewal service, which then adopts that identity when renewing leases.

We felt that this mechanism was too open to abuse, in that the identity of the user or authorized agent was transmitted to and stored on the physical system hosting the lease renewal service, thereby opening an additional avenue of attack on the Jini system.

Our present system provides first that the lease renewal service authenticates with and receives authorization from the original lessee, and that it is then granted powers to renew the lease. When it comes time to renew the lease, the lease renewal service then presents its own credentials to the grantor of the lease, rather than the credentials of the original lessee. The grantor is then free to decide whether or not to grant the lease renewal, based on whether or not it trusts the lease renewal service.

This mechanism provides an additional layer of security, in the event that a lease renewal service is compromised: secured services can be told not to renew leases offered by it.

Implementation

Security in the PersonalGenie system is based on both code and user authentication. There are three services involved in secured operations: the Authentication Service, the Secured Lookup Service, and the Cryptographic Service. Much of the specifics of these services are proprietary to PersonalGenie, but we can examine the basics and some of the implementation concerns here.

Authentication Service

Jini services are typically based on a client-server model. To secure such a model, it is necessary to prove who the client is. PersonalGenie's authentication service recognizes two mechanisms for doing so:

- ❏ **A client attempting to authenticate with a certificate.** The client starts off by delivering a certificate to the service. The service then examines the certificate. First it verifies that it knows either the certificate signer, or the chain of certificates to a recognized signer. Next it checks to see if any of the certificates in the chain have been compromised. Finally it checks to see if the certificate appears on any revocation list. If the certificate fails at any stage it is deemed untrusted.

- ❏ **A client attempting to authenticate with a serial number**. In some cases it is possible that a Jini-aware device will be too small to hold its own certificate, or it may be cheaper to manufacture without a certificate. In that case a serial number can be used instead. A serial number by itself is not very useful, so added to that serial number is a signed URL of where the service's certificate can be obtained. The URL is signed by the device manufacturer. The authentication service verifies that the URL has not been tampered with, it then turns to the URL and requests the certificate that is associated with the provided serial number. Once a certificate is delivered the authentication proceeds as if the client had a certificate all along.

One of the concerns might be that someone may attack the connection between the authentication service and the certificate server. Since both systems are much less resource constrained it is possible to use some heavier cryptography software. SSL is employed between the systems to protect the communications. Both the authentication services and the certificate server authenticate themselves. This prevents such things as 'man in the middle' attacks, that is someone listening in to the communications back and forth.

The final step, after a client has been authenticated, is the authentication token. The authentication token proves to any future checks that the service has been authenticated, by a specific authentication service. One concern at this stage maybe that someone will take that authentication token and claim it to be their own. This problem has been addressed by having the authentication service sign the owner's name as part of the authentication token. The other concern some may have with this token is that someone gets the token, cracks the real client, and then masquerades as the client. To defeat – or at least blunt – this attack, a lease or timeout is signed into the token. This guarantees that the token has only a set life span.

This service is available to all other services so that they can authenticate each other. This makes it easier for services to communicate with each other securely.

The Secure Lookup Service

The lookup service plays the central role in Jini, and as such plays a central role in the security model that we have devised. At the heart of our implementation of the lookup service are two components: the security manager and the authentication module. The authentication module, for all purposes *is* the authentication service, but since we must have authentication available to the lookup service when the lookup service starts, the authentication service functionality has been integrated into our implementation of the lookup service.

Another important element of the lookup service is the security manager. The security manager is the next most important feature of the lookup service. It makes the actual decisions as to which clients are permitted to execute which methods. In order to make these kinds of decisions the security manager relies on a policy file, which is defined by the lookup services administrator.

The policy file that the security manager uses is not the same as the policy file that the JRE uses to define different policies. One of the shortcomings of the standard policy file is that it is a simple text file. This means that anyone who can gain access to the policy file could change it with minimal effort. The policy file we use is encrypted. This means that even if someone was able to get access to the file, they could not alter it without having the password. Typically, the password is entered as a command line parameter when starting the lookup service.

The other difference between PersonalGenie's policy file and the standard one is that our policy file understands exclusion as well as inclusion, so that permissions may be explicitly withheld from some entity, as well as granted. This makes things a little more complicated in the development of the security manager, but makes it easier for the administrator. By default the policy is to deny access to everyone for everything.

This policy is very flexible, as it allows the administrator to define a very broad or very narrow permission. For example, the administrator may choose to allow a specific service at a specific IP address on a specific port to have access to a specific method of the lookup service. Alternatively, the administrator may choose to be very broad and block an entire class of IP addresses from having access to the lookup service.

The security manager comes into play at two points, before the authentication of a client, and after the authentication of a client. We use client here to mean both a service wanting to register in the lookup service and a client looking to find a service.

First, the security manager comes into play just as a client attempts to talk to the lookup service. The security manager makes sure that the IP address of the client is permitted to talk to the lookup service. This process is transparent to the Jini discovery process in that when a client attempts to discover a lookup service, the service can ignore requests from clients that do not pass this check on the source IP address.

The authentication module then verifies the client's credentials. If the client has an authentication token, it's tested to make sure it has not been tampered with and that it's still valid. If the token is no longer valid, or the client lacks an authentication token the client's credentials are tested again. Failing authentication the client is disconnected from the lookup service.

Second, after the client has been authenticated, the security manager decides whether the client has access to the lookup service method it is attempting to use, such as `ServiceRegistrar.join()` or `ServiceRegistrar.notify()`. The security manager checks its list of permitted and denied services and methods. If the client is permitted to perform the action then the method is executed and the results returned to the client. If the client is not permitted to perform the action then the lookup service proxy returns a security exception to the client.

The Cryptographic Service and the Encryption of the Line

We have selected a powerful, fast, yet small cryptographic algorithm to build the cryptographic service: Twofish. Twofish is one of the final candidates selected by the US Government to replace the well-known DES encryption. Part of the requirements of this cryptographic algorithm is that it run well on both fast desktop computers and small devices, such as smart cards.

We have packaged up the Twofish algorithm, along with two stream classes, into a Cryptographic service. The service delivers the algorithm to the client's hardware, and executes it locally on their hardware. The two streaming classes, one an input and the other an output stream, make it extremely easy for two entities to communicate secretly with each other. Using this Cryptographic service, a service and its proxy could communicate secretly.

For the lookup service to communicate with its proxy it is necessary to encrypt the line of communication between the lookup service and its proxy. Since this is a necessary part for the lookup service to function properly this service has been integrated into the lookup service as a module. When the lookup service delivers its proxy to the client it is sent with a secret key. This key is then used by the lookup service and the proxy to conduct secret communications.

This style of cryptography/communications is known as a shared secret key. To avoid problems with the key being stolen, the lookup service rotates the key used every time. This ensures that the theft of a single shared key will have a minimal impact on the system. Keys are typically generated with the assistance of a thermal noise type random number generator attached to the PersonalGenie servers.

Class Services

One of the elements frequently noted by newcomers to Jini technology is the requirement of an external source of class information for service objects and attributes acquired from the lookup service.

This is generally regarded as a side effect of Jini technology's dependence on `java.rmi.MarshalledObject` for transmitting service items to the consumer of the service. While this technique and associated dependence certainly work, they frequently raise issues of security and portability. Many of the issues of security have been dealt with in the PersonalGenie implementation of a secured lookup service, described in the previous section. Here, we address the issues of code portability.

In the sense that this term is usually meant, portability refers to the capability of executing a particular piece of code on several different types of platforms. Here, the execution environment, Java, is consistent from host to host, but the specifics – items such as the host's name and capabilities – may differ dramatically.

Additionally, host services such as HTTP and FTP daemons may either crash, or may not have been started. Codebase annotations may point to the wrong server, or may be absent altogether. In distributed environments where components may be on servers or devices separated by extremely high latency, the possibility of failure increases with every new component or service added to the system.

In consideration of these things, and in working with certificates and authentication tokens in the secure lookup environment, we realized that a simple mechanism existed to deal with many of the complications of class management in highly distributed environments: make the class loading mechanism itself a Jini service, and thereby gain the Jini environment's self-healing and graceful failure mechanisms.

Once we had conceived of a Jini class loader or class management service, a number of possibilities for the future immediately came to mind; since this service presents a consistent interface for class loading, it may be used as a front end for many different sources of class information. For instance, class information could be drawn from a database where it was stored as a BLOB (binary large object), from a version control system, or from a secondary highly distributed file system.

Using a Jini Class Loader

In its expression, using a Class Loader Jini service is a combination of the techniques for using Jini services and class loaders. In its simplest form, a Jini service class loader is invoked thus:

```
PackageNameEntry[] peTemplate = { new PackageNameEntry("org.jini.mypackage") };
Class[] clTemplate = { Class.forName("java.lang.ClassLoader") };
ServiceTemplate st = new ServiceTemplate(clTemplate, peTemplate);
ClassLoader cl = (ClassLoader)serviceRegistrar.lookup(st);
Thread.currentThread().setContextClassLoader(cl);
```

The assumption made by this pattern, of course, is that the calling program knows the packages for which it will load classes, and that the current security manager will allow the instantiation of class loaders at run time. There are, of course, a number of other criteria that can be used to select a particular class loader; the example shown here searches for a class loader that 'knows' how to load classes in the package `org.jini.mypackage`.

A further criterion could be the inclusion of the address or location of the provider of the class information, so as to minimize network latency, for example "I want a class loader for this package, the server for which is located in my building of the corporate headquarters".

Implementation

As is so frequently the case with Jini services, a simple proof-of-concept implementation can be very simple indeed, and a robust implementation extremely complex.

We begin with the entries used in the selection of the package:

```
package com.personalgenie.jini;

import net.jini.core.entry.*;

public class PackageEntry implements Entry
{
    public String packageName;
}
```

And the entry used to transmit the byte codes that define the class:

```
package com.personalgenie.jini;

import net.jini.core.entry.*;

public class ByteArrayEntry implements Entry
{
    public byte[] bytes;
}
```

The code that implements the service is – following the normal Jini pattern – divided into the service object implementation and the provider implementation.

The provider implementation is considerably simpler, since it does not have to deal itself with the complexities of class loading in several different environments:

```
/*
 * ClassLoaderProvider.java
 */

package com.personalgenie.jini;

import com.personalgenie.servicebasics.*;
import net.jini.core.entry.*;
import java.util.*;
import java.net.*;
import java.io.*;

/**
   Provides class bytecode information to the service object via a simple socket-
based communication mechanism. This implementation is a straightforward proof-of-
concept for a Jini class loader, and only deals with .class files located in a
directory accessible to the process running the provider..
 */
public class ClassLoaderProvider extends BasicActiveProvider
{
    /**
        It's necessary to explicitly include the constructor for the class
        because the constructor throws IOException. Note that if your service
        depends on other Jini services being available, this is probably
        the place where you'll set up to establish contact with the lookup
        service. Actual contact, of course, will probably be deferred to
        the appropriate event handlers.
     */
    public ClassLoaderProvider() throws IOException
    {
```

```
        super();
    }


/**
    Simple override of the BasicActiveService class.
*/
public Object createServiceObject(Properties config, InetAddress host,
                                  int port)
{
    return new ClassLoaderService(host, port);
}


/**
    You can initialize the service attributes however you like; the superclass
    createAttributes method is convenient for initializing the ServiceInfo and
    Name Entries.
*/
public Entry[] createAttributes(Properties config)
{
    // In this instance, package.name is an entry in the .properties file for
    // this service provider.
    PackageEntry pe = new PackageEntry();
    pe.packageName = config.getProperty("package.name");

    // createAttributes creates a set of standard attributes
    // from the entries in this provider's .properties file.
    Entry[] basics = super.createAttributes(config);

    Vector entryVec = new Vector();
    for (int entryIndex = 0; entryIndex < basics.length; entryIndex++)
    {
        entryVec.add(basics[entryIndex]);
    }
    entryVec.add(pe);

    Entry[] completeEntries = (Entry[])entryVec.toArray(basics);

    return completeEntries;
}


/**
    This is the basic functionality override. Any processing specific to your
    service will take place here. Note that since, in general, ALL requests are
    channeled through this method, you will need to use some technique to
    dispatch various types of requests from different methods of the service
    object.
*/
public Serializable handleRequest(Object msg)
{
    ByteArrayEntry bEntry = new ByteArrayEntry();

    // In the case of the ClassLoaderService, the incoming request is a
    String...
    if (!(msg instanceof String))
    {
        byte[] empty = { };
        bEntry.bytes = empty;
```

```
                return bEntry;
        }

        String rawClassName = (String)msg;

        // Okay-- now we turn the class name into a file name...

        StringBuffer nameBuf = new StringBuffer(rawClassName);
        for (int charIndex = 0; charIndex < nameBuf.length(); charIndex++)
        {
            if (nameBuf.charAt(charIndex) == '.')
            {
                nameBuf.setCharAt(charIndex, File.separatorChar);
            }
        }
        String fileName = nameBuf.toString() + ".class";

        try
        {
            // Once we have the file name, we can read the file as
            // an array of bytes.
            File f = new File(fileName);
            bEntry.bytes = new byte[(int)f.length()];

            FileInputStream fis = new FileInputStream(fileName);
            fis.read(bEntry.bytes);
            fis.close();
        }
        catch (Exception ex)
        {
            byte[] empty = { };
            bEntry.bytes = empty;
        }

        return bEntry;
    }
}
/*
 * ClassLoaderService.java
 */

package com.personalgenie.jini;

import net.jini.lookup.ClientLookupManager;
import net.jini.core.lookup.*;

import java.io.*;
import java.net.*;
import java.rmi.*;


/**
   A simple example of the use of the BasicActiveService class.
 */
public class ClassLoaderService extends ClassLoader
{
    protected InetAddress providerHost;
    protected int providerPort;

    /**
```

```
      The superclass, BasicActiveService, does not have a default
      constructor, so we override the two-argument constructor here.
   */
   public ClassLoaderService(InetAddress host, int port)
   {
      providerHost = host;
      providerPort = port;
   }


   /**
      The basic override for a class loader in the delegation model of JDK 1.2
      and higher.
   */
   protected Class findClass(String className) throws ClassNotFoundException
   {
      Class foundClass = null;
      byte[] foundBytes;

      // Note that submit is susceptible to IOExceptions.
      try
      {
         ByteArrayEntry byteEntry = (ByteArrayEntry)submit(className);

         foundBytes = byteEntry.bytes;
         if (foundBytes.length > 0)
         {
            foundClass = defineClass(className, foundBytes, 0,
                                     foundBytes.length);
         }
      }
      catch (IOException ioEx)
      {
         // The following "if" clause will change this
         // into a ClassNotFoundException.
      }
      catch (ClassFormatError cfErr)
      {
         // The next clause will change this into a
         // ClassNotFoundException.
      }

      if (foundClass == null)
      {
         throw new ClassNotFoundException("Jini ClassLoader could not find "
            + className);
      }

      return foundClass;
   }

   /**
      Accepts a serializable object and submits it as a MarshalledObject to the
      known host and port.
      Then, reads a MarshalledObject returned by the Provider, unmarshals it, and
      returns it to the caller.
   */
   public Object submit(Serializable msg) throws IOException
   {
```

```
MarshalledObject outgoing = null;
MarshalledObject incoming = null;
Object response = null;

Socket s = null;

// Try to construct an outgoing object:
try
{
    outgoing = new MarshalledObject(msg);
}
catch (IOException ioex)
{
    // Outgoing message may not be serializable
    // Throw annotated exception
    throw new IOException("Exception marshalling outgoing message: "
        + ioex.getMessage());
}


// Try to connect to service provider
try
{
    s = new Socket(providerHost, providerPort);
}
catch (IOException ioex)
{
    // Could not connect to provider

    // Report conditions
    System.err.println("Exception: (" + providerHost.toString() + ":"
        + providerPort + ")");

    // Throw annotated exception
    throw new IOException("Exception connecting to provider: "
        + ioex.getMessage());
}

// Try to send message to provider
try
{
    ObjectOutputStream oos = new ObjectOutputStream(s.getOutputStream());
    oos.writeObject(outgoing);
}
catch (IOException ioex)
{
    // Failed to write our outgoing message

    // Throw annotated exception
    throw new IOException("Exception sending message: " +
                        ioex.toString());
}

// Try to receive response from provider
try
{
    ObjectInputStream ois = new ObjectInputStream(s.getInputStream());
    incoming = (MarshalledObject)ois.readObject();
}
catch (Exception ex)
{
    // Could not read response
```

```
                    // Throw annotated exception
                    throw new IOException("Exception reading response: " +
                                          ex.getMessage());
            }
            finally
            {
                try
                {
                    s.close();
                }
                catch (IOException ioex)
                {
                    // Could not close socket...
                }
            }

            // Try to unmarshal the provider's response
            try
            {
                response = incoming.get();
            }
            catch (Exception ex)
            {
                // Could not deserialize response

                // Throw annotated exception
                throw new IOException("Exception unmarshalling response: "
                    + ex.getMessage());
            }

            return response;
        }

    }
```

It was once said that no one – not event the people who implemented the system – really understands all of the intricacies and emergent behaviors of class loading in Java. This may well be true; however, for purposes of approaching the goals of object distribution and code mobility, Jini technology applied to class loading is a good approach.

Diagramming Technique

One of the interesting points about Jini technology in general – and JavaSpaces in particular – is the challenge it presents to visualization of the system in operation. In particular, the classes and attributes advertised by a service or expected by a process monitoring a JavaSpace can be cumbersome to document in notations meant to provide a more static view of the system emphasizing linear flow of control.

To this end, one of the innovations PersonalGenie introduced was a set of diagramming techniques that emphasize the unique nature of Jini and JavaSpace environments.

Services

A Jini service can be addressed in a number of ways, but the simplest representation is that of the class of its service object, and the classes and values of the attributes it advertises on the lookup service. Note that an attribute of a service is always of some class implementing net.jini.core.entry.Entry, as are entries in JavaSpaces; we use the term 'attribute' with reference to Jini services and 'entry' with respect to JavaSpaces.

At its core, the service object is a single instance of some specific class. We represent this with a rectangle, typically labeled with the colloquial name of the service. This is frequently (but not always) the value of the Name attribute of the service. The rectangle may also have the name of the class of the service object:

So far, we're not doing anything different from a number of design notations. Now, however, we introduce some of the unique nature of Jini services.

The left side of the basic rectangle or service icon indicates the interfaces that the service implements or the classes from which it inherits.

These are typically attached to the left side of the service icon by single lines. The lines may be perpendicular to the left side of the service icon, or they may be at an angle to it to allow for readability. Similarly, they may be of varying lengths.

The icons representing the interfaces and classes are typically just the names of those interfaces or classes. The package name may be omitted for clarity, but should be included in cases where there may be some ambiguity or where the distinction is relevant to the service. The interfaces and classes may also be represented by graphical designs in addition to the name. We have found this to be a useful mnemonic device when several services implement the same interfaces or descend from the same classes.

All classes and interfaces that are relevant to the expected operation of the service should be represented. The class java.lang.Object may always be omitted. The interface java.io.Serializable may also be omitted, as it can be assumed in a Jini service object.

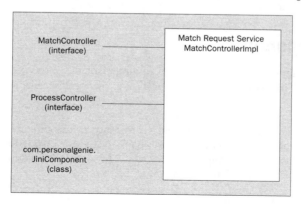

From the bottom of the service icon extend similar lines representing attributes. An attribute is typically given by the name of its class, such as `ServiceInfo`, `Name`, `Location`, etc. Attribute names may be followed by a colon and a string representation of the designated values of the attribute.

For many services, we find it useful to provide an `Address` attribute – an instance of `net.jini.lookup.entry.Address` – that describes the location of the server where the process is currently running. PersonalGenie is a fully distributed, full-time telecommute company, and in our development environment services are frequently running on machines located at each of our developer's facilities. The `Address` attribute helps us to track which developers are working with which services.

Similar to the classes and interfaces 'side' of the service icon, attributes may be represented solely as text, or they may be represented by a small decorative icon as an aid to memory and to relate them to similar attributes of other services. All expected attributes of a service should be represented: there are generally no attributes that can be omitted as trivial or obvious.

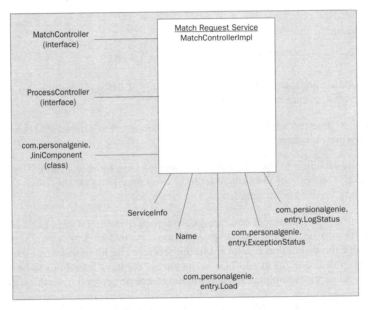

Fully decorated icons such as these are typically grouped in displays by their relationships to each other. For example, in PersonalGenie's system documentation, all of the process control services are grouped together, as are known device services, and messaging services.

JavaSpace Components

In addition to being Jini services, most components of the PersonalGenie system rely on JavaSpaces for inter-process messaging. This requires some modification to the basic service icon model given in the previous section.

In a JavaSpace, messages are extremely undirected. Conventional flow-of-control diagrams and descriptions tend to be overly complex when describing the activity – or possible range of activity – of a JavaSpace in operation. At the same time, the model of the JavaSpace itself, and the structure of components that interact with it, is relatively simple.

Most of PersonalGenie's components are built in such a way that they 'watch' a JavaSpace for entries that they understand or that are directed to them, and place their responses back into it. Some components are connected to the world outside the JavaSpace by other means – servlets, for example – and serve as a source of entries into the JavaSpace.

For a component's interaction with the space, there are two basic notational requirements: we indicate the classes and values of entries that are read or taken by the component, and indicate those entries that are written by the component back into the space.

For these purposes, we use a similar notation to that described for services, above, except that the left side of the component icon is decorated with the name and possibly the value of the entries for which the component 'watches' the JavaSpace, and the right side is used to describe the entries that the component will write to the JavaSpace.

We have found that representing entries with decorative images in this case is a great assistance in understanding the flow of entries among components that participate in the JavaSpace.

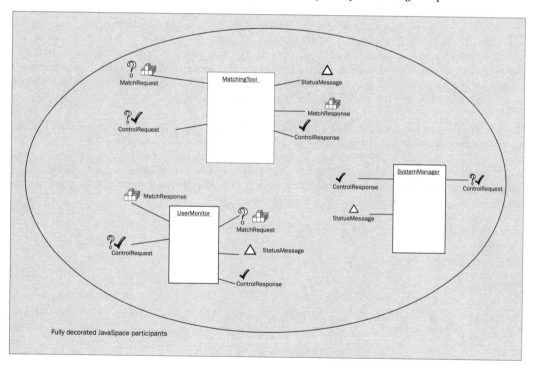

Fully decorated JavaSpace participants

Summary

Jini technology is a technology undergoing a rapid process of maturation. The promise of the technology is immense, and even the few applications that have been constructed using it to date have shown the power of a distributed infrastructure that intrinsically addresses issues of network latency and component failure.

Distributed architectures to date have focused on enterprise environments, where guarantees of quality of service – including low latency – can be met on a regular basis. Jini challenges this model by both recognizing and embracing the frequent *lack* of reliability in extremely sensitive or highly distributed networks where users expect results *in spite* of any issues with the network or its equipment.

The end user of the personal computer, who may be content with system failures or dropped connections of the order of once a day, is rapidly becoming the consumer of personal and home electronics, expecting reliability on a par with televisions and home lighting, with a mean time between failures of weeks or even months.

Jini technology – uniquely among widely accepted technologies for Java – accepts the notion of failure as a normative state of affairs, and by so doing makes it easier for software systems to behave in a graceful manner in the event of failure. For instance, by recognizing a communications fault in a home control environment, we can defer decisions about how the home should behave to simpler code running on the local system, rather than more complex and intuitive code running on a more powerful server – the end user may not even be aware that a fault has occurred.

The principal lesson that PersonalGenie has learned from our use of Jini technology is that this kind of lightweight, mobile code infrastructure can be built in an efficient and acceptable way.

In crafting what we believe to be the first comprehensive system for 'wish fulfillment', that is, for complete automated lifestyle support, we at PersonalGenie (http://www.personalgenie.com/) recognize the applicability of Jini technology to this environment.

Bob Flenner

17

JWorkPlace: the Fragment Repository

Imagine a world in which developers work together on their software projects, and share their knowledge, globally. Rarely (if ever) do these developers meet in person, but they are in constant communication, talking over IP, sharing ideas with digital images, and have constant access to a library of other developers' knowledge and ideas, conversations compressed and edited for their salient content. Small, portable devices, like Palm Pilots™, are used to build and maintain these relationships anywhere and everywhere. Imagine that you could request and access the information you needed – or simply satisfy your curiosity – instantaneously. You could be in touch with developments taking place anywhere in the world, as they happen.

It would be quite something – and it's possible even as we write. The recent proliferation of distributed technologies means this sort of communication is possible today.

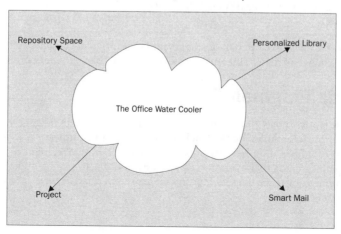

So what's stopping us? Currently, product and service development teams still tend to be localized development teams, using centralized communication principles instead of global ones. And, of course, we still have a long way to go with development processes themselves – most methodologies fail to incorporate 'learning and discovery' adequately. The wheel is being reinvented everywhere we look.

An Introduction to JWorkPlace

JWorkPlace is a foundation for learning, sharing, and collaborating using Jini and JavaSpaces technologies. The JWorkPlace is a virtual development center. This center revolves around a decentralized development team that enters and leaves the space at will, and participates at several different levels within the JWorkPlace community. The space is segmented into the following components:

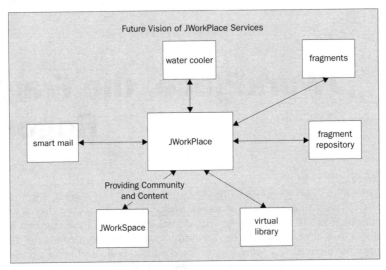

JWorkPlace is a complement project to JWorkSpace, being a simple Java source code editor. The editor simply marks up user selected source code into code fragments (see below) using XML definition for identification. The objectives are to promote re-use, and to formalize the common practice of copying code and learning by example.

> *'Example isn't another way to teach; it is the only way to teach.'*
> *Albert Einstein*

This case study focuses on the development of a fragment repository that supports code fragment exchange, and ultimately, the exchange of many different types of content and development project artifacts.

What is a Code Fragment?

A code fragment is a ready to use (but often incomplete) portion of code that serves as a programming template or example. Most technical books teach using fragment examples; JWorkPlace simply extends the reach of that sort of information-base by creating and maintaining fragment repositories of commonly used code fragments that everyone can access, in order to teach and accelerate the software learning and development process. The idea of fragments is extended as well, and takes on the more abstract form of 'digital content'.

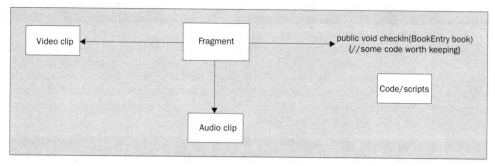

It's easy to envisage fragments flying through cyber space, being exchanged and modified by developers as they build their software solutions. There is, however, a little fine tuning needed – fragments flying through cyber space with little rhyme or reason isn't that distinct an idea from the situation that exists in many development communities today.

By bringing shape and order to this fragment development, we can begin to structure an environment that will facilitate more consistent and predictable results, fully incorporating code re-use. Because JWorkPlace is built from fragments already in use, developers everywhere can stop reinventing more and more approaches and definitions to problems. We can simply use something that has already been defined, and works.

JWorkPlace Conception

JavaSpaces, as we saw in Chapter 13, is not really designed to be a data repository or database management system. It's much more, and in fact much less, lacking too many of the capabilities of current relational database systems to be a really useful in this capacity for our purposes. However, it does integrate tightly with the Java language and provides lookup by association and type. In addition, as a Jini service, it supports the flexibility of location and distribution provided by Jini and RMI. This requirement is integral to our virtual development center. Service location transparency, and the ability to run on multiple platforms, current and future, makes these technologies the logical choices.

Most JavaSpaces examples demonstrate transient spaces in action. Such examples usually involve manager objects, such as workflow managers, working within a space or between spaces. These objects often act as coordinators between JavaSpaces, or as a mechanism to manage parallel processing. The JWorkPlace Fragment Repository will use **persistent** JavaSpaces, however, providing an 'active' and evolving object repository that responds to the needs of both development projects and the community as a whole.

We will not address repository issues here, because they relate to static objects persisted to a database or content management system. This could be implemented with any backend technology – simple serialization for small personal fragment repositories to relational database management systems, for example, leveraging XML for fragment access, semantics, and structure.

We'll begin by looking at the requirements for our development space, and then will step through the architecture and design of the application, looking at code fragments along the way.

General Requirements

Broadly speaking, the system must provide the capability to receive and process code fragments from any user authorized to update the fragment repository, or fragment space. This spawns further requirements:

Classification

The author of a fragment submits topic and category classifications, to facilitate retrieval, which the system maintains. A topic behaves like the chapter of a book, in that it organizes common themes across content. A category further refines the topic, in the manner of a section or subsection, and will be followed with a specific example. So examples developed for JavaSpaces would come under the topic 'JavaSpaces API'. One of the categories would be the 'read operation', and would include an example code fragment. This structure allows us to bring some order to the fragments that we currently use – from reference materials, publications and books, and web sites.

Collaboration

The system will enable multiple user collaboration within the fragment space. For instance, multiple authors might collaborate on a technical topic that provides fragment examples. The system will support the collaboration and coordination of this effort.

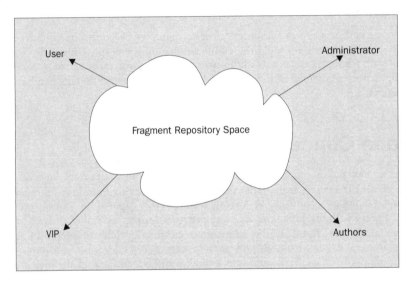

There are four user roles defined in the system. The first, the super user (or administrator), has the authority to start the system and maintain and administer user profiles. The second, the author, can publish works within the fragment space. This role is primarily responsible for bringing order to fragment spaces by classifying and publishing a collection of fragments into a cohesive and comprehensible document. The third role within the system is that of the registered user, who accesses and uses the space as a reference source. Finally, the VIP user is an identified expert in the domain of that fragment repository.

The system supports a 'space chat' capability for VIPs, authors, and registered users, allowing system users to exchange ideas and information about their development efforts. Many web site mailing lists and FAQs are currently filled with similar requests about deployment and installation problems. The capability to chat with an author or VIP in fragment space, and record that conversation, would prove invaluable to new users. The system would be able to playback chats that have taken place with VIPs and authors in the space for other users of the system. When a VIP enters a fragment space, all participants with an active session will be notified so that they can 'space chat' with the VIP.

On a similar note, the system allows users to request information on specific topics: information that may or may not be available in the current space location. Federated fragment repositories will either be able to satisfy the request immediately, or identify the need for information and issue a bid for it to other space systems or information brokers.

Users should have a visual and dynamic representation of the space, so the system will provide views of the space that are closely integrated with its overall architecture and dynamics. The system should also run continuously, and not shut down nightly or start up on demand. (Of course, a space that has little activity will present a rather mundane view.)

We also need to account for the fact that fragment spaces don't exist currently. So to incorporate more value, during the early stages at least, the system has the capability to integrate with current legacy-based web implementations. Initially this is accomplished by providing links (URLs) to relevant web sites. The capability to link a web site to a fragment and then view the site within the fragment space will have immediate information provision value.

Hopefully this brief overview of the requirements and services will give you an idea of the scope of the effort. We'll continue by focusing on some of the key components of this space:

- ❑ The overall architecture of JWorkPlace
- ❑ The entries that support the Fragment Repository
- ❑ The relationship of code fragments to XML
- ❑ Basic fragment scenarios
- ❑ Client-side architecture
- ❑ Server-side architecture
- ❑ System Administration

The Architecture of JWorkPlace

The requirements of this system mean that we need support for distributed processing and hierarchical data classification and structure. We've also emphasized the importance of viewing the space, and the dynamics of information exchange and collaboration. One document should be susceptible to editing by a number of individuals. Although we have only identified a limited number of roles, the distinctions between them impact the design and functionality significantly.

Our information architecture builds on the concept of a fragment. At each level additional meaning, structure and definition are imposed regarding the intended use and instructional capabilities of the fragment:

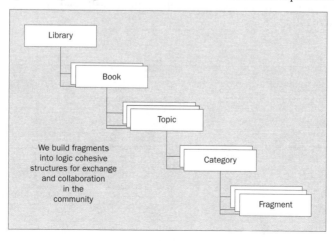

We therefore define workspace entries (which map onto the logical structure of fragments), categories, topics, etc. There is a one-to-many relationship between each data layer structure – just as a book contains many topics, and topics may contain many categories. This relationship builds on composition and recursive processing capabilities. The following might be a simple definition in the fragment repository:

Library: jworkplace.org

Book: Fragment Collections

Topic: Content Management

Category: Content Types

Fragment: JSP code example

Logical layers contain a controller for the user interface, an associated view, and access to a corresponding remote service – a library service, a book publication service, and so on. Event listeners can be plugged in at each layer to support entry processing and remote event notification.

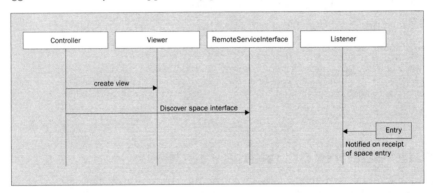

The controller is responsible for creating views, and resolving access to the JavaSpace. If the service interface is a remote interface then an authentication interface is implemented for access control. Layers may only interface with layers directly above or below, which both simplifies the design, and enables repetitive communication patterns (with the exception, in the current implementation, of fragment and category layers). Only code fragments are presented in this example. A production version would support many content types and each category may well contain many fragments. Each layer will have the capability to be defined as a separate space, so each controller will need to discover where on the network the JavaSpaces service resides.

The Library Layer:

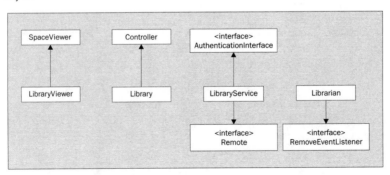

The Book or Document Layer:

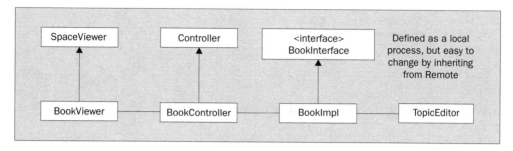

Viewers at each layer will be capable of viewing entries and providing a container for entry editing.

The event listeners will be notified when any event (an entry coming into the space, for example) occurs. Listeners may generate additional entries to notify adjacent layers. The listeners may be defined as remote objects, or may be contained in the same Java Virtual Machine. For instance TopicEditor is simply a class that is instantiated by the BookController, and accesses the space to retrieve and write entries to JavaSpace.

The Entries Defining JWorkPlace

WorkPlaceEntry is the base class for all entries written to JworkPlace, giving entries enough system time for their referencing and logging activities. This also makes administration of the space simpler by allowing browsers to find a single entry type, and inspect the status of the space. This is especially important during development. WorkPlaceEntry extends AbstractEntry which implements net.jini.entry.Entry, as all JavaSpaces entries must.

Collectively the entries in the class diagram below control the authentication and authorization requirements for the system. We'll look at some code as we walk though the system.

Authentication and Authorization

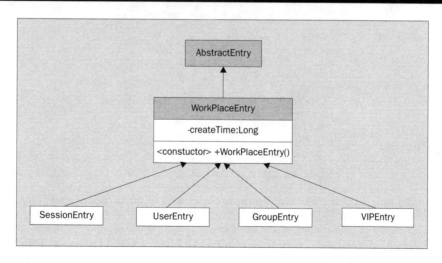

WorkPlaceEntry.java contains:

627

```
package org.jworkplace;
import net.jini.entry.AbstractEntry;

public class WorkPlaceEntry extends AbstractEntry {
    private Long creationTime;
    public WorkPlaceEntry() {
        creationTime = new Long(System.currentTimeMillis());
    }
}
```

`SessionEntry` is used to record a user's active session:

```
package org.jworkplace;
import net.jini.core.entry.AbstractEntry;
public class SessionEntry extends WorkPlaceEntry {
    public String userName;
    public Long loginTime;
    public SessionEntry(){
        this(null);
    }
    public SessionEntry(String userName){
        super();
        this.userName = userName;
        this.loginTime = new Long(System.currentTimeMillis());
    }
}
```

A `UserEntry` is defined for every user of the system, as it simply represents an account in JWorkPlace. Each user is also associated with one or more of the four roles we identified in the requirements – User, Author, VIP, or Administrator.

Structure and Layering of JWorkPlace Entries

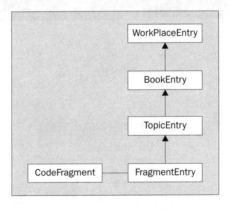

`FragmentEntry` provides the context and structure necessary to turn random code fragments into pieces of useful information. Although we are focusing on code fragments, these could also be images, audio, video, indeed any digital component used in the development process. In this example a simple `String` is returned from the `getContent()` method. An `Object` could just as easily be returned, providing a more flexible solution:

```
package org.jworkplace;
import net.jini.core.entry.Entry;
public class FragmentEntry extends WorkPlaceEntry {
    public String author;
    public String bookTitle;
    public String chapter;
    public String category;
    public String href;
    public CodeFragment content;
    public FragmentEntry() {
        this(null,null,null,null,null,null);
    }
    public FragmentEntry(String bookTitle, String chapter,
        String category, String href, String author,
        CodeFragment content) {
        super();
        this.bookTitle = bookTitle;
        this.chapter = chapter;
        this.content = content;
        this.category = category;
        this.href = href;
        this.author = author;
    }
    public String getContent() {
        return content.text;
    }
}
```

This is our book entry, which contains the title, the primary author name, and the collection of topics. BookEntry might also include an ISBN number:

```
package org.jworkplace;
import java.util.Hashtable;
import net.jini.entry.AbstractEntry;
public class BookEntry extends WorkPlaceEntry {
    public String bookTitle;
    public String author;
    public Hashtable topics;
    public BookEntry() {
        this(null,null,null);
    }
    public BookEntry(String bookTitle) {
        this(bookTitle,null,null);
    }
    public BookEntry(String bookTitle, String author) {
        this(bookTitle, author, null);
    }
    public BookEntry(String bookTitle, String author,
        Hashtable topics){
        super();
        this.bookTitle = bookTitle;
        this.author = author;
        this.topics = topics;
    }
    public Hashtable getTopics() {
        return topics;
    }
}
```

Defining Fragments Using XML

Our fragment repository can be thought of as an active content repository. Syndication involves the exchange of content, and syndicated systems are currently moving to define content using XML (Extensible Markup Language). We will use XML to define fragments 'outside' the virtual development community, in order to promote exchange, and allowing us to add instruction and context in a unified and consistent manner. It also means that all of the tools and services supporting XML will be available to us – parsers, viewers, translators, document models, and the rest.

We can map the structure of a code fragment directly to XML elements:

```
<!ELEMENT Author …>
<!ELEMENT Comments …>
```

Our fragments should be classified so that searches can be conducted on many areas of interest (for example, 'Show me all fragments that demonstrate reading, writing, and taking from a fragment space'). We can use the familiar reference to a URI in order to link the fragment to the virtual community and other sources of information:

```
<!ELEMENT Category …>
<!ELEMENT Reference …>
```

Here is our fragment XML with an embedded DTD:

```
<?xml version="1.0"?>
<!DOCTYPE fragment
    [
    <!ELEMENT fragment (author, category, reference, comments,
        code)>
    <!ELEMENT author (#PCDATA)>
    <!ELEMENT category (#PCDATA)>
    <!ELEMENT reference (#PCDATA)>
    <!ELEMENT code (#PCDATA)>
    ]>
```

So an example XML fragment might be:

```
</fragment>
    <author> Robert Flenner </author>
    <category> JavaSpaces </category>
    <reference> www.wrox.com/JavaSpaces/examples </reference>
    <code> any code here </code>
</fragment>
```

XML definitions, translations, and integrations are vital, in this model, for content definition and exchange. XML over HTTP will be used to provide structure between fragment space environments, JavaSpaces the active content repository, and XML the semantic integration between the spaces.

Building the Fragment Repository from JavaSpace Entries

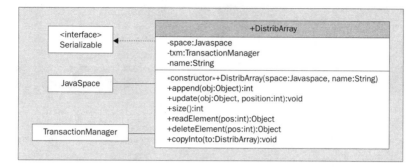

Central to our fragment repository is the `DistribArray` class. It has a reference to `JavaSpace` and a reference to the `TransactionManager`. This class contains the collection of books in JWorkPlace and provides the methods to create, read, update, and delete book entries. JavaSpaces uses the methodless 'marker' interface `net.jini.core.entry.Entry` to identify objects in a JavaSpace:

```
public interface Entry extends Serializable {}
```

The `Entry` specification stipulates that all entries must:

1. Have a public no-arguments constructor

2. Have at least one public non-static, non-final, non-transient field

3. Be of serializable types (in particular, not primitive types)

`net.jini.entry.AbstractEntry` implements `Entry` and the `equals()`, `toString`, and `hashCode()` methods.

In order to retrieve an entry from a space, a 'template' entry is supplied, which can contain wild cards in the any of null field values:

```
FragmentEntry template = new FragmentEntry();
template.author = 'Robert Flenner';
try
{
    FragmentEntry entry =
    (FragmentEntry)space.read(template, null, 10000);
}
catch ( Exception e )
{
    e.printStackTrace();
}
```

This will retrieve any `FragmentEntry` in the space with the given author. As you might remember from Chapter 13, JavaSpaces can make no guarantees about the object that will be returned if there are numerous `FragmentEntry` objects available, so subsequent readings might well return the same object.

One approach to this problem is to continually invoke `takeIfExists` within a transaction until `null` is returned, and then abort the transaction, allowing the space to revert to its previous state. This is, however, not a very good solution if hundreds of entries are involved.

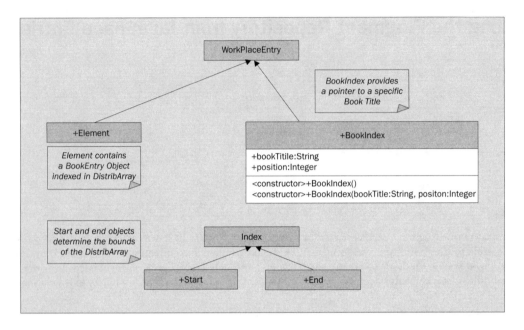

In JWorkPlace we create a distributed array to deal with the problem. This stores first and final indices as JavaSpace objects, keeping each element in a 'wrapper' JavaSpace object alongside its index. These JavaSpace objects also contain the array's name attribute, to allow multiple arrays to exist in the same space. Our `DistribArray` implementation uses the entry classes `Start`, `End` and `Element`:

```
public class DistribArray implements java.io.Serializable {
    private JavaSpace space;
    private String name;
    public Object readElement(int pos)
        throws RemoteException, TransactionException,
        UnusableEntryException, InterruptedException {
        Element template = new Element(name, pos, null);
        Element element = (Element)space.readIfExists(template,
            null, JavaSpace.NO_WAIT);
        return (element != null) ? element.data : null;
    }
    public int append(Object obj)
        throws RemoteException, TransactionException,
        UnusableEntryException, InterruptedException {
        // get the current last index
        End template = new End();
        template.name = name;
        End end = (End) space.take(template, null, 0);
        // increment it
        int position = end.increment();
        Lease lease = space.write(end, null, Lease.FOREVER);
        lrm.renewFor(lease, Lease.FOREVER, null);
        // wrap the array entry & write it to the space
        Element element = new Element(name, position, obj);
        lease = space.write(element, null, Lease.FOREVER);
        lrm.renewFor(lease, Lease.FOREVER, null);
        // return the index of the new entry
```

```
            return position;
    }
    // other methods
}
```

The distributed array structure also solves some of the basic problems of non-distributed data structure processing. Locking is implemented at entry level for accessibility, rather at than root level. This allows concurrent updates to be carried without compromising the integrity, or isolation, of the underlying data structure.

Because the objects stored in a distributed array are not themselves JavaSpace entries (allowing us to perform template matching on them – finding a book by its title, for example) we can create index entries for each array:

```
public BookEntry findBookByTitle(String title) {
    BookIndex index = null;
    BookEntry book = null;
    BookIndex template = new BookIndex();
    template.bookTitle = title;
    try
    {
        index = (BookIndex) space.read(template, null,
            Long.MAX_VALUE);
        book = (BookEntry)array
            readElement(index.position.intValue());
    }
    catch ( Exception e)
    {
        e.printStackTrace();
    }
    return book;
}
```

The combination of the distributed array structure together with entry-based indices is used to solve most access problems, both sequential and random. We can define as many indices as appropriate in the book array. It is important to note that maintaining additional indices will require synchronization and increase design complexity.

The `Element` entry is used to represent a collection of fragments, as an entire book would. The `String` name attribute is used for the book's name. The index allows us to step through the array (library) sequentially or use the associated `BookIndex` entry directly. The data actually references a `BookEntry`. This approach allows us to define and maintain many different indices into the array structure.

This is the file, `Element.java`:

```
package org.jworkplace;
import net.jini.entry.AbstractEntry;
public class Element extends WorkPlaceEntry {
    public String name;
    public Integer index;
    public Object data;
    public Element() {}
    public Element(String name, int index, Object data) {
```

```
            this.name = name;
            this.index = new Integer(index);
            this.data = data;
        }
    }
```

<h2 style="background:black;color:white">Providing Community Chat</h2>

Now that we have established some of the basic building blocks of JWorkPlace, let's begin to discuss the dynamics of collaboration and community. Community requires involvement, which requires a relationship, which requires communication.

Communication in this community is defined by a Message entry in JWorkPlace. Persistent communication differentiates our community from most implementations today, bringing together the benefits of email with the immediacy of conversation. Chat is an enabler of the community, and we use the community to define, refine, and instruct based on classified content types.

We define channels to enable communication. A channel is a unique name that identifies a chat session. An integer within the Message entry determines the sequence and ordering of messages during chat.

The text typed in is stored in the text variable:

```
package org.jworkplace;
import net.jini.entry.AbstractEntry;
public class Message extends WorkPlaceEntry {
    public String channel;
    public Integer position;
    public String text;
    public Message(){
        super();
    }
    public Message(String channel, Integer position,
        String text) {
        super();
        this.channel = channel;
        this.position = position;
        this.text = text;
    }
}
```

JWorkPlace Scenarios

In this demonstration, a simple user interface will be defined. A tabbed panel represents the documents that are available for use and update. Einstein sits on the left side of the library panel and the librarian (the book icon) sits on the right. You can select a book by selecting the associated tab. Clicking Einstein will start chat, and clicking the books will create a new book. Selecting a book immediately puts you in a chat session. Space, Time, Activity, and Resources are used to address workflow, and are under construction at this time.

Lookup and Discovery Scenario

`SpaceView` represents the high-level frame and view of JWorkPlace. It addition it supports the initial discovery of `JavaSpaces` and the `LibraryService`. The `LibraryService` is a remote service that implements `java.rmi.Remote`.

The file: `SpaceView.java` begins with this code:

```
package viewers;
import java.io.*;
import java.rmi.*;
import net.jini.core.entry.*;
import net.jini.core.lookup.*;
import net.jini.lookup.entry.*;
import net.jini.core.discovery.*;
import java.awt.*;
import java.awt.event.*;
import java.util.*;
import javax.swing.*;
import javax.swing.event.*;
import org.jworkplace.*;
public class SpaceView extends JFrame implements
    ActionListener {
    protected JDesktopPane spacePane;
    protected Library library;
    protected LibraryService li = null;
    protected LoginController sessionControl;
```

We pass a URI to the `SpaceView` constructor, which is used by the `net.jini.core.discovery.Locator` for unicast discovery. The `LookupLocator` will try to find the lookup service at the specified location. It will return a `ServiceRegistrar` using the `getRegistrar` method. The registrar uses a service template to find the appropriate service. In this case we are looking for the `LibraryService`. The `ServiceTemplate` takes three parameters, (all might all be `null`, indicating a match with anything). In our case we want any `LibraryService`:

```
public SpaceView(String url) {
    super("JWorkPlace");
    try
    {
        LookupLocator lookup = new LookupLocator(url);
        ServiceRegistrar registrar =
        lookup.getRegistrar();
        Entry entries[] = { new Name("LibraryService") };
        li = (LibraryService)registrar.lookup(new
            ServiceTemplate(null, null, entries));
```

Login Scenario

Once we have located the `LibraryService` we will attempt to login and open the library. The `LibraryService` implements the `ControllerInterface`, which defines the `openLibrary` method, and the basic `login` and `logout` methods.

Other layers such as `book`, may extend this interface.

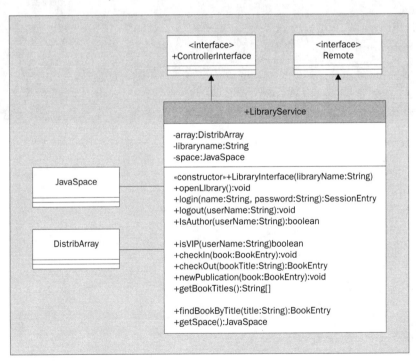

This code continues `SpaceView.java`:

```
            boolean result = login();
            if(result)
            {
                li.openLibrary();
                library = new Library(spacePane, li,
                    JWPNames.LIBRARY);
            }
            else
            {
                JOptionPane.showMessageDialog(this,
                    "Retries exceeded contact administrator");
            }
            addWindowListener(new WindowAdapter() {
                public void windowClosing(WindowEvent evt) {
                    logout();
                    System.exit(0);
                }
            });
        }
        catch (Exception e)
        {
            e.printStackTrace();
        }
    }
```

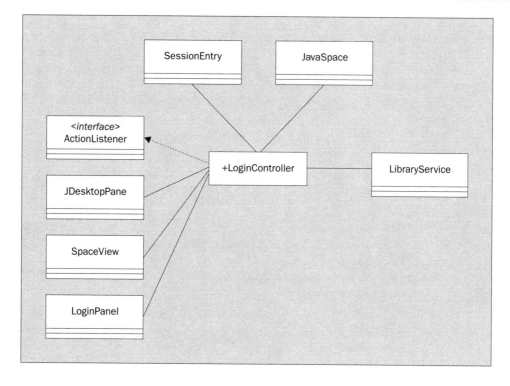

LoginController presents a standard request for username and password. Following three unsuccessful attempts, the controller takes the UserEntry from the system, at which point the System Administrator would have to be notified to reinstate the user entry.

More code from SpaceView.java:

```
boolean login() {
    sessionControl = new LoginController(this, spacePane, li);
    int count = 0;
    while(sessionControl.getResult() != true)
    {
        sessionControl.createView();
        count++;
        if(count > 2)
        {
            sessionControl.revoke();
            return false;
        }
    }
    return true;
}
```

LoginController calls the remote library interface to retrieve the UserEntry. If the entry does not exist or the password is invalid a rejection prompt is provided.

From LoginController.java:

```
public void actionPerformed(ActionEvent evt) {
    Object object = evt.getSource();
    if(object == viewer.ok)
    {
        authenticate();
    }
    else if(object == viewer.cancel)
    {

        result = false;
    }
    viewer.dispose();
}

void authenticate(){
    result = false;
    try
    {
        userName = viewer.getUserName();
        sessionEntry = li.login(userName,
            viewer.getPassword());
        if(sessionEntry == null)
        {
            JOptionPane.showMessageDialog(view, "Invalid
                user - password");
        }
```

```
            else
            {
                result = true;
            }
        }
        catch ( RemoteException e)
        {
            e.printStackTrace();
        }
    }
```

`LoginController` begins by trying to find a `UserEntry` corresponding to the given user name, and where one is found, validates the password. A `SessionEntry` is created to track the user's activity while logged in to the system.

One of our requirements was that when certain users logged into the system, their presence should be broadcast to all other users currently logged in. The check for `inGroup(name, group)` indicates whether the user belongs to the VIP group, and where he or she does, writes out a VIP entry to the system. This will in turn trigger a remote event notification, which every user logged in will then receive.

```
public SessionEntry login(String name, Char[] pword, String
    group) throws RemoteException {
    SessionEntry session = null;
    try
    {
        if(name != null)
        {
            UserEntry template = new UserEntry();
            template.name = name;
            UserEntry entry = (UserEntry)space.readIfExists(
                             template, null, JavaSpace.NO_WAIT);
            if(entry != null)
            {
                String password = new String(pword);
                if(password.equals(entry.password))
                {
                    session = new SessionEntry(name);
                    Lease lease = space.write(session, null,
                        30 * 10 * 1000);
                    lrm = new LeaseRenewalManager();
                    lrm.renewUntil(lease, Lease.FOREVER, null);
                    if(inGroup(name, group))
                    {
                        vip = new VIPEntry(name);
                        lease = space.write(vip, null, 30 * 10 * 1000);
                        lrm.renewUntil(lease, Lease.FOREVER, null);
                    } // of 4th if
                    return session;
                } // of 3rd if
            } // of 2nd if
        } // of 1st if
    } // of try
    catch ( Exception e)
```

```
    {
      e.printStackTrace();
    }
    return null;
  }
```

Our `SessionEntry` contains the user name and the time that the user logged in. The existence of this entry indicates a successful log-in and an active session.

This is the code in `SessionEntry.java`:

```
package org.jworkplace;
import net.jini.core.entry.AbstractEntry;
public class SessionEntry extends WorkPlaceEntry {
    public String userName;
    public Long loginTime;
    public SessionEntry() {
        this(null);
    }
    public SessionEntry(String userName)
    {
        super();
        this.userName = userName;
        this.loginTime = new Long(System.currentTimeMillis());
    }
}
```

We invoked a `readIfExists` to find the user entry. This will not block, as a read would, which ensures that we won't be kept waiting while the user is be defined in the system (and they might never be defined). We also used the `net.jini.lease.LeaseRenewalManager` to handle the renewing of our lease on the session and VIP entry. This class implements a utility that renews leases on resources for a specific period of time. It performs this function in the same process, by creating an internal thread that wakes up at the appropriate time. The session lease is initially set to thirty minutes. We then ask the lease manager to renew both entries forever, leases that we will in fact cancel when the user logs off the system. The `LeaseRenewalManager` has been deprecated in Jini 1.1 and moved to the `net.jini.lease` package.

Each group in the system is defined by a group entry. The name indicates the group type, for instance 'VIP'. A vector contains the user names in the group. The group entry is used to determine if a user is a member of a specific group. If group management became more complex, we would probably define a helper class to manage group entries to keep the entries as simple and concise as possible.

This is the code in `GroupEntry.java`:

```
package org.jworkplace;
import java.util.Vector;
import net.jini.entry.AbstractEntry;
public class GroupEntry extends WorkPlaceEntry {
    public String name;
    public Vector users;
    public GroupEntry()
    {
        this(null, null);
    }
```

```
        public GroupEntry(String name)
        {
            this(name, null);
        }
        public GroupEntry(String name, Vector users)
        {
            super();
            this.name = name;
            this.users = users;
        }
        public void addUser(String userName)
        {
            users.addElement(userName);
        }
        public boolean isMember(String userName)
        {
            return users.contains(userName);
        }
    }
}
```

Running the Space Browser

You can invoke the SpaceBrowser that comes with the JavaSpaces installation to look at the system after a VIP has entered the space.

To run the space browser, you would simply change \files in this code to your installation path:

```
java -cp \files\jini1_1\lib\space-examples.jar
-D java.security.policy=\files\jini1_1\example\browser\policy
-D java.rmi.server.codebase=http://localhost:8080/space-examples-dl.jar
com.sun.jini.example.spaceBrowser.Browser -admin
```

In this example we made the password public so that we could view the information (not recommended for obvious reasons).

We have collected enough information during the login scenario to meet some specific requirements.

The VIPEntry could be expanded to include information that the VIP would like to promote. Perhaps conferences, publications, or upcoming space engagements.

The mere presence of this entry in space triggers alerts to all active users. This could also be recorded so that an inactive user could be notified when they log in. Even the chat sessions are recorded and can be played back later. Chat sessions could be defined using XML and translation from text to other media would be possible (perhaps using XSL).

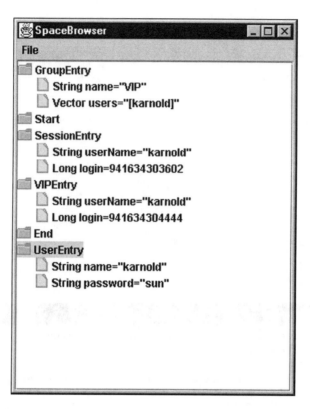

At this point you are logged into the system. If you are a member of the author group, you are able to create fragments and documents. Once you have successfully logged in, SpaceView will request the library to open through the LibraryService.

Initializing and Performing Space Operations

Let's look at the LibraryService. It initializes the distributed array for the client:

```
// code in LibraryService
public void openLibrary() throws RemoteException
{
    try
    {
        array = new DistribArray(space, libraryName);
    }
    catch (Exception e)
    {
        e.printStackTrace();
    }
    System.out.println("Exiting unable to open "+libraryName);
    System.exit(1);
}
```

The `LibraryService` has a method called `openLibrary` which is key to space access and collaboration. It uses the discovered space from `SpaceAccessor` (see below) and a unique name to create a distributed array structure. We give the array structure a unique name and define the start and end indices with the same name.

The `LibraryService` uses `SpaceAccessor` to find the specific `JavaSpaces` service identified by the constant `JWPNames.LIBRARYSPACE`. It also sets the supplied library name to be used to access the appropriate distributed array, which contains book entries. While constants are supplied, they could easily be changed from an administration panel.

This is the file `LibraryService.java`:

```
package org.jworkplace;
import java.rmi.*;
import java.util.*;
import net.jini.core.lease.*;
import net.jini.lease.*;
import net.jini.space.JavaSpace;
import util.SpaceAccessor;
public class LibraryService implements ControllerInterface,
    Remote {
    private DistribArray array;
    private String libraryName;
    private JavaSpace space;
    public LibraryService(String libraryName){
        this.libraryName = libraryName;
        space = SpaceAccessor.getSpace(JWPNames.LIBRARYSPACE);
    }
```

The `SpaceAccessor` should look familiar. It uses the lookup locator and service registrar just like our `SpaceViewer`. This time we are doing `unicast` discovery for a named JavaSpace. Each controller or implementation of an interface at each layer of the architecture uses `SpaceAccessor`. Therefore, we only look for space names that we have not discovered previously and cache the JavaSpace reference in a hashtable. If the implementation is on a single JavaSpace instance, such as in this case, `JWPNames.XXXLAYER` can be set to the same value, and a single `unicast` discovery will in effect resolve all addresses. This proves valuable when you are simply using the workplace for your own personal fragment repository.

This is the `SpaceAccessor.java` file:

```
package util;
import java.rmi.*;
import java.util.Hashtable;
import net.jini.space.JavaSpace;
import net.jini.core.entry.*;
import net.jini.core.lookup.*;
import net.jini.lookup.entry.*;
import net.jini.core.discovery.*;

public class SpaceAccessor {
  public synchronized static JavaSpace getSpace(String name){
    JavaSpace space = (JavaSpace)spaces.get(name);
    if(space != null) return space;
    try
    {
```

```
      if (System.getSecurityManager() == null)
      {
        System.setSecurityManager(new RMISecurityManager());
      }
      LookupLocator lookup = new
        LookupLocator(JWPNames.LOCATOR);
      ServiceRegistrar registrar = lookup.getRegistrar();
      Entry entries[] = { new Name(name) };
      space = (JavaSpace)registrar.lookup(new
        ServiceTemplate(null,null,entries));
      spaces.put(name, space);
      return space;
    }
    catch (Exception e)
    {
      System.err.println(e.getMessage());
    }
    return null;
  }
  public static Hashtable spaces = new Hashtable();
}
```

The `Library` is a client-side controller class that constructs the library view and communicates with the `LibraryService`. The architecture defined a controller and a viewer for each layer. The `Library` and `LibraryViewer` implement the controller-view model for the library layer.

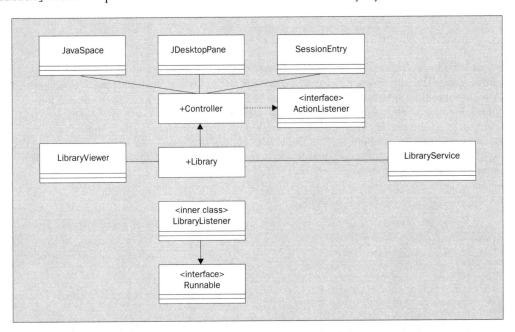

Creating New Book Scenario

The `LibraryService` supports a new publication method. It expects a `BookEntry`.

This is `LibraryService.java`:

```java
public void newPublication(BookEntry book) throws
  RemoteException {
  try
  {
     String title = book.bookTitle;
     // array is the distrib array
     int position = array.append(book);

     // Creating book index
     BookIndex index = new BookIndex(title, new Integer(position));
     Lease lease = space.write(index, null, Long.MAX_VALUE);
     lrm.renewFor(lease, Lease.FOREVER, null);
  }
  catch (Exception e) {
    e.printStackTrace();
  }
}
```

`BookEntry` is, as specified in the requirements above, is a collection of topics, and topics are collections of categories/fragments. There is a primary author defined in `BookEntry` and other authors defined within each fragment (they may or may not be the same). Writing a `BookEntry` to space causes a number of events to be triggered and it signifies the creation of a new book or the update to an existing book.

This is `BookEntry.java`:

```java
package org.jworkplace;
import java.util.Hashtable;
import net.jini.entry.AbstractEntry;
public class BookEntry extends WorkPlaceEntry {
    public String bookTitle;
    public String author;
    public Hashtable topics;
    public BookEntry()
    {
        this(null,null,null);
    }
    public BookEntry(String bookTitle)
    {
        this(bookTitle,null,null);
    }
    public BookEntry(String bookTitle, String author)
    {
        this(bookTitle, author, null);
    }
    public BookEntry(String bookTitle, String author,
        Hashtable topics)
    {
        super();
        this.bookTitle = bookTitle;
        this.author = author;
        this.topics = topics;
    }
    public Hashtable getTopics() { return topics; }
}
```

The append method of the distributed array takes the current end position, increments it, and then writes it back to the named space. It creates an `Element`, which contains our `BookEntry` (`Object obj`), and writes the named element using the current end position.

From `DistribArray.java`:

```
public int append(Object obj)
    throws RemoteException, TransactionException,
    UnusableEntryException, InterruptedException
{
    End template = new End();
    template.name = name;
    End end = (End) space.take(template, null, 0);
    int position = end.increment();
    Lease lease = space.write(end, null, Lease.FOREVER);
    lrm.renewFor(lease, Lease.FOREVER, null);
    Element element = new Element(name, position, obj);
    lease = space.write(element, null, Lease.FOREVER);
    lrm.renewFor(lease, Lease.FOREVER, null);
    return position;
}
```

So what you should see is:

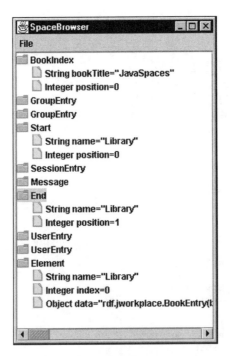

This is how the workplace looks after a book has been created.

Note the book index points to the position within the distributed array where the element resides. Start, End, and Element all refer to 'Library'. This is the unique name that we assigned in `JWPNames.LIBRARY`. Element contains an embedded reference to another `Entry`, `BookEntry`.

Selecting Books

Selecting a book opens the fragment tab panel and initiates a chat session. Anyone with the JavaSpaces book open is on the same chat channel.

The chat channel is initialized to the book title:

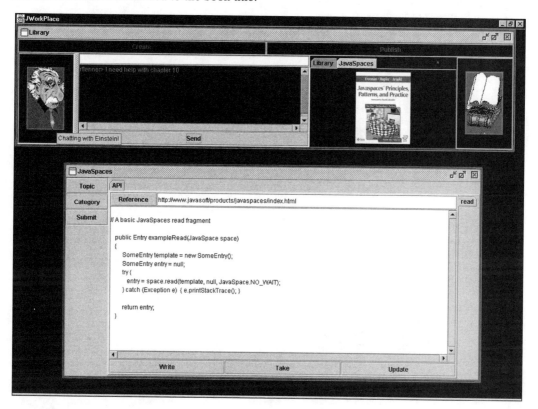

Client-Side Architecture – Events

One of the objectives of JWorkPlace is to allow collaboration. We want to ensure that as the space changes, users are advised of the changes and their views reflect the appropriate modifications. Community is the key here – we let users know that they are not alone!

So, if a new book is added through a book entry, every client view should reflect a new tab on the library panel. A more active space with thousands of books will require different views to be viable.

There are two basic approaches we use to stay in tune with the space. The first uses remote event notification, and the second spawns threads in the client process that wait for specific entries to be written into space. The BookEntry provides both forms of event notification.

Updating the View

A JTabbedPanel contains a tab for each book defined in the system. When an author adds a book to the system a BookEntry is written to JWorkPlace using the LibraryService. When the Library is instantiated on the client, it spawns a thread that reads BookIndex entries. How do we update the view to reflect the addition of new books? It's very straightforward, as you'll see from Library.java:

```
public class Library extends Controller{
    private LibraryViewer viewer;
    private LibraryService li;
    private ChatController chat;
    private EventRegistration registration;
    private SessionFilter listener;
    private String name;
    private String[] bookTitles;
    public Library(JDesktopPane spacePane, LibraryService li,
        String name) {
        super(spacePane, JWPNames.FRAGMENTSPACE);
        this.spacePane = spacePane;
        this.li = li;
        this.name = name;
        createView();
        new Thread(new LibraryViewSynchronizer()).start();
        createSessionAlerts();
    }
```

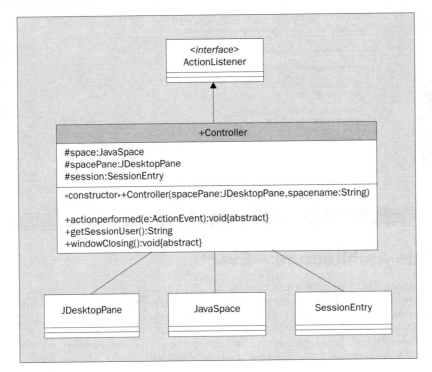

All client-side controllers (Fragment, Category, Topic, Book, etc.) extend the Controller base class. This is where the SpaceAccessor call resides and a reference to the SessionEntry that we created when we logged in is defined.

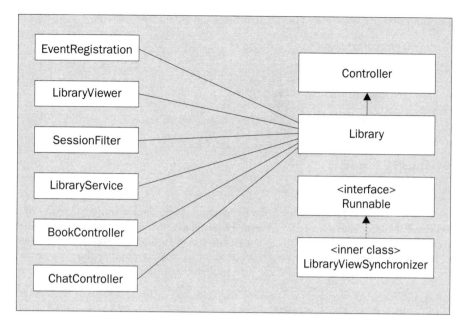

The `LibraryViewSynchronizer` is responsible for updating the library view and is an inner class of `Library.Java`:

```
class LibraryViewSynchronizer implements Runnable{

  int position = viewer.numberOfBooks();
  public void run(){
    BookIndex template = new BookIndex();
    BookIndex entry = null;
    while (true)
    {
      template.position = new Integer(position);
      try
      {
        entry = (BookIndex)space.read(template, null,
          Long.MAX_VALUE);
        viewer.addBookTitle(entry.bookTitle);
        position++;
      }
      catch (Exception e)
      {
        e.printStackTrace();
      }
    }
  }
}
```

`LibraryViewSynchronizer` gets the current number of books displayed and uses that count as a position index to read the next `BookIndex` entry that is written to the space. If there are three books currently displayed, it will wait for book four and then update its display and wait for book five. Because the read is a blocking call, it will patiently wait for next book index to be written. Admittedly this could be done through remote event notification leaving the view more loosely coupled with the `BookIndex` definition, but this works well on the client and serves as an example that could be expanded to give the listener a much more complex task.

When we instantiated the library we also created a session filter:

```
void createSessionAlerts(){
  try
  {
    listener = new SessionFilter(space, this);
    VIPEntry template = new VIPEntry();
    registration = space.notify(template, null, listener,
      Lease.FOREVER, null);
  }
  catch (Exception e)
  {
    e.printStackTrace();
  }
}
```

This is an in-use example of JavaSpaces's notify method, JavaSpace's implementation of the Jini Distributed Event Model. When an entry that matches the given template is written to space, the listener defined in the third parameter of notify is invoked. In this case we have requested notification of any VIPEntry into space to wake up our session filter object. Remember the requirement that all users of the system be alerted to the VIP? We accomplish that task in SessionFilter.java:

```
public class SessionFilter implements RemoteEventListener {

  private JavaSpace space;
  private Library controller;

  public SessionFilter(JavaSpace space, Library controller)
    throws RemoteException  {
    this.space = space;
    this.controller = controller;
    UnicastRemoteObject.exportObject(this);
  }

  public void notify(RemoteEvent event){
    VIPEntry template = new VIPEntry();
    VIPEntry entry = template;
    try
    {
      entry = (VIPEntry)space.readIfExists(template,
        null, Long.MAX_VALUE);
      if (entry != null)
      {
        controller.setVIP(entry.userName);
      }
    }
    catch (Exception e)
    {
      e.printStackTrace();
    }
  }
}
```

To receive remote notification you must implement the RemoteEventListener interface, which defines the single method notify. It uses the UnicastRemoteObject.exportObject method to register as a remote object. This method is part of the Java Remote Method Invocation package. This tells JavaSpaces to notify this object as a remote object. When a VIPEntry is written to JavaSpaces, a notification event will be sent to this remote interface which is running on the client. The Library will be updated by the setVIP method to reflect the VIP's user name. If we were to expand the functionality of the VIP entry, the setVIP method could be overridden.

Chat Scenario

Let's now turn our attention to the chat capabilities within JWorkPlace. The technique is based on similar patterns presented in *JavaSpaces: Principles, Patterns and Practice* by Addison Wesley. By default the channel is the active open book title. When you select a book from the library a chat controller is created and the channel is 'turned on'.

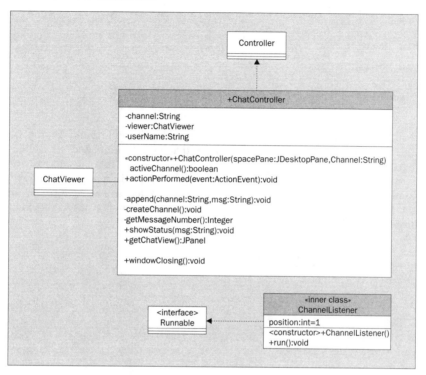

This is code from `ChatController.java`:

```
public class ChatController extends Controller{

    private String channel;
    private ChatViewer viewer;
    private String userName;

    public ChatController(JDesktopPane spacePane, String channel)
    {
      super(spacePane, JWPNames.CHATSPACE);
      if(session != null)
      {
        userName = session.userName;
        this.channel = channel;
        if(!activeChannel())
              createChannel();
        viewer = new ChatViewer(this,channel);
        new Thread(new ChannelListener()).start();
      }
    }
```

```
boolean activeChannel() {
  End template = new End();
  template.name = channel;
  try
  {
    End index = (End)space.readIfExists(template,
      null, JavaSpace.NO_WAIT);
    if(index == null)
      return false;
  }
  catch (Exception e)
  {
    return false;
  }
  return true;
}
```

We ensure that the channel does not already exist by checking for an End index entry with the channel name. The End entry signifies the end of the messages that have accumulated in the chat session. If a chat is in progress the ChannelListener will read all the messages that have already been created and bring you up to date within the session. If an End entry does not exist a new channel will be created. This is the same entry we used to signify the end of our distributed array structure for the library. Here it is being used to indicate the end of the messages in the chat channel for a specific book. It is initialized to zero on creation.

```
private void createChannel() {
  End index = new End();
  index.name = channel;
  index.position = new Integer(0);
  try
  {
    lrm = space.write(index, null, Lease.FOREVER);
  }
  catch (Exception e)
  {
    e.printStackTrace();
    return;
  }
}
```

Our channel listener is very similar to our LibraryViewSynchronizer only now we are waiting to read messages.

This is the code from ChatListener.java:

```
class ChannelListener implements Runnable {
  int position = 1;
  public void run(){
    Message template = new Message();
    template.channel = channel;
    Message msg = null;
    while (true)
    {
      template.position = new Integer(position++);
      try
      {
        msg = (Message)space.read(template, null,
          Long.MAX_VALUE);
```

```
        viewer.append(msg.text + newline);
      }
      catch (Exception e)
      {
        e.printStackTrace();
      }
    } // of while
  }
}
```

The `append` method simply retrieves the next message number from the `getMessageNumber` method and writes the chat message to the space. We are using similar communication patterns throughout the design. In this example our messages will exist in the space for 30 minutes and then be discarded.

```
private void append(String channel, String msg) {
  Integer messageNum = getMessageNumber();
  Message message = new Message(channel, messageNum, msg);
  try
  {
    space.write(message, null, 30 * 60 * 1000);
  }
  catch (Exception e)
  {
    e.printStackTrace();
    return;
  }
}
```

Reviewing the Layered Architecture

We started by defining listeners for every layer of the architecture. Actually the listeners below the `BookLayer` are local processes that get invoked based on user actions – submitting a new book to the library, for example.

The commands get routed down the hierarchy collecting information from each layer's associated space entry – `BookEntry`, `TopicEntry`, `FragmentEntry`, and so on.

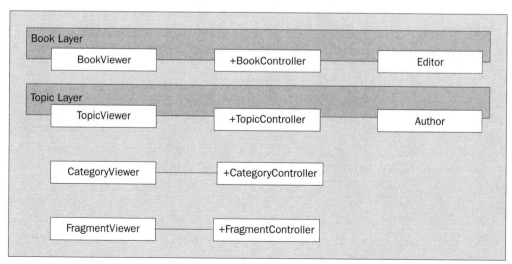

When a topic is added to a book, the `BookController` creates an associated `TopicController` for the new topic, and the `TopicController`, creates an associated `Author`. The `Author` is responsible for collecting `FragmentEntry` objects for the topic:

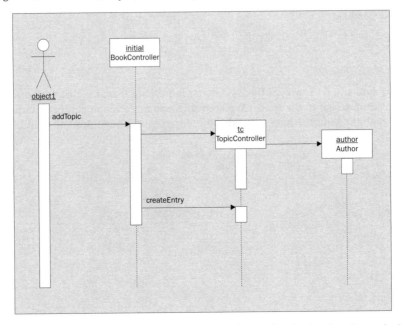

The `Editor` is responsible for collecting `TopicEntry` objects for the book, when a 'submit' request is received from the user. The write method of the `BookController` will loop through all associated `TopicControllers`, call the `Editor` to read the topics from JavaSpace, and then update the `Library` through the `BookImpl`:

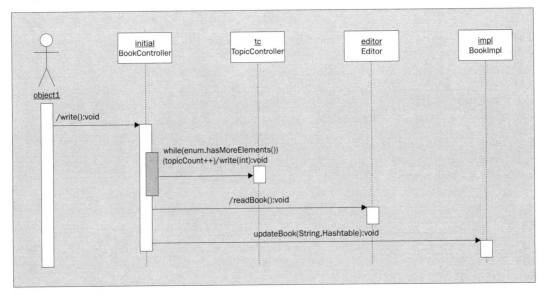

This code is from `BookController.java`:

```java
public void write(){
    int topicCount = 0;
    Enumeration enum = topics.elements();
    while(enum.hasMoreElements())
    {
        TopicController tc = (TopicController)enum.nextElement();
        tc.write(topicCount++);
    }
    // Read all Topic Entries - similar to Author
    editor.readBook();
    // call the BookInterface to write book to library
    impl.updateBook(bookTitle, session.userName,
        editor.getData());
}
```

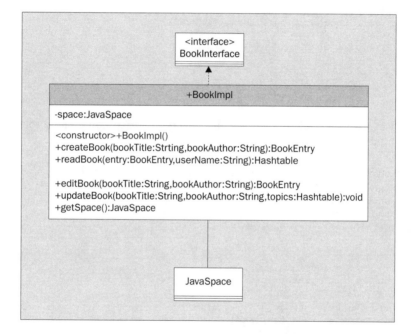

The `BookInterface` defines an update method, which takes a book title, the name of the primary author, and a `hashtable` of topics as parameters. It uses the size of the `hashtable` to determine how many topics have been written and uses that count to ensure that all lower layer functions have completed prior to writing a `BookEntry`. When a new book is created or an author selects a book, a `BookEntry` without topics is written to JavaSpace.

The exception handling in `updateBook` is not sufficient. If the update does not complete, we need a way to ensure recovery of this book update. We will discuss Transaction Management in another section and highlight some potential problems we have already glossed over.

This is code from `BookImpl.java`:

```java
public void updateBook(String bookTitle, String bookAuthor,
  Hashtable topics){
  try
  {
    LockEntry lock = new LockEntry("TOPIC-LOCK",
      topics.size());

    LockEntry lockEntry = (LockEntry)space.take(lock, null,
      Long.MAX_VALUE);
    BookEntry template = new BookEntry();
    template.bookTitle = bookTitle;
    template.author = bookAuthor;
    BookEntry bookEntry = (BookEntry)space.take(template,
      null, 30 * 60 * 1000);
    bookEntry.topics = topics;
    space.write(bookEntry,null,Lease.FOREVER);
  }
  catch (Exception e)
  {
    e.printStackTrace();
  }
}
```

Similar to the `Editor` for a book, the `Author` finds every `FragmentEntry` for a specific topic and puts them in a `hashtable`:

```java
public Author(JavaSpace space, String book, String topic) {
    this.space = space;
    this.book = book;
    this.topic = topic;
    this.categories = new Hashtable();
}

public void readTopics() {
    FragmentEntry template = new FragmentEntry();
    template.bookTitle = book;
    template.chapter = topic;
    FragmentEntry entry = template;
    try
    {
        while (entry != null)
        {
            entry = (FragmentEntry)space.takeIfExists(template,
                null, Long.MAX_VALUE);
            if(entry != null)
            {
                categories.put(entry.category, entry);
            }
        }
    }
    catch (Exception e)
    {
```

```
            e.printStackTrace();
        }
    }

    public Hashtable getData() {
        return categories;
    }
    }
```

Remember multiple users can be working on the same book at the same time. The distributed nature of the environment, and multiple threads running concurrently, mean that synchronization can become an issue.

We define a `LockEntry` to ensure that each `TopicController` waits for the lock prior to invoking its associated `Author` object. Remember the `Author` is out tracking down fragments in space. Topic zero initializes the lock process by writing the initial lock entry to space. Subsequent topic instances will use the count supplied by `BookController` to wait for their turn to invoke their `Author`, and then increment the lock counter so the next topic can process:

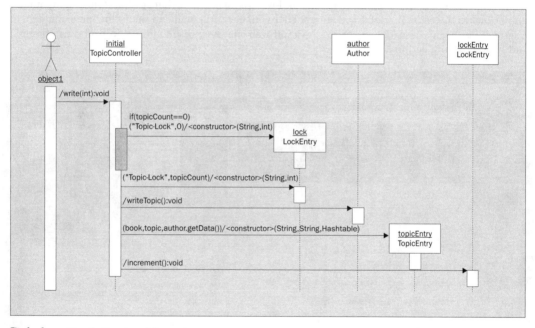

Code from `TopicController.java`:

```
void write(int topicCount){
    try
    {
        if(topicCount == 0)
        {
            LockEntry lock = new LockEntry("TOPIC-LOCK",0);
            space.write(lock, null, Long.MAX_VALUE);
        }
        LockEntry lock = new LockEntry("TOPIC-LOCK",
            topicCount);
        // block till available
```

```
        LockEntry lockEntry = (LockEntry)space.take(lock, null,
            Long.MAX_VALUE);
        author.writeTopic();
        // write out an associated Topic Entry to space
        TopicEntry topicEntry = new TopicEntry(book, topic,
            author.getData());
        space.write(topicEntry,null, 10*1000);
        // increment the lock count to release
        lockEntry.increment();
        space.write(lockEntry, null, Long.MAX_VALUE);
    }
    catch (Exception e)
    {
        e.printStackTrace();
    }
}
```

Once all topics have been written from the submit request, the fragment book view closes. If we select the JavaSpaces book, the book is re-opened and we are placed in a chat session. Our fragment entry definition has the capability of associating a URI with each fragment. In the following example a fragment has been associated with Sun's JavaSoft web site. As a result current web sites can be linked and retrieved from within Space View.

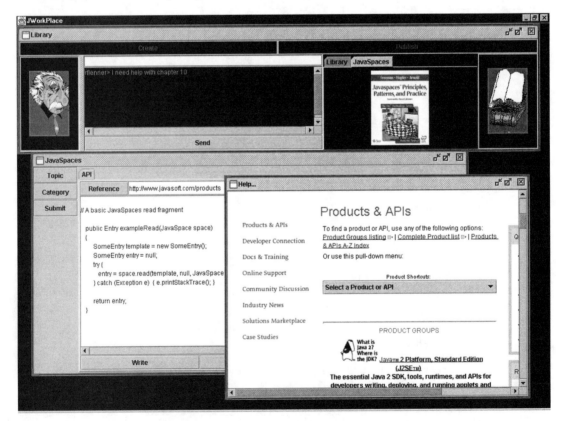

The Server-Side Architecture

We have spent a considerable amount of time putting together client interaction with JavaSpaces and developing an adapted and extended framework. Now let's put our attention to the server side of the LibraryServer and the administration of JWorkPlace.

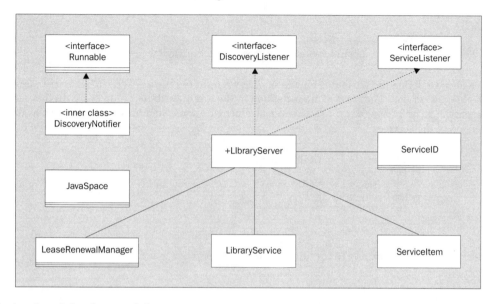

We developed the client and the supporting services using the Jini1.1 Beta implementation. The Join Manager in 1.1 differs slightly from the 1.0 distribution and has moved to the net.jini.lookup package. We will highlight some of the changes in the following section.

The Library Server implements the ServiceIDListener interface. It supports the serviceIDNotify method. We save the service ID so we can reuse it the next time we start the service. It is a common practice to reuse the service ID once it has been assigned, so clients that have saved that reference can reuse it, and be assured they are interfacing with the same service at a later time. We save it in our persistent JavaSpace in a LibraryEntry. In the main method we check for the existence of this entry and invoke the correct constructor on the JoinManager.

```
public class LibraryServer implements ServiceIDListener {

  protected static LeaseRenewalManager lrm = new
      LeaseRenewalManager();
  protected static JavaSpace space;
  // notified when a new service id is requested

  public void serviceIDNotify(ServiceID serviceID) {
    try
      {
        if(space != null)
        {
          LibraryEntry entry = new
            LibraryEntry(JWPNames.LIBRARY);
          entry.serviceID = serviceID;
          Lease lease = space.write(entry, null,
            Lease.FOREVER);
```

```
            lrm.renewFor(lease, Long.MAX_VALUE, null);
      }
      catch (Exception e) { e.printStackTrace(); }
  }

  public static void main(String[] args) throws
     InterruptedException, IOException {
     try
     {
        LibraryServer server = new LibraryServer();
        System.setSecurityManager( new RMISecurityManager());
```

First we need to define the attributes for the service we want to register. We will unicast discovery to find the lookup service. The class name is defined in the Name attribute of the entry. In this case we are registering the LibraryService.class. We also provide some standard attributes such as the name and version of the service.

```
      // Support the public group
      String[] groups = new String[] { "" };
      // Perform unicast discovery at the given url
      LookupLocator[] locs = {
         new LookupLocator(JWPNames.LOCATOR)
      };
      Entry[] entries = {
        new Name("LibraryService"),
        new ServiceInfo("JWorkPlace", "Robert Flenner",
          "Wrox", "1.0", "", "")
      };
```

We create an instance of the LibraryService and use it to locate the JavaSpaces service. We initialize the library and make the check for the existence of a LibraryEntry to indicate that the service has been run before. If it has, we pass the serviceID to the JoinManager constructor. LibraryServer implements the DiscoveryListener interface. It supports two methods. Discovered is called when a new lookup service is found, and discarded is called when a lookup service is no longer available or has changed the groups it supports.

```
      String libraryName = JWPNames.LIBRARY;
      LibraryService li = new LibraryService(libraryName);
      space = li.getSpace();
      li.openLibrary();
      LibraryEntry template = new LibraryEntry();
      LibraryEntry entry =(LibraryEntry)space.readIfExists
        (template, null,JavaSpace.NO_WAIT);
      if(entry != null)
      {
        serviceID = entry.serviceID;
        JoinManager jm = new JoinManager(li, entries,
          serviceID, null, lrm);
      }
      else
      {
        JoinManager jm = new JoinManager(li, entries,
           admin, null, lrm);
      }
```

We start two additional remote notification event handlers, the Publisher and the Librarian, and then ensure that the server runs forever by blocking until the current thread exits. The Publisher is under construction, and will be used as a mechanism to interface with other external entities, such as another FragmentRepository.

```
            server.startPublisher(space);
            server.startLibrarian(space, li);
            System.out.println("JWorkPlace ready");
            Thread.currentThread().join();
        }
        catch (Exception e) { e.printStackTrace(); }
    } // of main
```

We register the librarian for remote notification of all book entries coming into the space.

```
    void startLibrarian(JavaSpace space, LibraryService
      library) {
      try
      {
        Librarian listener = new Librarian(space, library);
        BookEntry template = new BookEntry();
        EventRegistration registration =
        space.notify(template,null,listener,Lease.FOREVER,
          null);
        lrm.renewFor(registration.getLease(), Long.MAX_VALUE,
          null);
      }
      catch (Exception e) { e.printStackTrace(); }
    }
  }
```

The librarian is responsible for checking books in and out of the library using the LibraryService. (A book entry with no topics defined is considered a request for a new book publication.)

```
  public class Librarian implements RemoteEventListener {

      private JavaSpace space;
      private LibraryService library;
      private Hashtable books;

      public Librarian(JavaSpace space, LibraryService library)
          throws RemoteException {
          this.space = space;
          this.library = library;
          this.books = new Hashtable();
          UnicastRemoteObject.exportObject(this);
      }

      public void notify(RemoteEvent event) {
        BookEntry template = new BookEntry();
        BookEntry book = template;
        try
        {
          book = (BookEntry)space.read(template, null,
              Long.MAX_VALUE);
```

```
        if (book.topics != null)
        {
          book = (BookEntry)space.take(template, null,
            Long.MAX_VALUE);
          books.put(book.bookTitle, book);
          BookEntry oldEntry =
            library.checkOut(book.bookTitle);
          if(oldEntry != null)
          {
            library.checkIn(book);
          }
          else
          {
            library.newPublication(book);
          }
        }
        else
        {
          // Do nothing for now this indicates a request
          // for a new book from the library
        }
      }
    catch (Exception e) { e.printStackTrace(); }
  }
}
```

System Administration of JWorkPlace

We have also defined an administration interface and implementation for our `LibraryService`. It allows us to add users to the groups we have identified, create new groups, and perform other miscellaneous housekeeping tasks.

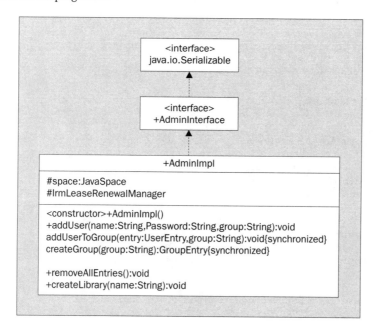

This code is from the file `AdminImpl.java`:

```java
public class AdminImpl implements AdminInterface {

  protected JavaSpace space;
  protected LeaseRenewalManager lrm = new
    LeaseRenewalManager();

  public AdminImpl() {
    space = SpaceAccessor.getSpace(JWPNames.FRAGMENTSPACE);
    lrm = new LeaseRenewalManager();
  }

  public void addUser(String name, String password,
    String group) throws RemoteException {
    try
    {
      if(name != null)
      {
        UserEntry template = new UserEntry();
        template.name = name;
        UserEntry userEntry = (UserEntry) space.readIfExists
          (template, null, JavaSpace.NO_WAIT);
        if(userEntry == null)
        {
          // new user
          template.password = password;
          Lease lease = space.write(template, null,
            Lease.FOREVER);
          lrm.renewFor(lease, Lease.FOREVER, null);
          addUserToGroup(template, group);
        }
      }
    }
    catch ( Exception e) { e.printStackTrace(); }
  }

  synchronized void addUserToGroup(UserEntry entry,
    String group){
    try {
      GroupEntry template = new GroupEntry(group);
      template.users = null;
      GroupEntry groupEntry =(GroupEntry) space.takeIfExists
        (template, null, JavaSpace.NO_WAIT);
      if(groupEntry == null)
      {
        template = createGroup(group);
        groupEntry = (GroupEntry)space.take(template, null,
          JavaSpace.NO_WAIT);
      }
      groupEntry.addUser(entry.name);
      Lease lease = space.write(entry, null, Lease.FOREVER);
      lrm.renewUntil(lease, Lease.FOREVER, null);
    }
```

```
    catch (Exception e) { e.printStackTrace(); }
  }

  synchronized GroupEntry createGroup(String group){
    GroupEntry entry = new GroupEntry(group, new Vector());
    try
    {
      Lease lease = space.write(entry, null, Lease.FOREVER);
      lrm.renewUntil(lease, Lease.FOREVER, null);
    }
    catch (Exception e) { e.printStackTrace(); }
    return entry;
  }
```

The following utility method allows us to reinitialize the library space by removing all entries. We use the `WorkPlaceEntry` type, which all of our entries are derived from, and then use the `snapshot` API to create the template. `Snapshot` is ideal for situations that will reuse a template many times, because it avoids repeatedly re-serializing the template object. You can use this anytime you have matching criteria that are not going to change.

```
  public void removeAllEntries() throws RemoteException {
    WorkPlaceEntry template = new WorkPlaceEntry();
    WorkPlaceEntry entry = template;
    try
    {
      Entry snap = space.snapshot(template);
      while (entry != null)
      {
          entry = (WorkPlaceEntry) space.takeIfExists
            (snap, null, Long.MAX_VALUE);
      }
    }
    catch (Exception e) {}
  }
```

The last method in `AdminImpl` is important because it actually initializes the `DistribArray` structure that we use for our `Library`. The `create` method on the array is where the `Start` and `End` indices are initially created and set to zero. If this fails we must exit.

```
  public void createLibrary(String name) throws
    RemoteException {
    try
    {
      DistribArray array = new DistribArray(space, name);
      array.create();
    }
    catch (Exception e) { e.printStackTrace();
    System.out.println("Exiting unable to create "+ name);
    System.exit(1);
    }
  }
}
```

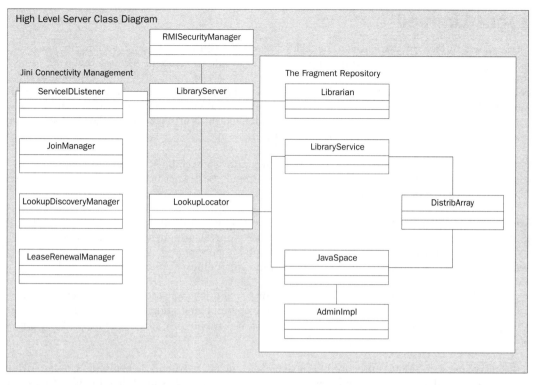

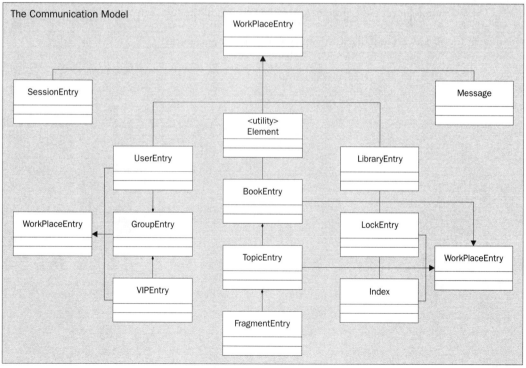

Lessons Learned

There were a number of challenges to be tackled when were building this application. Jini and JavaSpaces environments can be difficult to configure, and there are many services that need to be started separately. Of course once they are started and using RMI's auto activation capabilities this becomes less of an issue. However the initial release of the startup service had a bug causing RMID to not shut down properly. Registration of services failed and subsequent automatic activation did not work. In effect there was no persistence to the persistent space. Starting each service from a script and stopping RMID from the command line solved the problem.

Leasing resources is a new programming paradigm. It also seems to be contradictory to a persistent space! LeaseFOREVER does not, in fact, lease forever at all, but rather leases for the length of time that the service is willing or able to commit resources.

Much of this design is based on the 'self-healing' aspects of the Jini network. From another angle, then, Jini networks are designed to work with the unreliability prevalent in networks today. However, persistent space or 'I want forever space' may be a valid requirement. I certainly would not want to introduce another technology behind my object store with a different programming model.

The lack of collection classes defined specifically for Jini and JavaSpaces does impair development productivity. Collections are fundamental to defining common operations on data structures and objects. Little has been done in this area. The node class was only just introduced in the 1.1 Alpha release.

Last but not least, you should prepared for a steep learning curve when you begin developing with Jini and JavaSpaces. Many concepts are likely to be new to you, but rest assured that it really is worth the effort. These technologies are the precursors to the systems of the future.

Good luck. I look forward talking with you to you in fragment space!

JWorkPlace: Appendix A

Core methods supporting the Library Service

The following methods summarize the implementation of the `LibraryService`.

Logs client into library and determines group membership:

```java
public SessionEntry login(String name, Char[] pword) throws
  RemoteException {
    SessionEntry session = null;
    try
    {
      if(name != null)
      {
        UserEntry template = new UserEntry();
        template.name = name;
        UserEntry entry = (UserEntry) space.readIfExists
          (template, null, JavaSpace.NO_WAIT);
        if(entry != null)
        {
          String password = new String(pword);
          if(password.equals(entry.password))
          {
            session = new SessionEntry(name);
            Lease lease = space.write(session, null,
              30 * 10 * 1000);
            LeaseRenewalManager lrm = new
              LeaseRenewalManager();
            lrm.renewUntil(lease, Lease.FOREVER, null);
            if(isVIP(name))
            {
              VIPEntry vip = new VIPEntry(name);
              lease = space.write(vip, null, 30 * 10 * 1000);
              lrm.renewUntil(lease, Lease.FOREVER, null);
            }
            return session;
          }
        }
      }
    }
    catch ( Exception e)
    {
      e.printStackTrace();
    }
    return null;
}
```

Logs client out of library:

```
public void logout(String userName) throws RemoteException {
  SessionEntry template = new SessionEntry(userName);
  template.login = null;
  try
  {
    SessionEntry entry = (SessionEntry) space.takeIfExists
      (template, null, JavaSpace.NO_WAIT);
    if(isVIP(userName))
    {
      System.out.println(userName);
      VIPEntry vipTemplate = new VIPEntry(userName);
      VIPEntry vipEntry = (VIPEntry) space.takeIfExists
        (template, null, JavaSpace.NO_WAIT);
    }
  }
  catch (Exception e) {}
}
```

Determines group membership:

```
public boolean inGroup(String userName, String groupName) {
  try
  {
    GroupEntry template = new GroupEntry(groupName);
    GroupEntry groupEntry = (GroupEntry) space.readIfExists
      (template, null, JavaSpace.NO_WAIT);
    if(groupEntry == null) {
      return false;
    }
    return groupEntry.isMember(userName);
  }
  catch (Exception e) { e.printStackTrace(); }
  return false;
}
```

Checks a book into the library:

```
public void checkIn(BookEntry book) throws RemoteException {
  BookIndex index = null;
  BookIndex template = new BookIndex();
  template.bookTitle = book.bookTitle;
  try
  {
    index = (BookIndex) space.read(template, null,
      Long.MAX_VALUE);
    array.update(book, index.position.intValue());
  }
  catch (Exception e) { e.printStackTrace(); }
}
```

Checks a book out of the library:

```
public BookEntry checkOut(String bookTitle) throws
   RemoteException {
   BookIndex index = null;
   BookEntry book = null;
   BookIndex template = new BookIndex();
   template.bookTitle = bookTitle;
   try
   {
     index = (BookIndex) space.readIfExists(template, null,
       Long.MAX_VALUE);
     if(index != null)
       book = (BookEntry) array.deleteElement
         (index.position.intValue());
   }
   catch (Exception e) { e.printStackTrace(); }
   return book;
}
```

Get the list of all books currently available in library:

```
public String[] getBookTitles() throws RemoteException {
   Object element = null;
   String[] bookTitles;
   Vector titles = new Vector();
   titles.addElement(new String(JWPNames.LIBRARY));
   try
   {
     // references the DistribArray structure
     for(int i=0; i<array.size();i++)
     {
       element = array.readElement(i);
       BookEntry entry = (BookEntry)element;
       titles.addElement(entry.bookTitle);
     }
   }
   catch(Exception e) {}
   bookTitles = new String[titles.size()];
   titles.copyInto(bookTitles);
   return bookTitles;
}
```

Find a book by a specific title:

```
public BookEntry findBookByTitle(String title) throws
   RemoteException {
   BookIndex index = null;
   BookEntry book = null;
   BookIndex template = new BookIndex();
   template.bookTitle = title;
   try
   {
     index = (BookIndex) space.read(template, null,
       Long.MAX_VALUE);
     book = (BookEntry) array.readElement
       (index.position.intValue());
   }
   catch (Exception e) { e.printStackTrace(); }
   return book;
}
```

`com.sun.jini.outrigger` is the Sun implementation of the Jini JavaSpaces service. The examples that ship with the Sun reference implementation define the default space as 'JavaSpaces'. There are two implementations of JavaSpaces provided. One is referred to as Transient Space and the other as FrontEnd or Persistent Space. The Transient Space does not survive across system restarts. Transient Space is an implementation of JavaSpaces that is not an activatable service. The persistent implementation is the one that we start and configure for JWorkPlace. It uses `rmid` and should have reasonable resiliency over crashes.

Once you have access to JavaSpace, as in the reference to 'space' above, you can begin to perform the basic operations on the named space.

At this point let's show how the space was started. Starting a space is as simple as defining a named parameter in the JavaSpace service startup script. This assumes all the necessary Jini infrastructure (`rmid`, `reggie`, and an `httpd` server) are already started:

```
java -jar
-Djava.security.policy=\files\jini1_1\example\fragmentspace\policy.all
-Dcom.sun.jini.outrigger.spaceName=FragmentSpace \files\jini1_1\lib\outrigger.jar
http://172.16.1.2:8080/outrigger-dl.jar
\files\jini1_1\example\fragmentspace\policy.all \tmp\js_log public
```

The parameter `-Dcom.sun.jini.outrigger.spaceName=FragmentSpace` provides the name for the space that outrigger creates when the service starts. Outrigger can be configured to register with lookup servers in one or more specified groups and/or in one or more specific lookup servers (designated by hostname:port number pairs) as done in the above example. In the group case, Jini multicast discovery protocol is used, so the outrigger server and the lookup services have to be on the same Local Area Network.

Once you have a reference to the outrigger server you can use its admin interface to change the set of groups and/or provide a set of specific lookup servers to the join admin interface.

JWorkPlace: Appendix B

Steps and Scripts used to Start JWorkPlace

Windows NT

1. Start the HTTP server

   ```
   java -jar h:\files\jini1_1\lib\tools.jar -port 8080 -dir d:\files\jini1_1\lib
   -verbose
   ```

2. Start rmid

   ```
   rmid
   ```

3. Start reggie (Lookup Service)

   ```
   java -jar -Djava.security.policy=h:\files\jini1_1\example\lookup\policy.all
   h:\files\jini1_1\lib\reggie.jar http://your.ip.address:8080/reggie-dl.jar
   h:\files\jini1_1\example\lookup\policy.all h:\tmp\reggie_log public
   ```

4. Start mahalo (Transaction Service)

   ```
   java -jar -Djava.security.policy=h:\files\jini1_1\example\lookup\policy.all -
   Dcom.sun.jini.mahalo.managerName=TransactionManager
   h:\files\jini1_1\lib\mahalo.jar http://your.ip.address:8080/mahalo-dl.jar
   h:\files\jini1_1\example\txn\policy.all h:\tmp\txn_log public
   ```

5. Start JavaSpaces (Front End) outrigger

   ```
   java -jar -
   Djava.security.policy=h:\files\jini1_1\example\jworkplace\policy.all -
   Dcom.sun.jini.outrigger.spaceName=JavaSpaces
   h:\files\jini1_1\lib\outrigger.jar http://your.ip.address:8080/outrigger-
   dl.jar h:\files\jini1_1\example\books\policy.all h:\tmp\js_log public
   ```

6. Start WorkPlace Administration:

   ```
   java -Djava.security.policy=h:\files\jini1_1\example\jworkplace\policy.all -
   Doutrigger.spacename=JavaSpaces -Dcom.sun.jini.lookup.groups=public -cp
   h:\files\jini1_1\lib\space-examples.jar;h:\files\jini1_1\lib\jini-
   core.jar;h:\files\jini1_1\lib\jini-ext.jar;h:\files\jini1_1\lib\jworkplace.jar
   -Djava.rmi.server.codebase= http://your.ip.address: 8080/jworkplace-dl.jar
   viewers.WorkPlaceAdmin
   ```

7. Start the LibraryServer:

   ```
   java -Djava.security.policy=\files\jini1_1\example\jworkplace\policy.all -
   Doutrigger.spacename=JavaSpaces -Dcom.sun.jini.lookup.groups=public -cp
   h:\files\jini1_1\lib\space-examples.jar;h:\files\jini1_1\lib\jini-
   core.jar;\files\jini1_1\lib\jini-ext.jar;h:\files\jini1_1\lib\jworkplace.jar -
   Djava.rmi.server.codebase= http://your_ip_address:8080/jworkplace-dl.jar
   viewers.LibraryServer
   ```

8. Start the client SpaceView

   ```
   java -Djava.security.policy=\files\jini1_1\example\jworkplace\policy.all -
   Doutrigger.spacename=JavaSpaces -Dcom.sun.jini.lookup.groups=public -cp
   \files\jini1_1\lib\space-examples.jar;h:\files\jini1_1\lib\jini-
   core.jar;h:\files\jini1_1\lib\jini-ext.jar;h:\files\jini1_1\lib\jworkplace.jar
   -Djava.rmi.server.codebase= http://your.ip.address:8080/jworkplace-dl.jar
   viewers.SpaceView
   ```

Milé Buurmeijer

Eric Hol

18

Jini on Wheels – the Car as a Mobile Infrastructure

This case study is about cars, GPS Navigation systems, route planners, Jini, JavaSpacs and a business application that uses these elements. Technology providers, like Sun, IBM, or Ericsson call this application area **Ubiquitous Computing** or **Pervasive Computing** referring to seamlessly integrated devices in futuristic environments like the 'smart house' and the 'electronic cookbook'. The ingenious technology bit is true, but the rather idealistic setting is replaced with the more ordinary, but nonetheless appealing, business environment of *scheduled trips* as part of the customer services division of a company.

We'll show how we transform an in-car navigation system into a network service and integrate it with a company route planner service. By doing this we achieve a distributed planning and control system for customer service employees so that customers experience a better level of service when they make an appointment with a repairman. Of course this is all glued together with Jini Connection technology, which is exemplified with UML diagrams and code snippets of the essential integration based on Jini. The complete demo including source code is downloadable from the Wrox website.

Everybody who would like to see a suitable application area for applying Jini Connection technology should read this chapter. We, of Cap Gemini Ernst and Young, introduce a simple but innovative business case and show how Jini makes it a flexible and open solution. Based on the presented case solution we generalize the crucial issues tackled in the design and draw some conclusions from the generalizations. This case study makes things more tangible and is written for technology consultants and engineers who are new to the field of 'integration of various environments'.

Why This Case Study?

This chapter explains the reasons for doing a case study and the case itself.

As a systems integrator, Cap Gemini Ernst and Young is always looking for new challenges ahead. To exemplify the new IT environments we have to integrate, we present a case that shows a typical application that will live in this post-PC era. The case will be defined in terms of a problem domain, solution, and design process (architectural overview and discussion of design decisions).

How did we select the business case? It had to have several characteristics. We posed three criteria that had to be fulfilled by a successful case:

- ❑ It has to show the benefits of Jini Connection Technology. This means when laymen (preferably clients of Cap Gemini Ernst and Young) get to know the case they will also conclude that Jini Connection Technology is a benefit to the problem solved, hence they grasp the problems Jini Connection Technology can solve. It is especially interesting to show the spontaneous integration of software by combining several usually disconnected environments into one case.

- ❑ It should solve a relevant business issue. By having this criterion, we expect to see projects coming in more easily due to the clients' ability to place Jini Connection Technology in its business environment (for example, do not present things like refrigerators connected to the Internet, since most clients are not into home appliances).

- ❑ It should be relevant in more than one business branch to make it applicable.

There are several environments, like home, car, or office, identified that could be used to situate a case study. Because it is our understanding that the first glimpse of ubiquitous computing will pop up in certain environments before it becomes ubiquitous over these environments, we looked for a case that exceeds a single environment. The following figure shows this estimated evolution of post-PC era applications (the big arrow on the left indicates progress in time):

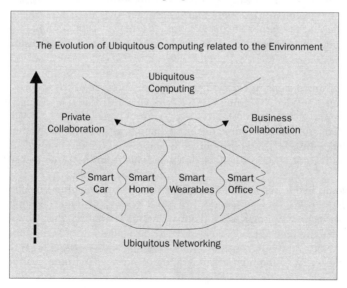

The first wave towards ubiquitous computing is labeled 'ubiquitous networking' and can be described as the Internet being everywhere and at anytime (this is almost reality). The next evolution wave shows the conversion of individual environments with the Internet. Thus smart means that the objects in that environment have communication capabilities (that is, the devices become smart through 'think and link'). Then these environments migrate into one ubiquitous computing environment. This private and business collaboration timeframe will show applications or services that exceed the individual environment and integrate services (for example, services provided by devices or services on the Net) found in the underlying environments.

We decided to focus on the combination of smart wearables, offices, and cars to visualize some of the things to come in the era of business collaboration. As we waded through all kinds of developments in the transportation sector we found that In-Vehicle Telematics and Intelligent Transportation Systems (ITS) are gaining popularity at the moment. Cap Gemini Ernst and Young's vertical divisions indicated that this market is in change and that there is a market for pervasive solutions in this sector. Therefore without further ado we present the case.

Case Description – Graded Ubiquitous Trip Support

Many companies have employees on the road to visit clients, service customer appliances or deliver goods. Most of these client contacts are planned far in advance with great time margins. Everybody has experiences of making appointments with a service company and having to take a day off work to wait for the repairman to show up. Calling the service center and asking for a more precise schedule is a waste of time. In the same way, many of us have also encountered the problem from the opposite point of view when you have an appointment with someone elsewhere and face all the things that can go wrong. The traffic conditions are hopeless and previous appointments tend to take longer than expected (or appointments are at least not very predictable).

So there are two problems that one can determine from the description above. One is that visibility of processes taking place outside the office (in terms of who is where doing what) is poor and the other is that the planning and control of the travelling part of outdoor trips is guesswork.

Problem Statement

The visibility problem leads to our case, the Graded Ubiquitous Trip Support (GUTS). The outdoor processes and their links to the company and customers are depicted in the figure below:

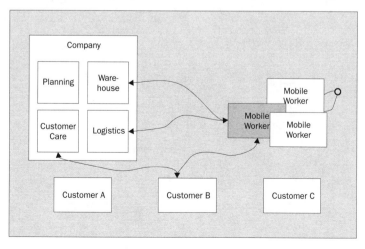

The mobile workers on the road usually do not communicate until there is an event that causes a change in plans for that day. Then they need to notify both the company and their customers. In the meantime, if customers telephone the call center (customer care) to inquire on the status of the delivery, they will not get an answer. The call center simply will not know the status unless they call the employee on their mobile phone.

The business process that plans and controls activities outside the company's walls (such as, visiting clients to deliver services or products) needs to be more dynamic and to be visible to all participating parties (employees on the road, the relevant business processes, the customers). This means that changes in the planning due to events that occur while on the road need to be communicated back and forth.

Also, events not happening on the road influence the outdoor process and are badly in need of a dynamic planning system. Think of customers canceling appointments or a last minute hiccup in the logistic chain.

So, what types of mobile workers are planned by the company to visit customers or deliver products to customers? The following list shows some of the lines of work in mind. The list is far from exhaustive, but gives an impression of the generality of the problem.

Traveling salespeople	Real estate brokers
Agents	Service employees
Couriers	Damage experts
Postal services	Insurance inspectors
Roadside assistance	

Solution

As was said earlier the planning of a trip is hardly predictable, due to variable traffic conditions. What can be done is that the consequences of relevant planning events, whether they come from within the company, on the road, or the client, are handled in a consistent manner. All participants of the GUTS service need to communicate the relevant events and can request up to date status information.

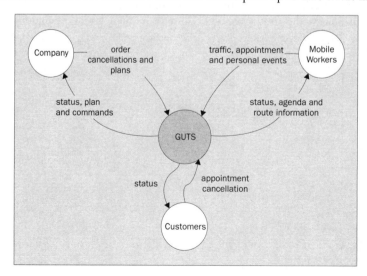

We make the assumption that it is of no interest to any party to send over exact details of the whereabouts of the employee. To reveal unnecessary details is command and control at too detailed a level. For both company and customer it is sufficient to know if things are still on schedule and if not what the consequences are (for example, skip an appointment or have a delay of half an hour). This requirement sets the outline of the GUTS system. It will influence the design a great deal. It gives us the opportunity to implement the command and control in a distributed approach.

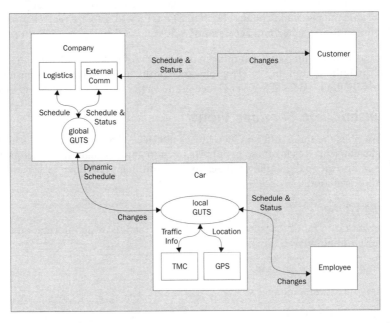

The above figure focuses on the information flow between company, car, customer, and employee entities. The information shared between the entities is a schedule. This schedule needs to be dynamic to handle the changes gracefully for command and control purposes. A schedule consists of a list of appointments and a route description between the locations of the appointments. It is the product of the central resource allocation process.

Company Interaction with GUTS

Within the company, an existing planning process produces a schedule and makes it available to the GUTS system. Within this planning process there is also a route planning system that determines an optimal route from appointment to appointment. The GUTS system can request rescheduling if the deviation measured while executing the plan (or schedule) is too large or the plan is impossible to perform due to changes or events.

Customer Interaction with GUTS

The customer has many ways to interact with the company. This could be a mobile phone with information access capabilities (WAP phone), the internet, or the company's call center. All the underlying media should be consistent when it comes to the status of the schedule and changes to it. The customer receives the schedule in terms of agenda items with appointment details in his/her e-mail inbox. Status and changes can be requested (this is real-time information). Based on this the customer doesn't have to take the day off work to be at home. He/she only needs to check the schedule regularly, or notification of changes can be sent automatically. The allowed variations in planning could even be part of the service level agreement ('I don't mind taking the morning off' versus 'I insist on a one hour margin').

Employee or Driver Interaction with GUTS

The employee in the car interacts with the system via its in-car component. This in-car component handles the command and control for the trip the employee has to make. It supports the employee with navigational directions and it communicates with the company regarding progress of the plan and might report deviations from the plan in terms of delay. The actual measurement of progress is based on the input of two other components that are available in the car. These are the global positioning system (GPS) and the traffic management channel (TMC). The GPS will provide real-time positioning info and such related information as speed and acceleration.

The TMC is usually transmitted as a sub-information stream of radio broadcast signals and is therefore an interface of the radio unit of the car. The relevance of the traffic info that is transmitted via the TMC can be evaluated by the local GUTS system since it knows the addresses it needs to visit.

Graded Ubiquitous Trip Services Views

This section describes the three different views (user interfaces) for the participants in the GUTS system. To be able to develop services for these people we need to get an insight into each party's point of view. Each party has their own goal that they can achieve by fulfilling predefined tasks; and to fulfill these tasks they need information.

View of the Mobile Worker

For the mobile worker to fulfill their task they need to get the following information (presented as requests the worker might give GUTS):

- ❏ Give me today's route right now.
- ❏ Give me my next destination.
- ❏ Give me directions to the destination.
- ❏ Give me the status please. Am I on schedule?
- ❏ Give me the reason for this change.

The user interface designed for the mobile worker looks like this:

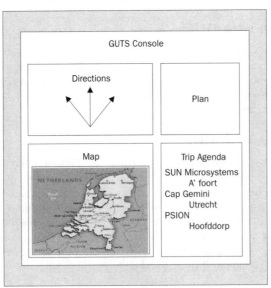

The in-car set of components is not unique to this service. For example the GPS or the TMC might be used for other services as well. Or the communication means between car and company might be used for synchronizing data the employee is generating in their job with back-end systems.

The employee accesses the GUTS service via their PDA. The employee uses this PDA for their daily work and uses it in the car as an interface to the GUTS system. GUTS will present the user with a navigation aid, agenda, and plan progress indicator. The PDA represents the wearable environment we want to integrate in this system and is very likely to exist.

View of the Company

From a company point of view certain information is needed to streamline the overall process. They need answers on the following issues:

- ❑ Give me an overview of my fleet right now.
- ❑ Report if one of my drivers is delayed.
- ❑ Report on incoming events that might influence a route of one of my drivers.
- ❑ Inform me on the reason for a certain change.

The back office of the company the mobile worker works for consists of a real-time console to monitor the actual status of ongoing trips at that time and their related plans. To make the office ubiquitous we introduce information appliances that can plug into the network anywhere and discover all relevant services that control the trips. Most notably this is the user interface of GUTS itself. The GUTS application is made out of separate services that also spontaneously integrate, for example the planning and more specific route planning systems are found by exploring the service on the network via querying a directory of services. By this we mean that it is not foreseen in the near future that legacy systems will be equiped with a Jini service interface, but that these can be found for example in an LDAP directory service.

The user interface for the company is shown below:

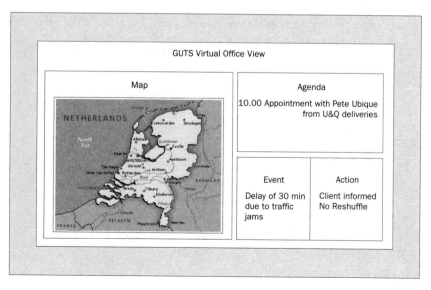

View of the Customer

The customer wants to be informed on the following:

- ❑ What time will I receive my product or service?
- ❑ Will I receive all I ordered?
- ❑ Is there a delay?

The customer perspective looks like the views we have seen for the central office and mobile workers:

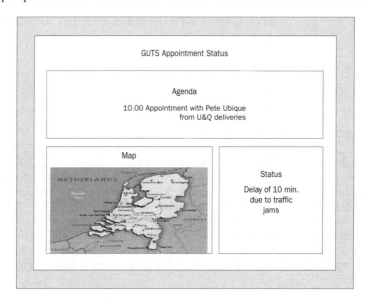

The interface for the customer is viewed within a browser. Therefore the client requirements are standard PIM (Personal Information Management) components, browser, agenda, and mail, only. Currently we have implemented the user interface as an applet that actually does Jini interaction towards GUTS instead of via an application server that does the back yard Jini. This applet solution with Jini is not something you want to deploy, but for demo purposes we did want a simple solution and not a heavy application server for doing something so simple.

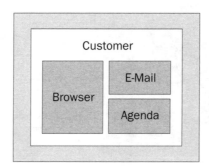

Wrap Up of Requirements

The combined list of requirements is therefore:

- ❑ Legacy integration (existing logistics)

- ❑ Multi-channel infrastructure for consistent information access (customer to company)

- ❑ Open in-vehicle infrastructure (multiple use of components by in-vehicle services)

- ❑ Dynamic and real-time scheduling and navigation (company, customer, and car)

- ❑ Multiple environments (car, company, and wearables)

Technological View of the Solution

When choosing technologies for the GUTS environment it is obvious that there is no single environment and that the platforms, network infrastructures, and application environments are very distinct. For example, in-vehicle automation has its own networking technology and does not support remote network services like Internet access yet. The car environment is mainly focussed on small systems that do not communicate with each other. The Ubiquitous systems we envision are fundamentally based on communication and therefore have other requirements of the network infrastructure. Also the level of abstraction in the car environment in terms of OS APIs and Network APIs is much simpler then in the Internet environment due to the limited processing and communication needs found in car components. When introducing networking à la Internet technology and applications, the infrastructure needs more capabilities than currently found in cars. Also the car environment is often based on single purpose devices. For example, this means that a GPS cannot be shared between systems.

> *An interesting article on in vehicle network development can be found at* http://www.ednmag.com/ednmag/reg/1999/081999/17cs.htm *and the proceedings of the 1999 ITS workshops on research subjects for in-vehicle automation – Transportation Research Circular E-C009. "Research Directions for In-Vehicle Computing" – can be found at* http://www.nas.edu/trb/publications/ec009.pdf.

How valid would it be to take the TCP/IP network layer as bare minimum for the car environment? Surely the prices of TCP/IP network components are dropping sharply and Ethernet bandwidth (10 Mb/s) is, for the time being, enough. Also is there a lot of knowledge, experience, and components available for developing services based on this network technology? Will it integrate well with the Inter-networked world found in companies and at the customer's end? Another requirement is that it should be implemented as a second network alongside all the safety systems on the main car network. Via GSM (Global System for Mobile communications) wireless networks one can setup easily a TCP link to the company network. Currently GSM has rather low bandwidth (9600 b/s), but the next generation, called GPRS (General Packet Radio Services), is packet switched (more efficient for data communication) and has higher bandwidth (max 171 kb/s).

Above the network layer we need a middleware layer that abstracts from all the networking fuss and platform idiosyncrasies. Currently, company systems are web-enabled and XML message based, but in-car systems are usually proprietary and not open for other systems. The new devices and systems introduced in cars should at least be open and network enabled. On top of that the middleware should enable easy integration of the devices and services on an application level, but have little resource consumption on the target platforms. Jini is just such a middleware technology that provides hassle free integration and has a small code base that can be implemented in embedded systems of sizes found in cars. Jini is a rather new technology, but is very small in terms of code, API size and computing requirements. It is also well designed. The programming model is very clean and easy to understand. The underlying network layer is based on TCP/IP and Java Remote Method Invocation (RMI). Although Jini is based on Java and therefore expects a Java Virtual Machine the complete Jini interface could be implemented in hardware for the smallest devices.

Both choices (TCP/IP and Jini) also work well for PDAs. These are usually TCP/IP enabled (on a serial line) and on most PDAs there is a JVM available for running Java and Jini programs. Of course there are some version issues when it comes to existing JVMs on devices. Most of these devices have a porting skew compared to desktop JVMs. Currently most of the JVMs out there (embedded, J2ME) are based on subsets of the JDK1.1 APIs, which makes it impossible to run Jini since Jini depends on a few JDK1.2 enhancements to RMI. Our assumption is that it is only a matter of time, since no manufacturer of these devices or appliances that have bet on Java want to miss the Jini opportunities.

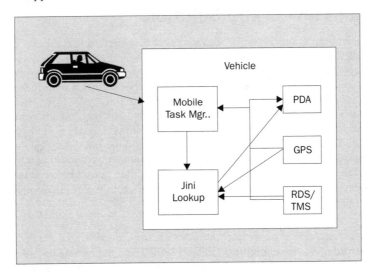

In the above figure the basic components of the car infrastructure are depicted. The PDA is not permanently available but only when the driver is in the car. The other components are quite straightforward. The Mobile Task Manager is, in GUTS terminology, the local-planning-and-control component or processor. It contains the routines to deduce the progress and to estimate the severity of the low-level traffic events that happen. The GPS and TMC are small devices that serve their services to the Jini infrastructure by registering themselves in the Jini lookup service. (The figure shows RDS/TMC, because the traffic information (TMC) is filtered out of the digital radio signal (RDS) of the car stereo set.) The PDA will find the Mobile Task Manager via the same lookup service. Also part of the infrastructure is the communication layer to the company (not shown in the figure). Based on simple GSM data calls an IP link is set up when needed.

The company infrastructure (next figure) is far more like what can be found in today's companies. Back office systems like planning or logistic systems are the legacy we have to integrate into the solution. Also the company's standard web interface (based on a web application server) needs to be integrated for the various channels to the customer. These channels are, apart from the Internet access, a call center that will use the web interface and wireless connections to mobile phones based on WAP servers. For sake of simplicity only the web connection is shown.

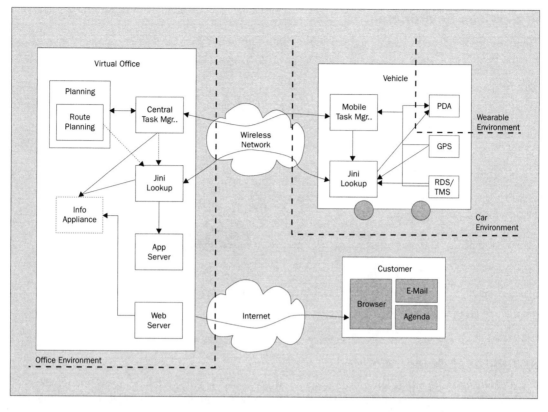

The need for Jini Connection Technology at the company side of the GUTS system needs some explanation. We choose to combine three different environments (car, company, and wearables). This means the GUTS service needs transparency over these environments. Parts of it will run in the car environment, some of it on the PDA, and the rest of it in the company environment. Each part of GUTS needs to be able to find the other parts spontaneously in an easy way. So the parts in the company that need to be visible to the other environments need to be Jini enabled as well.

Application Architecture and Jini Services

As stated earlier the GUTS application has a strong distributed nature. It is build around four specific Jini services that together form the GUTS system. Three of these services run in the car. The fourth service and one demo only service are running on servers somewhere in the network. This demo service, called Wizard, controls the demo.

The Services Environment

The following figure shows the services in their environment:

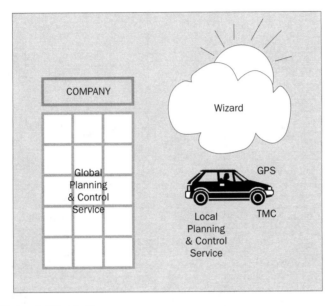

The Top-Level Object Model

First we focus on the top-level object model of GUTS, then on the car, company, and client part of GUTS. The core object model of GUTS is shown below. It contains the packages that form the different components of GUTS.

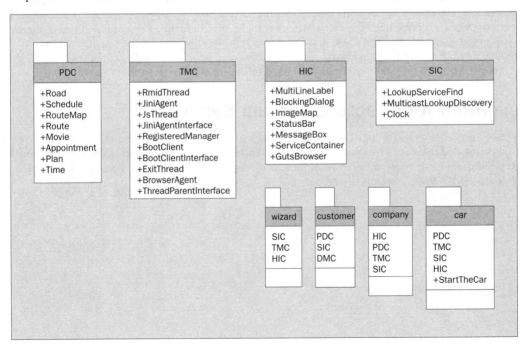

The componentization is based on Cap Gemini's object oriented analysis methodology. It is an extension of the well-known Model View Controller (MVC) design pattern. The Model part of MVC is called Problem Domain Component (PDC), the Controller part is called Task Management Component (TMC). The View part of Model-View-Controller is differentiated towards three distinct domains: human and system interaction (Human Interaction Component (HIC) and System Interaction Component (SIC), and data management (Data Management Component). Jini services can be categorized as SICs or TMCs depending on the nature of the service (if the Jini service is merely an interface to another system then it ends up in a SIC package; if it is task oriented (like agents) then it ends up in a TMC package). At the top level UML model of GUTS, the mentioned components (PDC, TMC, HIC, and SIC) are common between the use case specific parts of GUTS car, company, customer, and wizard.

The PDC package contains the core classes that are transferred between the car, company and customer part of GUTS. These are Plan, Appointment, Time, Schedule, Route, RouteMap Road, and Movie. The latter class is only there for demo purposes. The video server part of the demo shows movie clips of the roads that are traversed. This part of the demo cannot be downloaded.

The TMC package contains supporting Jini classes. Most interesting are the `BootClient` and the `JiniAgent`. `JiniAgent` starts the ClassServer, RMID daemon process, Lookup Service and the JavaSpaces service. The `BootClient` facilitates remote starting and stopping of Jini services. These `BootClient` services can be run on all participating platforms and can be controlled by the `GutsBrowser` (part of the HIC package). This browser makes it possible to select the GUTS Jini services together with the discovered `BootClients` in the network and start or stop these GUTS services. Initially we built the demo without `BootClients` and `JiniAgent`, but that made the demo startup process rather lengthy and error prone. We wanted to make starting and stopping the various demo components as simple as possible. This helps show Jini as the enabling technology it is.

The `BootClient` interface definition is shown below:

```
package com.capgemini.sba4.guts.TMC;

/**
 * Interface definition of the BootClient service. A BootClient service
 * enables remote starting and stopping of Jini Services. The BootClient
 * process itself can also be stopped remotely. It unregisters all running
 * Jini services threads
 */
public interface BootClientInterface extends java.rmi.Remote {

    public void startService(String serviceName) throws RemoteException;
    public void stopService(String serviceName) throws RemoteException;
    public void stopBootClient() throws RemoteException;

}
```

The implementation is very straightforward and not optimized to facilitate remote updates of local classes or the like. Below the initialization part of the `BootClient` implementation is shown:

```
public static void main (String[] args) {
    // use current System properties as parent
    Properties props = new Properties(System.getProperties());
    // get the Guts properties
    // Load from a file
    try {
```

```
        props.load(new BufferedInputStream(new FileInputStream(
            System.getProperty( "guts.properties")))));
    System.setProperties(props);
}
catch (Exception e) {
    System.out.println("Could not read properties file ");
    e.printStackTrace();
}
BootClient client;
Entry[] aeAttributes;
JoinManager joinmanager;
ServiceRegistrar registrar;

try {
    String localhost = InetAddress.getLocalHost().getHostName();
    System.out.println("Starting up BootClient " + localhost + "...");

    if (System.getSecurityManager() == null)
        System.setSecurityManager (new RMISecurityManager ());

    client = new BootClient();
    try {
        aeAttributes = new Entry[3];
        aeAttributes[0] = new Name("BootClient " + localhost);
        aeAttributes[1] = new ServiceInfo("BootClient " + localhost,
                            "Cap Gemini, Warp11",
                            "Cap Gemini, CGI",
                            "2.0",
                            "",
                            "");
        aeAttributes[2] = new Location(localhost,
        "Warp11", "Galgenwaard");
        ServiceItem serviceItem = new ServiceItem(null,
        client,aeAttributes);
        LookupLocator[] lookupLocators =
            MulticastLookupDiscovery.getLocators();
        if (lookupLocators.length == 0) {
            System.out.println("Lookup service not running! ");
            System.exit(0);
        }
        registrar = lookupLocators[0].getRegistrar();
        ServiceRegistration registration =
            registrar.register(serviceItem , 10000);
        client.lease = registration.getLease();
        client.lmgr =
            new LeaseRenewalManager(client.lease, Lease.FOREVER, null);
        System.out.println("BootClient " + localhost + "started!");

    } catch (Exception e1) {
        System.out.println("BootClient: main(): Exception " + e1);
        try {
            client.stopBootClient();
        } catch (Exception e2) {
        }
    }
```

```
            } catch (Exception e3) {
            }
        }
    }
package com.capgemini.sba4.guts.TMC;

import sun.rmi.server.*;

import com.capgemini.sba4.guts.SIC.*;
import com.capgemini.sba4.guts.car.SIC.*;
import com.capgemini.sba4.guts.wizard.TMC.*;
import com.capgemini.sba4.guts.company.TMC.*;
import com.capgemini.sba4.guts.car.TMC.*;


/**
 * The BootClient class serves a startup service for other services on this
 * local computer. The services are passed as java class name strings. Currently
 * it can start the following services: GPS, TMC, Wizard, GPCS, LPCS & MoviePlayer
 **/
public class BootClient extends UnicastRemoteObject
    implements BootClientInterface, ServiceIDListener, Serializable {

    private Wizard aWizard = null;
    private GPS aGPS = null;
    private GPCS aGPCS = null;
    private TMC aTMC = null;
    private MoviePlayer aMPS = null;
    private LPCS aLPCS = null;
    private Thread httpThread = null;
    private RmidThread rmidThread = null;
    private JsThread jsThread = null;
    private Lease lease = null;
    private LeaseRenewalManager lmgr = null;

    public BootClient() throws RemoteException {
        super();
    }

    public void startService(String serviceName) throws RemoteException {
        if (serviceName.compareTo("GPS Service") == 0) {
            aGPS = new GPS();
        } else if (serviceName.compareTo("Wizard Service") == 0) {
            aWizard = new Wizard();
            aMPS = new MoviePlayer(); // temporary fix, need to change this in
                                      // browseagent
        } else if (serviceName.compareTo("GPCS Service") == 0) {
            aGPCS = new GPCS();
        } else if (serviceName.compareTo("LPCS Service") == 0) {
            aLPCS = new LPCS();
        } else if (serviceName.compareTo("TMC Service") == 0) {
            aTMC = new TMC();
        } else if (serviceName.compareTo("MoviePlayer Service") == 0) {
            aMPS = new MoviePlayer();
        }
    }
```

```
public void stopService(String serviceName) throws RemoteException {
    if (serviceName.compareTo("GPS Service") == 0) {
        aGPS.stopService();
        aGPS = null;
    } else if (serviceName.compareTo("Wizard Service") == 0) {
        aWizard.stopService();
        aWizard = null;
    } else if (serviceName.compareTo("GPCS Service") == 0) {
        aGPCS.stopService();
        aGPCS = null;
    } else if (serviceName.compareTo("LPCS Service") == 0) {
        aLPCS.stopService();
        aLPCS = null;
    } else if (serviceName.compareTo("TMC Service") == 0) {
        aTMC.stopService();
        aTMC = null;
    } else if (serviceName.compareTo("MoviePlayer Service") == 0) {
        aMPS.stopService();
        aMPS = null;
    }
}

public void stopBootClient() throws RemoteException {
    if (aGPS != null) {
        aGPS.stopService();
        aGPS = null;
    }
    if (aGPCS != null) {
        aGPCS.stopService();
        aGPCS = null;
    }
    if (aLPCS != null) {
        aLPCS.stopService();
        aLPCS = null;
    }
    if (aTMC != null) {
        aTMC.stopService();
        aTMC = null;
    }
    if (aMPS != null) {
        aMPS.stopService();
        aMPS = null;
    }
    if (aWizard != null) {
        aWizard.stopService();
        aWizard = null;
    }
    httpThread = null;
    rmidThread = null;
    //jsThread = null;
    try {
        this.lmgr.cancel(this.lease);
        System.out.println ("Bootclient canceled.");
        ExitThread et = new ExitThread();
        et.start();
    } catch (Throwable exception) {
```

```
            System.err.println("Exception occurred in
                Bootclient.stopBootClient()");
            exception.printStackTrace(System.out);
            System.exit(0);
        }
    }
    public void serviceIDNotify (ServiceID serviceId) { } // ServiceIDListener
}
```

The rest of the `BootClient` implementation code is shown above. This code needs some cleaning and optimization, but is very straightforward. The current implementation is based on String identifiers for the Jini Services to manage. This should be changed to Java classes.

The In-Car Part of GUTS

The UML model of the in-car side of GUTS is shown below:

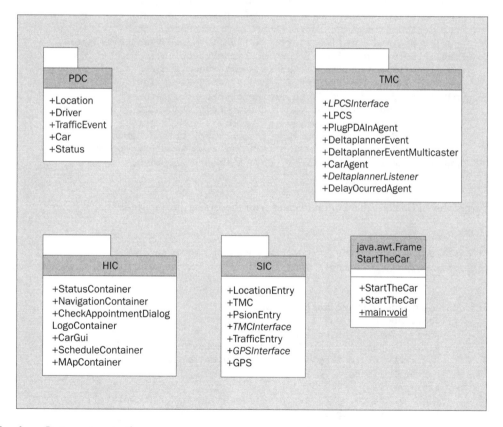

The three Jini services in the car are:

❑ GPS for determining the current location of the car,

❑ TMC for receiving traffic info via the car radio's traffic management channel (TMC)

❑ LPCS (Local Planning and Control Service) for monitoring progress of the car driving from appointment to appointment by gathering info from GPS and TMC and comparing these samples to the interpolated position. The LCPS receives the schedule with appointment from its global counterpart (GPCS).

The GPS and TMC services are rather low-level wrappers around the actual native implementations and are therefore placed in the SIC package. In the demo setup these are simulated services. In the TMC component there is the Local Planning and Control Service (LPCS) for keeping track of progress on the road. This LPCS is modeled as a Jini Service so that the Global Planning and Control Service (GPCS) can find it for receiving schedules. The LPCS itself receives crucial information indirectly from the GPS and TMC Jini Services. The GPS and TMC services post their info into a JavaSpace so that this info is available to other services as well. The JavaSpace is used as buffer between the LPCS service as receiving entity and the TMC and GPS service as data producing services. The LPCS interface is shown below.

```
public interface LPCSInterface extends java.rmi.Remote {
    public RouteMap getRouteMap() throws RemoteException;
    public Status getStatus()      throws RemoteException;
    public Schedule getSchedule() throws RemoteException;
    public boolean setDriver(Driver aDriver) throws RemoteException;
    public Driver getDriver() throws RemoteException;
    public void clearDriver() throws RemoteException;
    public void setFactor (int f) throws RemoteException;
    public void startDemo () throws RemoteException;
    public String getClockString() throws RemoteException;
    public void markAppDelivered(int appNr) throws RemoteException;
    public void setAppointment(Appointment app) throws RemoteException;
    public void setLocalPlan(Plan aPlan) throws RemoteException;
    public Location getLocation() throws RemoteException;
}
```

The part of the LPCS class that communicates with the In-Car JavaSpace is shown below:

```
/**
 * getCarJavaSpace tries locates the JavaSpace with the name
 * "CarJavaSpace" by doing a Jini Lookup. It returns null if none can be found.
 */

private JavaSpace getCarJavaspace() {
    if (carJavaSpace == null) {
        Entry[] aeAttributes = new Entry[1];
        aeAttributes[0] = new Name("CarJavaSpace");
        ServiceTemplate template = new ServiceTemplate(null, null,
            aeAttributes);
        try {
            carJavaSpace = (JavaSpace)registrar.lookup(template);
        } catch(Exception e) { }
        if (carJavaSpace != null)
            System.out.println("LPCS: CarJavaSpace found");
    }
    return carJavaSpace;
}

/**
```

```
 * The run method endlessly tries to read Traffic or Location object from the
 * "CarJavaSpace". If either of them succeeds in reading an objects then it is
 * further processed.
 */
    public void run () {
        while (true) {
            try {
                LocationEntry locTempl = new LocationEntry();
                LocationEntry locResult = (LocationEntry)js.read(locTempl, null,
                    1000);
                if (locResult != null) {
                    actualLocation =
                        new Location(locResult.location.x, locResult.location.y);
                    calcDeviation(
                        actualLocation, ((Long)locResult.timestamp).longValue());
                }
            } catch(Exception e) {
            }
            try {
                TrafficEntry traTempl = new TrafficEntry();
                TrafficEntry traResult = (TrafficEntry)js.take(traTempl, null,
                    1000);
                if (traResult != null) {
                    handleTrafficEvent(traResult.message);
                }
            } catch(Exception e) {
            }
            try { Thread.sleep(2000); } catch(Exception exc) { }
        }
    }
```

The code snippet above reveals that the JavaSpace interaction is implemented with a polling design pattern. Since JavaSpaces supports notifications it is likely that in a non-demo setting this would be changed to the use of notifications.

The part of the GPS service that posts LocationEntry objects into the Car JavaSpace looks like this:

```
/**
 * findJavaSpace performs a Jini Lookup of the JavaSpace.
 */
    protected void findJavaSpace(ServiceRegistrar reg) {
        try {
            javaSpace = (JavaSpace)reg.lookup(tmpl);
            while (javaSpace == null) {
                System.out.println("Found no space!");
                try { Thread.sleep(5000); } catch(Exception e) { }
                javaSpace = (JavaSpace)reg.lookup(tmpl);
            }
            System.out.println("Found a space!");
        } catch(Exception ex) {
            System.err.println("Error doing lookup: " + ex.getMessage());
        }
    }
```

```
/**
 * setGPS writes a LocationEntry object with a certain timestamp into the
 * JavaSpace
 */
    public void setGPS (Location aLocation, Long aTimestamp) throws
        RemoteException { //let GPS write new location to javaspace
        try {
            LocationEntry entry = new LocationEntry();
            carLocation = new Location(aLocation.x, aLocation.y);
            entry.timestamp = new Long(aTimestamp.longValue());
            entry.location = carLocation;
            javaSpace.write(entry, null, 1000);
        } catch(Exception ex) {
            System.err.println("Error writing to JavaSpace: " + ex.getMessage());
        }
    }
```

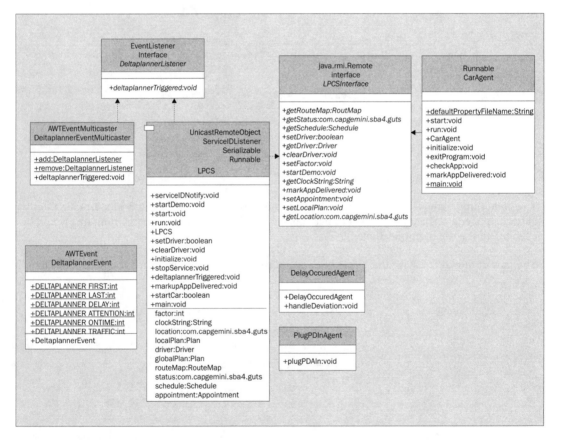

The UML model above states which events are handled by the LPCS. It also shows the actual process that controls user interaction in the car called CarAgent (By the term Agent we do not mean the concept of artificial intelligence, but merely an object with a task like role). This CarAgent communicates via the LCPS with GUTS. It allows the mobile employee to signal that an appointment took place or was dropped from the schedule. It also shows the mobile employee in the car the status of the schedule and in case of a delay the estimated length of the hold up.

There are many more pieces of code to show, but when we filtered out the relevant Jini code we found that most of the code is about getting the GUTS application to work. The complex part is the distributed application logic that tries to keep the state visible to customer, company and service employee consistent. The Jini code to tie these distributed processes together is copied almost right from the textbook and from a programmer's point of view is very easy to implement. So the difficult part was to divide this distributed app into the right Jini services. This means building distributed applications with Jini Connection Technology is accelerated, but designing these apps should still be given the right amount of attention. This became apparent when we designed the functionality for the demo setting. Then it must run like a simulation, i.e. the GPS coordinates and TMC traffic events need to be simulated. So we came up with one extra service called the Wizard Service that controls the simulation. It starts the company's GPCS process that triggers the in-car LPCS process. When the service employee starts the mentioned CarAgent process the Wizards starts sending LocationEntrys to the GPS service, which in turn places them into the JavaSpace as described. The Wizard service can also generate traffic events at will and send these to the TMC so that the TMC can publish these in the JavaSpace. Setting all this up takes a while and shouldn't be rushed by pushy project leaders or hasty programmers who want to start coding with Jini.

Technical Infrastructure

Earlier we saw that part of the services run in the car on an on board application platform. This platform must be a Java/Jini compatible platform, most likely a Java 2 Micro Edition with the Automotive profile. In our demo setting we have been running the demo on various sets of ordinary PC's and Unix servers.

> *For an overview of J2ME see the JavaOne2000 presentation TS-763:*
> *http://jsp.java.sun.com/javaone/javaone2000/pdfs/TS-763.pdf*

In-car networks have high robustness requirements since safety and security are of utmost importance when driving vehicles. To make it a safe environment the car industry is working towards separate in-car networks that have a kind of gateway that connects the highly robust and "closed" network to the relatively less robust and "open" multimedia network. The closed network links all safety and driving assistance components and the open counterpart the more ICT related components and services. Ford motor company presented an overview of these networks at JavaOne2000. Their architecture was also based on Jini Connection Technology. The presentation depicted embedded server as a kind of general-purpose application platform, for example based on Java Embedded Server or any OSGi compliant platform for running services (see http://www.osgi.org). This server could run the in-car GUTS processes. External communication can be done via the user's mobile phone. The phone integrates itself into the network with its Bluetooth RF communication and discovery capabilities. All these developments are beginning to get feasible and it will be interesting to see them progress. The communication to the user could be based solely on speech recognition and synthesis technology or be augmented with a non-obtrusive user interface.

> *Ford's JavaOne presentation is at http://jsp.java.sun.com/javaone/javaone2000/pdfs/BUS-1631.pdf*

Learning Jini by Adding Complexity

Don't try to use all Jini features right from the start. It has helped us a great deal starting by using a named lookup service (i.e. unicast `LookupDiscovery`). We were able to start up the http server, the RMI-daemon and a lookup service (don't forget to setup the classpath properly) based on the examples that came with the Jini packages. By looking into the batch file we figured out the name of the lookup service. Hence we could show this service in a `main()` method and `LookupLocator` using `System.out.println`.

The next step was to build a service ourselves (e.g. the GPS service), that would return its GPS position upon every call made. This GPS service has a method named `getLocation()`, returning the actual position (`Location` is a user-defined object, where `getActualGps()` calculates and stores the right position)

```
public Location getLocation() throws RemoteException {
    return new Location(getActualGps().getX(), getActualGps().getY());
}
```

This method must also be declared in the `IGps`-interface, which is revealed as a proxy in the lookup service.

The GPS service identifies itself in the lookup-service, running on a server called `our_servername`. This can be done by programming the following:

```
try {
    System.setSecurityManager (new RMISecurityManager());
    LookupLocator lookup = new LookupLocator("jini://our_servername");

    ServiceRegistrar registrar = lookup.getRegistrar();

    Entry[] aeAttributes = new Entry[2];
    aeAttributes[0] = new Name("GPS Service");
    aeAttributes[1] = new ServiceInfo("GPS Service",
                        "Cap Gemini, Warp11", "Cap Gemini, CGI", "v1.0",
                        "Global Positioning System", "111111");
    ServiceItem serviceItem = new ServiceItem(null, this, aeAttributes);
    ServiceRegistration registration = registrar.register(serviceItem, 10000);
    lease = registration.getLease();
    lmgr = new LeaseRenewalManager(lease, Lease.FOREVER, null);

    try {Thread.sleep (2000);} catch (Exception e) {}

} catch (Exception e) {
    System.out.println("GPS: Exception " + e);
}
```

In this method we use the `LeaseRenewalManager` from Sun, that automatically takes care of the integrity of the proxy registration in the lookup service)

Calling the GPS service is done in the following way:

```
try {
    System.setSecurityManager (new RMISecurityManager());
    LookupLocator lookup = new LookupLocator("jini://our_servername");
    ServiceRegistrar registrar = lookup.getRegistrar();
    Entry[] aeAttributes = new Entry[1];
    aeAttributes[0] = new Name("GPS Service");
    ServiceTemplate tmpl = new ServiceTemplate(null, null, aeAttributes);
    IGps gpsInterface = null;
    while (gpsInterface == null) {
        System.out.println("Looking for the GPS-service");
        gpsInterface = (GPSInterface) registrar.lookup(tmpl);
        try { Thread.sleep(2000); } catch (Exception e) {};
    }
```

```
        Location actualGPSLocationFromService = gpsInterface.getLocation();
        System.out.println("GPS location is X=" +
            actualGPSLocationFromService.getX() + ", y=" +
            actualGPSLocationFromService.getY());
        );
    } catch (Exception e) {
        System.out.println("client: exception: " + e);
    }
```

When you want to switch to a multicast LookupDiscovery (querying all available lookup services for a GPS service), the only line that needs to be replaced is the following:

```
    LookupLocator lookup = new LookupLocator("jini://our_servername");
```

Replace it with:

```
    LookupLocator[] locators = OurMulticastLookupDiscovery.getLocators();
```

All these locators now need to be queried for the presence of the desired GPS service. The mentioned class OurMulticastLookupDiscovery is implemented al follows:

```
public class OurMulticastLookupDiscovery implements DiscoveryListener {
    java.util.Vector v = null;

    public void discarded(DiscoveryEvent de) {
        /* empty. One could respond here whenever the lookup service is no
        longer available */
    }

    public void discovered(DiscoveryEvent de) {
        /* Is called when one or more lookup-service-registrars are found */
        LookupLocator lookupLocator;
        try {
            ServiceRegistrar[] registrars = de.getRegistrars();
            for (int i = 0; i < registrars.length; ++i) {
                lookupLocator = registrars[i].getLocator();
                v.addElement(lookupLocator);
            }
        }
        catch (Exception e) {
            System.out.println("discovered exception:" + e);
        }
    }

    public static LookupLocator [] getLocators() {
        try {
            System.setSecurityManager(new RMISecurityManager());
            v.removeAllElements();
            LookupDiscovery ld = new LookupDiscovery(LookupDiscovery.NO_GROUPS);
            ld.addDiscoveryListener(new OurMulticastLookupDiscovery());
            ld.setGroups(LookupDiscovery.ALL_GROUPS);
            Thread.currentThread().sleep(5000L);
        }
```

```
    catch (Exception e) {
        System.out.println("OurMulticastLookupDiscovery exception:" + e);
    }
    LookupLocator[] locators = new LookupLocator[v.size()];
    v.copyInto(locators);
    return locators;
    }
}
```

Design and Implementation Issues

The benefits and concerns of the proposed system are discussed at two levels. The first level is about the case specific issues. The second level generalizes some of these ideas. The issues are:

- ❑ Effects of Events on Schedules

- ❑ Human-Computer Interaction

- ❑ In Vehicle Automation

- ❑ Linking Real-World Events to Real-Time ICT Systems

- ❑ Communication Costs

- ❑ Other Value Added Services

Effects of Events on Schedules

Delegating tasks to software components rather than to humans is a delicate issue. In GUTS the local traffic events are interpreted and the severity verified against the plan. Thus the human factor in assessing the severity is skipped in this solution in favor of an assessment made by software. This means that this component has to take into account many factors that influence a correct assessment of this severity. For example the traffic management channel might report a traffic jam that is on the current route, but in one of the last segments of it. Then the decision to neglect this event for the time being could be wise or stupid depending on prior knowledge about the usual traffic jams and their favorite time to appear and disappear. This knowledge or experience is not built into the current solution, but could be part of it when you augment the route information with traffic flow statistics of the road segments within the route.

Another aspect that has to do with delegation is the visibility of what is going on to the driver or employee. When most things are handled without consulting the driver, he or she might not trust the system and its decisions. As soon as doubt is introduced, the trust in the system slides away and will influence the acceptance of these kinds of technologies. The balance between visibility and the avoidance of information overflow is contradictory. The win-win situation could be reached when visibility is available on request. The user can then decide when they want to know what is going on (preferably when it is safe to focus their attention at this system).

Human-Computer Interaction

Especially in a car environment, user interaction is directly related to safety. Too many interactions will distract the user too much and therefore will reduce his or her attention needed for driving the vehicle. There are many ways to interface with in-car computers. Think of the in-helmet projection system used by pilots in military aircraft.

Another observation is that the user interfaces themselves can minimize the interference to a great extent. For example the use of speech technology could reduce distractions a lot. How this behaves in car environments is not very well understood yet, but technology providers are developing prototypes.

One of the largest car electronics manufacturers has developed a Bluetooth component prototype. See the news release at:
http://www.johnsoncontrols.com/CorpPR/Releases/asg/release170.asp.

Linking Real-World Events to Real-Time ICT Systems

In an ICT model of reality it is hard to cope with all the noise that is generated by measuring the real world. These systems require Java based, real time solutions, that are currently still in development. Also getting the mapping accurate enough to base an entire planning and control system like GUTS on mere GPS coordinates is a bit tricky. Combined solutions like GPS and stationary radio antennae make a very reliable and accurate positioning system possible.

In Vehicle Automation

As explained in the human computer interaction paragraph, the safety of car driving is at stake when the car is seen as just another computer environment. This is due to the driving and information processing nature of tasks that we envision are going to be combined a lot more in the near future.

This also means that in-vehicle systems need to be aware of each other in terms of user interaction priorities. We are not sure we need regulations for introducing these kinds of systems into cars, but it is quite likely that we will soon need supervisory components in cars that control user interaction in relation to traffic events.

In vehicle automation is a hot subject nowadays. Many technology providers are actively developing prototypes of in-vehicle services.

Over the next five years, the number and variety of computer-based applications within the in-vehicle environment will escalate dramatically. Some Driver Assistance (DA) systems, such as adaptive cruise control and curve warning systems, are already available in world markets. Computer-based Mobile Services & Information (MSI) products are already available, such as in-vehicle navigation, emergency roadside assistance services, and other convenience-enhancing applications for travelers.

In the next two paragraphs we summarize some Driver Assistance systems and some Computer-based Mobile Services & Information (MSI) products to give an overview of existing, mainly standalone products. This text is based on the proceedings of an in-vehicle telematics workshop that is held by the major players in the automotive industry.

See the Transportation Research Circular E-C009. "Research Directions for In-Vehicle Computing," hosted by the Transportation Research Board Committee on Intelligent Transportation Systems at http://www.nad.edu/trb/publications/ec009.pdf.

Driver Assistance (DA) Systems

These locally focussed systems operate from within a vehicle and receive their input from within a small radius of the vehicle. They offer a significant change in the orientation of safety-related technologies.

The GUTS system cannot be characterized as a driver assistance system. Although the name suggests otherwise, navigation systems are not part of DA systems. For instance adaptive cruise control or curve warning systems are basic safety systems, but will not have much effect on dynamic route planning.

Integrating the following DA applications might have some positive impact on a dynamic route although they are of relative minor importance:

- ❏ Automated Mayday warnings
- ❏ Collision warnings
- ❏ Parking assistance
- ❏ Road condition sensing

Mobile Services & Information (MSI)

These global network based services can provide drivers, shippers, and carriers with vital information. They give travelers the ability to plan and follow routes, secure routine and emergency roadside assistance, and connect the vehicle and its occupants to the National and Global Information Infrastructure for a variety of travel and business purposes, such as:

- ❏ Dynamic Route Guidance (Real-time traffic information)
- ❏ Travel Information
- ❏ Roadside Assistance requests
- ❏ Smart Vehicle GUI
- ❏ Emergency Assistance
- ❏ User-initiated Mayday requests
- ❏ Voice mail
- ❏ E mail
- ❏ Concierge Services
- ❏ Parking space locations and reservations
- ❏ Vehicle diagnostics
- ❏ Driver preference adjustment
- ❏ Location (fleet management)
- ❏ Roadway driving information
- ❏ Local transactions
- ❏ Address book/calendar access and management

Communication Costs

The costs of having the car on line all the time cannot be justified, because there's no direct need to update the status of the schedule all the time for every little detail. The control structure makes it possible that communication costs can be tuned. When you want highly accurate status information from the cars your communication cost will be high. One can set a threshold level for the deviation of the plan. If the deviation rises above this threshold value the deviation will be communicated to the company. By this you have the means to keep the communication cost within limits.

Use of In-Car or External Route Planners and Navigators

In-car route planners and navigators are not lightweight applications. On top of this these systems are based on proprietary technology and not open to other systems. Most of them have an integrated GPS that is not accessible to other services. Another issue is the link between the company's route planner and the in-car navigation system. These are not based on the same map data or route planning software so routes are not easily interchangeable. This means that integrating in-car navigation systems is not really an option. The solution is somewhere in the middle. Use the company route planner for generating plans for the cars on the road. Distribute this plan to the cars complete with relevant segments of the mapping database. This extract shouldn't be too large to send over to the car. This results in an easy to update system (only centrally) instead of a complex system with map databases on CD-ROM, which need to be updated regularly. Doing this means the other components like GPS and TMC are easy to integrate as well.

Other Value Added Services

Having this Jini infrastructure in the company means that introducing other services is very simple. We will give a few examples that use the same services as the GUTS service, but for totally different applications.

❑ Think of the administration task of recording the hours driven by the drivers that most transport companies have. Based on the GPS Jini service in the car an-in car process could gather the data and send it once in a while to the company.

❑ The same data could be used to calculate the environmental load the trips have generated.

❑ Or when the data gets certified as legitimate, it could be used for paying toll charges implemented as a backend process instead of online when passing the booth.

Separation Between Infrastructure and Services

The separation of infrastructure and service is key to ubiquitous scenarios. Having an open infrastructure is the panacea for rolling out many services based on lower level services (GUTS is partly based on the GPS service in the cars). By that you get an infrastructure well suited for value added services, but it will be hard to distinguish this when doing initial implementations of these services. The load of the infrastructure on the initial project budget will be relatively high. It's like introducing an intranet in a company with multiple sites and a poor network infrastructure. The initial services provided by the intranet will be hard to sell when you see the total project costs due to the expensive infrastructure investments needed. To prove the benefits of this approach the initial pilots should focus on environments that have an existing infrastructure; but then again the benefits are harder to explain.

Level of Delegating Tasks to Software Components

Delegation is a complex issue that needs more investigation. Human reactions to delegation are hard to predict. Some will delegate tasks and completely rely on the software to which the task is delegated. Others will delegate, but monitor the progress excessively. Delegating tasks to software will become the unique selling point of ubiquitous solutions and is therefore a possible threat. The risk is that terminology like agents, smart, and intelligent will boost expectations far too high.

Delegation is related to the research subjects Intelligent Agents and even Artificial Intelligence (a case study on agents is the next chapter in this book). Thus delegation is not unique for ubiquitous computing, but when implementing ubiquitous services, delegation of command and control tasks is often the case, as in GUTS. GUTS will support the driver with navigation. The company delegates most of the command and control for outdoors activities to GUTS.

Security and Safety

Safety is usually not a subject that attracts a lot of attention in IT system development. In a post-PC era this issue is quite often real. Take for example the GUTS system. You don't want to interfere with the crucial safety systems of a car with your services. Other safety issues arise when physical processes are controlled by software services. Many of those systems have real-time characteristics and demand almost mathematical proof of the stability and robustness of the system before safety can be guaranteed. This mixes quite hard with distributed computing.

Security in this world is something else. Many papers have been written about security for Mobile Computing. Security is the protection of information, systems, and services against disasters, mistakes, and manipulation so that the likelihood and impact of security incidents is minimized. Will this result in different security issues when applied to a fully connected world of objects including code moving around from services and devices to client applications running on devices or resident on the network?

Lets see what is different by going through the three basic security topics. IT security is comprised of:

❑ **Confidentiality**
Sensitive business objects (information & processes) are disclosed only to authorized persons. Controls are required to restrict access to objects. In a ubiquitous world confidentiality is not different, but it is harder to achieve. Since there are many layers or computing platforms involved the confidentiality of each need to be guaranteed for the complete solution. The more components the solution contains, the harder it is for this criterion to be met. Authorization and authentication of users and components are the two concepts to regulate confidentiality. Think of the complexity of user authentication in a web of interacting components. Also authorization is complex when there are many access control lists and security policy files lying around all the services.

❑ **Integrity**
The business needs to control modification to objects (information and processes). Controls are required to ensure objects are accurate and complete. Integrity in such a distributed environment asks for robust distributed computing concepts that handle system integrity.

❑ **Availability**
Availability stands for the need to have business objects (information and services) available when needed. Controls are required to ensure reliability of services. Think of the GPS service in cars. This service might be used by more than one application. It is very easy to see that one application can influence the availability of the other by completely claiming the GPS service (also-called "denial of service attacks"). The smaller a device is the less robust resource scheduling is supported by it.

Other security issues are also introduced in heterogeneous environments. In Java/Jini environments mobile code or distributed code is transferred between computing devices all the time. This imposes extra security risks. Can the code be trusted by the receiving platform and can the code trust the platform it runs on? These are easy questions with hard answers.

In this case Jini related security was not taken into account. Security in Jini needs more research and development although much activity is going on in this area.

Lessons Learned

This section describes our learning experiences during the development of the case. Most of these lessons tell us things about the applicability of the Jini Technology in customer environments, rather than technicalities of Jini itself. A reason for that is (this is a lesson as well!) that Jini Technology is actually simple and robust: it works.

So, what have we learned?

Possibility of Outsourcing Part of the Services

As mentioned earlier, Cap Gemini Ernst & Young is a systems integrator. For SI's in general it is usually a requirement to use as many things already there as possible, or to outsource part of the work. Starting off with brand new technology is generally a big project risk. Not many reusables can be found or bought. Outsourcing parts of the development work usually does not mitigate the identified risk. It is our experience, however, that by using Jini Technology this risk is not likely to occur. A requirement is a good architecture for a distributed (possibly real-time) system, based on Jini principles (spontaneous, transparent). The robustness and high level of standardization of the technology take care of the rest.

Shortened Development Cycle

Although it is a bit presumptuous (based on a single case) to say that by using Jini Technology you can develop systems faster, all signs are pointing in the right direction. Once the Jini infrastructure (lookup service and underlying communications structures) is set up, services can be developed in a fairly straightforward manner. Another thing that helps is that you don't need to build all services at once. In a Jini environment services and service consumers can never be dependant on each other to the extent that a system will fail whenever one or the other is not there. This facilitates iterative development in a great way. Iterative development does not necessarily shorten the development cycle (as compared to linear application development) but is used to make a better system for out clients. Jini promises to be the technology to deliver distributed systems on time.

We Didn't Build a New Case, But We Built it Better

The case itself is not new. Many commercial applications can be obtained that more or less show the same functionality. This makes it hard for us, and probably also for you, to convince others of the benefits of Jini technology. Our statement is: we didn't build a new case, we built it better. However most of these products do not have an open structure or a standardized interface. Using them would have built a system based on several dedicated interfaces and specialized middleware. This is clearly not as flexible, extendable, or transparent, as we want it to be.

The Connection is Made

The first thing we did when we started this project was call Sun to ask them for the available devices. As a true systems integrator we intended to tie up the devices, add a little Java, implement a lookup service and off we go. Along the way we (both the team and Sun) found out that there were few devices available. This affected how we implemented our case study. Since it seemed that it wasn't about hardware, we had to think about another way to build up the case. So, if it is not hardware, it must be software. We found out that Jini Technology is perfect for connecting various software-based environments, especially components that are not normally connected.

Jini and Bluetooth Make the Perfect Couple

In a lot of cases we see that Jini and Bluetooth, and sometimes other technologies, are compared as if they are truly compatible. We think that Jini and Bluetooth are not competing, but rather are complementary technologies. Together they make a perfect couple. Bluetooth will provide in-car devices with wireless communication facilities. Based on this we can build a Jini service architecture. In the case we have right now, all communication is done via a standard (wired) Ethernet. (Jini is the software layer you need on top of TCP/IP and Bluetooth fits very well below the TCP/IP layer in the mentioned environments.)

Easy Skills Development from Java to Jini

The project members who took part in the project were all more or less skilled Java developers. We assumed that they would need training before they could start working on the case. Due to the lack of availability of training courses in the Netherlands, we had to start without them. We have learned that this will not cause major problems. The only real prerequisite is knowledge of Java (although knowledge of distributed computing would be beneficial). Jini Technology is easy to learn.

Risk Analysis

We developers are usually very eager to start coding directly. Especially when we can work with brand new technology like Jini. We should not, however, neglect basic project management principles. One of which is risk analysis.

Evidently we did not do this. It turned out that one of the most challenging tasks was to get the video player up and running. The video part of our demo was not designed and implemented as a service, nor did we use Java Media Framework. We had problems before with video streams in applications, so we could have anticipated this. The lesson learned here is that whenever you start working with something new, don't think that the old problems are over.

Partners and the Jini Community

Get your partners involved as soon as possible. We asked Sun for assistance right from the start. They were able to introduce us into the Jini community. Although this didn't bring us as many reusables as we had hoped for, it gave us a headstart in terms of knowledge. Don't try doing it all by yourself. The Jini community process is going strong, so get attached.

In addition to the Jini Community's home page at http://www.jini.org there is also a directory of Jini resources at http://www.litefaden.com/sv/jd/.

Tools

Don't bother about the tools. It is our experience that customers often require a specific development environment. Although this might be valid for numerous reasons, it is not so important when you want to build a demo case. Java and Jini are both properly standardized, so most development tools will work as we expect them to work. We used the following tools:

❑ Java

❑ For GUI-design we have used VisualAge for Java 3.0

❑ We used the Kawa editor for class editing, set to use JDK 1.2.2

❑ The Jini package used was version 1.0

❑ The Customer-applet used in the browser was designed and programmed with the aid of Borland's JBuilder

Test Environment

In the first phase of the project every developer had their own development environment running on their PC. This included a lookup service, and all services developed. Since all PC's were connnected via the LAN, this led to heavy and sometimes confusing network traffic. Every application discovered all the other lookup services, via which similar services were provided. Don't try this at home, it will not work. We solved the problem by installing a separate server where we ran the lookup service and the services we were building. Although it may sound trivial now, it kept us going for a while.

Summary

We hope this case study has given you an insight into what we were trying to achieve by designing the GUTS system, and the way we went about implementing it. It gives just a glimpse of what may be achieved in the future using Jini and related technologies.

Ronald Ashri

19

Using Jini to Enable a Framework for Agent-Based Systems

Introduction

What is a chapter about agents doing in a book about Jini?

The short answer is that agents are very close to being the next *big thing* to hit the area of distributed computing (some would say that agents have hit already), making them interesting to anyone working in this area, and Jini may very well hold the key to that breakthrough. The main drivers for such a development are the growth of consumer-based computing and the spread of the Internet. New areas always create the potential for new 'killer apps' and agents provide a way to embody the right set of ideas, such as distributed problem solving, to enable the new generation of such applications, while Jini can provide the platform on which they are developed. The slightly longer answer, as well as all the justification accompanying it, hopefully, lies within the pages of this chapter.

We begin by providing a brief introduction to the ideas that characterize systems designed with interacting agents (agent-based systems) and explain why such an approach is necessary to provide solutions to the increasingly complex situations developers are faced with. Having provided some motivation we then go on to explain why Jini can speed the take-up of these ideas, and present Paradigma, a Jini-based framework for developing agents. Paradigma serves as our point of reference, giving flesh to the ideas discussed and aids in explaining how an agent system can be integrated with Jini. It has been developed as a 'proof of concept' system based on a strong theoretical framework aimed at providing a generic description of directly implementable agents. As a result the presentation relies on illustrative diagrams and code snippets as opposed to complete class descriptions. The focus is, of course, placed on the role Jini plays in the system, while the actual agent code is presented is much less detail.

What Are Agents and Why Are They Needed?

Softbots (short for software robots, usually web crawlers), knowbots (knowledge-based software robots), interface agents (such as the (in)famous Microsoft paper clip), and e-mail filters are all different instances of some type of agent. Within all these different approaches lies the power of agents but also the difficulty in providing a hard and fast definition. In this section we attempt to provide an understanding of the notion of agents and their scope as well as some justification for the use of agents. This will hopefully give the necessary incentive to move on and read how Jini can make the realization of such systems possible in short space of time.

Defining an Agent

So, how do we come to understand the notion of an agent?

Well, we can begin by examining what we consider real-life agents, including, amongst others, estate agents, insurance agents, travel agents, and even secret agents! All use their specialized knowledge of the world to perform some tasks on our behalf. One aspect of "agenthood", therefore, must be that an agent *acts on behalf of others*. Furthermore, we can say that another characteristic of such agents is that they have a degree of freedom in performing their tasks. For example, we do not normally tell travel agents how to go about their work and they try to use their own initiative in telling us about a special offer if they believe it might appeal to us. Therefore, some agents can even *act autonomously*.

These two main characteristics, "acting for another" and "autonomy", can be used as the basis for defining computational agents and help us in deriving other attributes that these entail. We begin by offering a general description of an agent as a software program *situated in an environment*, able to perceive the environment through a set of *sensors* and able to cause changes to the environment through a set *effectors*. Now, in order for an agent to act on our behalf it might be required to have a certain degree of *social ability* so that it can negotiate and cooperate with other agents and humans. In time-critical environments it needs to be *reactive* so as to respond to changes in the environment in a timely fashion and adaptive so as to handle unexpected situations. Agents can also be *pro-active* by pursuing particular goals. In addition, agent software differs from more conventional software in that it tends to operate over long-term periods so that it has *temporal continuity*. This is especially true in cases such as remote site control, network monitoring or information gathering. Another attribute often mentioned in the literature, but not so much related to the notion of agenthood as to the ideas of distributed computation, is agent mobility, which refers to an agent's ability to cease operation on one machine and transfer state and code to another, where it can resume operation.

An agent-based system is one developed using the abstraction of an agent that displays some or all of the above characteristics in very much the same way that object-oriented software is software developed using the abstraction of an object. The term *multi-agent system* is used to differentiate between a system with just one agent and systems with two or more interacting agents. Such systems are more closely related to distributed computing and are the type of systems we will focus on with Jini.

Agents Versus Traditional Approaches

Agent-based ideas often come under fire from those who believe that they offer nothing new to the developer. Most often the arguments are based on the fact that agent definitions are too susceptible to multiple interpretations based on the interpreter's point of view. For example, we could claim that a light switch is an agent because it turns on the light when we assign to it the goal of creating light by pressing the switch!

However, that does not buy us anything since it does not provide us with more information or descriptive power; it is so simple that nothing more than its operating algorithm is required for a programmer to reason about it. Caution, therefore, is required because although practically anything can be defined using agent characteristics we should only attempt such an analysis when it aids in our understanding of the problem.

Sometimes, however, it might be beneficial to temporarily assign agent status to an object in the environment because it will help us in understanding its operation. So, for example, we might find it easier, in some circumstances, to reason about the operation of a printer as an agent with the goal of printing our document when requested to do so, thus *agentifying* the device. However, it would not be always beneficial to consider the printer as an agent as that would unnecessarily complicate matters. Therefore, when the printer satisfies the goal of printing our document we can *de-agentify* it and consider it as simply another object in the world. This is something that we will consider in presenting the concepts at the heart of Paradigma as well as giving precise definitions for the notions of agency and autonomous agency.

The Reasons for Using Agents

There has been a lot of talk (and hype) about the potential of agent-based systems in recent years. This has led, as usual, to promises that have never been met and has made developers wary of such ideas. Yet, underneath it all lie truly powerful ideas that, if effectively developed, could reap enormous benefits. In an information environment that is highly interconnected, interdependent, and heterogeneous, plagued by an explosion of available services, we need methods that will enable us to form dynamic, self-adapting solutions. Agent-based systems allow us to do just that, through a natural development of object-oriented programming and distributed computing. The level of abstraction is moved higher than objects into the dimension of entities able to communicate and reason about each other in a dynamic environment, each one attempting to satisfy its own goals. It is no surprise that the roots of agents can also be traced to the fields of Distributed Artificial Intelligence (DAI) and Computer Supported Cooperative Work (CSCW) which *required* such notions in order to begin providing solutions to the problems presented to them. From business workflow management and telecommunications network management to electronic commerce and intelligent homes, the agent paradigm can aid in providing solutions.

Exactly why are we facing a problem in handling the increase in information and services? The causes are to be partly found in the style of interaction between humans and computers. Currently, the de-facto method is *direct manipulation*, which is used to describe the situation where a user must explicitly guide the computer in performing tasks by manipulating objects on the screen such as windows, buttons, list boxes, etc. This was a great advance from the previous paradigm of command-line instructions where cause and effect were not clearly related and the user needed to memorize arcane instructions (even though some Unix die-hards would disagree). However, the increasing number of tasks to perform and the complexity of those tasks now make interaction much harder. With the aid of agent software a new style of interaction has emerged called *indirect manipulation*, in which the agent takes it upon itself to perform tasks for us as well as monitor events and react to them in an appropriate fashion. This can relieve the user's workload, allowing for the more creative use of time.

The benefits of the agent paradigm do not stop at the level of human-computer interaction. Thinking in terms of agents can help us model problems in ways that are more intuitive, yielding better solutions. In Sweden, for example, a multi-agent system is being developed as an answer to the problem of load balancing on the electricity grid. The project, named ISES (Information, Society, Energy, and Systems), is a joint University-Industry project which aims to provide efficient systems for communities, where utilities can be intelligently manipulated to gain the best price/performance ratios.

Intelligent home-appliance agents, either located on each appliance or responsible for the entire house, negotiate and cooperate for service provision with utility agents representing the power supply companies, and achieve optimal performance since the companies will not need to produce more power than there is demand for. Interestingly, the power grid also acts as a connection to the Internet so eventually people will be able to log into their appliances and manipulate them remotely, increasing home safety by allowing users to remotely disable appliances (*Rune Gustavson, Agents With Power, Communications of the ACM, Vol 42(3), pp 41-47*). An alternative example in the UK involves British Telecom where a multi-agent system, based on an architecture named Advanced Decision Environment for Process Tasks (ADEPT), has been developed for providing a customer price quote service (*N. R. Jennings, T. J. Norman, and P. Faratin (1998) "ADEPT: An Agent-based Approach to Business Process Management" ACM SIGMODRecord 27 (4) 32-39*). Customer service division agents accept the quotes and send the information to the design, legal and surveyor departments while simultaneously requesting a credit check on the client. The agents accepting the information do the necessary processing by calling on resources in their respective departments before a final co-operation stage between agents from all departments leads to an answer for the client that requested the quote.

All these examples show how the agent paradigm makes the solutions of complex problems easier by allowing us to bring into our toolkit the notions of multi-agent negotiation and cooperation, decentralization and a perspective from multiple sides. But the most powerful element of agent-oriented techniques is that it brings the unit of analysis closer to the natural organization of the real physical world, with the problem now broken down in terms of interacting entities, each with its own agenda to pursue by setting goals and implementing plans based on desires and beliefs about the environment. However, until now, agent-based system developers have had to construct proprietary infrastructures in order to create mechanisms for the discovery of other agents, the communication between agents or the movement of agent code in the case of mobile agent systems. The Jini connectivity technology can relieve the agent developer from such worries by providing the biggest part of that required infrastructure. Agents, just as any other service, can use the Lookup, Discovery, and Join protocols to make their existence known or to allow code mobility.

What Can Jini Offer an Agent-Based System

Now, in order to evaluate Jini's contribution to a multi-agent system it is useful to consider what we require to build a generic system and how Jini can provide it.

Agent discovery: If one is to build a multi-agent system the first worry is how agents can discover each other. In this respect Jini is an ideal platform. From its inception the focus has been towards mechanisms that would allow for the dynamic discovery of entities on the network and the possibility to manipulate those entities once they have been discovered. One of the patterns that has emerged from agent-system design is the concept of a place where agents find each other. Jini provides this place via the lookup service.

Agent management: Another important aspect is that of managing agents and making sure that lookup services do not become inundated with lingering agents that consume resources. Jini's distributed leasing mechanisms provide a solution to these problems by allowing for registered entities to be discarded from the lookup service. In addition, the administration utilities provided in the `net.jini.admin` package allow for the monitoring of any Jini service (including, of course) the lookup service.

Agent description & identification: Here Jini truly shines through the provision of the Jini Attribute Schema specification, which can allow agents, or any service, to advertise their attributes and capabilities to anyone interested and able to access the lookup service.

Furthermore, all registered services get a universally unique identifier which can serve for subsequent identifications, and the Jini specification actually demands it if the service is to be a well-behaved one.

Transaction support: One of the powers of a multi-agent system is the ability of a number of problem-solvers to come together in order to solve problems that are beyond each individual's capabilities. However, in order for that to be achieved we need some mechanisms that can assure reliable execution in the presence of concurrency and occurrence of failure. Jini provides for such situations through the Jini Transaction Specification and, furthermore, Sun provides an implementation of a transaction manager through mahalo (the transaction service provided with Jini).

Agent communication: Java is almost undoubtedly the most network-aware language available. As a result, there is a number of methods available for agent communication that we will expand upon in the subsequent sections, as well as explain how Jini can allow agents to provide not just one but many mechanisms for communication.

Security and Agent Authentication: This is an area where Jini fails to provide adequate support, in that it does not go beyond the existing mechanisms for security through RMI. However, there are a number of efforts currently underway to provide Jini with the necessary data encryption and authentication capabilities. The interested reader is directed to www.jini.org where a security project is currently underway.

Agent information sharing: Although JavaSpaces is not a part of the Jini system it is a service that has a lot to offer multi-agent systems and so is worth a mention. It can provide a distributed space in which to share information in a distributed fashion, and even exchange code and enhance each other's capabilities.

As you can see, it is hard to fault Jini as an environment upon which to build multi-agent systems. With the exception of security the necessary infrastructure is there to power the system. Of course, this is just half the story! What we need now is a framework through which to reason about agents, one that will extract the basic patterns and will allow for the development of different types of agents.

The Paradigma Agent Implementation Environment provides a way to describe agents through their attributes and their capabilities as well as mechanisms for registering with a Jini lookup service. It allows for the interaction of autonomous agents with simpler entities through the use of the notion of a 'server agent', a simple entity acting in order to fulfill a goal for another agent. Finally, it provides for a mechanism through which services can be used without need to resort to well-know service interfaces, a departure from usual Jini practice.

The next sections introduce the concepts at the heart of Paradigma in more detail and provide a prototype application that was developed using Paradigma. Subsequently we take a brief peek under the hood of Paradigma and see how all the functionality comes together at code level.

The Concepts Behind Paradigma

In this section we explain, in more detail, some of the concepts briefly hinted at above. These concepts form the basis of a formal agent framework developed by Michael Luck and Mark d'Inverno, in an attempt to bridge the gap between agent theories and real-life agent systems by providing precise definitions in a way that is more easily translatable to real systems (*Luck, M. and d'Inverno, M. (1995). A Formal Framework for Agency and Autonomy. In proceedings of the First International Conference on Multi-Agent Systems:254-260. AAAI Press/MIT Press*).

The framework aims to capture the complete scope of possible entities within a domain, and differentiate between the notions of agenthood and autonomy. What is proposed is a hierarchical four-tiered world that builds from simple objects to autonomous agents by making entities increasingly more complex. The structure is shown in the figure below;

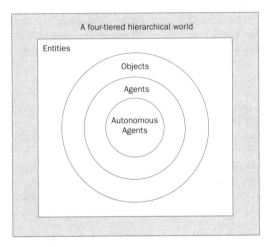

Everything in the world, according to the diagram above, is an *entity* with a number of associated *attributes*, where attributes are describable features of the world such as the size and color of a car or the printing speed and resolution of a printer. *Objects* are entities with certain *capabilities* or actions that have an effect on the state of the environment. For example, a printer executes its capability to print the required document, thus changing the state of the world from one where our document was not printed to one where it is. The natural position of typical Jini services in this framework is as objects, since they expose a number of methods you can call (their capabilities) as well as provide some description of their state (their attributes).

Agents are objects with a set of *goals*, where goals are defined as a set of desirable attribute values. A goal could be to change the attribute that describes the status of our document from not printed to printed. Finally, *autonomous agents* are agents that are able to generate their own goals through a set of *motivations* that drive them. Motivations can be thought of as preferences or desires of an autonomous agent that lead it to produce goals to satisfy those desires. This table gives an overview of the features at each level of the framework:

Features of the formal framework	Entities	Objects	Agents	Autonomous Agents
Attributes				
Capabilities				
Goals				
Motivations				

Thus agenthood is ascribed to any entity in the world that acts in order to satisfy some goal. When those goals are self-generated we have autonomous agents. In order to further facilitate the understanding of the framework we provide the additional definitions of *neutral objects* as those objects in the world that are not agents, and *server agents* as those agents in the world that are not autonomous.

The distinction is illustrated in the diagram below:

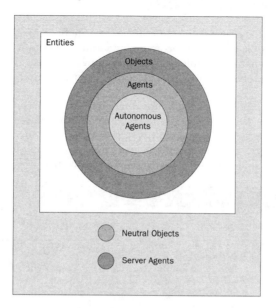

Neutral objects give rise to server agents when they are ascribed goals. Once those goals are achieved or pursuing those goals is no longer feasible, the server agent reverts back to a neutral object.

In order to make these abstract notions clearer, however, we can illustrate them with an example. Suppose that you are looking for the best train ticket to visit London this weekend. You give your personal agent (PA) the task of finding such a ticket for you. Now, your PA is an autonomous agent with motivations such as minimizing on line connection time, saving money, and providing comfort. Given this task, it generates appropriate goals according to its motivations. One of the most important goals generated is to get a list of all the travel agencies that provide train tickets to London, and it tries to achieve this by locating an object in the environment with the capability of providing updated lists of such agencies. The PA engages the object and thus instantiates a server agent from it with the goal of providing the required information. Now, the actions of the object required to accomplish this may be nothing more than a multicast announcement on the network requesting all active travel agencies to register their presence. Having received the list, the PA attempts to contact the travel agencies through an interaction of a different kind, requiring the PA to communicate via some form of communication language with the travel agency. Having acquired the required information (limiting the number of calls so as to satisfy the motivation of minimizing on line time, and getting a cheap ticket according to the other motivations), the PA reports the results and waits for further instructions.

It is important to note the differentiation between autonomous agents, which generate their own goals, and server agents, which have goals ascribed to them. As the example illustrates, the ability to consider the world in such terms makes the understanding of situations more intuitive and allows for a society of interacting entities that is dynamic and adaptive.

With the main ideas now explained, we present a prototype application developed using Paradigma with the goal of testing the ideas and giving us a way to demonstrate them.

A Home Appliances Agent

Appliances with all sorts of *enhanced* and *additional* features are becoming increasingly prevalent in homes today. The result is that users are becoming increasingly frustrated attempting to juggle more and more controls while on an initially simple quest of preparing breakfast. What is really required are devices that are able to do some of the work themselves, a perfect application area for agents.

The scenario for our prototype system is a house where help is at hand in the form of an autonomous agent that is responsible for keeping track of the appliances in the house, after having discovered them in the home lookup service they are supposed to register with. More specifically we have two appliances, one of which is a refrigerator and the other a security monitor. The appliances are represented as two Java graphic interfaces that are shown in the figures below:

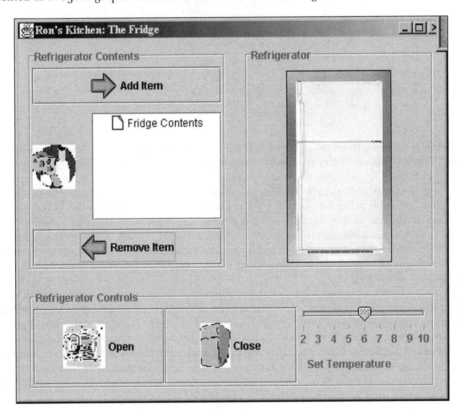

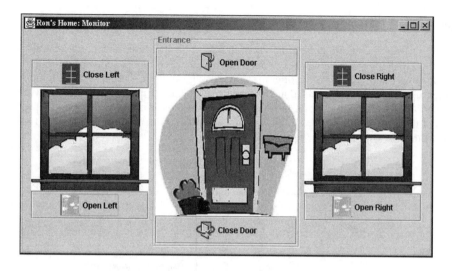

These graphic interfaces serve to provide a more realistic situation by allowing the devices to be manipulated both via the autonomous agent and their graphical interface. Our agent's task is to discover the two available services and set them under its control so that it will be able to monitor their behavior. An autonomous agent, in this case, adds value to our solution because it provides a central point of reference for the working of all the devices in the home, thus creating the indirect style of manipulation we require, as described in the introduction to agents. Eventually, the agent could be used to communicate with agents outside the house in order to arrange maintenance checks or replenish our supplies of standard groceries.

When the refrigerator is activated (the equivalent of plugging the fridge into the home network) it initializes itself for operation and then attempts to locate a Jini lookup service that it can register with. Once registered, it is available to be remotely manipulated by a human or software agent. Upon discovery of the refrigerator, the autonomous agent activates a thread within its own JVM that is responsible for monitoring that device.

The interesting point here is that the devices can be controlled without a device specific interface, but rather through a generic `NeutralObject` interface. What is the reason for this departure from device specific interfaces? Well, although the ideal situation would be to have standard interfaces for every possible type of device and, indeed, the efforts of the Jini community are all directed towards that goal, there is still a lot of work to be done before such a situation becomes reality. In any case, there will always be new types of services available and a method is required to enable their integration into a system immediately. That is why we propose a generic interface to complement standard interfaces that will enable the integration of services into the system immediately and without needing to tamper with the service user's code. To achieve this we make use of Jini entries to describe the service's attributes and capabilities and the agent framework with its provision for goals and plans to control the behavior of the service. The exact methods used become apparent by stepping through the example and the details are given in the next section.

Service Creation

The first step towards creating our devices is to define their attributes and their capabilities. For example, the refrigerator has attributes such as temperature, contents, status of door, and capabilities such as adjusting the temperature or opening and closing the door. It is important to note that capabilities are actually Java classes that conform to a `Capability` interface, which will be described later on, and are dynamically loaded into the JVM at run time. The XML file merely provides a *description* of those capabilities so as to allow other software agents and human users to read them and derive any information they may require.

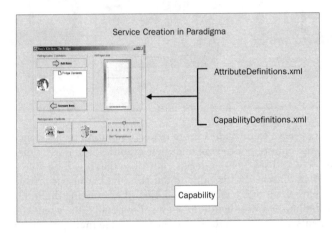

Service Registration

After a service has been created, it is passed to an `ObjectPublisher` class that takes care of registering it to a Jini lookup service. It extracts all the relevant information and creates Jini Entries that will be attached to the service proxy that will be made available in the Jini community. The `ObjectPublisher` needs to know the *static* attributes of the service, that is, those attributes that will not change over time, as well as the capabilities of the service. All this information allows others to use it without having a service-specific interface. In terms of the ideas described in the previous section the refrigerator and the security monitor are neutral objects in the world because they have some attributes and capabilities but are not doing anything at the moment.

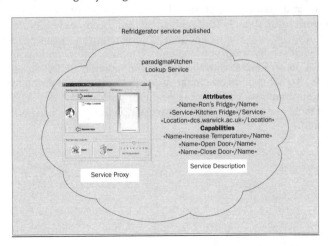

Service Discovery

Now, with both services (refrigerator and security system) ready for use we can turn our attention to the workings of the autonomous agent. Autonomous agents also possess attributes and capabilities like neutral objects. In addition to that however, autonomous agents have motivations that drive them to select goals according to the motivation utility of the goal. Once a goal is executed it will move on to the next one and so on. In our example the first goal will be to discover available lookup services and, having achieved that, it will be able to download and control the available services. When the services are under the control of the autonomous agent they change from neutral objects to server agents since they are assigned goals to achieve by our autonomous agent.

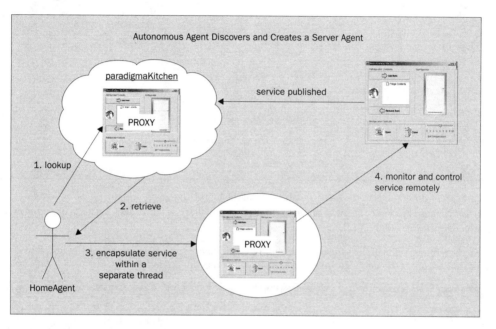

Controlling the Service

Now that the autonomous agent has control of the devices it begins the implementation of the goals and plans that control their behavior. In our example the goals and plans are simple and easy to understand. Whenever the door of the refrigerator is left open it must be closed, the temperature should be retained at 6 °C, and all the contents of the refrigerator should be monitored. The security monitor server agent should simply make sure that doors and windows remain closed. All this work is delegated to a `ServerAgent` class that is a separate thread within the autonomous agent's JVM. The `ServerAgent` class creates a view of the world, as seen from the refrigerator or security system, by polling the device for information on all the *changing* attributes, which have not been published in the Jini lookup service. Whenever there is a deviation from the required setting the appropriate goal is activated and the necessary plan implemented. An example of the graphical interface that allows us to visualize this behavior is shown next.

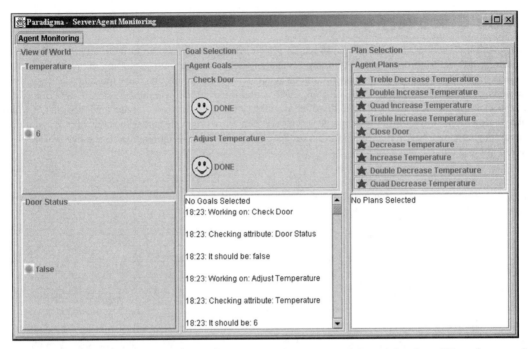

There are three components to the interface: the view of the world, the goals, and the plans. When the state of the refrigerator changes the server agent of our autonomous agent will sense it and activate the required plan or, simply, update the view of the world.

Next we show an example of the situation where some items have been placed in the refrigerator, thus changing its attributes and meaning the temperature must be regulated and the door closed.

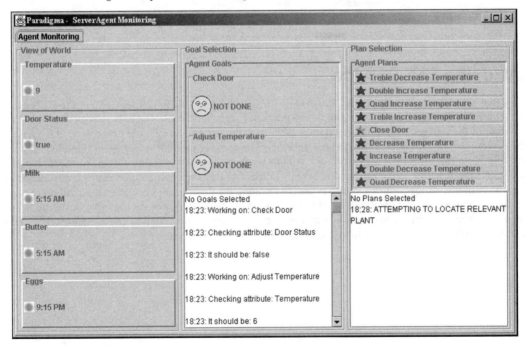

Why Do It This Way?

Until now there has been only brief justification of the techniques used in Paradigma, which were illustrated in the example. Why use XML to define and describe services? Why register, as entries in a lookup service, the names of the service's capabilities in order to use them and not use standard interfaces or reflection? Why not simply follow the 'standard' Jini model of defining interfaces for each device? The answer to these questions is simple: simplicity, expandability, and as an alternative.

The XML files for a service's (our neutral objects) attributes and capabilities are a useful way to initially describe the service. After the service has been created there is no need for them, since all the information is encapsulated within Java classes and can be updated or changed programmatically either locally or remotely. What it buys us is simplicity in developing the services. It becomes extremely easy to produce different versions of a service simply by editing the XML files and choosing which attributes and capabilities to provide it with. For example, a company wishing to market three progressively more complicated versions of a refrigerator does not usually change the hardware in the device, but only the parts that are actually wired in (some may recall the Intel's 486SX which had a math co-processor in silicon that was de-activated, but you could add a new chip if you needed such a capability). Similarly, the interface to the refrigerator need not change, what can change is the description of the refrigerator in a Jini lookup service and the capabilities that come with the software.

Continuing with our example we could also have situations where not only do the devices have more capabilities but they also exhibit different kinds of behavior, based on their surrounding environment. The more complex the devices, the more complex this behavior might be. This is where the notions of goals and plans come in handy.

When the proud master of a home agent plugs in the brand new device not only will the home agent be able to control it, it can also update itself with new goals and plans that will allow it to assign to the device the right kind of goals. All without having to stop the agent or change any of its code.

Of course, there are some drawbacks to this approach. Using a generic interface deprives us of the strong type-checking capabilities of Java. However, this can be regained in the form of a lexicon that the agent uses to verify the names of the capabilities. Eventually a simple lexicon might evolve into an ontology that describes the terms that are valid in a domain along with certain rules as to the constraints imposed by certain terms. This can add semantic information and lead to the use of more deliberative agents that perform extensive reasoning in an environment.

Nevertheless, we need to note that this approach is not proposed as a way to stop developing standard interfaces for devices. It should be thought of as an alternative that can co-exist with other approaches. Let us not forget that there is nothing to stop us from providing an agent with a capability that makes use of a standard interface to manipulate a device. What is important are the ideas of agents that can adapt and evolve without needing to be recompiled and that can act autonomously with little or no human intervention.

In the next section we have a closer look at the Paradigma framework, and focus on how it uses Jini to enable the creation of a distributed system.

Paradigma Agent Hierarchy

The most basic structure in Paradigma is the class relationship that translates the four-tiered hierarchical framework (explained previously) into a Java implementation of it. The initial intuition would be to provide a hierarchical structure of abstract classes, adding at each stage the extra methods required by the successively more complex entities in the world. The problem encountered in such an attempt, however, is that server agents are entities that exist in the world only as long as goals are ascribed to them. A hierarchical structure would make the framework too rigid and would not allow for the instantiation of server agents dynamically. The preferred, compositional, relationship is illustrated below:

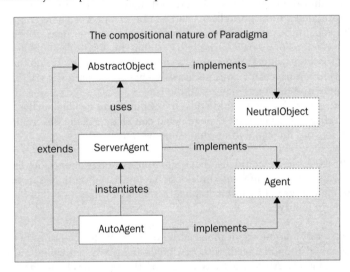

The `NeutralObject` interface defines method signatures that all objects in the framework should implement. These methods find a concrete implementation in the `AbstractObject` class that can then be extended by all actual neutral objects or autonomous agents. The `Agent` interface defines the method signatures that agents should implement. Autonomous agents get concrete definitions of these methods through the `AutoAgent` class.

However, autonomous agents require all the functionality of neutral objects, so they extend the `AbstractObject` class as well. The compositional nature of the structure comes from the fact that while all autonomous agent instances extend the `AutoAgent` class and therefore implicitly `AbstractObject`, server agents only implement the `Agent` interface and *wrap* around a neutral object by accepting it as an argument in their constructor. Server agents are instantiated by autonomous agents and disappear as soon as the objective has been met. This is how Paradigma allows for the dynamic creation of server agents as the situation demands it.

A small note needs to be made on the naming of the classes. The ideal name for the `NeutralObject` interface would be plain `Object` as the methods defined therein refer to the behavior of all objects, including agents. However, `Object` is reserved as the base class for all Java classes and so cannot be used! `AbstractObject` on the other hand signifies that this is an abstract class, which means it cannot be instantiated but can only be extended by other classes. The rest of the classes do not interfere with Java naming conventions and therefore can take the exact names of the entities they refer to.

Neutral Objects

Neutral objects are the most basic entities in the Paradigma framework. (Although the conceptual hierarchy begins with entities, they are an aid for a complete theoretical description and do not have any affects at the level of implementation.). Specific instances are created based on two XML files, one containing definitions for their attributes and the other one containing descriptions of their capabilities as well as the address from which those capabilities can be read in order to load them into the JVM.

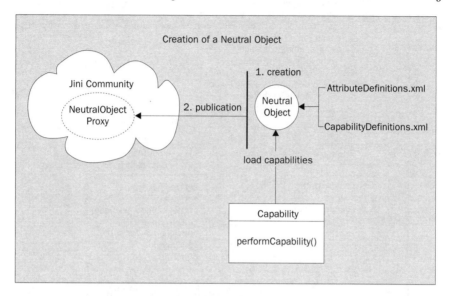

The object model overleaf illustrates the relationship between the `NeutralObject` and its attributes and capabilities. There are two types of capabilities and two types of attributes. Basic attributes are objects of the `Attribute` class and do not change frequently. If it is required that they change it can be done through a setter method. Attributes that change frequently extend the `ChangingAttribute` class.

Capabilities that might cause changes to the neutral object extend the `CapabilityWithEvents` class, which enables anyone to register as interested in listening to changes.

Such capabilities are often the sensors of an entity.

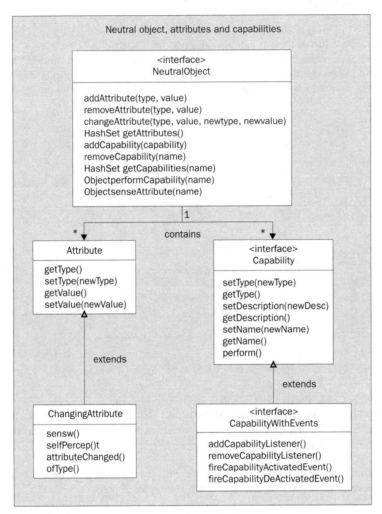

Publication of a neutral object is done through an `ObjectPublisher` class that takes care of discovering the required Jini communities and registering it with those communities, as well as translating attributes and capabilities to entries to be attached alongside the neutral object. Entries are created for static attributes and for all capabilities. These entries will help other agents to decide whether it is useful to engage the neutral object by eventually retrieving its implementation. Of course, more selective `ObjectPublishers` could be used for devices that do not wish to expose the full range of their attributes or capabilities.

Attributes

Attributes are describable features of the environment. The set of all attributes in an environment would give a description of that environment. The kinds of attributes that exist in a world depend on the entities of that world and the type of the world. If we take an example of a restaurant service it could be characterized by the kind of food it serves and perhaps delivery times, location, name and prices. In other instances there might be more complex attributes such as the kind of life-support systems on a spacecraft and the ways in which they can be manipulated. Some attributes may never change or change so infrequently that we can consider them constant while others may change continuously. What is important is that the framework will allow for handling of any form of attribute and will allow for a change in the way attributes are described with minimal effect on the rest of the framework.

In Paradigma attributes are defined by their type, their value and whether they are static or variable. Attributes are described in an XML file, which is read and parsed producing a Document Object Model (DOM) object that is passed through an attribute factory producing a number of attribute objects that are attached to the entity as a collection within a `HashSet` container. A Document Type Definition (DTD) document describes how these XML files should be structured and the attribute factory needs to have some knowledge of this DTD in order to know how to handle the DOM object.

However, the structure remains dynamic through the use of the factory pattern that is illustrated in the figure below. Different factory implementations can be provided, with no effect on the rest of the framework, which could cater for different DTD documents or be able to produce new kinds of attribute objects.

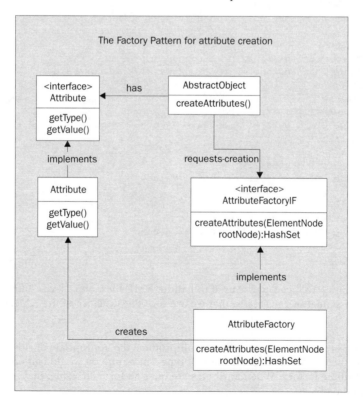

A basic DTD document that can accommodate our needs is shown below:

```
<!-- Sample Agent Attribute Definition DTD -->
<!ELEMENT Attributes (Definition+)>
<!ELEMENT Definition (Type,Value)>
<!ELEMENT Type (#PCDATA)>
<!ELEMENT Value (#PCDATA)>
<!ATTLIST Value Changing (yes|no) "no">
```

This DTD states that an attribute XML files contains a series of definitions, with the + sign denoting that at least one or more definitions must be included. Each definition represents an attribute, which has a type and a value, with values carrying an attribute indicating whether it is static or variable. Based on the above DTD the following XML file defines the attributes a neutral object interfacing to a kitchen fridge might carry:

```
<?xml version="1.0"?>
<!DOCTYPE Attributes SYSTEM "Attribute.dtd">
<Attributes>
    <Definition>
        <Type>Name</Type>
        <Value Changing="no">Ron's Fridge</Value>
    </Definition>
    <Definition>
        <Type>Service</Type>
        <Value Changing="no">Kitchen Fridge</Value>
    </Definition>
    <Definition>
        <Type>Location</Type>
        <Value Changing="no">http://dcs.warwick.ac.uk</Value>
    </Definition>
    <Definition>
        <Type>Availability</Type>
        <Value Changing="yes">Boolean</Value>
    </Definition>
    <Definition>
        <Type>Door Status</Type>
        <Value Changing="yes">Boolean</Value>
    </Definition>
    <Definition>
        <Type>Temperature</Type>
        <Value Changing="yes">Integer</Value>
    </Definition>
</Attributes>
```

In Paradigma the Sun JAXP package is used to handle XML files. Sun's JAXP offers a validating parser that is absolutely essential in our case so that we are sure the structure of the XML document conforms to the DTD.

Attribute factories, based on the type defined, will produce the appropriate attribute objects. For example if you wished to produce an attribute of type Integer you would call on an Integer attribute method of the attribute factory. When attributes are queried for their value, they will return the appropriate attribute object.

If an attribute is variable it must, of course, change in accordance with changes in the entity it is bound to. The problem we are faced with is how to update the attribute objects to reflect these changes. One possible technique would be to have a polling mechanism whereby the attribute objects *ask* the entity if anything has changed and accordingly change. However, Java offers a more flexible mechanism through event notification. When a change occurs the entity raises an event that carries as an ID the attribute concerned with that change as well as the updated value for the attribute. The classes and methods involved are illustrated in the figure below:

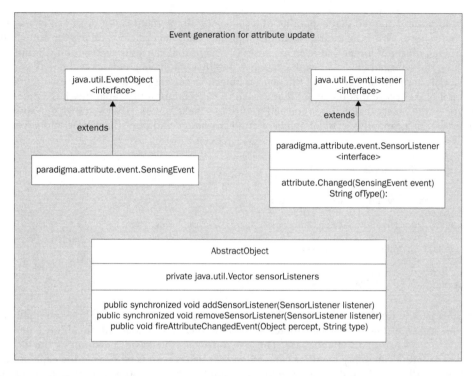

As the diagram shows, `AbstractObject` is able to update attributes by firing sensing events. Only the attributes of the type associated with the event are affected, since that type is passed as an argument to the `fireAttributeChangedEvent` method.

The final major issue that concerns attributes is their actual publication to a Jini community so that other agents can read them and decide if they wish to engage with the neutral object or contact the autonomous agent. Variable attributes are not published as the overhead of updating entries in a Jini community is too great and the information that would be gained cannot justify it. (However, one might choose to publish the fact that certain changing attributes exist, as it might aid an agent in deciding whether or not to use the device). Static attributes or attributes that change very infrequently can be sufficient in describing the entity by giving information such as the name, type of service, availability, capacity for further work, etc.

Capabilities

Through capabilities, entities act in the environment, changing or sensing attributes of the environment. Like attributes, they are described in XML files and capability factories take care of instantiating capability objects. The difference is that these capabilities are objects that are instantiated from classes are dynamically loaded into the entity's JVM. Such classes make themselves accessible through the `Capability` interface.

The most important method that capability objects need to implement is the `perform()` method that returns an `Object`. This is, of course, a simple approach that, nevertheless, allows for quite interesting behavior. One must not forget that in many cases the agent that causes the execution will not need to do *any* work on the returned object since the action is one that will have an effect in the real world and will be visible only through the sensors of the neutral object. In the case where the returned object is important it makes sense that the agent that caused the execution of the capability has some knowledge of the type of the object that will be returned in order to make use of it. Such knowledge would be contained within a capability class of an agent and can change and develop as time and needs require it to.

Below we show the `Capability` DTD:

```
<!-- Capability Definition DTD -->
<!ELEMENT Capabilities (Definition+)>
<!ELEMENT Definition (Path,Filename,Name,Description,Type)>
<!ELEMENT Path (#PCDATA)>
<!ELEMENT Filename (#PCDATA)>
<!ELEMENT Name (#PCDATA)>
<!ELEMENT Description (#PCDATA)>
<!ELEMENT Type (#PCDATA)>
```

We define a path to the file, its fully qualified filename, the name of the capability, and finally a description and type. The first two attributes are so as to enable it to load the capabilities into the JVM and provide in essence a sort of codebase. The actual place of the classes need not be the local file system and different capability factories can call on different methods of loading the capabilities, either remotely or locally. The final three are used to describe the capability to prospective users of the entity. Continuing on our fridge example here is a possible XML file for such an entity:

```
<?xml version="1.0"?>
<!DOCTYPE Capabilities SYSTEM "Capability.dtd">
<Capabilities>
    <Definition>
        <Path>/dcs/97/esvafweb/ProjectDev/Bin/</Path>
        <Filename>paradigma.capabilitybase.OpenDoor</Filename>
        <Name>Open Door</Name>
        <Description>Opens the fridge door</Description>
        <Type>Action capability</Type>
    </Definition>
    <Definition>
        <Path>/dcs/97/esvafweb/ProjectDev/Bin/</Path>
        <Filename>paradigma.capabilitybase.CloseDoor</Filename>
        <Name>Close Door</Name>
        <Description>Closes the fridge door</Description>
        <Type>Action capability</Type>
    </Definition>
    <Definition>
```

```
            <Path>/dcs/97/esvafweb/ProjectDev/Bin/</Path>
            <Filename>paradigma.capabilitybase.IncreaseTemperature</Filename>
            <Name>Increase Temperature</Name>
            <Description>Increases the fridge temperature</Description>
            <Type>Action capability</Type>
        </Definition>
        <Definition>
            <Path>/dcs/97/esvafweb/ProjectDev/Bin/</Path>
            <Filename>paradigma.capabilitybase.DecreaseTemperature</Filename>
            <Name>Decrease Temperature</Name>
            <Description>Decreases the fridge temperature</Description>
            <Type>Action capability</Type>
        </Definition>
    </Capabilities>
```

The Neutral Object Interface

The `NeutralObject` interface extends the `Remote` interface of the `java.rmi` interface so it is tagged as an interface that can be invoked from a remote JVM.

```
package paradigma.neutralobject;

//Import required Java classes
import java.util.*;
import java.rmi.*;

//Import Paradigma classes
import paradigma.capability.*;
import paradigma.attribute.*;


public interface NeutralObject extends Remote
{
```

The following method will activate a capability of a `NeutralObject`. The activation of capabilities can cause an answer to be returned to the party that caused the activation. As mentioned previously, the current approach does not allow for a great amount of control since no arguments can be passed to the capability we wish to activate. The reason is because the focus was on getting a complete system up and running, allowing for refinements to be done with the aid of experience.

```
    public Object performCapability(String name)
        throws RemoteException, NoSuchCapabilityException,
        NoCapabilitiesLoadedException;
```

This method allows an agent to query individual attributes on their current value.

```
    public Object senseAttribute(String name)
        throws RemoteException, NoAttributesDefinedException,
        NoSuchAttributeException;
```

The following methods allow the manipulation of individual attributes:

```
public void addAttribute(String type, String value)
    throws RemoteException;

public void removeAttribute(String type, String value)
    throws RemoteException, NoAttributesDefinedException,
    NoSuchAttributeException;

public void changeAttribute(String oldType,String oldValue,
    String newType, String newValue)
    throws RemoteException, NoAttributesDefinedException,
    NoSuchAttributeException;

public HashSet getAttributes()
    throws RemoteException;
```

Similar methods are available for capabilities. Care needs to be taken in this instance when remotely calling the getCapabilities() method. The developer needs to ensure that those capabilities are actually serializable, because, as we saw, although attributes go through a more standardized creation process through attribute factories, capabilities are loaded dynamically and unless checks are placed one cannot guarantee their behavior.

```
public void removeCapability(String name)
    throws RemoteException,NoSuchCapabilityException,
    NoCapabilitiesLoadedException;

public void addCapability(Capability capability)
    throws RemoteException;

public HashSet getCapabilities()
    throws RemoteException;
```

The current interface for NeutralObject is as you can see quite *open*, since it allows complete remote control of a neutral object. For the current development phase such a situation is acceptable; however, the interface would eventually need to be more restrictive enabling the execution of certain methods only to agents that have the authority to perform so. In others words there should be levels of administrative power, based on an agent authentication process.

Publishing a Neutral Object

A neutral object is published in a Jini community so that other agents can discover and use it. Therefore, it needs to provide a suitable description of itself to allow others to judge its utility to their own goals. The ObjectPublisher class accepts the neutral object as an argument in its constructor and extracts the information of static attributes and the description of capabilities, preparing entries for publication into the Jini community. The use of the Jini APIs make this job relatively easy.

Since this class makes use of Jini we will have a closer look at it.

We begin with the necessary class imports.

```
package paradigma.publisher;

//Import required Java classes
import java.io.*;
import java.rmi.*;
import java.util.*;
import javax.swing.*;

//Import Jini classes
import net.jini.core.entry.*;
import net.jini.core.lease.*;
import net.jini.entry.*;
import net.jini.core.lookup.*;
import net.jini.discovery.*;
import net.jini.lookup.*;
import net.jini.lease.*;

//Import Paradigma classes
import paradigma.publisher.event.*;
import paradigma.neutralobject.*;
import paradigma.capability.*;
import paradigma.attribute.*;
```

The class is a thread object, since registration to a Jini community is not a one-off process but one that requires close monitoring as lookup services come and go.

```
public class ObjectPublisher implements Runnable
{

    /* The neutral object to be published*/
    private NeutralObject publication;

    /*The set of attributes*/
    private HashSet attributes;

    /*The set of capabilities*/
    private HashSet capabilities;

    /*The array of entries to be published*/
    private Entry[] publicationEntries;

    /*Handles joining into the Jini community*/
    protected JoinManager manager = null;

    /*Handles the discovery of paradigma lookup services*/
    protected LookupDiscovery paradigmaDiscoverer = null;

    /*The groups to be dicsovered*/
    String[] groups = {"paradigma"};

    /*A vector of listeners to publication events*/
    private Vector publicationListeners = new Vector();


    /*The number of attributes published*/
    private int publishedAttributes = 0;
```

So, following the preliminary definitions, we have below the constructor of the `ObjectPublisher`. It accepts a `NeutralObject` as an argument. By having our interface defined we can forget all about the actual entity we are dealing with and focus on the considerations for taking care of its publication.

```java
public ObjectPublisher(NeutralObject object)
{

    //Set a security manager
    if (System.getSecurityManager() == null)
    {
        System.setSecurityManager (new RMISecurityManager());
    }

    //Retrieve object information
    try
    {
        this.publication = object;
        this.attributes = object.getAttributes();
        this.capabilities = object.getCapabilities();
    }
    catch (RemoteException excpt)
    {}

}
```

The method below simply calculates how many entries are actually going to be required to describe the neutral object in a Jini community. As mentioned before, static attributes and capability descriptions are what gets published.

```java
/*Returns the number of entries*/
private int numberOfEntries()
{
    int size = 0;
    int notForPublication = 0;

    Iterator collector = attributes.iterator();
    for (int i = 0; i<attributes.size(); i++)
    {
        Object current = collector.next();

        if (current instanceof ChangingAttribute)
        {
            notForPublication++;
        }
    }

    size = (attributes.size()-notForPublication) + capabilities.size();
    return size;
}
```

The following methods translate the attributes and capabilities to entries which are then added to the entry set that will be published:

```
/* Collect all the attributes to be published*/
public void getAttributeEntries ()
{
    Iterator collector =  attributes.iterator();
    for (int i = 0; i<attributes.size(); i++)
    {
        Object current = (Object) collector.next();

        //Check what type of attribute it is and load the
        //appropriate entry class
        if (! (current instanceof ChangingAttribute))
        {
            Attribute attribute = (Attribute) current;
            //Create an attribute entry
            AttributeEntry newEntry = new AttributeEntry(attribute.getType(),
            attribute.getValue());

            publicationEntries[publishedAttributes] = newEntry;
            publishedAttributes++;
        }
    }
}

/* Collect all the capabilities to be published*/
public void getCapabilityEntries()
{
    Iterator collector = capabilities.iterator();
    for (int i= publishedAttributes; i<(capabilities.size() +
            publishedAttributes); i++)
    {
        Capability current = (Capability) collector.next();
        CapabilityEntry newEntry = new
        CapabilityEntry(current.getName(),current.getType(),
        current.getDescription()); publicationEntries[i] = newEntry;
    }
}
```

Finally, the publish method uses the `JoinManager` to handle the publication of the neutral object. The `JoinManager` makes things much easier by handling almost all details of publication, relieving the developer from many responsibilities and minimizing the code required.

The constructor of the `JoinManager` we are using is:

```
JoinManager(java.lang.Object obj, Entry[] attrSets, ServiceIDListener callback,
    DiscoveryManagement discoverMgr, LeaseRenewalManager leaseMgr)
```

For discovery management `LookupDiscovery` is used, which can accept an array of groups to perform discovery on. Within `ObjectPublisher` there is a class that implements the `ServiceIDListener` interface and is used to listen for service ID notifications. No `LeaseRenewalManager` is defined, but one is created by `JoinManager` and handles the renewing of leasing to the lookup service.

Readers should note that currently, services are not well-behaved, since the service ID is not saved. As mentioned before, Paradigma is still at a development stage with the focus on a running system and not a market-ready one.

```
/*Publishes the object*/
public void publish()
{
    System.out.println("Attempting to publish...");
    try
    {
        //Create a discovery thread
        paradigmaDiscoverer = new LookupDiscovery(groups);

        //Create the join manager
        manager = new JoinManager(publication, publicationEntries,
            new IDListener(), paradigmaDiscoverer, null);

    }
    catch (IOException excpt)
    {
      System.out.println("IO exception in joining Jini community");
      System.out.println();
      excpt.printStackTrace();
    }
}
```

If publication needs to be canceled the `retrievePublication()` method can be called which will terminate the operations of the `JoinManager`. Upon expiry of the lease the neutral object will be cleaned up by the lookup service.

```
/*Retrieves the publication*/
public void retrievePublication()
{
    manager.terminate();
}
```

As mentioned at the start, `ObjectPublisher` implements `Runnable` so that it can run in a thread of its own. Currently nothing actually happens in this thread since `JoinManager` handles all the hard work. However, eventually one might want to be able to effect changes to the registered services following periodic checks, so as to change the entries attached to the service, handle leasing directly, etc.

```
public void run()
{

    publicationEntries = new Entry[numberOfEntries()];

    this.getAttributeEntries();
    this.getCapabilityEntries();
    this.publish();

    while (true)
    {
```

```
            try
            {
                Thread.sleep(10000);
            }
            catch (InterruptedException excpt)
            {
                System.out.println("Publisher interrupted");
            }
        }
    }
```

Finally, `ObjectPublisher` implements the `ServiceIDListener`:

```
    /**
     * IDListener is an inner class that listens
     * for ID events from the Jini community.
     *
     */
    class IDListener implements ServiceIDListener
    {

        public void serviceIDNotify(ServiceID serviceID)
        {
            String message = "Got service ID for object: " + serviceID;

            JOptionPane.showMessageDialog(null,message ,
            "Object publication message", JOptionPane.INFORMATION_MESSAGE);

            //This event notifies other interested classes that
            //are not related to Jini about publication.
            firePublicationEvent();
        }
    }
}
```

The final item that requires to be shown is the structure of the `CapabilityEntry` and `AttributeEntry` classes:

```
package paradigma.capability;

import net.jini.entry.*;


public class CapabilityEntry extends AbstractEntry
{

    /*The name of the capability*/
    public String name;

    /*The type of the capability*/
    public String type;

    /*The description of the capability*/
    public String description;
```

```
    public CapabilityEntry()
    {}


    public CapabilityEntry(String name, String type, String desc)
    {
        this.name = name;
        this.type = type;
        this.description = desc;
    }


    public void setDescription(String capabilityDescription)
    {
        description = capabilityDescription;
    }


    public String getDescription()
    {
        return description;
    }

    public void setType(String capabilityType)
    {
        type = capabilityType;
    }

    public String getType()
    {
        return type;
    }

    public void setName(String capabilityName)
    {
        name = capabilityName;
    }

    public String getName()
    {
        return name;
    }
}


package paradigma.attribute;

import net.jini.entry.*;

public class AttributeEntry extends AbstractEntry
{

    /*The type of the Attribute*/
    public String type;

    /*The value of the Attribute*/
    public String value;

    public AttributeEntry()
    {}

    public AttributeEntry(String Type, String Value)
    {
```

```
            this.type = Type;
            this.value = Value;
        }


    public void setType(String attributeType)
    {
        type = attributeType;
    }


    public String getType()
    {
        return type;
    }


    public void setValue(String attributeValue)
    {
        value = attributeValue;
    }

    public String getValue()
    {
        return value;
    }

}
```

We have now covered all the issues involved in the creation of a neutral object. If anything is to be learned from how Jini can aid in developing a system, it is the ease with which it can be integrated into the system. The biggest problems faced are usually the first steps of making sure all the required components such as http server and rmid are up and running, and that a security manager and permission files are correctly configured. Following such worries and once the concepts of how Jini works are understood you are two steps away from a distributed system, as far as coding is concerned. The real challenges, as ever, are in actually designing the system.

Creating a Neutral Object

In order to glue all the ideas presented above together, we will briefly illustrate how the, by now famous, refrigerator was put together.

The first step is for our `Fridge` class to extend the `AbstractObject` class and implement the `CapabilityListener` interface so that it can be notified for capability events:

```
    public class Fridge extends AbstractObject implements CapabilityListener
```

The constructor of our class should call the constructor of `AbstractObject` so as to create attributes and capabilities from the supplied XML files and then load the classes that actually implement those capabilities:

```
    public Fridge(String attributeDoc, String capabilitiesDoc)
            throws RemoteException


    {
        this.super(attributeDoc,capabilitiesDoc);

    }
```

Further initialization is done in an `init()` method. Capabilities that need to notify the `Fridge` class add the class as a listener to them and attributes that need to be notified by the class are registered as listeners.

Finally, we show the code required to instantiate the fridge and register it with Jini lookup services:

```java
public void createObject(String attributeDoc,String capabilityDoc )
{

    try
    {
        //Create the object
        fridge = new Fridge(attributeDoc,capabilityDoc);
        //Initialise it
        fridge.init();
    }
    catch (RemoteException excpt)
    {
        System.out.println("REMOTE EXCEPTION!");
        excpt.printStackTrace();
    }

    try
    {
        String[] groups = {"paradigmaKitchen"};
        ObjectPublisher publisher = new ObjectPublisher(fridge,groups);
        new Thread(publisher).start();
    }
    catch (Exception excpt)
    {
        System.out.println("Error in publication");
    }

}
```

The following print out, which occurs during the creation of a neutral object, illustrates the steps the process goes through:

```
C:\ProjectDev>ECHO OFF

Static attribute added
Static attribute added
Static attribute added
Changing attribute added
Changing attribute added
Changing attribute added
Attempting to load class: paradigma.capabilitybase.OpenDoor
Attempting to load class: paradigma.capabilitybase.CloseDoor
Attempting to load class: paradigma.capabilitybase.IncreaseTemperature
Attempting to load class: paradigma.capabilitybase.DecreaseTemperature
Listening to:Open Door
Listening to:Increase Temperature
Listening to:Decrease Temperature
Listening to:Close Door
Notifying attribute: Temperature
```

```
Notifying attribute: Availability
Notifying attribute: Door Status
There are :7 to be published
Attribute added to entry set of type Name and value Ron's Fridge

Attribute added to entry set of type Service and value Kitchen Fridge

Attribute added to entry set of type Location and value http://dcs.warwick.ac.uk

Capability added to entry set with name Open Door of type Action capability

Capability added to entry set with name Increase Temperature of type Action capa
bility

Capability added to entry set with name Decrease Temperature of type Action capa
bility

Capability added to entry set with name Close Door of type Action capability

Attempting to publish...
```

Browsing Neutral Objects

In order to aid in the easy deployment of neutral objects such as the ones above we have build a small administration tool that acts as a browser and capability activator for our neutral objects. The tool has a thread of execution that is continuously looking for lookup services that belong to the Paradigma group via a multicast call. Once such a service is discovered the information is kept in a `ServiceInfo` object and is added to a `JTree`.

The developer can then select the required lookup service and ask for a search to be performed and any registered services that implement the neutral object interface to be retrieved. In this case the lookup service is re-discovered using a unicast call. The following screenshot illustrate the execution of the Neutral Object Tester:

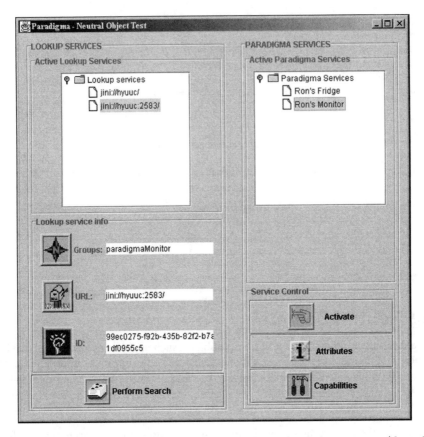

In the above case, our `NeutralObject` tester has discovered two lookup services (the information shown is that of the highlighted lookup service). Once a search was performed on them the refrigerator and home security services are discovered.

The class used for discovery is shown. The code is also used by the agents that wish to collect information on available Jini services.

```
package paradigma.discovery;

//Import required Java classes
import java.io.*;
import java.rmi.*;
import java.util.*;


//Import Jini classes
import net.jini.discovery.*;
import net.jini.core.lookup.*;

//Import Paradigma classes
import paradigma.discovery.event.*;

public class Discoverer implements Runnable
{
```

```
        /*The groups the discoverer is meant to locate*/
        private String[] groups = null;

        /*The LookupDiscovery object that will perform the lookups*/
        private LookupDiscovery jiniDiscover = null;

        /*The listeners to events from Discoverer*/
        private Vector discoveryListeners = new Vector();

        /*The time the discoverer should wait before beginning discovery*/
        int initialSleepTime;

        public Discoverer(String[] lookups, int sleepTime)
        {

            //Set a security manager
            if (System.getSecurityManager() == null)
            {
                System.setSecurityManager (new RMISecurityManager());
            }
            this.groups = lookups;
        }
```

The `discover()` method initiates discovery by passing an array of Jini community group names to a `LookupDiscovery` class of Jini:

```
        public synchronized void discover()
        {

            try
            {
                jiniDiscover = new LookupDiscovery(groups);
            }
            catch (IOException excpt)
            {
                System.out.println("DISCOVERY FAILURE.");
                excpt.printStackTrace();
            }
            jiniDiscover.addDiscoveryListener (new DiscovererListener());
        }

        public void run()
        {

            this.discover();

            while (true)
            {

                try
                {
                    Thread.sleep(10000);
                }
                catch (InterruptedException excpt)
                {
                    System.out.println("Publisher interrupted");
                }
```

```
        }//End while

    }//End run
```

The `Discovery` class fires an event upon discovery of the lookup service. This event carries to the registered parties the required information for them to attempt to relocate the service performing unicast discovery.

The reason for this is quite simply that once all the lookup services have been discovered we can then selectively proceed to query the ones we are specifically interested in. Agents may wish to know what lookup services are available but not be interested in actually using them, so we opted for a notification mechanism that is not based on agents implementing `DiscoveryListener`.

`Discoverer` itself, of course, implements `DiscoveryListener` in order to receive notification of discovered lookup services. Once a lookup service has been discovered, the required information is extracted and relayed to interested parties in the form of a `ParadigmaDiscoveryEvent`, the code of which is not shown since all it does is encapsulate the discovered lookup service's information.

```java
class DiscovererListener implements DiscoveryListener
{

    public void discovered( DiscoveryEvent event)
    {

        ServiceRegistrar[] registrars = event.getRegistrars();

        for (int i=0; i<registrars.length; i++)
        {
            try
            {
                String id = registrars[i].getServiceID().toString();
                firelookupServiceDiscoveredEvent(getGroups(registrars[i]),
                        getURL(registrars[i]),id);
            }
            catch (RemoteException excpt)
            {
                System.out.println("Error:" +  excpt.getMessage());
            }
        }
    } //end discovered

    public void discarded(DiscoveryEvent event)
    {} //end discarded
```

Below are the methods that perform the necessary information parsing to retrieve the Jini URL, group name, and ID of the discovered lookup service:

```java
/* Returns the JINI URL of the discovered lookup service*/
public String getURL(ServiceRegistrar reg)
        throws RemoteException
{
    return reg.getLocator().toString();
}
```

```java
                    /*Returns the groups of the discovered lookup service*/
                    public String getGroups(ServiceRegistrar reg)
                                throws RemoteException
                    {
                        String groups[] = reg.getGroups();

                        if (groups.length == 0)
                        {
                            return "<none>";
                        }


                        StringBuffer buf = new StringBuffer();
                        for (int i = 0; i<groups.length; i++)
                        {
                            if (groups[i] == null)
                            {
                                buf.append("NULL");
                            }
                            else if (groups[i].equals(""))
                            {
                                buf.append("PUBLIC");
                            }
                            else
                            {
                                buf.append(groups[i]);
                            }
                        }


                        return buf.toString();
                    }//end getGroups


        }//End Listener

} //End Discoverer
```

A class registered with `Discoverer` can keep information about discovered lookup services and use that information to retrieve an interface to the lookup services via unicast discovery. In the example of our Neutral Object test utility this is what happens when we perform a search on a listed lookup service.

A `ServiceDiscoverer` object is instantiated with the task of querying those lookup services for registered services, that implement the `NeutralObject` interface. The code for the `ServiceDiscoverer` is shown below:

```java
package paradigma.discovery;

//Import required Java classes
//Import required Java classes
import java.io.*;
import java.rmi.*;
import java.util.*;
import java.net.*;
```

```
//Import Jini classes
import net.jini.core.lookup.*;
import net.jini.discovery.*;
import net.jini.core.lookup.*;
import net.jini.core.discovery.*;
import net.jini.core.entry.*;
import net.jini.entry.*;


//Import Paradigma classes
import paradigma.discovery.event.*;
import paradigma.neutralobject.*;
```

Once more it implements the `Runnable` interface so that it can be run within its own thread of execution.

```
public class ServiceDiscoverer implements Runnable
{

    /*The LookupLocatorDiscovery object that will perform the lookups*/
    private LookupLocatorDiscovery jiniDiscover = null;


    /*The locator object to be passed to the LookupLocatordiscovery*/
    private LookupLocator[] jiniLocators = null;


    /*The service template to be used for retrieving services*/
    private ServiceTemplate serviceTemplate = null;


    /*The listeners to events from ServiceDiscoverer*/
    private Vector serviceListeners = new Vector();


    /*Set to true if service discovery will be repeated*/
    private boolean keepRepeating;
```

The constructor for service discoverer creates a number of `LookupLocators`, which correspond to each of the Jini lookup services that belong to the same group. These lookup locators will then be passed to the `LookupLocatorDiscovery` class that will perform the necessary work for unicast discovery of each of the required services.

```
    public ServiceDiscoverer(String[] jiniURL, boolean repeated)
    {

        //Set a security manager
        if (System.getSecurityManager() == null)
        {
            System.setSecurityManager (new RMISecurityManager());
        }

        jiniLocators = new LookupLocator[jiniURL.length];
```

```
        for (int i = 0; i<jiniURL.length;i++)
        {
            try
            {
                jiniLocators[i] = new LookupLocator(jiniURL[i]);
            }
            catch (MalformedURLException excpt)
            {
                System.out.println("MALFORMED URL.");
                excpt.printStackTrace();
            }
        }

        this.keepRepeating = repeated;
    }

    /**
     * This method will initiate discovery.
     *
     */
    public synchronized void discover()
    {

        try
        {
            jiniDiscover = new LookupLocatorDiscovery(jiniLocators);
        }
        catch (Exception excpt)
        {
            System.out.println("DISCOVERY FAILURE.");
            excpt.printStackTrace();
        }
        jiniDiscover.addDiscoveryListener(new ServiceDiscovererListener());
    }
```

The following method prepares the necessary service template. In our case it simply requests that the service implement the NeutralObject interface.

```
    public ServiceTemplate createServiceTemplate()
    {

        Class[] serviceType = new Class[] {NeutralObject.class};
        ServiceTemplate template = new ServiceTemplate(null,serviceType,null);
        return template;
    }



    /* The run method in accordance to the runnable interface
     */
    public void run()
    {

        serviceTemplate = this.createServiceTemplate();
```

```
            this.discover();

        while (true)
        {
            try
            {
                Thread.sleep(25000);
            }
            catch (InterruptedException excpt)
            {
                System.out.println("Publisher interrupted");
            }

            if (keepRepeating)
            {
                this.discover();
            }
        }//End while

    }//End run
```

Once a suitable service has been discovered, listeners to the ServiceDiscoverer classes are notified via a ParadigmaServiceEvent. The event carries to the listening party the Jini ServiceItem for the discovered service. With the service item we can then proceed to make use of the service object as well as the entries attached to it.

Finally, an inner class implements the DiscoveryListener interface, which will be notified from the LookupLocatorDiscovery class upon discovery of a suitable service:

```
    class ServiceDiscovererListener implements DiscoveryListener
    {

        public void discovered(DiscoveryEvent event)
        {

            ServiceMatches matches = null;
            ServiceRegistrar[] registrars = event.getRegistrars();

            for (int i=0; i<registrars.length; i++)
            {

                System.out.println("Lookup service rediscovered.");
                try
                {
                    matches = registrars[i].lookup(serviceTemplate,5);
                }
                catch (RemoteException excpt)
                {
                    System.out.println("REMOTE EXCEPTION");
                }

                if (matches.totalMatches>0)
                {
```

```
                          ServiceItem[] newItem = matches.items;
                          fireParadigmaServiceDiscoveredEvent(newItem);
                  }


          }
          }//end discovered

          public void discarded(DiscoveryEvent event)
          {}//end discarded


      }//End Listener


  } //End ServiceDiscoverer
```

When a service implementing the `NeutralObject` interface has been discovered, the Neutral Object Test UI can extract all the necessary information and display the service's attributes and capabilities as shown below:

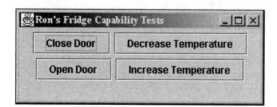

However, because our service describes itself through its entries, that information can be used to create the panel shown below, which allows for the manipulation of the service through its `NeutralObject` interface:

This concludes our brief overview of the neutral object browser application. The aim was to provide a way to discover lookup services and store that information for later use, including rediscovering the lookup services through a unicast call. The description published with the `NeutralObject` interface then allows us to manipulate the service remotely through a generic interface that is specialized via the description of the capabilities attached as entries to the service proxy. In the next section we will see how agents can control these services by executing plans in order to achieve their goals.

Agents

There are many ways one can go about designing agents. They range from the most basic control structures to complicated reasoning entities that use Artificial Intelligence techniques. Therefore, when attempting to develop a general framework for autonomous agents some common ground had to be found that would allow the exact implementation of that behavior to be as simple or as exotic as one wished.

Agents are ascribed goals by other agents or, in the case of autonomous agents, generate goals themselves. Goals are achieved through the implementation of plans that call on the execution of an agent's capabilities. Goals and plans are supplied to an agent via XML files. Both files are passed through a factory structure (as described for attributes) in order to create the *goalbase* and *planbase*, respectively, of the agent. An example of a simple goal and the accompanying plan is shown below:

```
<Definition>
    <Name>Adjust Temperature</Name>
    <Attribute>
        <Type>Temperature</Type>
        <Value>6</Value>
    </Attribute>
</Definition>
```

The goal calls for the temperature to be set at six degrees and the plan below will be activated in the case that the temperature is higher than six degrees.

Plans have four parts: Their name, under which conditions they are to be invoked, what needs to be true for them to be applicable, and finally the actions that need to be performed:

```
<Definition>

    <Name>Decrease Temperature</Name>

    <InvocationCons>
        <Goal>Adjust Temperature</Goal>
    </InvocationCons>

    <PreCons>
        <Attribute>
            <Type>Temperature</Type>
            <Value>7</Value>
        </Attribute>
    </PreCons>

    <Perform>
        <Action>Decrease Temperature</Action>
    </Perform>

</Definition>
```

An agent will know if a goal has been successful, following execution of a plan, by creating a view of the environment and *seeing* that the attribute in question has been set to the desired value.

Agents have all the functionality of neutral objects since they are nothing more but an extension of them. However, this functionality can come through two paths. In the case of autonomous agents it is acquired by extending the `AbstractObject` class and in the case of server agents by *wrapping* around a neutral object that is passed as an argument in their constructor. Both types of agents implement the `Agent` interface, which we describe below. A lot of details have been omitted, especially as far as plans and goals are concerned. The aim is to give the reader a qualitative understanding of the framework instead of detailed explanations of all its aspects.

```
package paradigma.agent;

//Import required Java classes
import java.util.*;

//Import Paradigma classes
import paradigma.capability.*;
import paradigma.decision.*;
import paradigma.plan.*;
import paradigma.goal.*;
```

The interface extends the `Runnable` interface, indicating that agents can execute is a separate thread:

```
public interface Agent extends Runnable
  {
```

The first method is called whenever an agent has been requested to achieve some goals for another agent. It *adopts* the other agent's goals and will place them in its goalbase until the situation allows it to pursue them.

```
public void adoptGoals(Goal[] goal);
```

The method `assessGoals()` is called in order to decide which goal the agent is going to pursue next. In the case of an autonomous agent the next goal will be the one offering the greatest motivational utility, while in the case of a server agent it is simply the next goal in the queue. Once a goal has been achieved it is marked as successfully achieved, but it is not removed from the goalbase as a change in the environment might cause the goal to be relevant again. For example the refrigerator server agent may close the door to conserve energy, but at a later point in time the door may once more be left open for too long.

```
public Goal assessGoals();
```

The following methods can be called to add and remove goals from the goalbase. In this case the actions are due to the agent itself and not due to external forces as in `adoptGoals()` above.

```
public void addGoal(Goal goal);

public void removeGoal(Goal goal);
```

Now, for the agent to be able to act in an environment it should have some model of that environment. The `canPerceive()` method tells the agent which of its capabilities it can use to perceive attributes of the environment.

```
public HashSet canPerceive(HashSet capabilities);
```

745

The willPerceive() method tells the agent which of those *perception* capabilities it will actually activate. The reason for not activating the complete range of perception capabilities is either to save on computational cycles or simply because it does not make sense in the agent's current execution cycle.

```
public HashSet willPerceive(HashSet capabilities);
```

The following method causes the activation of those perception capabilities, as well as the sensing of the agent's own attributes. The sum of these attributes forms the *view* of the world as seen by the agent. The structure returned is a set of attribute-value pairs.

```
public Hashtable getView();
```

Having created a view of the agent's environment the agentAct() method can be called in order to select a Plan from *planbase* that is applicable in order to achieve the current goal based on the current view of the world.

```
public Plan agentAct(Goal currentCoal, Hashtable currentView);
```

The following method actually commits an agent to performing a plan:

```
public void willDo (Plan currentPlan);
```

Finally, the agent can keep a log of its activities via the updateHistory() method. This log may be useful for deciding what to do next or simply for tracking the agent's behavior.

```
public void updateHistory(Object newInfo);
}
```

This interface allows for a wide range of implementations but provides a solid base upon which to build.

Instantiating Server Agents from Neutral Objects

There are a number of ways of interacting with neutral objects ranging from simply downloading and instantiating them locally to the smart use of a combination of RMI (Remote Method Invocation) and client local execution. These methods are well know to Jini developers but here we explain how they can be understood in the case of agent-based systems and more specifically the Paradigma framework.

Execution in the Engaging Agent's JVM

In this case the neutral object publishes the actual implementation of the NeutralObject interface that is downloaded by the client. The client will then instantiate a ServerAgent to wrap around the NeutralObject. All calls to the capabilities of the neutral object are executed locally. This behavior is useful if the available service represents a required extension to the agent engaging the neutral object, for example a network administration agent that requires a new module to control a device such as a router.

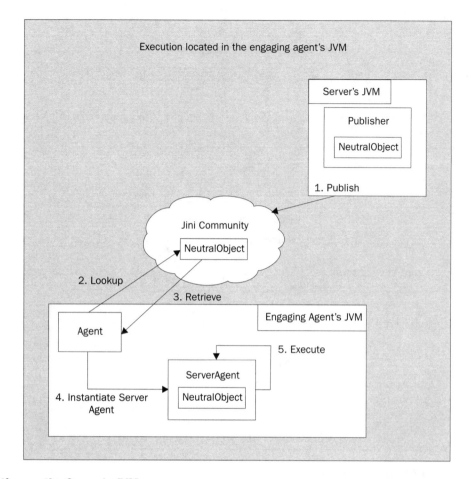

Execution on the Server's JVM

The neutral object will publish an RMI-based interface to act as a proxy to the actual implementation that resides in the server's JVM. As far as the engaging agent is concerned the behavior is the same in that it will once again instantiate a server agent to wrap the neutral object. All calls, however, will be communicated to the remote JVM. This is useful in instances where the neutral object serves as a channel to information on a database, or an interface for a remote sensor, or for the purposes of distributing computing power. Our prototype application uses this form of interaction since it involves the remote control of a device.

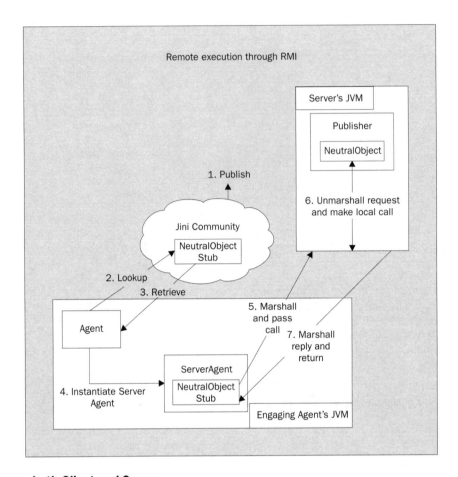

Remote execution through RMI

Execution on both Client and Server

Here we have what is often called a smart proxy. The neutral object publishes an implementation of the `NeutralObject` interface where some of the processing is done in the engaging agent's JVM and some on the remote JVM. Such an implementation is useful in instances where it is more profitable to distribute the processing over both machines. Such a decision will be taken based on the processing power of the machines and the cost of transferring information over the network as well as security issues.

Autonomous Agents

Autonomous agents give meaning to an agent-based system through their ability to generate their own goals, driven by their motivations. The selection of goals through motivations can be done in any number of ways from the very simple to the very complicated. The decision is up to the developer to select or devise mechanisms that suit him or her best. In Paradigma we have opted for a basic but powerful structure called an m-triple <m, v, b>; motivations have a name <m>, a strength <v> and a boolean variable <b> which indicates whether the motivation is static or variable. Motivations, along with an agent's goals and plans, completely define the agent's behavior. Upon instantiation of an autonomous agent XML files are read to create all attributes, capabilities, motivations, goals, and plans. (At the current stage of development we use different files for each aspect but eventually it would be more appropriate to have a single file that contains all the required information.)

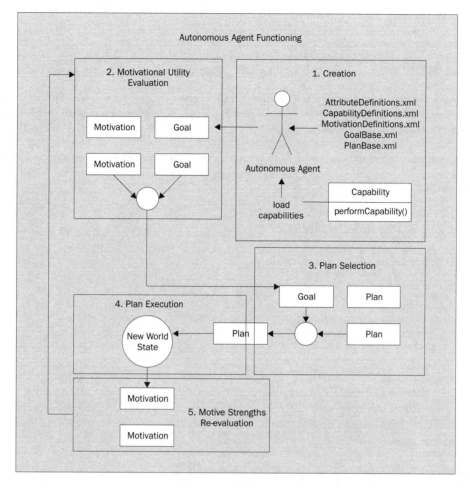

The set of goals and set of plans form, respectively, the *goalbase* and *planbase* of the agent. Based on its motivations the agent will choose the goal that offers the greatest motivational utility. This will lead to the attempt to select and implement a plan that will in turn lead to the activation of a certain number of the agent's capabilities or the engagement of other agents or neutral objects in order to achieve its goals. Once a goal has been obtained the autonomous agent will re-adjust its motivations and attempt the next best goal from its goalbase.

Below we show an example of motivation definitions for our autonomous agent:

```
<Definition>
    <Name>Be Connected</Name>
    <Value>1.0</Value>
    <Variable>Yes</Variable>
</Definition>

<Definition>
    <Name>Obey Commands</Name>
    <Value>1.0</Value>
    <Variable>No</Variable>
</Definition>
```

```
    <Definition>
        <Name>Control Kitchen Utilities</Name>
        <Value>0.0</Value>
        <Variable>Yes</Variable>
    </Definition>
```

The above example has the motivation for controlling kitchen utilities set to zero. This value will change once the motivation for being connected has caused the goal of beginning a lookup on the discovered lookup services for kitchen appliances.

The goal below is one of the first to be called since its motivational utility to be connected is 1.0:

```
<Definition>

    <!--The name of the goal->
    <Name>Find Kitchen</Name>

    <!-- The motivation utilities of this goal -->
    <Motivation>
        <ID>Be Connected</ID>
        <Utility>1.0</Utility>
    </Motivation>
    <Motivation>
        <ID>Obey Commands</ID>
        <Utility>1.0</Utility>
    </Motivation>

    <!-- The desired attribute change -->
    <Attribute>
        <Type>Found Kitchen</Type>
        <Value>true</Value>
    </Attribute>

</Definition>
```

This above goal will cause the execution of the following plan:

```
<Definition>

    <Name>Find Kitchen Appliances</Name>

    <InvocationCons>
        <Goal>Find Kitchen</Goal>
    </InvocationCons>

    <PreCons>
        <Attribute>
            <Type>Found Paradigma Kitchen</Type>
            <Value>true</Value>
        </Attribute>
    </PreCons>

    <Perform>
        <Action>Discover Appliances</Action>
    </Perform>

</Definition>
```

The complete behavior cycle of the autonomous agent is contained within the run() method that we show below:

```java
public void run()
{

    Plan planToExecute = null;

    Goal currentGoal = null;

    while (agentActive)
    {
        //Attempt to locate the best goal and the relevant plan
        while (planToExecute==null)
        {

            currentGoal = assessGoals();
            if (!(currentGoal==null))
            {
                //Create a view of the world
                Hashtable view = getView();
                //Based on the current goal and the
                //view of the world locate a suitable plan
                planToExecute = agentAct(currentGoal, view);
            }

            try
            {
                Thread.sleep(3000);
            }
            catch (InterruptedException excpt)
            {
                System.out.println("Agent interrupted");
            }

        }//planToExecute loop

                try
        {
            Thread.sleep(5000);
        }
        catch (InterruptedException excpt)
        {
            System.out.println("Agent interrupted");
        }

        //Attempt to execute that plan
        willDo(planToExecute);

        updateHistory(currentGoal);
        updateHistory(planToExecute);

        planToExecute = null;

        //Readjust motivations based on the current state of the world
        motiveController.getCurrentView(getView());

        HashSet currentMotivations;

        motivations = motiveController.adjustMotivations(motivations);
        }
    }//agentActive loop

}//end run
```

Autonomous Agent Capabilities

The autonomous agent presented at the start of the chapter was able to discover lookup services, perform a search on them and activate server agents. All of those actions come from the activation of the agent's capabilities. These capabilities use the same classes we discussed for the Neutral Object Test application in order to accomplish their tasks.

For example, upon instantiation of the agent the `HomeAgentDiscoverer` capability begins a thread of execution that discovers lookup services using the `Discoverer` class. Once lookup services have been discovered the attributes of the autonomous agent change to reflect this.

```
package paradigma.capabilitybase;

//Import java classes
import java.util.*;


//Import paradigma classes
import paradigma.capability.*;
import paradigma.discovery.*;
import paradigma.client.*;
import paradigma.information.*;
import paradigma.discovery.event.*;

public class HomeAgentDiscoverer extends AbstractEventCapability
        implements ParadigmaDiscoveryListener,InfoProvider
{
    private Discoverer discoverer;

    private Hashtable discoveredServices;

    private Vector infoConsumers;


    public HomeAgentDiscoverer()
    {
        discoveredServices = new Hashtable();

        infoConsumers = new Vector();

        String[] groups = {"paradigmaKitchen","paradigmaMonitor"};

        discoverer = new Discoverer(groups);

        discoverer.addParadigmaDiscoveryListener(this);
        new Thread(discoverer).start();
    }
```

The capability implements two interfaces. The `ParadigmaDiscoveryListener` interface, which we met before, is used to notify this class of lookup service discovery events. The `InfoProvider` interface indicates that this capability provides information for the autonomous agent to use in other capabilities that will implement the `InfoConsumer` interface. All information is stored in the `InfoCenter` class. Capabilities wishing to retrieve information must registered with the `InfoCenter` as `InfoConsumers` and capabilities that wish to post information must register as `InfoProviders`, while certain capabilities may need to register as both.

The diagram below illustrates the structure of the `InfoCenter`:

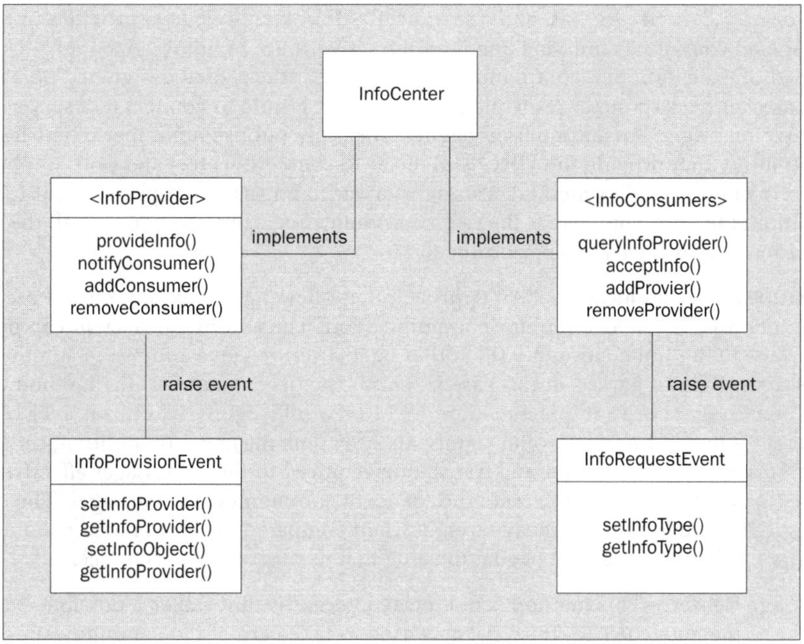

When our `HomeAgentDiscoverer` capability is notified of the discovery of lookup services it changes the required attributes and also posts the information in the `InfoCenter`. Once the information has been posted the other capabilities can use it to discover specific services. One of those capabilities is responsible for discovering the services the home agent is interested in and will also register the information with the info center.

The discovery of appliances will cause the agent to choose to create server agents and it can achieve this by calling a specific capability class for each server agent it wishes to create. For example, our home agent will have a capability for each device it wishes to handle and since capabilities can be loaded dynamically at run time it can keep extending itself as needs require.

Interacting with Other Agents

Until now we have discussed the creation of neutral objects and autonomous agents and then described the mechanisms of interaction between agents and neutral objects via the instantiation of server agents.

An autonomous agent that chooses to make itself available for cooperation with other autonomous agents needs to join a Jini community so that it can be discovered. The agent could facilitate such communication in a number of ways. We will outline some of the main ones giving their relative benefits and disadvantages.

❑ **Socket-based communication** – Sockets are logical connection points between hosts; they provide high-level abstraction mechanisms for communication. With the `java.net.ServerSocket` and `java.net.Socket` classes, Java provides in-built support for socket communication, making it an attractive route to follow. A server socket can begin a thread of execution that continuously listens for messages on a designated port number and can answer back to messages while a client socket is able to connect to a server and send and receive messages. An autonomous agent can simply publish a number of entries to the Jini community that provide the URL (Universal Resource Locator) and port number other agents need to contact it. This method is straightforward and easy to implement but it offers no additional features and leaves the two communicating agents to perform all the required work in order to guarantee a proper protocol.

❑ **RMI-based communication** – An approach that offers more flexibility is the use of RMI (Remote Method Invocation) for communication. The autonomous agent can publish an interface to the Jini community that other agents can retrieve and use to communicate their messages. What is gained in this case is that the actual signature of the method can form part of the message. For example a method `tell()` would signify that this is a TELL type message whereas a method `ask()` would signify an ASK type message. In addition, different interface implementations could offer any translation required to those messages effectively allowing the agent to communicate in different types of agent communication languages. The disadvantage of using RMI is that it is more heavy weight when compared to socket-based communication and agents still have to take care of guaranteeing that messages have been received.

❑ **Message Router** – This method is not a true alternative but rather a possible extension of either of the above two. A third party is used to take care of the communication between two agents. This third party can make guarantees that it will keep re-trying until messages go through as well as make sure that at least the structure of the message is in the right format. The best current metaphor would be a mail server. When we sent e mails to another person we do not send it directly to that person's computer but to a mail server that will then take care of transmitting it to its final destination and will also notify us if it is unable to transmit that message. The disadvantage of this method is that it is the most heavyweight; however, in terms of reliability it offers the best option and certainly any large scale agent-based systems would eventually require such a facility. The Jini `EventMailbox` uses exactly this ideas to notify objects of remote events they registered an interest in.

All three methods have their place within an agent framework and in Paradigma the wish is to abstract above the method by making the communication method transparent to the agents.

A Snapshot of Paradigma

We will conclude our look at the Paradigma Agent implementation environment by having a look at a situation that illustrates all aspects of the system:

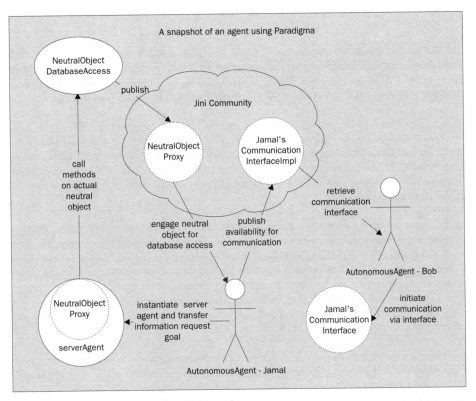

In the illustration we have an autonomous agent (Jamal) that wishes to access a database in order to gain some information. Jamal can achieves this goal by locating a neutral object that provides such a service. The neutral object is engaged and transformed into a server agent with the goal of querying the database. Because this neutral object has a description of its capabilities attached as entries to the proxy in the Jini lookup service Jamal is able to formulate the right type of goals and plans for the neutral object to achieve. In the meantime, Jamal also makes itself available for contact by other agents through the publication of a communication interface implementation. Another autonomous agent (Bob) that wishes to communicate with Jamal does so by retrieving the implementation of the communications interface. This communication interface can be though of as a special kind of neutral object whose capabilities are geared towards relaying messages to Jamal. These communications may eventually evolve into any one of the methods discussed previously.

Conclusions

Paradigma has been developed as a result of very practical concerns – supporting the development of agent-based systems. In order to achieve that it needs to be immediately accessible to developers. Therefore, it needed to be constructed using appropriate underlying technologies that were widespread and largely standardized.

Jini fits the bill perfectly for these purposes. It provides the developer not only with a set of ideas that are easy to understand and integrate into the design of a system but also with code that one can use immediately to have a working system. It is a network-aware environment that is likely to find widespread use and thus act as an enabler for the further evolution of the framework.

The final ingredient that it is hoped will make Paradigma dynamic and expandable is the use of XML as the description language for all entities within the problem domain. Attributes, capabilities, motivations, goals, and plans are all described using XML. This allows for the dynamic redefinition of agents without, necessarily, having to resort to Java code. It also enables the use of diverse capabilities by different agents. One can imagine libraries of goals, plans, and capabilities that can be used to construct agents as the circumstances require.

Several issues have not been addressed in this chapter, partly due to space constraints, partly due to focus, and partly because they have not yet been tackled in the context of Paradigma. We should note, however, that the scope for extending this work to address many other such issues is considerable. For example, the issue of payment for services rendered by agents, whatever the form of the engagement, is likely to be a key concern for the broader acceptance of systems developed in this way. Jini could provide for such cases via an extension of its leasing mechanisms. Services themselves could grant leases through the same mechanisms to consumers of their resources including, for example, the payment of some amount towards the use of the service.

We are entering a new phase of agent research and development in which the focus must be less on the exciting and inspirational issues, and more on the mundane but fundamental issues of consolidation that underlie any serious technological effort. These include the integration with, and use of, existing technology that is tried and tested, the application of agent solutions to pre-existent problems, the linkage of agent theory and practice, and the augmentation of the technology with facilities for development. These are exactly the issues that we are beginning to address through the Paradigma implementation environment described in this chapter.

Paradigma is still in its infancy, but the underlying ideas are proving fertile ground for further development and research. The experience and knowledge gained by the attempt will, unavoidably, lead to the final goal of a complete framework within which one can describe and solve problems using the agent paradigm.

Resources

For those wishing to delve deeper into the theoretical aspects of the agent framework presented above please point your browsers at the Agent-Based Systems Group at the University of Warwick, Department of Computer Science:

> http://www.dcs.warwick.ac.uk/absg/html/publications.html

Other attempts for agent frameworks using Jini are:

> Control of Agent Based Systems: http://coabs.globalinfotek.com/

The Ronin Framework: http://gentoo.cs.umbc.edu/ronin

General information on Multi-Agent Systems can be found at the following URL:

> http://www.multiagent.com

The home of FIPA, the body attempting to provide standards for agent systems is at:

> http://www.fipa.org

Finally, the writers can be contacted at:

> Ronald Ashri: r.ashri@europe.com

> Michael Luck: Michael.Luck@dcs.warwick.ac.uk

Types of Agent Systems

Based on the agent characteristics introduced above and the number of agents within an agent system we will introduce a possible classification of agent-based systems into three large categories of information management agents, user-interface agents and finally cooperation agents. The differences are due to the focus and number of agents within the system.

Information Management Agents

Information management agents are focused on processing large amounts of information using techniques that will allow them to classify that information according to the desired attributes. A typical example is that of a webcrawler roaming the Web, classifying sites. A similar type of application is that of maintaining distributed hypertext information structures by making sure that all links are valid, and then updating links when sites move. An army of such agents can be deployed to maintain either company-wide intranets where information and people move and change locations continuously or portals such as Yahoo! Lately, there has also been an increased interest in the use of agents for routing data in a network by continuously roaming the network and locating the optimum paths for data to take. Mobility is an important characteristic of such agents, as they tend to travel to the point of information thus achieving a distribution of computation and reducing information overload at the servers.

Information agents are not highly visible and work mostly in the background. Here, a technology such as Jini can be used to provide a port of call for such mobile agents. A possible scenario is one where webcrawlers roam the network collecting information and then join their Jini community when a quota of classified sites has been reached. Agents responsible for maintaining the websites for users can then *buy* the information of the webcrawlers and use it to update their own sites.

User-Interface Agents

Interface agents have a special appeal, as they will directly transform the way we interact with computers and there has been extensive research on the topic. Maes, at MIT, wrote an influential paper on the topic appropriately called "Agents that reduce work and information overload "(*Maes, P. (1997). Agents that Reduce Work and Information Overload. In Bradshaw, J.M. (ed) Software Agents, 145-164. AAAI Press/MIT*). Maes's definition of an interface-agent is one that uses "(..) Artificial Intelligence techniques to provide active assistance to a user with computer-based tasks". Such agents watch us as we go about our tasks and pro-actively intervene in order to aid us either by instruction or by carrying out part of the task for us. A real-life example of such agents are the (in)famous Microsoft Office agents which pop up offering assistance whenever they believe we require it. The Microsoft agents, however, are currently much simpler than the ones envisioned by Maes as they only react to simple queues and have no real understanding of their users.

The use of artificial intelligence is an important issue in the construction of such agents since the ability to understand their user and reason about the tasks at hand would be extremely useful. In such a case they would need to have a large amount of domain-specific knowledge and the ability to communicate their suggestions to the user in a clear manner. The tasks such agents might deal with range from e mail or news filtering to personalized help and meeting scheduling, including collaboration with other users' agents.

In any case, the importance of an infrastructure such as Jini is evident, since it would allow for the seamless interaction of such agents. Imagine the scenario where a project manager decided to schedule a team meeting and so simply by noting the meeting in an agenda that is monitored by a personal agent. The agent, being a part of a larger Jini community, could then take the initiative and notify the personal agents of the other team members about the meeting, which might lead to a negotiation between agents in the case of a clash of timetables and a new time being agreed upon, leading to an update of all the members' agendas. If there are more problems, the process may be repeated until the issue is settled. With Jini the same agent that resides on your desktop machine can find you when you are using a portable device such as the Palm V and when you are using you home computer.

So, interface agents lead us to a new user-interface paradigm of indirect manipulation and technologies such as Jini enable the interaction of agents over organization-wide networks. They can range from relatively simple agents, such as the Microsoft ones, to more complex agents that use AI techniques while attempting to resolve issues such as learning the user's preferences, adapting to changes in those preferences (as we do tend to change our mind), learning to obey user instructions, reasoning about the task being performed and, in addition, communicating with the user and understanding the user's needs through natural language processing. Perhaps the most challenging issue, however, is how such agents gain our trust and convince us to use them without checking their every move.

Cooperative Distributed Problem Solving Agents

Although interface agents could partly be thought of as distributed problem-solvers, their focus is on directly making the interaction of a user with a computer easier, and they might never use a network (although in today's world that is highly unlikely). Distributed problem solving agents, on the other hand, gain their utility exactly because of their distribution over a network, enabling them to maximize the use of computational power.

This category refers to agents that are focused on resolving problems by taking advantage of a decentralized approach to the issue. Such problems may range from commercial transactions to workflow management and manufacturing process coordination.

The most important characteristics of such multi-agent systems are the ability of agents to negotiate, cooperate and, in cases like workflow management and manufacturing, coordinate with other agents. The need for coordination becomes immediately clear if we consider the example of a car manufacturing plant with agents representing each automated machine in the plant. The agents would need to coordinate their actions in order to maximize the throughput of the plant and avoid a chaotic situation were each machine is operating with no concept of what other machines are doing.

Such agents may reside in diverse platforms and communicate via what is called an Agent Communication Language (ACL). The use of standardized ACLs enables any type of agent to communicate with other agents as long as it is able to understand the ACL used by all. Efforts are already underway to provide a standard ACL by the Foundation of Physical Agents (FIPA). FIPA is a standard-setting body that is concerned with the establishment of standards for agent-based systems and believes in the utilization of technologies such as Jini for agent-based systems, something that is illustrated by the active participation of Sun in FIPA, with Geoff Arnold on the members' board.

The benefits Jini has to offer to these types of agent systems is the ability to spontaneously create agent communities that come together to solve a problem. Services make use of other services and can in turn be used by others, each trying to achieve their own specific goals. By taking this perspective Jini technology encourages the construction of systems of high complexity and robustness.

Enabling Technologies

Having gone through an overview of the motivations for and types of agent-based systems, we now examine which technologies are required to enable the development of such systems. We begin with Artificial Intelligence (AI), a field that has a lot to offer towards the construction of intelligent agents. Although, AI is not *necessary* for agent-based systems its use would undoubtedly enhance their capabilities. Subsequently, we discuss OO languages and what requirements they should fulfill in order to be suitable for agent-based systems.

Artificial Intelligence

*"The job of AI is to design the **agent** program: a function that implements the agent mapping from percepts to actions".*

(Stuart Russell and Peter Norvig. Artificial Intelligence: A Modern Approach. Prentice Hall. 1995)

Artificial Intelligence (AI) is a largely fragmented field since researchers have traditionally focused on specific subfields with little or no integration between them. However, the attempt to create what Russell and Norvig call the "agent program" has motivated the desire for all the different aspects of AI to be integrated under one heading. As mentioned earlier AI does not need to be considered as a necessary discipline for the development of agents; however, in the next paragraphs we will explain the gains that are to be had through its use by describing some of the most important issues AI can answer.

Problem Solving and Planning

Typically, an agent program may need to perform some amount of problem solving. We can consider this activity as the search for a solution within a state space of all the possible outcomes. The answer will be a series of actions that will lead us from the current state to the desired state, or *goal state*, for our agent.

So, for example, if an agent had the goal of locating the hotel its user booked in an unfamiliar city it could consider the map of the city as the state space, with the solution being the path from the current location to the hotel. AI provides us with efficient algorithms to perform this search, including the very important notion of search using heuristics. Heuristics are rules of thumb that act as guides to our search in situations where the state space is so large that it is practically impossible to review every single situation. The most well known example is that of a chess game where the state space is of the order of 35^{100}, making it impossible for a computer to play chess without the use of heuristics.

However, in the real world information is very often incomplete and search techniques cannot be applied since the state space is impossible to define and, even if it possible, it would turn out to be too big.

Planning takes the approach that most of the time big parts of the world are not related, making it expensive and unnecessary to go through a series of unrelated states until we find the desired one. Plans describe exactly which actions we need to execute when in a specific state in order to achieve the desired state. They allow us to use a "divide and conquer" technique where a problem is taken apart into sub-plans that are individually pursued through a specification of series of actions. We will examine plans in more detail as they are used by agents in Paradigma to achieve their goals.

Learning

We have talked of agents that know user's preferences and employ them to make decisions about what the user might like to know or do. We also talked about agents that control business processes, coordinating their actions to achieve goals such as increased production or a customer quote service. The question now is how can such agents improve their capabilities in order to better execute their tasks? The field of machine learning provides some answers.

In the previous section we introduced the example of an agent searching a map in order to find the route to the hotel its user wanted to go to. If that agent had a learning capability it would be able to store the route in a knowledge base, effectively *learning* that route, thus enabling the agent simply to recall it from its knowledge base the next time it is required to provide those directions.

The above is one of the simplest examples of learning; a more complex agent would have a more ambitious learning capability consolidating knowledge gained over a long period of time in order to come to conclusions about traffic movement or anticipating that if it is evening and we are in that city we would like to go to the restaurant, thus taking the initiative to autonomously recall the route for us. The possibilities are practically endless, making learning one of the most exciting fields of AI and certainly the field where breakthroughs are required for a revolution in intelligent agents.

Expert Systems

Until now we have seen how agents can use AI to solve problems and even learn new things, but how do they learn to act in environments where large amounts of pre-existing knowledge is required, and for that matter, how do we extract that knowledge in order to encode it for our agents to use?

Knowledge engineering concerns itself with extracting that knowledge from the experts that possess it and formalizing it using an appropriate logic language. A reasoning mechanism for that language can then be employed to allow us to make inferences from the knowledge base.

Expert systems largely depend on correct knowledge engineering in order to aid users. As their name suggests, they are software systems that are able to manipulate knowledge in a certain domain to a high degree of accuracy. They usually consist of a long set of *if-then-else* rules used to deduce what actions should be taken in response to a number of facts relating to the current situation. A software agent could use such an expert system in order to handle complicated situations on its own without human guidance, since knowledge may already be encoded in its database.

Communicating Agents

We have repeatedly mentioned that the ability to communicate is vital for multi-agent systems. Research in linguistics and AI has enabled a better understanding of agent communication languages (ACLs). A message in an ACL is typically composed of two parts, the communicative act and the content of the message. The communicative act forms the outer skeleton of the message and defines the nature of the system such as ASK, TELL, INFORM. These are based on a linguistic analysis of the way we communicate where parts of the language can be considered as actions, such as "I declare that..." and are therefore called communicative acts.

The actual content of the message is the domain specific component that complements the communicative act to complete a message. So, a simplified example might be a message such as "ASK ABOUT current-stock-price FOR xyz" where ASK ABOUT is the communicative act and current-stock-price the content.

So, agents need to use the same ACL in order to be able to communicate, as well as have the same definitions of terms in the contents of the message. Such definitions are captured in what are called ontologies. They can be thought of as databases of definitions that can be used to resolve the exact meanings of agents.

Another aspect of communication for agents is that of communicating with humans. This aspect is addressed by research in natural language processing, a field that has received a lot of publicity with commercially available systems. There is still work to be done before we can communicate naturally with software agents but there is rapid progress and the target will eventually be reached.

Jini Client or Service	JavaSpaces and Helper Services

Jini Client and Service Support Helper Utilities

Jini Discovery Management Helper Utilities

Jini Protocol Helper Utilities

Jini Network Protocols	
	RMI and Rich Object Semantics
	Java VM and Networking

Network Protocols

Section 4

Appendices

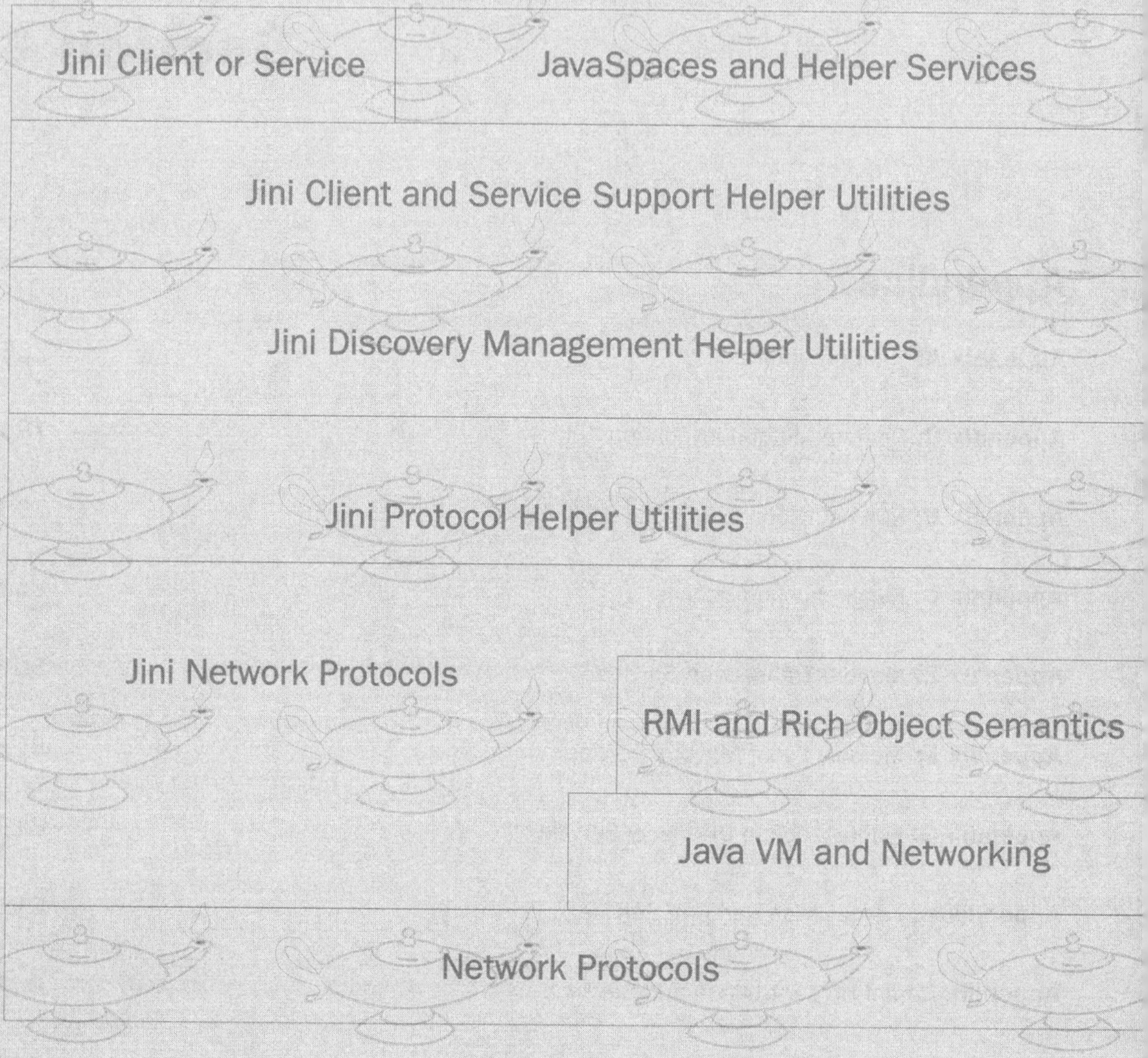
Jini Client or Service
JavaSpaces and Helper Services
Jini Client and Service Support Helper Utilities
Jini Discovery Management Helper Utilities
Jini Protocol Helper Utilities
Jini Network Protocols
RMI and Rich Object Semantics
Java VM and Networking
Network Protocols

Online discussion at http://p2p.wrox.com

Jini Core Interfaces

This appendix presents an overview of the Jini core packages and interfaces. The Jini Technology Starter Kit includes package and interface documentation in the form of JavaDoc HTML documents. In a similar way to the JavaDoc documentation for the Java Development Kit (JDK), the Jini JavaDoc documentation is the authoritative source of API information when programming Jini services. Rather than simply repeat all of that information, this appendix will focus on providing a linear presentation of only the most important interfaces and classes of the core Jini packages. Packages are therefore discussed in order of dependency and, within each package, only selected interfaces and classes are presented. Package and interface descriptions are meant to complement JavaDoc information: common uses of each interface or method are presented, with examples where appropriate, along with warnings about common errors.

The interfaces presented are based on the Jini 1.1 (beta) specification and documentation available at http://www.sun.com/jini/. The compiled class files for the core packages described are available in the jini1_1\lib\jini-core.jar archive file; source code is available in the jini1_1\source\vob\jive\src\net\jini\core directory.

Core Package Overview

The Jini core packages are part of the net.jini.core package. The figure overleaf shows a UML class diagram highlighting the dependencies between the core packages. The lease and event packages contain the core definitions for distributed events and leases. These packages are used to build the core Jini lookup functionality. Discovery and entry package interfaces, as indicated by the arrows, are used by the lookup service in naming and attribute declarations, respectively. Finally, the core transaction interfaces are included in the transaction package, presented last because it is not directly used by the other core packages.

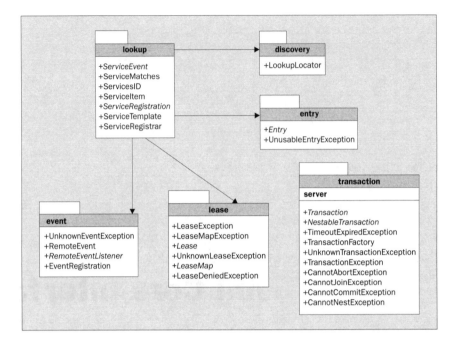

net.jini.core.lease

The Jini core `lease` package contains interface and exception definitions related to distributed leasing. A lease represents a contract between a server and a client concerning the provision of a certain service. Leasing is also the primary distributed garbage collection mechanism of the Jini architecture. The package contains two interface definitions, `Lease` and `LeaseMap`, and several lease-related exceptions:

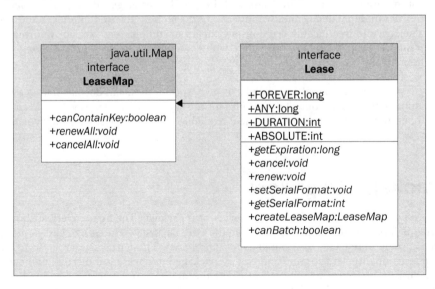

Lease

```
public interface Lease {
```

The `Lease` interface is implemented by objects returned from distributed services ('lease grantors') in response to a resource request. Unlike other Jini interfaces, implementing objects must be proxies, and not simple RMI stubs – this restriction is due to the fact that some `Lease` methods do not throw `RemoteException`. Lease proxies are serializable objects encapsulating the remote communication primitives used to contact the lease grantor. Proxies may employ any communication mechanism built on the Java 2 sockets mechanism (RMI, CORBA, etc.). Clients receiving a lease must check its expiration, as it may not match the one requested. There are two notable lease durations:

```
long FOREVER;
long ANY;
```

The constant `FOREVER` indicates a request for an assignment of an infinite lease; `ANY` indicates a request for a lease of any duration the granting service has available.

Lease expiration time is measured in milliseconds relative to the local clock:

```
long getExpiration();
```

So the lease duration can be calculated by using `(lease.getExpiration()` – `System.currentTimeMillis())`.

A leased resource can be cancelled early:

```
void cancel() throws UnknownLeaseException,
                     RemoteException;
```

Upon return, the lease grantor should no longer send any leased-resource related events to the subscriber.

A lease can be renewed for a given duration (in milliseconds):

```
void renew(long duration) throws LeaseDeniedException,
                                 UnknownLeaseException,
                                 RemoteException;
```

As long as there are no exceptions thrown, the renewed expiration time may be obtained by invoking `getExpiration()`. As noted earlier, the lease grantor may grant a shorter lease than that requested.

Leases are exchanged between distributed systems running independent clocks that may not be synchronized. The `Lease` interface provides a method for storing the duration time when the lease object is serialized using the constants `DURATION` and `ABSOLUTE`:

```
int DURATION;
int ABSOLUTE;
```

The default mechanism, DURATION, stores the lease duration in milliseconds. This is useful for transmitting an instance over the network. In such cases, the uncertainty introduced by the network transmission delay is considered smaller than the uncertainty introduced by the absence of clock synchronization between clients.

The ABSOLUTE mechanism serializes the lease expiration in absolute time. This mechanism is useful when serializing a lease for persistent storage. In such cases, it is assumed that the deserialization will occur on the same machine (therefore clock skew should be small), but that storage duration may be arbitrary.

The default serialization format for leases is DURATION and therefore new Lease instances may be directly exchanged between networked hosts. Before writing a Lease to a persistent storage, users must invoke the setSerialFormat() method for ABSOLUTE. Do not forget to reset the format to DURATION if the lease is to be subsequently sent over the network, especially after reading the lease from persistent storage.

```
void setSerialFormat(int format);
```

The serialization format of this lease (DURATION or ABSOLUTE) is retrieved using:

```
int getSerialFormat();
```

Lease maps are used to batch the renewal of related leases for more efficient bandwidth handling. The following creates a new lease map containing this lease:

```
LeaseMap createLeaseMap(long duration);
```

The final method here can be used to check if this lease can be renewed together with the lease passed as a parameter:

```
boolean canBatch(Lease lease);
```

Batching supports efficient renewal of multiple leases granted by the same service. The above method is usually invoked by utility lease renewal classes, such as the LeaseRenewalManager described in Appendix I.

```
} // Lease
```

net.jini.core.event

The Jini core event package contains the classes relating to distributed events. The package contains the RemoteEventListener interface, the classes EventRegistration and RemoteEvent, as well as the exception UnknownEventException:

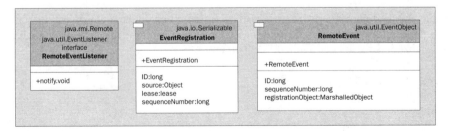

RemoteEvent

```
public class RemoteEvent extends java.util.EventObject {
```

RemoteEvent is the parent class of all distributed events. Users may directly instantiate objects of this class, or extend it for additional functionality. Distributed events are significantly different from local (within a single Java VM) events. This appendix focuses on the distributed event interface. RemoteEvent extends the java.util.EventObject to comply with the JavaBeans event model.

This is the constructor of a new RemoteEvent object:

```
public RemoteEvent(Object source, long eventID, long seqNum,
    MarshalledObject handback);
```

Source is a serializable object representing the event source (an RMI stub or a service proxy). The eventID identifies the type of event relative to the source object. The event sequence (seqNum) hints at the number of occurrences of this event relative to some earlier sequence number. Sequence numbers are guaranteed to differ if and only if the events represented by this object are distinct. Stronger guarantees may be made by objects but are not required by the interface. Finally, handback is the marshalled object that the client provided at registration time and is returned here opaquely (may be null).

The ID describing this event relative to the source object can be obtained using:

```
public long getID();
```

The source is obtained by the inherited method getSource().

The sequence number of this event, relative to some previous event (see constructor description), may be obtained using:

```
public long getSequenceNumber();
```

The marshalled object associated with the registration of this event is retrieved using:

```
public MarshalledObject getRegistrationObject();
```

```
} // RemoteEvent
```

RemoteEventListener

```
public interface RemoteEventListener extends java.rmi.Remote,
                                        java.util.EventListener {
```

Classes wanting to receive notification of remote events implement this interface. Unlike the JavaBeans/AWT event model, where listener interfaces are tied to particular event types, Jini defines a generic listener interface. This means that generic event-handling objects, such as event mailboxes and event forwarders, may be easily coded. It also means that objects must perform their own demultiplexing (categorization) based on the event class, source, and event ID.

Registration for remote event notification is invoked like this:

```
void notify(RemoteEvent theEvent) throws UnknownEventException,
                                    java.rmi.RemoteException;
```

Note that if the event class, source, or ID is unknown, then the method may throw an `UnknownEventException` exception; this will result in the removal of the event subscription.

This notification is synchronous, so the caller will have to wait for this method to return. This design simplifies the verification of successful remote event notification. Unfortunately it also means that event notification services depend on well-behaved client implementations. If your implementation needs to perform remote or other slow or blocking operations upon event notification, these should be performed in a separate thread.

```
}  // RemoteEventListener
```

net.jini.core.discovery

The Jini core `discovery` package contains a single class called `LookupLocator` which encapsulates the unicast discovery URL of a Jini service, and provides utility methods for contacting the service and obtaining a `ServiceRegistrar` (discussed in the `lookup` package section below).

LookupLocator

Jini services support unicast discovery by listening for TCP connections at a given port, by default port 4160. It is therefore possible to describe the location of a Jini service by combining its IP address with its unicast discovery port. The `LookupLocator` encapsulates that information and provides two utility methods that perform the unicast discovery and return a `ServiceRegistrar` object. Notice that because `LookupLocator`s encapsulate the address of a Jini service, they may be invalidated if the service is moved, or assigned a new IP address by some mechanism such as DHCP (Dynamic Host Configuration Protocol).

```
public class LookupLocator implements Serializable {
```

The `LookupLocator` class implements `Serializable` and can therefore be used to store Jini service references persistently, or send references over the network.

```
public LookupLocator(String url) throws MalformedURLException;
```

This constructs a new `LookupLocator` instance storing the unicast discovery address of the Jini service contained in the URL. Jini unicast discovery URLs use the protocol name `"jini"`. For example, the URL `"jini://demo.wrox.com:8000/"` represents the Jini service running on host `"demo.wrox.com"` and listening to the standard port 8000. If the URL does not include a port number, the default port 4160 is used.

```
public LookupLocator(String host, int port);
```

This constructs a new `LookupLocator` instance for the Jini service running on the specified host and listening at the given port.

```
public String getHost();
public int getPort();
```

These are accessor methods for obtaining the host and port number of the Jini service referred to by this locator.

```
public ServiceRegistrar getRegistrar()throws IOException,
                                        ClassNotFoundException;
```

Resolve this `LookupLocator` by contacting the Jini service using unicast discovery, and return a `ServiceRegistrar` proxy (discussed in the `lookup` package below). The result of this method is not cached, therefore a unicast discovery is performed every time.

```
public ServiceRegistrar getRegistrar(int timeout)throws IOException,

ClassNotFoundException;
```

Perform unicast discovery to obtain a `ServiceRegistrar` object, as above, but within a certain timeout. If the timeout is reached before unicast discovery can be completed, an `IOException` is thrown.

```
public String toString();
```

The string representation of a `LookupLocator` object is a Jini URL.

```
} // LookupLocator
```

net.jini.core.entry

The Jini core `entry` package contains interface and exception definitions used in describing service attributes. The package consists of a single interface called `Entry` and the exception `UnusableEntryException`.

Entry

```
public interface Entry extends java.io.Serializable {
}
```

Marker interfaces imply a certain semantic behavior by implementing objects, but do not explicitly define any methods or static attributes. The Entry interface is such a marker interface and extends `java.io.Serializable`. Objects implementing this interface may be attached to a Jini service during registration, or used to help lookup a particular service. Entries support simple exact-match lookup semantics. Exact-matching means that one may lookup instances of an entry with the name attribute "FooBa", for example, but not "any name starting with 'Foo'" (e.g. "Foo*"). Despite its simple appearance, there are several constraints on the structure and behavior of classes implementing this interface:

❑   Entry classes must have a no-argument (default) constructor

❑   Entries may not have primitive and non-public fields

❑   Each entry object public field is serialized separately, as a `MarshalledObject` instance

These constraints are not, however, checked by the compiler, and may not even be verified at run-time, so developers have to be rigorous about the correct use of objects that implement this interface. Notice that the exclusion of private fields prevents encapsulation, usually encouraged in object-based designs.

net.jini.core.lookup

The Jini core `lookup` package contains interfaces and classes used in performing the Jini service lookup. This package builds on the distributed events and leasing packages that were described earlier. The most important interface in this package is the `ServiceRegistrar` interface. Along with the low level discovery and join specifications, this interface forms the glue that holds together a Jini federation. The package also contains classes and interfaces used to describe lookup templates, return lookup match results, and to supply asynchronous notification of service matches.

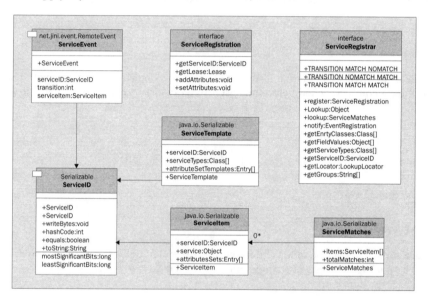

ServiceItem

A Jini service is programmatically viewed as a serializable Java object that may implement one or more service-specific interfaces. Clients locate service objects by contacting Jini lookup services implementing the `ServiceRegistrar` interface (discussed below). Services are assigned a globally unique service ID upon initial registration with a lookup service. In order to assist clients in locating appropriate services, service registrations are annotations with entry objects describing attributes such as location, name, capabilities, etc.

```
public class ServiceItem implements java.io.Serializable {
```

Instances of `ServiceItem` describe the registration attributes of a Jini service. Service items are used by Jini services registering with lookup services, and are returned as part of a query result, or asynchronous event notification.

The `serviceID` attribute contains the unique ID of the Jini service:

```
public ServiceID serviceID;
```

The service ID is assigned at initial registration time by the first lookup service discovered. Jini services are required to store their service ID persistently and use the same ID in all registrations of a given service object. `ServiceID` is a 128-bit value built using a combination of time, random number, and node identification making the creating of two equal IDs by different lookup services virtually impossible.

The service attribute contains a reference to a proxy object or RMI stub used to communicate with the Jini service:

```
public Object service;
```

The serializable `service` object implements one or more service-specific interfaces, as well as standard Jini interfaces such as `net.jini.admin.Administrable` (see Appendix I).

The `attributeSets`, below, is an array of `Entry` objects used to describe the Jini service's characteristics:

```
public Entry[] attributeSets;
```

It may contain standard Jini entries contained in `net.jini.entry` (see Appendix I), as well as other service-specific entry instances.

A simple constructor for `ServiceItem` instances is:

```
public ServiceItem(ServiceID serviceID, Object service, Entry[] attrSets);

} // ServiceItem
```

ServiceTemplate

```
public class ServiceTemplate implements java.io.Serializable {
```

Instances of `ServiceTemplate` are used in the lookup of Jini services and subscription for asynchronous notification of Jini service changes.

The semantics of template matching are limited to an exact match. There are three attributes to a service template: the service ID, interfaces implemented or extended by the service object, and an array of attribute entries:

```
public ServiceID serviceID;
public Class[] serviceTypes;
public Entry[] attributeSetTemplates;
```

Any and all of these attributes may be `null`, indicating wildcard status. For example, consider the task of locating all administrable services. A service template with both `serviceID` and `attributeSetTemplates` values set to `null` can be created, but with `serviceTypes` assigned the one-element array containing your search criteria: `net.jini.admin.Administrable.class` in this case. If the `attributeSetTemplates` array is not `null`, the template will match service items with entries of the same type whose attributes match the non-null attributes of the entries in the array. Note that because a null `Entry` attribute is interpreted as a wildcard, there is no way to specifically match entries with null values. For example, it is not possible to look for services with entries of type `net.jini.lookup.entry.Name` whose name value is `"null"`. Whenever such functionality is required, one possible solution is to include a boolean attribute called `isNameNull`.

A simple constructor for service template objects:

```
public ServiceTemplate(ServiceID serviceID, Class[] serviceTypes,
    Entry[] attrSetTemplates);


} // ServiceTemplate
```

ServiceRegistrar

```
public interface ServiceRegistrar {
```

The ServiceRegistrar interface is a non-remote interface used to communicate with a Jini lookup service. Lookup services provide proxy objects that implement this interface. This enables clients and services to access the lookup functionality of the Jini federation. Instances may be obtained by implementing the Jini discovery protocol, or by using the net.jini.lookup.JoinManager utility (see Appendix I).

A service described by the service item, is registered for at most leaseDuration milliseconds, like this:

```
ServiceRegistration register(ServiceItem item, long leaseDuration)
    throws RemoteException;
```

This requests registration of the Jini service described by the service item for the given initial maximum duration.

When a lookup service receives a registration request with a null item.serviceID, it checks to see if the service object is equal to one registered by another service. If a matching service is found, its registration is first deleted, and then the new registration parameters (item.attributeSets) are used with the old serviceID. Otherwise, if no matching service object is found, a new unique ID is assigned. Calls to register(...) are idempotent, meaning that repeated invocation following a communication failure is safe and will result in a single registration. Registering a service again results in the old service item being removed and the new one being added. It is recommended that users avoid invoking this method directly, by having the net.jini.lookup.JoinManager utility handle discovery and registration (see Appendix I). Use of JoinManager will ensure correct implementation of the join semantics.

The lookup service looks for a service object belonging to a service that matches the template, returning null if none is found. Note that this lookup method returns the service object directly, and requires additional calls to determine the associated service ID and items:

```
Object lookup(ServiceTemplate tmpl) throws RemoteException;
```

If the template matches more than one service item registered with the lookup service, the method returns a single match chosen arbitrarily (choice is implementation dependent). This means that successive invocations cannot be used to iterate over all matches. Instead, the lookup() method below should be used:

```
ServiceMatches lookup(ServiceTemplate tmpl, int maxMatches)
    throws RemoteException;
```

This method will look up the service items of at most maxMatches services matching the template, and return the results in an array of ServiceItem objects contained in a ServiceMatches object. The ServiceMatches object also contains an attribute representing the total number of matches, allowing callers to check if more services could be matched by increasing maxMatches. If no matching services are found the result is an empty array. If a service item cannot be deserialized, the corresponding ServiceMatches.items entry is set to null. It is therefore important to check for null values in the items array and handle them appropriately. Similarly, errors in deserializing service attributes (Entry objects) may result in null values stored in the service item Entry array.

Three transition constants are used to look up change notification registrations:

```
int TRANSITION_MATCH_NOMATCH;
int TRANSITION_NOMATCH_MATCH;
int TRANSITION_MATCH_MATCH;
```

❑ TRANSITION_MATCH_NOMATCH: receives notification if a service item that used to match the template no longer does. Events of this type may be triggered by the removal of a service from the federation, or by the modification of a service's attributes.

❑ TRANSITION_NOMATCH_MATCH: receives notification of service items that match the service template. Events of this type will be triggered when new matching services register, or when appropriate modifications are made to the attributes of existing services.

❑ TRANSITION_MATCH_MATCH: receives notification of changes in matching service items that don't affect the fact that the service matches. For example, if one looked for all Jini services implementing a given interface, independent of lookup entries, they would receive notification if one of these services had its net.jini.lookup.entry.Name entry value changed. This may be useful in applications such as browsers where entry changes may need to be reflected in the graphical presentation.

These transition constants may be used individually, or in combination using the Boolean OR operator. For example, to receive notification of all possible transitions one would pass (TRANSITION_MATCH_NOMATCH | TRANSITION_NOMATCH_MATCH | TRANSITION_MATCH_MATCH) to the notify() method described below.

```
EventRegistration notify(ServiceTemplate tmpl, int transitions,
    RemoteEventListener listener, MarshalledObject handback,
    long leaseDuration) throws RemoteException;
```

This method registers interest in remote notification of changes to services matching the service template. The types of changes are characterized by the transitions parameter using the constants just described. Callbacks are made to the listener object (a serializable proxy, or an RMI stub). The marshalled object is returned opaquely (unmodified and unexamined) to the listener as part of the callback (see previous discussion of RemoteEvent.notify()). The returned EventRegistration object includes the event ID and the source that will be used in remote event notification, as well as the current event sequence number and lease object.

This code uses lookup to locate the entry classes, used in service registration, that match the given service template:

```
Class[] getEntryClasses(ServiceTemplate tmpl) throws RemoteException;
```

The returned array may be empty (not `null`) if there aren't any matches, or the matching services do not have any attribute entries. Elements of the returned `Class` array may be `null` due to errors in deserializing one or more of the returned values.

The `getFieldValues()` method allows you to directly obtain field values from the entry attributes of services matching the `ServiceTemplate`:

```
Object[] getFieldValues(ServiceTemplate tmpl, int setIndex, String field)
    throws NoSuchFieldException,
        RemoteException;
```

First, the lookup service finds the service items matching the service template. Among these items, it looks for services having entries of the class stored in the `setIndex` location of the template (for example, entries of type `net.jini.lookup.entry.Name`). Finally, from the set of entries matching type entries, it picks up the value of the `field` attribute (for example `"name"`) and returns them stored in arbitrary order within an array. Internally, the lookup service uses the Java reflection API to access the named attribute of the `Entry` class. If the name is mistyped or incorrect the error will only be detected at run-time and a `NoSuchFieldException` will be thrown.

Here's a short example to clarify the use of the `getFieldValues()` method. Consider a print service that wants to find out the room location of other print services without downloading the service proxies. The service would create a service template object with null `serviceID` and `serviceTypes` attributes and a single-element array of entries containing an arbitrary `net.jini.lookup.entry.Location` entry (note that the array can contain other entries as well since the location entry will be identified by an index). At that point, the service invokes the `getFieldValues()` method on the registrar with the created service template, a `setIndex` value of zero (or the value where the `Location` class instance is stored) and `"room"` as the `field` descriptor. The returned array will then contain zero or more `String` objects with the room descriptions of the other printers.

The `getServiceTypes()` method is used to discover additional types (classes or interfaces) implemented by services matching the service template:

```
Class[] getServiceTypes(ServiceTemplate tmpl, String prefix)
    throws RemoteException;
```

For example, if your template matches all services implementing a given `Printer` interface, the returned array will contain all the other interfaces implemented by these services in addition to the `Printer` interface. Additionally, the returned classes may be filtered by name using the `prefix` value. In the example we're using, we could specify interest in additional classes whose name start with `"com.somePrinterManufacturer.jini"`. Note that this method allows you to work around the strict exact match semantics of `ServiceTemplate`, but will only work on service class names.

The local method returning the service ID of the lookup service is:

```
ServiceID getServiceID();
```

Here, a lookup descriptor for this lookup service is obtained using unicast discovery:

```
LookupLocator getLocator() throws RemoteException;
```

The lookup descriptor encapsulates a Jini URL of the form
`jini://hostname.domainname:optionalPort`.

Finally, this is how to retrieve the list of groups that the lookup service currently belongs to:

```
String[] getGroups() throws RemoteException;


} // ServiceRegistrar
```

net.jini.core.transaction

The Jini core `transaction` package contains interfaces and classes supporting client-side distributed transactions with default **ACID** (**A**tomic, **C**onsistent, **I**solated, **D**urable) semantics (see Chapter 9 for more details). Note that the server-side distributed transaction interface does not prescribe specific semantics (such as ACID) when performing two-phase commit. However, use of the classes and interfaces contained in the `net.jini.core.transaction` package does indeed guarantee default ACID semantics. If your Jini service does not require default semantics, it should not use a transaction manager returning transaction objects defined in this package. This is a subtle point that can be easily missed when reading the JavaDoc documentation.

The interfaces `Transaction` and `NestableTransaction` are used to allow clients to communicate with the server. Both interfaces declare an inner class called `Transaction.Created` which is used to return the lease-transaction pair when creating a new transaction. Finally, the `TransactionFactory` enables the creation of `Transaction` and `NestableTransaction` instances using the Factory design pattern.

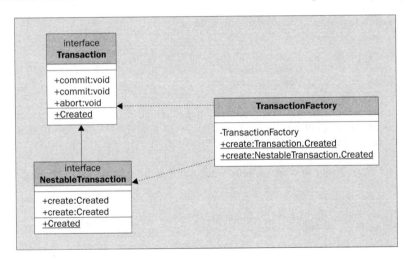

Transaction

```
public interface Transaction {
```

`TransactionManager` returns an object that implements the `Transaction` interface. The interface represents the client's view of a transaction. Use of `Transaction` and `NestableTransaction` provides the server with a framework within which to implement ACID properties.

This is a request for a transaction commit:

```
void commit() throws UnknownTransactionException,
                     CannotCommitException,
                     RemoteException;
```

The request will initiate the two-phase commit voting procedure at the server. The method only returns if the transaction reaches the NOTCHANGED or COMMITTED state; otherwise, an exception is thrown. If a remote exception is thrown, the client will have to inquire about the status directly with the transaction manager.

This is a request that a transaction be committed only after a decision has been made and, if there is time, all participants have been notified:

```
void commit(long waitFor) throws UnknownTransactionException,
                                 CannotCommitException,
                                 TimeoutExpiredException,
                                 RemoteException;
```

Adding the time limit complicates the results of this method. If the transaction manager reaches a decision, and all participants have been notified before the specified timeout, then the method behaves as commit(). If the transaction has reached a decision but has not notified all participants before the specified timeout, then it throws the TimeoutExpiredException. Finally, if the timeout expires before a decision is made, the method does not return until it is made, and then throws the TimeoutExpiredException.

Here, the transaction manager makes a decision to abort:

```
void abort() throws UnknownTransactionException,
                    CannotAbortException,
                    RemoteException;
```

If a decision has not been made, the transaction manager sets its state to "abort", and the method returns. Participants are notified (to roll-back state) asynchronously. If a commit decision has been made the CannotAbortException is thrown.

Here, the transaction manager decides to abort, and wait for the participants to be notified after waitFor milliseconds.

```
void abort(long waitFor) throws UnknownTransactionException,
                                CannotAbortException,
                                TimeoutExpiredException,
                                RemoteException;
```

So if one or more of the participants haven't been notified by the specified timeout, the TimeoutExpiredException is thrown.

This inner class is used by the transaction manager to return a lease-transaction pair:

```
public static class Created implements java.io.Serializable {
    public final Transaction transaction;
    public final Lease lease;
    public Created(Transaction transaction, Lease lease);
} // Created


} // Transaction
```

NestableTransaction

```
public interface NestableTransaction extends Transaction {
```

NestableTransaction extends Transaction and is implemented by transaction objects that can be nested. In contrast to Transaction, however, NestableTransaction provides factory methods for creating new NestableTransaction objects nested within the current one.

Here, a new NestableTransaction is leased using the same nestable transaction manager with the current transaction as its parent:

```
Created create(long leaseTime) throws UnknownTransactionException,
                                       CannotJoinException,
                                       LeaseDeniedException,
                                       RemoteException;
```

Here, however, a new NestableTransaction is leased again with the current transaction as its parent but this time using the specified nestable transaction manager:

```
Created create(NestableTransactionManager mgr, long leaseTime)
    throws UnknownTransactionException,
           CannotJoinException,
           LeaseDeniedException,
           RemoteException;
```

Created is an inner class used to return NestableTransaction and Lease pairs:

```
public static class Created implements java.io.Serializable {
    public final NestableTransaction transaction;
    public final Lease lease;
    public Created(NestableTransaction transaction, Lease lease);
}

} // NestableTransaction
```

TransactionFactory

```
public class TransactionFactory {
```

The factory class is used to create top-level transactions with default semantics (ACID). Clients should use this factory method to create transactions rather than invoking create() directly on the transaction manager because use of factory objects greatly simplifies the program-wide customization transaction manager selection criteria.

Here, a new top-level transaction is created with default semantics, returning a transaction-lease granted pair:

```
public static Transaction.Created create(TransactionManager mgr, long
            leaseTime) throws LeaseDeniedException,
                        RemoteException;
```

The factory method contacts the transaction manager to create the new transaction ID, and returns it encapsulated within an object that implements the `Transaction` interface. Note that if the transaction manager supports nested transactions, the transaction may be cast to `NestableTransaction`.

This creates a new top-level nestable transaction with default semantics. This factory method is called in order to avoid having to cast the transaction returned:

```
public static NestableTransaction.Created create(NestableTransactionManager mgr,
            long leaseTime) throws LeaseDeniedException,
                        RemoteException;


} // TransactionFactory
```

net.jini.core.transaction.server

The core transaction `server` package contains interfaces and classes for implementing the distributed two-phase commit protocol. The two-phase commit protocol is controlled by a transaction manager and cooperating participants. Note that the server classes do not make any guarantees on semantics (as was the case in the `net.jini.core.transaction` classes).

TransactionParticipant

```
public interface TransactionParticipant extends Remote, TransactionConstants {
```

The `TransactionParticipant` interface must be implemented by services wishing to export transactional access to their resources.

The transaction manager requests the participant to prepare to commit the transaction and vote on the outcome:

```
int prepare(TransactionManager mgr, long id)
                            throws UnknownTransactionException,
                                RemoteException;
```

The participant can vote one of three ways: PREPARED, ABORT, or NOTCHANGED. If the participant votes PREPARED, it waits for the manager's commit() or abort() call. Transactions that support the default semantics (ACID) require that the participant persistently store the results of its work within the transaction before returning. If the participant chooses to ABORT then its state should be rolled back, and can then discard information about the transaction. Similarly, for NOTCHANGED, the participant can also discard knowledge of the transaction upon return.

Following the participant's PREPARED vote, the transaction manager signals that the effects of the transaction should be made visible and the effected resources unlocked:

```
void commit(TransactionManager mgr, long id)
    throws UnknownTransactionException, RemoteException;
```

The participant should record the final decision in its logs and return; the participant may then discard knowledge of the transaction upon return.

When one or more participants have PREPARED, but another participant has voted ABORT, the transaction manager signals to the prepared participants that their transaction preparations should be rolled back:

```
void abort(TransactionManager mgr, long id)
    throws UnknownTransactionException,
        RemoteException;
```

When there is only one participant in the transaction, or only one participant that has voted PREPARED but the others NOTCHANGED, or this is the last participant notified after everyone else has voted COMMIT, then the transaction manager invokes this method:

```
int prepareAndCommit(TransactionManager mgr, long id)
    throws UnknownTransactionException,
        RemoteException;
```

This method is added for efficiency to avoid the overhead of two remote invocations (prepare(); commit()). Implementation should be equivalent to calling prepare() and, if the result is PREPARED, invoking commit(). The returned value should be one of ABORT, NOTCHANGED, or COMMITTED.

```
} // TransactionParticipant
```

TransactionManager

```
public interface TransactionManager extends Remote, TransactionConstants {
```

The TransactionManager interface is implemented by objects managing the two-phase commit protocol.

A Factory method is used to create a new transaction that is to be leased for a given duration. The method returns an instance of Created (shown below) containing the transaction ID (a long integer), and the lease granted:

```
Created create(long lease) throws LeaseDeniedException,
                                   RemoteException;
```

A transaction participant that wishes to join an ongoing transaction uses:

```
void join(long id, TransactionParticipant part, long crashCount)
    throws UnknownTransactionException,
        CannotJoinException,
        CrashCountException,
        RemoteException;
```

The potential participant provides its crash count, as well as the transaction ID and the callback reference. This crash count uniquely identifies the version of the participant's storage. Every time the participant loses storage as the result of a crash, the crash count must be updated. Additional join requests with the same crash count from the same participant for a given transaction are ignored. If a request arrives from a participant who has already joined with a different crash count, then the manager throws `CrashCountException`.

The transaction manager queries the current state of a transaction. This is used by participants to check the status of a transaction for which they voted PREPARED but never received notification of commit() or abort():

```
int getState(long id) throws UnknownTransactionException, RemoteException;
```

The manager is asked to initiate the voting process with the transaction participants, and reach a decision:

```
void commit(long id) throws UnknownTransactionException,
                           CannotCommitException,
                           RemoteException;
```

Returns are made once all the votes have been returned indicating PREPARED or NOTCHANGED, or at least one participant has voted ABORT. After returning, the manager notifies the transaction participants asynchronously of the voting decision.

The manager is asked to initiate the voting process with the transaction participants, reach a decision, and wait for the participants to be notified of its decision or the timeout to expire:

```
void commit(long id, long waitFor) throws UnknownTransactionException,
                                          CannotCommitException,
                                          TimeoutExpiredException,
                                          RemoteException;
```

Returns once a decision has been made (COMMIT or ABORT) and all participants have been notified. If the timeout expires before all participants have been notified then the `TimeoutExpiredException` will be thrown.

The transaction manager is asked to abort the transaction:

```
void abort(long id) throws UnknownTransactionException,
                          CannotAbortException,
                          RemoteException;
```

This throws the `CannotAbortException` if a decision to commit has already been made. The method returns once the manager has recorded the abort decision, without waiting for all participants to be notified.

The transaction manager is requested to abort the transaction and wait for either all the participants to be notified, or for the timeout to expire:

```
void abort(long id, long waitFor) throws UnknownTransactionException,
                                         CannotAbortException,
                                         TimeoutExpiredException,
                                         RemoteException;
```

If a decision to commit has already been made, a `CannotAbortException` is thrown. The method returns once the manager has recorded the abort decision, and all participants have been notified. If the timeout expires before all participants have been notified the `TimeoutExpiredException` is thrown.

An inner class is used to return the transaction ID and lease pairs by the `create(...)` factory methods:

```
public static class Created implements java.io.Serializable {
      public final long id;
      public final Lease lease;
      public Created(long id, Lease lease);
   } // Created


} // TransactionManager
```

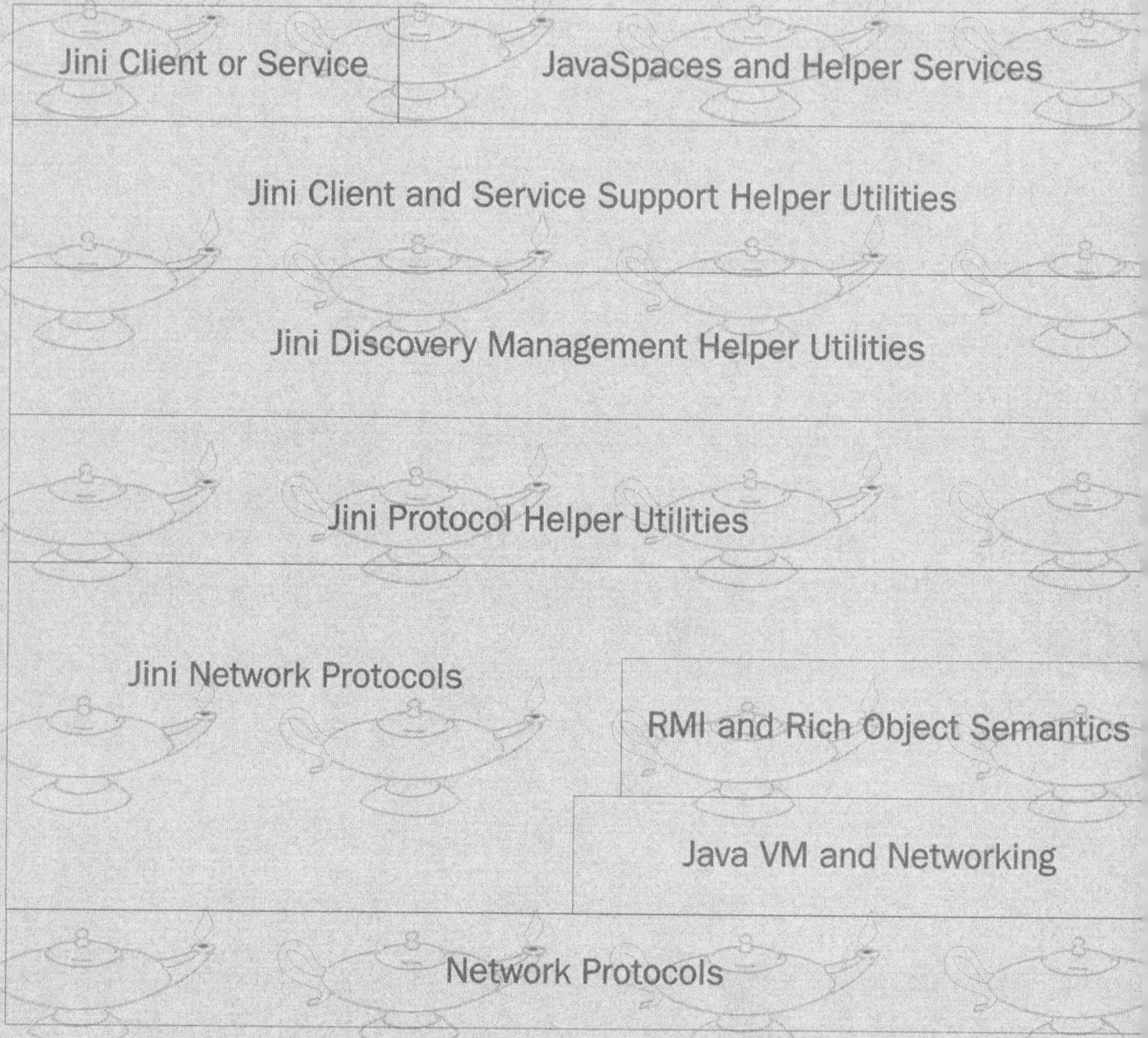

Jini Client or Service
JavaSpaces and Helper Services
Jini Client and Service Support Helper Utilities
Jini Discovery Management Helper Utilities
Jini Protocol Helper Utilities
Jini Network Protocols
RMI and Rich Object Semantics
Java VM and Networking
Network Protocols

Online discussion at http://p2p.wrox.com

B

Remote Method Invocation API

This section presents an overview of the Remote Method Invocation (RMI) API. The discussion is focused on the core interfaces and class implementations that are key to creating both non-persistent and persistent remote objects. The API is based on the JDK 1.2.2 release of Java 2, with comments on differences introduced in JDK1.3 where applicable. This appendix section provides a linear presentation of the RMI interfaces and complements information available in the Java 2 Development Kit JavaDoc documentation. Additional documentation and examples are available from Sun's RMI page at http://java.sun.com/products/rmi.

java.rmi

The **java.rmi** package contains the core Java Remote Method Invocation (RMI) interface and class definitions. It includes a definition of the Remote marker interface, and class definitions of MarshalledObject, Naming, and RMISecurityManager. These are used by the four subpackages: activation, dgc, registry, and server. Selected package classes and interfaces are shown in the UML class diagram overleaf.

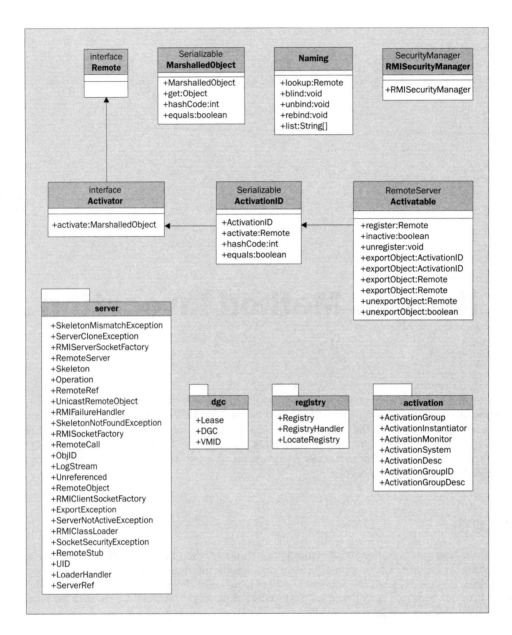

Remote

```
public interface Remote {}
```

Remote is a marker interface used to identify interfaces that may be invoked from a non-local Java Virtual Machine. Interfaces extending Remote must include java.rmi.RemoteException in the throws clause of *all* their methods. From this point on, we will use *remote interface* to refer to a Java interface extending Remote, and whose methods throw the remote exception.

Although a class may implement the `Remote` interface directly, technically speaking, none of its methods will be exportable. Programmers must define an interface extending `Remote` as described, and then implement that interface in their `server` class. Finally, note that the RMI compiler must be invoked on all compiled classes implementing remote interfaces in order to generate the stub and skeleton classes needed at run time.

RMISecurityManager

```
public class RMISecurityManager extends SecurityManager {
    public RMISecurityManager();
} // RmiSecurityManager
```

An instance of the RMI security manager must be installed by programs requiring the download of code and data as part of a remote method invocation. Forgetting to install the RMI security manager is a very common error (happens to seasoned programmers) and may result in silent and inexplicable failures in some of the Jini utilities (described below). The security manager may be installed by adding the following lines to your code (either in the main method, or in the service object constructor):

```
if(System.getSecurityManager() == null) {
    System.setSecurityManager(new RMISecurityManager());
}
```

Note that applets cannot install their own security managers because they are running under the browser's security manager, but the browser's security manager may permit downloaded code to be executed in the applet sandbox.

MarshalledObject

```
public final class MarshalledObject implements Serializable {
```

`MarshalledObject` is used as a container for exchanging objects in a serialized state. Sometimes referred to as a pickled object, instances of this class are used to pass an object opaquely between Java Virtual Machines, without deserializing it at the intermediary points.

For example, consider a Jini remote event subscription request. Part of the request includes an object that will be returned opaquely every time an event notification is made. If a reference to the regular object were passed, the object would have to be serialized at the client and then deserialized at the event server, and its class possibly downloaded. Every time an event occurred, the server would have to serialize the handback object and return it as part of the remote event notification. This is an inefficient process both due to the overhead of serializing a complex object, and to the requirement that the server load the class files for the handback object. By creating an instance of `MarshalledObject` at the client, containing the serialized state of the handback object, this overhead can be avoided.

When creating a marshalled object, its classes are annotated with a codebase URL so that when the object is retrieved (potentially at a different Java VM), the appropriate classes may be retrieved.

```
public MarshalledObject(Object obj) throws IOException;
```

787

This creates a new `MarshalledObject` instance containing the serialized state of the given object. It may throw an `IOException` if that object is not serializable.

```
public Object get() throws java.io.IOException,
    java.lang.ClassNotFoundException;
```

The above method de-marshals (de-serializes) the serialized object contained in this `MarshalledObject`, and may throw `IOException` if a deserialization error occurs, or `ClassNotFoundException` if the object class cannot be loaded.

```
public boolean equals(Object obj);
```

This returns `true` if the argument is a `MarshalledObject` containing the same serialized representation of an object, ignoring the class codebase annotation.

```
} // MarshalledObject
```

Naming

```
public final class Naming {
```

The `Naming` class provides static methods for performing remote object lookup, registration, and deregistration. Users will need to install an `RMISecurityManager` before invoking these static methods.

```
public static Remote lookup(String name) throws NotBoundException,
    java.net.MalformedURLException, RemoteException;
```

Looks up a reference to the remote object referred to by the name RMI URL. For example, a program may invoke `Naming.lookup("rmi://myhost:1099/Printer")` to obtain a reference to the remote object registered as `"Printer"` in the RMI registry running on `"myhost"` and listening on port 1099. Note that pre-Java2 JDK implementations did not accept the protocol identifier, but this has now been fixed. This method invocation may fail for various reasons:

❑ an `RMISecurityManager` has not been installed

❑ the URL is malformed (for example, it includes a protocol specifier)

❑ the hostname cannot be resolved (unknown host)

❑ the remote host is unreachable

❑ the RMI registry is not running (or is not listening to the given port)

❑ the registry has been contacted, but no object is bound to that name

❑ the object was found, but an error occurred during deserialization (for example, the object's stub is not in the classpath and its codebase has not been set, or the class files may not be retrieved)

Now let's look at `bind()`:

```
public static void bind(String name, Remote obj)
    throws AlreadyBoundException, java.net.MalformedURLException,
    RemoteException;
```

Binds an object to the given RMI URL. For example, a program may invoke
`Naming.bind("//myhost:1099/Printer", myPrinter)` to bind `myPrinter` to the name
`"Printer"` in the RMI registry running on `"myhost"` and listening on port 1099. This method
invocation may fail for similar reasons to those listed for lookup. An additional restriction is that the RMI
registry must be running on the same host as the Java VM registering the object (for security reasons).

```
public static void unbind(String name) throws RemoteException,
    NotBoundException, java.net.MalformedURLException;
```

Unbinds the object bound to the given RMI URL. This method will also fail if invoked from a Java VM
running on a different host from the RMI registry.

```
public static void rebind(String name, Remote obj)
    throws RemoteException, java.net.MalformedURLException;
```

Rebinds an object to the given RMI URL. Why would an object need to be rebound? RMI objects
extending `UnicastRemoteObject` (covered later) have to be re-exported every time the Java VM is
restarted. Thus, every time such an RMI server is restarted, it must rebind to the RMI registry. Rebind
will succeed even if no object had been previously bound to the given name. It is therefore a common
substitute for using `bind()` when programmers do not care about overriding previous bindings.
`Activation` objects (covered later in this appendix) are automatically rebound by the activation daemon.

```
public static String[] list(String name) throws RemoteException,
    java.net.MalformedURLException;
```

Obtains a list of all names (as URLs) bound to the RMI registry referred to by name. For example,
`Naming.list("//myhost:1099")` will return an array possibly including the string
`"//myhost:1099/Printer"`.

```
} // Naming
```

java.rmi.server

The RMI **server** package contains classes used in supporting RMI at the server side. There are many
classes and interfaces defined in this package, but we will focus on the few commonly used to
implement RMI server objects. The remaining classes may be used to implement custom RMI server
objects, an advanced topic. Selected interfaces and classes of the server package are shown in the
UML class diagram overleaf.

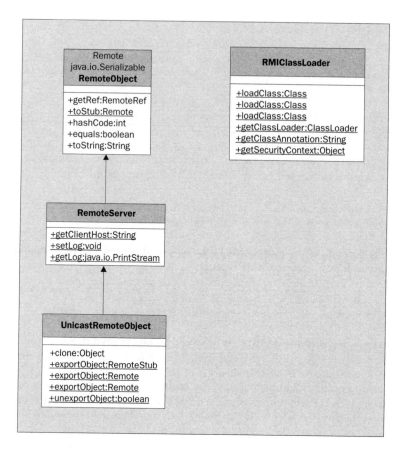

UnicastRemoteObject

```
public class UnicastRemoteObject extends RemoteServer {
```

The UnicastRemoteObject class provides a non-replicated and non-persistent implementation of RemoteServer. The term Unicast refers to the one-to-one communication pattern between clients and the single server. Objects implementing one or more remote interfaces may extend this class to inherit support for the remote server methods and remote semantics of hashCode, equals, and toString. Alternatively, the static exportObject(...) methods may be used if the remote object needs to inherit from some other class.

UnicastRemoteObject and the Activation class discussed below are the only RemoteServer implementations available currently. Users may implement their own RemoteServer functionality – for example, if they require replicated object services – but must be careful to comply with RMI semantics.

```
protected UnicastRemoteObject() throws RemoteException;
```

A protected constructor that creates and exports a UnicastRemoteObject instance bound to an anonymous (arbitrary) port. Since this is the default constructor, subclasses do not need to invoke it, but it is better practice to invoke super() as the first line in your constructor.

```
protected UnicastRemoteObject(int port) throws RemoteException;
```

A protected constructor for creating and exporting a `UnicastRemoteObject` instance bound to the provided port. If the port number is zero then an anonymous (arbitrary) port is chosen.

```
protected UnicastRemoteObject(int port,
    RMIClientSocketFactory csf, RMIServerSocketFactory ssf)
    throws RemoteException;
```

A protected constructor enabling users to supply their own socket client and server factories to be used in exporting the `UnicastRemoteObject`. As shown in Chapters 2 and 3 on RMI, this constructor may be used to secure RMI communications by providing Secure Socket Layer (SSL) socket implementations. Either of the factories may be null, resulting in use of the default socket factory.

```
public static RemoteStub exportObject(Remote obj)
    throws RemoteException;
```

Static method used in exporting an object implementing a remote interface and not inheriting from `UnicastRemoteObject`. Note that the object must implement the `hashCode`, `equals`, and `toString` methods in a manner complying with RMI semantics. The object is bound to an anonymous port.

```
public static Remote exportObject(Remote obj, int port)
    throws RemoteException;
```

The above is similar to `exportObject(Remote obj)` with an extra parameter for specifying the port number used in exporting the object.

```
public static Remote exportObject(Remote obj, int port,
    RMIClientSocketFactory csf, RMIServerSocketFactory ssf)
    throws RemoteException;
```

Static method similar to `exportObject(Remote obj, int port)` with the addition of explicit socket factories whose functions were described earlier.

```
public static boolean unexportObject(Remote obj, boolean force)
    throws java.rmi.NoSuchObjectException;
```

Static method used to unexport (unbind) a remote object from the RMI runtime. If `force` is `true` then the object is immediately unexported and all pending calls are terminated. Otherwise, if `force` is `false`, the object is only unexported if no calls are pending.

```
} // UnicastRemoteObject (some methods not shown)
```

java.rmi.activation

The Java RMI **activation** package contains classes and interfaces supporting the activation framework introduced in Java 2. As mentioned, `UnicastRemoteObject` objects are not persistent. Thus, upon exit of the Java VM that registered a remote object extending or using `UnicastRemoteObject`, the reference becomes stale. Besides limiting resiliency to errors, this behavior increases resource consumption when several infrequently used remote servers need to be instantiated in the VM's memory.

The activation framework offers a mechanism for persistent registration of remote servers. Briefly, remote object registration is a two-phase process:

1. The remote object is instantiated within a Java VM, and then registered with the `activation` daemon, at which point the Java VM may exit.

2. Based on parameters passed at registration time, the registration daemon 'activates' (wakes-up) the object upon the first request. Depending upon registration parameters, the object may be executed in a dedicated Java VM, or may share it with other `activation` objects. The remote server may also be put to sleep after a certain period of inactivity (configurable).

For further details please refer to Chapters 3 and 4 on RMI.

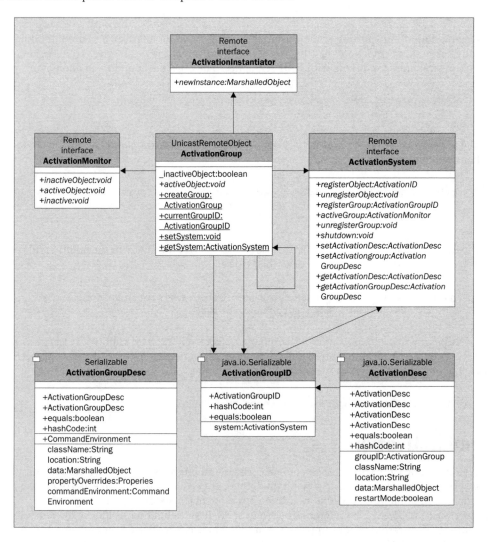

ActivationDesc

```
public final class ActivationDesc implements java.io.Serializable{
```

The `ActivationDesc` class contains the information necessary to activate an object. In particular, the descriptor includes:

- ❏ the object's activation group ID
- ❏ the object's fully-qualified class name
- ❏ the object's codebase
- ❏ the object's restart mode (following failure, restart immediately, or on-demand)
- ❏ a marshalled object used at initialization time

First, the constructor:

```
public ActivationDesc(String className, String location,
    MarshalledObject data) throws ActivationException;
```

Construct a new activation description object. The `className` string contains the name of the class (for example, `"com.wrox.ActivatablePrinter"`). The `location` string contains the codebase for loading the `activatable` class. Finally, `data` is the marshalled object: this is handed back to the object at activation time. When using this constructor, the group ID is set to the default group ID for this VM. Restart mode is set to `false` by default.

According to the JDK JavaDoc documentation, if no default group has been created the constructor will throw `ActivationException`. This is in conflict with the documentation of `ActivationGroup` stating that a new group is implicitly created by this constructor if one has not been created (Bug ID 4344646). Indeed, the JDK1.2.2/1.3 constructor implementation does create a new default activation group if one has not been manually created. Default groups may be manually created using the `ActivationGroup.createGroup` method.

```
public ActivationDesc(String className, String location,
    MarshalledObject data, boolean restart)
    throws ActivationException;

public ActivationDesc(ActivationGroupID groupID, String className,
    String location, MarshalledObject data);

public ActivationDesc(ActivationGroupID groupID, String className,
    String location, MarshalledObject data, boolean restart);
```

The above are variations on the previous constructor allowing the definition of parameters that were assigned default values. Notice that when the groupID is explicitly specified, the `ActivationException` is removed from the throws clause.

```
public ActivationGroupID getGroupID();
```

Returns the activation group ID of this descriptor.

```
        public String getClassName();
```

Returns the class name of the activation object.

```
        public String getLocation();
```

Returns the codebase containing the class files of the activation object.

```
        public MarshalledObject getData();
```

Returns the marshalled object supplied to the activation class at construction time.

```
        public boolean getRestartMode();
```

Return the activation restart mode of this descriptor. When `true`, the object is restarted immediately following the crash of its Java VM or the activation daemon. Otherwise, the object is activated on-demand. Notice that at initial registration time, the object is always activated on-demand. This causes problems for some Jini designs that depend on performing Jini service registration at activation time (the service will never be woken up since no-one will ever know how to contact it). One possible solution is to invoke a method on the object as part of the registration process.

```
    } // ActivationDesc
```

Activatable

The `Activatable` class provides a *persistent* implementation of `RemoteServer`. Objects implementing one or more remote interfaces may extend this class to receive support for the remote server methods and remote semantics of `hashCode`, `equals`, and `toString`. Alternatively, the static `exportObject(…)` methods may be used if the remote object needs to inherit from some other class.

Unlike `UnicastRemoteObject`, remote object export does not happen directly through `Activatable`. Instead, the `Activatable` implementation registers the remote object with the activation daemon, and the object is then instantiated in a separate Java VM.

Complicating this description is the fact that the protected `Activatable` constructors and the static `exportObject()` methods allow users to register and immediately export an activatable object from within the current Java VM. Therefore, it is important to remain aware of the two distinct functions performed by this class:

1. **Registering** the remote object with the activation daemon

2. **Exporting** the object to the RMI runtime

Objects extending `Activatable` or being registered using the static `Activatable` methods, must have a constructor with the following signature:

```
    // Must be implemented by objects that want to be activatable
    public ActivatableImplementation(ActivationID id,
        MarshalledObject data) throws RemoteException {
        // sample implementation :
        super(id, 0); // bind to anonymous port (see explanation below)
        // … other initializations
    }
```

This constructor will be invoked by the `activation` daemon upon first use of the remote server, or following a crash (when the restart option is set to `true`).

We now discuss the `Activatable` class interface:

```
public abstract class Activatable extends RemoteServer {

    protected Activatable(ActivationID id, int port)
        throws RemoteException;
```

The constructor above does not perform object registration. Instead, it is used on the activation daemon side to export the activated object to a given port (may be 0 to indicate an anonymous port). Therefore, it should be invoked from the special constructor (the one invoked by the activation daemon) of objects extending `Activatable`, as shown in the sample implementation above.

```
    protected Activatable(ActivationID id, int port,
        RMIClientSocketFactory csf, RMIServerSocketFactory ssf)
        throws RemoteException;
```

Similar to the previous constructor, with the socket factories added for providing custom mechanisms, such as SSL.

```
    protected Activatable(String location, MarshalledObject data,
        boolean restart, int port)
        throws ActivationException, RemoteException;
```

Constructor used to register and export an object on a specified port. This constructor may be invoked by a subclass of `Activatable` in order to effect registration and immediate export of the object (on the current Java VM).

```
    protected Activatable(String location, MarshalledObject data,
        boolean restart, int port,
        RMIClientSocketFactory csf, RMIServerSocketFactory ssf)
        throws ActivationException, RemoteException;
```

This is similar to the previous constructor but with the addition of custom socket factories.

```
    protected ActivationID getID();
```

Protected method used by subclasses to obtain their activation ID.

```
    public static Remote register(ActivationDesc desc)
        throws UnknownGroupException, ActivationException,
            RemoteException;
```

Static method used to register objects that do not inherit from `Activatable`. Returns the stub for the remote object.

```
    public static boolean inactive(ActivationID id)
        throws UnknownObjectException, ActivationException,
            RemoteException;
```

Static method informing the activation system that the remote object of the given activation ID is inactive.

```
    public static void unregister(ActivationID id)
        throws UnknownObjectException, ActivationException,
            RemoteException;
```

Static method used in deregistering the remote object described by the given activation ID.

```
    public static ActivationID exportObject(Remote obj,
        String location, MarshalledObject data,
        boolean restart, int port)
        throws ActivationException, RemoteException;

    public static ActivationID exportObject(Remote obj,
        String location, MarshalledObject data,
        boolean restart, int port,
        RMIClientSocketFactory csf, RMIServerSocketFactory ssf)
        throws ActivationException, RemoteException;
```

Static methods used in registering and exporting objects that do not extend `Activatable` but wish to support `Activatable` semantics.

```
    public static Remote exportObject(Remote obj, ActivationID id,
    int port) throws RemoteException;

    public static Remote exportObject(Remote obj,
    ActivationID id, int port,
    RMIClientSocketFactory csf, RMIServerSocketFactory ssf)
    throws RemoteException;
```

Static methods used to export a remote object with the RMI runtime. Only objects that do not extend `Activatable` need to invoke one of these methods.

```
    public static boolean unexportObject(Remote obj, boolean force)
        throws java.rmi.NoSuchObjectException;
```

Removes the remote object from the RMI runtime. If `force` is true, then the export occurs independent of pending calls, resulting in termination of such pending calls. Otherwise, if `force` is false, the object is only removed if no calls are pending.

```
    } // Activatable
```

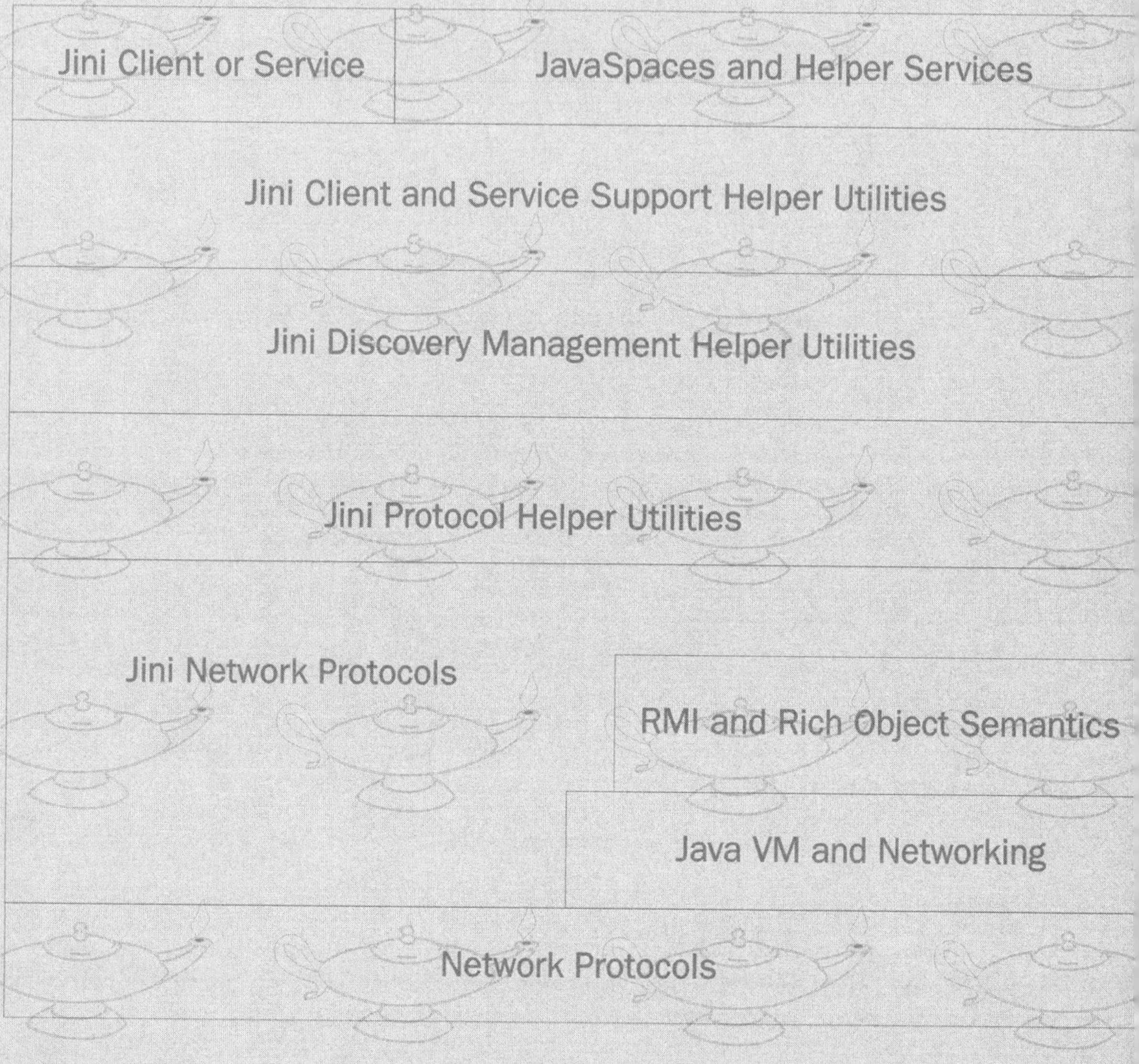

Jini Client or Service
JavaSpaces and Helper Services
Jini Client and Service Support Helper Utilities
Jini Discovery Management Helper Utilities
Jini Protocol Helper Utilities
Jini Network Protocols
RMI and Rich Object Semantics
Java VM and Networking
Network Protocols

Online discussion at http://p2p.wrox.com

C

RMI Activation Daemon

The RMI activation daemon (rmid) is part of the Java Development Kit (starting with JDK1.2/Java 2), and is responsible for the activation of all registered activatable objects. Upon invocation, rmid creates an internal registry on the default port 1098, and binds an ActivationSystem instance with the name java.rmi.activation.ActivationSystem. Note rmid also invokes a Java Virtual Machine (JVM) as a sub-process for each activation group, and monitors these JVMs for failure.

Unlike the other Jini sample services, the RMI daemon is not invoked using the Java interpreter. Instead, Sun provides an executable called rmid (rmid.exe in Windows, rmid in Unix) that starts the RMI daemon in the foreground.

There has been a significant change in RMI daemon behavior starting with JDK 1.3. Because of the flexibility in JVM invocation given to activation groups, the daemon can be used to execute arbitrary programs. Clearly this is non-desirable behavior since any program can potentially use this loophole to break the Java security model! This security issue was previously addressed by restricting access to sensitive functions to only those programs running on the same host. Starting with JDK 1.3, rmid is equipped with a security execution policy.

The rmid execution policy specifies which programs can be executed by rmid, and the command-line parameters that may be provided. For example, an execution policy for the Jini reggie lookup service would look like:

```
grant {
  permission com.sun.rmi.rmid.ExecOptionPermission
    "-Djava.security.policy=c:\\jini1_1\\example\\lookup\\policy";

  permission com.sun.rmi.rmid.ExecOptionPermission
    "-Djava.rmi.server.codebase=*";
```

```
    permission com.sun.rmi.rmid.ExecOptionPermission "-cp";

    permission com.sun.rmi.rmid.ExecOptionPermission
      "c:\\jini1_1\\lib\\reggie.jar";
  }
```

This execution policy allows the reggie registration program to request that the RMI daemon invoke the Java VM with a flag for setting the security policy (to the given file), assigning any codebase, even specifying the JAR file to be executed. By default, a `com.sun.rmi.rmid.ExecPermission` is given for the Java VM executable found in `rmid`'s `java.home` property. Clearly this is a very narrow policy, which restricts the RMI daemon for use with a single service. Other, less restrictive policies may also be defined (refer to Chapter 14 for a discussion on security).

Assuming that the above policy file is stored in a file called `c:\myproj\rmid.policy` it may be installed by adding the following command-line parameter to `rmid` (be careful not to mistype the policy filename because `rmid` will not issue a warning if the file is not found):

```
  -J-Djava.security.policy=c:\myproj\rmid.policy
```

It is important to note that the default behavior of `rmid` has been changed, and if no execution policy is provided at invocation, activation will fail! For the security lax programmers out there, Sun has provided a method for reverting to pre-JDK1.3 behavior (not recommended):

```
  -J-Dsun.rmi.activation.execPolicy=none
```

RMID Usage

`rmid` accepts the following command line parameters:

- ❑ `-port`: optional flag for specifying the port to which the internal RMI registry is bound (default is 1098)

- ❑ `-log <dir>`: optional flag for specifying the directory where daemon log files will be kept (default is the current directory)

- ❑ `-stop`: stops the currently running daemon cleanly (can be called as part of the host shutdown procedure). This flag may be used in conjunction with `-port` to identify an RMI daemon bound to a non-standard port

- ❑ `-C<runtime flag>`: passes an argument to the child process (activation group) at invocation time

- ❑ `-J<runtime flag>`: passes an argument to the Java interpreter executing the RMI daemon

For example, `rmid` may be invoked as follows to emulate pre-JDK1.3 behavior:

```
  rmid -log c:\tmp\rmid_log -J-Dsun.rmi.activation.execPolicy=none
```

The above line invokes the RMI daemon specifying the directory for storing log files, and using the `-J` flag to include the `-Dsun.rmi.activation.execPolicy=none` flag as part of the RMI daemon Java Runtime Environment invocation.

The JRE –D flag allows users to modify the environment properties of the Java VM. In this case, the property sun.rmi.activation.execPolicy is bound to the value none which, as previously mentioned, sets the rmid security policy to pre-JDK1.3.

Simple HTTP Daemon

The Jini distribution includes a simple pure-Java HTTP server. It may be used during development, but should not be seen as a replacement for a robust web server such as Apache (see http://www.apache.org).

The HTTP server is part of the jini1_1\lib\tools.jar archive file, and its command-line usage is:

```
java –jar <tools-jarfile> [-port <port-number>] <-dir document-root-dir> [-trees]
[-verbose]
```

- ❑   <tools-jarfile>: the path to the tools.jar file
- ❑   -port <portnumber>: an optional flag for specifying the server port (default is 8080)
- ❑   -dir: an optional parameter specifying the root HTTP directory (defaults to current directory)
- ❑   -trees: an optional flag to enable individual downloading of class files contained within Java archive files
- ❑   -verbose: a flag that is useful when debugging errors in codebases

For example, the following command line :invocation will start an HTTP server on port 8080, serving files from the c:\jini1_1\lib directory:

```
java –jar c:\jini1_1\lib\tools.jar -port 8080 –dir c:\jini1_1\lib
```

For example, the Reggie lookup service could set its code base to http://hostname:8080/reggie-dl.jar in order to export its client-side class files. Note that hostname would have to be replaced by the name or IP address of the host where the HTTP daemon is running. Users should never use localhost or 127.0.0.1 as a hostname since this will result in unexpected failures when code and startup scripts are moved from the development host to the deployment network.

Jini Client or Service	JavaSpaces and Helper Services

Jini Client and Service Support Helper Utilities

Jini Discovery Management Helper Utilities

Jini Protocol Helper Utilities

Jini Network Protocols	
	RMI and Rich Object Semantics
	Java VM and Networking

Network Protocols

Reggie Lookup Service

Reggie is Sun's reference Jini lookup service implementation. It can be used to create a Jini federation. Reggie is an activatable service registered with the RMI activation daemon.

The *Reggie* service class files are included in the executable Java archive file `jini1_1\lib\reggie.jar` and the client class files in `jini1_1\lib\reggie-dl.jar` (relative to the Jini 1.1 installation directory). There are several requirements for running this service:

1. Reggie is an activatable service and therefore requires a running **RMI activation daemon (RMID)**.

2. Reggie needs to **export** class libraries to clients, and therefore the `reggie-dl.jar` archive file must be accessible through a URL codebase.

3. The **codebase** command-line parameter to reggie must point to the URL from step 2.

4. Reggie employs **multicast** network transmission, therefore the Java VM host must have its network interface configured for multicast, and a multicast route must be available. In Microsoft Windows machines this is usually performed automatically; Unix and Linux hosts may need to be configured (see Appendix J).

5. Reggie needs to maintain a persistent state across activations, and therefore must be configured with a **storage directory.**

6. Finally, reggie requires permissions to perform network operations, Jini discovery, and file operations within the storage directory. An appropriate **policy** file must be provided. Using the `policy.all` file is *strongly discouraged* since the registry will be downloading and deserializing `Entry` classes allowing malicious users to execute arbitrary code on the lookup server (by defining a `readObject(...)` method). See Chapter 14 for more security details.

The reggie command line parameters are listed below. Note that arguments must be specified in the order listed:

```
java -jar [setup_jvm_options] jini1_1\lib\reggie.jar codebase_arg
security_policy_file_arg log_directory_arg [groups] [server_jvm] [server_jvm_args]
```

❑   **setup_jvm_options**: optional parameters for the Java VM used to register *Reggie* with the activation daemon (usually none).

❑   **codebase_arg**: URL for downloading the `reggie-dl.jar` client side file. Notice that this is a simple string argument and should *not* use the `-Djava.rmi.codebase=` definition. This is because the URL is not used in this VM but in the Java VM created by the activation daemon.

❑   **security_policy_file_arg**: path to the security policy file to be used in creating the Java VM at activation time (just the filename with a `-D` flag). A sample restricted policy file is available in `jini1_1\example\lookup\policy`.

❑   **log_directory_arg**: path to a directory that will be used to store the *Reggie* persistent state information.

❑   **groups**: optional string containing the set of groups to be handled by *Reggie* (empty signifies all groups). The group names must be enclosed by a 'global' quote, with names separated by commas but no spaces. For example `"com.wrox.uk,printgroup,securitygroup"`.

❑   **server_jvm**: optional path to the Java VM executable that is to be used by the activation daemon when activating *Reggie*.

❑   **server_jvm_args**: optional list of flags to be passed to the `server_jvm`.

For example, on a clean machine (without any other running services) *Reggie* may be started as shown below. The example assumes that the JDK 1.2.2 binary directory is in the search path (otherwise prepend each command with the path). Note that we start the RMI daemon with an empty security policy (`-J-Dsun.rmi.activation.execPolicy=none`; the inclusion of this extra flag ensures that the example will also work in JDK 1.3, should you be using it), and that we use the restricted policy provided in `jini1_1\example\lookup`. The policy file was first edited and the file permission strings were modified as follows (for the Microsoft Windows back-slash path separator; notice the escaping required since these are Java strings; alternatively the single forward-slash path separator may be used):

```
permission java.io.FilePermission "c:\\tmp\\reggie_log", "read,write,delete";
permission java.io.FilePermission "c:\\tmp\\reggie_log\\-", "read,write,delete";
```

The following three command-line invocations are made on separate command prompt windows (enter as one line each; multiple lines are shown for readability):

```
rmid -log c:\tmp\rmid_log -J-Dsun.rmi.activation.execPolicy=none

java -jar c:\jini1_1\lib\tools.jar -port 80 -dir c:\jini1_1\lib -verbose

java -jar c:\jini1_1\lib\reggie.jar
http://hostname:80/reggie-dl.jar
c:\jini1_1\example\lookup\policy
c:\tmp\reggie_log
```

Once the reggie registration program (`reggie.jar`) completes execution, the lookup service will always be available as long as the RMI daemon is running, and the file system does not corrupt the RMI daemon and reggie logs.

New users commonly find this confusing, as even after a reboot, another attempt to start reggie results in an error. Some resolve this by removing all RMI daemon and reggie logs. Users should never really have to perform such deletions (since most users do not modify reggie's source code). You should become used to the fact that reggie, and all other activation services, are persistent. When developing activatable services, you should write a small utility class that deregisters the activatable object from the RMI daemon when needed.

Configuration

Reggie may be configured using the following properties (using the –D flag at activation registration time):

❑ **net.jini.discovery.announce**: number of milliseconds between multicast announcements (default 120000 milliseconds, or two minutes)

❑ **com.sun.jini.reggie.unicastTimeout**: number of milliseconds before attempts to perform unicast discovery with a client or service are timed-out (default 60000 milliseconds, or one minute)

❑ **com.sun.jini.reggie.proxy.debug**: if set (to any value) reggie's proxy will output debugging information to System.err. You may use this property to debug clients receiving null responses to lookup service calls. This is a useful mechanism for discovering security policy misconfigurations, and codebase errors

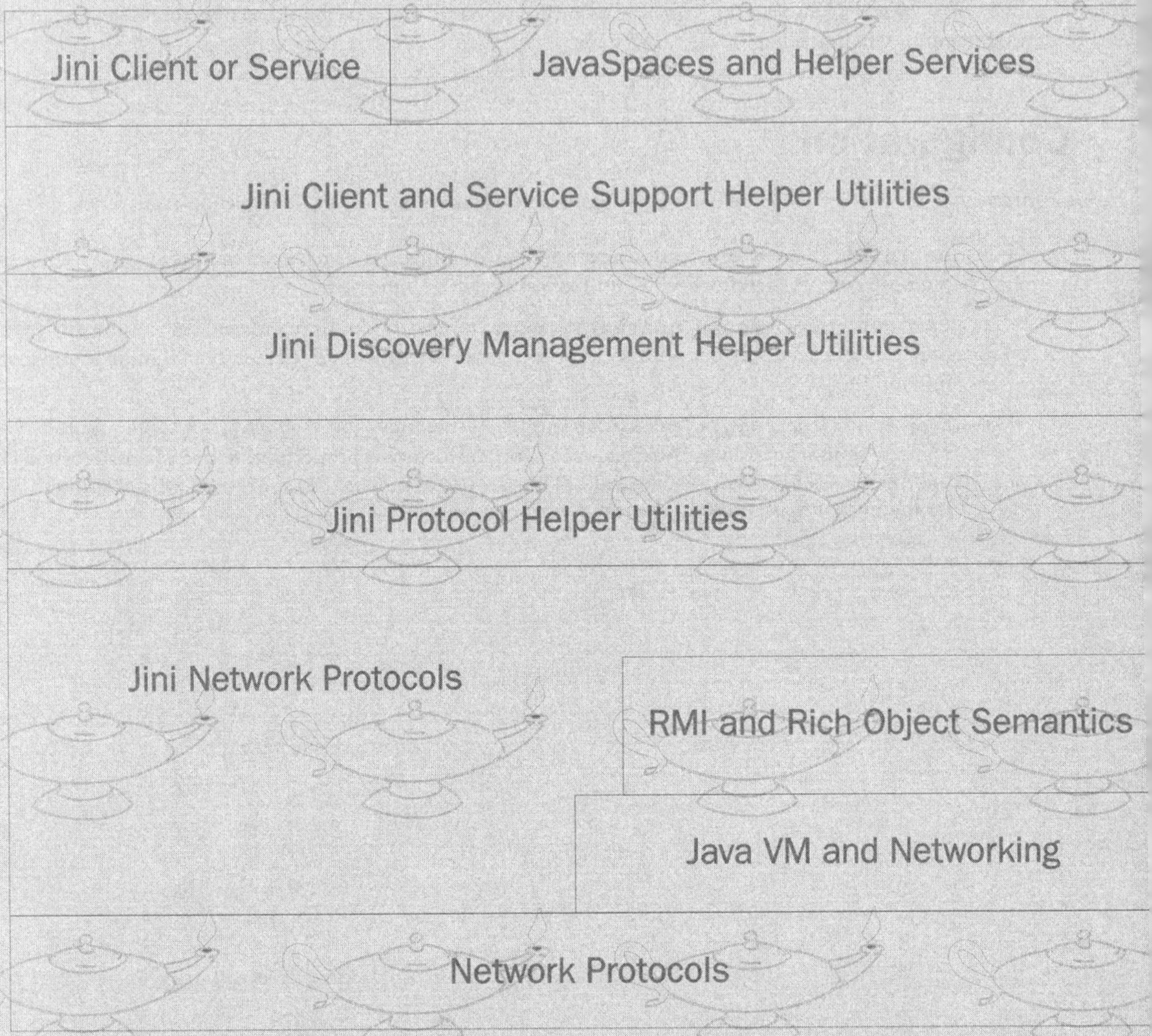

Jini Client or Service	JavaSpaces and Helper Services

Jini Client and Service Support Helper Utilities

Jini Discovery Management Helper Utilities

Jini Protocol Helper Utilities

Jini Network Protocols

RMI and Rich Object Semantics

Java VM and Networking

Network Protocols

Mahalo Transaction Service

Mahalo is Sun's reference Jini transaction service implementation. It may be used as a manager for two-phase commit transactions performed according to the Jini specification. *Mahalo* is an activatable service registered with the RMI activation daemon. *Mahalo* supports the Jini transaction semantics and API and should not be confused with transaction managers supporting the CORBA Java Transaction Service (JTS).

The *Mahalo* service class files are included in the executable Java archive file jini1_1\lib\Mahalo.jar and the client class files in jini1_1\lib\Mahalo-dl.jar (relative to the default installation directory). There are several requirements for running this service:

1. *Mahalo* is an activatable service and therefore requires a running **RMI activation daemon(RMID)**

2. *Mahalo* needs to **export** class libraries to clients, and therefore the **mahalo-dl.jar** archive file must be accessible through a URL codebase

3. The **codebase** command-line parameter to *Mahalo* must point to the URL codebase from step 2

4. *Mahalo* needs to maintain a persistent state across activations, and therefore must be configured with a **storage directory**

5. Finally, *Mahalo* requires permissions to perform network, discovery, and file operations within the storage directory. An appropriate **policy** file must be provided (using the policy.all file is strongly discouraged See Chapter 14 for more security details).

The *Mahalo* command line parameters are listed below (similar to Reggie). Note that arguments must be specified in the order listed:

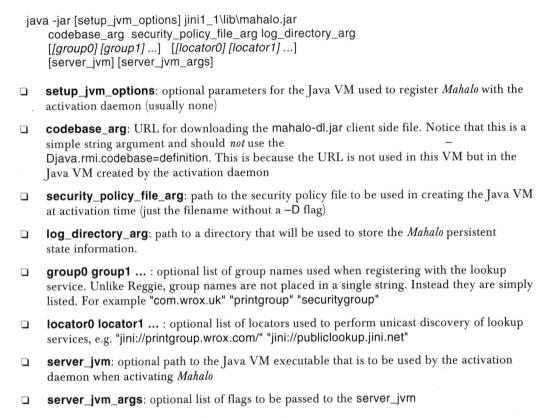

```
java -jar [setup_jvm_options] jini1_1\lib\mahalo.jar
    codebase_arg security_policy_file_arg log_directory_arg
    [[group0] [group1] ...]  [[locator0] [locator1] ...]
    [server_jvm] [server_jvm_args]
```

❏ **setup_jvm_options**: optional parameters for the Java VM used to register *Mahalo* with the activation daemon (usually none)

❏ **codebase_arg**: URL for downloading the mahalo-dl.jar client side file. Notice that this is a simple string argument and should *not* use the $-$ Djava.rmi.codebase=definition. This is because the URL is not used in this VM but in the Java VM created by the activation daemon

❏ **security_policy_file_arg**: path to the security policy file to be used in creating the Java VM at activation time (just the filename without a $-$D flag)

❏ **log_directory_arg**: path to a directory that will be used to store the *Mahalo* persistent state information.

❏ **group0 group1 ...** : optional list of group names used when registering with the lookup service. Unlike Reggie, group names are not placed in a single string. Instead they are simply listed. For example "com.wrox.uk" "printgroup" "securitygroup"

❏ **locator0 locator1 ...** : optional list of locators used to perform unicast discovery of lookup services, e.g. "jini://printgroup.wrox.com/" "jini://publiclookup.jini.net"

❏ **server_jvm**: optional path to the Java VM executable that is to be used by the activation daemon when activating *Mahalo*

❏ **server_jvm_args**: optional list of flags to be passed to the server_jvm

For example, on a clean machine (without any other running services) *Mahalo* may be started as shown below. The example assumes that your JDK 1.2.2 binary directory is in the search path (otherwise prepend each command with the path). Note that we start the RMI daemon with an empty security policy ($-$J-Dsun.rmi.activation.execPolicy=none; the inclusion of this extra flag ensures that the example will also work in JDK 1.3, should you be using it), and that we use the policy provided in jini1_1\example\txn\policy.all.

The following three command-line invocations are made in separate command prompt windows (enter as one line each; multiple lines shown for readability). If you have previously registered Reggie as described, you may skip the first two steps, since the RMI daemon is already running with an empty security policy, and the HTTP daemon exports all Jini archive files in the lib directory.

```
rmid -log c:\tmp\rmid_log -J-Dsun.rmi.activation.execPolicy=none
```

```
java -jar c:\jini1_1\lib\tools.jar -port 80 -dir c:\jini1_1\lib -verbose
```

```
java -jar c:\jini1_1\lib\mahalo.jar
        http://hostname:80/mahalo-dl.jar
        c:\jini1_1\example\txn\policy.all
        c:\tmp\txn_log
```

Once the *Mahalo* registration program (mahalo.jar) completes execution, the transaction service will always be available as long as the RMI daemon is running, and the file system does not corrupt the RMI daemon and transaction logs.

Configuration

Mahalo may be configured with the following properties using the −D flag at activation registration time:

- ❏ **com.sun.jini.mahalo.managerName**: if this property is set in the activation registration Java VM, its value will be used to set the name attribute of the net.jini.lookup.entry.Name entry value. If this name is known to clients, they may identify the particular *Mahalo* service instance when performing Jini lookup.

- ❏ **com.sun.jini.use.registry**: this is a deprecated property and will be removed in future *Mahalo* versions. If set, it will instruct *Mahalo* to bind to an RMI registry

- ❏ **com.sun.jini.rmiRegistryPort**: is also a deprecated property. When used in conjunction with the com.sun.jini.use.registry property, it may be used to set the port of the RMI registry used to bind *Mahalo*.

Jini Client or Service	JavaSpaces and Helper Services

Jini Client and Service Support Helper Utilities

Jini Discovery Management Helper Utilities

Jini Protocol Helper Utilities

Jini Network Protocols	
	RMI and Rich Object Semantics
	Java VM and Networking
Network Protocols	

Mercury Event Mailbox Service

Mercury is Sun's reference Jini event mailbox service implementation. Clients may use it as a persistent proxy of remote events as described in the helper services appendix (see net.jini.event.EventMailbox, Appendix I). mercury is an activatable service registered with the RMI activation daemon.

The mercury service class files are included in the executable Java archive file jini1_1\lib\mercury.jar and the client class files in jini1_1\lib\mercury-dl.jar (relative to the Jini 1.1 installation directory). There are several requirements for running this service:

1. Mercury is an activatable service and therefore requires a running **RMI activation daemon (RMID).**

2. Mercury needs to **export** class libraries to clients, and therefore the mercury-dl.jar archive file must be accessible through a URL codebase.

3. The **codebase** command-line parameter to mercury must point to the URL codebase from step 2.

4. Mercury needs to maintain a persistent state across activations, and therefore must be configured with a **storage directory.**

5. Mercury requires a **Jini lookup service** in order to make its services available.

6. Finally, mercury requires permissions to perform network, discovery, and file operations within the storage directory. An appropriate **policy** file must be provided (using the policy.all file is strongly discouraged). See Chapter 14 for more security detail.

The mercury command line parameters are listed below (similar to reggie and mahalo). Note that arguments must be specified in the order listed:

```
java -jar [setup_jvm_options] jini1_1\lib\mercury.jar
        codebase_arg  security_policy_file_arg log_directory_arg
        [[group0] [group1] ...]   [[locator0] [locator1] ...]
        [server_jvm] [server_jvm_args]
```

❑ **setup_jvm_options**: optional parameters for the Java VM used to register mercury with the activation daemon (usually none).

❑ **codebase_arg**: URL for downloading the **mercury-dl.jar** client side file. Notice that this is a simple string argument and should *not* use the -Djava.rmi.codebase=definition. This is because the URL is not used in this VM but in the Java VM created by the activation daemon.

❑ **security_policy_file_arg**: path to the security policy file to be used in creating the Java VM at activation time (just the filename without a -D flag).

❑ **log_directory_arg**: path to a directory that will be used to store the mercury persistent state information.

❑ **group0 group1 ...**: optional list of group names used when registering with the lookup service. Unlike Reggie, group names are not placed in a single string. Instead they are simply listed. For example "com.wrox.uk" "printgroup" "securitygroup".

❑ **locator0 locator1 ...**: optional list of locators used to perform unicast discovery of lookup services. Example: "jini://printgroup.wrox.com/" "jini://publiclookup.jini.net".

❑ **server_jvm**: optional path to the Java VM executable that is to be used by the activation daemon when activating mercury.

❑ **server_jvm_args**: optional list of flags to be passed to the server_jvm.

For example, on a clean machine (without any other running services) mercury may be started as shown below. The example assumes that your JDK 1.2.2 binary directory is in the search path (otherwise prepend each command with the path). Note that we start the RMI daemon with an empty security policy (-J-Dsun.rmi.activation.execPolicy=none; the inclusion of this extra flag ensures that the example will also work in JDK 1.3, should you be using it), and that we use the policy provided in jini1_1\example\txn\policy.all.

The following three command-line invocations are made on separate command prompt windows (enter as one line each; multiple lines shown for readability). If you have previously registered Reggie as described, you may skip the first two steps, since the RMI daemon is already running with an empty security policy, and the HTTP daemon exports all Jini archive files in the lib directory. Note that the mercury event mailbox service will not be made available to other Jini services if no lookup service is available in the network.

```
rmid -log c:\tmp\rmid_log -J-Dsun.rmi.activation.execPolicy=none

java -jar c:\jini1_1\lib\tools.jar -port 80 -dir c:\jini1_1\lib -verbose

java -jar c:\jini1_1\lib\mercury.jar
        http://hostname:80/mercury-dl.jar
        c:\jini1_1\example\txn\policy.all
        c:\tmp\mercury_log
```

Once the mercury registration program (mercury.jar) completes execution (it may take some time), the event mailbox service will always be available as long as the RMI daemon is running, and the file system does not corrupt the RMI daemon and event mailbox logs.

Configuration

The mercury service may be configured using the following properties:

- ❑ **com.sun.jini.mercury.debug**: Enables debugging output of a given subsystem and optionally specifies a log file to be used. Available subsystems include: `leases`, `delivery`, `admin`, `init`, `receive`, `expiration`, `recovery`, and `logs`. The property's syntax is:

    - ❑ `subsystem[:subsystem_log],...,subsystemN[:subsystemN_log]`

- ❑ **com.sun.jini.mercury.eventsPerLog**: specifies the number of events stored per log file (default 10). Files are deleted after all events are delivered, so large capacity will waste space, and small capacity will create many files.

- ❑ **com.sun.jini.mercury.eventsPerLog**: specifies the number of event log input/output streams (default 10). You may improve logging concurrency by increasing this value if *Mercury* is I/O bound. Note that for some operating systems, maximum file handling limitations may restrict your choice of values.

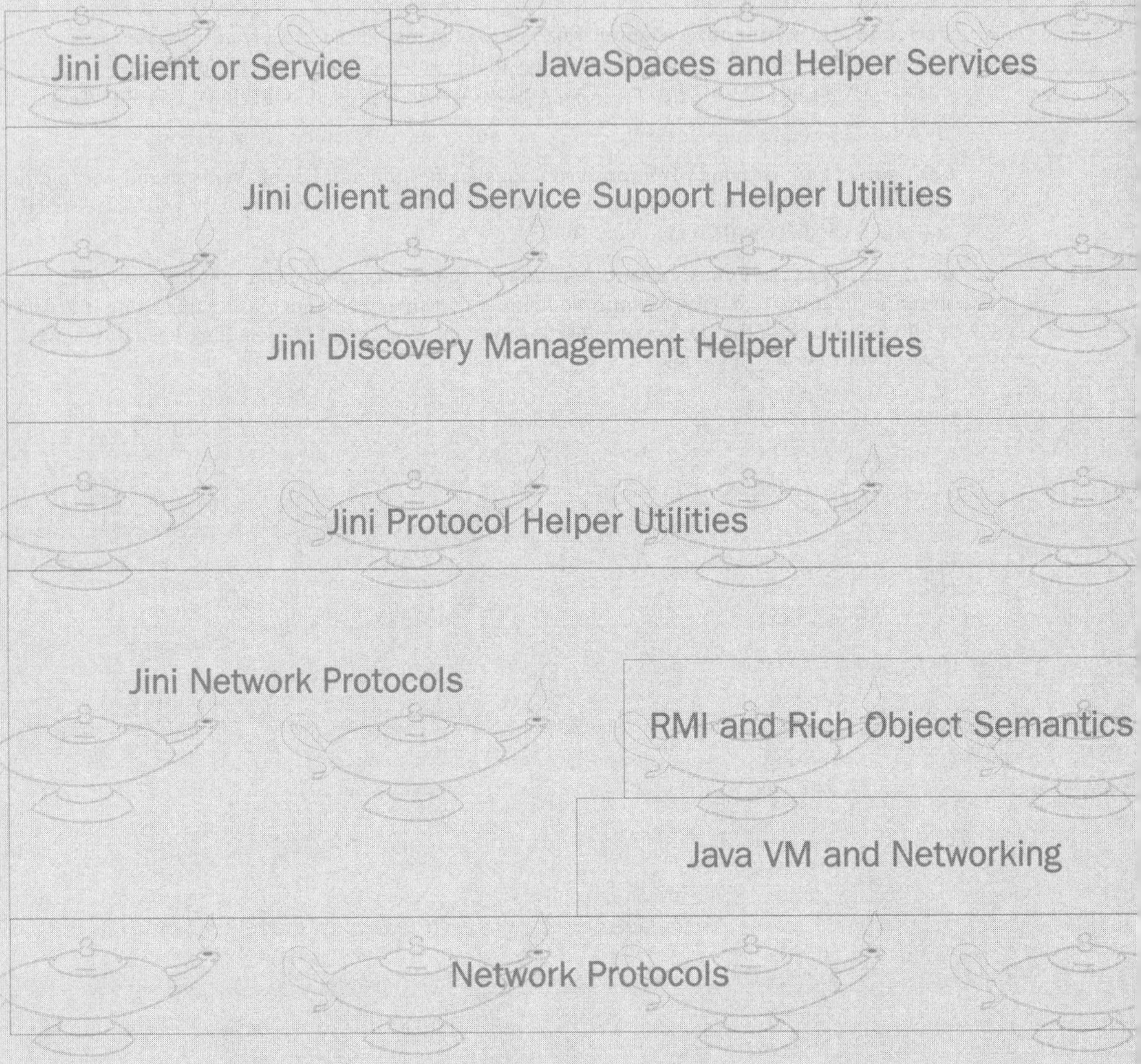

Jini Client or Service	JavaSpaces and Helper Services

Jini Client and Service Support Helper Utilities

Jini Discovery Management Helper Utilities

Jini Protocol Helper Utilities

Jini Network Protocols

RMI and Rich Object Semantics

Java VM and Networking

Network Protocols

Fiddler Lookup Discovery Service

Fiddler is Sun's reference Jini lookup discovery service implementation. Lookup discovery services perform discovery on behalf of Jini clients (see net.jini.discover.LookupDiscoveryService). As a Jini service, Fiddler requires the presence of a Jini lookup service (such as reggie).

Unlike the other contributed Jini service implementations, fiddler may be used either as an activatable service, or as a transient service. The activatable version is recommended for use in deployment, while the transient version may be useful during development.

The fiddler service class files are included in the executable Java archive file jini1_1\lib\fiddler.jar and the client class files in jini1_1\lib\fiddler-dl.jar (relative to the Jini 1.1 installation directory). There are several requirements for running this service:

1. Fiddler's activatable version requires a running **RMI activation daemon (RMID)**. (Note that this is not required when using the transient version, or when no other services such as reggie are running on the same host).

2. Fiddler needs to **export** class libraries to clients, and therefore the **fiddler-dl.jar** archive file must be accessible through a URL codebase.

3. The **codebase** command-line parameter to Fiddler must point to the URL codebase from step 2.

4. Fiddler needs to maintain a persistent state across activations, and therefore must be configured with a **storage directory** (also required for the transient version; transient refers to the service restart mechanism, not its state).

5. Fiddler requires a **Jini lookup service** in order to make its services available.

6. Finally, fiddler requires permissions to perform network, discovery, and file operations within the storage directory. An appropriate **policy** file must be provided (using the `policy.all` file is strongly discouraged. See Chapter 14 for more details about security).

The activatable fiddler command line parameters are listed below (similar to reggie and mahalo). Note that arguments must be specified in the order listed:

```
java -jar [setup_jvm_options] jini1_1\lib\fiddler.jar
     codebase_arg  security_policy_file_arg log_directory_arg
     [[group0] [group1] ...]   [[locator0] [locator1] ...]
     [server_jvm] [server_jvm_args]
```

❑ **setup_jvm_options**: optional parameters for the Java VM used to register fiddler with the activation daemon (usually none).

❑ **codebase_arg**: URL for downloading the `fiddler-dl.jar` client side file. Notice that this is a simple string argument and should *not* use the `-Djava.rmi.codebase=definition`. This is because the URL is not used in this VM but in the Java VM created by the activation daemon.

❑ **security_policy_file_arg**: path to the security policy file to be used in creating the Java VM at activation time (just the filename without a `-D` flag).

❑ **log_directory_arg:** path to a directory that will be used to store the fiddler persistent state information.

❑ **group0 group1 ...:** optional list of group names used when registering with the lookup service. Unlike reggie, group names are not placed in a single string. Instead they are simply listed. For example `"com.wrox.uk" "printgroup" "securitygroup"`.

❑ **locator0 locator1 ...:** optional list of locators used to perform unicast discovery of lookup services. Example: `"jini://printgroup.wrox.com/" "jini://publiclookup.jini.net"`

❑ **server_jvm:** optional path to the Java VM executable that is to be used by the activation daemon when activating fiddler.

❑ **server_jvm_args**: optional list of flags to be passed to the `server_jvm`

The transient fiddler command line parameters are listed below:

```
java -cp classpath [jvm_options]
     com.sun.jini.fiddler.TransientFiddler log_directory_arg
     [groups and locators]
```

As can be observed, the transient version of fiddler cannot be invoked directly as part of an executable Java archive (`.jar`) file. Instead, the Java interpreter is invoked and the class containing the transient `main()` method is specified. The `TransientFiddler` class is included in the `jini1_1\lib\fiddler.jar` file. Also, since the RMI daemon is not invoked, the code-base and security policy files must be defined within the invoking Java VM. In particular:

- ❑ **classpath**: must contain `jini1_1\lib\fiddler.jar`
- ❑ **[jvm_options]**: must minimally include definitions of
  - ❑ `-Djava.rmi.server.codebase=` [URL for obtaining `fiddler-dl.jar`]
  - ❑ `-Djava.security.policy=` [pointing to a Java security file]
- ❑ **log_directory_arg**, `group` and **locator** arguments as in the activatable version.

For example, on a clean machine (without any other running services) the activatable version of fiddler may be started as shown below. The example assumes that your JDK 1.2.2 binary directory is in the search path (otherwise prepend each command with the path). Note that we start the RMI daemon with an empty security policy (`-J-Dsun.rmi.activation.execPolicy=none`; the inclusion of this extra flag ensures that the example will also work in JDK 1.3, should you be using it), and that we use the policy provided in `jini1_1\example\txn\policy.all`.

The following three command-line invocations are made on separate command prompt windows (enter as one line each; multiple lines shown for readability). If you have previously registered reggie as described, you may skip the first two steps, since the RMI daemon will already be running with an empty security policy, and the HTTP daemon exports all Jini archive files in the lib directory. Note that the fiddler transaction service will not be made available to other Jini services if no lookup service is available in the network.

```
rmid -log c:\tmp\rmid_log -J-Dsun.rmi.activation.execPolicy=none

java -jar c:\jini1_1\lib\tools.jar -port 80 -dir c:\jini1_1\lib -verbose

java -jar c:\jini1_1\lib\fiddler.jar
        http://hostname:80/fiddler-dl.jar
        c:\jini1_1\example\txn\policy.all
        c:\tmp\fiddler_log
```

Once the fiddler registration program (`fiddler.jar`) completes execution (it may take some time), the lookup discovery service will always be available as long as the RMI daemon is running, and the file system does not corrupt the RMI daemon and lookup discovery logs.

Similarly, the transient version of fiddler may be invoked by starting the RMI activation daemon and HTTP server, as shown above (and if needed), and then invoking the transient fiddler main class:

```
java -classpath c:\jini1_1\lib\fiddler.jar
        -Djava.security.policy=c:\jini1_1\example\txn\policy.all
        -Djava.rmi.server.codebase=http://hostname:80/fiddler-dl.jar
        com.sun.jini.fiddler.TransientFiddler c:\tmp\fiddler_log
```

The transient fiddler version does not normally exit, unless explicitly asked to shutdown using the Jini administration interface.

Configuration

The fiddler service may be configured using the property:

- ❑ **com.sun.jini.fiddler.server.debug**: Enables `debugging output of a given subsystem and optionally specifies a log file to be used. Available subsystems include:` all, startup, tasks, events, groups, locators, discard, registration, lease, log, `and` off. This property's syntax is:
  - ❑ `subsystem[:subsystem_log],...,subsystemN[:subsystemN]`

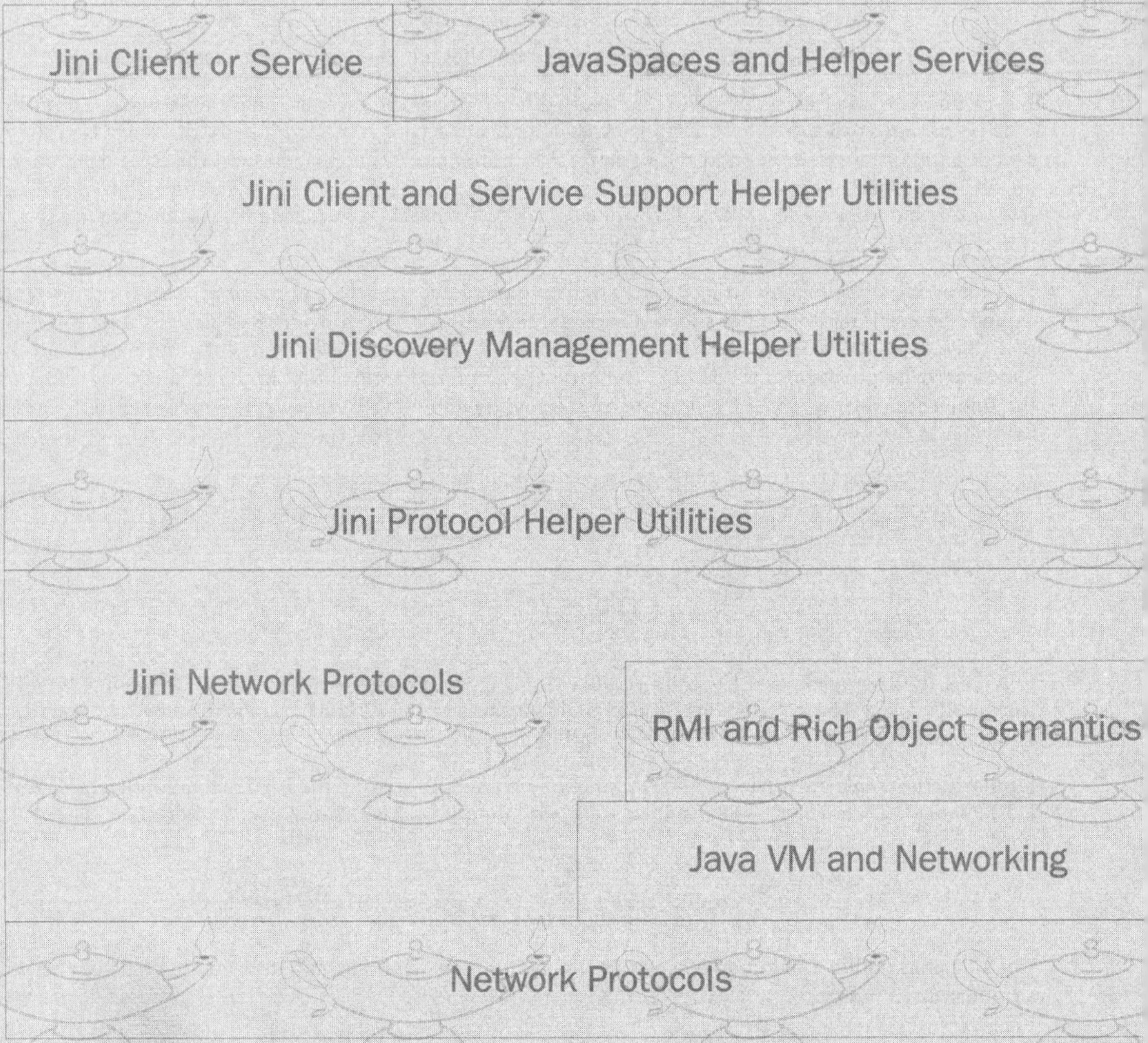
Jini Client or Service
JavaSpaces and Helper Services
Jini Client and Service Support Helper Utilities
Jini Discovery Management Helper Utilities
Jini Protocol Helper Utilities
Jini Network Protocols
RMI and Rich Object Semantics
Java VM and Networking
Network Protocols

Online discussion at http://p2p.wrox.com

Norm Lease Renewal Service

Norm is Sun's reference Jini lease renewal service implementation. Clients may use its lease registration proxy services as described in the helper services appendix (see net.jini.lease.LeaseRenewalService, Appendix I). Norm is an activatable service registered with the RMI activation daemon.

The Norm service class files are included in the executable Java archive file jini1_1\lib\norm.jar and the client class files in jini1_1\lib\norm-dl.jar (relative to the Jini 1.1 installation directory). There are several requirements for running this service:

❑   Norm is an activatable service and therefore requires a running **RMI activation daemon (RMID)**

❑   Norm needs to **export** class libraries to clients, and therefore the norm-dl.jar archive file must be accessible through a URL codebase

❑   The **codebase** command-line parameter to norm must point to the URL codebase from step 2

❑   Norm needs to maintain a persistent state across activations, and therefore must be configured with a **storage directory**

❑   Norm requires a **Jini lookup service** in order to make its services available

❑   Finally, norm requires permissions to perform network, discovery, and file operations within the storage directory. An appropriate **policy** file must be provided (using the policy.all file is strongly discouraged see Chapter 14 for more security details.

The norm command line parameters are listed below (similar to reggie and mahalo). Note that arguments must be specified in the order listed:

```
java -jar [setup_jvm_options] jini1_1\lib\norm.jar
     codebase_arg  security_policy_file_arg log_directory_arg
     [[group0] [group1] ...]   [[locator0] [locator1] ...]
     [server_jvm] [server_jvm_args]
```

❑ **setup_jvm_options**: optional parameters for the Java VM used to register norm with the activation daemon (usually none)

❑ **codebase_arg**: URL for downloading the **norm-dl.jar** client side file. Notice that this is a simple string argument and should *not* use the `-Djava.rmi.codebase=`definition. This is because the URL is not used in this VM but in the Java VM created by the activation daemon

❑ **security_policy_file_arg**: path to the security policy file to be used in creating the Java VM at activation time (just the filename without a −D flag)

❑ **log_directory_arg**: path to a directory that will be used to store the *norm* persistent state information

❑ **group0 group1 ...**: optional list of group names used when registering with the lookup service. Unlike reggie, group names are not placed in a single string. Instead they are simply listed. For example `"com.wrox.uk"` `"printgroup"` `"securitygroup"`

❑ **locator0 locator1 ...**: optional list of locators used to perform unicast discovery of lookup services. Example: `"jini://printgroup.wrox.com/"` `"jini://publiclookup.jini.net"`

❑ **server_jvm**: optional path to the Java VM executable that is to be used by the activation daemon when activating norm

❑ **server_jvm_args**: optional list of flags to be passed to the `server_jvm`

For example, on a clean machine (without any other running services) norm may be started as shown below. The example assumes that your JDK 1.2.2 binary directory is in the search path (otherwise prepend each command with the path). Note that we start the RMI daemon with an empty security policy (`-J-Dsun.rmi.activation.execPolicy=none`; the inclusion of this extra flag ensures that the example will also work in JDK 1.3, should you be using it), and that we use the policy provided in `jini1_1\example\txn\policy.all`.

The following three command-line invocations are made on separate command prompt windows (enter as one line each; multiple lines are shown for readability). If you have previously registered reggie as described, you may skip the first two steps, since the RMI daemon is already running with an empty security policy, and the HTTP daemon exports all Jini archive files in the lib directory. Note that the norm event mailbox service will not be made available to other Jini services if no lookup service is available in the network.

```
rmid -log c:\tmp\rmid_log -J-Dsun.rmi.activation.execPolicy=none

java -jar c:\jini1_1\lib\tools.jar -port 80 -dir c:\jini1_1\lib -verbose

java -jar c:\jini1_1\lib\norm.jar
        http://hostname:80/norm-dl.jar
        c:\jini1_1\example\txn\policy.all
        c:\tmp\norm_log
```

Once the norm registration program (`norm.jar`) completes execution (it may take some time), the lease renewal service will always be available as long as the RMI daemon is running, and the file system does not corrupt the RMI daemon and lease renewal logs.

Configuration

The norm service may be configured using the following property, by using the -D command line flag to the Java VM executing the norm registration program (for example, `"-Dcom.sun.jini.norm.debug=snapshot"`):

❑ **com.sun.jini.norm.debug**: Enables debugging output or a given subsystem and optionally specifies a log file to be used. Available subsystems include: snapshot, renewalFailure, renewal, renewals, and clientLeaseCodebase. The property's syntax is:

   ❑   subsystem[[:subsystem_log],...,subsystemN[:subsystemN]]

Jini Client or Service	JavaSpaces and Helper Services
Jini Client and Service Support Helper Utilities	
Jini Discovery Management Helper Utilities	
Jini Protocol Helper Utilities	

Jini Network Protocols	
	RMI and Rich Object Semantics
	Java VM and Networking
Network Protocols	

Jini Helper Utilities and Services

This appendix covers the Jini helper utilities and services covered in depth in Chapters 10 and 11. Further documentation may be obtained by reading the specification '*A Collection of Jini Technology Helper Utilities and Services Specifications*' (available as part of the Jini Technology Starter Kit in the directory `jini1_1\doc\specs\jxp-spec`) and the JavaDoc API reference (also part of the Starter Kit at `jini1_1\doc\api\index.html`). The helper utilities and interfaces have changed significantly between Jini versions 1.0 and 1.1. This appendix presents the interfaces defined in the Jini 1.1 beta specification.

The Jini helper utilities consist of classes and interfaces for assisting Jini clients and services in performing Jini operations according to the Jini specifications. These utilities are executed in the same address space (Java VM) as the Jini client or service, possibly on the same thread, or using separate threads. For example, `JoinManager` is a helper utility used by Jini services to perform Jini discovery and join according to the specification. Unlike the core Jini interfaces, use of the helper utilities is optional. However, it is strongly recommended that Jini clients and services take advantage of these implementations to ensure specification-compliant behavior.

The helper services consist of interfaces that may be implemented by Jini services that provide utility services. For example, the `EventMailbox` interface enables Jini clients and services to identify other services that may be used as event mailboxes. The helper services, as defined in `net.jini.*`, consist of interfaces, not implementations. Sun provides sample implementations as sub-packages of `com.sun.jini.*` described in the previous appendices (see the mahalo, fiddler, and mercury appendices). The UML class diagram below presents an overview of the `net.jini.*` packages and the classes and interfaces defined in each (the core package is also shown for completeness). Some of the packages (such as `net.jini.admin`) are not formally part of the Jini Helper Utility and Services specification, but are nonetheless discussed in this appendix.

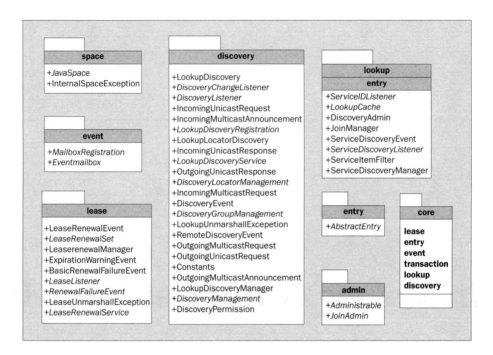

Administration Utilities (net.jini.admin)

The Jini **admin** package contains interface declarations related to Jini service administration. Currently, only two interfaces are defined: Administrable and JoinAdmin. It is recommended that Jini service objects implement these interfaces to provide consistent Jini service administration. Note that this package is not formally part of the Jini Helper Utilities and Services specification, and is therefore likely to change in future releases. The lookup discovery administration (DiscoveryAdmin) interface is included in net.jini.lookup and is discussed as part of the lookup package. Additional administration-related interfaces are defined in the com.sun.jini.admin package.

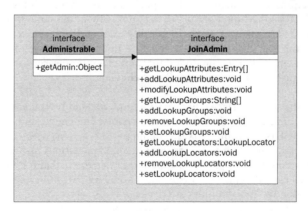

Administrable

```
public interface Administrable {
```

Objects supporting remote administration should implement the Administrable interface. The interface does not extend java.rmi.Remote and therefore may not be directly exported using an RMI stub. Users must either use a service proxy object or create a new interface extending Administrable and Remote (because all Administrable methods include RemoteException in their throws clause).

```
java.lang.Object getAdmin() throws java.rmi.RemoteException;
```

The above method obtains a reference to an object implementing the service's administration functionality. Callers may use the Java reflection mechanism to discover all the interfaces implemented by the administration object, or use instanceof to check against particular ones. The package defines a single standard interface, called JoinAdmin, which is described below.

```
} // Administrable
```

JoinAdmin

```
public interface JoinAdmin {
```

The JoinAdmin interface provides external control to Jini discovery and join attributes. Normally, the interface will be implemented by the administration object returned by Administrable.getAdmin(). This interface does not extend Remote and cannot be directly implemented by RMI stubs. As in Administrable, users may create an interface extending JoinAdmin and Remote for that purpose.

```
Entry[] getLookupAttributes() throws RemoteException;

void addLookupAttributes(Entry[] attrSets) throws RemoteException;

void modifyLookupAttributes(Entry[] attrSetTemplates,
    Entry[] attrSets) throws RemoteException;
```

The above are methods used to obtain and modify the entries used in joining the Jini federation. Following an add or modify call, the service will update its registration with currently joined lookup services, and use the entries in all future joins (therefore the added entries are stored persistently). Modify works similarly to ServiceRegistration.modifyAttributes().

```
String[] getLookupGroups() throws RemoteException;

void addLookupGroups(String[] groups) throws RemoteException;

void removeLookupGroups(String[] groups) throws RemoteException;

void setLookupGroups(String[] groups) throws RemoteException;
```

These can be used to obtain and update the lookup groups for this service. Remember that an empty groups array signifies that the service does not perform any joins, and that the reserved 'all' group must be used to signify all groups' registration.

```
LookupLocator[] getLookupLocators() throws RemoteException;

void addLookupLocators(LookupLocator[] locators)
    throws RemoteException;

void removeLookupLocators(LookupLocator[] locators)
    throws RemoteException;

void setLookupLocators(LookupLocator[] locators)
    throws RemoteException;
```

These are the `LookupLocators` used by the unicast lookup discovery process of this Jini service.

```
} // JoinAdmin
```

Discovery Utilities (net.jini.discovery)

The Jini discovery utilities provide interfaces and classes used for performing Jini discovery as described in the Jini Technology Core Platform specification.

The three primary interfaces defined in the Jini **discovery** package are `DiscoveryManagement`, `DiscoveryGroupManagement`, and `DiscoveryLocatorManagement`. These interfaces are implemented by the `LookupDiscoveryManager` and their methods will be described as part of that discussion.

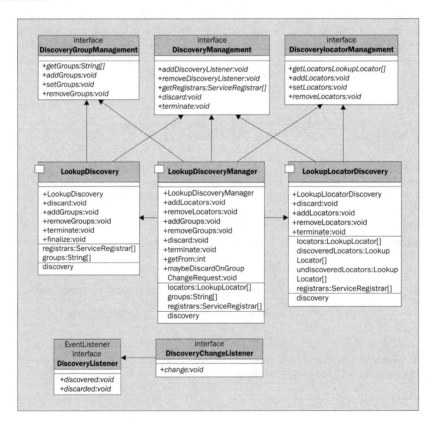

LookupDiscoveryManager

```
public class LookupDiscoveryManager implements DiscoveryManagement,
    DiscoveryGroupManagement, DiscoveryLocatorManagement {
```

`LookupDiscoveryManager` is the main class of the discovery package. It is used to assist Jini services in performing lookup discovery in accordance with the Jini specification.

```
public LookupDiscoveryManager(String[] groups,
    LookupLocator[] locators, DiscoveryListener listener)
    throws IOException;
```

This constructs an instance of the lookup discovery manager. The constructor starts a thread performing Jini lookup discovery in the background. The first parameter sets the groups to be used during lookup (use the `DiscoveryGroupManagement` constants `ALL_GROUPS`, and `NO_GROUPS` for special cases). The second parameter includes an optional list of Jini lookup locators used to perform unicast discovery. Notification of lookup discovery or discard events is made asynchronously through the listener object. The manager uses the groups provided.

```
public LookupLocator[] getLocators();

public void addLocators(LookupLocator[] locators);

public void removeLocators(LookupLocator[] locators);

public void setLocators(LookupLocator[] locators);
```

These are used to obtain and update the lookup locators used in performing unicast discovery. The `getLocators()` method returns the set of lookup locators used, including those for which no corresponding service registrar has been discovered. Note that this method only returns unicast lookup locators, and does not include the lookup locators of services discovered through multicast discovery (see `getRegistrars()` below). Removal of current lookup locators may result in the generation of service registrar discarded events.

```
public String[] getGroups();

public void addGroups(String[] groups) throws IOException;

public void removeGroups(String[] groups);

public void setGroups(String[] groups) throws IOException;
```

These methods are used to manipulate the groups used in performing lookup discovery. Note that the null array is used to signify all groups (constant `DiscoveryGroupManagement.ALL_GROUPS`). Group removal may result in service registrar discard events for registrars no longer matching any of the remaining groups.

```
        public void addDiscoveryListener(DiscoveryListener listener);

        public void removeDiscoveryListener(DiscoveryListener listener);
```

These add or remove a listener for service registrar discovery and discard events.

```
        public ServiceRegistrar[] getRegistrars();
```

This returns an array of service registrars discovered through unicast or multicast lookup discovery.

```
        public void discard(ServiceRegistrar proxy);
```

This instructs the lookup discovery manager to discard a service registrar from its list of managed services. This method may be invoked by a Jini service when a remote exception is thrown during communication with a lookup service. Once the lookup service becomes available again (could be immediately) the service will be discovered and registered and the listener's discovered method will be invoked.

```
        public void terminate();
```

This terminates all threads involved in discovery processing.

```
    } // LookupDiscoveryManager
```

DiscoveryListener

```
        public interface DiscoveryListener extends EventListener {
```

This interface is implemented by objects subscribing for discovery event notification from LookupDiscoveryManager instances.

```
        void discovered(DiscoveryEvent e);
```

Invoked when one or more service registrars has been discovered. The method should return quickly, without making any remote calls (that is, a separate thread to communicate with the service registrar). The DiscoveryEvent class contains an array of service registrars, and a map used to identify the groups served by each registrar.

```
        void discarded(DiscoveryEvent e);
```

Invoked when one or more service registrars have been discarded. The method should return quickly, without making any remote calls. Note that registrars may be removed because they are no longer available, or because the group registration or lookup locator list has changed.

```
    } // DiscoveryListener
```

Entry Utilities (net.jini.entry)

The Jini **entry** package contains utility classes related to Jini Entries. Currently, the package contains a single abstract class called AbstractEntry.

```
public abstract class AbstractEntry implements Entry {
```

AbstractEntry is an abstract class implementing the net.jini.core.entry.Entry interface. Entry classes may extend AbstractEntry to inherit appropriate equals() and hashCode() and toString() implementations. In cases where inheritance is not appropriate, AbstractEntry provides static versions of these methods, taking an entry as parameter.

```
public boolean equals(Object other);
```

This returns true if the argument is an entry of the same class as this entry, and all fields are equal. Null fields are considered equal, and non-null fields are compared using the equals() method. Remember that Entry objects must only have public fields and cannot store primitive types. If you violate this assumption, some of the AbstractEntry methods will quietly fail resulting in difficult-to-trace errors.

```
public static boolean equals(Entry e1, Entry e2);
```

This is a static method for comparing two entries using the equals() semantics presented above. Note that the parameters do not have to be instances of AbstractEntry. Any two entries that comply with the Jini Entry syntax and semantics, and implement the net.jini.core.entry.Entry interface, may be used.

```
public int hashCode();
```

This returns a hash code for this entry. The code is computed by performing an exclusive or (XOR) of the hash codes of all non-null fields. This guarantees that if two entries are equal, their hash codes will be equal.

```
public static int hashCode(Entry entry);
```

Static equivalent of the previous hashCode() method. It will calculate the hash code of any Entry object as described above (the parameter does *not* have to be an instance of AbstactEntry).

```
public String toString();
```

Returns a string containing the entry class name and the values of its fields.

```
public static String toString(Entry entry) {
```

This is the static equivalent of the previous method for creating a string out of any entry object.

```
} // AbstractEntry
```

Event Mailbox Service (net.jini.event)

An Event Mailbox Service is a Jini service that may be used as a proxy for remote events. Jini services or clients may use this service to store remote event notifications (for example, when off-line), and retrieve the stored remote events on demand.

EventMailbox

```
public interface EventMailbox {
```

Services implementing the `EventMailbox` interface support third-party storage and retrieval of remote events. Users may locate event mailbox services using the Jini lookup interfaces. Sun provides a sample event mailbox service called mercury, covered in a Appendix F.

```
MailboxRegistration register(long leaseDuration)
    throws RemoteException;
```

Event mailbox services implement a single method called `register()`. Invoking `register` results in the leasing of an event mailbox at the remote service (details shown below). It is the responsibility of the registering client to maintain renewal of the returned lease. Since event mailboxes are usually created by services that are not always connected to the network, the use of a lease renewal service is usually also required.

```
} // EventMailbox
```

MailboxRegistration

```
public interface MailboxRegistration {
```

Proxies implementing `MailboxRegistration` are returned by event mailbox services (RMI stubs cannot be used because some methods don't throw `RemoteException`). The mailbox registration interface provides access to the mailbox lease, and methods for obtaining the mailbox handler (listener), as well as methods for retrieving stored events.

```
public Lease getLease();
```

This returns the event mailbox lease object (local method).

```
public RemoteEventListener getListener();
```

This returns the remote event listener associated with this event mailbox. Clients use the listener reference to subscribe to the required remote events.

```
public void enableDelivery(RemoteEventListener target)
    throws RemoteException;
```

This initiates delivery of stored events to the remote event listener provided. If a listener has already been specified in a previous call, it will be replaced.

```
public void disableDelivery() throws RemoteException;
```

This stops the delivery of a stored notification to a target listener specified in the last enableDelivery() call. This is equivalent to invoking enableDelivery(null).

```
} // MailboxRegistration
```

Lease Utilities & Services (net.jini.lease)

The Jini **lease** package contains interfaces and classes used to support local as well as third-party lease renewal. We will focus on LeaseRenewalManager and LeaseListener for local lease renewal, and LeaseRenewalService and LeaseRenewalSet for third-party (Jini service) lease renewal.

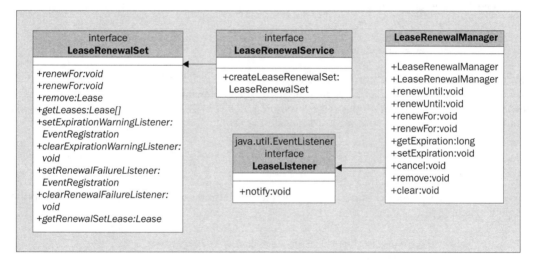

LeaseRenewalManager

```
public class LeaseRenewalManager {
```

LeaseRenewalManager is a utility class for performing Jini lease renewals. Instances start a thread, which renews managed leases in the background. Users are only notified when a lease renewal fails. Lease renewal is performed efficiently by renewing batchable leases as a set. The manager is non-persistent, which means that if the Java VM exits, leases will no longer be renewed; this is the desired behavior in most cases. Persistent renewals may be made using the LeaseRenewalService utility service described overleaf.

```
public LeaseRenewalManager();
```

This creates a lease renewal manager that does not initially handle any leases.

```
public LeaseRenewalManager(Lease lease, long desiredExpiration,
    LeaseListener listener);
```

This constructs a lease renewal manager initially handling the `lease` provided. The `desiredExpiration` enables callers to specify an *absolute* expiration of lease renewals (may indicate `Lease.FOREVER`). The manager will repeatedly renew the lease until the specified expiration time. Finally, the `listener` object is used for notification of lease renewal failures.

```
public void renewUntil(Lease lease, long desiredExpiration,
    LeaseListener listener);
```

This adds a lease to be renewed. Similar to the constructor above, the parameters include the lease to be renewed, the *absolute* expiration time of renewal efforts (may be `Lease.FOREVER`), and the listener to be notified on lease renewal failure.

```
public void renewUntil(Lease lease, long desiredExpiration,
    long renewDuration, LeaseListener listener);
```

This is similar to the previous `renewUntil()` method, with the addition of the `renewDuration` parameter: `renewDuration` contains the time used when renewing the lease. Renew duration may be a positive integer or `Lease.ANY` if desired expiration is `Lease.FOREVER`; otherwise, it has to be smaller than (`desiredExpiration - currentTimeMillis`).

```
public void renewFor(Lease lease, long desiredDuration,
    LeaseListener listener);
```

This is the relative version of `renewUntil()` where the desired renewal time is given *relative* to the absolute system time.

```
public void renewFor(Lease lease, long desiredDuration,
    long renewDuration, LeaseListener listener);
```

This adds a parameter for specifying renewal duration; the relationship between `desiredDuration` and `renewDuration` is the same as for `desiredExpiration` and `renewDuration` in the `renewUntil()` method.

```
public synchronized long getExpiration(Lease lease)
    throws UnknownLeaseException
```

The above method returns the desired (*absolute*) expiration time associated with the lease parameter.

```
public synchronized void setExpiration(Lease lease,
    long expiration) throws UnknownLeaseException;
```

This updates the desired absolute expiration time of the given `lease`. If the requested `expiration` is before the end of the leased expiration, then no action is taken (in other words, the lease cannot be cancelled this way).

```
    public void cancel(Lease lease) throws UnknownLeaseException,
        RemoteException;
```

The above removes a lease from the managed set and cancels it.

```
    public synchronized void remove(Lease lease)
        throws UnknownLeaseException;
```

This removes a lease from the managed set but does *not* cancel it.

```
    public synchronized void clear();
```

This removes all leases from the managed set. The leases are *not* canceled.

```
    } // LeaseRenewalManager
```

LeaseListener

```
    public interface LeaseListener extends java.util.EventListener {
        void notify(LeaseRenewalEvent e);
    }
```

Classes implement the `LeaseListener` interface in order to be able to subscribe for notification of lease renewal failure events. The lease renewal event contains references to the lease and exception that caused the failure. Notice that although the callback method is called `notify()`, `LeaseRenewalEvent` does *not* extend `RemoteEvent` and is not related to the `RemoteEventListener.notify()` method.

LeaseRenewalService

```
    public interface LeaseRenewalService {
```

Jini services implementing the `LeaseRenewalService` interface may be used as third-party lease renewal proxies. Clients use lease-renewing proxies when they may not be able to renew their leases on their own (for example, using a `LeaseRenewalManager`) because their connectivity may be intermittent. In such cases, it may be desirable to obtain an effective lease time which is longer than the leasing resource is willing to grant. Sun's contributed implementation (known as norm) is a sample lease renewal service implementing this interface (see Appendix H).

```
    public LeaseRenewalSet createLeaseRenewalSet(long leaseDuration)
        throws RemoteException;
```

Creates a new lease renewal set used to group leases. In most cases, the lease duration will be longer than the duration usually granted for the leases that will be added to the set.

```
    } // LeaseRenewalService
```

LeaseRenewalSet

```
public interface LeaseRenewalSet {
```

LeaseRenewalSet instances are proxies of Jini services implementing LeaseRenewalService. The lease renewal set (referred to as set), is a container of leases to be renewed by the third-party service. The set itself is leased, and failure to renew that lease will result in termination of lease renewal by the service. Usually, the lease duration for the renewal set is longer than the duration of the individual leases it contains.

```
public void renewFor(Lease leaseToRenew, long desiredDuration,
    long renewDuration) throws RemoteException;
```

The above method is similar to the LeaseRenewalManager.renewFor() method.

```
public void renewFor(Lease leaseToRenew, long membershipDuration)
    throws RemoteException;
```

This is equivalent to calling renewFor(leaseToRenew, membershipDuration, Lease.FOREVER). The membership duration would have been better termed desired duration.

```
public Lease remove(Lease leaseToRemove) throws RemoteException;
```

This removes the lease from the set of managed leases. The lease is *not* cancelled, and expires normally.

```
public Lease[] getLeases() throws LeaseUnmarshalException,
    RemoteException;
```

The above method obtains the leases managed as part of this set.

```
public EventRegistration setExpirationWarningListener
    (RemoteEventListener listener, long minWarning, MarshalledObject
    handback) throws RemoteException;

public void clearExpirationWarningListener()
    throws RemoteException;
```

These are a second mechanism for detecting lease set expiration. When a lease renewal set is created by the service, a lease is provided. In addition, clients may subscribe for remote event notification in advance of the lease set expiration. The minWarning parameter specifies the number of milliseconds before LeaseRenewalSet expiration that the first event should be sent. There may only be one expiration warning listener, which may be removed using the clear version of the method. If a renewal failure listener has already been registered, it will be replaced with the one specified.

```
public EventRegistration setRenewalFailureListener
    (RemoteEventListener listener, MarshalledObject handback)
    throws RemoteException;
```

This registers for remote events using the equivalent of the local `LeaseListener` renewal failure notification. Because the lease renewal service is remote, registration and notification for lease renewal failures have to use the Jini distributed events mechanism.

```
public void clearRenewalFailureListener() throws RemoteException;
```

This removes the remote event listener notified when lease renewals fail.

```
public Lease getRenewalSetLease();
```

This obtains the lease for this set to be used in renewal.

```
} // LeaseRenewalSet
```

Lookup/Join Utilities (net.jini.lookup)

The Jini **lookup** package contains interfaces and classes assisting Jini services in implementing the Jini discovery and join specification. There are several interfaces and classes defined, but here we focus on the main ones: `JoinManager` (used by services) and `ServiceDiscoveryManager` (used by clients that may also be services).

JoinManager

```
public class JoinManager {
```

`JoinManager` is a utility for implementing the Jini discovery and join specification. It is strongly recommended that Jini services that want to perform discovery and join use this class. Clients should use the `ServiceDiscoveryManager` since they do not need to join the federation.

```
public JoinManager(Object obj, Entry[] attrSets,
    ServiceIDListener callback,
    DiscoveryManagement discoverMgr, LeaseRenewalManager leaseMgr)
    throws IOException;
```

This constructs a new `JoinManager` instance, which attempts to add the service to the discovered lookup services. This constructor should be used by services that have never been assigned a service ID. The `JoinManager` operates on a separate thread and notifies the service ID listener asynchronously once a service ID has been assigned by a lookup service. The parameters are:

❑ `obj`: the service proxy or RMI stub

❑ `attrSets`: the set of attribute entries with which the service will be registered

❑ `callback`: the listener object to be notified upon service ID assignment

❑ `discoveryMgr`: an optional shared discovery manager (if null a new `LookupDiscoveryManager` is constructed)

❑ `leaseMgr`: an optional shared lease renewal manager (if null a new `LeaseRenewalManager` is constructed)

```
public JoinManager(Object obj, Entry[] attrSets,
    ServiceID serviceID, DiscoveryManagement discoverMgr,
    LeaseRenewalManager leaseMgr) throws IOException;
```

This constructs a new `JoinManager` for services that have previously been assigned a service ID. The parameters are the same as for the previous constructor.

```
public DiscoveryManagement getDiscoveryManager();
```

The above returns the discovery manager used by this join manager, so that it may be shared with other objects (such as `ServiceDiscoveryManager`). Be aware that the `JoinManager terminate()` method will terminate discovery management if the object was created by the constructor (passed as null). It is therefore not recommended that automatically generated discovery managers be shared.

```
public LeaseRenewalManager getLeaseRenewalManager();
```

The above returns the lease renewal manager used by this join manager, so that it may be shared with other objects (such as the service itself, or the `ServiceDiscoveryManager`).

```
public ServiceRegistrar[] getJoinSet();
```

This returns the set of service registrars with which the service is currently registered.

```
public Entry[] getAttributes();
```

This returns the entry set currently used when joining the service in a lookup service.

```
public void addAttributes(Entry[] attrSets);
```

This modifies the join entry attributes for the service represented by this join manager (for current and future joins). Upon return, the join manager notifies any currently joined lookup services asynchronously of the change (there are no guarantees about success of these updates). There is a subtle danger of introducing inconsistencies if the entries are further modified before all the lookup services have been updated (see the JavaDoc documentation).

```
public void addAttributes(Entry[] attrSets, boolean checkSC);
```

This is a variation of the previous `addAttributes()` method with the addition of a check for service controlled entries. Services should use this method when adding attributes on behalf of other clients or services (for example, through calls to the `JoinAdmin` interface). In such cases the value of `checkSC` should be `true`.

```
public void setAttributes(Entry[] attrSets);
```

This sets the join attributes of the service managed by this join manager. Similar to the `addAttributes()` method, the method returns once the change has been committed to persistent storage, but before all lookup services have been notified of the entry modification (notification is asynchronous).

```
    public void modifyAttributes(Entry[] attrSetTemplates,
        Entry[] attrSets);
```

This modifies the join attributes of the service managed by this join manager (also performed asynchronously for the currently joined lookup services).

```
    public void modifyAttributes(Entry[] attrSetTemplates,
        Entry[] attrSets, boolean checkSC);
```

This is a variation of the previous `modifyAttributes()` method which rejects service-controlled entry modifications. It should be called when propagating changes originating from `JoinAdmin` calls (from external sources to the service).

```
    public void terminate();
```

This terminates join management and cleans up state. It should be noted that the `DiscoveryManagement` object will also be terminated if it was created by this join manager (i.e. the constructor parameter was null). This is dangerous because the `getDiscoveryManager()` method may have been used to obtain a reference (and potentially used in starting a `ServiceDiscoveryManager`). The lease renewal manager is never terminated, independent of who created it.

```
    } // JoinManager
```

ServiceDiscoveryManager

```
    public class ServiceDiscoveryManager {
```

`ServiceDiscoveryManager` instances assist Jini clients (which may also act as services) in discovering services they want to use. The class supports three usage patterns:

1. Creates a `LookupCache` object to be used as a cache for lookup services, enabling clients to perform multiple lookups efficiently (for example, when narrowing-in on a particular service).

2. Discovers lookup services and registers to receive notification of service modifications matching the template, and locates current matching services.

3. Simple interface for performing advanced searches (client-side) on entries including arbitrary comparisons, such as finding a printer with resolution between 600 and 1200 dpi (explained below).

There is one very unusual requirement for using this utility class. Because the class encapsulates remote event registration through an inner class, users must export that class through the client DL jar file. This requirement breaks the object encapsulation abstraction but is required since otherwise the discovery manager would have to start an HTTP daemon using its own security manager (to handle codebase re-writing). If the required classes are not exported correctly (added to the .jar file; HTTP server started; codebase set appropriately) then methods requiring remote event registration (such as create cache) will fail.

```
public ServiceDiscoveryManager(DiscoveryManagement discoveryMgr,
    LeaseRenewalManager leaseMgr) throws IOException;
```

This constructs a new service discovery manager using the given discovery and lease managers (both may be null).

```
public ServiceItem lookup(ServiceTemplate tmpl,
    ServiceItemFilter filter);
```

This locates a single service item matching the service template and item filter provided. Service template matching is handled as in `ServiceRegistrar.lookup()`. `ServiceItemFilter` is a client-side filtering mechanism allowing arbitrary filtering on a service entry. The `ServiceItemFilter` has a single method `boolean check(ServiceItem item)`. Classes implementing this interface may perform any arbitrary computation in deciding whether to accept or reject a particular item. This lookup method returns at most one service item matching the lookup criteria. If more than one item matches, the method returns an arbitrary one. This is a non-blocking service. If a service is not found, either because it does not exist or because communication with the service registrars fails, the method returns `null`. Also note that the method does not throw `RemoteException`, and can therefore fail silently.

```
public ServiceItem lookup(ServiceTemplate tmpl,
    ServiceItemFilter filter, long wait)
    throws InterruptedException, RemoteException;
```

This is a blocking version of the lookup method shown above. A single service item is returned immediately if found, as earlier. However, if no service matching the search criteria is found immediately, the method will wait for the given milliseconds before returning. If a matching service is discovered during the wait period, it is returned immediately; otherwise, at the end of `wait` milliseconds `null` is returned. Clients that decide they no longer want to wait may use the thread interrupt mechanism (see `java.lang.Thread.interrupt()`).

```
public ServiceItem[] lookup(ServiceTemplate tmpl, int maxMatches,
    ServiceItemFilter filter);
```

This non-blocking lookup method may be used to locate multiple service items matching the search criteria. The maximum number of matches required is specified as a parameter.

```
public ServiceItem[] lookup(ServiceTemplate tmpl, int minMaxMatch,
    int maxMatches, ServiceItemFilter filter, long wait)
    throws InterruptedException, RemoteException;
```

The blocking version of the multiple service lookup supports the setting of the minimum as well as the maximum number of matches. Blocking lookup proceeds in two phases. In the first phase, all discovered lookup services are checked for matching items. If this step identifies at least maxMatches matching entries, the method returns immediately. Otherwise, lookup moves to phase two, where it blocks until either minMaxMatches have been found, or the wait timer expires.

```
public LookupCache createLookupCache(ServiceTemplate tmpl,
    ServiceItemFilter filter, ServiceDiscoveryListener listener)
    throws RemoteException;
```

This is a factory method used to construct a `LookupCache` instance. Lookup caches are used to perform multiple searches on a service item efficiently. They can be of use when multiple services match a given template and increasingly narrower searches are introduced to narrow the selection.

```
public DiscoveryManagement getDiscoveryManager();
```

This returns the discovery manager provided or created at construction time.

```
public LeaseRenewalManager getLeaseRenewalManager();
```

This returns the lease manager provided or created at construction time.

```
public void terminate();
```

This terminates the threads responsible for service discovery, event notification, and cache management. Note that if the discovery manager was created by this object, then it will also be terminated (independent of whether you have obtained a reference using `getDiscoveryManager()`).

```
} // ServiceLookupManager
```

Standard Lookup Entries (net.jini.lookup.entry)

The Jini lookup **entry** package contains common lookup entry and entry-bean definitions. For details of entry attributes, please refer to the JavaDoc specification and documentation. The UML diagram below shows the entry classes defined:

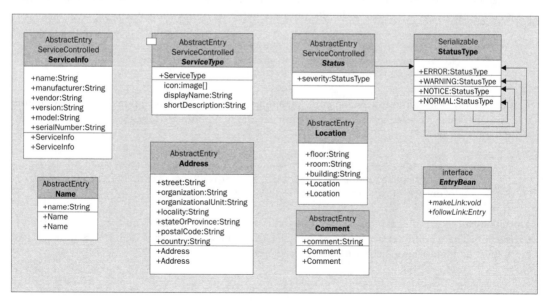

JavaSpace Service (net.jini.space)

The Jini **space** package contains the interface implemented by JavaSpaces services.

```
public interface JavaSpace {
```

JavaSpace is an interface implemented by JavaSpace service proxies.

```
Lease write(Entry entry, Transaction txn, long lease)
    throws TransactionException, RemoteException;
```

The above method writes an entry into the space (under lease) in the context of a transaction.

```
Entry read(Entry tmpl, Transaction txn, long timeout)
    throws UnusableEntryException, TransactionException,
    InterruptedException, RemoteException;
```

This reads an entry matching the template from the space. If a matching entry does not exist, or is locked by another transaction, the method blocks until one is written/unlocked, or the timeout expires (may be zero).

```
Entry readIfExists(Entry tmpl, Transaction txn, long timeout)
    throws UnusableEntryException, TransactionException,
    InterruptedException, RemoteException;
```

This reads an entry matching the template if one already exists in the space and has not been locked by a transaction. If the entry does not exist, the method returns immediately with a null value. In this call timeout is used to control the maximum wait for competing transactions to complete.

```
Entry take(Entry tmpl, Transaction txn, long timeout)
    throws UnusableEntryException, TransactionException,
    InterruptedException, RemoteException;
```

This atomically reads and removes an entry matching the template in the context of the transaction. The timeout parameter is used as in read() to indicate the maximum wait for a matching entry to be written (may be zero).

```
Entry takeIfExists(Entry tmpl, Transaction txn, long timeout)
    throws UnusableEntryException, TransactionException,
    InterruptedException, RemoteException;
```

This atomically reads and removes an existing entry matching the template in the context of the transaction. The method returns null immediately if no matching entry is found; timeout is used to mark the maximum wait in acquiring a lock on the entry.

```
EventRegistration notify(Entry tmpl, Transaction txn,
    RemoteEventListener listener, long lease,
    MarshalledObject handback)
    throws TransactionException, RemoteException;
```

This requests asynchronous remote notification of matching entry writes into the space.

```
Entry snapshot(Entry e) throws RemoteException;
```

This returns an entry snapshot. Snapshots provide efficient entry representations when performing multiple searches using the same entry.

```
} // JavaSpace
```

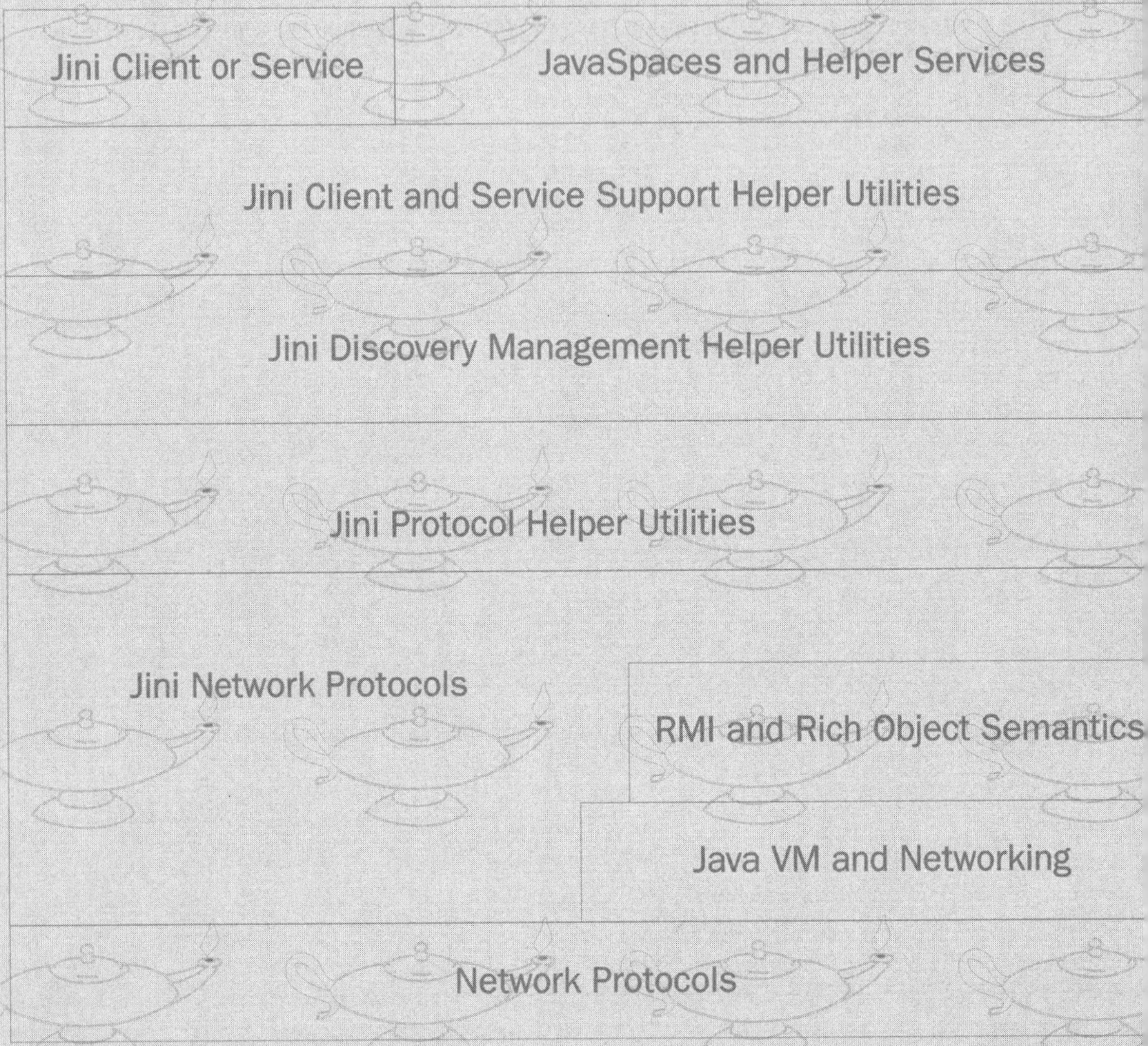

Jini Client or Service	JavaSpaces and Helper Services

Jini Client and Service Support Helper Utilities

Jini Discovery Management Helper Utilities

Jini Protocol Helper Utilities

Jini Network Protocols

RMI and Rich Object Semantics

Java VM and Networking

Network Protocols

Using Jini in Linux

Linux is a kernel supporting UNIX Posix interfaces and distributed under the open source GNU public license (http://www.gnu.org). The Linux kernel is usually packaged with various open source programs, such as the GNU utilities (compilers, editors, command-line utilities), in what are called Linux distributions. Readers may be familiar with popular Linux/GNU distributions such as RedHat, Caldera, Corell, SuSe, Slackware, etc. Linux was developed for the Intel x86 family of processors, but has since been ported to most computing platforms including Compaq Alpha, Motorola PowerPC, etc.

Recently, Linux has emerged from relative obscurity to become a popular platform for internet services, and in fewer cases a desktop environment. Linux has benefited from the open source development model, otherwise known as the bazaar model (see http://www.tuxedo.org/~esr/writings/cathedral-bazaar/). Source code for the Linux kernel and all GNU public license programs is freely available to everyone, and can be modified provided that all modifications are provided in source form without charge. Thanks to the development model, and the contribution of thousands of volunteers, the UNIX-type kernel written by a Finnish student called Linus Torvalds has become a stable platform used to run mission critical internet servers.

Linux initially found its way into corporations through the back door, as systems administrators installed popular internet servers (such as Apache) on machines running Linux. In the case of Java support, the porting effort was similarly pushed by a grass-roots effort lead by the Blackdown porting team (http://www.blackdown.org). The Blackdown team of volunteers was granted access to the Solaris port of the Java Development Kit under non-disclosure agreement with Sun and produced ports of the JDK 1.1.x and 1.2.x series. For several years, the Blackdown port (along with two individual port efforts) was the only platform for running Java on Linux. With the increase of developer interest in the Linux platform, developers pressured Sun to provide an officially supported Linux Java JDK. Indeed, the Linux JDK was for a long time the highest requested feature in Sun's Java bug-parade.

The widespread corporate adoption of Linux as an 'official' internet platform prompted Sun to release a supported version of Java 2 (1.2.2 and 1.3 Standard Edition and 1.2.2 Enterprise Edition) for Linux built on the Blackdown port. Sun recently announced that the Linux port of the Java 2 v1.4 will be released at the same time as the Windows and Solaris releases. IBM has also released a supported Java 1.1.8 JDK/JRE for Linux and has announced support for a JDK 1.3 port currently released as a beta version. Compiler vendor Tower-J also supports a Linux-native Java compiler. The Blackdown team continues to release its JDK/JRE ports, and will focus on support of optional interfaces, such as Java3D. Finally, the Kaffe open source clean room Java implementation also supports Linux, although support for Java2 is currently partial. It should be noted that with the exception of Kaffe and the Blackdown port, all other ports are for the Intel x86 architecture and that the future of supported non-Intel ports is unclear.

Given the number of JDK/JREs supporting Java 2 available, issues to consider while selecting one include support, stability, performance (JIT vs. Hotspot), threading model (green vs. native threads), and JPDA (debugging) support. The relative performance and characteristics of these ports changes with each release, and readers are encouraged to check the latest benchmarks, such as the Volcano benchmark (see http://www.volcano.com/benchmarks.html). Various Java development environments are also available to Linux, from smart editors such as GNU Emacs, to full-blown IDEs such as Inprise JBuilder, IBM VisualAge for Linux, Sun Forte for Java, etc. IBM provides an open source compiler called jikes that supports very fast compilation, but at the time of writing does not optimize code very well (use javac for release code).

Jini and Linux

In that Linux is a stable, open source operating system, it is a good match for Jini service deployment. Efforts are currently underway to use embedded versions of Linux in low-cost internet appliances (several recent announcements have been made). All versions of Jini are known to work with the Java 2 Linux JDKs from Sun, IBM, and Blackdown. There is no Java 2 Micro Edition runtime environment available for Linux at the time of writing (J2ME is currently not compatible with Jini).

Jini usage in Linux is similar to usage under Solaris. Most Jini and Java documentation examples applying to Solaris should work directly in Linux. For the examples listed in this book, you'll need to convert command-line path names to the forward-slash (/) file separator used in UNIX systems, and convert classpath sequences to use the colon (:) path separator. Also, policy files may need to be edited to reflect changes in file separator arguments. There are a few Linux-specific configuration checks you must perform before using Jini:

❑ Most Java2 Linux ports are built using version 2.1 of the GNU C library (glibc). Some older Linux distributions are packaged with an older glibc version (2.0). The only known workaround is to upgrade your Linux distribution (Linux upgrading has been significantly eased in most distributions).

❑ Linux (and most UNIX systems) restricts user processes to using ports above 1024. This restriction does not affect rmiregistry and rmid as their default ports are above 1024. However, if you decide to start an HTTP daemon listening to the standard port 80 you'll either have to execute as root (not recommended), select another port, or use the Apache daemon included in most distributions (there is a bug in the Jini 1.1beta reggie service that results in an exception being thrown when downloading classes served by the Apache server; however, this bug will be fixed in the Jini 1.1 FCS).

❑ Most Linux distributions include a kernel compiled to support multicast (required by Jini). However, many distributions (including RedHat) do not enable multicast on network interfaces by default. Also, many distributions do not add a route to the multicast network in the Linux routing table.

You can check to see if multicast is configured for your network interface by invoking:

```
$ /sbin/ifconfig -a
eth0      Link encap:Ethernet  HWaddr xx:xx:xx:xx:xx:xx
          inet addr:xxx.xxx.xxx.xxx  Bcast:xxx.xxx.xxx.xxx
Mask:xxx.xxx.xxx.xxx
          UP BROADCAST RUNNING MULTICAST  MTU:1500  Metric:1

lo        Link encap:Local Loopback
          inet addr:127.0.0.1  Mask:255.0.0.0
          UP LOOPBACK RUNNING  MTU:3924  Metric:1
```

Some values have been modified and part of the output removed for brevity. The path to the ifconfig program may be different for some distributions, and the -a flag may not be accepted (try it without the flag). In the example above, we have verified that the eth0 interface is configured for multicast (see bold "MULTICAST" tag in eth0). If the MULTICAST flag is not printed, you'll need to enable it as shown below. Interface configuration is a privileged access, and you'll need to have super-user (root) privileges.

```
# /sbin/ifconfig eth0 multicast
```

Replace eth0 with name of the interface connected to the multicast network. Some distributions may include a version of ifconfig that requires a different syntax for enabling multicast; check your Linux manual page (man ifconfig).

Once multicast is enabled on one of the network interfaces, a route must be provided. You may list the current routing table using:

```
$ /sbin/route
Kernel IP routing table
```

Destination	Gateway	Genmask	Flags	Metric	Ref	Use	Iface
xxx.xxx.xxx.xxx	*	xxx.xxx.xxx.xxx	UH	0	0	0	eth0
127.0.0.0	*	255.0.0.0	U	0	0	0	lo
224.0.0.0	*	240.0.0.0	U	0	0	0	eth0
default	xxx.xxx.xxx.xxx	0.0.0.0	UG	0	0	0	eth0

The multicast block of addresses is 224.0.0.0, and as can be seen in the table above, it is already routed through the eth0 interface. If the route does not appear in your host you may add it as shown below. Route configuration is a privileged access, and you'll need to have super-user (root) privileges.

```
# /sbin/route add -net 224.0.0.0 netmask 240.0.0.0 dev eth0
```

The command line arguments may differ for some Linux distributions; check your Linux manual page (man route).

If you have added the multicast flag and/or route manually, you will need to repeat these steps after every reboot. You may make these additions permanent by editing your distribution-specific network configuration files. RedHat users may edit the /sbin/ifup-local file. It is also possible (but not recommended) to add these two commands to your local initialization file (/etc/rc.d/rc.local in many distributions).

❑ Another Linux issue involves the IP address returned by `java.net.InetAddress.getLocalHost()`. In some distribution/JDK combinations, the result may be the loop-back address (127.0.0.1) and may cause problems if you use the result to export RMI code bases. One workaround is to edit the `/etc/hosts` file and place the name and IP address of your non-loopback interface before the loopback name-address pair. You should be aware that this modification might affect some Linux programs such as talk.

❑ Finally, the one area where Linux Java ports have been shown to have a weakness in the past has been in thread handling. JDK/JRE native thread support under current Linux kernel versions may not scale as well as in other platforms. Some JDK/JRE Linux ports support only one threading model, and it is understood that Sun will only support native threads in version 1.4. Users of the Java Native Interface (JNI) should use native threads.

Getting Help

The Blackdown team maintains an e-mail list called `java-linux`, which is subscribed to by the JDK porters and many Linux developers. If you have a Linux-specific Java question, you're likely to receive a knowledgeable response. Before posting, please verify that your question has not been answered before by scanning the archives. You should also verify that the error is Linux-specific and not a generic Java bug, ideally by running your code on another platform. As the Linux JDKs have matured the number of Linux-specific bugs has decreased significantly. General Java question posting is frowned upon and your message is likely to be ignored. The `java-linux` archives and registration instructions are available at the Blackdown site (http://www.blackdown.org), under documentation. Finally, Wrox publishes several Linux related references (see `http://www.wrox.com`), and there are also online discussion groups at http://www.p2p.com.

Jini Client or Service	JavaSpaces and Helper Services

Jini Client and Service Support Helper Utilities

Jini Discovery Management Helper Utilities

Jini Protocol Helper Utilities

Jini Network Protocols	
	RMI and Rich Object Semantics
	Java VM and Networking

Network Protocols

UML Notation

Classes and Objects

A class is represented in the UML like this:

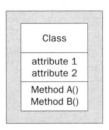

The rectangle representing the class is divided into three compartments, the top one showing the class name, the second showing the attributes, and the third showing the methods.

An object looks very similar to a class, except that its name is underlined:

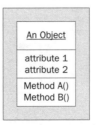

Relationships

Relationships between classes are generally represented in class diagrams by a line or an arrow joining the two classes. UML can represent the following, different sorts of object relationships.

Dependency

If A depends on B, then this is shown by a dashed arrow between A and B, with the arrowhead pointing at B:

Association

An association between A and B is shown by a line joining the two classes:

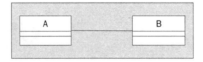

If there is no arrow on the line, the association is taken to be bidirectional. A unidirectional association is indicated like this:

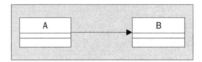

Aggregation

An aggregation relationship is indicated by placing a white diamond at the end of the association next to the aggregate class. If B aggregates A, then A is a part of B, but their lifetimes are independent:

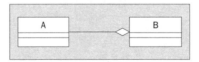

Composition

Composition, on the other hand, is shown by a black diamond on the end of association next to the composite class. If B is composed of A, then B controls the lifetime of A.

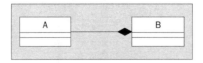

Multiplicity

The multiplicity of a relationship is indicated by a number (or *) placed at the end of an association.

The following diagram indicates a one-to-one relationship between A and B:

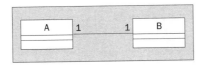

This next diagram indicates a one-to-many relationship:

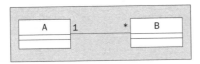

A multiplicity can also be a range of values. Some examples are shown below:

1	One and only one
*	Any number from 0 to infinity
0..1	Either 0 or 1
n..m	Any number in the range *n* to *m* inclusive
1..*	Any positive integer

Naming an Association

To improve the clarity of a class diagram, the association between two objects may be named:

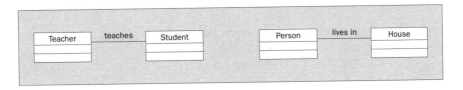

Inheritance

An inheritance (generalization/specialization) relationship is indicated in the UML by an arrow with a triangular arrowhead pointing towards the generalized class.

If A is a base class, and B and C are classes derived from A, then this would be represented by the following class diagram:

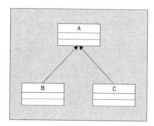

Multiple Inheritance

The next diagram represents the case where class C is derived from classes A and B:

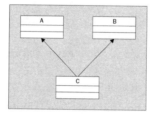

States

States of objects are represented as rectangles with rounded corners. The *transition* between different states is represented as an arrow between states, and a *condition* of that transition occurring may be added between square braces. This condition is called a guard.

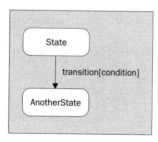

Object Interactions

Interactions between objects are represented by interaction diagrams – both sequence and collaboration diagrams. An example of a collaboration diagram is shown below. Objects are drawn as rectangles and the lines between them indicate links – a link is an instance of an association. The order of the messages along the links between the objects is indicated by the number at the head of the message:

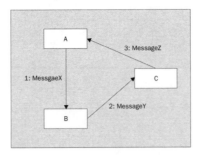

Sequence diagrams show essentially the same information, but concentrate on the time-ordered communication between objects, rather than their relationships. An example of a sequence diagram is shown below. The dashed vertical lines represent the lifeline of the object:

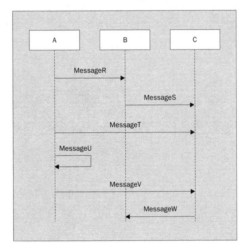

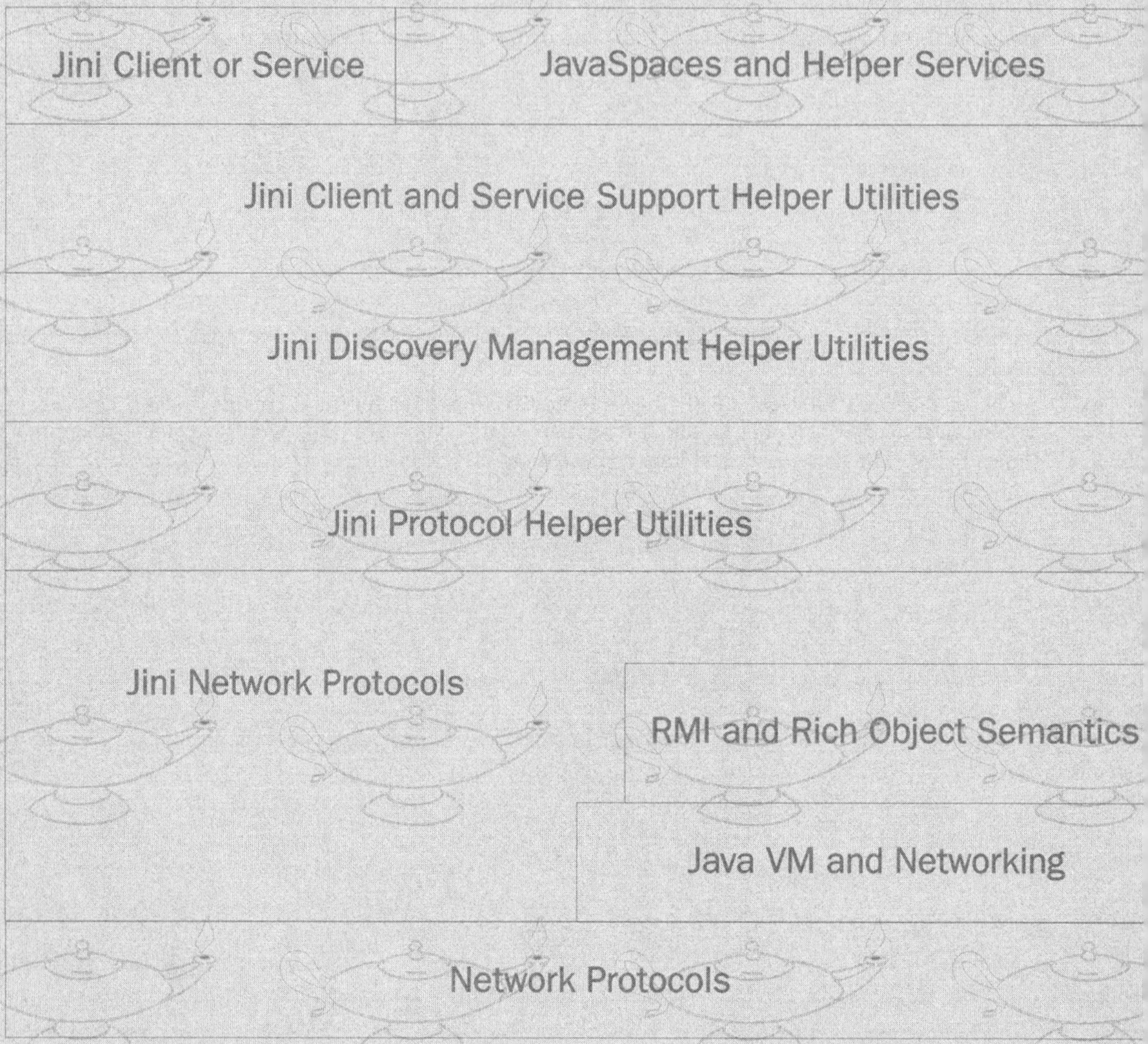

Jini Client or Service
JavaSpaces and Helper Services
Jini Client and Service Support Helper Utilities
Jini Discovery Management Helper Utilities
Jini Protocol Helper Utilities
Jini Network Protocols
RMI and Rich Object Semantics
Java VM and Networking
Network Protocols

Online discussion at http://p2p.wrox.com

Support, Errata and p2p.wrox.com

One of the most irritating things about any programming book is when you find that bit of code you've just spent an hour typing simply doesn't work. You check it a hundred times to see if you've set it up correctly and then you notice the spelling mistake in the variable name on the book page. Of course, you can blame the authors for not taking enough care and testing the code, the editors for not doing their job properly, or the proofreaders for not being eagle-eyed enough, but this doesn't get around the fact that mistakes do happen.

We try hard to ensure no mistakes sneak out into the real world, but we can't promise that this book is 100% error free. What we can do is offer the next best thing by providing you with immediate support and feedback from experts who have worked on the book and try to ensure that future editions eliminate these gremlins. We also now commit to supporting you not just while you read the book, but once you start developing applications as well through our online forums where you can put your questions to the authors, reviewers, and fellow industry professionals.

In this appendix we'll look at how to:

❑ Enroll in the **Programmer To Programmer**™ forums at http://p2p.wrox.com

❑ Post and check for errata on our main site, http://www.wrox.com

❑ E-mail technical support a query or feedback on our books in general

Between all three support procedures, you should get an answer to your problem in no time flat.

The Online Forums at p2p.wrox.com

Join the Pro Jini mailing list for author and peer support. Our system provides **Programmer To Programmer**™ support on mailing lists, forums, and newsgroups all in addition to our one-to-one e-mail system, which we'll look at in a minute. Be confident that your query is not just being examined by a support professional, but by the many Wrox authors and other industry experts present on our mailing lists.

How To Enroll For Support

Just follow these simple instructions:

1. Go to http://p2p.wrox.com in your favorite browser.
   Here you'll find any current announcements concerning P2P – new lists created, any removed and so on:

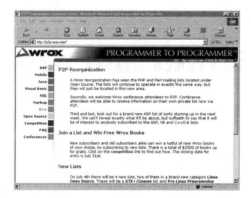

2. Click on the Java button in the left hand column.

3. Choose to access the pro_jini list.

4. If you are not a member of the list, you can choose to either view the list without joining it or create an account in the list, by hitting the respective buttons.

5. If you wish to join, you'll be presented with a form in which you'll need to fill in your e mail address, name, and a password (of at least 4 alphanumeric). Choose how you would like to receive the messages from the list and then hit Save.

6. Congratulations. You're now a member of the pro_jini mailing list.

Why This System Offers The Best Support

You can choose to join the mailing lists to receive mails as they are contributed, or a daily digest, or you can receive them as a weekly digest. If you don't have the time or facility to receive the mailing list, then you can search our online archives. You'll find the ability to search on specific subject areas or keywords. As these lists are moderated, you can be confident of finding good, accurate information quickly. Mails can be edited or moved by the moderator into the correct place, making this a most efficient resource. Junk and spam mail are deleted, and your own email address is protected by the unique Lyris system from web-bots that can automatically hoover up newsgroup mailing list addresses. Any queries about joining, or leaving lists, or any query about the list should be sent to: support@wrox.com.

Checking the Errata Online at www.wrox.com

The following section will take you step by step through the process of posting errata to our web site to get that help. The sections that follow, therefore, are:

- ❑ Wrox Developer's Membership
- ❑ Finding a list of existing errata on the web site
- ❑ Adding your own erratum to the existing list
- ❑ What happens to your errata once you've posted it (why doesn't it appear immediately)?

There is also a section covering how to e-mail a question for technical support. This comprises:

- ❑ What your e-mail should include
- ❑ What happens to your e-mail once it has been received by us

So that you need only view information relevant to yourself, we ask that you register as a Wrox Developer Member. This is a quick and easy process that will save you time in the long-run. If you are already a member, just update membership to include this book.

Wrox Developer's Membership

To get your FREE Wrox Developer's Membership click on Membership in the top navigation bar of our home site – http://www.wrox.com. This is shown in the following screenshot:

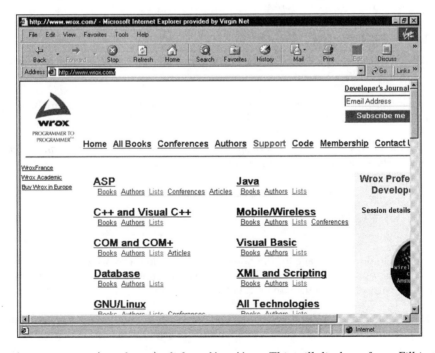

Then, on the next screen (not shown), click on New User. This will display a form. Fill in the details on the form and submit the details using the Register button at the bottom.

Before you can say 'The best read books come in Wrox red' you will get the following screen:

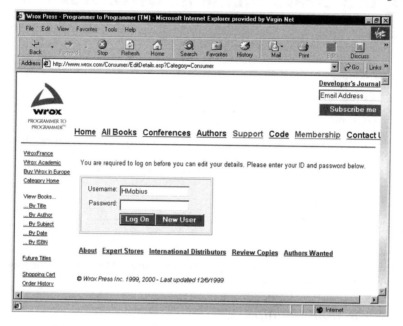

Type in your password once again and click Log On. The following page allows you to change your details if you need to, but now you're logged on, you have access to all the source code downloads and errata for the entire Wrox range of books.

Finding an Erratum on the Web Site

Before you send in a query, you might be able to save time by finding the answer to your problem on our web site – http://www.wrox.com.

Each book we publish has its own page and its own errata sheet. You can get to any book's page by clicking on Support from the top navigation bar.

Halfway down the main support page is a drop down box called Title Support. Simply scroll down the list until you see Professional Jini. Select it and then hit Errata.

This will take you to the errata page for the book. Select the criteria by which you want to view the errata, and click the Apply criteria button. This will provide you with links to specific errata. For an initial search, you are advised to view the errata by page numbers.

If you have looked for an error previously, then you may wish to limit your search using dates. We update these pages regularly to ensure that you have the latest information on bugs and errors.

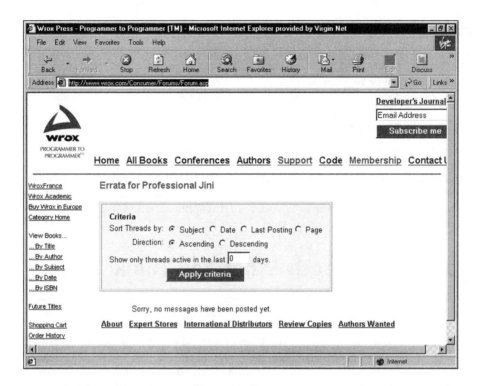

Add an Erratum : E-Mail Support

If you wish to point out an erratum to put up on the website or directly query a problem in the book page with an expert who knows the book in detail then e-mail support@wrox.com, with the title of the book and the last four numbers of the ISBN in the subject field of the e-mail. A typical e- mail should include the following things:

❑   The **name**, **last four digits of the ISBN** and **page number** of the problem in the Subject field.

❑   Your **name**, **contact info** and the **problem** in the body of the message.

We won't send you junk mail. We need the details to save your time and ours. If we need to replace a disk or CD we'll be able to get it to you straight away. When you send an e-mail it will go through the following chain of support:

Customer Support

Your message is delivered to one of our customer support staff who are the first people to read it. They have files on most frequently asked questions and will answer anything general immediately. They answer general questions about the book and the web site.

Editorial

Deeper queries are forwarded to the technical editor responsible for that book. They have experience with the programming language or particular product and are able to answer detailed technical questions on the subject. Once an issue has been resolved, the editor can post the erratum to the web site.

The Authors

Finally, in the unlikely event that the editor can't answer your problem, they will forward the request to the author. We try to protect the author from any distractions from writing. However, we are quite happy to forward specific requests to them. All Wrox authors help with the support on their books. They'll mail the customer and the editor with their response, and again all readers should benefit.

What We Can't Answer

Obviously with an ever-growing range of books and an ever-changing technology base, there is an increasing volume of data requiring support. While we endeavor to answer all questions about the book, we can't answer bugs in your own programs that you've adapted from our code. So, while you might have loved the chapters on file handling, don't expect too much sympathy if you cripple your company with a routine that deletes the contents of your hard drive. But do tell us if you're especially pleased with the routine you developed with our help.

How to Tell Us Exactly What You Think

We understand that errors can destroy the enjoyment of a book and can cause many wasted and frustrated hours, so we seek to minimize the distress that they can cause.

You might just wish to tell us how much you liked or loathed the book in question. Or you might have ideas about how this whole process could be improved. In which, case you should e-mail feedback@wrox.com. You'll always find a sympathetic ear, no matter what the problem is. Above all you should remember that we do care about what you have to say and we will do our utmost to act upon it.

Jini Client or Service	JavaSpaces and Helper Services

Jini Client and Service Support Helper Utilities

Jini Discovery Management Helper Utilities

Jini Protocol Helper Utilities

Jini Network Protocols	
	RMI and Rich Object Semantics
	Java VM and Networking

Network Protocols

Index

A Guide to the Index

The index is arranged hierarchically, in alphabetical order, with symbols preceding the letter A. Most second-level entries and many third-level entries also occur as first-level entries. This is to ensure that users will find the information they require however they choose to search for it. Page number references adjacent to major first and second-level entries (i.e. those containing several sub-entries), indicate important text mentions such as definitions, descriptions and overviews.

S

wrox
PROGRAMMER TO PROGRAMMER™

Wrox writes books for you. Any suggestions, or ideas about how you want information given in your ideal book will be studied by our team.
Your comments are always valued at Wrox.

Free phone in USA 800-USE-WROX
Fax (312) 893 8001

UK Tel. (0121) 687 4100   Fax (0121) 687 4101

Professional Jini - Registration Card

Name _____

Address _____

_____

_____

_____

City_____ State/Region _____

Country_____ Postcode/Zip _____

E-mail _____

Occupation _____

How did you hear about this book? _____

☐ Book review (name) _____

☐ Advertisement (name) _____

☐ Recommendation _____

☐ Catalog _____

☐ Other _____

Where did you buy this book? _____

☐ Bookstore (name)_____ City _____

☐ Computer Store (name)_____

☐ Mail Order _____

☐ Other _____

What influenced you in the purchase of this book?

☐ Cover Design

☐ Contents

☐ Other (please specify) _____

How did you rate the overall contents of this book?

☐ Excellent   ☐ Good

☐ Average   ☐ Poor

_____

What did you find most useful about this book? _____

_____

What did you find least useful about this book? _____

_____

Please add any additional comments. _____

_____

What other subjects will you buy a computer book on soon? _____

_____

What is the best computer book you have used this year?

_____

Note: This information will only be used to keep you update about new Wrox Press titles and will not be used for any oth purpose or passed to any other third party.

wrox

PROGRAMMER TO PROGRAMMER™

NB. If you post the bounce back card below in the UK, please send it to:

Wrox Press Ltd., Arden House, 1102 Warwick Road,
Acocks Green, Birmingham B27 6BH. UK.

Computer Book Publishers